CAMBRIDGE STUDIES IN
MEDIEVAL LIFE AND THOUGHT

Edited by M. D. Knowles, Litt.D., F.B.A.
Fellow of Peterhouse and Regius Professor of Modern History in the University of Cambridge

NEW SERIES VOL. IX

THE PROBLEM OF SOVEREIGNTY IN THE LATER MIDDLE AGES

NEW SERIES

1 *The Abbey and Bishopric of Ely* by EDWARD MILLER

2 *Tavistock Abbey* by H. P. R. FINBERG

3 *Crusading Warfare* by R. C. SMAIL

4 *Foundations of the Conciliar Theory* by BRIAN TIERNEY

5 *Bradwardine and the Pelagians* by GORDON LEFF

6 *Matthew Paris* by R. C. VAUGHAN

7 *Early Franciscan Government* by ROSALIND B. BROOKE

8 *Wyclif and the Oxford Schools* by J. A. ROBSON

THE PROBLEM OF SOVEREIGNTY IN THE LATER MIDDLE AGES

THE PAPAL MONARCHY WITH AUGUSTINUS TRIUMPHUS AND THE PUBLICISTS

BY

MICHAEL WILKS

Lecturer in History, Birkbeck College
University of London

CAMBRIDGE
AT THE UNIVERSITY PRESS
1963

PUBLISHED BY
THE SYNDICS OF THE CAMBRIDGE UNIVERSITY PRESS

Bentley House, 200 Euston Road, London, N.W.1
American Branch: 32 East 57th Street, New York 22, N.Y.
West African Office: P.O. Box 33, Ibadan, Nigeria

Printed in Great Britain by The Broadwater Press Ltd
Welwyn Garden City, Hertfordshire

CONTENTS

PART IV
VICARIUS CHRISTI

PART V
CHANGING CONCEPTIONS OF UNIVERSAL AUTHORITY

PART VI
THE CONCILIAR THEORY

PREFACE

THE problem of sovereignty is a permanent feature of organised political society, and at no time in European history has this been more apparent than in the perplexed conditions of the thirteenth and fourteenth centuries. Not only was the fading dream of universal government giving way to the new conception of the national state, but the whole ideological basis of medieval thought was being reorientated by the influx of Aristotelian ideas. The most striking effect of the new learning was the growth of a belief in the natural, innate capacity of the human individual to regulate his own affairs in the light of a rationalistic interpretation of life. This reacted with explosive effect upon the established philosophical and political order, whose principles were determined by the traditional tenets of the Christian faith. It meant the end of what Gierke has since termed the 'Middle Age proper'. The keystone of this order, which presupposed the incorporation of all Christians into a single political-ecclesiastical society, was the medieval papacy, a divine right monarchy which had laboriously cultivated its title to a universal and sovereign government over mankind during the preceding millennium. And it was this claim to sovereignty which became the immediate focus for the attack of the medieval Aristotelians upon the existing Christian order. In this book I have endeavoured to define the nature of this sovereignty, particularly as seen through the eyes of Augustinus Triumphus of Ancona, unquestionably one of the most important political thinkers of the medieval period. I have also tried to show that the attack upon the medieval papacy was twofold. The frontal assault of the radical lay writers demonstrated that the real issue at stake was the survival of a thoroughly Christian conception of society when faced with a completely antagonistic pagan ideal of natural, human competence. But the eventual success of this frontal assault was aided by the concealed undermining of the papal supremacy at the hands of the moderates, who were pursuing the ideal of a Christian humanism.

As a result the real issue was largely obscured by their insistence that the two opposed systems could be harmoniously combined into a great synthesis, in which the problem of sovereignty was by no means the least of the difficulties which could be effectively solved and forgotten.

Whilst therefore this study is primarily concerned with what we should now term political theory, theology, philosophy and law come equally within its scope. This reflects the attitude of the medieval publicists, and their contribution is of particular importance in view of the attempt by some modern commentators to suggest that there was no theory of sovereignty in the Middle Ages. Yet the publicists were convinced that they were dealing with precisely this problem. They understood that a ruler who saw himself, by virtue of his office, as a visible representation of God upon earth was forced to regard himself as an absolute governor. In this sense absolutism was the 'orthodox' theory of kingship. Since the government under consideration was the papal monarchy, it became a religious duty for the more conservative theologians, the Augustinians, to elaborate a doctrine of papal omnicompetence based upon a totalitarian conception of society. Whilst similar aspirations were certainly not lacking with the other European princes, it was the papacy which was above all responsible for developing the medieval theory of sovereignty. What can be said however is that many of these theologians were promptly horrified at the implications of the principles which they were propounding. Recoiling from the Leviathan which they had done so much to uphold, they deftly inserted into their work a series of grossly incompatible statements in a desperate attempt to mitigate its rigours. Even Augustinus Triumphus himself provides a glaring example of this subconscious capacity to advocate fundamentally opposed notions of authority. Indeed at times the extreme papalist becomes almost indistinguishable from his most savage lay opponent. This was made easier by the degree to which so many of the lay writers, with the notable exception of Marsilius of Padua, were prepared to accommodate themselves to compromise solutions. But what is even more remarkable is the apparent inability of the publicists to appreciate their own talent for contradicting themselves. Consistency is the quality most conspicuous by its absence in the thought of the period, and the student of the publicistic literature must quickly accustom himself to finding the same writer advocating totally opposite points of view. Thus, whilst it is relatively easy to discern the lines of conflict between the main schools of thought in the later Middle Ages, it would be historically inaccurate to make any rigid allocation of writers into specific groups when so many thinkers exemplify so many different standpoints. Since I have tried as far as possible to give an accurate account of these controversies, the reader must sometimes share with me the difficulty of accepting an almost incredible situation in which the same tract provides the best answer to its own propositions. The conflict between the opposing systems was fought out not only between writer and writer, but to an even larger extent within the mind of one and the same author. This was due partly to an attempt to find a new meaning for certain standard words and phrases without discarding them altogether; partly to an excessively legalistic approach which assumed that the amassing of precedents, however contradictory, was a sufficient substitute for a logical explanation; partly to a desire to escape censure by quoting all possible opinions in the assurance that one of them would be right. But more than anything else this was due to the workings of the great synthesis, which engendered the belief that thoroughly contradictory positions could be taken together by the employment of subtle distinctions. The net result was that the Ages of Faith were eventually converted into an Age of Reason only after the intervention of an Age of Confusion, during which both faith and reason were confounded by the attempt to prove that there was no conflict between them.

To illustrate this welter of ideas I have drawn upon a large number of tracts and treatises, roughly covering the years 1250–1350. Some are only a few pages in length; others run to many thousands of words. Many of them are rarely read; and new editions are urgently required. Much of the material is scattered; and some difficult to obtain. Even with the better known writers a close analysis of the relevant texts is necessary to establish the points which are of most significance. And I am not unaware that many of the matters discussed here are still the subject of fierce debate. These considerations have persuaded me that the evidence should be presented as fully as possible. Even so it has usually been necessary to make a choice from the wealth of material available. Where the modern writer can often convey his point in a few sentences, the medieval theologian was constitutionally incapable of writing less than a chapter, viewing the matter from every conceivable angle, and darting off along fascinating but irrelevant by-paths on the way. Inevitably this has resulted in footnotes of inordinate length, and I can only hope that the gain in convenience to the reader may offset any annoyance that this may cause. Some brief notes (for which no originality is claimed) on the various publicists and anonymous works are included in Appendix III.

Most of the work for this book was completed in the summer of 1957, although pressure of other duties has since prevented me from making more than spasmodic attempts to prepare it for publication. It does not therefore claim to have taken into account all the relevant literature published since that date. Undoubtedly the most serious omission is that of Professor E. H. Kantorowicz' monumental study, *The King's Two Bodies* (Princeton, 1957) which is particularly important for its discussion of the later development in lay thought of many of the themes discussed here. As far as possible I have attempted to remedy this deficiency by adding references in the footnotes under the abbreviation *KTB*. It is however my pleasant duty to record my debt to many other scholars in the field of medieval political theology: 'Dicebat Bernardus Carnotensis nos esse quasi nanos gigantium humeris insidentes, ut possimus plura eis et remotiora videre, non utique proprii visus acumine aut eminentia corporis, sed quia in altum subvehimur et extollimur magnitudine gigantea'. In particular I would like to tender my grateful thanks for their valuable advice and assistance to Professor B. Tierney, Professor E. F. Jacob, Professor H. Chadwick, Professor R. R. Darlington, and especially to Professor M. D. Knowles, who has done so much to make possible the publication of this volume. But above all I would like to thank Walter Ullmann, who has for so long been a constant guide and friend, and perhaps I alone can appreciate how much this study owes to his unfailing kindness and generosity. I would also wish to express my appreciation of the encouragement given to me by my colleagues at Trinity College, Cambridge, and Birkbeck College, London; and I must mention my wife, who, both by her labours and her forbearance, has done so much to help me. Finally I am glad to have this opportunity to acknowledge the generous financial assistance afforded me by the Syndics of the Cambridge University Press, the Adjudicators of the Prince Consort Prize Fund, and by Trinity College and Birkbeck College. Again I can only say how grateful I am to all concerned.

I am indebted to the Editors of the *Journal of Theological Studies* for permission to reprint material now included in Part IV.

M. J. W.

LONDON
13 October 1959

LIST OF ABBREVIATIONS

AKKR	*Archiv für Katholisches Kirchenrecht.*
Baluze	S. Baluzius, *Vitae Paparum Avenionensium* (ed. G. Mollat: Paris, 1914–27).
CSEL	*Corpus Scriptorum Ecclesiasticorum Latinorum.*
DDC	*Dictionnaire de droit canonique.*
DHGE	*Dictionnaire d'histoire et de géographie ecclésiastique.*
DTC	*Dictionnaire de théologie catholique.*
Dupuy	P. Dupuy, *Histoire du différend d'entre le Pape Boniface VIII et Philippe le Bel* (Paris, 1655).
EHR	*English Historical Review.*
Gratian	*Decretum Gratiani*, ed. A. Friedberg, *Corpus Iuris Canonici*, i (Leipzig, 1879).
KTB	E. H. Kantorowicz, *The King's Two Bodies: A Study in Medieval Political Theology* (Princeton, 1957).
Mansi	J. D. Mansi, *Sacrorum Conciliorum Nova et Amplissima Collectio* (Florence and Venice, 1759–98).
MGH	*Monumenta Germaniae Historica.*
MHP	*Miscellanea Historiae Pontificiae.*
MIOG	*Mitteilungen des Instituts für österreichische Geschichtsforschung.*
PG	J. P. Migne, *Patrologia Graeca.*
PL	J. P. Migne, *Patrologia Latina.*
Raynaldus	O. Raynaldus, *Annales Ecclesiastici* (Lucca, 1750).
SBAW	*Sitzungsberichte der bayrischen Akademie der Wissenschaften.*
Winkelmann	E. Winkelmann, *Acta imperii inedita saeculi XIII et XIV* (Innsbruck, 1885).
ZSSR	*Zeitschrift der Savigny-Stiftung für Rechtsgeschichte.*

INTRODUCTION

AUGUSTINUS TRIUMPHUS OF ANCONA

THE original aim of this book was to investigate the political ideas of Augustinus Triumphus of Ancona. However it soon became apparent that this must entail a consideration of the views of a very large number of his contemporaries, and as a result the book has become an attempt to clarify the more important problems in the political outlook of the later Middle Ages. For this purpose I have taken into account the opinions of a wide variety of authors—politicians, philosophers, theologians, canonists, civil lawyers and many others—and have compared them with the views expressed by the different rulers of the time. But on the whole I have tended to concentrate upon that class of writers usually known as the publicists, and in particular those who flourished in what I believe to be a vital period in the development of European political life, very roughly the century between 1250 and 1350. There was a reason for emphasising the publicistic contribution to the thought of this period. The lawyers, and even more the rulers themselves, tended to take it for granted that their readers were familiar with the principles under discussion, and with the very technical vocabulary and style used in those discussions. Princes have no time to explain themselves: lawyers generally prefer to remain unintelligible except to other lawyers. The publicists on the other hand, whilst dealing with the same subjects and employing the same technicalities, were prepared, sometimes at any rate, to assume a profound ignorance on the part of the reader and would often go to a great deal of trouble to explain what they had in mind. No doubt, since so many of them were clerics and schoolmen, they benefited in this respect from their preaching and teaching experience. And this means that the works of the publicists do enable the modern historian to gain a very much clearer and more accurate picture of the issues involved in the political and religious history of the thirteenth and fourteenth centuries. Moreover the publicists appreciated that these issues could be posed in terms appropriate to every scholastic discipline. Many of them were men of extraordinary academic attainment, and one can find in their works a cross-section of all the theological, philosophical, legal and political opinions of the age: indeed there is very little point in trying to distinguish between the various categories of knowledge. An excellent example of this is provided by Augustinus Triumphus himself, and since he continues to be the central figure in this book, he should not be allowed to slip unnoticed into the narrative.

The *Summa de potestate ecclesiastica* of Augustinus Triumphus has been described as 'one of the half dozen most influential and most important books ever written' on the nature of the papal supremacy in the Middle Ages,[1] and to disregard his work is to neglect and obscure some of the outstanding features of a crucial moment in the genesis of modern political ideas. Not only was Augustinus Triumphus a political thinker of the highest calibre, but it is also perhaps true to say that he alone amongst the publicists of the thirteenth and fourteenth centuries gives a really complete and adequate account of the maturer stages of papal-hierocratic doctrine. And whilst the importance of Augustinus Triumphus has long been recognised, it has been customary for most textbooks to dismiss his views in a few perfunctory pages. Only a very small number of modern works have devoted their attention to him. Two Dutch historians, van Moé in 1928 and van Gerven in 1947, dealt with his views in doctoral dissertations, although only the latter has reached publication.[2] In 1938 Jean Rivière published a short survey well calculated to stimulate further research.[3] But in general little has been done to dispel the clouds of uncertainty which still envelop his political theories. Traditionally regarded as a 'fanatical hiero-

[1] C. H. McIlwain, *The Growth of Political Thought in the West* (London, 1932), p. 278.

[2] E. van Moé, *Les Ermites de St. Augustin au début du XIVe siècle: Agostino Trionfo et ses théories politiques:* see the *Position de thèses* (Paris, 1928), pp. 101–14; R. van Gerven, *De wereldijke macht van den paus volgens Augustinus Triumphus* (Antwerp-Nijmegen, 1947).

[3] J. Rivière, 'Une première "Somme" du pouvoir pontifical: le pape chez Augustin d'Ancone', *Revue des sciences religieuses*, xviii (1938), pp. 149–83.

crat',[1] closely allied to such extremists as Aegidius Romanus or Alvarus Pelagius,[2] we are informed by some recent commentators either that he was a great deal more moderate than they were,[3] or that, since they themselves were not extremists, it would be incorrect to regard Augustinus Triumphus as one either.[4] Indeed the real attitude adopted by all the so-called extremists of the early fourteenth century is equally a matter of complete uncertainty, and this ambivalence of opinion has only served to complicate an already complex subject. Accordingly it is hoped that this study may serve to redefine the position of not only Augustinus Triumphus but also of the other prominent thinkers of the period by setting them in their right relationship to each other against the background of contemporary developments in political thought.

The generally accepted version of Augustinus Triumphus' career, deriving from his sixteenth-century editor, Augustinus Fivizanius,[5]

[1] G. Pilati, 'Bonifacio VIII° e il potere indiretto', *Antonianum* viii (1933), pp. 350–1; similarly R. L. Poole, *Illustrations of the History of Medieval Thought and Learning* (London, 1920), pp. 221, 223.

[2] Rivière, *art. cit.*, pp. 149–52, 181; R. Scholz, *Die Publizistik zur Zeit Philipps des Schönen und Bonifaz' VIII* (Stuttgart, 1903), p. 150; P. Munz, *The Place of Hooker in the History of Thought* (London, 1952), pp. 120–4.

[3] A. Gwynn, *The English Austin Friars in the Time of Wyclif* (Oxford, 1940), pp. 40, 63.

[4] For example van Gerven, *op. cit.*, although this attempt to moderate Augustinus Triumphus' views dates back to the great apostle of the indirect power theory, Cardinal Bellarmine: *De potestate summi pontificis*, v. 5 (cited van Gerven, p. 4 n. 1), 'Neque difficile esset alios theologos qui contrariam sententiam tueri videntur ad concordiam cum caeteris revocare. Nam ipse etiam Augustinus Triumphus, qui apertissime tribuere videtur summo pontifice temporalem potestatem in orbem terrarum universum, explicat se tamen in *quaest.* i, *De potestate pontificis*, *art.* 7, in responso ad ultimum, ubi dicit potestatem temporalem aliter esse in pontifice ac in rege: in pontificem enim esse ut in confirmante et corrigente, in rege vero ut in administrante; et clarius *art.* 8 scribit papam habere spiritualem potestatem, sed per eam disponere etiam de temporalibus, et *art.* 9 demonstrat Christum non fuisse regem temporalem sed spiritualem'. For the deliberate attempt to reinterpret the hierocratic writings see Part III, Chapters II and III below.

[5] In his preface to the 1582 edition of the *Summa*. See also Scholz, *Die Publizistik*, pp. 172–3; J. Rivière, *Le problème de l'église et de l'état au temps de Philippe le Bel* (Paris–Louvain, 1926), p. 156; and his articles in *DDC*, i. 1416–22; *DTC*, xv. 2. 1855–60; M. T. Disdier, *DHGE*, v. 487–9; P. Glorieux, *Répertoire des maîtres en théologie de Paris au XIIIe siècle* (Paris, 1932), ii. 321; E. Lewis, *Medieval Political Ideas* (London, 1954), p. 384.

has recently been totally demolished. According to Fivizanius' elaborate account, Augustinus Triumphus was born in 1243, entered the Augustinian Hermit Order of friars at the age of eighteen through the good offices of his uncle, and was almost immediately sent to Paris with Aegidius Romanus. Here he studied under Bonaventure and Aquinas, took his mastership in 1270, and was of such great brilliance that he was sent to attend the Council of Lyons of 1274 as a replacement for Aquinas himself, who had died on the way to the council. Thereafter he preached at Padua and Venice, and was eventually installed as court preacher to Charles II of Naples and tutor to the young prince Robert, subsequently becoming a trusted adviser to both monarchs. He is however said to have been in Paris in the first decade of the fourteenth century, and it is suggested that he read the *Sentences* at the unlikely age of sixty and became regent master in 1314–16, apparently in conjunction with his duties at Naples. Following this pious myth the *Summa* was written at the advanced age of seventy-seven, and he eventually died at the age of eighty-five. An imaginary portrait on the title page of Fivizanius' edition depicts him as a hale and hearty old man nearly thirty years older than he can have been at death. But following up the queries raised by Mariani[1] and Perini,[2] a very different biography has been convincingly established by Father Blasius Ministeri, O.E.S.A.[3] This lacks much of the romantic detail of the earlier legend, but the main events of his life are now clear. Augustinus of Ancona—the surname Triumphus appears to be unknown before the sixteenth century[4]—was born *c.* 1270–3, became a mem-

[1] U. Mariani, 'Scrittori politici medioevalia Egidio Romano e Dante, Agostino Trionfo', *Giornale Dantesco*, xviii (1925), pp. 147–67; xix (1926), pp. 111–40; *Scrittori politici agostiniani del secolo XIV* (Florence, 1927); *Le teorie politiche di S. Agostino e il loro influsso nella scuola agostiniana del secolo XIV* (Florence, 1933).

[2] D. A. Perini, 'Trionfo, Fr. Augustino', *Bibliographia Augustiniana: scriptores itali* (Florence, 1937), iv. 20–8.

[3] In a doctoral thesis of 1942 published in two parts in the *Analecta Augustiniana*, xxii (1951–2), and republished separately as *De vita et operibus Augustini de Ancona, O.E.S.A. (*1328)* (Rome, 1953). Cf. now U. Mariani, *Chiesa e stato nei teologi agostiniani del secolo XIV* (Rome, 1957), pp. 89–93.

[4] For the sake of convenience I have retained the title, although Ministeri, *op. cit.*, pp. 10–11, denies Fivizanius' statement that Triumphus is the name of an old Ancona family.

ber of the Augustinian Order at the normal age of fourteen, and was sent to Paris *c.* 1297–1300. He read the *Sentences* of Peter Lombard in 1302–4 or 1304–6,[1] and probably returned to the Ancona province as lector in the Augustinian school at Padua. He became a master of theology at Paris in 1313–15, and is next heard of at Naples in late 1321. He there gained the favour of Charles, son of King Robert of Naples, and was appointed 'in consiliarium et capellanum' in October 1322.[2] He died on 2 April 1328, at the age of fifty-five to fifty-eight, and was buried in the church of St Augustine at Ancona.

Of his personal characteristics we know nothing, and little insight is to be gained from the rigidly impersonal style of his writings. These on the other hand were numerous, and quickly gained him a reputation for academic brilliance at Paris: 'varius et multiplex atque copiosissimus ex theologis augustinianae scholae XIV saeculi'.[3] Whilst a definitive list of his works may never be compiled, due to the large number of spurious works attributed to him in the fifteenth and sixteenth centuries, the traditional figure of thirty-six *opera* would seem to be reasonably accurate.[4] Of these the majority are purely philosophical and theological treatises, and it is only necessary to mention here his five or six 'political' treatises. The *Tractatus contra articulos inventos ad diffamandum Bonifacium*,[5] written in defence of Boniface VIII and containing scathing references to Clement V and his French allies, and the *Tractatus de facto Templariorum*,[6] concerning Philip the Fair's persecution of the Knights Templar, can safely be ascribed to the period 1307–9. The next two pamphlets, the *Tractatus de potestate collegii mortuo papa*[7] and the

[1] H. Denifle, *Chartularium Universitatis Parisiensis* (Paris, 1889–91), ii. 85 n. 1.

[2] *Regestum Angioninum*, n. 244, fo. 11v: see Ministeri, *op. cit.*, pp. 4–5, 47; cf. Mariani, *Chiesa e stato*, pp. 91–3.

[3] M. Grabmann, *Storia della teologia cattolica* (Milan, 1939), p. 151.

[4] For a complete list see Ministeri, *op. cit.*, pp. 136–8.

[5] Ed. H. Finke, *Aus den Tagen Bonifaz' VIII* (Münster, 1902), pp. lxix–xcix.

[6] Ed. R. Scholz, *Die Publizistik*, pp. 508–16; and X. P. D. Duynstee, *'S pausen Primaat in de latere Middeleeuwen en de Aegidiaansche Schoul. I. Philips de Schoone* (Hilversum, 1935), pp. 340–5.

[7] Ed. R. Scholz, *Die Publizistik*, pp. 501–8; and W. Mulder, *Studia Catholica*, v (1928), pp. 40–60.

Tractatus de duplici potestate praelatorum et laicorum,[1] in which Augustinus Triumphus begins the real formulation of his political ideas, are, as Ministeri reasonably suggests, in reality two *quaestiones* taken from a now lost *Quodlibet*, which may be assigned to *c.* 1315.[2] Some mention should also be made of the *De origine ac translatione et statu Romani imperii* which was probably written a year or two earlier. Although often attributed to Augustinus Triumphus,[3] it now seems more likely that it is the work of Tholemy of Lucca.[4] The 'historical' passages in this tract bear a very close resemblance to certain passages in both Tholemy's *Determinatio compendiosa* and Augustinus Triumphus' *Summa*, and it might well be the work of either writer. But in default of further evidence I have continued to accept the authorship of Tholemy.

Finally we come to the enormous *Summa de potestate ecclesiastica*, completed in 1326,[5] which quite overshadows all his other political opuscules. This egregious work, as Cardinal Bellarmine termed it,[6] represents the full flowering of Augustinus Triumphus' political ideas, and comprises nearly half a million words. It is as much a theological as a political treatise—a distinction which its author would not have appreciated[7]—and throughout we are kept con-

[1] Ed. R. Scholz, *Die Publizistik*, pp. 484–501; and X. P. D. Duynstee, *'S pausen Primaat. I.*, pp. 331–40.

[2] Ministeri, *op. cit.*, pp. 76–80. Mulder, on the basis of Fivizanius' life, dated it at 1268–71. The philosophical tract *De cognitione intuitiva et abstractiva* is suggested as a possible third *quaestio*.

[3] Noted by Scholz, *Die Publizistik*, p. 174 n. 6; Glorieux, *Répertoire*, p. 326; Mariani, *Scrittori politici*, p. 213. This has been rejected by Ministeri, *op. cit.*, p. 125 and Mariani, *Chiesa e stato*, p. 97 as being the tract of the same title by Engelbert of Admont. This would seem to be true of the Rome text, Bibliotheca Angelica Codex lat. 739; but Ministeri is mistaken in assuming that this is the same as the text of Paris, B.N. lat. 4046, ff. 34–6, which bears no resemblance to Engelbert's much longer work.

[4] According to its editor, M. Krammer, in the appendix to his edition of Tholemy of Lucca, *Determinatio compendiosa* (Hanover–Leipzig, 1909). Krammer uses the Parisian text, and suggests a date of *c.* 1308–14.

[5] This date may be gauged from John XXII's letter of thanks (*Ep.* 104: *Reg. Vat.* 114, fo. 19v): see Ministeri, *op. cit.*, pp. 49, 112. Fivizanius gave the date as 1320, *Summa*, p. 563.

[6] Bellarmine, *De script. an.* 1301, 'Scripsit egregiam summam de potestate ecclesiae'.

[7] For example Augustinus Triumphus, *Summa*, cviii. 3, p. 536, 'distinctio

stantly aware that theology is the 'finis et domina omnium scientiarum'.[1] It is, he declares, the only truth, and his many philosophical arguments are designed simply to support its exposition.[2] When he does refer to matters outside the theological-political sphere, social matters for example such as the legality of usury, he does so only incidentally and his opinions on them are rarely explicitly stated. Nevertheless theology is given its widest interpretation, and it may be pointed out that for writers of the time a superb legislator like Innocent III was essentially a 'magnus theologus',[3] which is certainly not so if theology is taken in the modern much narrower sense. And so whilst the bulk of the second and third sections of the *Summa*, dealing with dispensations, apostolic poverty and the states of perfection, are of primarily theological interest, they stem quite naturally from Augustinus Triumphus' discussion of the papal plenitude of power, which comprises the first section. He makes it clear however that his main purpose is the defence of the papal supremacy: to inform the ignorant and to denounce those who, puffed up with worldly pride, seek to reject it.[4]

unius scientiae ab alia non accipitur penes rem quae cognoscitur, sed penes diversum modum sciendi. . . Illa ergo eadem quae tractantur in theologia tractantur in iure canonico; et illi iidem canones qui recipiuntur in theologia recipiuntur in iure canonico; et quae respuuntur ibi respuuntur hic. . . Differunt tamen in modo considerandi'. In spite of this description of law as juristic theology, his preference for theology over canon law comes out in iii. 5, pp. 32–3, where he declares himself to be strongly in favour of electing a theologian rather than a canonist as pope. The same tendency in Ockham has been noted by E. F. Jacob, *Essays in the Conciliar Epoch* (Manchester, 1953), p. 94, and has been discussed by M. Grabmann, 'Die Erörterung der Frage, ob die Kirche besser durch einen guten Juristen oder durch einen guten Theologen regiert werde bei Gottfried von Fontaines (*1306) und Augustinus Triumphus von Ancona (*1328)', *Eichmann Festschrift* (Paderborn, 1940), pp. 1–19. Note also Marsilius of Padua's complaint about the lack of theologians in the *curia*, *Defensor pacis*, II. xxiv. 2–10, pp. 452–8.

[1] Augustinus Triumphus, *Summa*, xxxvii. 6 ad 3, p. 224; cf. iii. 5, p. 33, 'Constat autem quod sacra scriptura est illa quae praefertur omnibus legibus et scientiis'.

[2] Augustinus Triumphus, *Summa*, lxxi. 1 ad 3, p. 372, 'per studium et exercitium scientiae credibilia explicantur et declarantur'.

[3] E.g. Aegidius Spiritalis, *Libellus*, p. 108, 'papa Innocentius III, qui fuit mirae prudentiae et sapientiae et magnus theologus'.

[4] Augustinus Triumphus, *Summa*, *Dedicatio*, 'In quem quandoque multi labuntur dictae potestatis ignorantia; quae cum sit infinita, eo quod 'Magnus

It is true that the papal power is of such magnificence that it cannot be subject to human scrutiny: to doubt its fullness is to cast aspersions upon the power of God himself—the *potestas Dei et papae* is one. But he does not presume to question its nature, merely to elucidate it. Has not Aristotle himself said that by doubting we attain to truth? The declaration of anti-papal theses will serve to bring out by contrast the true glory of the Roman sovereignty.[1] So widely does Augustinus Triumphus cast his net over the works of the various anti-hierocratic writers that it seems improbable that the *Summa* was composed in refutation of any specific doctrine.[2] Nor can it be certain that it was written at the direct request of John XXII.[3] But it is dedicated to that pontiff, and Augustinus Triumphus' literary activities had already gained him a handsome pension from the papal *curia*.[4] There seems however to be no truth in the

est Dominus, et magna virtus eius, et magnitudinis eius non est finis' [*Ps.* cxliv. 3], omnis creatus intellectus in eius perscrutatione invenitur deficere. Multi vero hominum complacentia, quia sic multa de divino cultu et Christi reverentia usurpata sunt, quae honoribus deferuntur humanis, sive humilitate nimia sive adulatione pestifera. Multo magis hac duplici causa multa subtrahuntur de Christi vicario dominio et potentia. Multi autem curiosa scientia et utinam non elata superbia cupientes ex quibusdam novis, videri potius quam videre, et sciri potius quam scire; imitantes in hoc illos curiosos et superstitiosos Athenienses qui ad nihil aliud vacabant nisi audire vel discere aliquid novi'.

[1] Augustinus Triumphus, *Summa*, i. 10, pp. 15–16; x. 3 ad 3, p. 79; xxviii. 1, pp. 168–9; similarly Alvarus Pelagius, *De planctu Ecclesiae*, ch. 59, p. 168. See also the debate over the legality of discussing papal power in John of Paris, *De potestate regia et papali*, ch. 22, pp. 248–9, and Ockham, *Breviloquium*, i *passim*. This followed several papal prohibitions: in 1194 Roger of Hoveden, *Chronicon* (ed. W. Stubbs, London, 1868–71), iii. 230, spoke of Celestine III 'de cuius amplitudine disputare fas non est'; Innocent III said that no one might be judge of the privileges of the Roman church, *Decretales*, II. i. 12: 'Cum super privilegiis sedis apostolicae causa versatur, nolumus de ipsis per alios iudicari'; and Innocent IV had subsequently described it as sacrilege to dispute about papal power. This prohibition, later repeated at the Council of Trent, was borrowed from Roman law: *Cod.* IX. xxix. 2, 'Disputari de principali iudicio non oportet: sacrilegii enim instar est dubitare an is dignus sit quem elegit imperator'. See further *KTB*, p. 158, n. 209.

[2] Mariani, *Scrittori politici*, pp. 236–8, regarded it as a direct answer to Marsilius of Padua's *Defensor pacis* of 1324, whilst Disdier, *DHGE*, v. 488, saw it as an attack upon the Franciscan anti-pope Nicholas V.

[3] According to Fivizanius, *Summa*, p. 563.

[4] The pension consisted of ten ounces of gold annually and a lump sum of 100 gold florins 'pro scribendis libris', 28 January, 1326 (Denifle, *Chartularium*, ii. 280).

suggestions that they also earned him either a bishopric or canonisation.[1]

To attempt to assess the very great debt which Augustinus Triumphus owes to earlier writers is a difficult and unrewarding task. Most of his sources are the stock in trade of any late hierocratic writer. Quotations from Augustine are as numerous as those from the Bible itself, and like most of his school, Augustinus Triumphus believed that he was simply restating the principles of the great doctor himself. There are many passages taken from the other Church Fathers, Cyprian, Jerome, Chrysostom, Gregory and Cyril of Alexandria. So too Isidore and Dionysius the Pseudo-Areopagite are well represented, although it need not be inferred that he was necessarily directly familiar with the works of these early writers. He appears however to have had a thorough knowledge of Bernard of Clairvaux' *De consideratione* and Hugh of St. Victor's *De sacramentis*. The same is true of all the canon law books, and many of his theories are derived from the canonists. Of these only Huguccio of Pisa is mentioned by name, but the derivation of other canonistic doctrines cannot be attributed solely to his use of Guido de Baysio's *Rosarium*. Many references are made to Innocent III and Boniface VIII, and he was clearly familiar with the opinions of Innocent IV. It is also obvious that he had a good working knowledge of the writings of Aquinas and Tholemy of Lucca,

[1] 'Beatus Augustinus Triumphus' according to Fivizanius, who also remarks that members of the Augustinian Order were accustomed to carry miniature pictures of him: see Ministeri, *op. cit.*, pp. 8–10. The tradition that Augustinus Triumphus was a bishop goes back to the fifteenth century, but is not discussed by Ministeri. See Laurentius Aretinus, *Liber de ecclesiastica potestate* (as printed by K. Eckermann, *Studien zur Geschichte des monarchischen Gedankens im 15. Jahrhundert* (Berlin–Grunewald, 1933), pp. 161–8 at p. 163), 'Post quos Augustinus de Ancona, sacrae paginae doctor eximius, librum illum *De potestate papae* composuit de factis concilii inter parum et nihil se immiscendo, ex quo libro quia papalem causam favit, in Ariminensem [Rimini] episcopum est promotus, cum beati Bernardi sententia sit quod obsequium regni regis amicus habet'. Neither Gams, *Series Episcoporum*, p. 722, nor Eubel, *Hierarchia Catholica*, i. 107, confirm this. According to J. F. von Schulte, *Die Geschichte der Quellen und Literatur des canonischen Rechts* (Stuttgart, 1875–80), ii. 193–4, and S. Riezler, *Die Literarischen Widersacher der Päpste zur Zeit Ludwigs des Baiers* (Leipzig, 1874), p. 286, Augustinus Triumphus died as archbishop of Nazareth: this was *in partibus infidelium*, but there was a real see at Barletta. Again no confirmation of this can be found.

and in particular the *De renuntiatione papae* of Aegidius Romanus, although it is virtually impossible to say to what degree he was influenced by other near-contemporaries. Perhaps however the most striking feature in this respect is his cautious use of Aristotelian and Roman law ideas. Whilst he largely resists the temptation to assimilate these alien views with orthodox teachings, a popular pursuit which was engaging the attention of most of his contemporaries, Augustinus Triumphus does not deny that there was much that could be useful in the new learning. Might it not, he asks, be utilised with sufficient circumspection to avoid the acceptance of its final intent?[1] Why lose an opportunity for spoiling the Egyptians?[2] And like his contemporaries he seems to have remained quite unaware of the danger attendant upon even this limited acquaintance with 'those infernal men', as the English Franciscan Roger Marston described the pagan philosophers at the end of the thirteenth century. One of the tragedies of medieval history is to watch the undermining of a system by the very men who believed that they were doing everything in their power to build it up, and it must be acknowledged that Augustinus Triumphus unwittingly played his part in this process. On the other hand it was his willingness to countenance certain anti-monarchical tendencies, however much they did violence to his basic principles, which undoubtedly contributed to his extensive influence upon later writers of widely differing opinions. This again is hard to calculate in view of our still limited knowledge of the later fourteenth and fifteenth centuries, but his theories appear to have been adopted in various ways by both supporters of the late medieval papacy and its opponents alike. Of immediate use to writers like Alvarus Pelagius and Conrad of Megenberg, the *Summa* also had its attractions for the conciliarists at the

[1] Augustinus Triumphus, *Summa*, xliv. 7 ad 1, p. 245, 'non ut in eis sistat eorum finalis intentio'.

[2] Augustinus Triumphus, *Summa*, xliv. 7, p. 245, 'eo modo licet uti legibus imperatorum quo modo licet uti doctrinis philosophorum . . . sicut Aegypti non solum idola habebant et onera gravia quae populus Dei detestabatur, sed habebant vasa atque ornamenta de auro et argento, quae populus ille exiens de Aegypto sibi potius tamquam ad usum meliorem clanculo vindicavit'. This was the standard contemporary argument, and derives from Augustine, *De doctrina Christi*. ii. 60 (*PL*. xxxiv. 63).

turn of the century, and, as will be seen, Augustinus Triumphus had in fact anticipated almost the whole of William of Ockham's conciliar theory. Nevertheless it is as a defender of papal monarchy that Augustinus Triumphus is of prime importance, and the high reputation which the *Summa* enjoyed in the fifteenth century is attested by the large number of manuscripts still extant.[1] This popularity was maintained by the rapid reprinting of the *Summa* in the later years of the century,[2] and the book became a standard work of reference in the papal *curia* for use against the onslaught of the Reformation. In the last quarter of the sixteenth century he became regarded as the greatest product of the Augustinian school of political thinkers, and a new impression of the *Summa* appeared every year for four years in succession.[3] It is one of the ironies of history that it was only when it was already too late that full recognition was accorded to what was rightly described during the nineteenth century as a 'Klassische Darstellung der Papstmacht'.[4]

[1] Ministeri, *op. cit.*, pp. 112–15, lists 47 manuscripts.

[2] Augsburg, 1473; Cologne, 1475; Lyons, c. 1479; Rome, 1479; place unknown, 1484; Venice, 1487; Lyons, 1489.

[3] Rome, 1582, 1583, 1584, 1585. All references used here are to the 1584 version except when noted otherwise.

[4] J. F. von Schulte, *Die Geschichte*, ii. 194.

PART I
THE UNIVERSAL SOCIETY

I. SOCIETAS CHRISTIANA

THE problems which confronted the political theorists of the early fourteenth century were to a very large degree the result of the growth of monarchic principles of government and the steady centralisation of lay and ecclesiastical authority which had been taking place during the previous two hundred years. European society had now become more highly organised than at any time since the end of the old Roman empire, and was in consequence suffering from all the complaints attendant upon too much government and too many governors. The question of the right relationship of powers, so necessary for the maintenance of the *harmonia mundi*, became the prime consideration of the age. It remained however an age of permanent crisis, a fact due not only to the multiplication of novel and disturbing theories of the position of the ruler in the community, but also to the multiplicity of rulers itself. Popes, kings, bishops and emperors vied with each other in their attempts to bring about fundamentally incompatible versions of the universal order, and the promotion of their own interests in particular. Moreover this clash of interests amongst rulers was sharpened and supplemented by the growth of ideas which threatened the autonomy of any prince, whoever he might be. Whilst it is true that the development of Roman law principles in the twelfth century had given immense support to the rise of the European monarchies, and above all to the emergence of the papacy as the dominant force in Western society, the balance was to be redressed with a vengeance by the introduction of Aristotelian principles into medieval thought in the thirteenth century. Aristotelianism revitalised old doctrines of the supremacy of the popular will and of an ideal of limited government which had all but disappeared beneath the encroachments of the absolute monarchs, and provided a radically different answer to the problem of the origin of political authority. From the time of Aquinas, who had done more than anybody else to secure acceptance for the new learning, we can begin to distinguish between three main schools of political thought. In the first place there are those who continue to favour the omnipotence of a divinely constituted ruler, and these can be fairly sharply divided off from those who seek an alternative source of power in the community at large. Whilst between them there now appears an ever-increasing number, headed by Aquinas himself, who endeavour to unite both parties in an ideal of the ruler who is both absolute and limited at the same time. By the second quarter of the fourteenth century this latter attractive but inadequate theory has gained the field, and writers like Augustinus Triumphus and Marsilius of Padua, the exponents of sovereignty papal and popular, are left as lonely and isolated giants on the fringes of the main body of late medieval political thinkers.

As with all attempts to separate writers and thinkers into groups and categories, such distinctions are necessarily of an arbitrary nature and exhibit a certain degree of artificiality. It would be dangerous to suppose that there were three quite separate blocs: as always, views merged into each other and dividing lines are hard to draw. The political philosophy of most of the papalists became an uneasy blend of orthodox papalism and Thomist novelties; the theories of many lay writers were vitiated by an incongruous mixture of Christian and pagan Aristotelianism. By the fourteenth century political writers had become heir to far too many divergent traditions to remain rigidly consistent. It was now perhaps too late for any writer to put forward a completely Christian system unalloyed by naturalistic tendencies, just as it was as yet too early for any thinker to propound a purely secular social ideal shorn of all religious considerations. But if this is borne in mind, it still remains possible to discern three alternative views of the proper structure of authority in medieval society. In spite of being publicised as a panacea for all political ills, the system evolved by Thomas and his followers could never in a final analysis be integrated into either the conservative hierocratic doctrine or the radical Marsilian thesis. And each of these three points of view provided conflicting but characteristic answers to all the problems of political obligation current in the thirteenth and fourteenth centuries. Moreover in tracing these lines of thought it becomes more and more apparent that the divergencies were caused by totally dissimilar conceptions of the nature of medieval society itself. Although there remained a superficial resemblance, there was in reality a bottomless ideological gulf fixed between the Christian body of Augustinus Triumphus and the Christian unity of Aquinas, between the *societas christiana* of the hierocrat and the *societas humana* of the Averro-Aristotelian. Such divisions have tended to become obscured because every writer, even Marsilius and the French lawyers, paid lip service to an all-embracing universalism and employed a common terminology. But there was no more genuine agreement about the nature of medieval society than there was about the problem of universals or the exact relationship of reason and faith. Indeed the failure to find a universally acceptable philosophical system was itself the root cause of the conflicts in medieval political thought. The constitutional theories of the age were no more than an expression in terms of government of all the discordant elements in contemporary philosophy.[1] Most of the great publicists were first and foremost philosophers and theologians, and their political systems were at bottom metaphysical exercises in a more secular guise. Extreme realism, moderate realism and nominalism, the three main streams of medieval scholasticism, were paralleled by three opposed assumptions about the essential character of political society and political obligation. Conversely it was the fact that these underlying philosophical principles had inescapable political implications and were to be translated into concrete theories of government that lent such vigour to the disputes over universals and caused them to rage unabated throughout the medieval period.

The main current of medieval thought up to the thirteenth century was predominantly Christian and Neoplatonic, permeated with a rigid Stoicism.[2] Although isolated attempts to preach nom-

[1] See the very pertinent remarks of M. Grabmann, 'Studien über den Einfluss der aristotelischen Philosophie auf die mittelalterlichen Theorien über das Verhältnis von Kirche und Staat', *SBAW, Phil.-Hist. Abt.* (Munich, 1934), Heft 2. Grabmann distinguished between a theory of the supremacy of faith leading to papal supremacy, a balance between reason and faith which characterises Thomism, and the autonomy of reason which supports a lay monarchy based on popular consent. For an application of this see P. Munz, *The Place of Hooker in the History of Thought* (London, 1952).

[2] For the medieval belief in the fundamental agreement between Platonic and Christian doctrines see R. Klibansky, *The Continuity of the Platonic Tradition* (London, 1939), pp. 23–7, 33–4.

inalism had been made, and the moderate realism of Abelard and the later Chartrain masters already heralded a new philosophical movement, the great clash of antithetic principles had not yet developed. Orthodox philosophy retained the realistic character which it had been given by St. Augustine and which was handed on by the great ecclesiastics like Anselm and Bernard. When translated into terms of political organisation, this marriage of Christianity and Platonic realism could only produce the idea of an essentially totalitarian society founded on the principles of the Christian faith. Realism and revelation in philosophy were united to theocracy in politics in the conception of a single monarchically governed Christian society which was the Universal Church. In the words of the classic Augustinian formula as interpreted by James of Viterbo, there was no State but the ecclesiastical one:

Nulla communitas dicitur vera respublica nisi ecclesiastica, quia in ea sola est vera iustitia et vera utilitas et vera communio.[1]

To the papalist the medieval Church had been expanded into a comprehensive whole which included not only religious but equally all political and social institutions. It came near to being a practical realization of the ideal of Plato's *Republic*, that is, of the rule of the wise over a unified society built up organically in ranks, and of the ideal of the Stoics whose universal commonwealth was to contain the whole of mankind without distinction in one universal right-minded and right-living community. It was this idea of *Ecclesia*, the assumption that all Christians and potentially all men formed a single corporate political entity, which provided the basis on which the entire hierocratic system rested.[2] And so to Augus-

[1] James of Viterbo, *De regimine christiano*, i. 4, p. 127; cf. Anon., *Somnium viridarii*, i. 53, p. 75, 'Ille principatus est summus principatus et *solus in universo terrestri* qui attingit omnem gradum ultimae perfectionis in via: talis est principatus Ecclesiae'. For the principle that a 'respublica regni christianorum' must be equated with the whole *universitas christianorum* in the thirteenth century, see the Franciscan writer Hugo de Digna (d. 1255–6), *De finibus paupertatis*, ch. 1, ed. C. Florovsky, *Archivum Franciscanum Historicum*, v (1912), pp. 277–90, at p. 281: cf. Bonaventure, 'respublica universalis Ecclesiae', *De perfectione evangelica*, ii. 3 (ed. Quaracchi, v. 161); also Hervaeus Natalis, *De potestate papae*, fo. 141, 'sed praesidens universaliter reipublicae in communitate christiana est papa'.

[2] On this see in particular W. Ullmann, *The Growth of Papal Government in*

tinus Triumphus, although the same may well be said of all the papal-hierocrats, the *Ecclesia* normally signifies the universal body of Christians, which embraces both clergy and laity: 'omnes fideles tam laici quam clerici sunt membra Ecclesiae'.[1] The works of the publicists abound with phrases like the *totus populus christianorum* or the *tota humanitas Christi* and many other similar expressions intended to demonstrate that all Christians are gathered together into one gigantic community, the congregation of the faithful. As Alvarus Pelagius repeatedly informs his readers, the world forms a single society of which both ordained and unordained Christians have membership, a *societas omnium christianorum*.[2] The term *Ecclesia* then, in its most general sense, stands for the corporate union of the whole Christian people into one body, the *unum corpus* of the Pauline epistles.[3] It is a society resting upon and orientated by the tenets of the Christian faith. But it is not merely a spiritual unity: it is just as much a civil society, a universal body politic. For this reason it is commonly described as a city or kingdom, or, as Augustinus Triumphus aptly puts it, the *principatus mundi*.[4] In short it is a Christianised version of the universal empire of the Romans:

the Middle Ages (London, 1955). Reference may also be made to Gierke-Maitland, *Political Theories of the Middle Age* (Cambridge, 1927), pp. 1–30; Troeltsch-Wyon, *The Social Teaching of the Christian Churches* (London, 1931), i. 203–52; A. H. Chroust, 'The Corporate Idea and the Body Politic in the Middle Ages', *Review of Politics*, ix (1947), pp. 423–52; E. Lewis, 'Organic Tendencies in Medieval Political Thought', *American Political Science Review*, xxxii (1928), pp. 849–76.

[1] Augustinus Triumphus, *Summa*, lxi. 3, p. 323; ci. 5, p. 497, 'Papa praeest contemplativis et activis viris de Ecclesia, quia praeest pastoribus et ovibus, religiosis et clericis, litteratis et laicis'.

[2] E.g. Alvarus Pelagius, *De planctu Ecclesiae*, ch. 37, p. 46; ch. 59, p. 175; also Augustinus Triumphus, *Summa*, xxv. 2, p. 151. The related terms *societas*, *populus* and *multitudo* derive from Cicero through Augustine, and are equated with *respublica*.

[3] Augustinus Triumphus, *Summa*, xx. 2, p. 122; ii. 6, p. 24, 'tam ad laicos quam ad clericos, qui sunt de corpore Ecclesiae'; also lxxi. 2, p. 372. Cf. *Romans*, xii. 5.

[4] Augustinus Triumphus, *Summa*, xxii. 3, p. 131; similarly Hervaeus Natalis, *De potestate papae*, fo. 143v. For 'politia christiana' see Alvarus Pelagius, *De planctu Ecclesiae*, ch. 40, p. 60; cf. Hermannus de Schildiz, *Contra haereticos*, ch. 3, p. 133, 'Christus... Ecclesiam disposuit ad modum politiae monarchicae'; also Anon., *Disquisitio theologico-iuridica*, ii. 14, p. 1350, 'politia subcoelestis seu ecclesiastica'; v, p. 1360, 'politia seu universitas fidelium'.

'istud imperium catholicum' as Clement VI described it in 1346 as he bestowed his approval upon Charles IV's imperial election, and laboured to instruct the callow Bohemian about the nature of the society over which the pope was shortly to invest him with universal powers.[1]

The universalism of this society is seen to be not merely territorial but to cover every aspect of social and political life. The *Ecclesia* is an expression of corporate and indivisible unity, and the preservation of its essential wholeness is the prime purpose of government. To detract from its oneness is to destroy the very fabric of an organism in which no part can ever be complete in itself or experience a separate existence. It is, declares Aegidius Romanus, as indivisible as the seamless garment of Christ.[2] Whatever their standpoint, the publicists were agreed that there could be a direct transfer of philosophical principles into the political field. As Aquinas said,

> Manifestum est autem quod omnes qui sub communitate aliqua continentur, comparantur ad communitatem sicut partes ad totum.[3]

Here the extreme realistic relationship of universal and individual is believed to govern man's relationship to society. Since to the Augustinian the whole was always prior to the parts, the entire *Ecclesia* correspondingly becomes infinitely more important than any of its members, and exists over and above them. In this highly realistic conception the individual has no great significance except in so far as he assists towards the functioning of the whole.[4] Politically speaking the well-being of one person, ultimately even his existence, is of no account in comparison with the well-being of the whole towards which all things are ordered. This produces a real *mystique* of the political community. The common good of the society is not merely the sum of the individual goods of its members:

[1] *MGH*, *Const.*, VIII, n. 100, p. 152.

[2] Aegidius Romanus, *De renuntiatione papae*, ch. 25, p. 64; also Henry of Cremona, *De potestate papae*, p. 469; cf. *John*, xix. 25.

[3] Thomas Aquinas, *Summa theologica*, II, II. lviii. 5.

[4] Augustinus Triumphus, *Summa*, xliv. 3, p. 242, 'quae sunt omnia iusta . . . ordinantur ad bonum commune et ad promotionem reipublicae . . . nullo privato bono considerato'.

the *Ecclesia* is something other than a mere aggregate of the persons who compose it. It is a mystical entity really existing outside the world of particulars, and is therefore best described as a universal: it is on a level with the species and genera which alone have true reality.[1] This is all the more apparent when we appreciate that the universal essence of this society is nothing less than Christ himself, whom the Fathers had commonly characterised as *species*.[2] Christ not only gives being and identity to the *Ecclesia*, but literally is the *Ecclesia* in its mystical or heavenly form: 'all Christians form one body of Christ in Christ.'[3] The *Ecclesia* then, like Plato's Ideal, is a society situated in heaven, having a spiritual personality in the heavenly Christ. As Augustine had explained, this essence is given a terrestrial presentment in the shape of an earthly society, but this earthly society exists only as a reflection of a being in heaven, a person in whom all its human members must seek to be incorporated.[4] The prime purpose of this attribution of a mystical personality,

[1] Alexander de S. Elpidio, *De ecclesiastica potestate*, ii. 1, p. 13, 'Non est multitudo non participans uno, sed quae sunt multa partibus sunt unum toto; quae sunt multa accidentibus sunt unum subiecto; quae sunt multa numero sunt unum specie; et quae sunt multa specie sunt unum genere . . . multitudo credentium est anima una et cor unum in Deo [*Acts*, iv. 32] . . . sancta Ecclesia est una sicut unum corpus ex multis membris et sicut unum totum ex multis partibus'; similarly Alvarus Pelagius, *De planctu Ecclesiae*, ch. 63, pp. 200–1, 203; *Collirium*, p. 505, 'Nam Ecclesia genus est, imperium vel regnum species de genere praedicto, ut Ecclesia contineat imperium sicut genus speciem'.

[2] This is to be found in Peter Lombard, *Sententiae*, I. xxxi. 2 §19, which cites Augustine and Hilary as its sources. Augustine, *De Trinitate*, vi. 10 (*PL*, xlii. 931), had used the term to describe the undying nature of Christ: see L. Sweeney, 'Lombard, Augustine and Infinity', *Manuscripta*, ii (1958), pp. 24–40.

[3] E.g. Anselm, *Meditationes*, i. 6 (*PL*, clviii. 714). For Augustine see now S. J. Grabowski, *The Church: An Introduction to the Theology of Saint Augustine* (St. Louis, 1957), especially pp. 6–19.

[4] Augustine, *De civitate Dei*, xxii. 18 (*PL*, xli. 779), 'Ecce qui est vir perfectus, caput et corpus, quod constat omnibus membris'; and note also his use here of *Ephes.*, iv. 13–16, 'occurramus omnes . . . in virum perfectum . . . qui est caput Christus ex quo totum corpus *compactum* et connexum'. Cf. *Sermo* i. 1 (*PL*, xxxix. 1943); *Enarrationes in Psalmos*, x. 7 (*PL*, xxxvi. 135); xc. 1 (*PL*, xxxvii. 1150); also xliii. 1 (*PL*, xxxvi. 476), 'Esurit Ecclesia, esurit corpus Christi, et homo ille ubique diffusus, cuius caput sursum est, membra deorsum'; cxxii. 2 (*PL*, xxxvii. 1630), 'Quis unus homo diffusus est usque ad fines terrae?' Similarly Innocent III, *De sacro altaris mysterio*, iv. 44 (*PL*, ccxvii. 886), 'Et sicut unum corpus, una persona, Christus cum suis membris'.

identified with Christ, to the Universal Church is to denote the function for which the Christian community is created. It emphasises the prevailing belief that the purpose of a political society is to pursue the good, an ideally right way of life. The mysterious essence of the society is, again like the Platonic *polis*, a divine pattern of existence: Christ is *via* as well as *veritas*. The human community must necessarily mirror the essential way of life: it exists to bring men into contact with true reality and so enables them to attain the supreme good. Only by doing this, as Augustine had emphasised, does it become a true *respublica*. Understood *simpliciter*, the *Ecclesia* is more correctly defined as a universal mode of right living rather than as the actually existing community of mortals which endeavours to follow it. Correspondingly, as we shall see, the supreme function of the ruler, representing the *Ecclesia*, is to give practical effect to this way of life by translating the divine pattern into the material form of positive law. To act as the *Ecclesia* or as *vicarius Christi* means above all that the pope shall be a universal legislator, abstracting the principles of divine righteousness and remitting them in the form of coercive measures required to make the *Ecclesia* a reality upon earth.

From all this the society emerges as the *instrumentum Christi*, the earthly image cloaking the divinity, by which man and God are brought together. The *Ecclesia* as an institution is the structure in which the Christian essence of goodness assumes a visible nature, and it is this intricate theological doctrine which the publicists endeavour to convey by their repeated references to the community as the mystical body of Christ: 'Ecclesia quae corpus Christi mysticum est'.[1] The terminology is basically Pauline: St. Paul had laid particular stress upon the incorporation of all the faithful into a

[1] Augustinus Triumphus, *Summa*, xxv. 1, p. 150; also i. 6, pp. 9–10; vi. 5 ad 3, p. 61; *De potestate collegii*, p. 504, 'Cum igitur papa sit caput in toto corpore mystico quod est Ecclesia'. Similarly Alvarus Pelagius, *De planctu Ecclesiae*, ch. 37, p. 48, 'in mundo mystico, id est in congregatione hominum et maxime fidelium', 'in mundo mystico qui est universalis Ecclesia'; also ch. 19, p. 33; ch. 24, p. 33; ch. 31, p. 35; ch. 37, p. 57; ch. 38, p. 58; ch. 54, p. 139; ch. 67, p. 238; Alexander de S. Elpidio, *De ecclesiastica potestate*, i. 10, p. 12; ii. 1, p. 13; ii. 4, p. 18; ii. 5, pp. 19–20; Tholemy of Lucca, *De regimine principum*, iii. 10, p. 259; *Determinatio compendiosa*, ch. 15, p. 33.

unity with Christ, and this idea was considerably developed in Patristic writings, where the sacraments were frequently held to symbolise the organic unity between head and members of the *Ecclesia*.[1] Accepted at first as the Eucharist itself, the term *corpus Christi mysticum* was not however directly applied to the *Ecclesia* before the twelfth century. But in response to those, like Berengar of Tours, who sought to spiritualise and mystify the sacraments, it became necessary to emphasise the real presence of Christ in the Eucharist. The sacraments now became known as the *corpus Christi verum*,[2] whilst the expression *corpus mysticum* was transferred after about 1150 to the *Ecclesia* itself and eventually received official approbation from Boniface VIII.[3] By this it was intended to show not only the unified nature of the *Ecclesia* but equally the fact of its more important non-material existence, the idea of it as a body with an essence or personality of its own, which transcended that of its members. And when this is put into legal phraseology, the *Ecclesia* is immediately recognisable as a corporation.[4] By the Roman law theory of corporations a corporate group of individuals becomes a single person for legal purposes, and the publicists were able to make full use of all the Roman law expressions for a corporation to apply to the *Ecclesia*. As the canonist Johannes Andreae explained, 'Ista vero nomina, universitas, communitas, collegium, corpus,

[1] E.g. Augustine, *In Ioannis evangelium tractatus*, xxvi. 15 (*PL*, xxxv. 1614), 'Hunc itaque cibum et potum societatem [Christus] vult intelligi corporis et membrorum suorum quod est sancta Ecclesia'; and see also *Sermo* ccxxvii (*PL*, xxxviii. 1100), which follows Cyprian, *Ep.* lxiii. 13 (*PL*, iv. 383–4). For further references Grabowski, *op. cit.*, pp. 184–7; and G. Lecordier, *La doctrine de Saint Augustine sur l'eucharistie* (Paris, 1930), p. 73.

[2] E.g. Augustinus Triumphus, *Summa*, i. 1, p. 2; i. 6, p. 9; iv. 2, p. 41. On the development of the idea of the true and mystical bodies of Christ see H. de Lubac, *Corpus mysticum: l'eucharistie et l'église au moyen âge* (Paris, 1944); E. Mersch, *Le corps mystique du Christ* (Paris, 1936); M. Roberti, 'Il *corpus mysticum* di S. Paolo nella storia della persona giuridica', *Studi in onore di Enrico Besta* (Milan, 1939), iv. 37–82; A. Ehrhardt, 'Das *Corpus Christi* und die Korporation im spät-röm. Recht', *ZSSR*, *Rom. Abt.*, lxx (1953), pp. 299–347; and now *KTB*, especially pp. 193f.

[3] *Extrav. Comm.*, I. viii. 1, 'unum corpus mysticum cuius caput Christus'.

[4] See further P. Gillet, *La personnalité juridique en droit ecclésiastique* (Malines, 1927). For the corporation theory as an example of realistic philosophical principles see the remarks of M. H. Carré on St. Augustine's realism, *Realists and Nominalists* (London, 1946), pp. 32–8.

societas, sunt quasi unum significantia'.[1] To describe the society as the mystical body of Christ is simply an alternative way of saying that it forms a single corporate entity, one being or person: 'universitas est quoddam individuum'.[2] This combination of Roman law and Pauline teaching had already been adopted by Augustine. The juridical person of the Roman *respublica* becomes the mystical person of the Christian society, existing on a heavenly, spiritual level and to be identified with Christ.[3] On this authority the acceptance of the notion was secure for the rest of the Middle Ages. There was a legal fiction which distinguished the body taken as a single corporate whole from the members individually, and gave it the status of a *persona iuridica* in the public law of the society. Its basis was a unity of purpose, the actual individuals comprising the corporation playing only a secondary role to the body itself. The idea appears in Gratian, and was subsequently elaborated by Innocent IV, for whom the *Ecclesia* becomes a *persona ficta*, a juristic person.[4] That this personality is described as a fictitious one in no way detracts from its importance. As Augustine had said, it is the fiction which is the mark of truth,[5] and when the *figura veritatis* was Christ himself any denial of the true reality of mystical persons was virtu-

[1] Cited Gillet, *op. cit.*, p. 151. Cf. Augustinus Triumphus, *Summa*, xxvii. 7, p. 165; xl. 3 ad 1, p. 232. Note also Innocent IV, *Comm. ad Decret.*, V. xxxi. 14, sv. *unum corpus*, 'societas intellectualis et iuris'; *ad* V. xxxix. 53, sv. *consiliarios*, 'universitas sicut est capitulum, populus, gens et huiusmodi, haec nomina sunt iuris et non personarum'.

[2] Roffredus, *Quaestiones Sabbathinae*, cited Gillet, *op. cit.*, p. 102; Thomas Aquinas, *Summa theologica*, II. 1. lxxxi. 1, 'Omnes homines qui sunt unius communitatis reputantur quasi unum corpus, et tota communitas unus homo'.

[3] Augustine, *De doctrina Christi*, iii. 31 (*PL*, xxxiv. 82), 'Christi et Ecclesiae una persona nobis intimari'; *In Iob* (*PL*, xxxiv. 855), 'una persona Ecclesiae'; *In Ps. LXI* (*PL*, xxxvi. 730), 'Sed debemus intelligere personam nostram, personam Ecclesiae nostrae, personam corporis Christi'.

[4] Innocent IV, *Comm. ad Decret.*, II. xx. 57, 'cum collegium in causa universitatis fingatur una persona'. See also W. Ullmann, 'The Delictal Responsibility of Medieval Corporations', *Law Quarterly Review*, lxiv (1948), pp. 77–96, especially pp. 83–6, 93. For a discussion of the essentially realist character of Innocent's corporation theory see I. T. Eschmann, 'Studies on the Notion of Society in Thomas Aquinas', *Mediaeval Studies*, viii (1946), pp. 1–42 at pp. 33–6.

[5] Augustine, *De quaestionibus evangelistarum*, ii. 51 (*PL*, xxxv. 1362), and cited Thomas Aquinas, *Summa theologica*, III. lv. 4 ad 1, 'non omne quod fingimus, mendacium est . . . cum autem fictio nostra refertur in aliquam significationem, non est mendacium sed aliqua figura veritatis'. See further *KTB*, p. 306.

ally impossible. In conformity with this Aquinas takes the *persona mystica* which Augustine had applied to Christ and uses it to define the *Ecclesia*.[1] The mystical person is synonymous with the legal fictitious person which the *corpus mysticum* of the *Ecclesia* forms, an idea fully understandable only in terms of a thoroughly Christian and realistic approach to life. The juridical reality of the lawyer corresponds to the metaphysical reality of the philosopher and the divine reality of the theologian.

By this means the individual's relationship to society is transposed on to the higher plane of man's relationship to God, and it is clearly inconceivable to this way of thinking that the individual should be in a position to claim rights and privileges of his own at the expense of society itself. Every individual part must be totally subject to the whole into which it is absorbed and which alone really exists: 'Omne autem quod est per participationem subditur ei quod est per essentiam universaliter'.[2] The individual cannot bear comparison with the whole. Individuals have an ephemeral existence and must pass away, but the *Ecclesia* never dies. No change in its membership can affect its immutability.[3] It is a world removed, composed of yet remaining apart from its innumerable components. The denial of the individual in favour of the corporate reality of society is a commonplace of medieval thought, and is still frequently encountered in the fourteenth century, although the monastic fervour which nurtured it was ebbing away. But at every step in hierocratic writings we still meet the assumption that it is only in and through society that it is possible to achieve the good life. There can be no distinction between the good man and the good citizen, between the *fidelis* and the *civis*. True happiness therefore rests in

[1] Thomas Aquinas, *Summa theologica*, III. xlviii. 2 ad 1, 'caput et membra sunt quasi una persona mystica'. It may also be remarked that there are numerous Biblical allusions to Israel as a person, e.g. *Ps.*, cxxix. 8; *Hosea*, xi. 1, and cf. *Matthew*, ii. 15, which applies this to Christ.

[2] Tholemy of Lucca, *De regimine principum*, iii. 9, p. 258.

[3] Augustinus Triumphus, *Summa*, xxi. 4, p. 129; *De potestate collegii*, p. 503; Aegidius Romanus, *De renuntiatione papae*, x. 5, p. 26; xi, p. 34; Peter de la Palu, *De causa immediata ecclesiasticae potestatis*, ch. 6, fo. 69v. This stems from Aristotle, *Politics*, iii. 3, and from the Roman law theory that the *populus* (or *imperium*) cannot die; it was used by Augustine, *De civitate Dei*, v. 16 (*PL*, xli. 160), 'illa civitas sempiterna est', and cited Gratian, C. 24 q. 1 c. 33. See further Gillet, *La personnalité juridique*, pp. 79–99, 108–15; *KTB*, pp. 291–305.

service to the community. The point is very well illustrated in Clement VI's letter of approval to Charles IV which we mentioned earlier. After reciting a positively formidable list of imperial duties, the pope urges Charles to spare no effort to fulfil them. It is the empire itself which must be the supreme object of a man's desires; power must be wielded for the public, not private, good; and all things must be done for charity, the *amor communitatis*, not for personal glory. 'Et quando talis est imperator', the pope concludes, 'tunc potest vere dici felix'.[1] This principle of devotion to duty and so to the community constantly reappears in the literature of the period, and takes many and various forms of expression. It comes out most strongly in the widespread belief that a man must be willing to die for the sake of society. Although Augustinus Triumphus acknowledges that all men have a natural urge to preserve themselves, this natural tendency must be subdued when the faith and well-being of the Christian community are imperilled, and they must be ready to face death on its behalf. What is more, he implies that the good Christian should be prepared to imperil even his moral or spiritual welfare for this cause.

> Universaliter homo tenetur vitam suam conservare tam naturalem quam moralem quantum potest. Sed in casu fidei vel pro vitando maiori periculo seu pro utilitate reipublicae tenetur se mortis periculo exponere.[2]

But perhaps the classic example of this is that to be found with the Dominican preacher Remigio de Girolami. In his tract on the supremacy of the common good, Remigio emphasises that the whole is more real than any part. It is the whole which really exists, whereas the part has no more than a potential existence: in other words the individual may only obtain his full stature through the society to which he belongs.[3] From this point Remigio passes

[1] *MGH, Const.*, VIII n. 100 pp. 159–61. This incorporates Augustine's views in *De civitate Dei*, v. 24 (*PL*, xli. 170–1).

[2] Augustinus Triumphus, *Summa*, vi. 8 ad 3, p. 63.

[3] R. Egenter, 'Gemeinnutz vor Eigennutz: Die soziale Leitidee im *Tractatus de bono communi* des Fr. Remigius von Florenz (*1319)', *Scholastik*, ix (1934), 79–92 at p. 82. For this see also G. de Lagarde, 'Individualisme et corporatisme au moyen âge', *Recueil de travaux d'histoire et de philologie, 2e série*, xliv (1937); *KTB*, pp. 478–80.

easily to one at which he advocates that a citizen must sacrifice his whole being, even his immortal soul, for the preservation of the universal society.[1] Man is indeed the image of God, but the *civitas* is a more perfect image of God than man; and although the *civitas* is a *minor mundus*, there is a still more perfect image, the whole world itself. Consequently a man is bound to love the universal whole more than himself: he must love it like God himself to the extent of dying for it.[2] Remigio, it is true, does not always go to the extreme lengths with which he is sometimes credited. He had been a pupil of Aquinas, and Thomas' pupils did not usually go to extremes. He did not believe that God would in the end really allow a man to lose his soul for so righteous a cause; he was even prepared to permit the individual a potentially worthwhile existence apart from society; and in general he seems to have been much more concerned with his own *civitas* of Florence than with the larger whole of which he declared it to be part. But his remarks are significant in that they portray the ancestry of his views. In particular we may note his declaration that the universal society is the *imago Dei* and must be loved like God himself. What Remigio was seeking to express was the hierocratic conception of society as the *corpus Christi*, that is, as the earthly image or projection of God himself. God and his Church are in essence one and the same thing, or, more precisely, the *Ecclesia* has a spiritual personality which is Christ. Concern for the well-being of society thus becomes the perfect expression of Christian charity, since it is the love of Christ himself. 'Amor patriae', says Tholemy of Lucca, 'in radice charitatis fundatur'.[3] Love of the fatherland, we might say, becomes love of the Father. And this is all the more strongly apparent when it is appreciated that the term *patria* does not in this connection relate to any local kingdom, but to the universal society which is a reflection of heaven on earth.[4] Defence of the Christian community against

[1] Egenter, *art. cit.*, pp. 89f. [2] Egenter, *art. cit.*, p. 84.

[3] Tholemy of Lucca, *De regimine principum*, iii. 4, p. 253.

[4] This derives from Augustine, *De civitate Dei*, v. 16 (*PL*, xli. 160), and from Roman law: *Inst.*, I. xxv. *proem.*, states that those who die in defence of the empire live for ever in glory. Aquinas also maintains that the good citizen should be ready to die for the Christian society: *Summa theologica*, I. lx. 5, 'Est enim virtuosi civis ut se exponat mortis periculo pro totius reipublicae con-

its enemies to the point of death, or martyrdom, is not only the supreme political obligation but equally a religious necessity, an idea closely related to and stimulated by the crusading movement, and then slowly transferred to the national kingdom as an expression of patriotic sentiment.[1]

The philosophical, theological and legal principles on which the idea of the *Ecclesia* rested are in this way seen to have a direct political importance, and this partly explains the zeal with which the scholastics plunged into their interminable wrangles. Up to the period under discussion the whole of medieval life was inevitably dominated by the unifying reality of the *Ecclesia*, within which numerous institutions, the papacy, the regional churches, the monastic and religious orders, the schools, towns, guilds and manors, and many other corporate personalities emphasise the general confidence in realistic conceptions. The pope, says Augustinus Triumphus, is *rector totius collegii*,[2] the head of a comprehensive political whole which embraces all men and all lesser corporate institutions. The *Ecclesia* is both a single corporation itself and the greatest of a hierarchy of corporations stretching from the whole world down to the lowest political unit, the village or manor, by way of the kingdom, the province and the city. Each of these communities is at the same time as much a civil as an ecclesiastical corporation: the universal church is the universal empire, the kingdom is equally an episcopal province, the city is a bishopric, and the village is a parish.

Ordines episcoporum sunt plures . . . propter plures communitates et administrationes quibus praesunt. Distinguuntur enim per Philoso-

servatione', and elsewhere equates this *patria* with Heaven, II. II. lxxxiii. 11; II. II. ci. 1–3; III. viii. 3. Cf. Innocent III, *De quadripartita specie nuptiarum* (*PL*, ccxvii. 941), '. . . secundum statum triumphantis Ecclesiae quem habet in patria'.

[1] On the whole subject see now *KTB*, pp. 232–64, and here further literature and references.

[2] Augustinus Triumphus, *Summa*, ii. 1, p. 18; viii. 2, p. 69; viii. 3, p. 70; ix. 3 ad 2, p. 74; x. 1, p. 77, 'papa est rector totius Ecclesiae'; cf. v. 6, p. 54, 'collegium universalis Ecclesiae'. Similarly Hervaeus Natalis, *De potestate papae*, fo. 149v, 'Ecce ipse [Christus] expresse dicit Petrum esse institutum caput totius collegii; caput autem dicitur secundum influentiam ad membra; influentia autem non potest intelligi nisi per derivationem potestatis, quae potestas aliorum a potestate Petri derivatur'.

phum quinque communitates, quarum prima est communitas vici, quae resultat ex pluribus domibus. Alia est communitas civitatis, quae constituitur ex pluribus vicis... Tertia est communitas provinciae, quae insurgit ex pluribus civitatibus. Quarta est communitas regni, quae resultat ex pluribus provinciis. Quinta est communitas totius orbis, quae constituitur ex *omnibus* regnis. In prima ergo communitate praesunt presbyteri parochiales, quorum quilibet regit unum vicum et unam parochiam. In secunda vero praesunt episcopi... In tertia vero communitate praesunt archiepiscopi vel metropolitani. In quarta praesunt patriarchae et primates. Sed in quinta communitate praeest summus pontifex quia ... omnes qui sunt in toto orbe sint sub potestate papae.[1]

Thus each lesser community mirrors the corporate nature of the greater whole. There is no divorce of temporal from spiritual, of Church from State, since all such distinctions are lost in the unity of the universal society. Each inferior community is no more than an administrative unit. The kingdom is at the same time a church; the king is subject to his primate as the emperor is to the universal bishop; and each bishop and chapter are strictly analogous to the pope and his college of cardinals.[2] Kings and bishops are integral parts of one and the same body politic, which is itself an integral part of the universal principate. Each lower *societas publica*, whether it is the *civitas* or the community of the realm (*communitas regni*), is bound into the framework of the *Ecclesia*, and has neither right nor ability to exist apart from it.[3] It is not a separate entity subject to a

[1] Augustinus Triumphus, *Summa*, i. 6 ad 1, p. 10. Various versions of this can be found in most of the writers of the time: e.g. Anon., *Disquisitio theologico-iuridica*, ii. 4, p. 1350; Aegidius Romanus, *De renuntiatione papae*, x. 4, p. 25; Alexander de S. Elpidio, *De ecclesiastica potestate*, i. 10, p. 12; Alvarus Pelagius, *De planctu Ecclesiae*, ch. 54, p. 136; Dante, *Monarchia*, i. 3, p. 342; Engelbert of Admont, *De ortu imperii*, ch. 14, p. 763; James of Viterbo, *De regimine christiano*, ii. 5, p. 205; Johannes Branchazolus, *De principio imperatoris et papae*, ii. 1, p. 49; John of Paris, *De potestate regia et papali*, ch. 25, p. 258; Thomas Aquinas, *Comm. in Sent.*, III. xxiv. ii. 3; *De potentia*, v. 6 ad 3; Tholemy of Lucca, *De regimine principum*, ii. 7–8, p. 243. The number of *communitates* ranges between three and six. Although the usual reference here was to Aristotle, the principle may be traced back to Augustine, *De civitate Dei*, xix. 7 (*PL*, xli. 633), 'Post civitatem vel urbem sequitur orbis terrae, in quo tertium gradum ponunt societatis humanae, incipientes a domo atque inde ad urbem, deinde ad orbem progrediendo venientes'.

[2] Augustinus Triumphus, *Summa*, iii. 9 ad 2, p. 37; lxi. 5, p. 325.

[3] Augustinus Triumphus, *Summa*, cv. 3, p. 519.

greater, but simply part of a chain of incomplete corporations which, as one writer puts it, adds up to the figure one of the *Ecclesia*.

Principatus autem catholicus sive politia christiana est quoddam unum numerale, non habens sub se partes subiectas, sed integrales.[1]

Hence, although it is possible to consider each community as a theoretical unit, just as it is possible to divide up the lay and ecclesiastical governors within that unit, any distinctions of this kind can have only a limited application, and must eventually be absorbed into the all-inclusiveness of the universal ecclesiastical corporation.

In many ways then some such term as Christian principality or polity gives a more accurate description of medieval society than such modern notions as Church and State. It is quite erroneous to regard the Church of the hierocrat as a spiritual unity distinct from the political organisation. It is in every respect a civil society, and like any other civil society requires law and government. By its very nature, writes Augustinus Triumphus, it is a jurisdictional structure: 'Ecclesia est nomen iurisdictionis'.[2] That it is a mystical body means that it is a legislative body: 'potestas . . . respectu corporis Christi mystici . . . vocatur potestas iurisdictionis vel administrationis'.[3] The *Ecclesia* is not merely an ethereal substance, but very much an earthly community. It must therefore be governed by men. As Innocent IV pointed out, incorporeal things require

[1] Anon., *De potestate Ecclesiae*, p. 252. The partial nature of each lesser community in the descending derivative hierarchy of corporations could be graphically described by comparing it to a part of the natural body: e.g. Johannes Andreae, *Novella ad Decretales*, I. i. 13, 'Ecclesia universalis est unum Christi corpus . . . cuius caput est Romana ecclesia . . . inferiores ecclesiae sunt *huius capitis membra*, quae sunt vel membra ex capite vel membra ex membris, sicut in corpore humano a brachio manus, a manu digiti, a digitis ungulae, proveniunt'. Using the same idea Nicholas of Cues, *De concordantia catholica*, iii. 1, described each lay ruler or official as having a clerical counterpart who represented the soul in each particular member: the pope is the soul in the brain, the patriarch the soul in the senses, the archbishop the soul in the arm, and so on.

[2] Augustinus Triumphus, *Summa*, iii. 9 *prop.* 1, p. 37.

[3] Augustinus Triumphus, *Summa*, i. 6, p. 9; cf. iv. 1 ad 2, p. 41, 'potestas clavium . . . cum respiciat corpus Christi mysticum importat potestatem iurisdictionis'.

human beings through whom they may act on earth.[1] The mystical person, identifiable with Christ in that the *Ecclesia* is the *corpus Christi*, needs a terrestrial manifestation. There has to be a physical representation of the *persona Ecclesiae*, an earthly Christ. And just as Christ, the real head, represents the *corpus Ecclesiae*, so it is that the pope, as the present head of the society, stands for the *Ecclesia* itself. This had been made perfectly clear by Augustine,[2] and was subsequently repeated by writer after writer. Peter and his successors personify the Christian society: 'in ipso [Petro] omnes intelliguntur tamquam gerente personam totius Ecclesiae'.[3] All power is constituted in the pope *in persona Ecclesiae*, and is derived from him as head to all the other members of the society. The universal is incarnate in the individual. The pope becomes a *minor mundus*, the actualised image of the single and universal administration of all things. The head is a microcosm, in which is reflected the total ordering of the world.[4] Thus the ruler can be described as both head and whole of the community in the same way that Christ is not only the *caput Ecclesiae* but also forms the *corpus Ecclesiae* itself. The pope as vicar of Christ is similarly both head and body of the community, together making up the complete mystical man: 'corpus

[1] Innocent IV, *Comm. ad Decret.*, V. xxxix. 64, sv. *culpabiles*, 'quia capitulum, quod est nomen intellectuale et res incorporalis, nihil facere potest nisi per membra sua'.

[2] Augustine, *Sermo CCXCV*, ii. 2 (*PL*, xxxix. 1349), 'Inter hos [discipulos] pene ubique *solus* Petrus totius Ecclesiae meruit gestare personam. Propter ipsam personam quam totius Ecclesiae *solus* gestabat audire meruit 'Tibi dabo claves regni coelorum'. Has enim claves non homo unus sed unitas accepit Ecclesiae. Hinc ergo Petri excellentia praedicatur, quia ipsius universitatis et unitatis Ecclesiae figuram gessit. . .'. For numerous examples of this see S. J. Grabowski, 'Saint Augustine and the Primacy of the Roman Bishops', *Traditio*, iv (1946), pp. 89–113 especially pp. 97–9; and now *The Church*, pp. 129 f.

[3] Peter Olivi, *De renuntiatione papae*, p. 350; Innocent IV, *Comm. ad Decret.*, V. xxxix. 49, 'Hoc enim privilegium Christus Petro in persona Ecclesiae concesserit'; John XXII, Raynaldus, xxiv. 324, 'Constat enim quod a Christo Petro, et in persona Petri Ecclesiae, potestas coactiva concessa vel saltem promissa extitit'. Cf. Innocent III, *De sacro altaris mysterio*, i. 30 (*PL*, ccxvii. 786), 'Ille cuius pontifex iste gerit personam, scilicet Christus. . .'.

[4] Aegidius Romanus, *De ecclesiastica potestate*, iii. 4, p. 166; Francis de Meyronnes, *De principatu temporali*, ch. 7, p. 71; ch. 8, p. 73; Thomas Aquinas, *De regimine principum*, i. 12, p. 235. Again there is an Augustinian basis: see Chroust, *The Corporate Idea*, p. 426.

Christi mysticum ibi est ubi est caput, scilicet papa'.[1] This idea can perhaps only be satisfactorily presented in pictorial form, and indeed medieval artists were constantly drawing diagrams of the *Ecclesia* in microcosmic form. The microcosm was sometimes depicted as a head,[2] sometimes as both head and body forming a complete man. This man was usually Christ himself, but it was quite common to describe him as Adam, who had been the whole human race in one man,[3] whilst the publicist Opicinus de Canistris endeavoured to sum up the whole complex notion by labelling his microcosm 'papa'.[4]

Equally fertile were the papalists' discussions on the corporate nature of the ruler himself. As they pointed out, when the whole community is in its corporate nature represented by one man, that one man becomes himself a corporation, and there followed a direct transference to the papacy of the Roman law theory of the corporation sole: 'papa solus totius Ecclesiae gestat personam'.[5] In his solitude the pope epitomises the oneness of the *universitas fidelium*, and contains all that is necessary for the functioning of the universal body. Remonstrating with Dante, the Dominican Guido Vernani emphasises that mankind needs no other power than that of the pope for the conduct of life: 'non esset necessaria in hominibus potestas alia'.[6] The Christian faith, and its correlated thesis, the right government of the faithful, are concentrated in the head. The *Ecclesia* conceived of in terms of the pope alone lacks nothing es-

[1] Alvarus Pelagius, *Collyrium*, p. 506.

[2] J. Seznec, *The Survival of the Pagan Gods* (New York, 1953), pp. 64f.; F. Saxl, 'Macrocosm and Microcosm in Medieval Pictures', *Lectures* (London, 1957), i. 58–72.

[3] Cf. Thomas Aquinas, *Summa theologica*, III. 1. lxxxi. 1, 'omnes homines qui nascuntur ex Adam possunt considerari ut unus homo'. Dante, *Monarchia*, ii. 13, p. 363, uses the same idea in favour of the emperor.

[4] R. Salomon, *Opicinus de Canistris. Weltbild und Bekentnisse eines Avignonesischen Klerikers des 14. Jahrhunderts* (London, 1936), pl. xx. It is interesting to note that Opicinus specialised in producing maps of Christendom (Europe) drawn in the figure of a man.

[5] For examples see below p. 469. On the Roman origins see F. Schultz, *Classical Roman Law* (Oxford, 1951), pp. 90f.; and in general F. W. Maitland, 'The Corporation Sole' and 'The Crown as Corporation', *Selected Essays* (Cambridge, 1936), pp. 73–127.

[6] Guido Vernani, *De reprobatione Monarchiae*, ch. 1, p. 130.

sential, and for all practical purposes he may be regarded as acting as and on behalf of the whole Christian society. The *Ecclesia*, as Augustinus Triumphus says, can be either the whole body of the faithful or the pope alone: 'per Ecclesiam potest intelligi praelatus vel ipsa congregatio fidelium'; and somewhat later the Clerk in the *Somnium viridarii* is to be found describing the pope as 'papa qui est Ecclesia vel caput Ecclesiae'.[1] Most of the writers of the period were in fact eager to impress upon their readers that the actions of the ruler were the actions of the whole community, and that in his capacity as head the pope might simply style himself as the *Ecclesia*. Augustinus Triumphus' influential predecessor in the Augustinian order, Aegidius Romanus, gives an excellent example of this. The pope, he affirms, is the *dominus Ecclesiae*, and for this reason the power of the keys which is possessed by the whole *congregatio fidelium* is present only in the ruler. Hence what the society has, the pope has; and what the pope does is what the corporate body of Christians can be said to do.[2] According to Aquinas it is a matter of general principle that 'quod princeps civitatis facit, dicitur civitas facere', and he goes on to explain that the prelate, the supreme part of the community, adopts the *nomen* of the *Ecclesia* as a mark of rulership.[3] Similar expressions are frequently found with other

[1] Augustinus Triumphus, *Summa*, vii. 3 ad 1, p. 66; Anon., *Somnium viridarii*, i. 147, p. 115. Cf. a similar passage in Thomas Aquinas, *Summa theologica*, III. *suppl.* xcv. 3 ad 4, referring to Christ.

[2] Aegidius Romanus, *De ecclesiastica potestate*, ii. 12, p. 109, 'bene dictum est quod Ecclesia habet claves regni coelorum, et si habet haec Ecclesia, habet haec summus pontifex, qui adeptus est apicem totius Ecclesiae. Immo quod summus pontifex facit, dicitur Ecclesia facere, quia in eo reservatur auctoritas totius Ecclesiae'.

[3] Thomas Aquinas, *Comm. ad Rom.*, v. 3; *Comm. in Cant. Cantic.*, ch. 1, 'Ecclesia autem dupliciter potest accipi. Primo pro tota congregatione fidelium, secundo pro ipsis praelatis, quia quando aliquod *nomen* convenit omni congregationi, tale *nomen* dicitur de parte superiori totius . . . quia *nomen Ecclesiae* dicitur de tota congregatione fidelium, praelati qui supremum gradum in Ecclesia tenent dicuntur Ecclesia'. The idea that the head is representative of the essence or soul of the body, the source of its capacities, and therefore bears its name, can be traced back to Isidore, *Etymologiae*, XI. i. 25 (*PL*, lxxxii. 400), 'Prima pars corporis caput, datumque illi hoc *nomen*, eo quod sensus omnes et nervi inde initium capiant, atque ex eo omnis vigendi causa oriatur. Ibi enim omnes sensus apparent. Unde ipsius animae, quae consulit corpori, quodammodo *personam* gerit'.

publicists, and it is perhaps surprising that contemporary writers felt that the point needed so much elaboration. By this time we might well have expected them to take the *papa–Ecclesia* identification for granted. For many years canon law decrees had regularly referred to the *Ecclesia* when they meant the pope himself, and it was Gratian's *Decretum* which had asserted the principle that the bishop was in the church, and the church was in the bishop, an idea which the glossators had immediately applied to the pope and the Universal Church.[1] All the members are one with the head in the *corpus Ecclesiae*, and although we shall see that this could be reinterpreted to suggest that all the members contributed to the power of the head, this was the exact reverse of what the papalists were trying to say. For them the emphasis is always upon the single self-sufficient head to which the society may ultimately be reduced. They insist that the *reductio ad unum* should be maintained without exception, since it is the head alone which is the source of power in society. Some of them exercised considerable ingenuity in attempting to bring this point home. Henry of Cremona, for example, uses the papal tiara as symbolic of the society in general, in much the same way that the lay writers were even then referring to the king as the Crown, and therefore the representative of his kingdom.[2] From the pointed apex of this structure, says Henry, there extends outwards and downwards on all sides the ranks and offices of those who govern and administer to the needs of the universal society spread out beneath them. Perhaps it is better to allow Henry's words to speak for themselves:

[1] Gratian, C. 7 q. 1 c. 9, 'Scire debes episcopum in ecclesia esse, et ecclesiam in episcopo, et si quis cum episcopo non sit, in ecclesia non esse'. This derives from Cyprian, *Ep.*, lxvi. 8. For the Decretists' identification of pope and society see B. Tierney, *Foundations of the Conciliar Theory* (Cambridge, 1955), pp. 34–5; and for its application to lay rulers *KTB*, especially pp. 439–40.

[2] The insignia of the ruler symbolises his embodiment of the mystical personality of the community, by which he bears the *nomen* of that person, Christ, and the community itself: cf. Innocent III's description of the papal mitre as the *nomen Christi*, *De sacro altaris mysterio*, i. 44 (*PL*, ccxvii. 790); also *Sermones de tempore*, xxiii (*PL*, ccxvii. 417), 'Unde Petrus . . . coram regibus et principibus nomen Christi portavit, constanter affirmans quo[d] magis oportet Deo quam hominibus obedire [*Acts*, v. 29]'. Note also Peter's words in *Acts*, iv. 12, 'Nec est aliud *nomen sub coelo* in quo oporteat nos salvos fieri'; cf. *Phil.*, ii. 9–10.

Nam sunt diversae ordines et diversae potestates ecclesiasticae et saeculares, et ultimo est summus pontifex *in quo* omnes potestates aggregantur et ad quem tamquam in simplicissimum terminantur, et ad quod designandum summus pontifex in coronatione sua mitram seu coronam portat in capite, quae a base seu inferiori parte lata incipit et terminatur in simplici cornu, quia latitudo et diversitas omnium ordinum et potestatum in persona ipsius summi pontificis terminantur et ad eum reducuntur.[1]

This beautiful imagery can be paralleled by the idea of the pope as the source from which all the rivers of power and faith flow into the society. He is, writes Augustinus Triumphus, the 'fons et origo ad quem omnia reducuntur', the fount from which the life-giving waters pour out to irrigate the Universal Church.[2] None of the other members have any power other than that which is initially in the pope, and is subsequently derived in them from him. There is nothing that can be done on earth that he himself cannot do.[3] No one, in the view of the papalists, could deny that the *Ecclesia* existed essentially in Christ, and so therefore it was impossible to deny that the society similarly existed in his vicar. The power of the pope is the essence of the *Ecclesia* and is identifiable with it, bearing all the characteristics of a universal. It is perpetual, and incorruptible, and common to all the society.

[1] Henry of Cremona, *Non ponant laici*, pp. 474–5.

[2] Augustinus Triumphus, *Summa*, xxii. 3, p. 131. See also the dedication to John XXII, 'ut sicut talis potentia a vobis tamquam a fonte *derivatur in omnes* per universalem influentiam', and note the use of the passive voice to imply that it is the pope himself who causes this derivation to take place. Also Lambertus Guerrici, *Liber de commendatione*, ch. 5, p. 161, 'de cuiusque fontis rivulis universalis *irrigatur* Ecclesia'; cf. Innocent III, *Reg.*, II. ccviii (*PL*, ccxiv. 758).

[3] Augustinus Triumphus, *Summa*, i. 2, p. 4, 'Sicut ergo omnia entia causantur et *derivantur* ab uno ente, et sicut omnes substantiae *derivantur* ab una substantia, ita omnis principatus *derivatur* causaliter ab uno principe . . . Propter quod sicut omnes *rivuli derivantur* a fonte, sic omnis potestas derivatur a fonte primo'. Note the close connection between *rivuli* and *de-rivare*. Similarly Innocent III, *Reg.*, VII. i (*PL*, ccxv. 279), 'Petrum caput Ecclesiae . . . qui . . . in membra diffunderet ut nihil sibi poenitus deperiret, quoniam in capite viget sensuum plenitudo, ad membra vero pars eorum aliqua *derivatur*'; Anon., *Disquisitio theologico-iuridica*, ch. 7, p. 1345, 'idcirco a potestate vicarii Christi omnis potestas in terris oritur'; also Aegidius Romanus, *De ecclesiastica potestate*, iii. 9, p. 193, 'totum posse quod est in Ecclesia reservatur in summo pontifice'.

Dicemus enim quod papalis potestas est perpetua et incorruptibilis eo quod Ecclesia ipsa, cuius papa *sponsus* existit, mori non potest. Propter quod sicut Ecclesia est perpetua, sic potestas papae est perpetua.[1]

The pope thus becomes a common person, the common father of all Christians whose directives are universally binding. His law is the common law of the society;[2] his city, Rome, is the common fatherland of all believers; and his seat, the Roman church, is the common court of Christendom.[3] He who governs from Rome is the ruler of the world, the *dominus urbis et orbis*.

When the ruler takes on the personality and identity of the society, the superiority of that society over its members may then be orientated in favour of the head himself. In his discussion of the subject of monarchy, we find Guido Vernani expressly stating that the ideal relationship of whole to parts must also be applied to the ruler: 'rex . . . comparatur ad omnes subditos sicut totum comparatur ad partes',[4] and the justification for this is the common identity of ruler and society with Christ. Once it is agreed that union with Christ is the end for which man exists, and that this is something to be gained only by incorporation into the society

[1] Augustinus Triumphus, *De potestate collegii*, p. 503; Alvarus Pelagius, *De planctu Ecclesiae*, ch. 44, p. 77, 'Ad haec potestas papalis dignissima et utilissima est omnium potestatum quia composita et media et communis'; cf. Tholemy of Lucca, *De regimine principum*, ii. 7, p. 247, 'Natura autem status regalis quamdam habet universalitatem, eo quod communis est populo sibi subiecto'.

[2] Augustinus Triumphus, *Summa*, xxii. 4, p. 132, 'dominus communis omnium'; xxxv. 4 ad 2, p. 208, 'summus pontifex est pastor communis totius Ecclesiae'. Throughout the *Summa* canon law is regularly described as common law: cf. Peter Olivi, *Quaestio de infallibilitate*, p. 331, 'quod tota Ecclesia universalis unum generalem [rectorem] haberet qui communibus statutis et decretis ordinandis intenderet'; Aegidius Romanus, *De ecclesiastica potestate*, iii. 2, p. 152, 'Sicut ergo censendum est de Deo prout secundum legem communem gubernat totum mundum, sic etiam censendum est de vicario Dei prout secundum legem communem totam Ecclesiam gubernat et *inebriat* et rigat'.

[3] Benedict XII, Baluze, iii. 483, 'Olim nonnulli Romani pontifices, praedecessores nostri, attendentes et provida circumspectione pensantes quod ad Romanam curiam, quae communis patria existere noscitur, et ad quam cuncti fideles de universis mundi partibus possunt recurrere, securus haberi debet accessus'; cf. Guilielmus Durantis, *Speculum iuris*, ii. 397, 'unde Roma, quia communis patria est, convenitur cuilibet'. The idea of Rome as the *communis patria* goes back to Cicero and the Roman jurists: Ullmann, *The Growth of Papal Government*, p. 6 n. 1.

[4] Guido Vernani, *De reprobatione Monarchiae*, ch. 1, p. 128.

which is his body, then it may equally well be established that this end is obtainable only by means of the head who is the common bond between Christ and his Church. The good life should be sought not only in and through society, but also in and through the ruler himself, acting *vice Christi* and *loco Ecclesiae*. Or, as Augustinus Triumphus phrases it, it is through the pope that we live, move and have our being as good citizens:

motum directionis et sensum cognitionis papa influit in omnia membra Ecclesiae: in ipso enim vivimus, movemur et sumus.[1]

Unity with the head is the only way to achieve salvation, and in political terms this means absolute obedience to the ruler's will. Only by identifying himself with the commands of the head can the subject hope to lead the right way of life. True citizenship and membership of the Christian body, according to Augustinus Triumphus, must logically involve membership of the pope himself, '*in quo* tamquam in capite omnia membra Ecclesiae uniuntur'.[2] And this leads to the even more curious expression that all Christians form the body of the pope. The *caput-corpus* relationship of the society to Christ becomes directly applicable to his vicar. We might very well speak of the *Ecclesia* as the *corpus mysticum papae*. In spite of its esoteric appearance, this theory contains a principle of the highest importance, and demonstrates with striking force how far the hierocratic system went towards submerging the individual in society at large. It means that every individual action calculated to implement the right order in society must be attributed to the head. The subject does not act on his own behalf but for the community which the head represents: thereby he becomes *pars corporis papae*.[3]

[1] Augustinus Triumphus, *Summa*, xxxvi. 6, p. 217; cf. *Acts*, xvii. 28.

[2] Augustinus Triumphus, *Summa*, lix. 1, p. 309; xiv. 2, p. 96, '[Romanus pontifex] *in quo* uniuntur omnia membra Ecclesiae'; cf. Innocent III, *Reg.*, I. cccliii (*PL*, ccxiv. 327), 'ut oves Christi ab uno pastore regantur . . . et ut sub uno capite cuncta membra corpori connectantur'. The relative ease with which Augustinian statements of Christ's headship were transferred to the pope is apparent from the following example: *Enarrationes in Psalmos*, xliv. 3 (*PL*, xxxvi. 495), 'Assumpta est Ecclesia ex genere suo ut caput esset Ecclesiae ipsa caro Verbo coniuncta, et caeteri credentes membra essent illius capitis'.

[3] As applied to papal legates, e.g. Bernardus Parmensis, *Glossa ordinaria ad Decretales*, I. xxx. 9, fo. 110v, sv. *commissam*, 'Illi vero qui mittuntur de latere

There is no cleavage between head and members. We may no longer speak of the activities of this or that person, but only of the action of the whole. All act as one man, and this fictitious being, the irreducible minimum, is portrayed by the ruler. Whatever authorised duty the individual undertakes, its performance is credited to the pope. This point had been elaborated at some length by Innocent III when defining the position of papal legates—significantly they are termed legates of Christ[1]—with whom the idea is most commonly associated, although it has a much broader application to the whole society. The pope, he explains, has a universal duty to act on behalf of all. Admittedly his human condition prevents him from personally exercising all government, or as he phrased it the universality of care, himself. But this is immaterial since the ruler is successfully able to achieve the purpose of government, the implementation of the law of Christ, by acting through others who form the body of the pope. All act as members one of another, that is, as *unum corpus*, a single compact entity. Separate action by many individuals is not indicative of division but, provided of course that all remain in obedience to the head, the distinguishing mark of a society that is at one with itself. Conversely, as Innocent appreciated, this doctrine emphasises that the ruler becomes responsible for all his subjects' affairs: the pope has the care of all the churches daily, he writes, and it is this responsibility for the whole body which underlies the all-pervasive dominance which the head exercises over the community.[2]

domini papae, quia et ipsi pars corporis eius esse intelliguntur. . .'. Aquinas states that the ruler acting in place of God on earth 'reputat singulos, qui suo subsunt regimini, sicut propria membra', *De regimine principum*, i. 12, p. 235: that this is applicable to the pope follows, i. 14, p. 237.

[1] Innocent III, *Reg.*, I. cccxlv (*PL*, ccxiv. 320), 'legatum sedis apostolicae, immo Christi'.

[2] Innocent III, *Reg.*, I. cccxlv (*PL*, ccxiv. 319), 'Quia vero lex id humanae conditionis non patitur, nec possumus in persona propria gerere sollicitudines universas, interdum per fratres nostros, qui sunt membra corporis nostri, ea cogimur exercere quae, si commoditas Ecclesiae sustineret, personaliter libentius impleremus. Cum autem omnes unum corpus simus in Christo, singuli autem alter alterius membra, sic per singulos cum oportet iniunctae nobis sollicitudinis onera dispensamus, ut cum alter alterius onera supportarit, a singulis lex Christi laudabiliter impleatur. Non enim in uniformitate corporis Christi, quod est Ecclesia, sicut in humani corporis constitutione segregatio

It would be most incorrect, from the papal point of view, to suggest that this organic connection between head and members as contained in the conception of the *corpus papae* permitted the subject any participation in papal power. In a letter of the following year, Innocent had been careful to emphasise this. The inclusion of all in one means the supremacy of one over all: unity entails monarchy.[1] The incorporation of all in the head involves no division of sovereignty (which would thereupon cease to be sovereignty). By citizenship the subject acquires duties and obligations, but not rights: he is in the position of a wife whose identity, goods and legal rights are by law absorbed into those of her husband and lost to her personally. This analogy was in fact constantly employed by the publicists, for whom the pope, like Christ, figures as the *sponsus Ecclesiae*.[2] A mystical or spiritual marriage is deemed to exist between ruler and people, who no longer figure as two separate entities, but become essentially one person. There is a complete identification: as Aquinas said, the bridegroom comes to be the bride in

partium generat sectionem, sectio vero mortem vel deformitatem inducit; immo segregatio in obedientiae virtute consistens, unitas est signum . . . per quam multitudinis credentium erat, sicut legitur, cor unum et anima una. Sane licet instantia nostra quotidiana sit omnium ecclesiarum sollicitudo continua [II *Cor.*, xi. 28]'. Very similar passages can however be found in papal letters from the fourth century onwards: e.g. Siricius, *Ep.* i. 7 (*PL*, xiii. 1132), 'quanto nos possumus dolore percelli, cum eorum qui *in nostro* sunt *corpore*, compellimur deplorare, praecipue quibus secundum beatum Paulum instantia quotidiana et sollicitudo omnium ecclesiarum indesinenter incumbit. Quis enim infirmatur et non infirmor? Quis scandalizatur et ego non uror?'; also i, 15 (1146), 'ad Romanam ecclesiam, utpote ad caput tui corporis'; cf. Anastasius I, *Ep. ad Ioan. Ierosol.*, 5 (*PL*, xxi. 631), 'Mihi certe cura non decrit, Evangelii fidem circa meos custodire populos, partesque *corporis mei* per spatia diversa terrarum, quantum possum, literis convenire. . .'.

[1] Innocent III, *Reg.*, II. ccix (*PL*, ccxiv. 763), 'Ex omnibus [ecclesiis] una consistit tamquam ex particularibus generalis; et una praeeminet omnibus quoniam cum unum sit corpus Ecclesiae . . . illa velut caput caeteris membris excellit'.

[2] Innocent III, *Consec. serm.*, iii (*PL*, ccxvii. 662), 'Ergo qui habet sponsam, sponsus est. An non ego sponsus sum? [*John*, iii. 29]'; also Augustinus Triumphus, *De potestate collegii*, p. 503, 'Ecclesia ipsa, cuius sponsus papa existit'; *Summa*, xix. 1 ad 2–3, pp. 117–18; xix. 4 ad 3, p. 120; xxix. 5 ad 1, p. 178; Conrad of Megenberg, *Oeconomica*, III. iii. 1, p. 586, 'sponsus Ecclesiae militantis'. Cf. I *Cor.*, xi. 3; *Ephes.*, v. 23; and note the description of Israel as a wife, *Hosea*, xii. 12. See further *KTB*, pp. 212–23.

that he takes on her personality.[1] Like most of the other political analogies in general use during the thirteenth and fourteenth centuries, this device was susceptible of very different interpretations. But in this context it was designed to demonstrate the completeness of papal government. If the pope acts as and for the whole community, then there is clearly no absolute necessity for the community itself to act at all. The Christian society is always present in its head, and it is for this reason that the pope assumes a universal title, the *nomen* of the whole Christian body politic: as Gregory VII had put it, his is the only name in the world.[2] Alternatively it can be said that the pope is the *Ecclesia* because he is the rock upon which it is founded. Although the 'petra' of the Petrine Commission, as described in *Matthew*, xvi. 18, was more usually taken to refer to Christ himself, a conflation of 'petra' and 'Petrus' was inevitable, and appeared to have been deliberate on the part of Christ himself. Thus the rock becomes many things, which are all essentially one and the same thing: it is Peter, it is Christ, it is the pope, it is the Universal Church.[3] In that the same substance of power and personality is common to all, Christ, Peter, pope and *Ecclesia* may be indiscriminately identified with each other, and this leads contemporary writers to make what is at first sight the startling announcement that even the Christian religion takes its name from the pope, since he is the one who has founded it.

[1] Thomas Aquinas, *Summa theologica*, III. *suppl.* xcv. 3 ad 3, 'aliquando dicitur Christus sponsa, non est quia vere sit sponsa sed in quantum sibi assumit personam sponsae suae, scilicet Ecclesiae, quae est ei spiritualiter coniuncta'. This accords with Augustine, *De doctrina Christi*, iii. 31 (*PL*, xxxiv. 82), 'Non haesitemus quando a capite ad corpus, vel a corpore transitur ad caput, et tamen non receditur ab una eademque persona. Una enim persona loquitur dicens, sicut sponso imposuit mihi *mitram*, et sicut sponsam ornavit me ornamento, et tamen quid horum duorum capiti, quid corpori, id est, quid Christo, quid Ecclesiae conveniat, utique intelligendum est'. Cf. *Isaiah*, lxi. 10.

[2] Gregory VII, *Dictatus papae*, c. 11, 'Quod hoc unicum est nomen in mundo' cf. Tertullian, *Adversus Iudaeos*, 7 (*PL*, ii. 611), 'Christi autem regnum et nomen ubique porrigitur...'.

[3] Alvarus Pelagius, *De planctu Ecclesiae*, ch. 55, p. 140, 'Petra erat Christus', and p. 143, 'Petrus autem a petra, petra vero Ecclesia, ergo in Petri nomine figurata est Ecclesia'; Aegidius Romanus, *De ecclesiastica potestate*, ii. 4, p. 51, 'tunc dedit sibi claves Ecclesiae quando dixit 'Tu es Petrus', qui dicitur a petra, id est a Christo, super quem Ecclesia est fundata'. For the Patristic origins of this see Grabowski, 'Saint Augustine', pp. 92–3; *The Church*, pp. 124–8.

Tota religio christiana a papa nominatur, quia nominatur a Christo cuius vicarius ipse existit.[1]

Since the head is the concentrated embodiment of the *Ecclesia*, we may say that there would be no Christian society without him, or at least in the sense that made Alvarus Pelagius describe it as a single totality or oneness.[2]

The identification of the ruler with the society in whose name he acts is one of the most influential conceptions in the history of political thought, and is the basis of the modern theory that the government or its head represents 'the State'—an idea which is still liable to be surrounded with an aura of mysticism in more totalitarian regimes. This is however nothing more than the secularised offspring of the thoroughly Christian belief that the ruler must be equated with the whole congregation of the faithful, both having a common identity in the mystical personality of Christ. This theory is indeed ultimately unexplainable without a clear understanding of its central principle, namely, that the ruler is the human form of God. Again and again the exponents of the papal-hierocratic ideal were forced back to an assumption of the pope's identity with the divinity as the only means of safeguarding the permanent link between God and man in a society which Augustine had defined as a reflection of heaven. In much the same way that the theological conception of the *corpus verum* required a constant reappearance of Christ in the sacraments, so the political theory of the *corpus mysticum* demanded a personal manifestation of Christ in the pope. No doubt the effort of faith required here was too great for every occasion. It is not to be supposed that even his most ardent supporters were necessarily always aware of the pope *ut Deus*, any more than they were always capable of remembering that the Eucharist was

[1] Augustinus Triumphus, *Summa*, lxxiii. 3 ad 3, p. 373; also Anon., *Compendium maius*, p. 173; Conrad of Megenberg, *De translatione imperii*, p. 332; Hervaeus Natalis, *De potestate papae*, fo. 145v; Peter de la Palu, *De causa immediata ecclesiasticae potestatis*, i. 3, fo. 25v. This contention was rejected by Tholemy of Lucca, *De regimine principum*, iii. 10, p. 259, since he was unable to accept the full identity of pope and Christ implied by it.

[2] Alvarus Pelagius, *De planctu Ecclesiae*, ch. 63, p. 202, 'Primo enim dicitur una unitate *totalitatis*: est enim Ecclesia velut unum totum'. Its constituent parts, he adds, the *singuli fideles* and *particulares ecclesiae*, bear the same relationship to the whole as fingers to a hand.

the body of God: the pope looked like a man, just as the Eucharist looked like bread and wine, and, as Aquinas pointed out, the Christian did not automatically cease to be human just because he was a Christian. But when papal writers came to present the *rationale* of the Augustinian system and to analyse the prevalent ideal of rulership, the divinity of the ruler in a world permeated with Christian realism was inescapable. Even when the constitutional lawyers and the theologians of seventeenth-century England propounded a much more secular version of society as a corporate entity represented by the head, they still found it necessary to rest their theories upon the doctrine of kingship by divine right. Thus we may perhaps sum up the importance of these ideas by suggesting that they represent in an unfamiliar form what a modern writer would immediately recognise as a theory of State-sovereignty. The idea of the 'State' as an immaterial essence expressing itself through the political community is common under one form or another to all ages. Since the State, the body politic, is in this case a Church, the idea is presented in an ecclesiastical guise. The immaterial State-entity is not called the State—although we shall see that the term was beginning to emerge in the thirteenth and fourteenth centuries—but is expressed here as the *Ecclesia*. Roman law had cultivated the idea of the State-essence as an abstract or juridical person, and in the medieval period this mysterious entity, the *Ecclesia*, is similarly personalised and spoken of as a more really existing being, namely, Christ. Christ is the sovereign essence of the society, a proposition conveyed in the repeated assertion that he is the true and undying head of the community.[1] Although therefore it amounts to the same thing in practice, it is not strictly speaking correct to describe the earthly ruler, in this case the pope, as the sovereign. Sovereignty resides in the society itself in its ideal form: the ruler simply represents the *Ecclesia* or Christ. Hence the current formula 'vicarius illius qui etc., etc.' He becomes the human expression of the sovereign entity, and thus acts as the *Ecclesia* or Christ himself—in other

[1] E.g. Augustinus Triumphus, *De potestate collegii*, p. 504, 'Nam caput Ecclesiae *simpliciter* est ipse Christus. . . Sed caput Ecclesiae *simpliciter* est immortale'.

words he embodies the 'State'. Accordingly it is against the *Ecclesia*, the ideal essence of the society, that the capacity of each individual comes to be gauged. Similarly the Petrine Commission as related in *Matthew*, xvi. 18–19, is not simply the institution of a society, but the formation of its corporate personality or essence and the designation of its human representative, in this case Peter: a process which political thinkers would later endeavour to explain away in terms of the Social Compact. Here the State-entity is the 'mea Ecclesia' of verse 18, a sovereignty whose power content is defined in the next verse. It is not the political community itself but the rock or essence upon which the society will draw to gain realisation on earth, an entity now made actual in the person of the papal monarch.

Seen through the eyes of the papalists the arguments in favour of monarchy are overwhelming and irrefutable. If the *Ecclesia* is a society founded upon the tenets of the Christian faith and united by the common bond of that faith amongst its members, there must be some final authority which can determine exactly what constitutes the faith. With Augustinus Triumphus we meet a constant reiteration of the necessity for some agency which shall be the ultimate and only judge in matters of belief. He realised that without a supreme head there was nothing to safeguard the unity of the society. No doubt, he somewhat sardonically remarks, all Christians are bound together by love, but it is faith that cements them into one community.[1] The primacy of faith is unquestioned, but this still leaves the problem of actually determining what this faith shall be. Precise and explicit definitions of faith require *auctoritas*, a binding rule emanating from a single source whose position is such that it cannot be challenged. And for him the claim of the papacy to be able to give the necessary judgements and definitions is unassailable: as a result of the Petrine Commission papal pronouncements rest upon divine revelation and authority. The power of the keys, he points out, was given to Peter and his successors for the express purpose of preventing disunity following upon disputes over matters of belief.

[1] Augustinus Triumphus, *Summa*, xxv. 2 ad 1, p. 151.

Christus solum unum vicarium et unum caput voluit esse in tota Ecclesia ad quem diversa membra recurrerent si forte ab invicem dissentirent.[1]

We must bear in mind that the thirteenth and fourteenth centuries saw sporadic attempts to challenge institutionalised Christianity, its laws and traditions, and to supplant them by direct and personal contact with God. Such attempts meant a constant protest against the papacy as the sole repository of revealed truth. We may instance the revolt of the Fraticelli, whose views on apostolic poverty engaged the attention of most papal writers for a considerable time.[2] By the end of the thirteenth century their ideas had found ready acceptance in Southern France, where traces of the old Catharism still lingered, and had become characterised by the spread of an apocalyptic theology and political message markedly Joachist in inspiration. The leader of the movement, Peter Olivi, was seen by some of his most ardent followers to be Christ himself, or at least inspired by the Holy Ghost. God, it was claimed, could choose any man or any congregation as the direct recipient of the divine wisdom. Such movements as this inevitably tended to destroy the *harmonia universalis*, the orderliness and stability which was the expression of the idea that God had revealed himself once and left one institution as the guardian of that revelation on earth. The formula for so many hierocratic treatises in this period thus becomes the need for a *reductio in unitatem*, a constant stress upon the necessity for what Augustinus Triumphus calls a single 'caput et director fidei

[1] Augustinus Triumphus, *Summa*, i. 1, p. 2. He continues, 'potestas papae tamquam capitis universalis Ecclesiae ordinatur . . . ad omnium quaestionum et negotiorum solutionem et determinationem . . . ut ad unitatem nos invitaret. Ideo enim principem apostolorum Petrum constituit ut Ecclesia principalem Christi vicarium haberet . . . quia si diversa capita in Ecclesia essent, unitatis vinculum rumperetur'. Most of this is taken from the *Glossa Ordinaria* on *Matthew*, xvi. 19.

[2] See further F. Ehrle, 'Die Spiritualen, ihr Verhältniss zum Franciscanerorden und zu den Fraticellen', *Archiv für Litteratur- und Kirchengeschichte des Mittelalters*, i–iv (1885–8); D. S. Muzzey, *The Spiritual Franciscans* (New York, 1907); D. L. Douie, *The Nature and Effect of the Heresy of the Fraticelli* (Manchester, 1932); E. Benz, *Ecclesia Spiritalis: Kirchenidee und Geschichtstheologie der franziskanischen Reformation* (Stuttgart, 1934); W. H. May, 'The Confession of Prous Boneta, Heretic and Heresiarch', *Essays in Medieval Life and Thought* (ed. J. H. Mundy, R. W. Emery, B. N. Nelson, New York, 1955), pp. 3–30.

christianae'.[1] For him unity and monarchy are merely different aspects of the same principle. One body requires one head, and a plurality of rulers is to him a totally alien conception.

Entia nolunt male disponi: ideo unus princeps et unus principatus.[2]

To advocate anything else would be to turn the *Ecclesia* into a hydra-headed monstrosity.[3]

Closely associated with the idea of unity was the idea of order. It was felt that when the right order was established there would be unity, and this alone could give peace and stability to the Christian society: 'multitudo sine ordine confusio est'.[4] The conception of a *stabilitas mundi* or *pax ordinis*, which ought to exist and had once done so, was of Augustinian origin and is present in every writer of the period. Even the 'rebels' like Dubois and Marsilius harp upon this theme,[5] although perhaps the best statement of the close connection between monarchy and the right order is that of St. Bonaventure:

Licet diversi homines pluribus ligaminibus ad subiectionem obedientiae diversis sint adscripti secundum diversitatem graduum, officiorum et potestatum, tamen haec varietas ad unum reduci debet summum et primum antistitem, in quo principaliter residet universalis omnium

[1] Augustinus Triumphus, *Summa*, lxxi. 1, p. 371; cf. xlvii. 8, p. 258, where the pope is described as the 'unus magister' of *Matthew*, xxiii. 10.

[2] Augustinus Triumphus, *Summa*, xxii. 3, p. 131; cf. Dante, *Monarchia*, i. 9, p. 345, 'Entia nolunt male disponi; malum autem pluralitas principatuum; unus ergo princeps'. The quotation was borrowed from Aristotle, *Metaphysica*, xi. 10, probably by way of Thomas Aquinas, *Summa theologica*, I. ciii. 3, but note also Augustine, *De vera religione*, i. 24 (*PL*, xxxiv. 150).

[3] It is curious to find one of the best expressions of this in Peter Olivi, *De renuntiatione papae*, p. 361, 'tunc destrueretur unitas Ecclesiae et capitulum eius in plura capita et in plures ecclesias generales, et esset monstruosa forma et compositio, ut scil. una generalis Ecclesia haberet plura capita, essetque contra exemplar coelestis ierarchiae et totius universitatis creaturae, ibi qua solus unus et unus Christus est eius caput'.

[4] Alvarus Pelagius, *De planctu Ecclesiae*, ch. 62, p. 199.

[5] Pierre Dubois, *De recuperatione sanctae terrae*, ch. 130, p. 120, 'ubique debet esse ordo, praeterquam in inferno ubi, prout ait sanctus Iob (x. 22), nullus ordo sed sempiternus horror'. For the idea of a naturally existing order in Marsilius of Padua see A. Gewirth, *Marsilius of Padua* (New York, 1951–6), i. 14–16, 54–60, 200–3.

principatus, et non solum ad ipsum Christum, sed etiam iure divino ad eius vicarium: et hoc quidem congruentissime cum istud requirat ordo universalis Ecclesiae et stabilitas in utroque.[1]

All the Middle Ages looked back to a greater ancestral self, to a Golden Age when the right universal order had been laid down. For most papal writers this meant the rule of Christ himself upon earth, when, according to Francis of Meyronnes, there had been a universal monarchy, which was the best possible disposition for the powers of this world.[2] There had at this time been imposed upon mankind the framework of the universal society, the right relationship of powers, and the institutions necessary for its preservation. The Petrine Commission was itself the most important part in this process. It had not only created the universal whole as it was to be handed on from Christ to his successors, but it had also prescribed the organic interrelation between this divinely ordained whole and its parts, and the equally divinely determined relationship between the parts themselves. And since every part had been allocated position and scope, a mutually interlocking relationship with all the other parts and the society as a whole, harmony ought to prevail. This divinely imposed order should ensure the smooth functioning of the body politic, and although there had been a great falling away since the time of Christ, it was still held that under normal, under the right, circumstances this comprehensive order would naturally exist. It was this idea which motivated the medieval papacy, and incidentally allotted a plenitude of power to the pope. The papacy was not, in its own eyes at least, endeavouring to gain supreme power for itself—an idea which suggests an extension of claims—so as to create the right order. This was unnecessary since it was assumed that this supremacy and this order already existed by divine will. It was, as Aquinas said, an expression of God's plan, of the *logos* of the universe.[3] It was not a question of whether this

[1] Bonaventure, *De perfectione evangelica*, iv. 3 (ed. Quaracchi, v. 193).

[2] Francis de Meyronnes, *De principatu temporali*, ch. 1, p. 58.

[3] Thomas Aquinas, *Summa theologica*, II. 1. xci. 1. Cf. Peter Olivi, *Quaestio de infallibilitate*, p. 334, 'Nec vilem reputes formam hanc quae in terris est: formam habet in coelo. Viderat hoc qui dicebat, Vidi civitatem sanctam descendentem de coelo a Deo paratam [*Apoc.*, xxi. 2]', which follows St. Bernard, *De consideratione*, iii. 4 (*PL*, clxxxii. 768–9).

order ought or could be made to exist: it did exist so long as man would or could be forced to leave it to function of its own accord. Consequently the task of the papacy, and of every other ruler subject to it, was to preserve this order against infringement, to correct the subversion of order which produced disorder.[1] Evil-doers deformed the natural beauty of the divine order: they are those who, in the word of Peter de la Palu, 'non naturaliter agunt vel difformantur ad rectam rationem'.[2] Unhindered the various parts of the structure function in tranquillity, but every wrong act is an impediment to the maintenance of the natural peace. Government thus becomes simply a divinely appointed *poena et remedium peccati*, a removal of obstructions. Papal policy was not an attempt to create a new system, but simply to implement a system already in being. Its aim was the essentially negative one of preserving the existing order. In the eyes of the publicists the pope becomes a doctor, remedying the ravages of ill-health to bring back the body politic to its normal state of fitness, or a judge, introducing nothing new but correcting the abuses and infringements of the established system of government.[3]

[1] Hervaeus Natalis, *De potestate papae*, fo. 143v, 'ad ipsum [papam] pertinet corrigere in tota communitate christiana omnes abusus de *inordinatione* hominum'; fo. 144v, 'Ad eum pertinet corrigere omnem abusum de ordinatione hominum a Deo in tota communitate christiana ad quem pertinet tollere *impedimenta motionis* ad perfectum virtutem et unionem cum Deo; . . . ad eum pertinet tollere omne impedimentum tenendi ad finem, qui est Deus, et non solum pertinet ad eum corrigere omnem abusum ecclesiasticae potestatis sed etiam ad eum pertinet omnem abusum potestatum terrenarum eorum qui sunt de Ecclesia, quia sicut dictum est ad talem potestatem pertinet tollere omne impedimentum tenendi in Deum in populo christiano, et per consequens ad eum pertinet corrigere omnem abusum tam potestatis ecclesiasticae quam terrenae in quocunque existente de populo christiano'.

[2] Peter de la Palu, *De causa ecclesiasticae potestatis*, vi, fo. 70. Cf. Innocent III's description of wrong-doers as 'distorti', *De quadripartita specie nuptiarum* (*PL*, ccxvii. 957). All this is basically Augustinian: *De civitate Dei*, xiv. 13 (*PL*, xli. 421). 'Pax omnium rerum est tranquillitas ordinis; ordo est parium dispariumque rerum sua cuique loca tribuens dispositio'; see also *Enchiridion*, ch. 10 (*PL*, xl. 236).

[3] Anon., *Disquisitio theologico-iuridica*, ii. 11, p. 1348, 'Christus et eius vicarius est in medio totius populi christiani sicut medicus perfectissimus. Ad medicum autem perfectissimum spectat sanitatem inducere et ea quae sanitatem impediunt per remedia perfectissima tollere'; cf. ii. 13, pp. 1349–50, for the idea of the pope as *summus iudex*. Engelbert of Admont, *De officiis*, pp. 115–16, defines the duties of the universal ruler as 'orbem pacificare, regere et defendere, excessus

Of this system God was the founder and the supreme ruler: the whole organisation of the universal society was imposed from above, and was to be carried out in accordance with the revealed will of God. The *Ecclesia*, writes Augustinus Triumphus, is his house, whose perfect layout was symbolically foreshadowed in the exquisite arrangement of the Temple of Solomon,[1] and which since the time of the Petrine Commission has been posited on earth. The divine order of the universe is now paralleled by that of the divinely ordered Christian society,[2] which has been given a temporal existence but draws its very nature from above. This gives the *Ecclesia* a dual character. Christ, the God-man, who unites in his own person both human and divine natures, has founded it as a reflection of himself, as a divine-human organism. It is on the one hand an essentially spiritual body, the mystical body of Christ, yet on the other hand it is made up of men and women, an earthly, actually existing body with all the attributes of a terrestrial society—in the words of Augustinus Triumphus, an 'Ecclesia corporalis et temporalis'.[3] Although the society is heavenly in that its essence is the city of God laid up in heaven, there is a physical representation of it

principum corrigere, et omnia a statu debito dissoluta in integrum reformare'. It may be remarked that *understanding* the medical art is regarded as an even more important factor than the practical science of curing the disease—a point stressed by Plato: E. Cassirer, *The Myth of the State* (London, 1946), pp. 69–70. Cf. R. Arbesmann, '*Christus-Medicus* in St. Augustine', *Traditio*, x (1954), pp. 1–28.

[1] Augustinus Triumphus, *Summa*, lxxi. 2, p. 372; cf. Alvarus Pelagius, *De planctu Ecclesiae*, ch. 60, p. 186, 'Item domus Dei totus est mundus; domus Dei est Ecclesia catholica'; also p. 183, 'mystice autem templum Dei est Ecclesia Christi'. The idea that the layout of society is an expression of beauty is again thoroughly Platonic: Cassirer, *op. cit.*, p. 108. Cf. Aegidius Romanus, *De ecclesiastica potestate*, i. 5, p. 16, 'Et quod videmus in ordine et in gubernatione universi debemus ymaginari in gubernatione reipublicae et in gubernatione totius populi christiani . . . quod ordo universi, qui est ordo pulcherrimus'. Francis de Meyronnes, *Quaestio de subiectione*, ii. *proem.*, p. 87, denounces those who question papal supremacy as 'nonnulli, pulchritudinem ordinationis ierarchicae ignorantes.'

[2] Augustinus Triumphus, *Summa*, lxi. 1, p. 322. There are frequent comparisons of the organization of the *Ecclesia* to the arrangement of the universe, and of the systems of ranking in both lay and sacerdotal orders to the angelic hierarchies of heaven, e.g. Aegidius Romanus, *De ecclesiastica potestate*, ii. 13, pp. 126–7; Tholemy of Lucca, *Determinatio compendiosa*, ch. 7, p. 19. The starting point was invariably Dionysius the Pseudo-Areopagite, *De coelesti hierarchia*.

[3] Augustinus Triumphus, *Summa*, xix. 2, p. 118.

in the present *Ecclesia*.[1] Christ had said, 'My kingdom is not of this world', but as Augustinus Triumphus remarked, it is nevertheless *in* this world, a projection of the more really existing celestial *regnum*.[2] Once again we are made aware of how much this was a conception permeated with Augustinian realism. Man as we know him is essentially a corporeal reproduction of himself: he exists in a material body which represents on earth, is animated and given shape by, his true self which we term the soul. Similarly the essence of the *Ecclesia* is in Christ, whilst the earthly *Ecclesia*, although clothed in the mundane form of a body politic, is only an image of the perfectly existing Church Triumphant.[3] The *Ecclesia* exists on both planes, the material and the spiritual—'Ecclesia in praesenti et Ecclesia gloriae in futuro est eadem Ecclesia'[4]—and its aim is the reabsorption of the lower level into the higher. As Conrad of Megenberg puts it:

Descriptive igitur dicendo Ecclesia catholica sive universalis est totius orbis fidelium omnium christianorum monarchya in unum finem veritatis tendentium, scil. in felicitatem sempiternam... Et dico ad unum finem tendentium ut connotetur per hoc illa esse descriptio Ecclesiae Dei militantis in hoc mundo cuius finis, propter quem militat, est Ecclesia triumphans in coelesti paradiso.[5]

[1] Innocent IV, *MGH, Epp. select. xiii saec.*, ii, n. 301, p. 224; n. 665, p. 476; Thomas Aquinas, *Summa contra gentiles*, iv. 76.

[2] Augustinus Triumphus, *Summa*, i. 7 ad 1, p. 11, 'Christus ergo non dixit, Regnum meum non est in hoc mundo, quia et in hoc mundo et in futuro regnat super fideles suos . . . sed dixit, non est de hoc mundo'. This is followed by the fifteenth-century writer, Antonio Roselli, *Monarchia*, i. 41, p. 273, 'Papatus et sacerdotium non sunt de mundo, sicut nec Christus fuit de mundo . . . licet vicariatus papae sit in mundo, non tamen censendus est de mundo'. See also Durandus de S. Porciano, *De iurisdictione ecclesiastica*, ch. 3, fo. 7; Peter Bertrandus, *De origine iurisdictionum*, ch. 3, fo. 98v [misnumbered 79].

[3] Aegidius Spiritalis, *Libellus contra infideles*, pp. 112–13, 'Certum est quod militans Ecclesia ordinata est et constituta ad *effigiem* coelestis et triumphantis Ecclesiae. Hoc enim sic esse voluit ordinatio divina . . . quod Ecclesia militans *repraesentet* Ecclesiam triumphantem'.

[4] Thomas Aquinas, *Comm. in Ep. ad Coloss. I, lect.* 5; James of Viterbo, *De regimine christiano*, i. 1–2.

[5] Conrad of Megenberg, *Tractatus contra Occam*, ch. 7, p. 368; also the very Augustinian passage in Alvarus Pelagius, *De planctu Ecclesiae*, ch. 59, p. 175, 'Alio modo dicitur regnum terrenum illud idem quod coeleste, scilicet congregatio vel societas bonorum peregrinantium in terris, unde Greg. in homilia,

The *Ecclesia* can only exist ordered towards its creator. The divine ordering presupposes its orientation heavenwards, so that the criteria for every form of human activity are the principles of right living as embodied in the Christian faith. The society was founded upon faith, and every action within it is important only when taken in conjunction with the furtherance of the *cultus Dei*. It must, as Durandus of S. Porciano emphasised, be directed towards the end for which the society was created: 'omnes actiones christianorum sunt ordinati ad consequendam vitam aeternam'.[1] The *Ecclesia* is imposed on earth by God, and must strive always towards God. Only by constant reliance upon his commands and by identification with the divine will can the society find the fulfilment for which its nature intends it. Just as the soul of each individual Christian lives for its ultimate reunion with its maker in the *visio beatifica Dei*, so the whole *congregatio fidelium* must aim at reintegration with the *civitas Dei*.[2] And this, concludes Augustinus Triumphus, can only be achieved by making faith the measure of all things.[3]

It is the element of faith which determines the nature of the society and consequently singles out those who are qualified to guide it towards its end. To understand this we must return to the question of the composition of the *Ecclesia*. It is the *communitas omnium fidelium*, comprising all Christians whether members of the laity or the clergy, and forming a single polity. It is symbolised by Noah's Ark, or by Mount Sinai, both of which at certain times had

regnum coelorum praesentis temporis Ecclesia dicitur. Nam ex eo quod ad bona coelestia *finaliter* ordinatur dicitur regnum coeleste; ex eo autem quod adhuc conversatur in terris et ipsis bonis terrenis utitur dicitur regnum terrenum'. Cf. Hervaeus Natalis, *De potestate papae*, fo. 144v; Thomas Aquinas, *In symbolum apostolorum*, ch. 9.

[1] Durandus of S. Porciano, *De iurisdictione ecclesiastica*, q. 3, fo. 5.

[2] Alexander de S. Elpidio, *De ecclesiastica potestate*, ii. 1, p. 13, 'totum universum . . . dicitur unum unitate ordinis et unitate ipsius principis Dei, qui totius mundi est finis et principium, quia sicut omnia producuntur ab eo sicut a principio, ita omnia reducuntur in ipsum sicut in finem . . . qui est beatitudo aeterna sive Deus ipse in beatitudine possidendus'; Hervaeus Natalis, *De potestate papae*, fo. 142, 'Sciendum quod finis totius iurisdictionis ecclesiasticae, quae post Christum principaliter residet apud papam, est ordinare communitatem christianam ad impendum Deo cultum debitum et sibi acceptum, et per consequens vitae aeternae meritorium'.

[3] Augustinus Triumphus, *Summa*, lix. 4, p. 311.

held all the chosen people of God who sought salvation by faith.[1] Nevertheless the unity of this body does not prevent the drawing of distinctions between the various members. All are members of one body, but the members of any body have different functions. The first and most important separation of functions is between the governors and the governed, between those who have special qualifications for directing the society and the rest of the Christian body, in other words between the ordained and unordained members of the community. Just as the *Ecclesia universalis* has both a spiritual and an earthly nature, so it is what Augustinus Triumphus terms the 'tota multitudo et tota respublica vel spiritualis vel corporalis'.[2] The body is one, but each body has two sides, left and right. Hence the Christian body is made up of two orders, sacerdotal and lay, its spiritual and secular members.

Unius corporis mystici Ecclesiae duo latera sunt, quia ad dexteram sunt clerici et ad sinistram laici.[3]

The division of the two *ordines* is analogous to the separation of a man into body and soul, and that the *ordo clericalis* is superior and dominates the *ordo laicalis* logically follows, and was a useful weapon in the hierocratic armoury.[4] But nearly all writers, whatever their political persuasion, were agreed upon some sort of distinc-

[1] Augustinus Triumphus, *Summa*, viii, 1–2, pp. 68–9. According to Ministeri, *op. cit.*, pp. 81–4, his immediate source for this may have been the *Tractatus de Arca Noe* of Aegidius Romanus (ed. A. Bladus, *Primus Tomus Operum D. Aegidii Romani*, Rome, 1558); see also his *De ecclesiastica potestate*, ii. 1, p. 36. But it may be pointed out that most contemporary writers used Noah and the Ark as symbols for pope and *Ecclesia*, including Boniface VIII, and this may be traced back to Augustine.

[2] Augustinus Triumphus, *Summa*, vii. 4, p. 67.

[3] Augustinus Triumphus, *Summa*, xx. 2, p. 122. This is taken from Hugh of St. Victor, *De sacramentis*, II. ii. 3 (*PL*, clxxvi. 417). Similarly Conrad of Megenberg, *Tractatus contra Occam*, p. 367, 'Sed partes Ecclesiae primae sunt duo prima genera christianorum, scilicet, genus clericorum et genus laycorum', referring to Gratian, C. 12 q. 1 c. 7.

[4] For example Augustinus Triumphus, *Summa*, i. 3, p. 5, 'Patet hoc etiam per Hugonem de Sancto Victore, 2 *lib. de sacramentis*, 2 *par.*, *cap.* 4 [*PL*, clxxvi. 417–18], ubi distinguit duplicem vitam spiritualem et corporalem; duplicem populum laicorum et clericorum; duo bona spiritualia et temporalia; duplicem potestatem spiritualem et saecularem. Et postea subdit quod quantum vita spiritualis dignior est quam terrena, et spiritus quam corpus, tantum spiritualis potestas terrenam potestatem et saecularem et honore et dignitate praecedit'.

tion between the two classes of people who made up the community. This, it must be emphasised again, was not the modern distinction between Church and State, but between the ordained and unordained members of the same society. Nevertheless it was a distinction of fundamental importance. For although baptism might be enough to secure membership of the society, it did not give each member the right to participate in its government. Direction of the community was dependent upon an understanding of its real nature and the purpose for which it existed. Knowledge of the Christian faith therefore became the supreme criterion for government, and since every act had to be a Christian act, that is to say, orientated by faith, it followed that only those who knew the content of faith were entitled to rule, and in so ruling to dominate every aspect of human life. Direction and government by the *sacerdotium* becomes inevitable since they alone can tell what is and what is not Christian. Ordination gives not only the ability to administer the sacraments, itself a vital feature in a society which is the *corpus Christi*, but also the ability to expound the principles which Christ himself had taught. Besides being the culmination of a long period of training, it is also a divine mystery by which the eternal truths of God are revealed to man. As Alexander de S. Elpidio put it, ordination confers knowledge 'partim ex revelatione, partim ex subtillitate intellectus humani'.[1] Only the ordained members can decide what is in accordance with the faith, and are therefore functionally qualified to shape these decisions into the form of law, by which every political society must be governed. Ordination not only sharply distinguishes the *sacerdotium* from the rest of society, but qualifies the priesthood for the duty of directing the *Ecclesia* in accordance with its underlying purpose. The *regimen animarum* is indeed, Augustinus Triumphus declares, the *ars artium*.[2]

[1] Alexander de S. Elpidio, *De ecclesiastica potestate*, i. 2, p. 4; cf. Pierre Dubois, *De recuperatione Terrae Sanctae*, ch. 97, p. 78, 'Fertur quod sanctissimi Romani pontifices, non visis alias processibus, iudicare cum summa ratione et arte philosophica per eum qui sic primo facere cepit acquisita, vel innata sive divinitus gratis data, consueverunt'.

[2] Augustinus Triumphus, *Summa*, iii. 3 ad 3, p. 30. See also c. 27 of the Fourth Lateran Council decrees of 1215–16, and note the equation of lawgiver and priest in Roman law, *Dig.*, I. 1. i: on this see further *KTB*, pp. 118–24.

This setting apart of the members of the priesthood is emphasised by the application to them alone of the term *Ecclesia*, which we have hitherto seen used only of the head or the whole of society. Although this has inevitably tended to cause a good deal of confusion, the distinction between the *Ecclesia* as the *congregatio fidelium* and as the *sacerdotium* may be found throughout the medieval period and served to make the *clerici* a race apart. As William Amidani of Cremona explained it:

Uno modo accipitur Ecclesia pro communitate omnium fidelium, quae est corpus Christi. Alio modo accipitur Ecclesia pro *potiore parte* Ecclesiae primo modo dictae, scilicet pro clericis seu pro universitate clericorum, non quin laici non sint ecclesiastici, immo sunt, sed quia non sunt ita nobiles in Ecclesia sicut clerici.[1]

Just as the supremacy of the pope over the whole society was implied by referring to him as the *Ecclesia*, so the superiority of the clergy over the laity was suggested by the application to them of the same term.[2] By virtue of their ordination they have become the chosen people of the Lord, and the hierocratic writers strove to emphasise their exalted status by describing them as angels and gods.[3] The divinely instituted society can only be guided by those who have the understanding of divine things. Theirs is to know and to teach, writes Conrad of Megenberg, the duty of others is to learn. In a Christian society the laity are not and cannot be functionally qualified to govern, since they are ignorant of the very aim of the community. They cannot lead: they can only be led.[4] This point of

[1] William Amidani, *Reprobatio errorum*, ch. 1, p. 17.

[2] E.g. Conrad of Megenberg, *Tractatus contra Occam*, ch. 7, p. 367, 'dicimus genus clericorum quandoque ecclesiam, et principem eius nonnumquam scripture nominant ecclesiam, scil. papam'.

[3] Aegidius Romanus, *De ecclesiastica potestate*, ii. 2, p. 39, 'Clerici ergo non debent habere aliam sortem nec aliam partem quam Deum, quia Deus est eorum sors. Unde Ieronimus ait [Jerome, *Ad Nepotianum*: see Gratian, C. 12 q. 1 c. 5, also D. 21 c. 1] quod clerus graece, latine sors, appellatur, et dicit quod propterea dicti sunt clerici quia sunt de sorte Domini'; Conrad of Megenberg, *Tractatus contra Occam*, ch. 7, p. 367, 'Et dicuntur clerici, id est sorte electi, ipsos enim Deus in suos elegit'. Cf. *Ps.*, lxxxii. 6, *John*, x. 34 and I *Cor.*, vi. 3.

[4] Conrad of Megenberg, *Tractatus contra Occam*, ch. 7, p. 367, 'Item genus clericorum est tamquam lux christianae religionis, quibus Salvator in personis apostolorum ait, Vos estis lux mundi [*Matth.*, v. 14]. Genus autem laicorum est populus ignarus, qui potius doceri debet quam docere, potius duci quam

view is expressed in its extreme form by Augustinus Triumphus, who declares that in comparison with the *sacerdotium* the laity are illiterate idiots,[1] whilst Alexander de S. Elpidio describes the laity as the arms and feet of the body politic, which, being blind, need the head and eyes of the pope and the priests to show them what to do and where to go.[2] The people must be guided, since the society itself is in motion towards its heavenly end. It must always have a tendency towards and be orientated by this end or *finis*. To quote Conrad of Megenberg, the *Ecclesia* is one body with one end, a unity of purpose.[3] The functional qualification of the priesthood rests upon their comprehension of this purpose, which gives shape and form to the society. Whatever is good in public life can only be gauged by reference to this *finis* which is the *summum bonum*. In any society the idea of what constitutes the 'good' can only be seen against the purpose for which the society stands,[4] and in a Christian society this purpose must necessarily be the living of a Christian life in every possible way.

ducere. . . Istud genus hominum regere non debet clerum, sed potius regi ab eo, quoniam, Sapientis est regere, non autem regi, ut ait Aristoteles, prohemio *Metaphysicae* [i. 2]. Genus autem clericorum sapientiam scripturarum possedit, sed genus laicorum ignorantiam retinuit'.

[1] Augustinus Triumphus, *Summa*, ii. 7, p. 25.

[2] Alexander de S. Elpidio, *De ecclesiastica potestate*, ii. 1, p. 13, 'Et membra in hoc corpore sunt diversi fideles habentes diversa officia . . . quae membra invicem secundum quod diversas gratias a Deo datas habent se iuvare et protegere debent. Sicut videmus membra facere in corpore naturali, quia oculus qui pollet acumine visus videt sibi et manui. Pes autem in quo viget potentia gressiva et deficit in videndo, seipsum portat et alia membra, sicut et manus purgat pedem et oculum. Sic etiam suo modo est in unitate sanctae Ecclesiae, quia caput est princeps sive praelatus, unde praelati et principes dicti sunt capita populorum. Oculi possunt dici sapientes sive doctores, qui debet alios illuminare. Manus sunt milites sive defensores Ecclesiae. Pedes possunt dici populares sive simplices et rudes, qui etiam debent sua diversa officii exercere ad utilitatem corporis mystici Ecclesiae'.

[3] Conrad of Megenberg, *Tractatus contra Occam*, ch. 7, p. 368; also ch. 8, p. 375, 'Ecclesia etenim catholica non est una unitate hominum, qui sunt multi, sed unitate fidei ac *unione intentionis*'.

[4] Walter Burleigh (Burlaeus, d. 1343), 'Omnis communitas seu societas instituta est propter aliquod bonum, quia propter aliquem finem; et finis et bonum idem sunt': see M. Grabmann, 'Die mittelalterlichen Kommentare zur Politik des Aristoteles', *SBAW*, *Phil.-Hist. Abt.* (Munich, 1941), Band II, Heft 10, pp. 28–36.

The teleological approach to the problem of the right government of the Christian body was, as we have endeavoured to show, as much a living force in hierocratic doctrine in the fourteenth century as it had been at any other time in the medieval period. As with Plato, the hierocrat saw society not simply as a political and social institution requiring government, but as a conscious expression of a way of life, a pattern of human existence. It was something to be understood as much as manipulated: indeed one was impossible without the other. Consequently the knowledge of right and the means to enforce it were of necessity to be concentrated in the same hands. To all pro-papal writers it seemed transparently clear that the society, being a Christian one, must be directed by those whose knowledge of Christianity enabled them to appreciate the purpose of life and the way to obtain it, and thereby qualified them for the task of promulgating laws and governmental decrees. Nevertheless with Augustinus Triumphus, although the teleological principle is constantly stressed, we may notice a refinement of this doctrine in favour of monarchy. Whilst he did not attempt to deny the functional qualification of all *clerici*, the emphasis always falls upon the pope as head of the ordained members and so therefore the supreme interpreter of the nature of the Christian way of life:

... quia *solus* ipse habet considerare universalem Ecclesiae promotionem. Semper enim *artifex* supremum finem considerans habet omnes inferiores ad illum finem dirigere et ordinare. Et cum ipse supremum perfectionis gradum in Ecclesia teneat, ipse *solus* habet aliis vias ad perfectionem tenendi ostendere. Similiter *solus* ipse habet illa quae ad divinum cultum pertinent universaliter ordinare.[1]

Faced with increasing attempts by the bishops to claim parity with the Roman church, determined to emphasise the unity of the Christian *corpus* on the one body, one head principle, he brusquely thrusts aside anything which may detract from the idea of papal monarchy. In consequence he allows only the pope to be regarded as having a full understanding of the *telos* of the community. Had

[1] Augustinus Triumphus, *Summa*, lxxi. 3, p. 373; cf. xxxv. 4, p. 208, 'Ipse *solus* habet considerare finem totius Ecclesiae et ad dictum finem omnes ordinare'.

not Aristotle himself declared that government entailed direction by a single legislator in accordance with the purpose of the society? 'Intentio legislatoris semper est ut homines ad virtutem inducat',[1] and this implied that the ruler could only be he who had the right estimation of the end, and was therefore in a position to direct the society towards it:

Ille enim qui rectam existimationem habet de fine disponit et dirigit omnia in ordine ad ipsum.[2]

He alone is fully capable of taking the abstract principles of faith on which the *Ecclesia* rests and transforming them into the actual codes of law necessary for the administration of a political society. Although faith is the substance of this entity, the *Ecclesia* for Augustinus Triumphus is not a mere unity of faith, but very much a civil community. Its members cannot live by faith alone. Faith has to be converted into terms of real government, and accordingly the pope is not only the source of faith but of all law, government and jurisdiction as well. To Augustinus Triumphus the *Ecclesia* is a corporate political entity in which the monarchic idea is utilised to its fullest possible extent.

This emphasis upon the heavenly end of mankind underlines the transitory nature of human existence and gives the religious values of life complete supremacy. Man's relationship to the world is thus conceived of in terms of vocation and duty, and the society is pictured as a huge organism in which each member has been allotted a

[1] Augustinus Triumphus, *Summa*, xliv. 1 ad 3, p. 241; xliv. 4, p. 242: see Aristotle, *Ethics*, ii. 1. Cf. Peter de Lutra, *Liga fratrum*, ch. 7, pp. 59–60, 'Quia secundum Philosophum, II *Ethic.*, intentio legislatoris est cives facere bonos, et dominus papa in ordine ad finem supernaturalem aeternae beatitudinis est universalis *legislator* totius ecclesiasticae multitudinis, quae corpus Christi misticum constituit, ipse tenetur membra totius Ecclesiae in ordine ad finem et etiam inter se in debito ordine et regimine conservare... Et ideo summus pontifex membra Ecclesiae bene ordinat si cuique suum statum conservat'.

[2] Augustinus Triumphus, *Summa*, ci. 5 ad 1, p. 498; Andreas de Perusio, *Tractatus contra edictum Bavari*, p. 70, 'Ideo cum papa sit ultimo fini praepositus, sicut tenetur omnes ad finem dirigere iuxta posse, ita etiam a peccato, quod est finis contrarium, abvertere renitentem'; Thomas Aquinas, *Summa theologica*, II. 1. xc. 3, 'Quia et in omnibus aliis ordinare in finem est eius cuius est proprius ille finis'.

specific function, which he pursues for the sake of the common purpose.

Sicut ergo in corpore humano singula quaeque membra propria et discreta officia habent et unumquodque non sibi soli agit, sic in corpore Ecclesiae *dona* officiorum distributa sunt, et tamen unusquisque non soli sibi habet illud quod solus habet.[1]

Each member has a function or office within which he acts in accordance with the overriding purpose of the whole. The Pauline and patristic teachings demanding that one should remain in 'the calling to which one has been called' now assume as much a political as a social significance. Only when each person acts in his proper function will the natural tranquillity and order, the *pax Ecclesiae*, be obtained.[2] Therefore the right allocation of functions is a matter of the utmost importance, and can only be entrusted to the pope. The papal-hierocratic theory is essentially architectonic. The unity of the society is ascribed to the wisdom of a great architect, who orders the world according to a divine plan.[3] The well-ordered society depends upon the right apportioning out of the various offices, and entails a correct evaluation of the abilities of each member. There can be no unity in the body unless there is a true and harmonious coherence amongst the members themselves and between the members and the head. Within the framework of their assigned functions each member must supplement and support the others.

[1] Augustinus Triumphus, *Summa*, lxxi. 2, p. 372; similarly Thomas Aquinas, *Summa theologica*, II. II. clxxxiii. 2, 'Ad Ecclesiae Dei perfectionem et decorem convenit in ea diversorum officiorum et statuum munera diversis personis distributa inveniri pro necessitate multarum actionum quae in illa necessariae sunt'.

[2] Innocent III, *Reg.*, I. ccccIxxi (*PL*, ccxiv. 437), 'unusquisque maneat in ea vocatione in qua dignoscitur esse vocatus'; cf. I *Cor.*, vii. 24.

[3] Augustinus Triumphus, *Summa*, lxxiii. 3, p. 380, 'Planum est autem quod papa est omnis iuris interpres et ordinator tamquam *architector* in tota ecclesiastica hierarchia vice Christi'; lxxi. 3, p. 373, '*artifex* supremum finem considerans'. Cf. Clement VI, *MGH, Const.*, VIII n. 100 p. 157, 'Sic potestas spiritualis est architectonica'. Aquinas too had spoken of legislators 'sicut architectores in artificialibus', *Comm. in VI Ethic.*, lect. 7, and of *iustitia* as being 'in principe principaliter et quasi architectonice', *Summa theologica*, II. II. lviii. 6. This refers to the principle of *techne architectonice*, the subordination of ends and therefore of agents, in Aristotle, *Ethics*, i. 1.

Moreover a proper application of the teleological principle results not only in an ordering between the lay and sacerdotal orders, but also in a rigid hierarchical ordering within each order.[1] Since the nature and value of each function is determined by consideration of the end of society, there will appear a grading of functions from higher to lower. As one anonymous papal supporter put it,

Ordo totius universi seu totius mundi ... consistit in gradibus inferiorum et superiorum seu dominorum et subditorum ... sine quo ordine mundus stare non possit nec homines vivere.[2]

Without this, said Augustinus Triumphus, the right way of life in the society, which 'consistit in ordine [unius] ad alterum per respectum ad bonum reipublicae', cannot be achieved.[3] He does not doubt that all men were equal in a state of natural innocence, nor

[1] Augustinus Triumphus, *Summa*, i. 6, pp. 9–10, 'Nam in corpore mystico triplicem ordinem distinguere possumus: unum quo clerici ordinantur ad clericos, alium quo laici ordinantur ad clericos, tertium quo laici ordinantur ad laicos. Et quia ordinatio qua laici ordinantur ad laicos est potestas corporalis et temporalis, cum semper corporale et temporale debeant regulari per spirituale, necessarium est quod talis potestas laicorum reguletur per potestatem spiritualem qua ipsi clerici ordinantur ad laicos. Similiter potestas clericorum qua ordinantur ad laicos regulanda est et ordinanda per potestatem qua clerici ordinantur ad clericos et potissime per potestatem illam qua clerici ordinantur ad summum clericorum, qui est papa. Itaque papa *per unam potestatem* ordine quodam habet ordinare clericos ad clericos, et clericos ad laicos, et laicos inter se'. This is supported by a passage from Augustine, *De trinitate*, iii. 4, in which it is stated that corporeal things are arranged in a hierarchy and are governed by spiritual things, also arranged hierarchically and reaching up to God, so that 'universa creatura regitur per suum creatorem ex quo et per quem et in quo condita atque instituta est' (*PL*, xlii. 873).

[2] Anon., *Disquisitio theologico-iuridica*, v, pp. 1357–8; Peter de la Palu, *Articulus circa materia confessionum*, fo. 92v, 'Primo probatur de iure naturali quod ordo Ecclesiae et naturae hoc requirit ut sit mutua obligatio inter praelatum et subditum ut sicut praelatus praefertur subdito sic subditus subiiciatur praelato'. There is no suggestion of reciprocal rights in this arrangement. In the same way Augustinus Triumphus repeatedly affirms that the right order in society is 'in quodam ordine superioris ad inferiorem', which is designated the *ordo iustitiae* or *ordo iudicarius: Summa*, i. 2, p. 4; iv. 3, p. 43; xlv. 1 ad 3, p. 247. This again derives from the Augustinian view that the proper order and adjustment consists in the 'ordinata imperandi atque obediendi concordia civium', *De civitate Dei*, xix. 13 (*PL*. xli. 640).

[3] Augustinus Triumphus, *Summa*, xliv. 5 ad 3, p. 244; cf. Alvarus Pelagius, *De planctu Ecclesiae*, ch. 62, p. 199, 'multitudo sine ordine confusio est'.

that they will be in heaven,[1] but he believes that the various gifts given to men make the ascendancy of one over the other inevitable. Inequality is part of the divinely ordained natural order.[2] Thus he is able to make good use of the Aristotelian theory of natural rulers and natural slaves, a view which the earlier Aristotelian commentators had been able to combine fairly easily with the Augustinian notion of the depravity of man, whose corrupted nature requires the remediation of government and inequality.[3] Augustinus Triumphus strongly decries any suggestion that the people as a whole, which in general meant the laity, might be capable of looking after their own affairs. Direction of the society and a good deal of its administration must be left to the *sanior pars*, the priesthood, who, although numerically a minority, far outweigh the rest by virtue of their fitness for government.[4] An hierarchical ordering in the community must follow from the principle that men are not equal: equality is opposed to the whole order of the universe.

Quia ordo naturae hoc requirit ut sicut in rebus naturalibus superiora movent inferiora ad suas actiones per excellentiam naturalis virtutis diviniter eis collatae, sic in rebus humanis superiora imperant inferioribus per suam *voluntatem* ex ordine iustitiae diviniter ordinatae.[5]

An ordering is of itself intrinsically good by both divine and natural law. For Augustinus Triumphus the need to uphold the principle

[1] It was, he said, only in heaven that there would be no more 'dominatio vel praelatio', *Summa*, i. 2, p. 4. In a natural condition all men were equal in that they were all men, but a man cannot maintain himself in the state in which he is born, and so he needs government in the same natural way that he needs clothes, *Summa*, xxxvii. 2 ad 3, pp. 220–1. Likewise there was no private property in the prime natural state, but this became a matter of natural necessity for human needs, *Summa*, liv. 1 ad 2, p. 287. This distinction between the two forms of natural law had been developed by Aquinas working on Ciceronian and Augustinian bases: see further E. Lewis, 'Natural Law and Expediency in Medieval Political Theory', *Ethics*, l (1939–40), pp. 144–63 at pp. 145–52.

[2] Augustinus Triumphus, *Summa*, xxii. 6, p. 134.

[3] Augustinus Triumphus, *Summa*, xxiii. 3, p. 138; also Aegidius Romanus, *De renuntiatione papae*, xvi. 1, p. 41.

[4] Augustinus Triumphus, *Summa*, ii. 8, p. 26, 'populus sequendus non est in iudicio, sed doctores qui, licet sint pauciores numero, sunt tamen sanior consilio'.

[5] Augustinus Triumphus, *Summa*, xxii. 5, p. 133; cf. vi. 2, p. 58; *De duplici potestate*, pp. 496–7.

of order within the *Ecclesia* cannot be too highly stressed. To reject it, he says, is to disregard the will of God.[1]

The well-being of the *Ecclesia*, the maintenance of the jurisdictional ordering, and the supreme authority of the pope as the guarantee of the essential unity of the body, are all inseparable from each other in the hierocratic mind. Since the essential unifying factor in the *Ecclesia* is faith, its members are united both by the beliefs in which all share and by their common obedience to the head as the source of faith. There is then a double unity, one acting horizontally, the other vertically.

Est autem in Ecclesia, quae corpus Christi mysticum est, duplex unitas: una membrorum ad caput, et secunda membrorum ad invicem.[2]

This unity of the members amongst themselves was the constitutive feature of the body in the Pauline doctrine—'so we being many are one body in Christ and everyone members one of another' (1 *Cor.*, xii. 12)—in spite of the fact that different members were suited to widely diverse activities. Implicit in this view was the necessity for a dovetailing of functions to keep the body an integrated whole, and to Augustinus Triumphus it was apparent that the first unity was insufficient without that second unity in which all the members were brought together in obedience to one head.[3] The unity of the members to each other was not enough and, he pointed out, might merely pave the way for a series of warring sects and separatist groupings which would deny the whole idea of *unum corpus*.[4] And in their attempts to impress this organological conception of society upon their readers, the hierocratic writers re-

[1] Augustinus Triumphus, *Summa*, vi. 3, p. 59.

[2] Augustinus Triumphus, *Summa*, xxv. 1, p. 150; also xxvi. 4, p. 157; xliv. 5 ad 3, p. 243. Following Aristotle, Aegidius Romanus in the *De regimine principum* frequently distinguishes between the *iustitia commutativa* which regulates the relationships between the different members of a society, and the *iustitia distributiva* which proceeds from one central office and communicates vital energy and motion in due proportion to each member.

[3] Augustinus Triumphus, *Summa*, vi. 6, p. 61, 'Sed ordo iudicarius qui vertitur inter homines praesupponit auctoritatem papae'.

[4] Augustinus Triumphus, *Summa*, xxvi. 1 ad 3, p. 156, 'non sufficit in Ecclesia servare congregationem vel unitatem membrorum sine unitate capitis; immo ex hoc ipso quod tyranni uniunt eis membra Ecclesiae et dividunt ipsa ab unitate et ab obedientia capitis, cui simul cum eis deberent subiici, schismatici censendi sunt'.

sorted to every possible form of analogy. By far the most useful way of expressing the idea of the Christian community as a single whole directed by a single head was a comparison of the body politic of the *Ecclesia* with the natural body, an idea which had a special appeal to the sensualistic character of the medieval outlook. Again this was an example of the way in which the medieval attitude made the world of material things seem unreal in contrast with the real world of faith. All things were in a sense *signa rei sacrae*, expressions of the divine cosmology. It was felt that the political order did not differ substantially from any other aspect of the nature of things, and so any form of analogy could be used as a means of analysing political institutions. Not only was the employment of allegory and symbolism effective in conveying complex theories of society to even the slowest intellect, but it seemed to link up the material world with the immaterial, and gave vital spiritual principles a cloak of tangible significance and power. However large a part faith played in medieval thought, it was always necessary to be reconciling Christianity with reality, and to describe a complicated intellectual thesis like the idea of *Ecclesia* in such a way as to give it immediate political value required the use of some such device. Although Aquinas had pointed out the shortcomings of anthropomorphism, there was hardly a writer who did not fall back upon some sort of anatomical symbolism.[1] With Augustinus Triumphus the pope becomes successively the head, the heart and the soul of the political body, and whilst he plainly feels the incongruity of comparing him to so many organs at the same time, he points out that these are merely different ways of expressing the same idea.[2] It is the pope as the heart who pumps faith, the lifeblood of the Chris-

[1] Aquinas analysed the discrepancies between the natural and political bodies, *Commentum in Sententias*, III. xiii. ii. 2 *sol.* 2, but it is noticeable that he often used such comparisons himself: e.g. *Summa theologica*, III. viii. 1, 'Ecclesia dicitur unum corpus mysticum per similitudinem ad naturale corpus hominis'; III. xlix. 1, 'Sicut naturale corpus est unum ex membrorum diversitate consistens, ita tota Ecclesia, quae est mysticum corpus Christi, computatur quasi una persona cum suo capite, quod est Christus'.

[2] Augustinus Triumphus, *Summa*, xix. 2 ad 1, p. 118, 'in metaphoricis locutionibus non est inconveniens unum et idem diversis nominibus appellari secundum diversam similtudinem. Papa igitur est caput Ecclesiae propter similitudines superius dictas; potest tamen cor appellari propter alias conditiones'. This follows Thomas Aquinas, *Summa theologica*, III. viii. 1 ad 2 and 3.

tian society,[1] into all the other members to give them motion and force; he is the soul which vivifies the whole *corpus* in every way; he is the head without whose guidance the body would lose all sense of direction: 'influit enim caput in membra motum et sensum'.[2] Crude as these allegories may have been, they serve to give a mental picture which is far more illuminating than many pages of elaborate explanation. The *Ecclesia* appears as an articulated organism with its parts distributed according to the requirements of the whole, and united under one leader in a common purpose. As Augustinus Triumphus put it, the pope becomes the general of a Christian army, setting out his line of battle to gain the prize for which all Christians must fight their way through this earthly life: alternatively he appears as the captain of the ship of the *Ecclesia* piloting it to its destination.[3]

The initiation and maintenance of the whole system of ordering could, in Augustinus Triumphus' opinion, only be carried out by one who stood supreme over both laity and clergy. All the manifold offices and duties which assist the operation of the *Ecclesia* must be derived from and dependent upon the pope. In a telling phrase Aegidius Romanus describes the pope as disposing and ordering all things and all people according to their number, weight and measure.

Dicamus quod summus pontifex omnia quae sunt in Ecclesia disponit et ordinat in numero, pondere et mensura.[4]

[1] Augustinus Triumphus, *Summa*, xlvii. 1 ad 1, p. 253, 'Sine fide enim spiritualis vita haberi non potest'; cf. xxviii. 5, p. 172, 'fundamentum totius spiritualis vitae'.

[2] Augustinus Triumphus, *Summa*, cvi. 4, p. 529; cf. Tholemy of Lucca, *Determinatio compendiosa*, ch. 15, p. 33, and see I *Cor.*, ii. 16. We may also note Innocent III's statement that as head he possesses a *plenitudo sensuum* through which unity is given to the various functions of the other members, *Reg.*, I. cxvii (*PL*, ccxiv. 106). The whole of this theory has however a thoroughly Augustinian basis: see Grabowski, *op. cit.*, pp. 13–14.

[3] Augustinus Triumphus, *Summa*, xxii. 4 ad 3, p. 133; cf. Peter de la Palu, *De causa immediata ecclesiasticae potestatis*, ii. 2, fo. 27, 'Unde cum Ecclesia est terribilis castrorum acies ordinata, et apostoli fuerunt coelestis aulae milites, belli triumphales duces, habentes arma spiritualia et specialiter gladium spiritus quod est verbum Dei, debuerunt habere unum capitaneum, scilicet Petrum, quia propter hoc dictus est Cephas, quia caput aliorum a quo in acie ordinarentur'.

[4] Aegidius Romanus, *De ecclesiastica potestate*, iii. 12, pp. 207–8; cf. Alvarus Pelagius, *De planctu Ecclesiae*, ch. 54, p. 137; Opicinus de Canistris, *De prae-*

And since every function performed by any one member is simply a part of the function of the whole, a single centralised motive force has to be presupposed which enlivens, regulates and directs in unison the whole stratified system of the society. To Francis of Meyronnes the pope is the Universal One, the monad or pivot of spiritual and material forces which gives account for all existence. He is a mathematical and metaphysical 'point' at the centre of a universe conceived of in terms of a geometrical equation.[1] And passing from mathematical to mechanical symbolism we may see the universal society through the eyes of Augustinus Triumphus as a great machine, which requires a *summum movens*, a prime mover or motor, to put each part of the mechanism into operation and keep it going as it moves slowly but majestically towards its goal. It is the pope, the 'unum primum a quo alia regulantur', who is the motor which sets this machine in motion.[2] He is the political *deus ex machina*, controlling and regulating the harmonious movement of each part in the same way that the soul functions as the prime mover of the human body. In fact we are given a fascinating picture of the *Ecclesia* as a gigantic engine, whose smooth running owes all to the work of a great mechanic, who both supplies the power and endeavours to prevent this Juggernaut from shaking itself to pieces.[3]

eminentia spiritualis imperii, pp. 94, 103. By contrast the pope's power is described as immeasurable (*immensa*). This recalls Augustine's discussion of the infinity of God (*Enarratio in Ps.*, cxlvi. 5) contained in Peter Lombard, *Comm. in Ps.* (*PL*, cxci. 1275), and his description of God as the universal craftsman, *De Genesi contra Manichaeos*, i. 16 (*PL*, xxxiv. 185–6). Cf. *Sap.*, xi. 21; but note also *Dig.*, XII. i. 2, 1.

[1] Francis de Meyronnes, *De principatu temporali*, ch. 3, p. 60, 'per monarcham intelligitur unus princeps universalis omnium, quia monarcha dicitur a monade'. The term monad is commonly used in fourteenth-century theology to illustrate the nature of God as an indivisible essence which is the source of all created things. It derives from Dionysius the Pseudo-Areopagite.

[2] Augustinus Triumphus, *Summa*, lxxi. 4, p. 374; cf. i. 8, p. 12; xxxvi. 6, p. 217, 'Voluntas papae, qui est eius [scil. Dei] vicarius, est prima et summa causa omnium corporalium et spiritualium motionum'. Thomas Aquinas, *Summa theologica*, III. viii. 2, also referred to the soul as the *motor corporis* and applied this to the *Ecclesia* as *corpus Christi*.

[3] Augustinus Triumphus, *Summa*, xxii. 3, p. 131, 'Tota machina mundialis non est nisi unus principatus'; also Aegidius Romanus, *De ecclesiastica potestate*, i. 5, p. 16; Alvarus Pelagius, *De planctu Ecclesiae*, ch. 41, p. 70; *Conrad of Megenberg*, *Planctus ecclesiae in Germaniam*, *proem.*, p. 190; *De translatione imperii*,

ch. 1, p. 255; ch. 25, p. 343; Francis de Meyronnes, *De principatu Siciliae*, ch. 2, p. 103; Johannes Branchazolus, *De principio imperatoris et papae*, i. 3, p. 47; ii. 1, pp. 48–9; Tholemy of Lucca, *Determinatio compendiosa*, ch. 19, pp. 39–40. For its use by Benedict XII see Baluze, iii. 224–5, and by Henry VII, *MGH*, *Const.*, IV n. 801, p. 802. See also Innocent III, *Sermones de tempore*, xxvii (*PL*, ccxvii. 433), 'Universalis domus Dei est tota machina mundialis'; *Comm. in Psal. poen.*, 5 (1105). 'Terra ergo est machina mundialis'; and Frederick II, *Liber Augustalis*, i. 1, 'post mundi machinam'. The idea of the *Ecclesia* as an instrument or machine by which the soul is taken heavenwards is of early Christian origin, and was often applied to the Cross as a symbol of the Universal Church: W. Bousset, 'Platons Weltseele und das Kreuz Christi', *Zeitschrift für die neutestamentliche Wissenschaft*, xiv (1913), pp. 273–85 at p. 283, 'oder vielmehr das Kreuz selbst ist der wunderbare Mechanismus der diese ben Himmel führt': for this see E. S. Greenhill, 'The Child in the Tree: a study of the cosmological tree in Christian tradition', *Traditio*, x (1954), pp. 323–71 at pp. 333–4, 357–61. But cf. Aristotle, *Metaphysics*, iii. 8. For its use by Ignatius of Antioch and Greek writers in the fourth century, see H. Rahner, 'The Christian Mystery and the Pagan Mystics', *The Mysteries: Papers from the Eranos Year Books* (ed. J. Campbell, London, 1955), ii. 337–401 at pp. 337, 379. It is interesting to note that this concept was applied to France in the seventeenth century, and that Louis XIV was described by contemporaries in very similar terms: he is the highest central monad, the almighty *ingénieur* or *architecte de la machine*. This conception also leads on to the great machine of the Newtonian world and the Hobbesian state.

II. DIVIDE ET IMPERA

Two of the most common and confusing words in the medieval political vocabulary are 'temporal' and 'spiritual'. Although in general use, different writers give them very different implications, and their interpretation always depends upon the ideological standpoint of the user. To the hierocratic way of thinking the members of the Christian society can be divided into spiritual and temporal, ordained and unordained, in the same way that the community itself is believed to be an essentially spiritual society given a material existence on earth: 'tota multitudo et tota respublica vel spiritualis vel corporalis'.[1] But the use of a working distinction between temporal and spiritual is in no way intended to detract from the unity of one body of believers. Temporal and spiritual power merely describes that jurisdiction usually granted by the pope to laymen and clerics respectively. It does not signify that there are two powers, but that there is a *potestas duplex*, one power having twin aspects in the same manner that the *unum corpus Ecclesiae* has two sides. A passage from Alvarus Pelagius admirably illustrates this point:

cum dicitur potestas temporalis praeexistere in illo apud quem est spiritualis, non ita est intelligendum quasi per duas potestates diversas et distinctas habeat, sed quod *per unam suam potestatem super spiritualia et temporalia* potest. Nam inferiora sunt in superioribus unitive, et quod in inferioribus distinguitur, in superioribus unitur. Dicitur tamen in ipso esse *duplex potestas*. . . Sic *una potestas* habentis potentiam spiritualem dicitur temporalis et spiritualis et distinguitur circa officia.[2]

Beyond the advantage of having a settled allocation of functions there is no reason why a layman, the holder of 'temporal' jurisdiction, should not exercise the 'spiritual' jurisdiction normally re-

[1] Augustinus Triumphus, *Summa*, vii. 4, p. 67.

[2] Alvarus Pelagius, *De planctu Ecclesiae*, ch. 56, p. 157; cf. ch. 44, p. 77, 'potestas mixta de spiritualibus et temporalibus'.

served to a bishop, and vice versa.[1] The idea of a single juridical body must, according to Augustinus Triumphus, find its complement in the notion of *una potestas iurisdictionis*:

potestas papae est respectu Ecclesiae cuius administrationem gerit. Sed Ecclesia est una . . . ergo potestas papae similiter erit una.[2]

To be accurate therefore it is impossible to talk of 'the two powers', still less of such alien conceptions as Church and State. Lay power is simply a part of the whole; kings, as the papalists put it, 'intra Ecclesiam continentur sicut pars in toto'.[3] Baptism is as much a mark of citizenship as entry into the body of Christians; and religious obedience is identical with political obligation. In the true hierocratic conception of society there can be no real separation of earthly and spiritual matters, and the lay power, existing only to provide the Augustinian *pax terrena*, cannot have any independent existence. It is neither self-sufficient nor autonomous, because temporal things are not, and cannot be, an end in themselves: they have,

[1] Augustinus Triumphus, *De potestate collegii*, p. 502, 'potestas iurisdictionis sacerdotis aliquando potest esse et potest remanere in non-sacerdote, et potestas iurisdictionis episcopi esse potest et remanere in non-episcopo'. A layman could be granted any power normally appertaining to episcopal jurisdiction: *Summa*, lxxiv. 3, p. 385, 'ex commissione papae puto quod laicus potest excommunicare, beneficia ecclesiastica conferre, et omnia facere quae ex iurisdictione proveniunt'. This includes the right to preach (lxiv. 1, p. 337; lxiv. 2, p. 338; lxiv. 3 ad 2, p. 339; lxiv. 6, p. 341), to grant indulgences (xxix. 8, p. 180; xxix. 9, p. 181), and to excommunicate and deprive of the sacraments (xxvii. 1, p. 160; xxvii. 5, p. 163). This follows Thomas Aquinas, *Commentum in Sententias*, IV. xxv. i. 1 ad 3, 'Papa, qui habet plenitudinem potestatis pontificalis, potest committere non-episcopo ea quae ad episcopalem dignitatem pertinent, dummodo illa non habeant immediatam relationem ad verum corpus Christi'; but was derived from Decretist teaching, e.g. *Summa Et est sciendum, ad* D. 22 c. 3, 'Sed numquid potuit eis concedere papa? Ergo eadem ratione posset laico committere causam spiritualem determinandam et ita laicus posset excommunicare contumacem': F. Gillmann, 'Die Dekretglossen des Cod. Stuttgart. hist. f. 419', *AKKR*, cvii (1927), pp. 192–250 at p. 228.

[2] Augustinus Triumphus, *Summa*, i. 6, p. 9. He continues, 'Si vero loquimur de potestate papae respectu corporis Christi mystici, quae est potestas iurisdictionis, talis similiter est *una* in papa unitate cuiusdam ordinis. . . Itaque papa *per unam potestatem* ordine quodam habet ordinare clericos ad clericos, et clericos ad laicos, et laicos inter se'.

[3] Alvarus Pelagius, *Collyrium*, p. 504; also Augustinus Triumphus, *Summa*, i. 4 ad 3, p. 7; Gilbert of Tournai, *Eruditio regum*, II. i. 1, p. 44; cf. Gratian, C. 23 q. 5 c. 20.

as Augustinus Triumphus says, no *finalis intentio.*[1] The lay power is merely a derivative of the power of that ruler who knows and understands this aim: it is given to kings and princes by the pope, but ultimately it remains papal power. All temporal power is therefore spiritual power; lay jurisdiction is enveloped and embraced by the spiritual. The power of the pope is called spiritual power because he governs a fundamentally spiritual society: it is also called ecclesiastical power,[2] because the political institution over which he presides is an *Ecclesia*, but it includes all temporal power.

Et ideo qui concedunt summum pontificem habere plenitudo potestatis in spiritualibus, concedunt ipsum necessario habere plenitudo potestatis in corporalibus. Nam totus homo christianus spiritualis est iuxta sententiam Salvatoris.[3]

And those, added Augustinus Triumphus, who seek the kingdom of God have all earthly things given unto them.[4] Repeatedly, he and other papalists stress that when spiritual power is under discussion, it must be assumed as a matter of course that this includes all temporal power. Those who have spiritual power automatically hold temporal power, says Alexander de S. Elpidio—'Cui ergo concessa est potestas spiritualis, concessa est temporalis'—and Augustinus Triumphus can be found echoing his words.[5] The triad 'one society, one head, one power' beats like a refrain through the

[1] Augustinus Triumphus, *Summa*, lx. 3 ad 1, p. 315.

[2] Aegidius Romanus, *De ecclesiastica potestate*, iii. 12, p. 209, 'de potestate ecclesiastica sive de potestate summi pontificis'; cf. Innocent III, *Reg.*, I. cccxlv (*PL*, ccxiv. 319), 'plenitudo potestatis ecclesiasticae'.

[3] Anon., *De potestate Ecclesiae*, p. 254.

[4] Augustinus Triumphus, *Summa*, xxii. 2, p. 130, 'Principatus papae et omnis principatus ecclesiasticus est principaliter propter bonum spirituale. Per redundantiam autem et ex consequenti habet esse circa corporalia, quia vicarius illius existit qui dixit, Quaerite primum regnum Dei, et haec omnia adiicientur vobis [*Matth.*, vi. 33]'.

[5] Alexander de S. Elpidio, *De ecclesiastica potestate*, ii. 6, p. 21; Augustinus Triumphus, *Summa*, i. 8, p. 12, 'Papa ergo qui vicem Dei gerit in terris ex quo habet potestatem spiritualium habebit similiter potestatem temporalium et corporalium'; and cf. the use of I *Cor.*, ix. 11 in *Summa*, lxix. 4, p. 363. It may be noted that this applies not only to the pope himself but to all members of the clergy.

work of the publicists: and with Alvarus Pelagius this theme is reiterated at length. The civil power, he argues, cannot be distinguished from the ecclesiastical. They are not two separate species but integral parts of one governmental unit dominated by the ecclesiastical. All Christians form a single political community, since all are one body in Christ, and thus there is one ruler. It cannot be maintained that there are two separate authorities, spiritual and temporal, because neither ruler nor subject can have anything which does not pertain to the one Christian community. There cannot be a division of the society into spiritual and temporal because it is all one society. Again, the Universal Church is the one and only body politic, one people needing a monarch to direct and guide it.[1] Hence we see that in a society which is conceived of as *unum corpus* 'temporal' and 'spiritual' are really identical, and lose much of their significance as descriptive terms. All terrestrial power may be reduced to spiritual power,

Et eodem modo est in toto corpore Ecclesiae quod omnes potestates temporales et spirituales ad unam primam et summam reducuntur, in qua et sub qua clauduntur, per quam reguntur, et in suis actibus regulantur,

and if this was initially present in Christ, it has now passed into the sole keeping of his vicar on earth.[2] Consequently there is no other

[1] Alvarus Pelagius, *De planctu Ecclesiae*, ch. 40, pp. 60–1, 'Ex quo patet quod principatus civilis non distinguitur a principatu ecclesiastico sicut una species ab alia, sed sicut partes integrales unius principatus, intelligendo per civilem principatum saecularem potestatem, inter quas partes principalissima et superior est ecclesiastica potestas. . . Ecce unus principatus in politia christiana, et unus pastor. Ecce unus principalis rector et monarcha huiusmodi principatus, et secundum hoc sunt omnes fideles Christi unum corpus mysticum. . . Nec potest dici quod christiani sunt unius principatus quantum ad spiritualia et alterius quantum ad corporalia et temporalia, quia nullus princeps vel subditus christianus potest aliquid licite possidere vel acquirere nisi in eo quod militat sub principatu christiano. . . Ex quo liquido patet quod civilitas christiana et politia et quantum ad temporalia et quantum ad spiritualia ad eundem principatum pertinet, et hoc clamat tota sacra scriptura quod sumus omnes Christi fideles una communitas et unus populus. . . Viso autem quod politia christiana sit simpliciter una, tunc facile est videre quod unus est princeps regens et dirigens eam'.

[2] Anon., *Disquisitio theologico-iuridica*, ii. 13, p. 1350; also Tholemy of Lucca, *De regimine principum*, iii. 10, p. 259, 'Quod si dicatur ad solam referri spiritualem

source from which power can be obtained except the pope. The setting up of the papal vicariate of Christ has excluded any possibility of direct grant from God, and it follows that it is only the will of the pope which brings the lay power into existence at all.

Potestas papae est maior omnia alia maioritate causalitatis, quia eius potestas causat omnem aliam potestatem examinando, confirmando et iudicando . . . quia cuiuslibet ordinis dignitatem et potestatem Romanus pontifex habet *instituere* et confirmare; eius vero potestatem solus Christus fundavit et confirmavit.[1]

The very *esse* of the lay ruler, it may be said, stems from Peter and his successors. He becomes no more than a papal official, subject to the pope in every possible way. Every king, provided he is worthy of it, is instituted by the pope, says Augustinus Triumphus in an adaptation of the famous passage from Hugh of St Victor, and if he shall prove to be unworthy, the pope shall destroy him.[2] Lay rulers are the instruments of papal policy, created to assist the Roman pontiff in the government of the world and in the attainment of the end for which the *Ecclesia* was set up. As such they have a useful but necessarily auxiliary function. There can be no suggestion that they have any degree of autonomous existence or that they have in themselves a right to exist at all. Was it not for the papal commission of power to them, kings and emperors would have no place in a Christian society.

The question of whether the lay ruler has an inalienable right to govern in a Christian society is obviously a matter of paramount importance and requires much closer consideration. Nevertheless it can be seen that the full expression of the hierocratic theory leads

potestatem, hoc esse non potest, quia corporale et temporale ex spirituali et perpetuo dependet, sicut corporis operatio ex virtute animae. Sicut ergo corpus per animam habet *esse*, virtutem et operationem . . . ita et temporalis iurisdictio principum per spiritualem Petri et successorum eius'.

[1] Augustinus Triumphus, *Summa*, i. 3, p. 5.

[2] Augustinus Triumphus, *Summa* (Augsburg, 1473), xlvi. 1, 'spiritualis potestas terrenam potestatem habet instituere *ut sit*, et iudicare atque corrigere si bona non fuerit': see Hugh of St Victor, *De sacramentis*, II. ii. 4 (*PL*, clxxvi. 418). The operative phrase in this passage, which he uses many times, is 'ut sit'—so that it [the lay power] has being or existence. It is noticeable that those publicists who accept Aquinas' theory of the natural origin of lay power consistently omit this phrase. It is omitted in later editions of the *Summa*.

inexorably to the conclusion that the lay power is in the last resort superfluous. If the pope is the *Ecclesia*, then there is of necessity no room for other princes, and those that do exist can do so only by his permission. The lay power is thus effectively excluded from any major share in the direction of the *congregatio fidelium*. It is hardly necessary to point out that this conception of the value of lay government cut right across the claims of the kings and emperors themselves. Few amongst the European princes were prepared to acknowledge the papacy as a universal monarchy, still less to assist in making it a reality. At no time in the medieval period were the lay rulers willing to accept the very inferior status accorded to them in the hierocratic conception of the right order, and it was this which proved the most effective stumbling block to every attempt to put the hierocratic scheme into practice. It was appreciated that an acceptance of the papal claim to universal sovereignty would extinguish all royal and imperial aspirations to monarchy, and from the beginning the hierocratic idea had met with the fiercest opposition. But whilst the hierocratic idea in its early stages had appeared as a mere usurpation of an already established imperial right to control all men and all matters, the vigorous exposition and application of hierocratic principles since the age of Gregory VII had, for a time, made the papal position almost impregnable. Indeed it was the lay thesis which had now to find the means of justifying itself, and in the process a good deal of the old caesaro-papist elements in it had been forced underground. Although the ideal of a lay monarch who should have supreme control of all aspects of political and religious life never entirely disappeared, the majority of the papal opponents in the twelfth, thirteenth and fourteenth centuries confined themselves to demanding only an unworkable plurality of independent rulers within the framework of the one society. Faced with the assertion of a pope who was both priest and king, and who claimed to be the sole repository of God's truth and power on earth, the protagonists of imperial power were in reality on the defensive. Their immediate objective was not the total destruction of papal authority, but its limitation; and it was held that this might be best achieved by making a rigid separation between the provinces of pope and lay ruler, to create in effect autonomous spheres of temporal and spiritual in which emperor and pope could reign supreme. Inadequate as this contention was when viewed in the context of a society which was *unum corpus Christi*, the idea of a *dualitas* was generally accepted by every lay ruler in Europe during this period.[1] By the time of Louis IV of Bavaria it was firmly entrenched as the official imperial doctrine, and as such was defended by a veritable host of anti-hierocratic writers. To Louis himself the claim of John XXII to universal headship of the Christian body was an enormity and a perversion of the right ordering, which, he declares, ought to make the pope worthy of deposition.[2] There has been only one *caput Ecclesiae* with so much power, and this Christ himself. But even Christ was so convinced of the propriety of separating temporal and spiritual functions from each other that he renounced all his right to temporal power in favour of the Roman emperor:

Amplius Christus ipse se nolle imperatoris et sacerdotis officium insimul ab ullo eius vicario seu ministro ullatenus possideri per facti evidentiam propalavit, dum ipse, cui *soli*, quia verus Deus et verus homo, data fuit in coelo et in terra universa potestas, regnum seu imperium terrenum et omne dominium temporale a se penitus abdicavit.[3]

Whilst this does not deny the fact of the Petrine commission, it means that the emperor holds the secular government of the world

[1] This theory was first officially proclaimed by the emperor Henry IV: for this and the sources of the Henrician view see W. Ullmann, *The Growth of Papal Government*, pp. 345f. For its use in France, and a comparison of the theory with Frederick II and Philip the Fair see H. Wieruszowski, 'Vom Imperium zum Nationalen Königtum', *Historische Zeitschrift*, xxx (Munich and Berlin, 1933), especially pp. 89–108.

[2] Baluze, iii. 388, 'In quo etiam abutitur notorie plenitudine potestatis quae nonnisi ad aedificationem Ecclesiae datur. Et cum non possit iudicare nec debeat nisi secundum iustitiam, malitiose et iniuriose iuris pervertit ordinem, processus suos fundando super notoriis, quae tamen non solum sunt notoria sed manifeste falsa'. He accuses John of 'attentans et satagens, quamvis illicite, imperialem et sacerdotalem simul dignitatem et potestatem habere, quas Christus ipse in suppositos voluit esse distinctas', so that he becomes 'hunc misticum antichristum qui se papa nominat', whose maltreatment of imperial subjects earns him the title of 'vir sanguinum'. And he reminds the pope of the penalties attendant upon an attempt to detract from imperial power, citing the proscription of Robert of Naples 'propter crimen laesae maiestatis' (iii. 427–8).

[3] Baluze, iii. 428.

direct from God, in the same way that the pope rules the spiritual things of the society by the same divine right. Louis' successor, Charles IV, was to make the very same point in the Golden Bull when he styled himself *temporale caput populo christiano*.[1] Although this may in a sense be regarded as the beginning of the idea of Church and State in a society which conceived of neither, it must be made clear that the lay thesis was not intended to affect the actual nature of the Christian society, but only its internal organisation. A dualism was held to exist within the framework of the universal body, not to replace it. The imperialist still regards the *Ecclesia* as the one body of Christ which embraces all Christians; it is still both a Church and a civil society; but it is maintained that a separation can and must be made between the competence of the civil and ecclesiastical powers. The Knight in the *Somnium viridarii*, for example, takes one man as a microcosm of the *maior mundus*, and from this concludes that the whole world forms a single unit, of which it is acknowledged that the pope is head. However, he adds, this papal headship can only be understood in a spiritual sense, for the lay ruler is the foundation of the temporal life of his kingdom. Therefore the pope may no more interfere in temporal matters than the king in spiritual ones.

... sic in regimine maioris mundi omnes in Christo sumus unum corpus; huius corporis caput est Romanus pontifex ... qui omnibus praeesse noscitur *spiritualiter*... Dominus autem temporalis sicut rex in regno recte dicitur fundamentum... Sic nec Romanus pontifex debet se de temporalibus intromittere, nec rex de spiritualibus, ne alteruter eorum falcem imponat in messem alienam.[2]

[1] Golden Bull, ch. 2; ch. 3 'temporale caput mundo': K. Zeumer, *Quellen und Studien zur Verfassungsgeschichte des Deutschen Reiches in Mittelalter und Neuzeit*: II. 2 *Die Goldene Bulle Kaiser Karls IV* (Weimar, 1908), pp. 14–15.

[2] Anon., *Somnium viridarii*, i. 38, p. 71. For the dualists' acceptance of the idea of a unified Christian society cf. Johannes Branchazolus, *De principio imperatoris et papae*, ii. 1, pp. 48–9, 'machina mundialis est unum corpus' comprising all cities and provinces; and note the definition of *Ecclesia* and Roman empire as 'omnes christiani, omnes fideles' by Ugolinus de Celle, *De electione et coronatione regis Romanorum*, ch. 16, p. 78. Similarly Louis IV, Baluze, iii. 434, 438, 'in omnium fidelium'; 'Dei sive corporis eius mystici quod est Ecclesia'; 'ab universali Ecclesia recepta'. Henry VII had also described himself as acting in the name of a single universal body of Christians: R. Folz, *Le souvenir et la légende de Charlemagne* (Paris, 1950), pp. 400–1.

There are two swords: temporal and spiritual *are* distinct from each other, and can be shut up into relatively watertight compartments. But the Universal Church is still a political community. Even the French publicists, although they demanded that each king should be supreme in temporal matters, continue to regard the kingdom of France as a component of the universal society, and at times almost outbid the papalists in their entreaties for the basic unity of all Christians. The passage reading 'Sancta mater Ecclesia, sponsa Christi, non solum ex clericis sed etiam ex laicis . . . ex omnibus fidelibus una est Ecclesia,' which might be duplicated in any one of a hundred hierocratic tracts, does in fact form the starting point from which the author of the virulently anti-papal *Antequam essent clerici* sets out a series of propositions in favour of lay independence.[1] But even more interesting in this respect are the arguments put forward by William Nogaret, adviser to Philip the Fair and the perpetrator of the Anagni incident. A year after the death of the humiliated Boniface, Nogaret seeks to justify his actions by presenting them as having been taken in defence of the French kingdom. And since the French kingdom, he maintains, is an integral part of the *Ecclesia*, and the welfare of part and whole are inseparable, then the Anagni affair may be regarded as something undertaken for the benefit of the whole Christian society.[2] In the same fashion two years earlier, in 1302, a French priest had sought to justify his master's disastrous campaign against Flanders on the ground that it was undertaken in defence of peace—not only the peace of France but of the whole *Ecclesia*, since no real distinction could be drawn

[1] Anon., *Antequam essent clerici*, p. 21; also the *Rex pacificus*, ch. 3, p. 672; Pierre Dubois, *De recuperatione Sancta Terrae*, ch. 3, p. 3; ch. 4, p. 7; and Nogaret in Dupuy, p. 263. For Nogaret and Philip IV see further E. Boutaric, 'Notices et Extraits de documents inédits relatifs à l'histoire de France sous Philippe le Bel', *Notices et Extraits des manuscrits*, xx. 2 (1862), pp. 82–237 at p. 184; and Wieruszowski, *op. cit.*, p. 147, for a comparison with Frederick II.

[2] Dupuy, p. 241, 'Item proposuit quod, videns regnum Franciae venerabilem partem Ecclesiae sanctae Dei ac principalem columnam sententationis ecclesiae Romanae. . .'; p. 243, 'Item quod cum ad conservationem et defensionem corporis universi Ecclesiae catholicae necessaria sit conservatio ac defensio partium corporis ipsius, et maxime tam magnae partis quam egregiae corporis ipsius Ecclesiae ut est regnum Franciae, cum ipsa Ecclesia in partibus suis consistat'.

between them.[1] However much practical realities might demonstrate otherwise, and however much they argued for the supremacy of the ruler in his own kingdom, the lay writers were still very far indeed from shaking themselves free of the dominant concept of a universal community into which all lesser political societies were gathered.

But whilst these writers stress the necessary retention of the ultimate universality of the Christian body, they also urge that the sphere of secular things (*regnum* or *imperium*) can and ought to be divorced from those purely spiritual matters controlled by the *sacerdotium*, and, most confusingly, also covered by the term *ecclesia*.[2] This distinction, said Louis IV, is an act of God. *Imperium* and *sacerdotium* derive independently and immediately from Christ, and their respective rulers are subject to none but God. The Roman emperor is the heir of God in temporal matters, and as such cannot be held responsible for his actions to the pope.[3] In temporal

[1] J. Leclercq, 'Un sermon prononcé pendant la guerre de Flandre sous Philippe le Bel', *Revue du moyen âge latin*, i (1945), pp. 165–72 at p. 170, 'pax regis est pax regni; pax regni est pax Ecclesiae. . . Igitur qui contra regem invehitur laborat contra totam Ecclesiam'.

[2] It is noticeable that it is the dualists who at this time put most emphasis upon the distinction between the *Ecclesia* as the universal body of Christians and the *ecclesia* in the sense of the *sacerdotium*: e.g. Anon., *Rex pacificus*, ch. 3, p. 672, 'Et hoc intelligitur debet accipiendo ecclesiam non in generali, prout dicimus quod Ecclesia dicitur congregatio fidelium, sed secundum quod accipitur in speciali, scilicet, prout ecclesia distinguitur contra saeculum, et clerici et viri ecclesiastici contra laicos et saeculares'. This is the meaning of Frederick II's famous claim to be acting 'pro Ecclesia contra ecclesiam'.

[3] Louis IV in his condemnation of John XXII at Rome, 18 June, 1328: Baluze, iii. 425–6, 'Gloriosus Deus et sublimis dominantium dominus nulli secundus, qui universa propter semetipsum operatus est, impium quoque ad diem malum, sacerdotium et imperium independenter principians et conservans, ut hoc quidem divina exerceat, illud autem humanis praesideat rempublicam sibi traditam recte et magnifice gubernando, nos, Ludovicum quartum Romanorum imperatorem semper augustum, in imperialis culmine maiestatis constituit et in hoc quia nos *in principem super haereditatem suam inunxit*, ut de manibus inimicorum suum populum liberemus, exaltans nos *super gentes et regna*, ut pacis subversores disperdamus ubique, zelatores vero eiusdem *plantemus et aedificemus*, creans fructum labiorum nostrorum pacem hiis qui longe sunt et hiis qui prope. . .'. Note the use of the favourite papal text, *Jer.*, i. 10, and the influence of Justinian's decree in *Nov.*, VI *proem.* Cf. Frederick II, *MGH*, *Const.*, ii. 197, 'Gloriosus in maiestate sua dominantium dominus qui regna constituit et firmavit imperium . . . ad hoc nos supra reges et regna praeposuit et in imperiali solio sublimavit'.

things therefore the lay ruler becomes a real monarch ruling by divine right, a concept given expression in the idea of the *sacrum imperium*.[1] Similarly the pope is God's choice as ruler of the *sancta ecclesia*, the counterpart of the *sacrum imperium*, but this implies that he is *caput Ecclesiae* only in regard to spiritualities. He is the vicar of that Christ whose kingdom is not of this world, and who fled into a mountain when offered an earthly crown.[2] Consequently, said one French writer, it is positively frivolous that the pope should claim to have any temporal power in his own right;[3] and in general the dualists agreed that he could only exercise such jurisdiction if it had been granted to him by a lay ruler, and that he should remain subject to lay supervision whilst using it.[4] There are then at least two vicars of Christ, the lay ruler in temporals and the pope in spirituals, who stand upon an equal footing with each other: there are two heads to the one society.[5]

[1] Baluze, iii. 387; 388; 393, 'de iurisdictione temporali sacri imperii'; 429, 'quoniam sacrum Romanum imperium quoad temporalium administrationem noluimus nec debuimus recognoscere eidem [papae] fore subiectum'.

[2] Baluze, iii. 429, 445; cf. Pierre Dubois, *La supplication du pueuble de France*, p. 216, 'Dieu le Père bailla à deux personnes le gouvernement de son petit pueuble d'Israël, à un le temporel, à l'autre l'esperituel. . . Ce que tu lieras en terre sera liè au ciel [*Matth*., xvi. 19], ceste parolle d'esperitualité'; and compare this with Dante's denial that the papal power of binding and loosing is applicable to imperial laws, *Monarchia*, iii. 8, p. 369.

[3] Anon., *Disputatio inter clericum et militem*, p. 13, 'Et quemadmodum terreni principes non possunt aliquid statuere de vestris spiritualibus, super quae non acceperunt potestatem, sic nec vos de temporalibus eorum, super quae non habetis auctoritatem. Unde frivolum est quicquid statuistis de temporalibus, super quae potestatem non accepistis a Deo'.

[4] John of Paris, *De potestate regia et papali*, *proem*., p. 175, 'puto . . . quod scilicet praelatis ecclesiae non repugnat habere dominium in temporalibus et iurisdictionem . . . nec tamen eis debetur per se ratione status sui et ratione qua sunt vicarii Christi et apostolorum successores, sed eis convenire potest talis habere ex concessione vel permissione principum'; Anon., *Rex pacificus*, ch. 3, p. 672, 'Sic etiam qui nunc vocatus est ad iurisdictionem spiritualem . . . bene habet usum alicuius iurisdictionis temporalis sicut papa et praelati alii alicubi, sed nonnisi quantum sibi datum et permissum ab illis qui habent in hoc mundo temporalium potestatem, videlicet ab imperatoribus, regibus et aliis principibus'.

[5] Anon., *Rex pacificus*, ch. 4, p. 680, 'Sed quando dicitur papa est vicarius Christi, dico quod verum est in spiritualibus; sed bene habet alium vicarium in temporalibus, videlicet, potestatem temporalem, qua cum sit a Deo, sicut dicitur *Rom*., 13 [xiii. 1, 4], potest dici vices Dei gerere in regimine temporali'.

The separation of *imperium* and *sacerdotium* (or *ecclesia*) did not profess to give the lay ruler complete control of his lay subjects, whilst leaving the charge of his clergy to the pope. Like the society itself, each individual was subject to a divided jurisdiction: it was a separation of temporal and spiritual matters, not persons. Accordingly the pope was still the superior of both laity and clergy in spiritual cases, whilst the lay ruler remained the superior of the priesthood in temporal matters. 'To render unto Caesar', the favourite lay argument, did not deny the universality of papal power in respect of all Christians, but prohibited its extension into secular affairs. Both *imperium* and *sacerdotium* retained their universality, since these terms denoted spheres of competence rather than anything else. Nevertheless this functional separation inevitably tended to become a territorial one. The realities of the political situation in Europe after the death of Frederick II made for a distinction between the territorial extent of the Empire and those lands subject to the Roman church, and this separation seemed to be an example of dualism in practice.[1] This offshoot of the orthodox *dualitas* theory found a good deal of support from imperial adherents, since it ensured the inviolability not only of the lay sphere but of the territorial empire altogether. Papal influence was to be cut off from all interferences with the German clergy or imperial subjects in general,[2] although the 'right' of the emperor to coerce the laity subject to the Roman church (*in terra ecclesiae*) could still be urged by a reversion to the more usual dualist line. At the same time incipient

[1] For example the *Somnium viridarii*, ii. 294, p. 192, 'Hic est attendendum quod licet principatus orbis, attenta illa divina potestate limitata imperatoris habet potestatem, *territorium*, et messem suam distinctam a messe temporali limitata ecclesiae et a messe spirituali'. A distinction between the *terrae imperii* and the *terrae ecclesiae* is assumed in most imperialist tracts of the period: see further C. N. S. Woolf, *Bartolus of Sassoferrato* (Cambridge, 1913), especially pp. 75–8, 94–100, 322.

[2] Ugolinus de Celle, *De electione et coronatione regis Romanorum*, ch. 9, p. 75, 'quia a solo Deo habet [imperator] illam potestatem in temporalibus, papa vero in spiritualibus. Et sic divisa est iurisdictio . . . quia [papa] de subditis imperii non habet se intromittere'. Similarly Pierre Dubois, *Deliberatio super agendis*, p. 45, argued the fundamental right of the French king to appoint his own clergy and use the revenue from their benefices. Cf. John of Paris, *De potestate regia et papali*, ch. 10, pp. 94–5, 'immo sunt potestates distinctae episcopalis et temporalis non solum re sed subiecto'.

nationalism in Germany and Italy steadily strengthened the idea of two separate kingdoms, one imperial and the other papal.[1] But whilst a territorial separation might seem in many ways to be a practical compromise between the competing claims of popes and emperors to world monarchy, an adequate theoretical justification for any sort of two power doctrine was virtually impossible whilst the lay writers continued to work within the framework of the Christian society. They were in fact endeavouring to meet their opponents on their own ground, and were inevitably worsted in all the great debates on papal-imperial relationships. Undeterred by references to Manichees and monsters, the lay writers laboured on at their self-appointed task of proving that one plus one equalled one, and were consequently vulnerable to the impeccable logic of all the papal arguments in favour of unity, monarchy and functional qualification.[2] How could a society which was essentially one be composed of two autonomous parts? How could *unum corpus* have *duo capita*? In what way is the lay ruler functionally qualified to lay down the necessarily Christian law appropriate to a society based upon faith? And if temporal and spiritual can really be separated, exactly where and on what authority is the line of demarcation to be drawn? Such questions as these were unanswerable when the lay writers attempted to reply to the papalists in their own terms. The hierocratic doctrine, whatever its weaknesses in fact, was a system of universal right, and could only be destroyed by the overthrow of its central premise and postulate, the idea of a universal and unitary Christian society.

Because of their inability to deny this concept of society, in

[1] See Woolf, *op. cit.*, pp. 314–15, for the demand of the Italian poet Fazzio degli Uberti for a national kingdom in Italy. The empire, he says, has become a German thing, and is lost to Italy beyond hope of recovery.

[2] These arguments are to be found in most papal tracts: e.g. Francis de Meyronnes, *Quaestio de subiectione*, i. 2, p. 77, 'Si autem ponitur duo principes quorem neuter est sub altero universales, universum istius vitae tunc erit divisum, et tunc non erit optime dispositum; et confirmatur quia omne regnum in se divisum desolabitur, *Matth.* 12 capitulo [xii. 25]; et quanto divisio est magis intrinsica, tanto magis in regno sequitur detrimentum'; Alvarus Pelagius, *Collyrium*, p. 505, 'Nam haeresis est Manichaeorum ponere duo principia'; Anon., *De potestate Ecclesiae*, p. 251, 'sicut monstrum et contra naturam esset unum corpus habere duo capita distincta'.

reality the idea of one body and one head remained as attractive to the anti-hierocrat as to the papalist. The theory of the *dualitas* initiated by Henry IV had been a retraction from the old imperial idea in which the emperor held the place now taken over by the pope, but it never quite forgot its parentage. A close study of the dualist argument in the early fourteenth century shows that although the pope was theoretically permitted full spiritual jurisdiction over all Christians, the ultimate objective of imperial and French policy was to deprive him of all coercive power worthy of the name. Complete jurisdictional supremacy was to pass back into the hands of the lay rulers, and the successorship to Peter was to confer no more than a magisterial primacy, the power to decide purely moral and theological points. In support of this the Frenchman Pierre Dubois demands that the pope shall be stripped of all his possessions because 'papa, qui est caput ecclesiae et lux mundi consistens verbo magis et opere totum mundum debet docere'.[1] The ideal of nearly all contemporary princes was to deny the pope any real share in the government of the Christian society, and, by revitalising the proprietary church system, to ensure that the clergy rested totally subject to themselves. Half a century earlier Frederick II had in fact expressly stated that behind dualism lay a determination to shut out pope and clergy from all concern with governmental affairs. They are, he contemptuously remarked, suited only for the mystical and spiritual duties of holy men and miracle workers.[2] Much the same attitude emerges from Louis IV's elaborate exposition of dualism. The pope is denied both the right to condemn for heresy and the ability to promote the clergy,[3] whilst the emperor becomes

[1] Pierre Dubois, *Deliberatio super agendis*, pp. 46–7. For the same attitude in the *Rex pacificus* see W. Ullmann, 'A Medieval Document on Papal Theories of Government', *EHR*, lxi (1946), pp. 188–201.

[2] Winkelmann, ii. 50, n. 46, 'semper nostrae fuit intentio voluntatis clericos... ad hoc inducere et maxime maximos ut tales perseverarent in fine quales fuerunt in Ecclesia primitiva, apostolicam vitam ducentes, humilitatem dominicam imitantes. Tales enim clerici solebant angelos intueri, miraculis coruscare, egros curare, mortuos suscitare, et sanctitate non armis sibi reges et principes subiugare'. For a similar position with Frederick I see W. Ullmann, 'Cardinal Roland and Besançon', *MHP*, xviii (Rome, 1954), pp. 107–25 at pp. 118–19.

[3] He complains, Baluze, iii. 389, that John XXII 'archiepiscopatus, episcopatus et abbatias confert partialiter et indignis omnino, cuiuscunque aetatis sint,

defensor fidei in the fullest sense of the term: he has almost complete jurisdictional control of the priesthood, from which it follows that he should be able to appoint and depose its head. Thus Louis announces that he will personally concern himself ('in quo nos, favente Domino, intendimus personaliter interesse') with the removal of him 'qui se dicit Iohannem papae XXII'. This is not for reasons of personal spite but '*propter* zelum fidei et propter devotionem quam habemus et sanctam Dei *ecclesiam*, cuius defensor, patronus et advocatus existimus'.[1] But one thing is abundantly clear: the emperor is to be the real source of authority in the Christian society. As emperor of the Romans he is the chief of a royal priesthood, and the implication that he himself is *rex-sacerdos* is inescapable. We have come to Italy, declares the self-styled emperor in 1328, so that we may occupy our principal see as quickly as possible, and govern the chosen people with the invincible power that belongs to God and us. Those who have removed themselves from their natural overlord are to be forcefully corrected, whilst the yoke of the tyrant popes is to be lifted from the faithful. King and priest, the emperor is now to be seen as the true ruler of the world.[2]

qualiscunque vitae, dummodo sint imperio rebelles et inimici, quantuncunque sint *naturaliter* vassalli imperii. Nullus autem imperialis per ipsum potest quomodolibet promoveri . . .', and continues, p. 391, that the emperor must be the judge of whether his subjects were guilty of heresy, not the pope. If the pope was allowed to do this he would be acting as accuser and judge in his own case: 'cum ipse idem contra praedictos sit accusator simul et iudex'. John of Calvaruso, *Quaestio an Romanus pontifex potuerit treugam inducere principi Romanorum*, pp. 1313–16, acknowledges that the pope possesses *iurisdictio in spiritualibus*, but promptly denies him the power to excommunicate. For Philip the Fair's rejection of the papal right to excommunicate French subjects see R. Génestal, *Les Origines de l'Appel comme d'Abus* (Paris, 1950), pp. x–xi. The royal claim to judgement in matters of heresy is denounced by Augustinus Triumphus in the *De facto Templariorum*.

[1] Baluze, iii. 409. He will not however act directly himself but through the medium of a general council. This is a complete reversion to the Saxon idea of emperorship, and it is interesting to note that Louis compares his deposition of John XXII with Otto I's deposition of John XII (also effected through a synod), Baluze, iii. 431.

[2] Baluze, iii. 426, 'celeri cursu in Italiam venimus ad sedem nostram praecipuam, Romam videlicet, properantes . . . in qua siquidem urbe divina opitulante providentia caesareo diademate ac sceptro legitime susceptis per nostrum Romanum peculiarem populum (cf. p. 430, 'hanc sacratissimam gentem et urbem Romanam, videlicet quam Christus ipse in gentem sanctam, genus

In the previous century the German cleric Alexander of Roes had occupied himself during a visit to Rome in attempting to account for the imperial position.[1] Like most supporters of the empire Alexander began by defining the dual nature of the *imperium* and the *ecclesia* as divine institutions: 'sicut ecclesia Romana est ecclesia Dei, sic utique regnum Romanorum est similiter regnum Dei', although the superiority of the *imperium* could be gauged from Christ's injunction, 'Seek ye first the kingdom of God'. But he was not content to let the matter rest there, and went on to maintain that both emperor and pope derived their power from St. Peter, who had been put in possession of a *regale sacerdotium* by Christ. Having thus neatly sidestepped the problem of the Petrine commission, Alexander was now however faced with the difficulty of explaining how the emperor could be said to have gained power from St. Peter. To solve this he resorted to the legend of St. Peter's staff, popularised a century earlier by Godfrey of Viterbo.[2] The legend relates that this staff, which symbolised the apostolic jurisdiction, was given by the saint to those of his disciples who were sent to convert the Rhineland. From them it passed to the archbishops of Triers and Cologne. The top part was given to Cologne, the lower but longer part to Triers, to demonstrate that Triers was an older see than Cologne but inferior to it. Thus, according to Alexander, himself a canon of Cologne, it is these archbishops who now elect the emperor, and through them that St. Peter's jurisdiction devolves upon him. And what else can this be, asks Alexander, than the *regale sacerdotium*?

electum, regale sacerdotium ac populum acquisitionis incommutabiliter praeelegit [I *Pet.*, ii. 9]') Urbi et orbi Dei ac nostra potentia invincibili praesidemus, ut manus nostrae fortitudine triumphali rebelles, qui pro nunc a nobis suo domino *naturali* longe sunt, corripiamus potenter, fidelesque nostros ab angariis et persecutionibus tyrannicis insuperabili potestate Dei et nostra efficaciter eruamus'.

[1] Alexander of Roes, *De translatione imperii*, pp. 31–6, which he is said to have written whilst attending Cardinal James Colonna at the papal curia *c.* 1281.

[2] Godfrey of Viterbo, *Pantheon* (*MGH. SS.*, xxii. 156). The story is quoted by Innocent III, *De sacro altaris mysterio*, i. 62 (*PL*, ccxvii. 796–7). Aquinas, *Summa theologica*, III. *Suppl.* xl. 7 ad 8, also maintains that the pope does not use the staff because St. Peter had given it to the see of Triers. Alexander of Roes' argument recalls the scheme promoted by Frederick I for making the archbishop of Triers *primas*, ruling *vice Petri*, over an imperial church independent of Rome.

Sed quid per Petrum apostolorum principem et fundamentum Ecclesiae nisi regale sacerdotium intelligimus? Et quid per baculum pastoralem... nisi sacrum imperium, id est, sacerdotale regnum designatur?

In this way the old Staufen theory of the German archbishops as imperial popes is, provided one accepts Alexander's account, successfully knit up with an explanation of the German ruler's right to the empire predating the historical translation to Charlemagne. The emperor gains his authority from a purely German election and coronation, and it is an authority compounded of both royal and priestly elements. Hence it is immeasurably superior to that of 'the Italian bishop', that High Priest's servant who lost his ear to St. Peter's sword. But, argues Alexander, it is just as simple a matter to cut off the whole head as a single ear, and the pope is thereby left to conclude that his life is at the mercy of imperial power.[1] In spite of appearances, the dual vicariate is far from presupposing an equality of powers, and the same theme is uppermost in the mind of Johannes Branchazolus. Writing some thirty years later at the time of the emperor Henry VII, Johannes provides one of the best contemporary examples of the way in which dualism was little more than a reluctant and temporary retreat from a far more rigorous position. Johannes does indeed pay lip-service to the traditional *dualitas* idea, although he is careful to mention the priority of the lay power: 'Et sic ab eodem principio, scilicet a Deo, licet non eodem tempore, tam sacerdotium quam imperium processerunt'. He even acknowledges the status of both pope and emperor as *capita Ecclesiae*.[2] But increasingly he harks wistfully back to a remote past, before the time of Moses, when there had been a single supreme ruler over the whole world, combining all power in his own person. This king, who is as much priest as king, can hardly be more highly estimated: he is described as

[1] Alexander of Roes, *De translatione imperii*, pp. 32–3, 'Praesules siquidem Germaniae non sunt illius vicarii qui relicta sindone nudus abfugit [*Mark*, xiv. 52] sicut episcopi Italici, sed eius vicarii qui dixit, Domine paratus sum et in vitam et in mortem tecum ire [*Luke*, xxii. 33], et in tempore tribulationis eduxit gladium et amputavit servo pontificis auriculam; non amputavit ei pedicam sed auriculam, ut ostenderet quod ei caput libentissime amputasset'.

[2] Johannes Branchazolus, *De principio imperatoris et papae*, i. 4, p. 47; ii. 3, p. 49.

. . . super omnes gentes . . . a Deo datus est lex animata in terris . . . et a coelesti maiestate sibi traditur imperium . . . et post Deum communis pater omnibus appellatur . . . et sicut Deus est in terra . . . et a Deo condendi leges licentiam accepit. . . Talis itaque rex secundum humanam constitutionem omnia iudicabat quoniam, ut ait Seneca, *De IIIIor virtutibus*, nihil aliud est iustitia quam nostra constitutio; et talis rex appellabatur pontifex et sacerdos . . . et ideo dicitur in *Exodo* [I *Esdr.*, ix. 7?], Quot sacerdotes tot reges.[1]

Since this ruler is described in terms expressly adopted from Roman law—that divine law deriving out of the Mosaic law[2]—we need hardly take too seriously Johannes' subsequent disclaimer that from the time of Moses temporal and spiritual jurisdiction have been separated. Thus, whilst the Petrine commission is seen to have specially instituted the papacy *circa spiritualia*, we then learn that the emperor already holds and retains supreme spiritual power, being 'dominator in spiritualibus et divinis quoniam rex est omnium rerum, etiam divinarum, ut ff. De legibus, lege ii [*Dig*., I. iii. 2], cum caput sit Ecclesiae'.[3] Therefore, concludes Johannes, although the spiritual is *dignior*, the emperor must be the master of the pope in the same way that the body is the ruler of the soul: 'sic corpus animae dominatur . . . imperator apostolico dominatur'.[4] Beneath their romantic camouflage these examples clearly illustrate the tendency of contemporary imperial thought towards outright lay supremacy. In their more inspired moments most dualists threw dualism overboard and permitted the lay ruler to wield both swords.[5] The papal-imperial struggle in the fourteenth century remained what, fundamentally, it had always been: a struggle between two systems of universal monarchy. And, as Boniface VIII found out to his cost, when the interests of the French crown were involved, the dualism propounded by Philip the Fair and his supporters effectively deprived the pope of even spiritual jurisdiction

[1] Johannes Branchazolus, *De principio*, i. 2, p. 46.
[2] Johannes Branchazolus, *De principio*, i. 3, p. 47.
[3] Johannes Branchazolus, *De principio*, ii. 3, p. 49.
[4] Johannes Branchazolus, *De principio*, ii. 4, p. 50.
[5] For example the German writer Henry of Meissen (d. 1318) declared that the emperor derived his power from Charlemagne, who had possessed both swords: see Folz, *op. cit.*, pp. 403–4.

within the French kingdom, and gave rise to a concept of kingship in which the ruler was not only *imperator in regno suo* but pope as well.[1]

[1] The author of the *Quaestio in utramque partem*, p. 97, reminds the pope that he does not give temporal power to the French king, but rather that king has the power 'confirmandi papam et ordinandi sedem apostolicam' by virtue of his descent from Charlemagne and according to canon law (Gratian, D. 63 c. 22), to which the pope is subject. For the current French view that the king has the care of his subjects' souls see H. Kämpf, *Pierre Dubois und die Geistigen Grundlagen des Französischen Nationalbewusstseins um 1300* (Leipzig and Berlin, 1935), pp. 39–45.

III. SOCIETAS HUMANA

THE failure of the dualists to provide an adequate alternative to papal monarchy was fundamentally a philosophical rather than a political one. Because nearly all philosophical speculation up to the thirteenth century was realistic in character, the hierocratic conception of the Christian society was everywhere accepted, even by those who refused to accept papal supremacy as its logical implication. Consequently, in the great papal-imperial struggles which convulsed most of the Middle Ages the nature of society was not in dispute, but only the proper distribution of authority within it: and in the ceaseless paper war which went on alongside the political contest the lay writer could not hope to triumph whilst he fought the hierocrat on the latter's own ground. What he needed was not another theory of the right distribution of power but a totally new conception of society, and this could only come about when a philosophical revolution had taken place. This revolution occurred during the thirteenth century with the rediscovery of many of the lost works of Aristotle. Even the immediate impact of this new literature was disturbing, for it was revealed that on many vital points of Christian thought Aristotle's views were at variance with orthodox teachings, and this disparity was exaggerated by the way in which the Philosopher's thought had been interpreted by the great Arab scholars like Averroes and Avicenna. Aristotle was found to maintain views on providence, on natural causality, on the eternity of the world, on individual reality, on freedom and immortality which were all in direct opposition to Christian beliefs, and right from the beginning of the century there was a constant stream of papal prohibitions on the study of Aristotle,[1] whilst the more conservative theologians began a conscious 'back to Augustine' movement in philosophy. In politics this revolution was equally disastrous from the papal point of view, but came about

[1] M. Grabmann, 'I Papi del Duecento e l'Aristotelismo: I divieti ecclesiastici di Aristotele sotto Innocenzo III e Gregorio IX', *MHP*, v (Rome, 1941).

very much more gradually, and did not exert its full influence on political theory for several centuries. Although it is possible to detect a steadily increasing secular tone in the works of the lay apologists in the middle of the century,[1] the initial work on Aristotle's *Politics* and *Ethics* was confined to commentating,[2] and it was not until the great schools of what has been called Latin Averroism were established in the late thirteenth century that a laicalised and ultimately non-Christian conception of society began to be developed.[3]

Until the twelfth century it had been largely possible to combine the pagan tradition with Christianity on the assumption that the pagan formulae were merely Christian with Christ himself left out. The advent of the purer pagan learning, however, quickly demonstrated the unreality of this view, and for the first time an alternative system of thought could now be set up alongside the Christian outlook on the world. This system, especially as developed by the Averro-Aristotelians, introduced a frankly materialistic stream into medieval thought. For its adherents the material world now reigned supreme over the world of spirit, and since matter was held to have existed from the beginning the whole conception of a divinely ordained world, even the theory of creation, became doubtful. Aristotelian standards were in the last analysis finite: they regarded only the mortal happiness of the individual and the terres-

[1] For example, John of Viterbo, *De regimine civitatum*, ch. 3, pp. 218–19, 'non dico de civitate sancta Ierusalem coelesti, quae dicitur civitas magna, civitas Dei nostri, cuius interpretationem relinquo theologicis et divinis, quoniam non est meum ponere os in coelum; sed dico de civitatibus huius saeculi'. This was probably written about 1250.

[2] M. Grabmann, 'Die mittelalterlichen Kommentare zur Politik des Aristoteles', *SBAW, Phil.-Hist. Abt.*, ii. 10 (Munich, 1941); S. H. Thomson, 'Walter Burley's Commentary on the *Politics* of Aristotle', *Mélanges Auguste Pelzer* (Louvain, 1947), pp. 557–78; C. Martin, *The Commentaries on the Politics of Aristotle in the late thirteenth and early fourteenth century* (Oxford Thesis, 1949): on this see G. de Lagarde in *Revue du moyen âge latin*, vi (1950), pp. 329–33; and 'Some Medieval Commentaries on Aristotle's *Politics*', *History*, xxxvi (1951), pp. 29–44.

[3] For the Averro-Aristotelian schools in Northern Italy, especially Bologna and Padua, see H. Rashdall, *The Universities of Europe in the Middle Ages* (ed. Powicke-Emden, Oxford, 1936), i. 262–5; C. J. Ermatinger, 'Averroism in Early Fourteenth Century Bologna', *Mediaeval Studies*, xvi (1954), pp. 35–56.

trial welfare of political society. His mind shrank back from the indefinite and the limitless, and demanded to know only what humanity could achieve during life on earth. The Christian ideal of conduct on the other hand assumed the universal imperfection and infinite perfectibility of man, with eternity as the basis of his fulfilment. Consequently, with this premise, early medieval thought had been necessarily deductive, and there was a genuine abhorrence of empirical and inductive methods of reasoning. But Aristotle, basing his principles primarily upon observation, brought a new, inductive and naturalistic system into medieval philosophy. For Aristotle everything had a natural cause, which not only discounted direct divine intervention into human affairs, but gave even the *summum bonum* a purely natural, terrestrial meaning: the greatest good of mankind became first sheer survival and self-preservation[1] and beyond that the full development of human happiness on earth alone, the pursuit of social, political and economic self-sufficiency.[2] The end of life was contained in life itself, and could be measured entirely in temporal terms. Man was simply a social animal, needing and living in political society as a result of nothing more than natural inclination. Society was essentially a human and not a divine institution. The necessity for and justification of public authority was to be sought in human nature, not in any specific commission of power by God to individuals. And in face of this the idea of the Universal Church as the one form of desirable or legitimate social and political organisation open to men steadily faded away.

It must not however be imagined that there was any sudden and

[1] This was pointed out by Aquinas in his definition of natural law: *Summa theologica*, II. I. xciv. 2, 'ordinem inclinationum naturalium est ordo praeceptorum legis naturae. Inest enim primo inclinatio homini ad bonum secundum naturam in qua communicat cum omnibus substantiis: prout scilicet quaelibet substantia appetit conservationem sui esse secundum suam naturam. Et secundum hanc inclinationem pertinent ad legem naturalem ea per quae vita hominis conservatur et contrarium impeditur'.

[2] Again a point made by Aquinas, *Comm. in Eth. Nic.*, I. ii. 29–31, 'Finis politicae est humanum bonum, id est optimus in rebus humanis . . . unde ad ipsam [artem civilem] maxime pertinet considerare finem ultimum humanae vitae tamquam ad principalissimam. . . Dicit autem ad politicam pertinere considerationem ultimi finis humanae vitae'.

cataclysmic destruction of the papal-hierocratic edifice. It was a slow process and was never completed. Nor, with the possible exception of Marsilius of Padua, can it be said that any writer of the time adopted unmitigated Aristotelianism and propounded a thoroughly secular social ideal. At this stage all that can be shown is that certain aims and concepts were seeping, often unconsciously, into the political thought of the period, and were found to be consistently antagonistic to the hierocratic tradition. Those writers who exhibited the most marked tendency to accept unqualified Aristotelian ideas were few in number and, faced with almost universal condemnation, did not emphasise their partiality. The evidence of Averro-Aristotelian influence in the work of writers like John of Paris, Engelbert of Admont, Dante and Ockham is buried in much that was unprovocative and orthodox, and even Marsilius himself can be shown to have been a great deal more 'medieval' than has been generally thought.[1] On the other hand it would be wrong to consider Marsilius as the sole exponent of the extreme

[1] The shrewd judgement of G. Mathew, 'Boniface VIII to the Council of Constance', *Church and State* (London, 1936), pp. 87–8, on John of Paris, 'his premises are Aristotelian and his deductions Thomist', may equally well be applied to Dante, Engelbert and Ockham. For John's Averroistic tendencies see J. Leclercq, *Jean de Paris*, pp. 73–6. The view that there is a sharp division between Dante's Thomism and radical Aristotelianism has been propounded by F. Ercole, 'Per la genesi del pensiero politico di Dante', *Il pensiero politico di Dante*, ii (1928). On the question of Dante's Averroism see the survey of literature in A. P. d'Entrèves, *Dante as a Political Thinker* (Oxford, 1952), pp. 101–2, 107; and now *KTB*, pp. 472f.; and for Averroistic influences in Marsilius see in general Grabmann, *Studien über den Einfluss*; and 'Der lateinische Averroismus des 13 Jahrhunderts und seine Stellung zur christlichen Weltanschauung', *SBAW, Phil.-Hist. Abt.* (Munich, 1931); also A. Gewirth, *Marsilius of Padua* (New York, 1951–6), ii. 438–42. For similarities between Dante and Marsilius see d'Entrèves, *op. cit.*, pp. 8–15, 39; and Gewirth, *op. cit.*, i. 23–30. The influence of Dante on Ockham is noted by E. F. Jacob, *Essays in the Conciliar Epoch* (2nd ed., Manchester, 1953), p. 93, who also (pp. 89f.) surveys the literature on the correspondence between Ockham and Marsilius. His view that Ockham attempted to combine both Averroistic and Thomistic versions of Aristotle is supported by E. A. Moody, 'Ockham and Aegidius of Rome', *Franciscan Studies*, ix (1949), pp. 417–42 at pp. 434–8. Note also J. G. Sikes, 'A Possible Marsilian Source in Ockham', *EHR*, li (1936), pp. 496–504; and the remarks of P. A. Hamman, *La doctrine de l'église et l'état chez Occam* (Paris, 1942), pp. 183–8 on the close affinity between the theories of Ockham and John of Paris.

laical point of view or to think that with him there was a sudden eruption into prominence of a doctrine of popular sovereignty. As we have said, it is impossible to draw exact lines, and the work of several writers, whose thought was basically Thomist in inspiration, paved the way for the *Defensor pacis*. A clearcut separation can in fact be made between those passages in their treatises which favour human self-sufficiency, and those which advocate the supremacy of spiritual ends and consequently some measure of papal superiority. They alternate between the traditional lay dualist outlook, the Thomist version of papal monarchy, and a doctrine of popular sovereignty based upon the natural right of all men to govern themselves and a purely secular conception of human existence. And so in emphasising this latter aspect of their work it must not be forgotten that there is another side to the picture, and that much of what they said here was in other places heavily qualified and frequently contradicted. Nevertheless a naturalistic conception of society had an indisputable attraction for these writers, and it is with them that there is to be seen the genesis of a system of thought totally alien to the hierocratic way of life.

Although the old view of William of Ockham as the 'great destroyer' has in recent years come under heavy attack,[1] and his political theory proves upon examination to be disappointingly conservative, the importance of Ockham's part in the breakdown of the hierocratic system need not be underrated. Whilst there is little novelty to be found in his political tracts, Ockham, by a wholesale adaptation of Aristotelian principles, did succeed in providing a philosophical basis for the anthropocentric theory of society which had already been hinted at by earlier publicists. The key to this is to be found in his views on the relationship of God to the world and human existence. Although Ockham never attempted to deny the reality of God, he always maintained that absolutely nothing could be proved about God in the light of natural reason. The existence of God is an object of faith, not of demonstration: 'non potest sciri

[1] Notably by P. Boehmer in a series of articles in *Franciscan Studies* (1941–9), and J. B. Morrall, 'Some Notes on a Recent Interpretation of Ockham's Political Philosophy', *Franciscan Studies*, ix (1949), pp. 335–69. As a corrective see the exposition of the more traditional view in G. de Lagarde, *La naissance de l'esprit laïque au déclin du moyen âge*, iv–vi (Saint-Paul-Trois-Chateaux, 1942–6).

evidenter quod Deus est'.[1] It is, he said, indeed probable that there is a God, that he has endowed man with a soul, and that this soul is an incorporeal and immortal substance: but none of this can be shown in philosophy, and so, in spite of what the theologians may say, it cannot be demonstrated in theology. In short it cannot be demonstrated at all. Without faith Ockham's God was beyond the reach of human knowledge. Belief now becomes the only ground on which one can hold on to God, and this a belief which has as one of its motives the conviction that the philosophers can refute every argument for God that has ever existed. Thus God immediately comes for Ockham within the scope of the principle that beings shall not be multiplied without necessity. Empirically given things have to be considered in isolation: one has no right to place them against hypothetically given things whose existence cannot be verified. All that needs to be considered is that which really exists, that which can be actually appraised by human experience. And much the same result derives from a consideration of God's omnipotence. To ensure this omnipotence it must be said that what is may always be different, so that it becomes a waste of time to speculate upon the hypothetical causes of actually existing things. How can it be proved that God has decided conclusively in favour of this or that? How can there be a necessary intelligibility in anything? How can there be a divinely ordained natural order when there may not be any nature? Such an attitude inevitably worked in direct opposition to the hierocratic belief that God had created the closest link between himself and man by establishing his own vicariate on earth, that there was a divine order in the world, and that the world itself was only a reflection of heaven. For Ockham, as for Aristotle, man and God had become unrelated beings, two existent absolutes. But if man was to be absolute he could perfectly well be studied with-

[1] M. de Wulf, *History of Medieval Philosophy* (3rd ed., London, 1938), ii. 184. This has been contested by Boehmer, *Franciscan Studies*, i (1941), p. 71; ix (1949), p. 453: and it is probable that Ockham was forced to retract this view as a result of his interrogation at Avignon. However it is noteworthy that this is one of the propositions attributed to him and subsequently condemned by the papal commissioners in 1326: see A. Pelzer, 'Les 51 Articles de G. Occam', *Revue d'histoire ecclésiastique*, xxiii (1932), pp. 240–70. This is also accepted in opposition to Boehmer by Pegis, *Speculum*, xxiii (1948), pp. 452–63.

out reference to God. It was but a short step from this to denying not only the divine order but a divinity at all. In any case there was no need to consider them.

Applied to the hierocratic idea of the *Ecclesia* this doctrine was devastating. Indeed it destroyed the conception that political society was a Church, and substituted for this idea a purely naturalistic *societas humana*. If only the empirically proved actuality can be studied, it is only human society which can be considered, and this isolated from any consideration of heaven. One has no need, and so no right, to see it against the hypothetical existence of heavenly beatitude, of a Church Triumphant whose reality cannot be verified. The end for which mankind exists, and the way in which human society shall be organised, must be established by earthly criteria. This does not deny the conceptual existence of the *civitas Dei*, but only human society is known to have being. The idea of a Christian society striving towards a universal reality which exists elsewhere cannot be countenanced. It is the actual which has true existence, and this means individual realities, not universal ones. For Ockham universals may have a conceptual reality, so that the idea of the *Ecclesia* standing over and above its members can be imagined, but 'nihil est in rerum natura extra animam nisi singulare': only the individuals, the members themselves, have real existence. Moreover 'frustra fit per plura quod potest fieri per pauciora', and the acceptance of universal realities is not only confusing but violates the law of economy. Universals are not only unreal but in the last resort unnecessary: the individual alone exists, and the universal is essentially not an individual.[1] For both Ockham and Marsilius species and genera are not the names of substances but signs,[2] and

[1] 'Sufficiunt singularia et ita tales res universales omnino frustra ponuntur': cited M. H. Carré, *Realists and Nominalists* (Oxford, 1946), p. 107, cf. pp. 112f.; also R. I. Aaron, *The Theory of Universals* (Oxford, 1952), pp. 16–17.

[2] Although Marsilius declared that sacraments were necessary to avoid eternal death, *Defensor pacis*, II. xvii. 15, p. 370; cf. II. xvii. 12, p. 368, he regarded them as mere signs 'showing' what God already intended to do but contributing nothing real, II. vi. 6–7, pp. 202–4; II. xv. 10, p. 336. It was a similar nominalistic interpretation of the sacraments which had brought Roscellin's theory of universals into disrepute, and led to the Catharist doctrine that no priests were necessary for the administration of sacraments. It is used by Marsilius to imply that the priesthood has no necessary function in the community.

the *Ecclesia*, which to the Realist had all the properties of a universal, is reduced to a mere conception. It is no longer an actually existing entity but a myth, an artificial abstraction superimposed upon the existent realities of individual communities.

In this way the philosophical propositions of Ockham led straight to the political conclusions already reached by John of Paris. John does not deny the existence of a Universal Church, of a *congregatio fidelium*,[1] but he regards this as a purely spiritual entity, not a political society. His conception of the *Ecclesia* is essentially fideistic. If, he argues, Christ had ruled the world by faith alone, why should one attribute more power to his vicar? To make the *regnum Christi* into an earthly, political one would be to commit the *error Herodis*, for this was what Herod had mistakenly feared.[2] The pope and his bishops have nothing but spiritual power, that is, the power to give directions in matters of faith, unless it should so happen that they have been granted a measure of temporal rule from a lay prince.[3] Therefore it is only from the point of view of faith that all Christians can be regarded as living in one community and in need of the unity given by one head. It is a relatively easy matter, he remarks, to dominate the world in spiritual things, where only words are required. But it is a very different situation in secular things, where the sword must be used. And as regards temporal power, which John equates with governmental jurisdiction, there is no benefit to

[1] John of Paris, *De potestate regia et papali*, ch. 16, p. 223.

[2] John of Paris, *De potestate regia et papali*, ch. 9, p. 194, 'Nec est intelligendum quod Christus regnat per fidem in hominibus quasi ex eo quod aliquis convertatur ad fidem sit subiectus Christi vicario in temporalibus bonis sicut solent homines suis regibus subdidi'. To think, he continues, that the pope 'in quantum est loco Christi in terris habere dominium in temporalibus bonis principum et baronum et cognitionem et iurisdictionem' is to commit the 'error Herodis, qui, audiens Christum regem natum, credidit ipsum regem esse terrenum'. He then goes on to explain that Christ 'dicitur regnare per fidem quia id quod in hominibus est supremum et principale, scilicet intellectum, Christo subicunt ipsum in fidei obsequium captivantes. Et iste est intellectus sanctorum. Unde Christus per fidem non dicitur regnare in possessionibus sed in cordibus.' Cf. Anon., *Informatio de nullitate processuum papae*, p. 20, where the view is developed that Christ's kingdom is only over the souls of the faithful, not over the transitory things of this world. See further J. Leclercq, 'L'idée de la royauté du Christ au XIVe siècle', *Miscellanea Pio Paschini* (Rome, 1948), i. 405–25.

[3] John of Paris, *De potestate regia et papali, proem.*, p. 175.

be gained from having a common polity: 'non sic autem fideles necesse est convenire in aliqua politia communi'. Indeed men are far better provided for by living in their own regional kingdoms, with their own language, customs and constitutions:

. . . secundum diversitatem climatum et linguarum, diversi modi vivendi et diversae politiae, et quod virtuosum est in una gente non est virtuosum in alia. Non est igitur sic necesse mundum regi per unum in temporalibus sicut necesse est quod regatur per unum in spiritualibus.

For political virtue has little or no connection with religious virtue. Earthly and heavenly things can be measured by different standards. The former may almost be said to change with the climate; the latter are constant: and this is the extent of the dissimilarity between them. John of Paris in fact denies the whole idea of a single and uniform right way of life, and with it that of a universal body politic. In its place he substitutes a conception of the *Ecclesia* in which the universal Christian society becomes no more than a mere unity of faith.[1] So too for Marsilius of Padua the *Ecclesia* is a 'purely spiritual sacramental community', a 'purely spiritual congregation of believers connected by no ties but their common faith and participation in the sacraments'.[2] For Marsilius it is indeed the *universitas fidelium*, but he at once adds that this exists in every part, in every community, even the family.[3] Its universality and wholeness are distributive, and dependent upon its parts. Taken by itself the *Ecclesia* is a mere *nomen*, a word without substance. Faith may indeed be seen as a universal giving a specific or generic unity, and the unity of the *Ecclesia* follows from the oneness of its faith. But this is a mystical, insubstantial unity with no material consequences. In the world of fact the *Ecclesia* is not one thing, one body, but a multitude of singular bodies, and consequently does not even require the institution of monarchy.[4] It may be expedient to have one head in

[1] John of Paris, *De potestate regia et papali*, ch. 3, p. 181.

[2] Gewirth, *Marsilius of Padua*, i. 277, 279.

[3] Marsilius of Padua, *Defensor pacis*, II. ii. 3, p. 144, 'Rursum secundum aliam significationem dicitur hoc nomen Ecclesia . . . de universitate fidelium credentium et invocantium nomen Christi, et de huius universitatis partibus omnibus in quacunque communitate, etiam domestica;' cf. *Defensor minor*, xv. 8, p. 51.

[4] Marsilius of Padua, *Defensor pacis*, II. xxxviii. 13, p. 544; cf. William of Ock-

matters of faith, but his duties as *caput Ecclesiae* are confined solely to such matters as the definition of theological problems, whilst real government pertains to the citizens of the locality concerned.[1] This unity may also be desirable from the point of view of making easier the task of purely secular government, but this is not a matter of necessity: in this respect there can perfectly well be individual communities and kingdoms.[2] It is by his membership of the latter that a *civis* has a share in coercive government: by his membership of the *Ecclesia* the *fidelis* simply shares a common belief.[3] Consequently coercive power exists only in a civil community which is not the *Ecclesia*, whilst the pope as *caput Ecclesiae* is considered to have only an advisory capacity.[4]

The new philosophy however reacted not only upon the idea of society but upon the very nature and origin of political authority itself. For Ockham the cardinal principle of life is the belief that everything which exists is a single thing. To him *ens* and *unum*, being and one, are identical. To be one is to be a substance, and to be a substance is to exist: 'existentia et essentia idem omnino significant'.[5] This reduction of all existence to individual existence is the essence of nominalism, and it was this emphasis upon the individual in Ockham's thought which completely reversed the traditional hierocratic view of the relationship existing between the whole and its parts, between the community and its members, as well as transforming the idea of society itself. The *Ecclesia* is no longer for Ockham a body whose essence is a universal on a superior plane of reality: it is basically nothing more than a collection of actually existing people. No doubt it is convenient to ascribe a fictitious

ham, *Dialogus*, III. I. ii. I, p. 788, 'quamvis corpus naturale esset monstruosum si haberet duo capita . . . tamen corpus mysticum potest habere plura capita spiritualia'.

[1] Marsilius of Padua, *Defensor pacis*, I. xii. 3, p. 63, 'in communitate illa super quam lex fertur'.

[2] Note the passage in which Marsilius speaks of the 'regnum et quaevis altera quaecunque temperata civilis communitas', *Defensor pacis*, III. iii, pp. 612–13.

[3] Compare the definition of a *civis* in Marsilius of Padua, *Defensor pacis*, I. xii. 4, p. 64, with that of a *fidelis*, II. ii. 3, p. 145.

[4] Marsilius of Padua, *Defensor pacis*, II. xxii. 6, pp. 425–6; *Defensor minor*, ii. 6, p. 5; *De iurisdictione imperatoris*, pp. 1387–9.

[5] M. de Wulf, *op. cit.*, ii. 184; Carré, *op. cit.*, p. 118.

personality to this group as a whole, but it remains a fiction, a purely artificial device.[1] It may even be useful to attribute sovereign powers to this mystical entity, but since the myth has no reality apart from the human individuals who represent it, sovereignty unquestionably resides with the individual members of the community. The *Ecclesia* considered as a corporation is only a mental concept: its substance remains in the parts themselves. Hence Ockham refuses to accept the view that the *universitas* constitutes a juridical reality distinct from and prior to the individuals who compose it. The house is no more than a heap of stones: the *populus* is only the sum of its individual persons, a simple plurality. Although it is still possible to speak in general terms, it is the individual or part upon which the emphasis falls and which is of primary importance. This necessarily refutes the notion that the *Ecclesia* is essentially a wholeness, a totality imposed on earth from above: it implies that its organisation, even the source of political authority itself, is to be sought in the desires of the members themselves. If the universal society retains its character as a corporation, the will of this corporation is now simply a legal construct made up of the wills of its members acting collectively, *omnes ut universi* as opposed to *omnes ut singuli*, and the real subject of the rights and duties of the corporation is the members of it: 'every whole is nothing other than the sum of its parts taken together', and the common good is a mere collective term.[2] This highly individualistic doctrine, in stark contrast to the hierocratic view, means that each person has a value of

[1] William of Ockham, Addition to the *De imperatorum et pontificum potestate*, ch. 27, pp. 80–1. 'Ecclesia papalis ac multitudo ac ratione consimili ordo Fratrum scilicet Minorum potest habere actum realem et quod non sit persona ymaginaria et representata, sed est vera persona, quamvis non sit una persona, unde Apostolus ait ad Romanos 12 [xii. 5], multi unum corpus sumus in Christo'; also *Opus nonaginta dierum*, ch. 6, p. 361; ch. 11, p. 372; ch. 62, p. 1108.

[2] For the idea of the *Ecclesia* as a corporation in Ockham, B. Tierney, 'Ockham, the Conciliar Theory, and the Canonists', *Journal of the History of Ideas*, xv (1954), pp. 40–70; and 'A Conciliar Theory of the Thirteenth Century', *Catholic Historical Review*, xxxvi (1951), pp. 415–40, for some remarks on the influence of corporation theories on Marsilius. See also G. de Lagarde, 'Comment Ockham comprend le pouvoir seculier', *Scritti di sociologia e politia in onore di Luigi Sturzo* (Bologna, 1953), i. 593–612, who emphasises the nominalistic attitude of Ockham and Marsilius towards the community as a collection of real individuals.

his own and not merely because he is part of a whole. He is not just an instrument of the community, but is an end in himself. It is the individual members who are all-important. Instead of the divinely appointed head of the community being regarded as the source of all power and organisation, the way is now open for a theory of power dependent upon a contractual relationship between the individual members of the community and the popularly constituted ruler. Thus, having cited Aristotle to demonstrate that political authority has a natural basis, Engelbert of Admont goes on to define this *modus naturae* as the decision of the members of a community to elect one out of their own number (*unum aliquem ex se*) to govern and preserve the security of the others. Their acceptance of this ruler, he adds, takes the form of a compact between the prince and his subjects: they obey 'sub pacto et vinculo subiectionis'.[1] Marsilius and Ockham duly echo the same principle.[2] Political obedience is no longer enjoined by God, but becomes a matter for the members of the society themselves to decide,[3] even for each individual himself. Man, not God, now stands at the centre of the universe, and it is the needs and rights of man which become the supreme criteria for government. The Christian society in the Ockhamist philosophical system thus becomes earthbound and atomised, and it was this, the political implications of his philosophy

[1] Engelbert of Admont, *De ortu imperii Romani*, ch. 2, p. 755. Aegidius Romanus, *De regimine principum*, III. i. 6, explained Aristotle's theory of political evolution in similar terms: the *civitas* is formed when the *dispersi* contract with each other to live in society under one head in order to secure the necessities of life—'aliquando *concordabant* in unum constituentes sibi civitatem aliquam'—and then these communities 'simul *confoederarentur* et *concordarent* ut sub uno rege existerent'.

[2] William of Ockham, *Dialogus*, III. II. iii. 25, p. 923, '*Generale pactum societatis humanae* est obtemperare suis regibus in his quae spectant ad bonum commune'; Marsilius of Padua, *Defensor pacis*, I. xvii. 11, p. 120, 'Sic quoque unius civitatis aut provinciae homines dicuntur una civitas aut regnum, quia *volunt* unum numero principatum'. Ockham's phrase derives from Cicero and Augustine by way of Gratian, D. 8 c. 2. For the later medieval view that the term *societas* in itself implied a contract see J. W. Gough, *The Social Contract* (2nd ed., Oxford, 1957), p. 46.

[3] William of Ockham, *Dialogus*, III. II. iii. 25, p. 923, 'societas humana *obligat se* ad obediendum generaliter regibus et per consequens multo magis imperatori'; John of Paris, *De potestate regia et papali*, ch. 1, p. 178, 'homines . . . certis legibus ad vivendum communiter ligaverunt'.

rather than his political thought itself, which made Ockham into one of the most dangerous opponents of the papal system of government.

Whilst Ockham hesitated to draw the inevitable conclusions from his philosophical propositions, this had in fact already been done to a large extent by Marsilius of Padua. For Marsilius too the existence of God is not susceptible to rational proof: God therefore has for him no contact with human life, so that even his existence may be said to be in doubt.[1] Neither the fact of eternal happiness, the hierocratic *finis vitae*, nor the consequent necessity for a priesthood can be proved.[2] In accepting this Marsilius cuts right across the Christian tradition of a unitary theory of knowledge, the complement of the one society in which, by emphasising the necessary role of faith, it was considered possible to demonstrate the existence of divine things by natural reason. There is in this little to choose between Marsilius and Ockham. For both it becomes a matter of urgent importance to separate philosophy and theology, to prohibit the testing of reason by faith, and to restrict the sphere of rationally demonstratable truth. What reason can say concerning theological matters does not go beyond the order of mere dialectical probability. It must be remembered that by the end of the first quarter of the fourteenth century there was no great novelty attached to this view. For some time it had been commonly asserted in the schools that Christian dogmas could not be supported by reasonable proof; they were at best probable inferences, and at worst, when argument led to opposite conclusions, the Christian was expected to embrace by faith what his own reason rejected. This attitude was inevitably a precarious one, and heralded deep fissures in medieval culture. But once having postulated the absolute autonomy of the spheres of

[1] Marsilius of Padua, *Defensor pacis*, I. ix. 2, pp. 39–40; I. xii. 1, p. 62.

[2] Marsilius of Padua, *Defensor pacis*, I. iv. 3, p. 17, 'Quodque istud secundum vivere, sempiternum scilicet, non potuit philosophorum universitas per demonstrationem convincere, nec fuit de rebus manifestis per se, idcirco de traditione ipsorum quae propter ipsum sint, non fuerunt solliciti'; I. v. 10, p. 25, 'Superest autem nobis de sacerdotalis partis necessitate dicere de qua non omnes homines sic senserunt concorditer, ut de necessitate reliquarum partium civitatis. Et causa huius fuit quoniam ipsius vera et prima necessitas non potuit comprehendi per demonstrationem nec fuit res manifesta per se'.

revelation and reason, the only solution was the acceptance of two coexistent but contradictory truths.[1] In other words nature and supernature became two completely separate realms, and a proposition which was false in one could be perfectly true in the other: 'dicunt enim ea esse vera secundum philosophiam sed non secundum fidem catholicam'. The Averro-Aristotelians were forced into this position by the logic of the situation: as intellectuals their honesty prevented them from doing other than recognising the truths of Aristotle; but as Christians they were committed to revealed truth, and so could only take refuge in the notion that two truths could well contradict each other because they applied to totally different realms of thought. Certainly Marsilius accepted two completely contrary standards of values without making the slightest attempt to reconcile them, and it is difficult to believe that this was not merely a cloak for sheer atheism. He himself declares religion in general to have been invented by philosophers because it serves a quasi-necessary function in political society: its promises of eternal rewards and punishments are obviously useful as deterrents to wrongdoing and incentives to good works, and thereby preserve the peace of the community.[2] Nominalism indeed always skirted on the fringes of rationalism (we may recall Anselm's denunciation of Roscellin as a *pseudo-christianus*), and even if Ockham is exempted from the charge of agnosticism, it cannot be denied that he laid the foundations of religious scepticism. Certainly the authorities at Paris thought so: they condemned his teachings no less than four times between 1339 and 1347. What he

[1] For a general description of the problem of double truth in religious thought see F. Betzendörfer, *Die Lehre von der zweifachen Wahrheit* (Tübingen, 1924); see also de Lagarde, *La naissance de l'esprit laïque*, iii. 64, 255; E. Gilson, 'La doctrine de la double vérité', *Etudes de philosophie médiéval* (Strasbourg, 1921), pp. 51–75; R. A. Gauthier, 'Trois commentaires averroïstes sur l'Ethique à Nicomaque', *Archives d'histoire doctrinale et littéraire du moyen âge*, xvi (1947–8), pp. 187–336, especially pp. 278f. Definite evidence of the use of this stratagem by Boethius of Dacia is adduced by A. Maurer, 'Boetius of Dacia and the Double Truth', *Mediaeval Studies*, xvii (1955), pp. 233–9, with reference to his recently discovered *De aeternitate mundi*, ed. G. Sajo (Budapest, 1954).

[2] Marsilius of Padua, *Defensor pacis*, I. v. 11, pp. 26–7. For a discussion of this see Gewirth, *op. cit.*, i. 69–84; J. W. Allen, 'Marsilius of Padua and Medieval Secularism', *The Social and Political Ideas of Some Great Medieval Thinkers*, ed. F. J. C. Hearnshaw (London, 1923), pp. 167–91.

declared to be inaccessible to reason might easily tend in other hands to become condemned as contrary to reason, and it is probable that this was his own feeling in the matter. At all events there is a strong tendency in the more extreme lay writers towards a genuine dualism, towards the acceptance of Christian principles with the use of a purely secular theory of society. The supremacy of Christian doctrine becomes something held by faith alone, and is not therefore necessary in a consideration of the actual realities of political problems.[1] Faced with an exclusively Christian theory of society, elaborated by Christians for the benefit of Christians, told that if they did not believe they had nothing to understand, Ockham and Marsilius were forced either to deny their own philosophical principles or else to erect a form of society based exclusively on the principles of natural reason and independent of religious revelation. Although Ockham declared that his political thought was based upon 'reason rather than the assertions of the whole world of mortal men',[2] it may be said that he chose the former, and Marsilius the latter, alternative.

The specifically political outcome of these philosophical premises is to be seen in the completely secular approach to all religious and political matters which is so striking a feature of the *Defensor pacis*. Marsilius seems to have been determined to seek a basis for political society with the use of purely rational methods. Thus in *Dictio I* he omits all considerations of eternal life and the divine origin of political power on the grounds that such matters are not amenable to reasonable justification,[3] and although he subsequently 'confirms' his findings by revelation in *Dictio II*, he thereby demonstrates his independence of the teachings of faith, and consequently their superfluity. Like Machiavelli two centuries later, Marsilius was intent to show that it was unnecessary to garb one's

[1] Marsilius of Padua, *Defensor pacis*, II. xxx. 4, p. 593, 'sed in sola lege christianorum actio sacerdotum est aliarum perfectissima, quod tamen sola fide tenemus'.

[2] William of Ockham, *De imperatorum et pontificum potestate*, *proem*, pp. 3–4, 'in his quae fidei sunt et scientiae plus me monebit una ratio evidens vel una auctoritas scripturae sacrae sane intelligenda quam assertio totius universitatis mortalium'.

[3] Marsilius of Padua, *Defensor pacis*, I. iv. 3, pp. 17–18; I. v. 10, p. 25; I. ix. 2, pp. 39–40; I. xii. 1, p. 62.

politics in religious sanctions, which only gave entry to the political aspirations of the priests and deprived the lay ruler of his natural rights. These sanctions could be stripped away, and yet the same basic political principles would remain. They were unnecessary and, being unnecessary, could and should be ignored; or retained only on the grounds of evident utility, since the religious plea is the best method of securing subjection and obedience. The priesthood is useful, but plays no vital part in the life of the earthly community. Marsilius does indeed apply the Aristotelian teleological principle which was such an important feature of the hierocratic theory, but the end and purpose in view is only a terrestrial one. The separation of reason and faith in philosophy means the predication of two entirely unconnected ends of government in politics, and since the earthly end of human life is all that can be established by *experientia sensata*, the additional consideration of a hypothetically given celestial end offends against the law of economy and can be ignored. This axiom of the two autonomous ends of human existence is thus a marked feature of all the extreme anti-hierocratic tracts of the first half of the fourteenth century. First in the field were the French publicists. 'Ad alium finem ordinatur potestas spiritualis et ad alium temporalis', declares the author of the *Quaestio in utramque partem*, with the *Rex pacificus* and John of Paris following suit.[1] The latter indeed took this as the occasion on which to elaborate his distinction between the earthly and the heavenly virtues. Moral virtues, he says, can be perfect without reference to theological ones. Any perfection derived from theology is accidental.[2] All the Frenchmen admitted that the spiritual end of life was worthier than the temporal end, but since these ends were quite distinct, there could be a complete division between the respective jurisdictions of those rulers, the popes and the kings, whose duty it was to guide their subjects to each end.[3] Hard on the heels of the French writers

[1] Anon., *Quaestio in utramque partem, proem.*, p. 96; Anon., *Rex pacificus*, ch. 4, p. 678; John of Paris, *De potestate regia et papali*, ch. 5, pp. 183–4.

[2] John of Paris, *De potestate regia et papali*, ch. 19, p. 234, 'virtutes morales acquisitae possunt esse perfectas sine theologiciis, nec ab ipsis perficiuntur nisi quadam accidentali perfectione'.

[3] John of Paris, *De potestate regia et papali*, ch. 5, p. 184; Anon., *Quaestio in utramque partem*, ch. 3, pp. 100–1.

came Dante: infallible Providence has set up two *fines* to human life, two paradises, two states of blessedness. One is earthly and the other heavenly: both have their separate sets of virtues, which are complete in themselves, however much the heavenly may transcend the earthly. The terrestrial paradise is to be achieved by the use of human reason which, through the means of *philosophica documenta*, teaches mankind the way to acquire temporal virtue. Heavenly beatitude follows from the study of *documenta spiritualia*, which propound the virtues of faith, and whose meaning is revealed by the Holy Spirit.[1] From this Dante concludes that it is the task of the pope to lead men to salvation by the use of revealed truth, while he recommends that the emperor should direct them to temporal happiness by the use of philosophic truth.[2] Here again then the separation of the earthly and ecclesiastical societies seems complete: the empire rests upon human law, the *Ecclesia* upon the word of Christ—'Nam Ecclesiae fundamentum Christus est . . . imperii vero fundamentum ius humanum est'.[3] And in a letter written about the same time to the Roman people, the immediate political result is drawn: 'bifurcatur Petri Caesarisque potestas'.[4] Finally the ideal of the two separate ends of existence is taken over by Marsilius himself,

> Vivere autem ipsum et bene vivere conveniens hominibus est in duplici modo, quoddam temporale sive mundanum, aliud vere aeternum sive coeleste vocari solitum.[5]

It is Marsilius who brings out its graver implications. Gone is the suggestion that this is merely a novel way of justifying a duality of powers; gone is the need to preserve the façade of a system in which

[1] Dante, *Monarchia*, iii. 16, p. 375; cf. *Convivio*, iv. 4, pp. 416–17. This was the focal point of Guido Vernani's attack on Dante, *De reprobatione Monarchiae*, ch. 3, pp. 145–6.

[2] Dante, *Monarchia*, iii. 16, p. 376, 'Propter quod opus fuit homini duplici directivo secundum duplicem finem, scilicet summo pontifice, qui secundum revelata humanum genus perduceret ad vitam aeternam, et imperatore, qui secundum philosophia documenta genus humanum ad temporalem felicitatem dirigeret'. This characterisation of the emperor as the supreme philosopher stems from Roman law: *Cod.*, VI. xxxv. 11; *Nov.*, xxii. 19; lx. 1.

[3] Dante, *Monarchia*, iii. 10, p. 371.

[4] Dante, *Epistolae*, V. v, p. 53.

[5] Marsilius of Padua, *Defensor pacis*, I. iv. 3, p. 17.

pope and lay ruler might be expected to work in conjunction with one another. How can they work together, queries Marsilius, when their purposes are so totally unconnected? Two rulers having coercive power over the same people can only impede each other, particularly if they are in search of such different ends.[1] It is not only undesirable but unnecessary to permit jurisdiction to the priests.[2] If the temporal end of life is to be sought without reference to the spiritual, then the terrestrial order must be omnicompetent and sufficient unto itself. The natural end becomes as complete a good as the supernatural, and perfection may be achieved by the pursuit of either.[3] But for all practical purposes the natural end of society is all that matters, and the spiritual, having nothing to do with the purely earthly problems of government and political obedience, can be ignored.

By degrees this new approach enabled the lay writers to emancipate themselves from the idyllic notion that power could be shared between pope and lay ruler. But it could only be achieved at the price of stipulating a purely earthly conception of human happiness, and restricting the final and perfect end of life to one of material well-being. Consequently all the writers influenced by the Averro-Aristotelian approach tended to concentrate upon the sufficiency of what they termed 'living civilly', the sort of life to be led in a purely human society. From Engelbert of Admont through the French writers and Dante to Marsilius of Padua more and more stress is laid upon the merits and satisfactory nature of secular life taken in its own right.[4] Indeed for Marsilius it becomes the supreme good and the ultimate human activity:

[1] Marsilius of Padua, *Defensor pacis*, II. iv. 5, p. 162, 'Duo namque coactiva dominia non subinvicem posita ac respectu eiusdem multitudinis se impediunt'.

[2] Marsilius of Padua, *Defensor pacis*, II. v. 6, pp. 191–2; II. ix. 4, p. 235.

[3] Cf. Dante, *Monarchia*, i. 9, p. 345; ii. 8, pp. 357–8.

[4] Marsilius of Padua, *Defensor pacis*, I. iv. 1, p. 16, 'quoniam viventes civiliter non solum vivunt, quomodo faciunt bestiae aut servi, sed bene vivunt'. For the idea of the sufficient life in Marsilius see I. iv. *passim*: this is naturally desired by all men, I. iv. 2, p. 17; I. i. 7, p. 9; cf. Dante, *Monarchia*, i. 5, pp. 343–4, 'bene sufficienterque vivere'; John of Paris, *De potestate regia et papali*, c. 1, pp. 176–7; Engelbert of Admont, *De ortu imperii Romani*, ch. 8, p. 758, 'felicitas est vita per se sibi sufficiens'. The phrase 'vivere per se sufficienter' derives from William of Moerbecke's translation of Aristotle, *Politics*, i. 2; *Nich. Ethics*, i. 7.

. . . necessarium debentibus civili felicitate frui, quae *in hoc saeculo* possibilium homini desideratorum optimum videtur et *ultimum* actuum humanorum.[1]

It is something to be achieved by the use of reason alone, the practice of which was largely held to consist in an intensified study of Aristotle.[2] And Aristotle merely confirmed these writers in their belief that the purpose of society was no longer the achievement of salvation but the preservation of security on earth.[3] Political thought comes in this way to be more concerned with means than with ends. The question of the purpose for which individuals exist, other than that of being governed, does not warrant consideration. Because it produces peace and order on earth, *civilis pax sive tranquillitas* as Marsilius terms it,[4] government becomes an end in itself. This then leads straight on to the Machiavellian conception of politics, but it is the natural outcome of a deep absorption of Aristotelianism. To live well is the aim of all men *viventes civiliter*, and the good life can be conceived of in terms of civil life alone. There is

[1] Marsilius of Padua, *Defensor pacis*, I. i. 7, p. 9; cf. Boethius of Dacia, *De sompniis*, 'Summum bonum quod est homini possibile ex actionibus moralibus est felicitas politica', cited M. Grabmann, *Mittelalterliches Geistesleben* (Munich, 1936), ii. 217.

[2] Dante, *Convivio*, iv. 6, pp. 425, 427, 'Che Aristotile sia dignissimo di fede e d'obbedienza e che però le sue parole siano somma e altissima autoritade così provare. . . Ed a vedere come Aristotile è maestro e duca della gente umana in quanto intende alla sua *finale* operazione, si conviene sapere che questo nostro fine, che ciascuno disia naturalmente, antichissimamente fu per li savi cercato. . . L'ingegno quasi divino che la natura in Aristotile messo avea. . . Congiungasi la filosofica autorita colla imperiale a bene e *perfettamente* reggere'; cf. iv. 23, p. 489, 'il Maestro della nostra vita Aristotile'; *Monarchia*, iii. 16, p. 375; Engelbert of Admont, *De ortu imperii Romani*, ch. 3, pp. 755–6. Marsilius said that the means of attaining this natural end were self-evident, *Defensor pacis*, I. iv. 2, p. 17; III. iii, p. 613.

[3] Engelbert of Admont, *De ortu imperii Romani*, chs. 13–14, pp. 761–3, 'Habito igitur ex his quae praedicta sunt eo quod felicitas regni est finis intentus in constitutione et administratione sive regimine regum et regnorum, et quod ipsam felicitatem faciunt et perficiunt ista tria, videlicet, bonum regni sufficientia sine indigentia, et tranquillitas sine turbatione, et securitas sine timore . . . ex eo quod tale regnum solum possit esse sibi ex se sufficiens et securum, ideo quia magnum et tranquillum in se, et ideo quia iustum . . . omnia tamen ista sub una ratione et sub uno nomine pacis includuntur, quae est finis *ultimus* et principalis, ad quem tendunt omnes hominum communitates'.

[4] Marsilius of Padua, *Defensor pacis*, III. iii, p. 613.

therefore no need for a divinely instituted governing power: the basis of all political authority is a human and natural one because man is naturally a political and social animal.

Lo fondamento radicale della imperiale maestà secondo il vero e la necessita della umana civiltà, che a uno fine è ordinata, cioè a vita felice, alla quale nullo per sè è sufficiente a venire senza l'ajuto d'altrui, conciossiacosachè l'uomo abbisogna di molte cose, alle quali uno solo satisfare non puo. È però dice il Filosofo che l'uomo naturalmente è compagnevole animale.[1]

Those entrusted with political authority need no divine functional qualification: any lay ruler, provided that he ensures terrestrial peace, the general well-being, security and liberty of his subjects, is capable of directing the society over which he rules to its final and perfect end.[2] It is the lay ruler therefore, not the pope or the bishops, who is the immediate source of power: only he is capable of promulgating law worthy of the name, and he is concerned with the necessities of human life alone. 'Officium regis', says John of Paris, 'est ad vitae humanae civilis necessitatem'.[3] The only true law is that human law which deals specifically with life on earth.[4] For Marsilius divine law is a matter dealing solely with the after-life, and

[1] Dante, *Convivio*, iv. 4, pp. 415–16; cf. Engelbert of Admont, *De ortu imperii Romani*, chs. 1–2, pp. 754–5; ch. 8, p. 758; ch. 15, p. 764, 'naturale regnum et imperium'; John of Paris, *De potestate regia et papali*, ch. 1, pp. 176–8: on this Leclercq comments, p. 93, 'Le "regnum" n'est pas seulement pour Jean de Paris une forme de gouvernement entre bien d'autres, c'est la forme idéale de la vie politique; ... Le "regnum" est donc une institution strictement naturelle... Le "regnum" est la meilleure forme de gouvernement parce qu'il répond mieux que les autres régimes politiques aux exigences de la vie humaine'.

[2] Dante, *Convivio*, iv. 4, pp. 416–17.

[3] John of Paris, *De potestate regia et papali*, ch. 4, p. 183.

[4] Marsilius of Padua, *De iurisdictione imperatoris*, p. 1386, 'Dicunt ergo et scribunt seriosius in suis tractatibus iam dicti doctores quod Christi fideles reguntur et vivunt sub duplici lege, divina videlicet et humana. Lex autem proprie sumpta praeceptum coactivum est de fiendis aut omittendis humanis actibus sub poena transgressoribus infligenda. Verum lex divina est coactivum praeceptum a Deo factum immediate absque humana deliberatione propter finem in futuro saeculo consequendum, et sub poena transgressoribus infligenda in eodem tantum modo, non praesenti. Sed lex humana voluntate seu deliberatione procedens propter finem immediate in hoc saeculo consequendum, et sub poena in eodem solum modo transgressoribus infligenda'. Cf. William of Ockham, *Dialogus*, I. i. 8, p. 405.

although he did not deny the ultimate superiority of its dictates,[1] he regards them as simply moral precepts and not real law at all.

Et propterea quamvis sacerdotibus liceat condere seu facere ordinationes sive exhortationes circa bonos mores et opera fienda, et malos et crimina fugienda, non tamen nunc dici debent huiusmodi ordinationes leges sed potius documenta seu regulae. Neque ipsorum iudicium per tales regulas circa hominum actus debet appellari iurisdictio sive forum. Secundum vero legem humanam talis est principans auctoritate legislatorum humanorum coactivam habens potestatem arcendi per poenam realem aut personalem transgressores legis humanae in praesenti tantum saeculo, non in illo [futuro].[2]

A political society can be governed without reference to ecclesiastical rulings. Correspondingly, although most of the lay writers continue to assume the existence of a *caput Ecclesiae* having spiritual power in addition to the secular governor,[3] the type of power which one exercises will be, as Dante said, of a different species to that of the other.[4] But since the lay ruler is to deal with all matters concerned with earthly government, it is doubtful whether the

[1] Marsilius of Padua, *Defensor minor*, xiii. 6, p. 41; xv. 3–4, pp. 47–8; *De iurisdictione imperatoris*, p. 1390; *Defensor pacis*, II. xii. 8–9, pp. 268–9; II. xxiii. 3, p. 443. However human law may disagree with divine law and yet be fully valid, since it is not righteousness but coercive force which gives law its practical effect and value: *Defensor pacis*, I. x. 4–5, p. 50; II. x. 7, pp. 250–1; II. xii. 9, p. 269; II. xiii. 2, pp. 275–6. Although Marsilius cites Aristotle in support of this, *Defensor pacis*, I. x. 4, p. 50: Aristotle, *Ethics*, x. 14, this is now regarded as a misinterpretation of Aristotle: M. Grignaschi, 'Le rôle de l'aristotelisme dans le *Defensor Pacis* de Marsile de Padoue', *Revue d'histoire et de la philosophie religieuses*, xxxv (1955), pp. 301–40 at pp. 318–20. Aristotle had however acknowledged that a just law did not in itself constitute good government unless it could be enforced, *Pol.*, iv. 8.

[2] Marsilius of Padua, *De iurisdictione imperatoris*, p. 1389; cf. *Defensor pacis*, I. x. 4, pp. 49–50; II. ii. 8, pp. 151–2; II. x. 8, p. 252, 'Si enim peccata huiusmodi non essent humana lege prohibita, ea committentes nequaquam punirentur'.

[3] John of Paris, *De potestate regia et papali*, ch. 5, pp. 183–4; ch. 8, pp. 190–2; ch. 10, pp. 194–201; ch. 17, p. 227; ch. 18, pp. 229–30; Dante, *Monarchia*, iii. 16, p. 376; Engelbert of Admont, *De ortu imperii Romani*, ch. 18, p. 768; ch. 21, p. 771.

[4] Dante, *Monarchia*, iii. 12, pp. 372–3, 'Cum ergo papa et imperator sint id quod sunt per quasdam relationes, quia per papatum et per imperiatum quae relationes sunt, altera sub ambitu paternitatis, et altera sub ambitu dominationis . . . Non enim dicimus imperator est papa nec e converso. Nec potest dici quod communicent in specie, cum alia sit ratio papae, alia imperatoris in quantum huiusmodi'.

pope has any real power at all. What authority he has can be reduced to matters of faith and doctrine only, and even this cannot be enforced unless the lay ruler lends jurisdictional support for this purpose. Papal power is of the nature of divine power, and on earth that is immaterial. Papal law has no intrinsic binding force, but is rather a series of moral and theological ordinances and exhortations,[1] except in so far as its precepts are embodied in the *corpus* of civil law.[2] At best it is what Marsilius describes as quasi-political.[3] The same is true not only of ecclesiastical power but of the *Ecclesia* itself. For Dante there is the Roman empire and the *Ecclesia universalis*, but unlike the Roman empire which is, as we have seen, a natural or civil society, the *congregatio fidelium* is a mystical or supernatural conception: 'it is not an effect of nature but of God'.[4] It may be the *regnum Christi*, but it is not of this world: it is an insubstantial abstraction.[5] And whilst the lay writers still tend to preserve the idea of a single, universal body politic, they no longer regard it as necessary for this community to be an *Ecclesia*, a Christian society: it is essentially a human society, the *communitas mortalium*.[6] There is nothing fundamentally Christian about it. As Dante points out, this community includes all mankind, not only Europeans but also Africans and Asians.[7] The Universal Church, a specifically Christian body, becomes nothing more than a descriptive

[1] Marsilius of Padua, *De iurisdictione imperatoris*, pp. 1388–9: bishops are only 'doctores seu iudices doctrinales', having the power only to issue 'ordinationes sive exhortationes', 'documenta seu regulae'; also *Defensor minor*, xiv. 2, p. 45; *Defensor pacis*, II. v. 4, pp. 182–5; II. xxx. 6, pp. 597–8.

[2] William of Ockham, *Dialogus*, I. i. 8, p. 405, 'libri canonistarum . . . sunt mere positiva ex humana voluntate dependentia'; Marsilius of Padua, *Defensor minor*, xiii. 5–6, pp. 40–1; xv. 4, p. 50. On this reduction of canon law to purely human law see de Lagarde, *La naissance de l'esprit laïque*, vi. 195–6. This had however already been suggested by the canonist Damasus at the beginning of the thirteenth century: W. Ullman, *Medieval Papalism* (London, 1949), p. 42, n. 4.

[3] Marsilius of Padua, *Defensor pacis*, II. i. 3, p. 140; II. i. 5, p. 142; II. iii. 10, p. 155.

[4] Dante, *Monarchia*, iii. 14, p. 374.

[5] Dante, *Monarchia*, iii. 15, p. 375.

[6] Dante, *Monarchia*, iii. 11, p. 372, 'universum mortalium'; i. 2, p. 342, 'universalis civilitas humani generis'; i. 3, p. 342, 'humana universitas', 'universitas hominum', 'genus humanum universaliter'; *Convivio*, iv. 4, p. 415, 'umana civiltà'. Similar terms are used by Ockham in the *Dialogus* and the *Octo quaestiones*: also *Dialogus*, III. II. iii. 25, p. 923, 'societas humana'.

[7] Dante, *Monarchia*, iii. 14, p. 374.

term for the community of believers within a larger political unit. It is, said Ockham, a *principatus specialis* forming part of the *generalis principatus mortalium*,[1] but this does not give its members special rights, privileges or powers: logically a pagan is just as good a member of the body politic as a Christian.[2] In the eyes of these publicists a pagan society is a perfectly legitimate one,[3] and they emphasised this by contrasting the disturbed state of contemporary Christendom with the perfect society which was held to have existed when the Roman people, although pagan, ruled the world.[4] The hierocratic assumption that only the Christian could have full rights of citizenship is put aside. Kingdoms can be just without obedience to God or his vicar. Indeed for such trenchant opponents of the Roman church it is quite understandable that freedom of belief should be a vital matter of principle.

The main reason advanced for the legitimacy of the old pagan Roman empire was that it had been acquired by the Romans with the consent of the majority of those now subjected to it,[5] and this

[1] William of Ockham, *Octo quaestiones*, iii. 4, p. 106; iii. 5, p. 109; *Dialogus*, III. I. iv. 23, pp. 865–6.

[2] This was one of the charges made against Ockham in 1324: Pelzer, *art. cit.*, p. 252.

[3] Engelbert of Admont, *De ortu imperii Romani*, ch. 11, pp. 760–1; Marsilius of Padua, *Defensor minor*, xii. 3, p. 36, 'Ex quo sequitur quod unum imperium et iustum fuit et esse potest apud infideles'; *Defensor pacis*, II. xxii. 15, p. 434; John of Paris, *De potestate regia et papali*, ch. 19, p. 234; William of Ockham, *Breviloquium*, iii. 13, pp. 134–6; iv. 10, pp. 159–60, 'tendendum est pro certo quod Romanum imperium tempore Christi verum fuit et legitimum, non tyrannice usurpatum', although he adds in his usual manner, 'sed quando et qualiter coeperit esse verum imperium fateor me nescire . . . forte solus Deus novit'. Much of this relied upon Augustine's remark, *De civitate Dei*, v. 15 (*PL*, xli. 160), that the Roman conquest of the world was justified.

[4] Dante, *Monarchia*, i. 16, p. 350, 'non inveniemus nisi sub divo Augusto monarcha, existente monarchia perfecta, mundum undique fuisse quietum. Et quod tunc humanum genus fuerit felix in pacis universalis tranquillitate, hoc historiographi omnes, hoc poetae illustres, hoc etiam scriba mansuetudinis Christi testari dignatus est, et denique Paulus plenitudinem temporis [*Gal.*, iv. 4] statum illum felicissimum appellavit'. On this passage see further T. Silverstein, 'On the Genesis of *De Monarchia*, ii. 5', *Speculum*, xiii (1938), pp. 326–49. See also *Convivio*, iv. 5, pp. 419f.; and for his idealisation of Rome in general, C. T. Davis, *Dante and the Idea of Rome* (Oxford, 1957).

[5] E.g. William of Ockham, *Dialogus*, III. II. i. 27, p. 809; III. II. ii. 5, p. 905, 'consensu maioris partis mundi'.

leads on to another vitally important application of nominalism in political thought. The innate individualism of the theory of universals as expounded by Ockham threatened not only the papal monarchy but the whole theory of absolute rulership which Roman law doctrines had fostered during the previous two centuries. Since for Ockham the important part of any political whole is its individual members, since government exists for their immediate well-being and happiness, and since the structure of society is from this point of view a man-made thing, it follows that the source of authority can only be the individual members of the community.[1] The assent of the citizens of any society, of the whole world if the community is universal, must be the true cause of every valid and effective law.[2] To Marsilius the ultimate authority in any society rests with a *legislator* comprising all its members, and the will of this legislator is that expressed by the *universitas civium*. It is necessary for its own convenience that this legislator should establish a *pars principans*, which could represent it *quasi instrumentalis vel executiva*, and regulate the society in accordance with the fundamental laws laid down by the legislator.[3] But if the *pars principans* itself transgresses those laws it is subject to correction and deposition by the community as a whole,[4] and is therefore conceived of as the typical Aristotelian limited ruler.[5] The Aristotelian basis of all this was in fact common to both Marsilius and Ockham, and can be seen in the emphasis which they placed upon the good of the community. Ockham for example frequently asserts that the first thing requisite for the *optimus principatus* is that it shall be directed towards the common good of those subject to it. It is true that the hierocrat also taught that government should be in the interests of the *bonum commune*, but he saw this as an eternal celestial thing whose temporal and mundane aspect could only be understood in relation to the heavenly one. But to Ockham and Marsilius the perfect life is

[1] William of Ockham, *Dialogus*, III, II. i. 8; III. II. i. 29–31; cf. III. II. i. 27, p. 899; *Octo quaestiones*, iv. 8, p. 52; viii. 4, p. 192.

[2] William of Ockham, *Dialogus*, III. II. ii. 28, p. 924; I. i. 8, p. 405.

[3] Marsilius of Padua, *Defensor pacis*, I. xii. 3, p. 63; I. xv. 4, p. 87.

[4] Marsilius of Padua, *Defensor pacis*, I. xvi. 21, pp. 109–10; I. xviii. 2–7, pp. 121–4.

[5] Marsilius of Padua, *Defensor pacis*, I. viii. 4–11, pp. 41–7.

that governed according to natural right, that is to say, according to the dictates of reason which they felt was naturally present in all men.[1] Therefore all have to agree upon what the dictates of right reason are, and it follows that this duty lies with the whole community itself. Since it is the common good which is in question it is the concern of all. The entire community can judge its interests better than any ruler. Hence political authority assumes an essentially voluntarist character: all make the law so that all shall wish to obey it,[2] and the form of government is again ideally a matter for the general choice.[3] Nevertheless neither Marsilius nor Ockham ever really shook themselves free from the deeply ingrained medieval view that government was exercised for the people and not by the people.[4] In practice it was with them very much a case of government by consent (and often tacit consent at that), and they were never able to escape from Aristotle's contention that some are natural lords whilst the rest are fit for nothing but subjection. This is particularly true of Marsilius, for whom it was apparent that some men were always deficient in right reason, and that the real control of government should rest with the *valentior pars* of the community.[5] Marsilius was not in fact an individualist to the same extent that Ockham was. Legislation is best carried out by a few: the *valentior pars* is that numerical minority functionally qualified by their natural ability for government.[6] But although Ockham also

[1] See for example Marsilius' defence of the intellectual and moral competence of the *vulgus*, *Defensor pacis*, I. xii–xiii.

[2] Marsilius of Padua, *Defensor pacis*, I. xii. 6, pp. 66–7. To support this he uses Aristotle's idea of a community of free men, *Politics*, iii. 6.

[3] For Ockham the ultimate arbiter of the nature of the Roman empire is the *communitas mortalium* itself: *Dialogus*, III. II. i. 31, 'Romanum imperium non potest minui nec dividi, saltem absque consensu tacito vel expresso communitatis mortalium'.

[4] Thus Ockham defines a tyrant as one who disregards his subjects' interests not as one who disregards their wishes, *Dialogus*, III. I. ii. 6.

[5] E.g. Marsilius of Padua, *Defensor pacis*, I. xiii. 2, p. 71, 'Si ergo valentior hominum multitudo vult politiam manere, quemadmodum bene dictum videtur, vult idem etiam sine quo politia manere non potest'.

[6] Marsilius of Padua, *Defensor pacis*, I. xiii. 8, pp. 76–7. Similarly a general council, which is the *valentior pars Ecclesiae*, should consist of a few people, II. xx. 2, p. 393. On the question of the nature of the *valentior pars* see below at pp. 194f.

used the same concept of the *valentior pars*,[1] there were other occasions when his fierce individualism brought him out against the necessary rightness of any majority decision, whether that majority was one of quantity or quality.[2] In his own case, as we have already noticed, he was prepared to back his own opinion against the assertions of the whole world of mortal men. This could only mean that for Ockham truth was not something handed on by those who had in the past preserved it, but was to be tested by the mind in the light of present experience. The empiricism which is so notable a feature of Ockham's philosophy is here readily apparent. Judgement has to be made by the mind and can only be of real value when made by the individual himself. In the last resort it was a denial of all authority. At bottom Ockham was an anarchist, and it was this which led not only to his opposition to John XXII and Benedict XII, but eventually to a renunciation of his allegiance to the Franciscan order and the withdrawal of his obedience to the Roman church.[3]

In spite of their opposition to the papal monarchy, neither Marsilius nor Ockham expressed dislike for the idea of kingship as an institution. Indeed the idea of one ruler, even though ultimately subject to the whole community, commended itself to the doctrine of economy: 'what can be done by one is better done by one than by many'.[4] Consequently for both writers the *pars principans* is usually

[1] William of Ockham, *Dialogus*, III. II. iii. 17, p. 948, says that government should function 'ex consensu ipsorum vel saltem valentioris partis'; Dante, *Monarchia*, iii. 14, p. 374, 'Et quod etiam ab assensu omnium [mortalium] vel *praevalentium* non habuerit, quis dubitat?'

[2] William of Ockham, *Dialogus*, III. I. ii. 27, p. 816, 'non semper est standum maiori parti nec pluralitati'. In the same way he fiercely attacks Marsilius' view that many heads are better than one (*Defensor pacis*, I. xiii. 2–6, pp. 70–5; I. xii. 5, pp. 65–6; II. xvii. 14, p. 369) on the grounds that those who are fallible separately are fallible together, *Dialogus*, I. v. 25, p. 495; I. v. 35, p. 506.

[3] William of Ockham, *De imperatorum et pontificum potestate*, ch. 1, p. 5, 'ab obedientia ecclesiae Avinionicae et a societate multitudinis fratrum minorum me subtraho'. It should be pointed out that he doubted whether the Avignonese church could be called the Roman church, e.g. ch. 21, p. 38, 'isti Avinionenses . . . etiam si essent vera Romana ecclesia', but this is patently a subterfuge.

[4] William of Ockham, *Dialogus*, III. I. ii. 19, p. 804, 'quando tamen ad alicuius inventionem sufficit unus solus, qui tunc non indiget favore vel auxilio aut consilio plurium, melius est quod queratur et inveniatur ab uno quam a pluribus. . . Quando autem pauci sufficiunt ad vivendum perfecte, quid est

assumed to be one man, and more specifically, the Roman emperor. Moreover, although they often spoke in general terms, and occasionally flirted with the idea of a number of independent polities, both worked on the general assumption that their political theories were applicable to the Roman empire, which they identified with the *communitas mortalium*. Notwithstanding the fact that Aristotle had spoken only of the *polis*, which in medieval terms was normally equated with the *civitas* or *regnum*,[1] neither Marsilius nor Ockham, any more than Dante or Engelbert of Admont, were really capable of thinking in terms of anything but a single universal society with a single political head. If the perfect community was to be the *regnum*, then it should be a *regnum omnium mortalium*.[2] Marsilius cannot be said to have made this very clear in the *Defensor pacis*: although he does speak on at least one occasion of the 'humanus legislator Romani imperii',[3] and he expressly states that the book is written for the benefit of the *imperator Romanorum*, Louis of Bavaria.[4] But the *Defensor pacis*, completed in 1324, was followed within a year or two by a short tract on the various translations of the Roman empire. In this second work Marsilius refers directly to the *Defensor pacis* as an idealistic account of the way in which the Roman empire ought to be organised. The *De translatione imperii* is to provide a more realistic balance to this by retailing the actual way in which the seat of imperial Roman government has passed

agendum et quid omittendum non expedit multitudinem convenire ad tractandum, sed melius est quod conveniant pauci, sufficientes tamen. Et ideo quando unus sufficit, non oportet convenire multos'; Dante, *Monarchia*, i. 14, p. 349, 'Et quod potest fieri per unum melius est per unum fieri quam per plura'.

[1] The Aristotelian view of the *polis* as the perfect, because self-sufficient, community is widely quoted by the publicists, although the papalists tend to give it a specialised meaning. For example Augustinus Triumphus points out that the *civitas* is called a perfect community only in that it is the seat of that perfect priest, a bishop: *Summa*, i. 6 ad 1, p. 10, 'Alia est communitas civitatis... et ista est communitas perfecta secundum Philosophum, quia si civitas bene ordinata est, in ea debet inveniri quidquid necessarium est ad vitam humanam. . . In [ista] vero praesunt episcopi quia civitas quaelibet est communitas perfecta sicut quilibet episcopus est sacerdos perfectus, cum possit simile sibi generare'.

[2] William of Ockham, *Dialogus*, III. II. ii. 20, p. 917, 'imperator est dominus in temporalibus omnium immediatus, ita ut in his quae spectat *ad regnum mortalium* magis sit obediendum imperatori quam cuiuscunque domino inferiori'.

[3] Marsilius of Padua, *Defensor pacis*, II. xxx. 8, p. 601.

[4] Marsilius of Padua, *Defensor pacis*, I. i. 6, p. 8.

successively between Romans, Greeks, Franks and Germans.[1] Marsilius added that the same basic principles ought to be followed in any lesser community, and it is understandable therefore that he was not too precise in defining his terms in the *Defensor pacis*. The *pars principans*, for example, is at one point briefly referred to as consisting of one or several people,[2] and he was well aware that a city-state was as likely to be governed by an oligarchy as by a single head. But in general it is apparent that by the *pars principans* Marsilius has in mind the Roman emperor, whom he describes as the head of a universal, or very nearly universal, monarchy originating from Rome.[3] In the *Defensor minor*, written some fifteen years later, it is the Roman emperor who figures as the choice of the human legislator, the one to whom this legislator has transferred its powers.[4]

[1] Marsilius of Padua, *De translatione imperii*, ch. 1, p. 148, 'Quoniam in eo quem *Defensorem pacis* habemus tractatum fecimus de Romani et cuiuslibet alterius principatus institutione, nova translatione, ac alia quavis circa principatum mutatione, diximusque per quem et quomodo secundum rationem seu de iure fieri debet et potest'. In the present tract 'dicemus igitur de imperialis Romanae sedis translatione, per quem vel quos et qualiter de facto processerit a Romanis in Graecos; deinde vero a Graecis in Gallicos sive Francos; novissime autem a Francis in Germanos'.

[2] Marsilius of Padua, *Defensor pacis*, I. xvii. 2, p. 113. But even if composed of several people they were still 'unum secundum officium' in accordance with the general principle of unity: 'dico unum numero ex necessitate fore, non plures, si debeat regnum aut civitas recte disponi'.

[3] Marsilius of Padua, *De translatione imperii*, ch. 1, p. 148, 'Ante tamen oportet attendere quod Romanum imperium in una sui significatione quandoque significat monarchiam seu regalem principatum Romanae urbis vel civitatis tamen qualis fuit ab origine sua quemadmodum ex sequentibus apparebit. In alia vero acceptione significat imperium Romanum universalem et generalem totius mundi vel plurimarum saltem provinciarum monarchiam; qualis fuit Romanae urbis totius orbis principatus in eius processu secundum quem etiam acceptione de ipsius translatione tractare propositum magis est nobis'.

[4] Marsilius of Padua, *Defensor minor*, i. 7, p. 3, 'sed talem dispensationem seu relaxationem [praeceptorum aut prohibitorum humanae legis] ad Romanum principem in quantum legislatorem humanum et auctoritatem solummodo pertinere'; iii. 7, p. 8, matters of tithes 'ad auctoritatem Romanorum principum pertinere, ipsis ab humano et supremo legislatore traditam et concessam'; *De iurisdictione imperatoris*, p. 1388, 'Est etiam similiter secundum legem humanum legislator, ut civium universitas aut eius pars valentior, vel Romanus princeps supremus imperator vocatus. . .' The Marsilian terms *universitas* or *communitas mortalium* and *pars principans* are employed by Ockham in the *Dialogus* and the *Octo quaestiones* to refer to the Roman empire and the Roman emperor respectively.

This gives him authority over 'all the provinces of the world'—or most of them—and the legislator itself is seen to consist of all *Romani*, that is, all the members of the universal empire, or, as the name *humanus legislator* suggests, all mankind. This is the theory: for practical purposes, says Marsilius, the legislative powers, and the right to elect a prince to exercise them, were transferred to the inhabitants of Rome itself 'on account of their exceeding virtue'. There they will remain until the human legislator revokes them. For the present the geographical *Romani* represent or epitomise the universal *Romani*, the whole human race.

Inquirendum utique est quis sit supremus legislator humanus. . . Et quoniam haec potestas sive auctoritas per universitatem provinciarum aut ipsorum valentiorem partem, translata fuit in Romanum populum propter excedentem virtutem ipsius, Romanus populus auctoritatem habuit et habet ferendi leges super universas mundi provincias; et si populus hic auctoritatem leges ferendi in suum principem transtulit, dicendum similiter ipsorum principem habere huiusmodi potestatem, quorum siquidem auctoritas seu potestas leges ferendi, scilicet Romani populi et principis sui, tam diu durare debet et durata est rationabiliter quam diu ab eisdem per universitatem provinciarum a Romano populo vel per Romanum populum ab eius principe fuerit revocatae.[1]

In any case, in the *Defensor pacis* itself, Marsilius had concluded that his earlier remarks on the possibility of numerous communities as sufficient to ensure earthly peace were not to apply when a specifically Christian society was under consideration. Here only a universal ruler, provided that he was an emperor and not a bishop, could suffice, and was indeed necessary when considerations of salvation were to be taken into account.[2] In spite of the thoroughly secular ideals propounded in the course of his argumentation, Mar-

[1] Marsilius of Padua, *Defensor minor*, xii. 1, p. 35.

[2] Marsilius of Padua, *Defensor pacis*, II. xxviii. 15, p. 546, 'Concluderet enim ratio haec pariter oportere unum numero esse yconum in orbe universo, quod non est expediens neque verum. Sufficiunt enim ad convictum humanum quietum unitates numerales principatuum secundum provincias, quemadmodum diximus 17° primae. Unum autem esse iudicem coactivum omnium, nondum demonstratum, videtur esse de necessitate salutis aeternae, cum tamen *huius amplior videatur necessitas inter fideles* quam unius universalis episcopi, eo quod *universalis princeps* magis in unitate potest conservare fideles quam universalis episcopus'.

silius was quite unable to overcome the tacit assumption of his age that Roman and Christian should figure as alternative terms. So that although his views on the exact relationship between the 'humanus legislator Romani imperii', the human race itself, and the *congregatio fidelium* are shrouded in vagueness, it seems clear that Marsilius, far from emphasising the distinction, was inclined to assume their identity. The supreme legislator is for him not only a human one but also a Christian one: the community of the faithful is equated with the Roman people.[1] In spite of reducing the *Ecclesia* to a mere unity of faith concerning only the Christian members of the human race, in the end neither Marsilius nor any other writer of the time could escape from the overpowering influence of the ideal of a single, universal, and Christian, body politic. Indeed the overall impression given by all Marsilius' works is that he is simply describing a secularised version of the papal-hierocratic *Ecclesia*.[2] For all its illusion of modernity, the *Defensor pacis* is in many respects nothing more than an Aristotelianised version of the traditional medieval theory of the Christian Roman empire, with its constitution resting upon the *lex regia*.

But if Marsilius' society is still in a sense a Christian society, there has been a profound change of emphasis. The society does not exist for a Christian, religious end, but the Christian religion is permitted to flourish in the society for the purely secular end of internal security. It is the papal principle of the unity given by one faith adapted for purely political reasons. The human society of Marsilius is a complete inversion of the papally-inspired Christian society, and in nearly every way is an exact parallel to it. If Marsi-

[1] For example the 'humanus fidelis legislator', consisting of 'omnes fideles', in *Defensor pacis*, II. xxxi. 8, p. 410, is clearly the 'universalis legislatoris fidelis' and 'supremus humanus legislator' of II. xviii. 8, p. 382, which is again identifiable with the 'supremus imperii Romani humanus legislator' of II. xxx. 8, p. 601 and the *Defensor minor*, iii. 7, p. 8.

[2] E. Gilson, *Dante the Philosopher* (London, 1948), pp. 166, 179, describes Dante's description of the Roman empire as 'un décalque laïcisé de la notion de l'Eglise'; and his identification of *Ecclesia* and *imperium* has been remarked upon by C. H. McIlwain, *The Growth of Political Thought in the West* (London, 1932), p. 274; Woolf, *Bartolus of Sassoferrato*, p. 296; and Folz, *Le souvenir et la légende de Charlemagne*, p. 396. Certainly Dante uses Rome as a symbol common to both the Roman empire and the Universal Church: Davis, *op. cit.*, pp. 2–3.

lius regards the hierocratic view that all lay power derives from the ecclesiastical head as an *opinio perversa*,[1] his own conception of the right order is simply an *opinio reversa*. Although he does not permit ecclesiastical institutions, pope, clergy or general council, any jurisdiction in their own right, they may exercise whatever coercive power is granted to them by the *pars principans* on behalf of the human legislator.[2] Whilst the papalist emphasised the role of the lay power as an *instrumentum papae*, Marsilius went far towards making the priesthood into an *instrumentum imperii*. The clergy are simply a *pars communitatis*, and draw their being, and receive regulation, from the head of that community: a view which subsequently inspired Louis of Bavaria's Roman expedition of 1328 and lay at the basis of all the many imperial attempts to effect a *reformatio urbis et orbis*. Indeed the whole of Marsilius' very Aristotelian thesis of the six parts of the community[3] was little different from the hierocratic idea of society as a complex organisation of functions necessary for the well-being of social life and carried out by a hierarchy of orders and offices.[4] Each part is allotted a limited sphere of independent functioning—each to his own function—but is subject to the supervision and control of the ruler.[5] Similarly the natural adjustment of each part to the others is comparable to the co-ordination of the members of the animal body, whilst his doctrine of the constant clash of interests between individuals leads to the view of each as a cog whose constant friction against its neighbours makes for the functioning of the machine.[6] When each part is properly adjusted to the others and to the good of the whole body there will ensue the natural unity and order which spells *pax* and *tranquillitas*.[7] So too this order and unity is presumed to exist naturally, and that it does not do so in fact is attributed to the impedi-

[1] Marsilius of Padua, *Defensor pacis*, II. i. 1, p. 139.

[2] Marsilius of Padua, *Defensor pacis*, II. vi. 12–13, pp. 209–15; II. xxi. 8, pp. 410–11.

[3] Marsilius of Padua, *Defensor pacis*, I. v. 1, p. 20, based upon Aristotle, *Politics*, iv. 8.

[4] Marsilius of Padua, *Defensor pacis*, I. iii. 5, pp. 15–16; I. iv. 5, p. 19; I. v. 1, p. 20; I. v. 5, pp. 22–3.

[5] Marsilius of Padua, *Defensor pacis*, I. ii. 1–3, pp. 10–12; I. v. 7, pp. 23–4.

[6] Gewirth, *op. cit.*, i. 60–3; Gierke-Maitland, *Political Theories of the Middle Age* (Cambridge, 1927), pp. 26–7.

[7] Cf. Marsilius of Padua, *Defensor pacis*, I. xvii. 9–11, pp. 117–20.

ments to this natural order created by those 'qui non naturaliter agunt'.[1] The function of the *pars principans* is therefore essentially negative: the judgement of disputes and the remediation of injustice. The right order in society does not have to be created but already exists, needing however the constant attention of the political *medicus* to maintain it.[2] The interrelated concepts of peace, unity and universality in the work of Marsilius thus lead him into the corporate conception of the community which is to be found in the writings of any papalist. As Henry of Ghent had said, the teaching of the Averro-Aristotelians might lead to the supremacy of the individual good over that of the whole, but in practice the individual good is assimilated to that of the whole, and, since the destruction of the common good means the ruin of the individual good, the retention of the well-being of the whole remains paramount.[3] So too for Marsilius the collective good of all the individuals, the good of the whole, eventually becomes superior to that of its parts, and a semi-totalitarian view of a corporate political organism emerges.[4] In this way the Marsilian community tends to be closely analogous

[1] See in particular his reasons for allowing ultimate authority to be in the hands of the *valentior pars* rather than the whole community: e.g. *Defensor pacis*, I. xiii. 2, pp. 70–1. Some are deformed (*orbatum*) intellectually and so will impede the working of the natural order. As one might expect, the chief impediment to the maintenance of this *pax* and the *unitas ordinis* is the priesthood: I. xix. 3, p. 127. The idea of impediments in the naturally existing order is also Aristotelian: see William of Moerbecke's version of *Physics*, ii. 8, 'in physicis autem semper sic est nisi aliquid impediat'.

[2] Marsilius of Padua, *Defensor pacis*, I. xv. 11, p. 93, 'Quo modo conservabit in esse debito unamquamque partium civitatis et a nocumentis ac iniuriis praeservabit; quod si paciatur aut agat iniuriam ipsarum aliqua, curari debet per principantis actionem, inferens quidem iniuriam sustiendo poenam. Est enim poena sicut medicina quaedam delicti'; I. v. 7, p, 24, 'statuta fuit necessario in civitate pars aliqua seu officium per quam excessus talium actuum corrigantur et ad aequalitatem aut proportionem debitam reducantur. . . Haec autem pars ab Aristotele vocata est iudicalis seu principans'.

[3] Henry of Ghent, *Quodlibet*, xiv. 8: on this see G. de Lagarde, 'La philosophie sociale d'Henri de Gand et Godefroid de Fontaines', *Archives de l'histoire doctrinale et littéraire du moyen âge*, xiv (1943–5), pp. 73–142 at pp. 94–8.

[4] Marsilius of Padua, *Defensor pacis*, I. xiii. 2, p. 71, 'omne totum maius esse sua parte'; Engelbert of Admont, *De ortu imperii Romani*, c. 15, pp. 763–4, 'Item bonum commune melius est et magis curandum bono singulorum et respublica plus quam res privata . . . tamquam bonum particulare et privatum [ordinatur] ad bonum commune et publicum, et tamquam bonum minores ad maius, et naturaliter tamquam pars ad totum'.

to the hierocratic *Ecclesia*, even to the extent of having in its *valentior pars* a functionally qualified directorate of government closely allied to the position of the *sacerdotium*, the *sanior pars*, in the papal-ecclesiastical corporation. In spite of the situation of ultimate authority in the community as a whole, the general impression to be gained from the *Defensor pacis* is that Marsilius favours a single source for all power in the community, a conception in which the undertones of a Roman law theory of absolutism were not lacking,[1] although the premises on which he worked, necessary to the primary aim of destroying the papal-hierocratic system, effectively prevented him from developing it. Similarly the papalists' unitary notion of power is implied: the *ius sacrum* remains part of the *ius publicum*,[2] and no sharp distinction can be drawn between temporal and spiritual matters. For Marsilius every spiritual question has its temporal side if it is to have any significance in the earthly paradise, and therefore comes within the scope of imperial jurisdiction. Sin has become a crime; and heresy with Marsilius, as with the papalist, is equated with treason, although now punishable not as an offence against God, but as an offence against the political head using religious unity as a means of securing political unity. The nature of Marsilian society is essentially one and requires one head,[3] and this head combines within himself all the attributes of the priest-king permanently lurking behind the traditional imperialist ideology. In a final analysis Marsilius' separation of the spiritual and secular orders of life can be seen as mainly a defensive measure, which has to some extent obscured the real aim of his political philosophy,

[1] E.g. Marsilius of Padua, *Defensor pacis*, II. viii. 9, p. 230, 'Propter quod siquidem evitandum fateri oportet secundum veritatem iurisdictionem in episcopos seu presbyteros et clericos omnes legislatoris auctoritate principantem habere, ne principatuum etiam pluralitate inordinata politiam solvi contingat'; and note therefore his remark that the Roman people transfer *merum imperium* to the emperor: II. iv. 12, p. 172, 'vocatur haec iurisdictio [principis] a Romano legislatore merum imperium'. For a discussion of the absolutist elements in Marsilius see Gewirth, *op. cit.*, i. 248–59.

[2] *Dig.*, I. i. 2. This was used by both Marsilius and Ockham to justify imperial intervention into papal affairs.

[3] Cf. Engelbert of Admont, *De ortu imperii Romani*, ch. 15, p. 763; and ch. 18, p. 767: there will be 'multorum capitum unum monstrum' if several lay rulers are permitted 'in uno corpore christianae reipublicae'.

namely, the creation of one, essentially lay, society having a single temporal head who is both emperor and pope.[1] It was very largely this consideration which later commended itself to the defenders of the Tudor theory of State, where again an intrinsically nominalist, anti-papal, conception of society was woven into the making of an authoritarian community owing allegiance to a new vicar of God.[2] And it may be borne in mind that in the following century the nominalism of Hobbesian philosophy succeeded only in producing a Leviathan.

[1] This clearly emerges from his discussion of the ecclesiastical rights of the emperor, *Defensor pacis*, II. xxxv. 7, pp. 473–4. It may be mentioned that the term *pars principalis* is used with reference to the pope by Hostiensis. Cf. E. Gilson, *Dante the Philosopher*, p. 179, 'By a curious paradox Dante was able to raise up a universal monarch vis-à-vis to the universal pope only by imagining this monarch himself as a kind of pope'.

[2] For the influence of Marsilian thought on the Tudor political writers see P. Munz, *The Place of Hooker in the History of Thought*, pp. 93–111, 117, and Appendix C: and here further literature. Munz also shows how the Puritan theory of two societies in reality cloaked the basic aim of establishing a single theocratic state.

IV. VIA MEDIA

THE potential danger to the papal system of government in the new Aristotelianism was quickly recognised by the papacy itself. Consequently the initial reception accorded to the new learning in leading ecclesiastical circles was coldly hostile. Even at the very end of the thirteenth century the English Franciscan, Roger Marston, is to be found describing the pagan philosophers as 'those infernal men', and urging a return to the wisdom of the saints. But at the same time it was appreciated that much of what Aristotle had to say could be exceedingly useful, and in any case was not to be denied. Some Aristotelian principles, such as the teleological approach to government, had already in fact played a vital part in the building up of the hierocratic system. It was generally felt that Aristotle could not be ignored, but that in some way or other his teachings should be modified and harmonised with orthodox doctrine. This attitude seems to emerge from Gregory IX's prohibition on the use of Aristotle's books on nature in 1231. He acknowledges that these works contain 'both useful and useless matter', and commands the Dominicans at Paris that, 'examining these books in a way that is convenient, subtle and prudent, you entirely exclude anything which you may find there to be erroneous or likely to give scandal or offence to their readers, so that what is suspect being removed, the rest may be studied without delay or offence'.[1] In this way the duty of acting as official censors was largely entrusted to the Dominicans, and although the process of 'baptising' Aristotle went on for the rest of the Middle Ages, it was widely held by the early fourteenth century that most of this had been achieved. More than anyone else the man responsible was Thomas Aquinas. In spite of the fact that he was regarded during his lifetime with considerable disfavour for his constant use of Aristotle, one of the most important features of fourteenth-century political thought is

[1] *Chartularium Universitatis Parisiensis* (ed. Denifle-Chatelain, Paris, 1889), i. 143–4.

the rise of Aquinas' political principles to an almost sensational popularity. It was still felt to be safer to borrow from the Angelic Doctor without acknowledgement, but to some extent every political writer of the time was influenced by his doctrines. Even Augustinus Triumphus and Marsilius of Padua, respectively the great exponents of absolute papal and lay supremacy, did not escape tincture from the Thomist tar brush, whilst Ockham positively revelled in the task of demonstrating the *reductio ad absurdum* of Thomas' political expedients. And although it may be true to say that some of the canonists remained relatively free from infection, undoubtedly the civilians succumbed almost to a man.[1] The reason is not difficult to discover. Aquinas worked on the assumption that although there might be many forms of truth, because they were truth, all were ultimately reconcilable. It was not for him to accept one form and reject the others as necessarily incompatible: it was taken for granted that all had a certain if unequal degree of validity. And what he had discussed in general principles, he and his followers were convinced must logically apply to every discipline, above all to political science. The declared aim of what we may term the Thomist school of political thought was the acceptance of all the conflicting theories, hierocratic and anti-hierocratic, of society and government, and the demonstration of their final harmony with each other. It was a project highly acceptable to the medieval mind, with its tendency to assume a Platonic unity of knowledge, and when Aquinas and his supporters announced that this had been achieved their contemporaries were mesmerised into thinking that what they had always believed to be so actually was the case. Indeed, in so far as it was humanly possible, Aquinas had succeeded: and if the historian of today has reason to express his dissatisfaction, the attractiveness of the Thomist synthesis, especially to minds conditioned by their own innate beliefs to accept it, must not be underrated. To the majority of the publicists in the fourteenth century it seemed that Aquinas had pointed out the way in which Augustine

[1] H. D. Hazeltine in his introduction to W. Ullmann, *The Medieval Idea of Law* (London, 1946), pp. xxii–xxv. It was also the case that Aquinas employed many ideas which the Roman lawyers had themselves developed in the first place. For Aquinas' use of Roman law see J. M. Aubert, *Le droit romain dans l'oeuvre de Saint Thomas* (Paris, 1955).

and Aristotle could be combined in politics just as much as in philosophy. It was felt that they were attempting nothing new, but were only giving an explanation of what had always been. But in reality this combination of widely divergent streams of thought created a new trend in political thinking which reacted upon every problem that the political writer of the time was called upon to face. For whatever it set out to do, this political synthesising did not reproduce the authentic outlook of either the hierocrat or the extreme Aristotelian. The Thomist system of government included much that was Augustinian, much that was Aristotelian, and much else besides, but the result was neither recognisably Augustinian, Aristotelian nor anything else. It was simply eclectic, and stemmed from an essentially eclectic philosophical basis which had already led its author into conflict with both the Augustinian and Aristotelian schools of philosophy which were actively disputing by his side. And if it is certainly true that his preoccupation with the harmonising of contradictory opinions led Aquinas into making inexact interpretations, it might also be said that a Christian Aristotelianism was itself a contradiction in terms. But although the Thomist political philosophy exhibited certain inherent weaknesses, there can be no denying its authority amongst the publicists, not only because it purported to give an answer to every political problem, but also because it was expressly designed to give an explanation of life as it actually was, and to harmonise not only a set of inharmonious ideals with one another but also those ideals with the realities of the contemporary political situation. Thus Thomism was not quite a system in the sense that the hierocratic theory or the grand design of the *Defensor pacis* were systems. The latter were essentially idealistic, concentrating upon what their authors wished and thought should be rather than what was: their adherents could afford to ignore the wide and obvious discrepancies between reality and right, and the process of historical change played no vital part in their elaboration. They felt that there could be no alteration of basic principles, and that these principles were always applicable in every detailed and specific circumstance. Although this is still partly true of Thomism, the followers of Aquinas amongst the publicists were very much more concerned with the facts of the European situation in the early fourteenth century, and laboured to prove that this was what ought to be, and how and why it was so. Whatever the contradictions involved, they ended up with an explanation loose enough to cover most of the existing facts. Fact and theory, it seemed, could be combined as easily as reason and faith. Consequently the general tone of the Thomist writers was considerably more optimistic than of the hierocrat, who could only see the right order being rapidly reduced to confusion, or of the Averro-Aristotelian, who still seemed to be a midget pitting his strength against the might of the ecclesiastical Colossus. Hence it is in the works of Aquinas and Tholemy of Lucca that there can be found a quasi-historical treatment of the subject of monarchy, and indeed the whole theory of the natural law basis of civil power was fundamentally a rationalisation of already existing facts. The lay power was seen to have existed from 'the time to which memory does not run', and was therefore something to be explained away. Similarly the *de facto* independence of the lay kingdoms was indisputable, but yet had to be combined with the theoretical lordship of pope and emperor over a universal society. It was the same policy as that which defined the place of grace in the universe without detracting from the efficacity of nature and natural causes. Another result of this was that the Thomists made the first real attempt to combine feudal concepts with the political thought of the day. This is not to suggest that the hierocrats and the papacy itself had not made use of the prevailing feudal political and economic system for their own purposes,[1] but in general feudalism was something outside the hierocratic system, and the papalist could say with Innocent III that he did not concern himself with feudal matters.[2] But the Thomists did. Their whole view of the pope as *apex Ecclesiae* from whom ran out the two lines of temporal and spiritual power to the *populus* below suggested that the society was a feudal triangle. A feudal flavour was introduced into their theory of the bond of allegiance which bound emperor to pope. It appears again in their conception of a contractual theory of power in which both ruler and subjects had inalienable rights, and the view that the existing

[1] Ullmann, *The Growth of Papal Government*, pp. 332–43.
[2] Innocent III, *Decretales*, II. i. 13, 'Non intendimus iudicare de feudo'.

order could be overturned if those rights were infringed.[1] Thus the Thomists could plead a greater acquaintance with the realities of medieval political life and a genuine attempt to combine fact with ideal. For this reason the principle of utility was constantly emphasised, and there comes a very noticeable adaptation of ends to means. But it also suggested that events, having once occurred were practically immutable, and it was therefore the theory which required change. It tended to assume that what was done was just as important as what ought to be done, and so inevitably paved the way for a theory of politics based solely upon the immediate requirements of the *raison d'état*.[2]

For Aquinas and those publicists who elaborated his doctrines the main aim was the reduction of all knowledge, political, philosophical and theological, to a unity. They succeeded in reducing it to two terms, human and divine, reason and faith, and the reconciliation of these two became the *summum bonum* of scholastic activity. In his *Summa contra Gentiles* Aquinas had distinguished the two forms of truth and recognised each as a distinct *origo* of knowledge: revelation, the divine unveiling of ultimate truth through the media of the Scriptures, tradition, the Church Fathers and papal decrees; human philosophy, the system of natural right revealed in the human mind and contained *par excellence* in the dictates of Aristotle: a higher and a lower truth which had to be blended into each other: and it was with this end in view that Aquinas compiled the great *Summa theologica*. From this emerged the view that human nature had not been entirely corrupted by the Fall of man from grace, but was still able, within the purely natural order, to recognise those rules of conduct which suffice for right living.[3] And since

[1] See for example Tholemy of Lucca's very feudal definition of regal government, *De regimine principum*, ii. 10, p. 245.

[2] Something of this attitude can be seen in the apology offered by Bartolus, *Comm. in Dig. Vet.*, *Rubrica*, n. 13, 'Videte nos sumus in terris amicis ecclesiae, et ideo dico quod ista donatio [Constantini] valeat... volens favere ecclesiae, dico quod illa donatio valuit'. Bartolus may be reckoned as the leading exponent of Thomism amongst the Roman jurists: Woolf, *Bartolus of Sassoferrato*, p. 17; Hazeltine, *op. cit.*, p. xxiii.

[3] Thomas Aquinas, *Summa theologica*, II. I. xciv. 2, 'Tertio modo inest homini inclinatio ad bonum secundum naturam rationis, quae est sibi propria: sicut homo habet naturalem inclinationem ad hoc quod veritatem cognoscat de Deo

all good things had been created by God, reason itself was ultimately divine, so that by following reason man was still ultimately following the will of God rather than his own desires. In this sense, said Aquinas, he is co-operating with God, and is partaking in the divine government of the world.[1] Human nature is neither destroyed nor annulled by the fact that the ultimate end of life is the *visio beatifica Dei*,[2] nor the human mind rendered incapable of discovering the natural moral law. But it cannot discover for itself either the supernatural end of man or the means of attaining that end. Neither reason nor the natural order taken by themselves can be enough. Knowledge of the fullness of life can be acquired only by the addition of revelation, which transcends the immediate pursuit of human happiness. The right ordering of human society must therefore take account of both the natural order which all men can interpret and the divine order whose understanding is reserved only to the priesthood. Reason and revelation are two semi-independent sources of law, each of which is competent enough to guide man within its own sphere, but insufficient to cover the whole of human life. Philosophy and theology, the natural order and the supernatural, must be taken together, and will normally be found to exist side by side in an harmonious relationship.

In Thomist phraseology the natural order is potentially good, but because of the ultimate divine end of life it requires the divine order to give it realisation, to make it actual and complete. This principle can now be applied to anything, essence and existence, matter and form, body and soul, and, as every medieval writer was aware, this is analogous to the right ordering of society and the correct relationship existing between the lay and ecclesiastical authorities.[3] Man is a psycho-physical unity in which neither body nor soul is self-sufficient, even though the body has an imperfect, temporary, ex-

et ad hoc quod in societate vivat. Et secundum hoc ad legem naturalem pertinent ea quae ad huiusmodi inclinationem spectant'.

[1] Thomas Aquinas, *Summa contra Gentiles*, iii. 21, 'Dei sumus adiutores' [I *Cor.*, iii. 9]; cf. iii. 13; *Summa theologica*, II. I. xix. 4.

[2] Thomas Aquinas, *Summa contra Gentiles*, iii. 25.

[3] Thomas Aquinas, *Summa theologica*, II. II. lx. 6 ad 3; Aegidius Romanus, *De potestate ecclesiastica*, i. 7, pp. 22–7; i. 8, p. 29; Tholemy of Lucca, *Determinatio compendiosa*, ch. 7, p. 18.

istence when deprived of the motivating force of the soul. But since the body cannot act without the soul, it is the soul which is the guiding component of the body and stands superior to it. Man has a double nature in the same way that he has a double existence, first earthly and subsequently heavenly; similarly Aquinas stipulates a double purpose for human society. Initially the community exists to promote the fulfilment of the physical aspect of human life, economic self-sufficiency.[1] He adopted without hesitation Aristotle's dictum that man is naturally a political animal, and that civil government is a necessary consequence of man's innate social tendencies.[2] It is part of the natural order,[3] and may therefore be said to have divine approbation. Men have a natural right to form themselves into political communities, and sufficient natural reason to set up their own forms of government. Lay government is perfect in the sense that it is sufficient for the attainment of the good life on earth, and if this is all that matters there is no need for any rulers except kings, or any political society other than a human one. But to the Thomist the good life can only be understood with reference to the after-life: terrestrial well-being is not enough and cannot be an end in itself—'Non est possibile in hac vita esse ultimam hominis felicitatem'.[4] Lay rulers exist for the maintenance of the *pax terrena*,

[1] See the *De regimine principum*, ii. 1–4 of Aquinas and ii. 5–6 of Tholemy of Lucca, where 'omnia quae humanae vitae requirit necessitas' are dealt with in a very Aristotelian manner. Their achievement produces a 'societas perfecta', ii. 3, p. 240. Cf. Aegidius Romanus, *De regimine principum*, III. i. 2.

[2] Thomas Aquinas, *Comm. in Polit.*, i. 1, quotes Aristotle to the effect that man is naturally a social animal, and continues, 'Agit de institutione civitatis, concludens ex praemissis quod in omnibus hominibus est quidam naturalis impetus ad communitatem civitatis, sicut et ad virtutes. Sed tamen sicut virtutes acquiruntur per exercitium humanum, ut dicitur in secundo *Ethicorum*, ita civitates sunt institutae humana industria'; cf. Aegidius Romanus, *De regimine principum*, II. i. 1; III. i. 1–4; Alexander de S. Elpidio, *De ecclesiastica potestate*, ii. 10, p. 28; Alvarus Pelagius, *De planctu Ecclesiae*, ch. 52, p. 126.

[3] Aegidius Romanus, *De regimine principum*, I. i. 2: it is part of the 'ordo rationalis et naturalis'; Thomas Aquinas, *Summa theologica*, I. xcvi. 4 ad 4.

[4] Thomas Aquinas, *Summa contra Gentiles*, iii. 48; *De regimine principum*, i. 14, p. 237; *In lib. Boetii de Trinitate expositio*, i. 1, 'Id sine quo non potest conservari *humana societas* est homine maxime necessarium et toti humano generi, cum homo sit animale politicum, ut dicitur 8 *Ethicorum*; sed sine fide humana societas servari non potest. . . Ergo fides humano generi est maxime necessaria . . . igitur finis humanae vitae sit beatitudo'; Durandus de S. Porciano, *De*

but this must be used to further the *pax Christi*, since this 'pax mundi est imperfecta'.[1] Taken by itself civil government is, like the natural order, only potential: it is, said James of Viterbo, *inchoatus*, unfinished.[2] The imperfect must be subject to the perfect,[3] and the perfect, ultimate end of mankind is heavenly beatitude, which only divine grace can fathom. It is the spiritual government, the divinely instituted vicariate of Christ held by the successors of Peter, which alone can guide men to this celestial *finis*.[4] Papal government perfects civil government by making it actual and real.[5] There are two ultimate sources of power, human jurisdiction deriving from the *populus* and divine jurisdiction emanating from God through his vicar, and both must come together in the establishment of any complete political community.

Sed princeps spiritualium regit suum principatum secundum legem divinam, si bonus est, et princeps temporalium regit secundum legem

iurisdictione ecclesiastica, ch. 2, fo. 2v, 'Ex hoc ad propositum dicendum est quod si bona ad quae facienda homines debent induci et mala a quibus homines debent arceri pertinerent solum ad praesentem civilem vitam et politicam, sufficeret ad regimen populi potestas iurisdictionis saecularis, nec alia aliqua esset necessaria. . . Sed quia vita fidelium christianorum non tendit solum ad bona et mala praesentis vitae, [immo] principaliter tendit ad bona futurae vitae . . . ideo praeter eam inter christianos necessaria est alia potestas quae nomine potestas vocatur spiritualis'.

[1] Thomas Aquinas, *Comm. in Evang. Ioh.*, xiv. 27, *lect.* 7.

[2] James of Viterbo, *De regimine christiano*, ii. 7, p. 232.

[3] Thomas Aquinas, *Comm. in Polit.*, vii. 2; Alexander de S. Elpidio, *De ecclesiastica potestate*, ii. 9, p. 26, 'Dici potest quod temporalis potestas habet aliquid de veritate *potentiae*, cum sit ex iure humano, quod a natura oritur, tamen *imperfecta* et *informis* nisi *formetur* per spiritualem'.

[4] See the extended statement of this in Thomas Aquinas, *De regimine principum*, i. 14–15, p. 237, which centres on the following passage: 'Sed quia finem fruitionis divinae non consequitur homo per virtutem humanam sed virtute divina perducere ad illum finem non humani erit sed divini regiminis. . . Huius ergo regni ministerium ut a terrenis essent spiritualia distincta, non terrenis regibus sed sacerdotibus est commissum, et praecipue summo sacerdoti, successori Petri, Christi vicario, Romano pontifici, cui omnes reges populi christiani oportet esse subditos sicut ipsi Domino Iesu Christo'; cf. *Summa theologica*, II. 1. xc. 2.

[5] James of Viterbo, *De regimine christiano*, ii. 8, p. 232, 'Imperfecta quidem et informis est omnis humana potestas nisi per spiritualem formetur et perficiatur'; cf. Johannes Branchazolus, *De principio imperatoris et papae*, ii. 4, p. 50, 'licet [apostolicus] ei [scil. imperatori] det perfectionem ut potentialiter agat et vivat'.

humanam ut potest in civilibus . . . sicut virtutes politicae sunt *informes* nisi sint subiectae virtutibus theologicis, ita principatus temporalium est *informis* nisi principi spiritualium sit subiectus.[1]

The lay power must be ordered towards the spiritual kingship of the pope,[2] so that final authority remains with the papacy, but the two are mutually complementary and will normally function alongside each other in harmony. Since however the ultimate heavenly end of life is manifestly superior to mere earthly well-being, the *ordo finium*[3] demands that the lay rulers shall be generally subject to the pope, who is alone functionally qualified to interpret the nature and means of attaining this supreme end.

Spiritualis iurisdictio ecclesiae se habeat ad iurisdictionem saecularem sicut ars quae considerat finem se habet ad artem quae considerat illud quod ordinetur ad finem. . . Constant autem quod ars quae considerat finem imperat arti quae considerat illud quod est ad finem.[4]

And in those cases in which the lay ruler is found to be insufficient, even though a temporal matter is concerned, the pope must be permitted the right to intervene. In this way it was felt that both sides would be satisfied. The hierocratic teleological principle, although modified, had been preserved,[5] as had the idea of the functional qualification of the priesthood.[6] Moreover the final subjection of

[1] Francis de Meyronnes, *De principatu temporali*, ch. 4, pp. 64–5; cf. Thomas Aquinas, *Commentum in Sententias*, II. xliv. ii. 2.

[2] James of Viterbo, *De regimine christiano*, ii. 7, p. 230, 'Quia finis temporalis, qui est felicitas naturalis, ordinatur ad finem spiritualem, qui est beatitudo supernaturalis, et ideo temporalis est propter spiritualem finaliter. Et qui potestatem temporalem quam habent ad spiritualem non ordinant perverse ipsos agere non dubium est'; also Aegidius Romanus, *De ecclesiastica potestate*, ii. 4, pp. 49, 53; ii. 5, p. 59; Durandus de S. Porciano, *De iurisdictione ecclesiastica*, ch. 3, fo. 8.

[3] Aegidius Romanus, *De regimine principum*, III. ii. 27, p. 526.

[4] Durandus de S. Porciano, *De iurisdictione ecclesiastica*, ch. 3, fo. 5.

[5] Thomas Aquinas, *De regimine principum*, ii. 4, p. 241, 'Finis autem quam rex in civitate sui regiminis debet intendere ut vivere secundum virtutem: ceteris autem quilibet uti debent sicut his quae sunt ad finem et quantum est necessarium in prosequendo finem'.

[6] Thomas Aquinas, *De regimine principum*, i. 15, p. 237, 'Quae autem sit ad veram beatitudinem via et quae sint *impedimenta* eius ex lege divina cognoscitur, cuius doctrina pertinet ad sacerdotum officium'.

all lay rulers to papal control and supervision had been ensured;[1] the pope retained an overriding plenitude of power in temporals, although allowed only a casual exercise of it. The anti-hierocratic writers on the other hand were to be soothed into acquiescence by the knowledge that the lay power existed in its own divinely approved right: it did not depend upon papal institution, so that the ruler might still in a sense describe himself as the vicar of God: 'in quo considerare debetis quod principes terrarum sunt a Deo instituta'.[2] Whilst the lay power is undoubtedly inferior to papal power, its existence is a matter of necessity and is no longer dependent upon the *voluntas papae*.[3] The lay ruler is regarded as being normally competent to govern temporal matters, and in practice exercises a fair degree of autonomy. Although the pope has the overall direction of government, the use of temporal jurisdiction remains *regulariter* in the hands of the lay ruler as an inalienable right.[4] Thus an

[1] Aegidius Romanus, *De regimine principum*, I. i. 12, p. 38, 'Illud quod habet aliquid per participationem et imperfecte est instrumentum et organum eius quod habet illud essentialiter et perfecte; quia ergo vim regitivam et potentiam regandi habet principaliter et perfecte solus Deus, oportet quicunque principatur sive regnat sit divinum organum sive sit minister Dei'; Francis de Meyronnes, *Quaestio de subiectione*, i. 3, p. 78, 'Sed universitas rerum temporalium est subiecta universitati rerum spiritualium'; *De principatu temporali*, ch. 4, p. 65, 'Sed totus ordo et facultas rerum temporalium est ordinatus ad facultatem et ordinem rerum spiritualium sicut ad finem, cum corporalia sint propter spiritualia . . . ergo princeps temporalium principi spiritualium debet esse subiectus'.

[2] Thomas Aquinas, *De regimine Iudaeorum*, ch. 6; cf. *De regimine principum*, i. 9, p. 233; i. 12, p. 235, 'Hoc igitur officium rex suscepisse cognoscat ut sit in regno sicut in corpore anima et sicut Deus in mundo. Quae si diligenter recogitet, ex altero iustitiae in eo zelus ascenditur, dum considerat ad hoc se positum ut loco Dei iudicium regno exerceat'.

[3] E.g. Alvarus Pelagius, *De planctu Ecclesiae*, ch. 59, pp. 168–9, 'Necessitas autem et ratio distinctionis harum potestatum sumitur ex duplici populo, scilicet, clericorum et laicorum, qui sunt velut duo latera ecclesiasticae corporis. . . Nam ad potestatem spiritualem pertinet ea quae spirituali vitae attribuuntur. Ad temporalem autem illa quae temporali vitae sunt necessaria'. He continues, 'Potestas autem regalis cum ordinata est numquam discordat a sacerdotali sed ei concordat, et sicut vita terrena subministrat spirituali et vita spiritualis collaborat terrenae'. If there is discord this follows from one impeding the other 'ex inordinata voluntate'.

[4] The imperialists were quick to use this to deny that the emperor received his power from the pope: e.g. John of Calvaruso, *Quaestio an Romanus pontifex potuerit treugam inducere principi Romanorum*, p. 1310, 'vacante demum imperio,

harmonious dualism between temporal and spiritual rulers is to result, with the unity of the society preserved by the ultimate subjection of all men and all things to the papal monarchy. Although subject to separate temporal and spiritual government in the normal course of events, the Christian is not in reality a member of two societies but of one great social organization whose parts can indeed be distinguished, but which still possesses a final wholeness. And here, it was felt, was a philosophical justification for all beliefs and for the actual political situation of the time.

That this represented the true desires of neither the hierocrats nor their opponents is obvious. As one papal writer complained, Aquinas had avoided the abhorrent doctrine that one body could have two heads: but what he in fact now had was one head with two bodies, which was equally as bad:

sicut monstrum et contra naturam esset unum corpus habere duo capita distincta, ita monstrum et contra naturam esset unum caput habere duo corpora distincta.[1]

And certainly even the staunchest papal adherents amongst the followers of St. Thomas now operated on the assumption that there were two independent spheres of temporal and spiritual, and that temporal jurisdiction and spiritual jurisdiction were two quite different things.[2] Nor had Aquinas solved the fundamental problem of the dualists, namely, of where the line of demarcation ought to be drawn between temporal and spiritual. Where does nature end and grace begin? It was this problem which exercised the mind of nearly every publicist after Aquinas, and eventually demonstrated that the Thomist political system, in spite of appearances, suffered from severe leakage at the seams.

Nevertheless the limitation of lay autonomy and the use of the overriding prerogative of the pope in a few specific cases repre-

supplet ecclesia in temporalibus; ergo non vacante non debet se temporalibus immiscere . . . qui eius rei non habuit potestatem. Nemo enim dat quod non habet regulariter, licet casualiter hoc contingat'.

[1] Anon., *De potestate Ecclesiae*, p. 251.

[2] See for example Francis de Meyronnes who distinguishes between the 'duae universitates' which produce two kinds of subjection, temporal and spiritual, corresponding to the two types of jurisdiction: *Quaestio de subiectione*, i. 8, p. 81; *De principatu Siciliae*, ch. 1, p. 94.

sented about as much as the fourteenth-century papacy usually achieved in practice: and there was too close a similarity between St. Thomas' view that the pope *could* not normally intervene in secular matters, and St. Bernard's view that he *ought* not to do so, for the Thomist deviationism to be condemned out of hand. The elaboration of the theory of casual papal jurisdiction in temporal matters was to be the thin end of a very large wedge which held open the door for far more radical theories; but since the idea of casual jurisdiction had already been developed by the canonists, it was not this aspect of the Thomist system which came under immediate attack or was taken to be an outright threat to papal monarchy. A more present danger to the hierocratic system lay in the Thomist answer to the problem of universals and the relationship of part to whole, and it was here that a more definite break was made with the monistic realism which inspired the papal system of government. For the realist it was the universal which had real existence rather than the individual, and this had led straight to a totalitarian conception of society in which the preservation of the wholeness of the *Ecclesia* was the prime consideration. But since the twelfth century there had been a much more popular philosophical pursuit than the preaching of a rigidly logical and consistent system of thought into which all had either to be fitted or discarded. This new pursuit was the combination of realism and nominalism, the 'solving' of the problem of universals, and nearly every great scholastic thinker made his attempt and duly claimed to have found the answer. Nevertheless during the thirteenth century these solutions retained a moderately realistic flavour. Similarly in politics there was an attempt to combine completely opposed constitutional systems, more specifically an absolute and monarchic structure of government with one that contained more than a hint of popular sovereignty. In other words an attempt was being made to combine a realistic conception of the right order in the universe with a nominalistic one, and this had its effect in both philosophy and politics. The best example of this movement in our period is provided by Aquinas himself, whose moderate realism has enjoyed an immense popularity for many centuries after him. It was very much more moderate realism than moderate nominalism, and consequently all aspects of Thomas' political system were slanted in favour of papal supremacy. The conciliarist elements in Aquinas' thought, like his tendency to give the lay ruler more freedom of action, were not elaborated by Aquinas himself. They were a hint of what was to come, but only received real emphasis and development in the hands of later writers. Nevertheless those publicists who sought to strike a balance between papal monarchy and the view that full power resided in the *congregatio fidelium* looked to Aquinas' answer to the problem of universals for their philosophical justification. In this Aquinas had tried to lay an even stress upon both individual and universal. The universal was indeed the essence of a thing, but it could only exist in a specialised sense without the object itself. It had a potential existence, and consequently could be conceived of in isolation, but in general it required the individual manifestation of itself to become actual. One could not exist without the other except as a mental abstraction: only in this sense had the universal an existence over and above its individual examples. There was then no attempt to deny the reality of universals, but it was only in a special theoretical sense that they could be said to actually exist by themselves. An abstraction remains an abstraction even though we may occasionally use it as if it was a concrete thing on the material plane of being. When applied to society this idea produced a very novel conception of the nature of sovereignty. Since society did exist as an immaterial entity, even if only potentially and as a theory, it could be regarded as the seat of power. Sovereignty could be attributed to the abstract *Ecclesia*: it was not a myth. Indeed under special circumstances it could become immediately actual. Nevertheless it remained a largely abstract conception. As Aristotle had said, it was essentially the *notion* of a whole which was prior to the parts (*Politics*, i.2), and the hierocratic writers had made a serious error in assuming that the sovereign *Ecclesia* was always a direct and present reality. In fact it very rarely was. This meant that one could perfectly well imagine society as a spiritual entity possessing sovereignty, but this sovereignty was not to be manifested by any particular person or group of persons, except under certain circumstances and in a special limited sense. Generally speaking the sovereign essence could not be separated from the whole body of individuals related to it. The universal could have no permanent existence without its parts, which are therefore a vital element in its being. The *Ecclesia* can be regarded as something over and beyond its individual members; it can be represented by the pope: but neither pope nor *Ecclesia* are fully able to exist in isolation from the whole body of the faithful. Neither *Ecclesia* nor pope is self-sufficient, except in a very limited sense, without the individual *fideles*. The *Ecclesia* conceived of in terms of the pope alone as the embodiment of this sovereign essence is not enough. Hence for the Thomist the *Ecclesia* must signify the combination of both pope and *congregatio fidelium*. Papal power is the potential for all the activities of the community,[1] but the consent and use of it by each member as required are needed to make it actual. One therefore supplements the other, and ecclesiastical decrees are those made by the pope on behalf of the society in concurrence with the counsel and consent of all Christians acting through the medium of, for example, a general council. Harmony between head and members is assured by the knowledge that the end for which the whole exists is that for which the individuals exist.[2] Their common interest makes for a common cause between society and the individual, between the ruler and his subjects.

According to this there is no simple answer to the question of where the earthly source of authority in the Christian society is to be situated. Both the whole community of believers and the head who represents the whole may be classed as the source of law.[3] But the point is largely irrelevant since each will normally be seen to work in conjunction with the other in the interests of the common good. Nevertheless it is not to be forgotten that the universal is

[1] Note the frequent substitution of the term *potentia* for *potestas* when referring to papal power: e.g. Aegidius Romanus, *De ecclesiastica potestate*, ii. 13, p. 117; ii. 14, p. 132; Alvarus Pelagius, *De planctu Ecclesiae*, ch. 56, p. 157.

[2] Thomas Aquinas, *De regimine principum*, i. 14, p. 236, 'Idem autem oportet esse iudicium de fine totius multitudinis et unius'; Guido Vernani, *De reprobatione Monarchiae*, ch. 1, p. 125, 'Non est ergo alius finis unius hominis et totius humani generis'.

[3] Thomas Aquinas, *Summa theologica*, II. I. xc. 3, 'Ordinare autem aliquid in bonum commune est vel totius multitudinis vel alicuius gerentis vicem totius multitudinis. Et ideo condere legem vel pertinet ad totam multitudinem vel pertinet ad personam publicam quae totius multitudinis curam habet'.

still allowed a specialised existence over and beyond the individual. We may still say that there are occasions when the whole is superior to the part, when the individual must be ready to sacrifice himself, his rights and his possessions for the general good.[1] Translated into political terms we arrive at the stipulation that just as the universal has a theoretical existence superior to the parts, so the ruler representing the society holds certain *de iure* powers which permit him to act beyond the bounds of his normal co-operation with his subjects. In the last resort society may take any steps to preserve its well-being. It remains true then under certain circumstances that the whole is greater than the sum of its parts. On the other hand it is equally important to preserve the balance. And it was not lost upon later writers that to predicate the theoretical reality of universals in isolation was tantamount to presuming the equally theoretical reality of the parts by themselves. Only a slight change of emphasis is required. This too is susceptible of a more practical definition. Although the whole normally represents the wishes and desires of all, the value and importance of the individual is not denied, and may correspondingly, seen from another angle, be occasionally considered superior to the whole.[2] Under certain circumstances the individual members of society must be permitted the theoretical right to function independently and in their own right for the general benefit.[3] In sum this system follows the ideal of the golden mean which Aristotle so highly esteemed. The diverse origins of society are brought together in the common action of head and members. In practice each subordinates itself to the needs of the other for the promotion of the common good, and there is no conflict between whole and parts. On the other hand the identity of each is not totally submerged. The whole, represented by the

[1] Thomas Aquinas, *Summa theologica*, II. I. xcvi. 4, 'Cum enim unus homo sit pars multitudinis, quilibet homo hoc ipsum quod est et quod habet, est multitudinis: sicut et quaelibet pars id quod est, est totius. Unde et natura aliquod detrimentum infert parti ut salvet totum'.

[2] Thomas Aquinas, *Summa theologica*, II. II. clii. 4.

[3] Thomas Aquinas, *Comm. in Eth.*, I, 'ideo pars eius totius potest habere operationem quae non est operatio totius'. Similarly Dante, *Monarchia*, i. 3, p. 342, said that a partial whole such as mankind could have some independent actions ('opera propria universitatis humanae') which were not part of the actions of the complete whole of the universe.

head, is sometimes superior to the parts: at other times the parts themselves become individual wholes, and the greater whole recedes from view: it depends upon our mode of considering them, but in the long run both are true.[1] It must be added that Aquinas himself was not very much concerned with these ultimate potentialities. Since he was convinced that part and whole functioned best when there was a real identity between them, he saw little point in investigating the occasions when this identity failed to give satisfaction. In any case it was all as theoretical as the isolated existence of universals themselves. But the publicists were never so happy as when in the pursuit of theories, and would follow them as far as they could simply to find out where they went. They were also far more aware that these theories did have a practical significance. It was after all fairly well established by the late thirteenth century that on emergency occasions the ruler could act above the law against the rights and liberties of his subjects for the general welfare, and this was seen to be nothing but a practical application of Aquinas' thesis of the *de iure* capacity of the whole over the part. Similarly, when Aquinas in his innocence remarked that a man was not totally absorbed into society,[2] he can hardly be expected to have been aware that this was the signal for intensive speculation on the question of when a man could take political power into his own hands and defy established authority. The publicists agreed that normally the pope representing the whole acted for the common good and purpose of all the individual members of the *Ecclesia*. But they also held that no realistic political theory can assume that the interests of the whole necessarily coincide with all the interests of all the members all the time, and that there will consequently be occasions on which the community of individuals must take precedence. Indeed it seemed to the followers of Aquinas that here was an ideal way of striking a balance between the idea of the absolute power of the head embodied in the old hierocratic maxim that 'papa a nemine iudicatur', and the rampant conciliarism of those writers who saw the individual members of the society as the ulti-

[1] Thomas Aquinas, *Summa theologica*, I. lxxxv. 4 ad 3.

[2] Thomas Aquinas, *Summa theologica*, II. I. xxi. 4 ad 3, 'homo non ordinatur ad communitatem politicam secundum se totum et secundum omnia sua'.

mate source of all authority. If *regulariter* the pope personifies the common good of all, there may still be occasions when papal government of the *Ecclesia* ceases to be adequate for this good. On such occasions the individuals, the parts, can act of their own accord by supplementing, even replacing, government by the head. This was so attractive a proposition that even exponents of extreme realism and of nominalism in other political matters were ready to accept it: and we shall see that it was both discussed and adopted by writers of so very different standpoints as Augustinus Triumphus and William of Ockham.

But once it is admitted that the people as a whole can act contrary to the wishes of the head, even if only *casualiter*, it is but a short step to recognising that the individual members of the *populus christianus* are the ultimate source of power. When for example Augustinus Triumphus and Ockham adopted Thomistic principles, they both ended up by contemplating a system of popular control of the papacy which was not far short of Marsilius' conciliar theory. Some such result was almost bound to happen once Aquinas set out to correct the political Augustinianism of the hierocratic system. He had no intention of destroying it, but he sought to curb what seemed to him to be its worst excesses. Accordingly he derided the fear that to attribute any efficacity to man would be to detract from the power and glory of God, in the same way that he rejected its political equivalent of total human subjection to a God-like prince. He asserted that it was a mistake to forget that men were essentially the creatures of God, that man was *imago Dei*, and that one way of obeying God was therefore through the humanity which he had brought into being. God could be known through his people as well as directly, by natural as well as by divine law. The process was not of course to be taken too far. There should be a nice adjustment between direct obedience to the vicar of God and obedience to the will of God working through the natural reason of the individual. In fact the divine right of kings was to be balanced by the natural, and therefore divine, right of resistance. But unfortunately his disciples were not always so cautious. They lacked Aquinas' delicacy of touch. Some of them were even crude enough to demand a straight answer to the problem of sovereignty. And whilst Aquinas cannot be blamed for the use that others made of his principles, the probability was that in the ferment of ideas which characterises the early fourteenth century they would tend to be given a much more radical interpretation than Aquinas himself had desired. It was almost inevitable, once the individual and the whole were equated, that the emphasis would begin to fall upon the individual. This change of emphasis can be seen from a comparison of Aquinas' and Ockham's use of the theory that the good of the individual is the same as that of the whole community. Aquinas argues that since this is so, we must devote ourselves to the common good of the whole community, and the good of the individual will follow automatically. Ockham on the other hand uses exactly the same principle, but goes on to say that it is necessary to advance the particular good of the individual, thereby promoting the good of the whole.[1] Aquinas had himself hastened this process both by denying full existence to universals apart from individuals and by insisting on the excellence, freedom and self-sufficiency of the human person.[2] But as soon as the individual is held to be an important element in society, as soon as it is admitted that he has an innate natural ability to consider matters of government, the motivating influence in the constitution of political authority must logically be held to be the people themselves.[3] Political society is then founded upon human nature and those who form the society are sovereign. The maintenance of the ruler in his position of authority depends entirely upon his continuing ability to carry out the wishes of his subjects, which now constitute the *summum bonum*, the common good

[1] Thomas Aquinas, *Comm. in Ethic.*, i. 2; *De regimine principum*, i. 14, p. 236. William of Ockham, *Dialogus*, III. II. ii. 27: he is discussing the question of whether individual people or corporations can be given special privileges without obstructing the good of the whole society.

[2] Thomas Aquinas, *Summa theologica*, I. xxix. 3, 'Persona significat id quod est perfectissimum in tota natura, scilicet subsistens in rationali natura. Unde . . . conveniens est ut hoc nomen persona de Deo dicatur . . . sed excellentiori modo'; II. II. lxiv. 2 ad 3, 'homo est naturaliter liber et propter seipsum existens'.

[3] Durandus de S. Porciano, 'magis esse secundum naturam quod totus populus haberet rationem principis. . . Ergo potestas et dominium ad regendum populum est in hominibus secundum debitum rationis et divinae ordinationis': cited J. Koch, *Durandus de S. Porciano: Forschungen zum Streit um Thomas von Aquino zu Beginn des 14. Jahrhunderts*, i. 172–3.

of the society. Government is therefore to some extent immediately put on a contractual basis. The Thomist premise of natural law and the social principle of man as a political animal, given an individualistic emphasis, gave scope to the theory of contract and ultimate popular sovereignty.[1] Similarly the conception that man acts as the co-adjutor of God clearly illustrates the naturalistic and individualistic dangers of Thomist philosophy. God has given him the natural faculties for making law, and hence government established by men is in the last analysis established by God. But whereas Aquinas always laid the emphasis upon God, others, such as the extreme Aristotelians, would always stress the human element. In the hands of later publicists Aquinas' apparently innocuous remarks were given a radical political interpretation and were used to make man the absolute arbiter of his own life. If ultimate authority was in the hands of the people, then all men were the vicars of God.[2] A natural law theory of society led straight to the idea of the *sacra humana*,[3] and at this point the end of the Middle Ages was already in sight.

[1] Aquinas had in fact gone so far as to state that the *civitas* originated naturally with a 'quasi quoddam *pactum* inter regem et populum', *Comm. in Ep. ad Rom.*, xiii. 1. If the ruler broke his part of the contract by tyrannical government, the *multitudo* was justified in disregarding it also, whatever its terms, and could depose him: *De regimine principum*, i. 6, p. 230, 'Nec putanda est talis multitudo infideliter agere tyrannum destituens, etiam si eidem in perpetuo se ante subiecerat; quia hoc ipse meruit in multitudinis regimine se non fideliter gerens ut exigit regis officium, quod ei *pactum* a subditis non reservetur'.

[2] See for example the use made of the idea that all Christians are kings and priests: Thomas Aquinas, *De regimine principum*, i. 14, p. 237, 'ab eo, scil. Christo, regale sacerdotium derivatur: et quod est amplius omnes Christi fideles in quantum sunt membra eius reges et sacerdotes dicuntur': which is cited in one form or another by most of the publicists. Note the implication of self-government in this as expressed by James of Viterbo, *De regimine christiano*, ii. 10, p. 182, 'Quidam regunt semetipsos, ut singuli fideles . . . secundum illud I *Pet.*, ii [9], Vos estis genus electum, regale sacerdotium'. Initially a purely theological concept, this was given prominence in the ecclesiology of the Thomist writers, and during the course of the fourteenth century steadily received a more political interpretation: for the use of this by Wyclif to assert the vicariate of all Christians see M. Maccarrone, *Vicarius Christi* (Rome, 1952), pp. 213–14. On the theological aspect of this idea and for further examples see P. Dabin, *Le sacerdoce royal des fidèles* (Brussels and Paris, 1950). This leads on to the Reformation theory of 'every man his own priest'.

[3] This idea can be clearly seen in Philip the Fair's enfranchisement of the bondmen of the Valois demesne in 1311: 'Comme créature humaine, qui est formée

This combination of moderate realism in philosophy and naturalism in politics not only had serious effects upon the internal organisation of the hierocratic *Ecclesia*, but profoundly altered the conception of the universal society itself. Neither hierocrat, anti-hierocrat nor Thomist doubted that the *Ecclesia* had the nature of a universal, but the different opinions of the reality of universals seriously affected the character of this society. The reality of universals corresponded to the reality of the *Ecclesia* as the only true political and religious organism on earth; the unreality of universals reduced the Christian society to an other-worldly, unreal concept; but the subtleties of moderate realism were designed both to preserve the existing corporate political nature of the *Ecclesia*, and at the same time to put the emphasis upon its theoretical, mystical and spiritual quality. Just as the universal in Thomist philosophy becomes real only in the sense that it is a mental abstraction from the concrete realities of existent particulars, so the *Ecclesia* in this analogy becomes an abstraction out of human individuals who are neither specifically Christian nor specifically pagan. The initial organisation of men into political communities, or even a single *societas humana*, is possible without reference to any necessarily Christian conception of society. That these communities are insufficient to achieve the fullness of life, and consequently need to be supplemented by incorporation into a universal Christian society,[1] does not however deny the legitimacy of such 'natural' societies, since 'gratia non tollit naturam sed perficit'.[2] Whereas the hiero-

à l'image de Nostre Seigneur doie generalement estre franche par droit naturel', *Ordonnances des Rois de France de la troisième Race*, xii. 387: see further Sir F. Pollock, 'The History of the Law of Nature', *Essays in the Law* (London, 1922), pp. 31–79.

[1] Thomas Aquinas, *Expos. in Psal.*, xlv. 3, 'Secundum est quod habeat sufficientiam per se . . . in civitate oportet invenire omnia necessaria ad vitam. Et haec sufficientia est in Ecclesia, quia quidquid necessarium est ad vitam spiritualem invenitur in ea. . . Tertium est unitas civium, quia ab hoc, scilicet ab unitate civium, civitas nominatur, quia civitas quasi civium unitas. Et haec est in Ecclesia'; *Summa theologica*, II. I. c. 5, 'sicut praecepta legis humanae ordinant hominem ad quandam communitatem humanam, ita praecepta legis divinae ordinant hominem ad quandam communitatem seu rempublicam hominum sub Deo'.

[2] Thomas Aquinas, *Summa theologica*, II. I. cix. 2; II. II. x. 10; James of Viterbo, *De regimine christiano*, ii. 7, p. 232; Alexander de S. Elpidio, *De ecclesiastica potestate*, ii. 8, p. 24; Alvarus Pelagius, *De planctu Ecclesiae*, ch. 56, p. 152.

cratic conception embraced *all* kingdoms, and refused to recognise the right to exist of any community which was not part and parcel of the Christian body, every publicist who followed Aquinas was bound to admit the right of pagan societies to exist of their own accord.[1] Kingdoms could still be just without obedience to God or his vicar. And it was this suggestion that there were political societies, albeit imperfect ones, outside the *Ecclesia*, which both detracted from its corporate wholeness and implied that it was not so much a political entity as a unity of faith. It drove a wedge between the political and religious capacities of men, and entertained more than a hint of the idea that they now belonged to two societies, one real and political and the other mystical and spiritual. At best the *Ecclesia* is only something imposed upon already existing civil communities. It is these communities which are the real governmental units. As Francis de Meyronnes explained, although the *Ecclesia* is still in a sense a political society, and the priesthood still has therefore a supplementary function in temporal matters, the basic nature of the *Ecclesia* is spiritual only. For, according to Francis, there are four distinct types of society in heaven and earth. At one extreme is the purely secular and earthly society of the pagan state; at the other the purely celestial kingdom of Heaven. Between them stands first the civil community, essentially temporal but related to the spiritual society; and secondly the ecclesiastical society, essentially spiritual but maintaining its links with the temporal community.

Et secundum hoc est invenire quadruplicem principatum.

Primus est temporalis, ita quod nullo modo spiritualis nec per essentiam nec per participationem, sicut fuerunt ab initio principatus infidelium...

Secundus est temporalis per essentiam et spiritualis per participationem, sicut principatus fidelium regum, quia licet de sua natura respiciat tantum temporalia in quibus solum regnant, tamen participant spiritualia in eo quod subiciuntur Ecclesiae in spiritualibus.

[1] Thomas Aquinas, *Summa theologica*, I. xcvi. 4; II, II. x. 10; Alvarus Pelagius, *De planctu Ecclesiae*, ch. 52, pp. 126–7; ch. 56, p. 152; *Collyrium*, pp. 504–5; Alexander de S. Elpidio, *De ecclesiastica potestate*, ii. 8, pp. 24–5; ii. 10, p. 28; James of Viterbo, *De regimine christiano*, ii. 7, pp. 230–3; Durandus de S. Porciano, *De iurisdictione ecclesiastica*, ch. 3, fo. 4v; Tholemy of Lucca, *Determinatio compendiosa*, chs. 21–4, pp. 42–7.

Tertius est spiritualis quidem per essentiam sed temporalis per participationem, sicut est principatus subcoelestis ierarchiae, quae est militans Ecclesia . . . iste est per essentiam spiritualis quia de natura sua respicit spiritualia. . .

Quartus est ita spiritualis quod nullo modo temporalis, sicut est principatus coelestis ierarchiae.[1]

A Christian kingdom, for all its Christianity, remains as a political unit temporal *de sua natura*. Correspondingly the *Ecclesia*, whatever its political affiliation, is spiritual *per essentiam*. There is still no complete distinction between Church and State within Christendom, but it may now be considered permissible to use these terms.

In this way the Thomist distinction between men as men and men as Christians,[2] and the view that each lesser civil community has a purpose and mode of operation distinct from that of the universal whole,[3] made clear that there could be a sphere of life outside the cognizance of ecclesiastical government, and that the Christian society did not fully cover every aspect of human existence. Although the desirability of all men becoming Christians was never doubted, and the subjection of civil societies to the overall end of the Christian society was upheld, the Thomist theory of *Ecclesia* could not avoid giving each kingdom a certain independent political status. As Aquinas himself had remarked, a community is only a convenient generalisation made by the mind to cover many things, a mere collective term.[4] The universal order gives unity, but not

[1] Francis de Meyronnes, *De principatu Siciliae*, ch. 1, pp. 96–7.

[2] Durandus de S. Porciano, *De iurisdictione ecclesiastica*, ch. 3, fo. 4v, 'potestati temporali vel saeculari subsunt christiani non ut christiani, quia inter non-christianos potest esse et est vel fuit illa potestas legitima, sed solum ut cives. Potestati autem spirituali et ecclesiasticae subsunt ut christiani et fideles'; also fo. 5, 'omnes christiani in quantum sunt christiani pertinent ad forum Ecclesiae... quia quilibet laicus christianus est utrique iudicio subditus, uni ut civis, alii ut christianus'; Aegidius Romanus, *De regimine principum*, III. i. 2, p. 404; James of Viterbo, *De regimine christiano*, ii. 8, p. 233; John of Paris, *De potestate regia et papali*, ch. 7, p. 189; Pseudo-Thomas, *De eruditione principum*, ii. 12, p. 413.

[3] Thomas Aquinas, *Comm. in Nich. Eth.*, i. 1; *De regimine principum*, i. 1, p. 225; Aegidius Romanus, *De regimine principum*, III. i. 1; III. ii. 32; Dante, *Monarchia*, i. 3–5, pp. 342–4.

[4] Thomas Aquinas, *Commentum in Sententias*, I. xxxv. i. 3; cf. *Summa theologica*, I. xxxi. 1 ad 2: see further T. Gilby, *Principality and Polity: Aquinas and the Rise of State Theory in the West* (London, 1958), pp. 251–6.

that of a single substance. It is no more than the ordering of many parts which retain their identity without being absorbed into the whole: 'unum positione vel ordine cuius plurimae partes non sunt assumptibles'.[1] If therefore abstract realities, such as faith and natural law, continue to give a superior unity, there is no need to assume that this gives a total identity between parts in practice. There is for example no reason why different peoples should not observe different systems of positive law provided that they adhere to and apply the fundamental tenets of the supreme unwritten laws. Variety is the mark of all human things.

> ... principia communia legis naturae non eodem modo applicari possunt omnibus propter multam varietatem rerum humanarum; et ex hoc provenit diversitas legis positivae apud diversos.[2]

Thus a bridge is constructed between the papal and imperial conception of a single universal political society and the fast developing idea of the national sovereign state. Correspondingly the *Ecclesia* itself appears as not much more than a unity of faith, whose oneness is preserved, but mainly by a common bond of religion than of government. Whilst it would be most incorrect to attribute a deliberate spiritualisation and mystification of the *Ecclesia* to Aquinas (indeed his views on the matter were never coherently expressed in any one place), there is no doubt that this was the interpretation which other writers accepted. We have already seen how in his more radical moments John of Paris, 'un disciple fidèle de Saint Thomas',[3] managed to empty the idea of *Ecclesia* of practically all jurisdictional content, and even amongst the later supporters of papal monarchy Aquinas was held to have propounded a theory of the Christian society which considerably diluted the corporate wholeness upon which hierocratic writers laid so much stress. From the hierocratic point of view the dangerous part of Aquinas' theory of *Ecclesia* was not so much what he said as what he omitted to say, and the omissions could only lead others to assume that Aquinas had not accepted the points left out, particularly when his

[1] Thomas Aquinas, *Summa theologica*, III. iv. 1 ad 4; *Comm. in Ethic.*, i. 1.
[2] Thomas Aquinas, *Summa theologica*, II. 1. xcv. 2 ad 3.
[3] Leclercq, *Jean de Paris*, p. 84.

consideration of other matters was so voluminous. Conscious of the outcry raised up against the slightest unorthodoxy in so important a matter, Aquinas' discussion of the nature of the *Ecclesia* was one of eloquent silences. He indeed compared the unity of the *Ecclesia* to that of the natural body, but remarked only that it was a union of faith, hope and charity amongst its members. It had not that monolithic structure which the hierocrats likened to the figure one.[1] It could no longer be described as *unum corpus* except by analogy: rather it was a mere collection of individuals. In the words of Alvarus Pelagius, the *Ecclesia* is 'a multitude, but is more properly called united than one, and its connection is more properly called union than unity... It cannot be called one in the same way that a man is called one ... except perhaps by analogy ... but the *Ecclesia* is called one by collection'.[2] The moderate realist version

[1] See his *Commentum in Sententias*, III. xiii. ii. 2, where Aquinas discusses the similarity of the members of the natural body to the members of the Christian body. In the natural body, he says, there is a 'conformitatem naturae, quia omnia membra constat ex eisdem similibus partibus et sunt unius rationis, sicut manus et pes ex carne et osse, et sic dicuntur membra unum genere vel specie'. This too can be found in the mystical body, but it is to be understood only in the sense of sharing in a common faith, hope and charity: 'Prima autem dictorum unionum non est unio simpliciter, quia illud in quo est unio haec *non est unum numero* ... quia per fidem et caritatem in uno credito et amato secundum numerum uniuntur; similiter Spiritus Sanctus unus numero omnes replet'. Commenting on this Turrecremata, *Summa de Ecclesia* (Venice, 1561), ii. 71, fo. 195v, says that although there is a resemblance between the *Ecclesia* and the natural body, as for example both have many members, 'nihilominus multiplex est differentia et dissimilitudo'. To substantiate this he refers to Aquinas and points out that the latter had spoken only of a unity of faith: 'Quod ergo dicitur una fides Ecclesiae, una spes, una charitas, non accipitur unitas ex parte unius subiecti numero earum, quia nullum tale est, sed ex parte obiecti, quia videlicet omnes fideles . . . idem credunt, idem sperant, idem amant, sic dicit sanctus Thom. in 3 dist. decimatertia'. Therefore the members of the *Ecclesia* do not constitute 'aliquod *unum numero reale totum*'; and this, he concludes, will do away with the 'fantasiae canonistarum'. The inadequacy of this definition for the papalist, and its lack of political content, are made clear by Alexander de S. Elpidio, *De ecclesiastica potestate*, i. 4, p. 5, 'Ecclesia perfecte dicitur poni una, non solum unitate formali per fidem, spem et caritatem, seu unitate finis, quoniam ad unum finem ordinatur, sed etiam unitate dirigentis et regulantis, quod non esse posset nisi haberet unum universalem vicarium qui teneat universalem et plenam et immediatam potestatem a Domino'.

[2] Alvarus Pelagius, *De planctu Ecclesiae*, ch. 40, p. 63; cf. James of Viterbo, *De regimine christiano*, i. 3.

of the Aristotelian principle that nothing really exists except the individual could lead to no other conclusion: yet it was much too akin to the nominalist doctrine which defined the *Ecclesia* in simple additive terms for hierocratic tastes. And it is of the greatest significance that Marsilius of Padua used an almost identical definition of the *Ecclesia* to deny the need for having a pope at all.[1]

As the conception of the Christian society receded into the form of a purely spiritual brotherhood, so the emphasis was laid more and more strongly upon the material aspects of the good life for which the lay power was considered sufficient to provide.[2] During the course of the fourteenth century Aristotelianism ate its way deeper and deeper into the roots of the hierocratic system, and the danger of which Bonaventure had warned Aquinas became increasingly apparent: 'Attribuere quod est Dei creaturae periculosum est'.[3] Although the Thomist explanation of the structure of society appeared to be very comprehensive, the nature of medieval civilisation had been, if not changed, re-orientated. Aristotle had not been Christianised: rather the Christian society had become Aristotelianised. Secular things were no longer imbued with a pervasive, all-embracing Christian purpose: they were still dominated by the spiritual end of society, but they retained their basic secularity. Political virtues, said Aquinas, have a value in that their

[1] Marsilius of Padua, *Defensor pacis*, II. xxviii. 13, p. 544, 'Ad eam vero rationem qua deducebatur Ecclesiam unam esse et unum esse primum episcopum propter fidei unitatem secundum Apostolum ad *Ephesios* 4 [iv. 5], dicendum, sumendo Ecclesiam in propria significatione pro fidelium multitudine, sic esse unam Ecclesiam sicut fides est una. Et quoniam fides non est numero in omnibus fidelibus sed specie vel genere, idcirco non concludit argumentum, Ecclesiam aliter unam. Et cum additur Ecclesiam non esse unam nisi per unitatem numeralem alicuius episcopi caeteris superiorem, hanc nego: et si concederem ipsam ad aliam illationem quod hoc principium sive caput est Romanus episcopus institutione divina immediate, nego illationem hanc cum suis probationibus'.

[2] E.g. Tholemy of Lucca, *De regimine principum*, iii. 11, pp. 260–1, 'quia supposito quod humana societas sit naturalis, ut probatum est supra, omnia necessaria ad communem conservationem dictae societatis erunt de iure naturae. . . Sic et in necessitatibus regni quod pertinet ad conservationem socialis humanae vitae, rex, qui est *artifex architectus* dictae societatis, non debet deficere sed omnem defectum supplere cum ipsa societate'.

[3] E. Gilson, *The Philosophy of St. Bonaventure* (London, 1938), p. 476.

acts are good in themselves (*actus de se boni*), and are merely improved by the influence of theological virtues.[1] The lay ruler was no longer a papal official, but a governor in his own right acting under papal direction. Spiritual purpose and papal authority had become indirect rather than direct. The society was no longer Christocentric but influenced by Christianity, so that lay government was permitted a relative value. Faith and papal supremacy remained technically absolute, but by being united with natural reason and natural lay rule as relative ideals, they themselves became relative and deprived of their exclusiveness. As St. Augustine had said, to express any satisfaction with something less than the *summum bonum* was to deny its supremacy. The steady laicisation of medieval society was matched by the vicissitudes of fortune which befell the papacy in the fourteenth and fifteenth centuries. Nevertheless, apart from Marsilius of Padua, there was no other writer of the time who was prepared to launch a full-scale attack on the hierocratic system. If Thomistic influences made subtle changes in the hierocratic idea and contributed to its breakdown, those same Thomistic influences vitiated the work of nearly every contemporary lay thinker. In spite of the threads of radical Aristotelianism woven into the political systems of Engelbert of Admont, John of Paris, Dante and Ockham, none of these writers could avoid the powerful attractions of the Thomist synthesis. Both Dante and Engelbert ended up by equating their human monarchies with the Universal Church. For all his insistence on dualism,[2] there are occasions when Engelbert's tract on the Roman empire reads like a papal manifesto. There is only one true form of human law, he declares, and that which is in agreement with divine law, which is the Christian faith. There is only one true *populus*, and that the Christian *populus*. Consequently there is only one society, a Christian society, and he agrees with Augustine that 'extra Ecclesiam non est imperi-

[1] Thomas Aquinas, *Commentum in Sententias*, II. xl. i. 5: on this see O. Lottin, 'Les vertus morales acquises sont-elles de vraies vertus? La réponse des théologians de Pierre Abélard à Saint Thomas d'Aquin', *Recherches de théologie ancienne et médiévale*, xx (1953), pp. 13–39; xxi (1954), pp. 101–29.

[2] Engelbert of Admont, *De ortu imperii Romani*, ch. 21, p. 771, 'quia stante adhuc capite Ecclesiae in spiritualibus, scilicet apostolica sede, et capite in temporalibus, scilicet imperio Romano'.

um'.[1] Whilst he admits the separation of ends, Engelbert can only conclude that the temporal end of life is imperfect with respect to the celestial one.[2] It will therefore occasion no surprise when we learn that the true duty of the emperor is to obey the pope, and that the penalty for his disobedience can be nothing less than deposition.[3]

More surprisingly, Dante is impelled in a rather vague manner to the same conclusion. The problem of Thomistic influences in Dante remains a much disputed point, although it now seems reasonably certain that he was familiar with Aquinas' teachings through his master Remigio di Girolami, himself a pupil of Aquinas.[4] Certainly something like this is necessary to explain the almost contradictory nature of some parts of the *Monarchia*. In spite of his emphasis upon the autonomy of human reason, Dante is forced to acknowledge that there are occasions when reason is not enough, and true justice is discernible only by recourse to faith.[5] However much he stresses the secular integrity of ancient Rome, granting it its own merits, purpose and *raison d'être*, he is brought to

[1] Engelbert of Admont, *De ortu imperii Romani*, ch. 15, p. 764, 'Sed est unum solum in toto mundo verum ius divinum, videlicet unus cultus verus Dei, et unum solum verum ius humanum, scilicet canones et leges consonae iuri divino, quia ius humanum sumit auctoritatem et principium a iure divino, et non econtrario. Et est unus solus consensus populi in illud ius divinum et humanum, scilicet fides christiana, et unus solus populus, scilicet christianus populus, fide consentiens in illud ius divinum et humanum, et per consequens una sola respublica totius populi christiani. . . Ex qua ratione concludit etiam August. 19 *de civitate Dei*, quod extra Ecclesiam numquam fuit nec potuit nec poterit esse verum imperium'.

[2] Engelbert of Admont, *De ortu imperii Romani*, ch. 17, p. 766, 'Primo quod felicitas, quam beatitudinem appellamus et quam omnes optant et inquirunt, est duplex, scilicet praesens quae est temporalis et transitoria, et futura quae est vera et aeterna. . . Secundo quod felicitas praesenti vitae simpliciter est imperfecte respectu aeternae verae felicitatis'.

[3] Engelbert of Admont, *De ortu imperii Romani*, ch. 23, p. 772, 'videlicet quod imperatorum et regum Romanorum quidam reprobati sunt propter suam *inobedientiam* eo quod fuerint inobedientes et rebelles ecclesiae . . . propter imperatorum et regum inobedientiam quoad ecclesiam et propter ipsorum superbiam et avaritiam, ignaviam et malitiam quoad gubernationem reipublicae iuste gerendam, poterit fieri ipsorum depositio'.

[4] Davis, *Dante and the Idea of Rome*, pp. 80–2; and see the review of literature in d'Entrèves, *Dante as a Political Thinker*, pp. 101–2.

[5] Dante, *Monarchia*, ii. 8, pp. 357–8.

admit that it must be placed within the wider framework of a Christian ideal.[1] But the most striking evidence of a change of attitude appears in the last chapter of the *Monarchia*, where Dante, having just accepted the complete separation and self-sufficiency of the realms of reason and faith, of emperor and pope, suddenly adds that it is not in the last resort true to say that the emperor is completely free from subjection to the pope. To explain this *volte face* he goes on to acknowledge that the temporal end of life is, after all, ordered towards the spiritual, and thereby reaches the conclusion that the emperor must observe that reverence to the pope which is owed to a father by his eldest son.

Quae quidem veritas ultimae quaestionis non sic stricte recipienda est ut Romanus princeps in aliquo Romano pontifici non subiaceat, cum mortalis ista felicitas quodammodo ad immortalem felicitatem ordinetur. Illa igitur *reverentia* Caesar utatur ad Petrum qua primogenitus *filius* debet uti ad *patrem* ut, luce paternae *gratiae* illustratus, virtuosius orbem terrae irradiet.[2]

This suggests a complete breakdown of Dante's dualism. Not only was the father-son analogy a favourite hierocratic device, but Dante had an extensive knowledge of Roman law,[3] and was therefore perfectly familiar with the legal principle (*Dig.*, I. xvi. 9, 3) which involved absolute obedience on the part of a son to his father even to the point of death. The point is in fact conclusively proved by Dante himself in the *Convivio*, where reverence and obedience are more than once used as interchangeable terms.[4]

Nor can Dante's attitude be regarded as an isolated occurrence. The same phenomenon is plainly visible with John of Paris, otherwise one of the most vigorous and successful defenders of lay inde-

[1] Davis, *op. cit.*, p. 37. [2] Dante, *Monarchia*, iii. 16, p. 376.

[3] J. Williams, *Dante as a Jurist* (Oxford, 1906), especially p. 50; d'Entrèves, *op. cit.*, pp. 27–8; *KTB*, p. 452 n. 4.

[4] See Dante, *Convivio*, iv. 9, p. 440, where reverence (*reverenza*) is equated with subjection (*suggetti*); iv. 24, pp. 494–5, and iv. 25, p. 497, where it is repeatedly emphasised that sons must be *reverente* and that the proper disposition of a son to a father is one of obedience. To support this he quotes *Coloss.*, iii. 20, 'Children, obey your parents in all things'. Dante also describes himself, *Monarchia*, iii. 3, p. 365, as writing with the reverence of an obedient son towards his father and mother, Christ and *mater ecclesia*.

pendence. Indeed, having achieved a complete separation of temporal and spiritual, and pronounced the perfectibility of lay government, John is also to be found admitting to sacerdotal supremacy. Man, he says, is ordered not only towards the good that can be acquired by nature, but must further order his life towards the eternal and supernatural end which is the source of virtue.[1] Therefore a non-Christian government can have no validity.[2] In addition to the *rex humanus*, to whom is committed the care of earthly things, there must be a *rex divinus*, supreme over all other rulers. This divine ruler is, in the first instance, Christ himself. But Christ has appointed his ministers and mediators in the priesthood, which is the link between God and man. Thus the priests have not only what he terms spiritual power, but also *auctoritas*, whilst the pope as their head and vicar of Christ is the supreme ruler of the world:

In tota Ecclesia et toto populo christiano est unus summus, scilicet papa Romanus, Petri successor, ut sic Ecclesia militans per similitudinem a triumphante derivetur, ubi unus praesidet toti universo.[3]

John of Paris has no intention of allowing this monarch unrestrained power, but he is compelled to allow that under the necessary conditions the pope is to be permitted as much temporal jurisdiction as he requires for the maintenance of the overall well-being of the community and the good of the Christian faith.[4]

Finally we see that Ockham came to take up the same general position. Although he had in his way done as much as Marsilius to

[1] John of Paris, *De potestate regia et papali*, ch. 2, pp. 178–9, 'homo non solum ordinatur ad bonum tale quod per naturam acquiri potest, quod est vivere secundum virtutem, sed ulterius ordinatur ad finem supernaturalem qui est vita aeterna, ad quam tota hominum multitudo viventium secundum virtutem ordinata est'.

[2] John of Paris, *De potestate regia et papali*, ch. 18, p. 229.

[3] John of Paris, *De potestate regia et papali*, ch. 3, pp. 178–9.

[4] John of Paris, *De potestate regia et papali*, ch. 7, p. 189: the pope is described as 'supremum caput non solum clericorum sed generaliter omnium fidelium ut fideles sunt tamquam generalis informator fidei et morum', and may 'in casu summae necessitatis fidei et morum' do as he sees fit with all the possessions of the faithful. Similarly, ch. 16, pp. 223–4, the pope has superior jurisdiction over temporal rulers in all matters involving sin. This derives from Innocent III, *Decretales*, II. i. 13, and, as the papalists were quick to point out, virtually covered all illegal acts.

destroy the hierocratic system, Ockham was quite unable to consider the *Ecclesia* as anything but a papally-governed body politic. Pointing to the inevitable ruin which faces a divided society, he warns his readers of the perils which may stem from having one head for the clergy and another for the laity. The mark of a Christian society is essentially that of a single community, and it must therefore have one ruler. It cannot be well governed in either spiritual or secular matters until it has a supreme judge and rector whose jurisdiction extends, directly or indirectly, to every possible case.[1] Accordingly, like John of Paris, with whom he has much in common, Ockham is forced back to recognising a 'plenitudo potestatis qua papa praeeminet et praefulget'.[2] Although he grants that all Christians are not immediately subject to the pope, the latter must ultimately be seen as the arbiter on all matters, divinely appointed as the head of all the faithful.[3] In one way or another he can do all things necessary for the government of the community.

[1] William of Ockham, *Dialogus*, III. II. iii. 19–20, 'Non solum illa societas est propinqua desolationi et ruinae quae est contra se divisa, sed etiam illa quae ex modo regendi est disposita ad divisionem et divisioni propinqua. Sed si communitas fidelium habeat duas partes quarum una habeat iudicem summum, et alia alium, communitas illa est disposita ad divisionem et divisioni propinqua... Ergo non solum est periculosa societas fidelium si sint plures iudices super eosdam populos vel subditos, sed etiam periculosa est societas fidelium si in eodem loco etiam super diversos subditos fideles fuerint plures summi iudices constituti, et ita non expedit quod clerici habeant unum summum iudicem ecclesiasticum, scilicet papam, et laici unum summum iudicem, scilicet imperatorem. . . Nulla communitas simul viventium vita politica est optime ordinata nisi sit civiliter una. Unde fideles sicut sunt unum corpus in Christo, ita etiam debent esse corpus seu collegium in vita civili: sed communitas illa quae habet diversos summos iudices seu diversa capita sive rectores non est civiliter una, sicut illi qui non habent unum regem non sunt unum regnum... Concluditur ergo quod communitas fidelium non erit optime gubernata civiliter etiam quantum ad vitam politicam nisi tota et omnis pars eius habet unum iudicem et rectorem supremum, de cuius iurisdictione immediata vel mediata *in omni casu* ab eo vel a iudicibus inferioribus eo omnis alius *pro quocunque delicto* debeat iudicari'.

[2] William of Ockham, *De imperatorum et pontificum potestate*, ch. 10, p. 23.

[3] William of Ockham, *De imperatorum et pontificum potestate*, ch. 12, p. 26, 'Sic licet non omnes fideles sint immediate subiecti in omnibus papae, nec papa in multis casibus sit iudex ipsorum, tamen quia in omni causa necessario definienda per iudicium regulariter vel casualiter iure divino potest esse iudex, immo concedendum est quod papa sub Christo est caput et iudex summus omnium fidelium'.

Papa iure divino regulariter vel casualiter omnia facere potest quae sunt necessaria regimini et gubernationi fidelium.[1]

Thus Ockham finally emerges as the arch exponent of the theory of casual papal power in secular affairs. The Thomistic view of a moral naturalism proved in fact to be almost as dangerous to the concept of the *societas humana* as to that of the *societas christiana*. It still forced moral standards of political evaluation up into the theological sphere for their ultimate justification, and thereby ran counter to the basic determinism which underlay the Marsilian-Ockhamist system. Whilst Engelbert, Dante, John of Paris and Ockham were well acquainted with the principles of Aristotelian philosophy and politics, which, if employed without modification, could lead only to the idea of the purely natural State, they insisted upon orientating Aristotle's principles *finaliter*, that is to say, subordinating them to the idea of the best possible community dedicated to the highest possible end. They therefore preserved the traditional allegiance owed by politics to ethical and religious considerations, and for this reason failed to free the political community from the overriding structure of a universal Christian society.

[1] William of Ockham, *De imperatorum et pontificum potestate*, ch. 13, p. 27. For this dichotomy in Ockham's work between Thomism and a more extreme Aristotelianism see further C. C. Bayley, 'Pivotal Concepts in the Political Philosophy of William of Ockham', *Journal of the History of Ideas*, x (1949), pp. 199–218; M. A. Shepard, 'William of Occam and the Higher Law', *American Political Science Review*, xxvi (1932), pp. 1005–23; xxvii (1933), pp. 24–38; Jacob, *Essays in the Conciliar Epoch*, pp. 87–9, 103–4.

PART II

THE ORIGIN OF POLITICAL AUTHORITY

I. THE SOVEREIGN PRINCE

ALTHOUGH the ability of the papacy to control the activities of the European monarchs steadily declines during the course of the thirteenth and fourteenth centuries, this process is counterbalanced by the elaboration of a doctrine of power unparalleled since the days of imperial Rome, and destined to pass only with the greatest hesitancy into the political thought of the secular state in the sixteenth and seventeenth centuries. The less that the popes could achieve in the world of fact, the more far reaching were the claims of their supporters, who, relieved of the necessity for maintaining some sort of relationship between theory and practice, were able to give full expression to that juristic desideratum, the omnicompetent sovereign. As Maitland and Figgis pointed out half a century ago, the term may be used here in its strict Austinian sense,[1] and the more generally accepted view of modern scholars that a clear conception of legislative sovereignty was only hinted at in the medieval period and does not become fully apparent before Bodin, is quite unnecessarily cautious. But whilst the idea of true sovereignty had always been implicit in the papal claim to the *plenitudo potestatis*, it is correct to add that it was not until the thirteenth century that we begin to find anything approaching a thorough development of this principle. Then, in the 1270s, Guilielmus Durantis the Elder ably summarised the achievement of the canonists in a famous description of the papal office, which provided the basis from which the later expositors worked.

Ipse est successor Petri et vicarius Iesu Christi, vicem non puri hominis sed veri Dei gerens in terris . . . unde omnia regit et disponit et iudicat prout sibi placet . . . habet etiam papa plenitudinem potestatis ad quam vocatus est . . . in omnibus et per omnia potest facere et dicere quicquid placet; auferendo etiam ius suum cui vult, quia non est qui ei dicat, cur

[1] F. W. Maitland, *Roman Canon Law in the Church of England* (London, 1898), p. 48; J. N. Figgis, *Studies of Political Thought from Gerson to Grotius, 1414–1625* (2nd ed., Cambridge, 1916), p. 17.

ita facis? . . . nam et apud eum est pro ratione voluntas, et quod ei placet legis habet vigorem. Potest etiam omne ius tollere et de iure supra ius dispensare . . . item non habet superiorem . . . sed ipse super omnes est.[1]

But the views of the canonists were scattered and abruptly stated. All too frequently they omitted to explain themselves, and so whilst much of the credit for this development is due to the lawyers, it was left to the publicists of the early fourteenth century, above all to Augustinus Triumphus, to present a fully mature and systematic version of the theory. Far and away the most potent factor in this process was the assimilation of Roman law theories of rulership by the hierocratic writers and by the papacy itself,[2] and it will be seen that much of Augustinus Triumphus' account of papal power incorporates direct quotations from Justinian's Codex. Whereas in classical Roman times the emperor had in principle been bound by the law, Hellenistic writers had already propounded the idea that the law itself was embodied in the person of the ruler.[3] This was adopted by many Roman political writers of the later period, and by the time that the Codex was compiled the classical opinion tended to be completely overshadowed. And so it passed to the Middle Ages, where the Roman law 'renaissance' of the eleventh and twelfth centuries proved of inestimable benefit in giving shape and form to the aspirations of the European rulers. The idea of the king governing *vi et voluntate* became an established feature of the French and English monarchies in the late twelfth and thirteenth centuries,[4] and continued to receive a somewhat spasmodic treat-

[1] Guilielmus Durantis, *Speculum iuris*, i. 1, p. 51. This is followed almost word for word by the Italian canonist and publicist Aegidius Spiritalis in his *Libellus contra infideles*, p. 108.

[2] G. Le Bras, 'Le droit romain au service de la domination pontificale', *Revue historique de droit français et étranger*, xxvii (1949), pp. 377–98; Ullmann, *The Growth of Papal Government*, pp. 310–31, 367–73.

[3] Aristotle for example, *Politics*, iii. 13, had spoken of 'a single supremely virtuous ruler who would be regarded as a god among men: so that for men of pre-eminent virtue there is no law; they are themselves a law'. See further E. R. Goodenough, 'The Political Philosophy of Hellenistic Kingship', *Yale Classical Studies*, i (1928), pp. 55–102; C. Wirszubski, *Libertas as a Political Idea at Rome during the Late Republic and Early Principate* (Cambridge, 1950).

[4] J. E. A. Jolliffe, *Angevin Kingship* (London, 1955); and see the useful historical survey given by F. Schulz, 'Bracton on Kingship', *EHR*, lx (1945), pp. 136–76.

ment by the civilians themselves. But although we might reasonably expect to find the most thorough definition of the doctrine of ablsoutism at the hands of the medieval Caesars, and the intention was certainly not absent, the constant struggle of the German emperors with their princes made inexpedient and gave little opportunity for the promulgation of a fully fledged theory of sovereignty. Consequently the initiative in this matter passed into the hands of the other *domini mundi*, the popes themselves.[1] The identification of the universal *Ecclesia* with the Roman empire, and the view that the pope was in reality the *verus imperator*,[2] facilitated the application to the papacy of the Roman law ideas which, when wedded to the doctrine of the Petrine commission, produced a comprehensive and awe-inspiring conception of divine right monarchy.

At the same time it must be emphasised that the influence of Roman law doctrines, reinforced with Aristotelian ideas, was also largely responsible for the growth of other constitutional principles. Both the idea of popular sovereignty and of a 'mixed' government were in direct line of descent from Greek and Roman political theory, but their development in medieval thought was a slower process since they rested to a large extent upon the acceptance of an adequate theory of a higher or natural law. The belief in an unchanging fundamental law, of supreme ethical and moral criteria, of an absolute 'rightness' (*iustitia*, natural law, equity), leads inevitably to the idea of limited rulership, and it was no accident that conciliar theories of government received a sudden access of energy following the penetrating investigation of the idea of natural law by Aquinas and his successors. It means that there are absolute standards existing over and above the positive decrees of

[1] The idea that papal law is universally binding itself owed much to Roman law teaching: see for example Gratian in D. 12. On this Augustinus Triumphus comments, *Summa*, xcii. 3 ad 3, p. 455, 'posset tamen papa, si vellet, statutum universale facere . . . et tunc omnes universaliter per universum orbem essent ad hoc astricti'; cf. lxvi. 3, p. 350.

[2] It is commonly accepted by hierocratic writers that the *princeps* of the Roman law books refers to the pope: e.g. Augustinus Triumphus, *Summa*, xvii. 5, p. 111, 'sine consilio principis, id est papae', which follows the *glossa ordinaria* of Bernardus Parmensis *ad Decretales*, I. xxxiii. 2, fo. 108v, s.v. *Principi*. It may also be noted that Gregory VII had stated in the *Dictatus papae*, c. 8, 'Quod solus [Romanus pontifex] possit uti imperialibus insigniis'.

rulers against which all acts of government are to be tested. If they are found to be wanting and deficient in 'rightness', if they do not assist the maintenance of the 'right way of life', of the common good, then the subject has a positive duty to disregard them and the authority of the ruler who promulgates them. The logical inference from this must be that in the last resort all men, or at least all politically qualified men, are capable of deciding whether an act of government is in conformity with this fundamental 'rightness'. Such a theory is incompatible with any true conception of monarchy, and the only real alternative, as Augustinus Triumphus realised, is to make 'rightness' dependent upon the will of the ruler himself. Although a certain amount of camouflage is required to make this doctrine palatable, in practice all law becomes valid, technically just, not so much because it is intrinsically right but because it is the command of the sovereign. A governmental act is not binding because it seems good, but simply because the pope wills it.

Quod principi placet vigorem legis habet... Sed supremus *princeps* vice Dei in toto orbe est ipse papa. Omnes ergo humanae leges ab eius *voluntate* emanant.[1]

Thus there is only one act absolutely bad in itself—the rejection of the pope's authority, and the only absolute ethical norm is one of obligation to obey him. On the other hand the pope himself can say and do whatever he pleases: it grants him complete autonomy of action, and this is justified on the grounds that in the last resort this can be the only guarantee of preservation for the society and salvation for its members. In this respect the fully developed hiero-

[1] Augustinus Triumphus, *Summa*, lx. 4, p. 315; also v. 3, p. 51, 'sed quod sibi placet legis vigorem habet'. This is *Dig*., I. iv. 31, *Inst*., I. ii. 6. Similarly Anon., *Determinatio compendiosa*, ch. 33, p. 544; Aegidius Romanus, *De ecclesiastica potestate*, iii. 8, p. 187; Aegidius Spiritalis, *Libellus contra infideles*, p. 108. The same idea is used by Dante, *Monarchia*, i. 15, p. 350, 'Nec ista una potest esse nisi sit *princeps* unus omnium, cuius *voluntas* domina et regulatrix aliarum esse possit'; *Convivio*, iv. 4, p. 417, 'e quello che egli dice, a tutti è legge, e per tutti dee essere ubbidito, e ogni altro comandamento da quello di costui prende vigore e autorità'. Note again Bernardus Parmensis, *ad Decretales*, I. vii. 3, fo. 62v, 'In his quae vult ei est pro ratione voluntas'. Note also the use of the maxim 'hoc volo, sic iubeo, sit pro ratione voluntas' (Juvenal, *Satires*, vi. 223) in this context.

cratic theory approached the Greek ideal of *eunomia*, a vision of a world order based upon laws which were not necessarily good in themselves but superlatively good in that they upheld the universal order itself. And whilst contemporary writers fiercely disputed that this implied any real divorce between morals and politics, it is here that the historian must begin his search for the origin of the modern notion by which goodness tends to be divorced from a purely moral context and is seen in terms of political stability and unity, a higher goodness which is the only surety for inferior moral values.

In spite of the complaints of Cardinal Bellarmine three centuries later that this demand for absolute obedience was liable to end by obliterating any fixed conceptions about the realms of good and evil,[1] the publicists did not set out to deny the existence of ultimate rightness in the shape of divine and natural law as something standing over and beyond human law. As Augustinus Triumphus himself acknowledged,

> fundamentaliter lex humana ex naturali lege et divina sit composita, eo quod nulla lex iusta potest esse nisi super naturali et divino iure fundetur,[2]

and his whole theory of the derivation of human law out of divine law by way of natural law adheres closely to the classic exposition formulated by Aquinas in the *Summa theologica*. To Augustinus the pope remains an imitator of justice, simply observing, declaring and executing a higher law. His function as vicar of Christ is essentially that of maintaining and reproducing the ultimate canons of right conduct.[3] But even when this is borne in mind it is still true

[1] Bellarmine, *De potestate summi pontificis*, iv. 5, 'Si autem papa erraret praecipiendo vitia vel prohibendo virtutes, teneretur Ecclesia credere vitia esse bona et virtutes malas, nisi vellet contra conscientiam peccare'.

[2] Augustinus Triumphus, *Summa*, lvi. 3 ad 3, p. 295.

[3] Augustinus Triumphus, *Summa*, xxiii. 4, p. 139, 'Legis igitur aeternae et divinae papa debet esse imitator, quia ab ipso omnis lex et omnis iustitia derivatur'; lxiii. 1 ad 3, p. 333, 'Planum est enim quod utriusque legis [divinae et naturalis] papa est interpres et declarator tamquam vicarius Christi'; cf. xxii. 3, p. 132, lxxv. 1, p. 387, 'conservator et observator iustitiae'; xliv. 4, p. 242, 'executor legis divinae'; lxii. 5, p. 331, 'executor divinae iustitiae'. *Iustitia* (natural law) may be described as the norm of right conduct which stands behind positive law. It is potential law, which only becomes actual in specific legal codes: lxiii. 1, p. 333, 'praeceptum papae ligat potentialiter et actualiter,

for Augustinus Triumphus, and in striking contrast to Aquinas himself, that the only way in which this divine-natural mode of right living becomes known on earth is through the ruler. Definition of what is politically and ethically right does in effect depend upon the interpreter himself: 'qualiter in religione christiana vivendum est', and consequently the law which enforces it, he declares, hang upon his will and are matters in which he has no superior.[1] Those who produce laws must be permitted the right to say what they contain and how they apply: 'cuius est condere, eius est interpretari',[2] and since he sees the pope as the *armarium scripturae*, all knowledge of God's will and purpose can be derived from him alone. Only he therefore, remarks another writer, is capable of governing a society whose whole reason for existence is to be found in the knowledge and love of God.[3] He comes to be regarded as the human mouthpiece of the Almighty, so that superhuman authority may be ascribed to his rulings, which have all the qualities of divine law itself.[4]

It is obvious that in this conception of authority there can be

ligamen vero legis naturae potentialiter solum'; also lx. 4 ad 1, p. 316. For a further discussion of this idea in hierocratic thought see Ullmann, *op. cit.*, pp. 273–6.

[1] Augustinus Triumphus, *Summa*, xxii. 4, p. 132, 'Quantum vero ad religionis christianae conservationem tenetur omnis christianus papae obedire, quia ad ordinandum qualiter in religione christiana vivendum est, nullus est superior ipso'; and cf. xx. 2 ad 2, p. 122, where the pope is described as having 'omne rectum iudicium quod sit in Ecclesia'.

[2] Augustinus Triumphus, *Summa*, xxii. 1, p. 130. For *armarium scripturae* see lxvii. 3, p. 354; cf. Johannes Andreae, *armarium iuris* (Du Cange, *Glossarium*, i. 389).

[3] Anon., *Determinatio compendiosa, proem.*, pp. 540–1.

[4] Hervaeus Natalis, *De potestate papae*, fo. 142, 'potestas papalis includit id quod excedit omnem auctoritatem humanam'; cf. Innocent III, *Reg.*, I. cccxlv (*PL*, ccxiv. 320), 'ratam habebimus et faciemus auctore Domino inviolabiliter observari'; Alexander of Hales, *Summa theologica*, iv. 3, 'Spiritualis enim potestas non iudicat secundum hominem vel secundum humanam legem, sed in quantum residet vice Dei'. Note also the use of the Roman law phrase 'leges humanae sunt per ora principum divinitus promulgatae', *Cod.*, X. xviii. 1 (cf. *Prov.*, xvi. 10), subsequently included in Gratian, C. 16 q. 3 c. 17, and used by Augustinus Triumphus, *Summa*, xliv. 1 ad 2, p. 241, but with the comment 'mediante tamen ore papae': also lx. 4 ad 4, p. 316, from which he draws the conclusion that 'unde sicut papa praeest toti mundo auctoritate Dei, ita auctoritate Dei dispensat in omnibus'.

room for only one such ruler, and that this ruler is the keystone of the whole structure of civil government. It is no overstatement to say that without him there would be no community at all. And this idea leads inevitably into a thoroughly totalitarian view of society. Although Augustinus Triumphus does not hesitate to employ the common medieval concept of the *status* or common good of the whole society, he makes it clear that this good is embodied in the pope as *caput Ecclesiae*. This suggests the various transformations which the expression underwent. Originally *status* referred to one's standing or position in society, and since this depended upon one's activities, to a person's function or office.[1] This gave the term a positive quality in itself, which was greatly enhanced when applied to the ruler, in this case the pope, whose function was above all the transmission and delineation of ultimate goodness and rightness to and for the benefit of his subjects. He is Aristotle's supremely virtuous being, not necessarily in his own actions, but in that his function is to be the source of rightness and goodness (*iustitia*) in the community. Acting through his office as ruler, he becomes a manifestation of divine well-being, *iustitia* incarnate, and correspondingly the absolute 'good' of the society is located in his office or *status*. His is the supreme and original *status* as vicar of Christ from which all other *status* descend, and it thereby becomes synonymous with the general good of all. The *status Ecclesiae*, the welfare of the universal society, is in this way seen to exist in the ruler. The preservation of the head is the prime requirement of good government. The common good can be maintained only by upholding the papal good, with the result that, taken relative to the good of all the other members of the society together, the well-being of the pope is of infinitely greater importance. To illustrate this most of the publicists adapted a passage in Aristotle's *Metaphysics* in which Aristotle, using the analogy of an army, had enquired whether the good was to be found in the whole force or its leader. And whereas Aristotle had merely emphasised the importance of the head, the publicists had no hesitation in locating the good of the army in the general, and of the *Ecclesia* in the pope. As Augustinus Triumphus says,

[1] Thomas Aquinas, *Summa theologica*, II. II. clxxxiii. 1–4.

Quia cum bonum exercitus non sit nisi propter bonum ducis, et bonum Ecclesiae non nisi propter bonum papae, maius est bonum ducis quam totius exercitus, et bonum papae maius quam totius Ecclesiae.[1]

Hence any justification for the community as a whole to exercise jurisdiction over its head becomes a logical impossibility. The current view that the ruler can act above the law for the common good is here transformed into the view that the pope, as the personification of that good, is himself above all law. If necessity knows no restriction, neither can the pope as the one person supremely qualified to pronounce upon the nature and occasion of necessity.[2] Underlying this is the all-important hierocratic principle which identifies the head of the Christian body, Christ or the pope, with the community as a whole. The society, conceived of as a corporation, exists over and above its members as a juristic entity, and this abstract being is for all practical purposes represented by the ruler. The pope therefore with Augustinus Triumphus can be spoken of as the *Ecclesia* itself. Put into modern terminology this abstract being may be referred to as the 'State', that intangible representative of the community which is personified by the head of government. Since this abstract is the essence of the society it also incorporates the general good, and consequently the ruler in his public capacity equally personifies the good or *status* of the whole: 'omnis status reducitur ad caput unum ... ubicunque autem est capitis unitas, ibi est status'.[3] The pope becomes the *status Ecclesiae*. Just as he acts for

[1] Augustinus Triumphus, *Summa*, vi. 6 ad 2, p. 63; cf. Aristotle, *Metaphysics*, xii. 10, and note an implication of the same principle in the *Lex Visigothorum*, II. i. 14, 'Quod antea ordinare oportuit negotia principum, et postea populorum'. Similarly Aegidius Romanus, *De renuntiatione papae*, iv, p. 7; Aegidius Spiritalis, *Libellus contra infideles*, pp. 122–3; Francis de Meyronnes, *De principatu temporali*, ch. 3, p. 61; Hervaeus Natalis, *De potestate papae*, fo. 148. For the contrasting use of this passage with Aquinas see *KTB*, pp. 265–7.

[2] Augustinus Triumphus, *Summa*, xxxv. 3, p. 207, 'Ubi tamen evidens et manifesta apparet utilitas, potestati papae subesse dignoscitur mutare et innovare omne quod expedit reipublicae utilitati'.

[3] Augustinus Triumphus, *Summa*, lxxxviii. 1, p. 439. This has Byzantine precedents: e.g. the description of the *Basileus* as 'the common good of all his subjects' in the *Espanagoge*, ii. 1, of Leo VI (c. 883). But note that Cicero had also said that in a monarchy the rule of the king was the *status* of the community: *De republica*, I. xxvi. 42, 'cum penes unum est omnium summa rerum, regem

the good of all, so every act taken for the common good is primarily an act on behalf of the pope. Similarly every subordinate officer entrusted with the care of the common welfare exists *loco papae*, on his behalf. Any official activity in the *Ecclesia*, which is the *corpus Christi*, designed to promote its well-being must at the same time be pursued in favour of Christ, who for all earthly purposes is represented by the pope. In time this idea leads to the term 'state' being applied direct to the juristic entity which any corporate community is held to form, and so to the political society itself as the organisation through which this good and right manner of life may find expression. It is this conflation of the two ideas of 'state' which was later to be summed up in the classic dictum *l'état, c'est moi*. In this theory then may be seen the origin of the modern idea of the totalitarian state, which also sees in its ruler the embodiment of the good of the whole community. Correspondingly there is a tendency towards the development of a ruler cult. Whilst absolute obedience and reverence are technically paid to him in his official capacity as the representative of Christ, the *Ecclesia*, and the common good, there results in practice a virtual deification of the head of 'state'.

The pattern of government evolved from these principles is essentially paternalistic. The subject is permitted no initiative in the ordering of the affairs of the society: all good things come as gifts from above. Government is an act of grace, and this means, as St. Augustine had stressed, something granted as a reward for faith. And since only the ruler knows what is needed and what is to be rejected in the name of the 'good', implicit obedience to his commands is essential: 'omnis homo tenetur parere papae ad repellendam iniuriam pro conservatione iustitiae'.[1] In matters of faith and government all Christians according to Augustinus Triumphus

illum unum vocamus et regnum eius reipublicae statum'. Cf. Jerome, *Dialogus contra Luciferianos*, 9 (*PL*, xxiii. 165), 'Ecclesiae salus in summi sacerdotis dignitate pendet'.

[1] Augustinus Triumphus, *Summa*, lxxv. 1 ad 1, p. 387; and note xxii. 4, p. 132, where he illustrates this with a quotation from *Exodus*, xxiv. 7, 'Omnia quae locutus est dominus, faciemus et audiemus', on which he comments, 'sic omnes viventes in religione christiana debent dicere ipsi papae', adding that this 'omnes' means 'tam domini quam servi, et laici et clerici'.

are subject to the pope: they are like children in such things and must be obedient in the same way that sons are to a father.

Planum est autem quod omnes qui sunt in corpore mystico Ecclesiae comparantur ad papam sicut filii ad patrem... Nam filii tenentur obedire parentibus carnalibus in his quae sunt corporum, quia patres sunt corporum, non animarum. Sed papae tenentur oves Christi fideles parere in his quae sunt corporum et animarum.[1]

The pope, as the name suggests, is set up as a gigantic father-figure seated over the *Ecclesia* whilst he dispenses guidance and judgement in the manner of God himself. Indeed such a conception of rulership is tenable only if the ruler is believed to have the attributes of God. The idea that justness is in the will of the sovereign presupposes an act of faith in the right of the ruler to determine *iustitia* and in the permanence of his infallibility. In the last resort the basis of the whole hierocratic system of government was a matter of belief—in the essentially Christian nature of the political community, in the establishment of the Petrine primacy, and in the unfailing sufficiency of its direction. This had of course always been perfectly well understood by all the great thinkers of the early medieval period, and the controversies in the schools over the relationship of faith and reason had only served to emphasise this fact. The supremacy of faith over reason is expressed politically in the doctrine of the plenitude of power. As Hostiensis in the thirteenth century, and Alvarus Pelagius in the fourteenth, pointed out, the pope must be presumed to be acting in the manner of God: acceptance of the justness of a papal command is an act of faith.[2] The true hierocrat

[1] Augustinus Triumphus, *Summa*, ci. 8, p. 500; cf. xxii. 2 ad 1, p. 131, 'per illos duos filios intelliguntur laici et clerici'; xxvii. 1, p. 160, 'papa solus est pater omnium fidelium'; also Opicinus de Canistris, *De praeeminentia spiritualis imperii*, p. 96. The title *papa*, which, as Augustinus Triumphus points out, is a corruption of 'pater patrum', *De duplici potestate*, p. 493, 'papa idem sonat quod pater patrum', derives from the Roman imperial title *pater patriae*. For the God-like ruler of Roman law as *pater omnium* see *Nov.*, xcviii. 2, 2 and cf. *Nov.*, xii. 4, 'pater legis'. For paternalism with the thirteenth-century theologians see I. T. Eschmann, 'Thomistic Social Philosophy and the Theory of Original Sin', *Mediaeval Studies*, ix (1947), pp. 19–55, especially p. 43.

[2] Hostiensis, *Comm. in Decretales ad* I. vii. 3, argues that the pope may be judge in his own cause, 'Et est ratio quia non est praesumendum quod vicarius Dei aliter iudicet quam ipse Deus esset iudicaturus'; Alvarus Pelagius, *De*

could not really consider the possibility that the pope might be mistaken: to Augustinus Triumphus he is the elect of God, predestined to govern well and act justly. His entry into heaven is already certain.

Nam papa potest comparari ad suam vocationem, et speciali modo vocatus est a Deo ad regendum gregem suum... Si igitur solus pontifex habet specialem divinam vocationem et summi status perfectionem et singularem spiritus sancti gubernationem, solus ipse quodam speciale modo potest dici a Deo praedestinatus et aeterna dampnatione privatus.[1]

Conversely, since a matter of belief is involved, obedience becomes a vital qualification for salvation: 'sic omnes volentes consequi vitam aeternam tenentur eius mandato parere'.[2] As the Clerk says in the *Somnium viridarii*, obedience to the pope is a rule to be followed without exception,[3] and, we might add, without consideration or fear for the consequences. In this sense it was a most comfortable creed. On the other hand it was also an essentially authoritarian one. A conviction of the unswerving rectitude of the ruler

planctu Ecclesiae, ch. 26, p. 34. Cf. *Cod.*, II. lviii. 2. 8, 'iudex dicitur, immo creditur esse Deus in omnibus pro hominibus'. In Roman thought the same belief was expressed by the application of the term *Optimus* to the emperor: Wirszubski, *op. cit.*, pp. 153–4.

[1] Augustinus Triumphus, *Tractatus contra articulos*, i. 2, pp. lxxii–lxxiii.

[2] Augustinus Triumphus, *Summa*, xlix. 2, p. 264. In lxiii. 4, p. 336, he cites St. Bernard to support this, 'Salutare credas quicquid praelatus iniunxerit'. This had already been pronounced by Boniface VIII, *Extravagantes Communes*, I. viii. 1, 'Porro subesse Romano pontifice omni humanae creaturae declaramus, dicimus, definimus et pronuntiamus omnino esse de necessitate salutis', and it is significant to note its unqualified acceptance by a later pope, Clement VI, *MGH, Const.*, VIII n. 100 p. 156. See also Anon., *Commentarium in Unam sanctam*, ch. 1, pp. 127–8; Aegidius Romanus, *De ecclesiastica potestate*, ii. 1, p. 36; Thomas Aquinas, *Opusculum contra errores Graecorum*, ii. 38. It is interesting to find that Augustinus Triumphus considers the promise taken on behalf of a child by his godparents at baptism to be an oath of obedience to the pope: *Summa*, xxii. 4 ad 2, p. 133, 'Nec verum est quod homo praestat alicui iuramentum prius quam papae, quia papae praestat iuramentum in baptismo quando promittit vivere secundum fidem et ritum christianae religionis'. This is comparable to the modern assumption that one is subject to the law of the State from birth.

[3] Anon., *Somnium viridarii*, i. 158 [misnumbered 178], p. 120, 'papae autem oportet universitatem fidelium spiritualium atque saecularium absque omni exceptione in omnibus obedire'.

inhibits any real conception of the liberty of the subject beyond that perfect freedom to be found in service to the community and its head. In the same way that Augustinian theology in the fourteenth century emphasises the sovereign will of God to the extent of denying the intrinsic right of his creatures to power and existence,[1] so the political expression of this outlook sees in his vicar an all-embracing and absolute authority which denies his subjects any freedom of action or being of their own accord.

In short it may be said that during the course of the thirteenth and fourteenth centuries there develops alongside the idea of natural justice from which all law derives its validity the alternative notion that the will of the ruler is the only expression of legality. In both cases the same phraseology is employed, but with a profound difference in emphasis. An idea of the ruler as *lex animata*, law personified, is common to all writers of the period, but as used by the hierocratic writers in favour of the pope the term takes on a special significance.[2] No one, not even Augustinus Triumphus, would deny that he ought to set an example to his subjects, that he should be a 'speculum ante oculos omnium fidelium',[3] a mirror of law reflecting the divine righteousness of God. But we are brought dangerously near to the view that just because the pope is living law, any expression of his desire and pleasure is justified. So much had long been the official legal standpoint. As Innocent IV said in discussing his right to act above positive law, it is much better for the prince to adhere to his own legislation; but that law cannot be held to bind him when he is its source and may as easily destroy what he has created. In supralegal actions his will alone is sufficient justification and there need be no other cause.

In his enim dispensationibus in iure nempe positivo sufficit sola *voluntas* dispensatoris etiam sine causa, quia eius est destruere ius qui illud condidit,

[1] G. Leff, *Bradwardine and the Pelagians* (Cambridge, 1957), pp. 41–53.

[2] For the general principle Aegidius Romanus, *De renuntiatione papae*, xvi. 2, p. 43, 'Est enim praelatus quaedam lex et quaedam regula subditorum: non enim est differentia inter principem et legem nisi quod lex est inanimatus princeps, princeps est animata lex'; cf. Anon., *Determinatio compendiosa*, ch. 33, p. 544, 'Demum papa est ipsum ius et lex viva, cui repugnare non licet'. The phrase derives from *Nov.*, cv. 2, 4; also Cicero, *De legibus*, III. i. 2.

[3] Augustinus Triumphus, *Summa*, lxxiii. 5, p. 382.

nec tenetur princeps sua lege . . . ipse tamen bene facit si suam legem servat . . . et princeps suis legibus non ligatur, quamvis ipsas deceat observare.[1]

Moreover such a contention, we repeat, can only be held if the pope approximates to God himself, and the claim that the pope is *lex animata* or *vicarius Christi* is intended to suggest precisely this. The Pauline conception of Christ as the Law is united with the Roman law theory of the *lex animata* and developed for the benefit of the pope as Christ's vicar. As a personification of the law he is nothing else but a personification of Christ; it is his duty to transmute the precepts of the ethereal realm in which Christ and righteousness reign into practical government on the earthly level. The pope then represents the point at which heaven and earth meet: he is, says Augustinus Triumphus, the soul which provides the connection between the body politic and the Godhead.

Sicut corpus Christi fuit unitum personaliter divinitati mediante anima ita quod tota humanitas Christi coniuncta divinitati est, caput Ecclesiae et influit in ipsam, sic membra Ecclesiae spiritualia principaliter recipiunt huiusmodi capitis influxum.[2]

Once again the analogy of a mystical marriage between head and members presents itself. The papacy represents the mystical union between God and man by which the earthly society is given its divine power and content, and is thereby made capable of acting as a divine instrument. To borrow the publicists' own phraseology, the addition of the papal 'soul' to the *corpus Ecclesiae* completes the body and creates the whole mystical man by which the society becomes identical with Christ.[3] Through the ruler the *mundus* is raised to its status of Augustine's heavenly city: the pope becomes a political variant of the world-soul of the philosophers. But what this is

[1] Innocent IV, *Comm. in Decretales*, III. xxxv. 6. Cf. St. Bernard's famous statement that the *regnum coelorum* is governed by will: *Ep. CIII*, 1 (*PL*, clxxxii. 237), 'et est regiae potestatis beare *pro voluntate* amicos'.

[2] Augustinus Triumphus, *Summa*, xix. 2 ad 2, p. 118.

[3] This probably owes something to Seneca's description of the emperor, *De clementia*, I. v. 1, 'tu animus reipublicae tuae es, illa corpus tuum', which was a popular figure of speech with the fourteenth-century civilians: *KTB*, p. 215.

endeavouring to express is the urgent medieval belief that there must be some agency through which the divine order is brought into the human order, by which divine law becomes positive legal codes. And from this it followed that the agency itself must have not only divine but also human qualities.[1] This then is the justification for the papacy, for the existence of the pope as 'mediator inter Deum et hominem',[2] closer to God than any man.[3] He comes to be regarded as a Janus-like figure who provides the sole link between the divine world and the terrestrial, partaking on one side in the spiritual nature of God and on the other in the material nature of man: 'qui est Deus et homo, puta Christus, cuius vicarius est ipse papa'.[4] Innocent III, who perhaps may be credited with doing more than anyone except St. Bernard to develop the mediatory conception of the papacy, had endeavoured to explain exactly the same idea by referring to himself as less than God and more than man.[5] Just as God became man in Christ to provide this link and to

[1] According to A. H. Chroust, 'The Corporate Idea and the Body Politic in the Middle Ages', *Review of Politics*, ix (1947), pp. 423–52 at p. 433, the same idea is to be found with Remigio di Girolami. Remigio declares that God is the true head of the body politic, and that by comparison every other type of head is only an 'equivocal' one. Nevertheless since God is of a different genus than the earthly *Ecclesia*, and since he prefers to speak to man through a 'univocal' medium, it is necessary that there should be a 'highest man or univocal *caput*' who is both head and of the same genus as the body. This conception of God speaking to man through man comes from Dionysius the Pseudo-Areopagite, *De coelesti hierarchia*, ch. 10 (*PG*, iv. 275), but we may also note the influence of Aristotle, *Physics*, ii. 1.

[2] Augustinus Triumphus, *Summa*, vi. 2, p. 58; xxii. 4, p. 132, 'cum ipse sit sequester et medius inter Deum et hominem seu totum populum christianum'. St. Paul's statement that there is only one such mediator, I *Tim*., ii. 5 (quoted cx. 6, p. 551) serves to emphasise the papal identity with Christ.

[3] This is applied by Augustinus Triumphus to all priests in so far as they have a mediatory function: *Summa*, xciii. 2, p. 457, 'sunt enim ipsi quasi medii inter Deum et populum . . . sunt propinquiores Deo ratione officii quod ministrant'. Cf. *Numbers*, xvi. 9.

[4] Augustinus Triumphus, *Summa*, xliii. 1 ad 2, p. 238; cf. i. 1 ad 2, p. 3, 'verum est potestatem imperialem esse a Deo, quia non est a papa ut est homo, sed est a papa ut gerit vicem Christi in terra, qui est verus Deus et verus homo'; xxxviii. 4 ad 3, p. 327.

[5] Innocent III, *Consec. serm*., ii (*PL*, ccxvii. 658), 'inter Deum et hominem medius constitutus, citra Deum sed ultra hominem, minor Deo sed maior homine'; cf. Johannes Andreae, *ad Clementinas*, *proem*., s.v. *papa*, 'Nec Deus es

propound the divine way of life upon earth, so, now that Christ has reverted to heaven, the function of divine mouthpiece passes to the pope 'qui vice Dei gerit in terris'. And according to Augustinus Triumphus it is only through the pope that God now acts upon earth: 'sic, mediante papa, Deus facit in praesenti vita'.[1] Conversely mankind has no contact with God except through the agency of the pope.[2] Since the society is visible whereas God is invisible, he stresses that there can be no other conclusion but that the visible *Ecclesia* must have a visible head who is invested with all the majesty, power and competence of God. With him the papal curia becomes the seat of God, and it is here, he writes, that the judgement of God is delivered in the voice of God by one having the power of God.

Solus papa dicitur esse vicarius Dei, quia solum quod ligatur vel solvitur per eum habetur solutum et ligatum per ipsum Deum. Sententia igitur papae et sententia Dei una sententia est . . . unum consistorium est ipsius papae et Dei . . . una sententia et una curia Dei et papae.[3]

This is a full-blooded assertion of the ruler's divinity, but his way of

nec homo, quasi neuter es inter utrumque'. Again this has a Roman origin: Tertullian, *Apol.*, ch. 30, puts the emperor between God and man. Emperors are next to God, 'a quo sunt secundi, post quem primi, ante omnes et super omnes deos. Quidni? Cum super omnes homines, qui utique vivunt' (*PL*, i. 441–2).

[1] Augustinus Triumphus, *Summa*, vi. 2 ad 2, p. 58; also i. 9, p. 13, 'potestas Christi, qui nunc regnat mediante papa tamquam mediante suo vicario'; i. 5, p. 8, 'Significatur enim summus pontifex per montem Sinai . . . quia sicut mediante tali monte descendit Deus coram toto populo Iudaeorum, sic Christus mediante potestate summi pontificis in lege nova descendit super toto populo christianorum . . . quia sicut de illo monte data est lex, sic ab ipso papa omnes leges et omnia iura exquirenda sunt'. Cf. Innocent III, *De sacro altaris mysterio*, i. 46 (*PL*, ccxvii. 791), 'visibilis pontifex'.

[2] Augustinus Triumphus, *Summa*, vi. 1 ad 2, p. 57, 'in praesenti vita non discutitur a Deo via appellationis nisi mediante homine et mediante ordine iudicario a Deo instituto'; vi. 3, p. 59, 'non potest intrare ad Deum nisi mediante homine et mediantibus iudicibus institutis a Deo'.

[3] Augustinus Triumphus, *Summa*, vi. 1, p. 57; xlv. 2, p. 247, 'Idem est dominium Dei et papae'; also xxxvi. 1, p. 212; cf. lxiii. 1 ad 2, p. 333, 'praeceptum papae impressum est similiter a Deo, puta a Christo'; ix. 1 *prop.* 1, p. 71, 'una est potestas Christi secundum quod Deus et papae'; c. 1, p. 488, 'Unde eiusdem *auctor*itatis est doctrina summorum pontificum, cuius est doctrina Christi, sicut eiusdem *auctor*itatis est veritas principalis *auctoris* et eius vicem gerentis'.

expressing it is neither unique nor particularly novel. Within a few years his Franciscan imitator, Alvarus Pelagius, was saying much the same thing: 'in eius sede Christus sedet et eius vicarius loco eius'.[1] Both however borrowed this identification of the papal curia with the court of God from a well-known statement by the thirteenth-century canonist Hostiensis, and whilst Hostiensis himself was perhaps influenced by English examples,[2] it had become standard practice for the thirteenth- and fourteenth-century popes to assert something of the same sort. Innocent III, for example, repeatedly declared that when the pope exercised the power of binding and loosing it was not in fact a man at all, but God himself who acted,[3] and a

[1] Alvarus Pelagius, *De planctu Ecclesiae*, ch. 68, p. 244; ch. 29, p. 34, 'unum est consistorium et tribunal Christi et papae in terris . . . et Christum audit qui papam audit . . . cum enim Christus sit caput Ecclesiae . . . loco eius recedentis et in sede eius dominus papa pro capite'.

[2] Hostiensis, *Lectura ad Decretales*, I. vii. 3, 'Consistorium Dei et papae unum et idem censendum'. Hostiensis had been in service to Henry III of England before becoming chaplain to Innocent IV, and it is perhaps significant that it was his contemporary Robert Grosseteste, bishop of Lincoln, who told Innocent IV at the Council of Lyons that 'This most holy see is the throne of God', E. Brown, *Fasciculus rerum expetendarum et fugiendarum* (London, 1690), ii. 254: see W. A. Pantin, 'Grosseteste's relations with the papacy and the crown', *Robert Grosseteste* (ed. D. A. Callus, Oxford, 1955), pp. 178–215 at p. 186. At the same time Bracton was speaking of the prince 'in sede ipsius regis quasi throno Dei' (ed. Woodbine, ii. 20, 21), which followed the eleventh-century tradition of the English monarchy: e.g. the Anglo-Norman Anonymous, *MGH, Lib. de Lit.*, iii. 667, 'potestas enim regis potestas Dei est'; iii. 676, 'Summi coelestis imperatoris et secundi terrenique una eademque potestas est'. Cf. Henry II, 'Omnipotentis Dei malevolentia, ira et indignatio, et mea', L. Delisle, *Recueil des Actes de Henri II* (Paris, 1909–27), ii. 244.

[3] This was common Innocentian language: *Reg.*, I. cccxxvi (*PL*, ccxiv. 292), 'cum non humana sed divina fiat auctoritate quod in hac parte per summum pontificem adimpletur, qui non hominis puri sed veri Dei vicarius appellatur. . . Unde quos Deus spirituali coniunctione ligavit, non homo quia non vicarius hominis, sed Deus quia Dei vicarius, separat'; *Reg.*, I. cccxxxv (*PL*, ccxiv. 306–7), 'Non enim homo sed Deus separat quod Romanus pontifex, qui non puri hominis sed veri Dei vicem gerit in terris . . . non humana sed divina potius auctoritate dissolvit'; also *Reg.*, I. cxvii (*PL*, ccxiv. 106); *Reg.*, I. dii (*PL*, ccxiv. 462). On a similar passage put into the Decretals, I. vii. 2, the glossator, Bernardus Parmensis, comments, s.v. *divina*, 'Et sic quod fit auctoritate papae dicitur fieri auctoritate Dei'. See also Anon., *Determinatio compendiosa*, ch. 33, p. 544; Anon., *Somnium viridarii*, ii. 294, p. 191, 'in hoc gerit vicem seu vice Dei, cuius est plenitudo orbis universi, et possit quod Deus in terris'. For Innocent cf. II *Par.*, xix. 6.

century later we find Louis IV of Bavaria expressing considerable irritation at John XXII's use of the same idea.[1] Similar examples can indeed be added almost indefinitely, but all serve to illustrate the prevailing medieval acceptance of the immediate divine nature of political power.

Although then the pope's human nature is an important element in this idea, it no longer remained possible for the papalist to regard him as a mere man. Said Alvarus Pelagius, 'non homo simpliciter sed quasi Deus in terris',[2] and the supereminence of the divine over the human left little room for doubt that his Godliness swallowed up his humanity. When contemporary popes were fond of remarking that they existed in and through Christ, it was felt that there could hardly be any reason to dispute their Christlike nature.[3] And it followed, as Clement VI pointed out, that disobedience became heresy and the acceptance of an anti-pope idolatry.[4] Altogether, it

[1] Baluze, iii. 387, 'Ipse autem, Phariseorum sibi assumens supercilium, putat se absolvere quos Deus ligat et ligare quos Deus solvit, in hoc contra Deum et fidem catholicam et sacram scripturam et veritatem et iustitiam faciendo'. There appears however to have been no objection to the same idea when applied to the emperor: e.g. Lucas da Penna, 'non est homo qui ligat sed Deus, qui dignos facit homines tanti honoris': Ullmann, *The Medieval Idea of Law*, p. 52.

[2] Alvarus Pelagius, *De planctu Ecclesiae*, ch. 37, p. 47; ch. 68, p. 247; *Collyrium*, p. 513; also Aegidius Romanus, *De renuntiatione papae*, iii, p. 4, 'papa quodammodo est Deus, id est, Dei vicarius', which is repeated in the first Colonna memorandum, p. 510. See further J. Rivière, 'Sur l'expression *Papa-Deus* au moyen âge', *Miscellanea Francesco Ehrle*, ii (Rome, 1924), pp. 278–89.

[3] See the letter of Clement V, 26 March 1308, 'Christus est nobis via, vita et veritas. Quis ergo potest ipsum negare, *per* quem et *in* quo subsistimus, quin nos destruere satagat': K. Wenck, *Clemens V und Heinrich VII* (Halle, 1882), p. 99. Cf. Tholemy of Lucca, *Determinatio compendiosa*, ch. 15, p. 34, 'omnia tamen regimina et omnis actus dependet a papa *per* Christum'; and note the remark of Bracton (Woodbine, ii. 305), 'Ad hoc autem creatus est rex . . . ut *in* eo Dominus sedeat et *per* sua iudicia discernat'. See also the use of *Luke*, x. 16, by Alexander de S. Elpidio, *De ecclesiastica potestate*, ii. 8, p. 26; Alvarus Pelagius, *De planctu Ecclesiae*, ch. 24, p. 33; ch. 29, p. 35; and by Peter Roger (Clement VI) in Peter Bertrandus, *De iurisdictione ecclesiastica*, p. 1368.

[4] See H. S. Offler, 'A Political *Collatio* of Pope Clement VI, O.S.B.', *Revue Bénédictine*, lxv (1955), pp. 126–44 at p. 136, where after condemning disobedience to the pope as heresy he adds, 'antipapam creando, ydolum in Ecclesia constituendo'. Disobedience to the apostolic see had already been defined as heresy and idolatry (on the basis of I *Reg.*, xv. 23) by Gregory VII: e.g. *Reg.*, ii. 66 (ed. E. Caspar: Berlin, 1955), p. 222, and see here (n. 2) for a list of

was very much easier, the hierocrat found, not to think of the pope as a man but as God himself in human form miraculously present upon earth. As late as 1441 the abbot Andreas was telling Eugenius IV that 'Es namque Deus in terris et Christus et eius vicarius et Petri successor'[1]—although this constituted no fundamental change from the time seven centuries earlier when Gregory II reminded the emperor that St. Peter had been an earthly God[2]—and the whole process by which the papacy took over the divine characteristics of the Roman Caesars is summed up when the canonists addressed the pope as 'Dominus Deus noster papa'.[3] On this rests the ultimate justification for the papal theory of sovereignty, and nothing less can be adequate for so far-reaching a claim to power. Only by a deliberate deification of the ruler can there be any firm basis for unrestricted authority or any theoretically watertight guarantee against the possibility that he might misuse his power. Startling as this doctrine is to modern eyes, the attribution of divine infallibility to the pope in hierocratic thought is a logical and necessary extension of the idea of sovereignty. At the same time it is hardly surprising that, as the living law, the living God, the pope came to be seen as the wonder of the medieval world.[4]

similar passages. This was also usually inferred by the publicists from Gratian, C. 25 q. 1 c. 11. See also Hervaeus Natalis, *De potestate papae*, fo. 152; Sybert of Beek, *Reprobatio sex errorum*, ch. 6, pp. 14–15. Augustinus Triumphus says that disobedience is a crime worthy of being termed heresy, *Summa*, xxviii. 3 ad 3, p. 170, but generally describes it as mortal sin, xxvii. 10, p. 167; xlvii. 6, p. 256.

[1] Maccarrone, *Vicarius Christi*, p. 254; cf. pp. 237–8.

[2] Mansi, xii. 972.

[3] Zenzellinus de Cassanis, *ad Extravagantes Iohannis XXII*, xiv *ante* c. 5 (Lyons, 1517), fo. 34. On this see F. Gillmann, *AKKR*, xcv (1915), pp. 266f. For the Roman use of 'Dominus noster Deus Caesar' see F. S. Lear, 'The Idea of Majesty in Roman Political Thought', *Essays in History and Political Theory in honor of C. H. McIlwain* (Cambridge, Mass., 1936), pp. 168–98 at pp. 187–94. The same attribution of deity to the ruler is common with the Roman lawyers: e.g. Bartolus, *Super const. extrav., ad Reprimendum*, s.v. *Fidelitates* n. 2, 'Princeps est Deus in terris'; and see the example of Cynus cited in Ullmann, *The Medieval Idea of Law*, pp. 174–5. Cf. Baldus, *Comm. ad Cod., tit. Sententia rescindi non potest, lex* 3, 'Princeps legitime electus est in terris Deus, et maxime papa, sed non legitime electus est diabolus in terris et apostata'. Note also Gratian, D. 96 c. 7.

[4] 'Papa est stupor mundi'. This originates from a poem by the English writer

Once having stipulated the divine nature of the papacy there can be no real limitation of papal power without at the same time infringing the omnipotence of God. From the *plenitudo deitatis* which Augustinus Triumphus accords to the pope[1] there is a natural and straightforward transition to a genuine *plenitudo potestatis*,[2] and, as St. Bernard had maintained, this plenitude may be contrasted against and distinguished from the limited capacity of all other rulers.[3] It is sovereignty pure and simple, the power to do all things: 'Papa omnia potest',[4] and this must be the case, it is argued, when all matters affecting a society which is the *corpus Christi* take on the aura of divine matters.[5] As the papalists hastened to point out, there was nothing basically new in all this. Had not the terms

Geoffrey de Vinsauf, *Poetria nova*: ed. P. Leyser, *Hist. poetarum medii aevi* (1721), 826 v. 1. For examples and the use of the term *admirabilis* see Aegidius Spiritalis, *Libellus contra infideles*, p. 106; Alvarus Pelagius, *De planctu Ecclesiae*, ch. 54, p. 137; Conrad of Megenberg, *Planctus Ecclesiae*, i. 1, p. 190. The publicists probably took this from the *glossa ordinaria* to the Clementines by Johannes Andreae, *proem.*, s.v. *papa*; but note the list of terms in *Isaiah*, ix. 6; also *Luke*, ii. 47, v. 26. For the application of these terms to Christ see Innocent III, *De quadripartita specie nuptiarum* (*PL*, ccxvii. 955).

[1] Augustinus Triumphus, *Summa*, xix. 2, p. 118; Tholemy of Lucca, *Determinatio compendiosa*, ch. 6, p. 17, 'plenitudo divinitatis'. Cf. *Coloss.*, ii. 9, and Augustine, *Ep. CLXXXVII*, xii. 40 (*PL*, xxxiii. 847; *CSEL*, lvii. 116).

[2] E.g. Augustinus Triumphus, *Summa*, xxix. 5, p. 178, 'Romanus pontifex plenitudinem obtinet potestatis'.

[3] Bernard, *De consideratione*, ii. 8 (*PL*, clxxxii. 752).

[4] Augustinus Triumphus, *Summa*, xxi. 1 ad 1, p. 127; also Peter Bertrandus, *De origine iurisdictionum*, ch. 4, fo. 98v; Aegidius Romanus, *De renuntiatione papae*, vi, p. 13, 'totum est in potestate sua'; cf. *Luke*, i. 37; *Phil.*, iv. 13. The expression *papa omnia potest* was frequently used by the canonists, e.g. the *Summa Et est sciendum*: Gillmann, *AKKR*, cvii (1927), p. 214; Guilielmus Durantis, *Speculum iuris*, i. 1, p. 51; Hostiensis, *Comm. in Decretales*, *ad* I. vii. 3; Innocent IV, *App. ad Decretales* I. v. 4, s.v. *Requisitas*, and another example *ad* II. ii. 2 in VI, c. 7. Note also the reported statement of Urban VI, 'Omnia possum et ita volo', Baluze, ii. 660. It also appears with the imperialists: e.g. Ugolinus de Celle, *De electione regis Romanorum*, ch. 7, p. 74. It is curious to note that the expression was a well known maxim in the English law courts, at least according to Justice Hankford in 1410: he refers to the case of Rex v Bishop of St. David's, which the Year Book dates as 1322: see the brief discussion by P. Vinogradoff, 'Constitutional History of the Year Books', *Law Quarterly Review*, xxix (1913), p. 282. For its origin in the Roman expression 'Caesar omnia potest' see Wirszubski, *op. cit.*, p. 135.

[5] For the Roman law basis see *Inst.*, II. i. 10.

of the Petrine commission expressly permitted Peter the right to bind *whatsoever* he wished without reservation? Surely, then, its mighty *Quodcunque* must comprise everything and everybody—'nihil excipit'.[1] It is therefore true, says Augustinus Triumphus, that papal power is infinite and unquestionable, so great in fact that even the pope himself may not know all that he can do with it.[2] He is *dominus absolutus*, having total jurisdiction over both men and their possessions.[3] Everything belongs to him, the vicar of one 'cuius est terra et plenitudo eius,' and he can do with his inheritance as he pleases.[4] There is no sphere of activity, public or private, be-

[1] Augustinus Triumphus, *Summa*, xlv. 2, p. 247, 'nulla reservatione facta'; Aegidius Spiritalis, *Libellus contra infideles*, p. 107, 'quia Petro et successoribus eius ex generali commissione sibi facta . . . ex quo nihil excipit'. This is copied from Innocent III, *Decretales*, I. xxxiii. 6, but see also Gregory VII, *Reg.*, iv. 2 (Caspar, p. 295), 'nullum excipit, nihil ab eius potestate subtraxit'.

[2] Augustinus Triumphus, *Summa*, *Dedicatio*, 'quae cum sit [potestas papalis] *infinita*, eo quod magnus est dominus et magna virtus eius, et magnitudinis eius non est finis [*Ps.*, cxliv. 3], omnis creatus intellectus in eius *perscrutatione* invenitur deficere'; iv. 2, p. 41, 'papa qui *indefinitam* iurisdictionem habens. . .'; xxxii. 3, p. 194, 'Dico quod ignotum est mihi et puto quod ignotum sit cuilibet creaturae et ipsimet papae. Nec credo quod papa possit scire totum quod potest per potentiam suam'. This may be compared with Nero's statement that the emperor could not know how much power he possessed (Suetonius, *Nero*, xxxvii. 3).

[3] Aegidius Romanus, *De ecclesiastica potestate*, ii. 4, p. 51, 'quis ergo diceret quod quilibet fidelis secundum se totum et secundum omnia quae habet non sit sub regimine Petri?' See also Alvarus Pelagius, *De planctu Ecclesiae*, ch. 40, p. 61, 'politiae christianae est unus principatus absolute'. The title 'Dominus absolutus' was applied to Boniface VIII by the German ambassadors in the consistory of 30 April 1303: *MGH*, *Const.*, IV. i n.173, pp. 138–45. Note also the Roman imperial maxim 'hoc agamus ne quis quicquam habeat': Wirszubski, *op. cit.*, p. 159.

[4] Augustinus Triumphus, *Summa*, ci. 7, p. 499, 'planum est papam vice Christi *dominium et usum* rerum habere non solum clericorum immo omnium laicorum. Est enim ipse Christus dominus Ecclesiae et omnium illorum quibus Ecclesia plena est, sicut dicit glossa super *Psal.*, 23 [1], Domini est terra et plenitudo eius'; see also his use of I *Par.*, xxix. 11, 'Tua sunt Domine omnia et quae de manu tua accepimus dedimus tibi', ci. 4 ad 1, p. 497. Cf. Innocent III, *R.N.I.* 18, p. 30; Gregory VII, *Reg.*, vii. 14a (Caspar, p. 487), 'si potestis in coelo ligare et solvere, potestis in terra imperia, regna, principatus, ducatus, marchias, comitatus et omnium hominum possessiones pro mentis tollere unicuique et concedere'. This thesis was savagely attacked as heresy by Ockham, *Quoniam scriptura*, pp. 78–9, but it had in fact been developed in favour of the emperor on the basis of *Cod.*, VII. xxxvii. 3, 'Cum omnia esse principis intelligantur'. Dante's

yond his control: *voluntas* is the mainspring of all government, and he is subject to no limitation by his inferiors.

Ergo ita erit in corpore Christi mistico, cuiusmodi est Ecclesia Christi seu congregatio fidelium, cuius rector et gubernator eius qui est Christi vicarius habet plenitudinem potestatis super omnia membra, hoc est super omnes fideles, ut eis possit imperare diversos actus exercere et ea ab actibus etiam propriis quibus voluerit modis rationabilibus arcere, nec oportet eorum consensum requirere sicut nec anima seu voluntas requirit consensum membrorum, sed eis potest licite imperare.[1]

The *Ecclesia* is a true monarchy, and having been instituted in this form by Christ, must remain unchanged until the end of Time.[2] Even if this monarchy should seem to be a tyranny there can be no recourse to any other agency. The pope has no superior but himself, even when God is taken into consideration. For he himself is Christ, a personalisation of the mystical head, the human representation of that *persona Ecclesiae* which exists over and above its members. The pope is indeed on another plane of political existence, remote from and untouched by the individuals who make up the *congregatio fidelium*. By virtue of his power he has himself the character of a universal.

The whole conception of the papal vicariate of Christ seen in this light excludes any suggestion that the pope receives power from below or can be deprived of it by the people. Hervaeus Natalis, a

emperor was also a monarch 'tutto possedendo e più desiderare non possendo', *Convivio*, iv. 4, p. 416.

[1] Anon., *Disquisitio theologico-iuridica*, ii. 12, p. 1349: his power, the author continues, is a 'potentia voluntatis'. Cf. Hermannus de Schildiz, *Contra haereticos, proem.*, p. 130, 'In ditione tua, domine, cuncta sunt posita, et non est qui possit resistere voluntati tuae, *Hester* xiii [9]. Haec verba ad vicarium Iesu Christi congrue diriguntur, cuius ditione illud verbum, quo constructum est coelum et terra, terreni simul et coelestis imperii iura commisit, ut merito omnes filii hominum, praecipue tamen fideles, suo beneplacito pareant vice Dei'.

[2] Hervaeus Natalis, *De potestate papae*, fo. 144, 'Iste principatus est unus quia nulla auctoritate humana potest dividi, itaque nec papa cum tota Ecclesia istam monarchiam posset licite dividere'. Most hierocratic writings describe the *Ecclesia* as a *monarchia*: e.g. Augustinus Triumphus, *Summa*, lxiii. 4, p. 336, 'papa monarchiam tenet'; Anon., *De potestate Ecclesiae*, pp. 250, 253, 'Et maxime hoc habet monarcha ecclesiasticus apud quem est plenitudo potestatis ecclesiasticae, cum sit vicarius Iesu Christi in terra'. The term is used by Innocent IV, Winkelmann, ii. 698.

French Dominican and one of the most ardent papalists of his day, denies that papal power can come from anyone but Christ.[1] There is no passage in the Scriptures, he declares, which can be construed in such a manner as to suggest that the pope gains his power from the people, and he has therefore no hesitation in concluding that the papal 'dominium non dependet a communitate christiana'.[2] Equally forthright is his fellow countryman, Peter de la Palu, also a Dominican, who sets out to prove three propositions: that papal power does not stem from the *Ecclesia universalis*; that it derives straight from Christ; and that all the jurisdiction in the world belongs to the pope.[3] If the papal supremacy, he argues, rested upon the judgement of the whole society, then the *congregatio fidelium* could not only depose the pope, but even go so far as to change the location of the papacy. But since this is impossible, it cannot be said that the pope owes his power to popular sanction.[4] And Augustinus Triumphus, asking himself why Christ had fled into a mountain when offered a crown by the Jews, answers triumphantly, 'quia noluit rex per homines fieri'.[5] Indeed it is at this point that the *caput-corpus* analogy is felt to be imperfect, since the head in any natural body must derive some degree of sustenance from the body itself. But in the political body, he says, the head is autonomous, owing nothing to the members: rather they receive their all from him.

... non est de ratione capitis ut caput est aliquid recipere a membris sed semper influere. Unde caput in corpore naturali non recipit aliquid a membris ut caput, sed si recipit aliquid, hoc est ratione nutrimenti quo

[1] Hervaeus Natalis, *De potestate papae*, fo. 142, 'Sed potestas papae de qua loquitur est potestas qua ipse papa utitur ut vicarius Christi in terra: ergo istam potestatem instituere ad nullum alium pertinet nisi ad Christum'.

[2] Hervaeus Natalis, *De potestate papae*, fo. 143.

[3] Peter de la Palu, *De causa immediata ecclesiasticae potestatis*, iv *proem.*, fo. 44, 'de causa immediata potestatis papalis sunt tres conclusiones. Prima quod potestas papalis non est ab Ecclesia; secunda quod est a solo Christo immediate; tertia quod ab ipso est omnis iurisdictio ecclesiastica et spiritualis in toto mundo et in tota Ecclesia'.

[4] Peter de la Palu, *De causa immediata ecclesiasticae potestatis*, iv. 1, fo. 44v, 'Si praeeminentia papae esset ex statuto Ecclesiae, Ecclesia posset illam mutare et transferre et papa a papatu deponere; sed non potest, ergo non est ab ea'.

[5] Augustinus Triumphus, *Summa*, i. 7 ad 3, p. 11. On this see further Leclercq, 'L'idée de la royauté du Christ', p. 418.

indiget per digestionem factam in stomacho et in hepate et in corde, et quantum ad hoc deficit a ratione capitis. Sed summus pontifex sic est caput in toto corpore mystico Ecclesiae quod nihil virtutis et auctoritatis a membris recipit sed semper influit, propter quod habet completam rationem capitis.[1]

The participation of representative councils in the making or promulgation of papal law is not considered to be necessary for its validity. Nor is the basic private law operating in the society any less subject to his discretion than matters of immediate policy or necessity. Established law and custom can be overturned by deliberate papal legislation, and there is no one who can say, in the current stylised phrase, 'Cur ita facis?'[2] The pope cannot be bound by the enactments of his predecessors, since one pope has no authority over another: 'par in parem non habet imperium'. He is *supra ius* and *legibus solutus*, free from all legal restraints.[3] If any act committed by him is illegal, there is nothing to be done about it. In the first place there is no one who has the authority to correct him; and secondly he is the sole judge of what constitutes an illegal act, and it is hardly to be expected that a pope will consent to recognise the invalidity of his own actions. Moreover he is the source of all law, and there is no reason why he should not change the existing law to preserve the legality of his position. The law cannot be greater than the legislator: 'non potest esse magis lex quam legislator'.[4] Nor

[1] Augustinus Triumphus, *Summa*, vi. 5 ad 1, p. 61. This is developed from Thomas Aquinas, *Commentum in Sententias*, III. xiii. ii. 1 ad 6.

[2] Nicholas de Nonancour, 'quia vicem gerit illius in mundo de quo dicitur *Hiob* xi [10], si subverterit omnia . . . quis contradicet ei? aut quis potest ei dicere, Cur ita facis?': A. Maier, 'Due documenti relativi alla lotta dei cardinali Colonna contro Bonifazio VIII', *Rivista di Storia della Chiesa in Italia* (1949), pp. 344–64 at p. 363. See also Anon., *Determinatio compendiosa*, *proem.*, p. 542; ch. 33, p. 544; Aegidius Spiritalis, *Libellus contra infideles*, p. 108. Cf. *Ecclesiastes*, viii. 4.

[3] Augustinus Triumphus, *Summa*, v. 3, p. 51, 'ipse est supra ius et eum iura positiva non ligant; si enim imperator non ligatur iure, quia princeps legibus solutus est, ut dicit Iurisconsultus in principio Digestorum [Dig., I. iii. 31], multo fortius papa nullo iure ligari potest'; also lxviii. 1, p. 357, referring to Innocent III's 'supra ius' in *Decretales*, III. viii. 4. This is repeated many times. Cf. *Galat.*, v. 18.

[4] Augustinus Triumphus, *Summa*, lxvii. 3, p. 354; cf. lxvi. 3, p. 350, 'papa potest omnia iura confirmare, condere et relaxare'.

does this apply only to canon law. If, as the papalists maintain, all law is in the bosom of the pope,[1] he must logically hold supreme jurisdiction over any other legal code, whose binding force remains dependent upon papal approval:

...ita omnis lex, a quocunque feratur, per eum est comprobanda si bona sit, et per eum est corrigenda si bona non sit.[2]

In fact, observes Augustinus Triumphus, he can abolish the existing system of law in any particular kingdom and replace it by another of his own choosing.[3] And if the law itself, why not those whose task it is to administer it?

It is important in this respect to bear in mind the corporate nature of the *Ecclesia*. The lay ruler and his officials are as much a part of the hierarchy of officers through whom the ecclesiastical corporation is governed as are the bishops and clergy.[4] But since there is a very necessary distribution of functions a pattern of offices will emerge. On the one hand there is the broad distinction between those who are, and those who are not, additionally qualified to carry out the sacramental duties so essential in a civil society which is also a church. But this vertical delineation of the sacerdotal and lay orders is also transected by a whole declension of roughly comparable grades within each *ordo*. In the same way that the whole society is itself a mass of smaller corporations ranging from the kingdom to the lowest administrative unit, the manor, village or parish, so each community has its own appropriate body of lay and

[1] F. Gillmann, 'Romanus pontifex iura omnia in scrinio pectoris sui censetur habere', *AKKR*, xcii (1912), pp. 3f. The expression derives from *Cod.*, VI. xxiii. 19, and was used by Boniface VIII, *Sextus*, I. ii. 1.

[2] Augustinus Triumphus, *Summa*, xliv. 4 ad 2, p. 242.

[3] Augustinus Triumphus, *Summa*, lx. 4, p. 316, 'potest papa in omni humana lege dispensare: primo propter populi cui datur lex correctionem. . . Si vero idem populus postmodum paulatim depravetur, ut corruptus rem pravatam reipublicae praeferat atque habeat venale suffragium et ad flagitiosa atque scelerata opera convertatur, iuste tali lege privatur et alia lege flagellationis et castigationis gubernatur'.

[4] Augustinus Triumphus, *Summa*, lxxv. 3, p. 389, 'conservatores dati per papam requirunt . . . primo ut ad iurisconditorem, puta ad papam, habeant immediatam subiectionem. . . Secundo requiritur iuris executio . . . [quia] aliqua iura exequuntur mediantibus laicis, aliqua vero mediantibus clericis, secundum diversitatem status et conditionis personarum'.

clerical officials. There are then two parallel ladders of offices,[1] in which each office-holder acts *auctoritate papae*: his power descends to him like water running down the links of a chain. Each has the task of carrying out the more generalised papal directives according to the individual needs of his community. Although all governmental power is initially concentrated in the pope as the mediator between God and man, it is, Augustinus Triumphus explains, very much easier for him if there are subsidiary *medii* between him and the affairs of the local societies.[2] Just as God finds it useful to appoint the pope as his minister in earthly government, so the pope himself is in practice forced to shift most of the burden of administration on to the shoulders of lesser officials: 'per suos ministros sua potentia virtuali universum mundum debet visitare', says Augustinus, and as we have already had occasion to point out, there is no real distinction between this and a direct papal action. Like God he remains remote, and yet is virtually present everywhere.[3] And it goes without saying that the form taken by this hierarchy, even its existence, is—or should be—at the discretion of the pope.

[1] Augustinus Triumphus, *Summa*, xix. 5, p. 120, 'ordo qui servatur in potestatibus temporalibus multo fortius servandus est in potestatibus spiritualibus. Sed glossa super illo verbo *Rom.* 13 [1], omnis anima potestatibus sublimioribus subdita sit, sic dicit quod maiori potestati magis est obediendum quam minori: sicut proconsuli magis quam procuratori, et imperatori magis quam proconsuli; similiter magis obediendum est papae quam episcopo, et episcopo magis quam presbytero'. See also the extended account by Alvarus Pelagius, *De planctu Ecclesiae*, ch. 54, pp. 135–6. The parallelism between lay and sacerdotal rankings had always been a common feature of hierocratic thought: for early examples, including Walafrid Strabo, see E. H. Kantorowicz, *Laudes Regiae* (Berkeley and Los Angeles, 1946), p. 61 n. 164. The symbolic expression of the *Ecclesia* as a huge ladder and the representation of the cross, which designates the Christian society, as a series of grades is discussed by Greenhill, *art. cit.*, p. 348.

[2] Augustinus Triumphus, *Summa*, iii. 5, p. 32, 'papa . . . debet esse medius inter Deum et alios pastores et praelatos Ecclesiae'; lxi. 4 ad 3, p. 324, 'verum esse praelatos esse medios inter summum pontificem et inferiores subditos'; i. 6 ad 2, p. 10, 'Sic et papa sua potestate spirituali aliqua temporalia et corporalia regit per seipsum, aliqua vero mediante potestate aliorum principum saecularium quorum potestas corporalis et temporalis est'.

[3] Augustinus Triumphus, *Summa*, xxi. 3, p. 128. The use of similar expressions with Frederick II and the civilians is noted by *KTB*, pp. 142, 163, who suggests a possible influence of the pseudo-Aristotelian tract *De mundo*.

Vicarius autem Christi in tota praesenti vita est ipse papa, ad quem de iure spectat omnes praelationes et omnia dominia in toto humano genere ordinare vice Christi.[1]

It is he who is responsible for setting up and regulating the grades within each order, and who maintains the right relationship between the two *ordines* themselves. It follows, as Hervaeus Natalis said, that he can make any necessary alterations, expanding and decreasing the numbers and types of officials at will.

Sed papa *per se* immutat et facit variationes circa tales potestates *irrequisito consensu talis Ecclesiae*.[2]

Since this applies within both orders, all lay officials, however inferior, must consider themselves as papal nominees,[3] and indeed anyone holding a public function is to be classified in this manner.[4] Judges, notaries, physicians, as much as kings and emperors, bishops, priests and cardinals, are all officers of the great corporation appointed to carry out specific functions which, taken collectively, will ensure the administrative working of the *Ecclesia* in accordance with its underlying purpose. To describe these offices Augustinus Triumphus employs a wide variety of terms, *officium*, *beneficium*,[5]

[1] Augustinus Triumphus, *Summa*, lxxi. 4, p. 374; also Lambertus Guerrici de Hoyo, *Liber de commendatione*, ch. 1, p. 159, 'ad quem horum et omnium terrenarum dignitatum approbatio et confirmatio noscuntur de iure et approbata consuetudine tamquam ad Christi vicarium veraciter pertinere'.

[2] Hervaeus Natalis, *De potestate papae*, fo. 146.

[3] Aegidius Spiritalis, *Libellus contra infideles*, p. 107, 'Ipse namque summus pontifex privat laicos in dignitate et honoribus constitutos omni dignitate et honore'. This leads on to an interesting discussion of the question of whether the pope can confer nobility upon a commoner. See also Opicinus de Canistris, *De praeeminentia spiritualis imperii*, p. 98. The papal claim to set up counts and barons, even against the wishes of the king concerned, is castigated as tyranny by Ockham, *Quoniam scriptura*, pp. 78–9.

[4] See the definition of a person who is granted power 'in administratione reipublicae' as a *persona publica*, Augustinus Triumphus, *Summa*, lx. 3 ad 2, p. 315.

[5] He is at some pains to emphasise that the term *beneficium* does not have the purely clerical connotation of the modern benefice. The *beneficiatus* can be 'sive laicus sive clericus', *Summa*, cxi. 1 ad 1, p. 552; cf. lxix. 4, p. 363, 'duplex est beneficium, spirituale et temporale'. Its definition as an office is also made clear: lxviii. 1, p. 357, 'ut beneficium detur propter administrationem officii'; lxix. 6 ad 1, p. 365, 'ex qua commissione committitur eis potestas recipiendi a populo

ministerium, *stipendiarium*, but all are used to illustrate the same idea, namely that their holders are merely papal ministers or vicars.[1] This conception of office permits the holder no autonomous right to his function: he exists by the will and for the convenience of the pope, and his deposition from this office whenever the pope wishes it is implied as a matter of course. In the pursuance of his function he must always observe the strictest obedience to papal commands, and for this purpose Augustinus Triumphus regards it as desirable that all officials should take an oath before entering upon their office.

Illa potestas est in ministerium data alteri cui iuramentum fidelitatis praestat et ab ea cognoscit esse *omne quod habet*: sed omnis potestas saecularium principum, imperatorum et aliorum est talis.[2]

Either disobedience or inefficiency constitutes a breach of this oath and is punishable by loss of office. But provided these duties are faithfully performed, these agents are worthy of their hire. Augustinus Triumphus refers to them as *stipendiarii*,[3] and their stipends

christiano temporalia beneficia propter officia quae eis tenentur administrare'. For example emperorship is a *beneficium* (xxxvii. 4, p. 222; xxxix. 1, p. 228), which means that the emperor is a *persona publica* (xxxv. 2 *prop.* 2, p. 206) who functions 'ex suo officio' (xliv. 1 ad 1, p. 241). For the same principle applied to judicial and medical officers see *Quaestiones* cix–cxii.

[1] E.g. Augustinus Triumphus, *Summa*, i. 1, p. 3, 'Illa potestas est data in ministerium alteri per quam habet institui, regulari et ordinari atque confirmari si bona sit, et per quam habet iudicari et condemnari si bona non sit. Sed talis est potestas saecularium imperatorum, regum et principum, quia per potestatem papae habet institui' etc.; and in many other places. Note the definition of this term here: 'in ministerium quae est restringenda, amplianda et executioni mandanda'. Cf. Landulfus de Colonna, *De pontificali officio*, ch. 3, p. 539, 'Pascant ergo praelati . . . fideliter populum sibi commissum ut et Deum diligere et Petri legitimos vicarios se ostendant'.

[2] Augustinus Triumphus, *Summa*, i. 1, p. 3; also xxxviii. 4, p. 227; xlix. 2 ad 1, p. 264, 'sicut executores reipublicae faciunt iurare eorum ministros ut iniuncta eis officia fideliter exequantur'. During the thirteenth century the canonists had pointed out that the close similarity between episcopal consecration and royal coronation oaths denoted that both bishops and kings were to be seen as public officers: P. N. Riesenberg, *Inalienability of Sovereignty in Medieval Political Thought* (New York, 1956), pp. 51–3; and in general M. David, 'Le serment du sacre', *Revue du moyen âge latin*, vi (1950), pp. 5–272.

[3] Augustinus Triumphus, *Summa*, cix. 6, p. 543, 'tam diu iuste potest recipere suum stipendium quam diu exhibet in eius cura fidele ministerium'. Cf. his *Tractatus contra divinatores et sompniatores*, ch. 7 (ed. Scholz, *Unbekannte Kirchen-*

may take the form of other lucrative offices,[1] although in the case of royal and episcopal rulers they normally consist of the right to levy taxes and tithes.[2] Nothing could suggest more forcibly that the pope is the effective owner of all the material wealth of the community.

This very novel idea once again brings out the overwhelming influence of corporation theories upon the outlook of the publicists. One of the supreme advantages of the corporation was its ability to hold property as a legal person, and the Roman lawyers had had little difficulty in determining that this applied equally to the political community itself. Given an absolutist interpretation, the doctrine emerged that the society, seen as a corporation, became the owner of all the property and possessions of the members, ownership being vested in the undying juridical person which the society formed in law. This legal entity was of course the abstract *imperium*, but since it was primarily financial considerations which were involved, the legal entity seen from this angle received the title of the *fiscus* or *aerarium*. As the medieval commentators put it, the fisc was the stomach of the juristic person, which absorbed and distributed all the materials needed for the functioning and government of the body politic.[3] But there was no real difference between the fisc and

politische Streitschriften, ii. 481–90), p. 489, 'praelati patres debent filiis thesaurizare'. Pierre Dubois, *De recuperatione Sanctae Terrae*, ch. 128, p. 119, refers to the French barons, counts and knights as *stipendiarii* of the king. The term was originally applied to a *populus subiectus* within the Roman empire.

[1] Augustinus Triumphus, *Summa*, lxviii. 4, p. 360. He suggests that when a cleric is granted additional offices for this reason it might be desirable for him to hold them 'tamquam laicus non sicut clericus' to avoid the canon law prohibitions of pluralism. For this he claims the support of Huguccio, *ad* C. 21 q. 1, although he is quick to point out that the pope is in no way restricted by the canon law provisions and can distribute offices as he pleases.

[2] Augustinus Triumphus, *Summa*, xxx. 2, p. 183, 'sustentantur enim ministri Ecclesiae de bonis temporalibus oblatis a populo'; lxii. 4 ad 3, p. 330, 'principes non sunt domini rerum subditorum nisi sint eorum servi, sed sunt tutores propter quorum tuitionem dantur eis redditus et stipendia'. This seems to have been derived from Thomas Aquinas, *De regimine Iudaeorum*, ch. 6, and had already been elaborated by Tholemy of Lucca, *Determinatio compendiosa*, ch. 16, p. 35; *De regimine principum*, iii. 11, p. 260; cf. Alexander de S. Elpidio, *De ecclesiastica potestate*, ii. 8, p. 25.

[3] Tholemy of Lucca, *De regimine principum*, ii. 7, p. 243, 'Amplius autem quodlibet regnum sive civitas sive castrum sive quodcunque collegium assimi-

the society itself, and their identity was emphasised by the fact that it was the ruler who personified the legal entity formed by the corporation, and so acted as the embodiment of the *imperium-fiscus*. In practice all the goods and lands of the empire came to rest in the possession of the prince—'cum omnia esse principis intelligantur' (*Cod.*, VII. xxxvii. 3)—and it now became possible to equate the emperor, the empire and the fisc indiscriminately. Then, as the hierocratic system was developed and took into its service a Christianised version of Roman law, these corporation tenets were applied to the *Ecclesia* as the continuation of the old Roman empire, and with them went the theory of the fisc. In course of time it underwent changes of nomenclature, which helped its assimilation with certain theological doctrines, but the basic principles remained the same, and it was the *Ecclesia* which now became the *fiscus Christi*. As Augustine had remarked, there can be no Christian society where Christ does not have his fisc: 'Si non habet rem suam publicam Christus, non habet fiscum suum', and elsewhere he equated the treasury of the Christianised Roman *respublica* with what he succinctly termed 'the Truth'.[1] This points to a most important development of the theory: the legal personality of the society is now identified as Christ himself, the head and mystical person of the *Ecclesia*. All the goods and possessions of the Christian society have their ownership vested in Christ—'Christus proprie habet domin-

latur humano corpori, sicut ipse Philosophus tradit et hoc idem in *Policrato* [John of Salisbury, *Policraticus*, v. 2] scribitur, unde comparatur ibidem commune aerarium regis stomacho, ut sicut stomacho recipiuntur cibi et diffunduntur ad membra, ita et aerarium regis repletur thesauro pecuniarum et communicatur atque diffunditur pro necessitatibus subditorum et regni'. For a very detailed account of the fisc theory in medieval Roman law see *KTB*, pp. 164–92. This should however be used with caution inasmuch as Kantorowicz does not distinguish between the 'absolute' version of the theory referred to here, and the dualistic version summed up in the maxim 'Quod non capit Christus, rapit fiscus' (cf. Gratian, C. 16 q. 7 c. 8), which implies a division of jurisdiction between the episcopacy (*Christus*) and the lay ruler (*fiscus*).

[1] Augustine, *Enarrationes in Psalmos*, cxlvi. 17 (*PL*, xxxvii. 1911); *De civitate Dei*, v. 16 (*PL*, xli. 160), 'Civitas [Dei] . . . ubi thesaurus communis est veritas. Proinde . . . Romanum imperium ad humanam gloriam dilatatum est'. Note also his description of Christ as the guardian of the great celestial bank (*horreum*); to which all earthly wealth should be entrusted, *Enarrationes in Psalmos*, xxxviii. 12 (*PL*, xxxvi. 423–4). Cf. Aristotle, *Politics*, iii. 3.

ium rerum Ecclesiae'[1]—and are distributed to the members as signs of divine grace. Ownership in the full sense of the term belongs only to Christ, the common or universal personality of the whole corporation, and in this way the divine-natural community of property described in the Biblical account of the primitive Christian community at Jerusalem,[2] and subsequently advocated as a necessity for the whole Church by the Fathers,[3] is preserved. Correspondingly the members of the community have no fundamental rights of ownership but are merely administrators or users of the divine gifts, and, it may be added, being devoid of true property rights, are properly described as the *paupertates Christi*.[4] Following up the patristic distinction between the heavenly and earthly *beneficia* deriving from God's grace,[5] the fourteenth-century publicists were able to speak of the double treasury of Christ, personal and mystical, or, in the words of John XXII, who cited Augustine as his

[1] Johannes Andreae, *ad Decretales*, II. xii. 4; *ad Sext.*, III. ix n. 7, 'Ecclesia, id est congregatio fidelium, cuius Christus est caput, habet dominium'. Innocent IV, *App. ad Decretales*, II. xii. 4, makes this very explicit: 'De hac materia potest notari quod non praelatus sed Christus dominium rerum Ecclesiae habet . . . vel Ecclesia habet possessionem et proprietatem . . . id est, aggregatio fidelium quae est corpus Christi capitis . . . dicimus quod quantumcunque moriatur praelatus et omnes clerici Ecclesiae, tamen proprietas et possessio remanet apud Christum qui vivit in aeternum vel penes universalem vel singularem Ecclesiam quae numquam moritur nec est unquam nulla'.

[2] *Acts*, ii. 44–5; iv. 32–7: particular emphasis is laid upon the fact that the multitude, whose members possessed nothing of their own, is described here as a single being, one heart and soul.

[3] Carlyle, *History of Medieval Political Theory in the West*, especially i. 132–8. Many of the patristic sources urging the need for communal ownership in a Christian society were quoted by Gratian: for details N. Cohn, *The Pursuit of the Millenium* (London, 1957), pp. 195–208; and now B. Tierney, *Medieval Poor Law: A Sketch of Canonical Theory and its Application in England* (Berkeley and Los Angeles, 1959), pp. 26–39.

[4] Note the use of this description by Innocent III, *Reg.*, I. ccclv (*PL*, ccxiv. 329). This follows the Biblical definition of the poor as all those who receive the Gospel and inherit God's kingdom on earth: *Matthew*, ii. 5; v. 3–5; *Luke*, vi. 20; *James*, ii. 5. In 1111 Pascal II had announced the poverty of the whole Church.

[5] E.g. Leo I, *Sermo X* (*PL*, liv. 164), 'Non solum enim spirituales opes et dona coelestia Deo donante capiuntur, sed etiam terrenae et corporeae facultates ex ipsius largitate proveniunt, ut merito rationem eorum quaesiturus sit, quae non magis possidenda tradidit, quam dispensanda commisit. Muneribus igitur Dei iuste et sapienter utendum est'.

authority, of the two *loculi Christi*,[1] whose wealth is distributed through the medium of the *Ecclesia*. The material resources of the community form the corporeal treasury, the earthly counterpart of Christ's spiritual treasury of sacramental grace.[2] Private possession by individual members of the society is not altogether denied, but is to be classified as stewardship rather than ownership, and is held by grace—or, in practice, according to the positive rulings of ecclesiastical law through which divine grace is transmitted to the faithful. Private possession, we may say, is established by law, but is in no sense a right inherent in the subject. In short, it is dependent upon the sovereign will of the legislator: whilst effective public ownership and control of the *thesaurus Ecclesiae* passes, as Augustinus Triumphus points out, into the hands of the pope, who is the human representment of Christ and the physical embodiment of the mystical, juridical *persona Ecclesiae:*

> ... dispensare thesaurum corporalem totius communitatis non pertinet nisi ad illum qui praeest toti communitati.[3]

[1] John XXII, *Extravagantes Ioannis XXII*, xiv. 5 (Venice, 1567), pp. 115–16, 'Et si quaeratur, propter quos infirmos istos loculos habuerit? Augustinus, cuius dictum insertum est in decretis [Gratian, C. 12 q. 1 c. 16], respondet dicens, Habebat Dominus loculos, a fidelibus oblata conservans, et suorum necessitatibus et aliis indigentibus tribuebat. Unde constat ipsum de suis discipulis hoc sensisse. Nec hoc, scilicet in communi et quo ad proprietatem aliqua habere, derogat'. Cf. Augustine, *Enarrationes in Psalmos*, cxlvi. 17 (*PL*, xxxvii. 1911), 'fiscus saccus est publicus. Ipsum habebat Dominus hic in terra quando loculus habebat; et ipsi loculi Iudae erant commissi'. The origin of this comparison of society to a purse may perhaps be traced back to the Cynic view that a man needed no State beyond the traveller's haversack, which gave him citizenship of the whole world: e.g. Crates, 'The wallet is a *polis*', *Fragmenta Philosophorum Graecorum*, ii. 295–341.

[2] The idea that indulgences are granted out of the spiritual treasury of sacramental grace is a familiar theological doctrine: this also is administered by the pope: Augustinus Triumphus, *Summa*, xxix. 1, p. 175, 'sic dispensare thesaurum spiritualem Ecclesiae pertinet ad illum qui praeest toti Ecclesiae'; cf. Aegidius Romanus, *De ecclesiastica potestate*, iii. 12, p. 208. See further E. Magnin, 'Indulgences', *DTC*, vii. 1594–1636; P. Galtier, 'Indulgences', *Dictionnaire Apologétique de la Foi Catholique* (Paris, 1924), ii. 718–52; and N. Paulus, *Geschichte des Ablasses im Mittelalter* (Paderborn, 1922–3), which deals with Augustinus Triumphus' theory of the spiritual treasury (*Quaestiones* xxix–xxxiv) at i. 363–71; ii. 30–1.

[3] Augustinus Triumphus, *Summa*, xxix. 1, p. 175; cf. xxx. 5, p. 185. See also Peter de la Palu, *De causa immediata ecclesiasticae potestatis*, i. 3, fo. 25,

From this is evolved the principle that the allocation of the financial resources of the *Ecclesia* is an act of papal grace, and the lay ruler who receives permission from the pope to collect taxes from his subjects is being paid for his services to the community out of the material *thesaurus Ecclesiae*.

Sunt reges et imperatores quasi ministri et stipendiarii ipsius papae et ipsius Ecclesiae, et per eum stipendiandi sunt thesauro corporali ipsius Ecclesiae pro pace et defensione eius secundum ipsius taxationem.[1]

Society governs itself by distributing its wealth, by way of the pope, to the officers who maintain it, protect it and administer it. The money or goods so received are not of course purely or primarily for the personal benefit of the ruler, although they may be used to uphold him in his proper state. But they are to enable him to exercise his office according to the requirements of the community. In this way the appointment of any official must react upon the distribution of wealth in the *Ecclesia*. Hence there is an extremely close link between the structure of offices in the corporation and the manipulation of its wealth, and accordingly some of the publicists speak as though the allocation of functions itself is an exercise of the papal guardianship of the treasury.[2] This gives the theory a wider application to the whole system of government in

'Tertio conclusio principalis est quod Petrus a Christo habuit plenitudinem potestatis quia . . . Christus super omnes thesauros regni coelorum, quae est Ecclesia iustorum, voluit esse unum universalem thesaurarium, qui haberet plenam dispensationem totius thesauri'.

[1] Augustinus Triumphus, *Summa*, i. 8 ad 1, pp. 12–13, where it is also explained that 'Imperatoribus autem et regibus reddenda sunt temporalia quasi pro stipendiis ipsorum, quia ministri Dei sunt, ut dicit Apostolus [*Romans*, xiii. 4]. Tenentur enim Ecclesiam Dei defendere et christianum populum gubernare et rempublicam in pace conservare, pro quo ministerio stipendiandi sunt thesauro Ecclesiae corporali, quia quodam iure naturae et divino pro tale ministerio debetur eis tale stipendium temporale'. This he interprets as the significance of 'Render unto Caesar', but adds a warning that the grant of *temporalia* to the emperor is not indicative of papal inferiority. This theory has a close connection with the later idea that God is the best paymaster.

[2] Alvarus Pelagius, *De planctu Ecclesiae*, ch. 54, p. 137, 'Hic [papa] est dispensator summus . . . et universalis ministeriorum Dei et thesaurorum Christi et Ecclesiae distributor et dignitatum et officiorum beneficiorumque ecclesiasticorum omnium'; cf. Conrad of Megenberg, *Oeconomica*, III. iii. 1 (Pelzer-Kaeppeli, p. 586), 'papa . . . thezaurarius Christi'.

the *Ecclesia*, and serves to emphasise that the current disputes over taxation only too frequently masked stages in the battle for sovereignty between the papacy and the lay princes. As the conflict between Philip the Fair and Boniface VIII demonstrated, there were much graver issues at stake than the right of the king to tax his clerical subjects. Nothing less than the whole nature of lay government in a Christian society was in question. Is the king or the emperor an independent ruler, acting entirely in his own right, or is he nothing more than a papal official, bound hand and foot to the imperial will of the vicar of Christ? For Augustinus Triumphus, as we might expect, there is only one answer: in the last resort the hierocratic theory reduces the lay ruler to a mere *instrumentum papae*, the very purpose of whose existence is the implementation of papal government.[1] This was however a position which none of the European monarchs of the fourteenth century was prepared to accept for a moment longer than political circumstances made necessary. And it was on the bedrock of lay intransigence that the ship of Peter eventually foundered.

[1] Augustinus Triumphus, *Summa*, xxxv. 1, p. 206, 'imperator est minister papae eo ipso quod papa est minister Dei, *Rom.*, xiii [4]. Deputavit enim Deus imperatorem tamquam ministrum summi sacerdotis... Est autem principaliter agentis eligere ministros et instrumenta ad suum finem . . . unde puto quod papa . . . possit imperatorem eligere'; xl. 3, p. 232, 'Est enim ipse imperator minister eius mediante quo [papa] administrat temporalia'.

II. PRINCELY LIBERTY AND THE 'VOX POPULI'

ONE great feature of the papal-hierocratic thesis was that it left its adherents in no doubt as to the immediate divine origin of political authority: the words of St. Matthew were in their eyes incontrovertible evidence on that point. But their opponents were unhappily torn between two ideals. They proclaimed that the king was the real repository of God's power on earth, and their assertions in this respect were daily reaching more frenzied heights. At the same time they were desperately eager to counteract the papal argument that if the lay ruler received power from God, then he could only have done so through the agency of God's vicegerent. And it was slowly borne in upon them that the only sure way of denying the papal claims was to stipulate the existence of an alternative source of power in the community at large. Consequently, whereas the papalist could afford to ignore the more republican aspects of Roman law teaching, the lay writers tended to give them greater attention. A case in point was *Institutes*, I. ii. 6. This indeed announced that the will of the prince had the force of law, but it added that this was possible only because the people had transferred their authority to him. Provided that this initial grant could be seen as an historical event with no further political importance, the idea of it seemed to offer the lay ruler a means of escape from papal control. The crucial point therefore was the question of whether the grant had in fact been irrevocable, or whether the Roman people or their 'representatives' still possessed the right to make law and, if necessary, retract the ruler's commission to govern. And although the emperors in the thirteenth and fourteenth centuries gave official recognition to an emasculated version of the *lex regia* theory, they did so with this vital matter still finally undecided. At first the debate had seemed to be a purely academic one. The right of the *Romani* to depose their ruler was acknowledged by several writers,[1] but it was not elaborated into a system, and the emphasis remained upon the absolute nature of Roman emperorship. Even in the mid-fourteenth century the great civilians remained opposed to the idea that the people could take the law into their own hands.[2] But by this time it would probably be true to say that they represented a minority opinion, particularly after Aquinas had lent weight to the opposing view by remarking that where the ruler derived his power from some initial popular grant, the right of the *populus* to depose a tyrant held good even when that initial grant was made perpetually irrevocable: 'etiam si eidem in perpetua se ante subiecerat'.[3] The situation had in fact been completely changed by the influx of Aristotelian ideas, which proved a powerful agent in refocusing attention upon the *lex regia* conception of authority. The thirteenth century saw the growth of a considerable reaction to absolutism, and one of the most striking features of our period is the emergence of a group of writers, Roman lawyers and publicists, who used the similarities between Aristotle and Roman law to

[1] E.g. Odofridus, *Comm. in Dig.*, I. iii. 32, 'Nam populus bene potest hodie legem condere sicut olim poterat. . . Item non obstat quod alibi dicitur quod populus omne imperium legis condere transtulit in principem . . . quia intelligo transtulit, i. concessit, non tamen a se abdicando'. The same position had previously been taken up by Hugolinus and Azo, and was adopted by Bulgarus and Martin Silimani, but practically the only writer prior to them to adopt this view was Manegold of Lautenbach, whose work has however the character of an isolated phenomenon.

[2] Bartolus, *Comm. in Cod.*, I. xiv. 11, 'Cum enim nihil sit de imperio remanserit eis [scil. populis], non video quod possint legem condere'; Baldus, *Comm. in Cod.*, I. xiv. 12, 'Quaeritur utrum hodie populus Romanus possit legem facere, dicendum est quod non'. This follows Irnerius, Placentinus and Guilielmus de Cuneo: on the other side Jacobus Butrigarius, Cynus and Jacobus de Arena. For a fuller discussion see Gierke-Maitland, *Political Theories of the Middle Age*, pp. 39–45; A. J. Carlyle, 'The Theory of the Source of Political Authority in the Medieval Civilians to the time of Accursius', *Mélanges Fitting*, i (Montpellier, 1906); R. W. and A. J. Carlyle, *A History of Medieval Political Theory in the West* (London, 1903–36), v. 64–7; vi. 13–22; Woolf, *Bartolus of Sassoferrato*, pp. 36–40; Ullmann, *Medieval Idea of Law*, pp. 48–9, 179. The debate was continued throughout the fifteenth century, but it is noticeable that the bulk of opinion is in favour of some form of revocation: Carlyle, *op. cit.*, vi. 145–56.

[3] Thomas Aquinas, *De regimine principum*, i. 6, p. 230. His subjects may break their contract of obedience just as the ruler has broken faith by failing to give good government: see above p. 136 n. 1.

justify a conception of the ruler as a mere delegate of the popular will, who could always in the long run be held responsible to it.

This idea of the ruler as the executive of the will of the people means that he is *lex animata* only in the sense that he activates the general principles of government authorised by the human legislator. It was an attitude most trenchantly expressed in the *Defensor pacis*, and although Masilius of Padua was one of the greatest of the medieval Aristotelians, it should be emphasised that his theory of government was basically only an elaboration of the *lex regia* idea. We have already had occasion to point out that Marsilius was thinking specifically of the Roman empire and the relationship between the emperor and the Roman people. The initial grant of authority by the people to the *pars principans* is revocable and the *legislator humanus*, as the name implies, retains the right to make law, even though in practice most of the administrative work of government falls into the hands of the prince.[1] However Marsilius was far from being alone in his adaptation of the Roman law idea as the answer to the hierocratic system, although it must be acknowledged that most of the other writers in this group made some attempt to come to terms with the papal theory. The early commentators on Aristotle's *Politics* were in fact the first to draw attention to the resemblance between Aristotelian 'democracy' and the *lex regia* text, and these combined authorities speedily led them to the conclusion that the equality of all men was a prime principle of natural justice.[2] All men therefore, said Durandus of S. Porciano, have a natural right to act as emperor, and must be considered as the source of the ruler's power.[3] Even if hereditary succession is the custom, the first ruler

[1] Marsilius of Padua, *Defensor minor*, xii. 1, p. 35, 'Romanus populus auctoritatem habuit et habet ferendi leges super universas mundi provincias; et si populus hic auctoritatem leges ferendi in suum principem transtulit . . . per Romanum populum ab eius principe fuerit revocata'.

[2] See C. Martin, 'Some Medieval Commentaries', pp. 39–40 for a discussion of the views of Peter of Auvergne, Walter Burley and in particular Albertus Magnus.

[3] For Durandus see above, p. 135 n. 3. For a discussion of Durandus' emphasis on the natural self-sufficiency of man see Leff, *Bradwardine*, pp. 165f. Cf. Hervaeus Natalis, *De potestate papae*, fo. 142, where he denies that any king is an 'explicit' vicar of Christ, because he has not been specifically appointed by God. But he adds that 'implicitly' any king is a vicar of God simply because he pos-

must have been elected, and the continued use of this principle requires popular sanction.[1] The prince may be head of the body politic, says the Pseudo-Thomas, but let him remember that it is the body which carries the head. If he forgets this he may find himself deprived of the power and right to rule.

Et si caput corpore humano sit altius, corpus tamen est maius; corpus regitur a capite, sed caput portatur a corpore: non minus indiget caput corpore quam corpus capite: caput habet a corpore quod sit in alto, corpore subiecto, quod quantum in se est esset in [altero]. Sic princeps a subditis habet potestatem et quod in alto sit; et cum eos despicit, aliquando potestatem et altitudinem suam amittit.[2]

For Ockham too the grant of authority made in the basically popular election of the emperor can always be revoked in the last resort on the grounds of public expediency: those who elect, he argues, can surely depose.[3] And although Ockham would permit the pope

sesses natural human reason: 'Possunt tamen principes dici vicarii Dei implicite in quantum Deus dedit naturae humanae rationem naturalem, per quam possit iudicare bonum esse aliquam potestatem in republica quam praeest'.

[1] Durandus de S. Porciano, *De iurisdictione ecclesiastica*, i. 1, ff. 1–2; John of Paris, *De potestate regia et papali*, ch. 10, p. 199, 'Ergo potestas regia nec secundum se nec quantum ad executionem est a papa, sed a Deo et a populo regem eligente in persona vel in domo', although he adds that in the Empire each emperor must be elected individually, ch. 19, p. 234, 'imperatores . . . in imperio non succedunt ut haeredes sed ab exercitu et populo rite eliguntur'.

[2] Pseudo-Thomas, *De eruditione principum*, i. 6, p. 397. This writer has been identified as William Perrault by L. K. Born, 'The Perfect Prince', *Speculum*, iii (1928), pp. 470–504 at p. 484; but see the discussion in W. Berges, *Die Fürstenspiegel des hohen und späten Mittelalters* (Leipzig, 1938), pp. 185–95, 308–13.

[3] William of Ockham, *Octo quaestiones*, ii. 8, p. 84, 'correctio imperatoris spectat ad Romanos'; and see the statement of popular election and deposition in the *Dialogus*, III. II. i. 8 and 29–31, 'Facilius sit populo emendere unum rectorem si taliter exorbitaverit ut sit puniendus vel amovendus quam plures'. Cf. also the *Tractatus pro rege Angliae*, ch. 4, p. 243, where the power of kings and 'aliae principales' is said to be 'a Deo non per auctoritatem papalem sed per auctoritatem hominum. . . Unde regalis potestas non est a papa sed est a Deo mediante populo, qui accepit potestatem a Deo praeficiendi sibi regem propter bonum commune'. See also Lupold of Bebenburg, *De iure regni Romani*, ch. 5, p. 352, 'Quod facere poterant de iure gentium, ex quo iure etiam regna condita sunt, scilicet, quod quilibet populus potest sibi regem eligere'; Anon., *De legibus*, ff. 13v–14, 'Translatio potestatis translatae in imperatorem est revocabilis ex una causa. Nam secundum quod dictum est, fundamentum eius est *expedientia publica*, et ergo statim quod cessaret expedientia posset revocari'.

certain rights over the emperor, even the right of deposition, he points out that the Roman people as the real source of power must be allowed to revoke and exercise all their original faculties.[1] Accordingly the right of any *populus* to determine its own form of government is now enshrined as a principle of the law of nations, 'natural law in the third sense', that rational system which men have universally inferred from the actual facts of life.[2]

The right of the members of the society to act in the creation and correction of the ruler with Marsilius of Padua is seen to be essentially that of a corporate group rather than the natural right of each man to share in determining his own government. The arguments which he employs to demonstrate the superiority of the collective mind and the superior force of the collective will are convincing only if they are used, as Aristotle originally used them, to support the active participation of the whole community in government.[3] But when that community is thought to be a universal empire, the idea as it stands is a patent absurdity. Admittedly from time to time minority groups within the Empire had declared that the whole Roman people had the right to elect the emperor. We may cite the example of the North Italian cities, especially Pisa, in 1256. To strengthen the position of Alphonso X they rejected the election of the German princes on the ground that this electoral power was derived from the whole Roman people, all of whom could therefore participate in the imperial election if they so wished. The same idea was also developed in the Swiss cities: in 1291 Berne declared that the imperial election was invalid until the citizens had approved of the candidate. The view also appears that the emperor has no authority over a city until he has personally visited it to receive the acclamation of the inhabitants, again a feeling particularly strong in the Italian communes, and possibly the source of Dante's theory that the emperor only gains imperial authority with his entry into Italy.[4] But all this was simply an attempt by the cities to gain for

[1] William of Ockham, *Octo quaestiones*, ii. 4–5, pp. 75–8; v. 6, pp. 161–3.

[2] William of Ockham, *Dialogus*, III. II. iii. 6, pp. 393–5.

[3] G. de Lagarde, *La naissance de l'esprit laïque*, ii. 164–94.

[4] C. C. Bayley, *The Formation of the German College of Electors in the Mid-Thirteenth Century* (Toronto, 1949), pp. 162, 208–9.

themselves some say in the imperial election and need not be taken too seriously. And although the author of the anonymous part of the *Determinatio compendiosa* mentions the existence of a theory, which he attributes to Michael of Cesena, that the emperor can be crowned not only by the pope 'sed etiam quocunque puro catholico',[1] most of the lay writers felt that in some way or other the power to act *vice omnium* had passed, or had always been, in the hands of either the German princes or the citizens of Rome itself. With Ockham and Marsilius, eager to bolster up the shaky claims of Louis IV to the imperial crown, and with the Bavarian himself, both alternatives are employed: the coronation of the *Romani* is complementary to the election of the German magnates. In neither case is the papacy to be permitted any part in the creation of the emperor.

Although less common, the device of regarding the Roman people as having the right to dispose of the imperial crown could be more easily justified. It had long been accepted in medieval thought that since the Universal Church was at the same time the universal or Roman empire, all Christians could be described as the *Romani*. And this led further to the idea that the inhabitants of Rome itself, the centre of the Roman world, were representatives of all *Romani*, i.e. all Christians, everywhere.[2] Thus the 'geographical' *Romani* may be held to epitomise all the members of the Empire, and their creation of the Roman emperor is the same as if all Christians had been able to participate in that act. This tradition, handed down in the idea that it was the acclamation of the Romans which was the constitutive feature of the imperial coronation,[3] was always likely to be resurrected at some suitably auspicious moment. In the mid-twelfth century Arnold of Brescia had sent envoys to Freder-

[1] Anon., *Determinatio compendiosa*, ch. 40, p. 549.

[2] Ullmann, *The Growth of Papal Government*, pp. 61–6, 163, 216, 276; Davis, *Dante and the Idea of Rome*, pp. 1–3; and for the development of the same principle in Roman constitutional law, Wirszubski, *Libertas as a Political Idea*, pp. 70f.

[3] For the early history of this idea see Kantorowicz, *Laudes Regiae*, pp. 76–120. The idea was still current in the fourteenth century and is referred to by Augustinus Triumphus, *Summa*, xlvi. 3 *prop.* 1, p. 251; Anon., *Determinatio compendiosa*, ch. 40, p. 549.

ick I to inform him that the emperor was the creature and servant of Rome, and owed his throne to her. Two centuries later Cola di Rienzo was telling Charles IV much the same thing. Both Barbarossa and Charles could afford to heap scorn on the idea, and it was mainly those pretenders to the imperial dignity who had already incurred the unremitting hostility of the papacy who welcomed the idea. In a manifesto of 1265 the uncrowned and illegitimate Manfred called upon the Roman prefect and pro-consuls to ignore the pope and place the elected Caesar in the imperial see by crowning him at Rome. In this way alone, he proclaimed, can there be a restoration of the sacred empire, whose head and mother is the Roman city, and whose authority resides in the senate and people.[1] It was this programme which was given practical effect with the coronation of Louis IV 'by the Roman people' on 17 January 1328.[2] Whether or not Louis was consciously influenced by Marsilius of Padua's contention that the geographical *Romani* had been given the right to elect the emperor by the *legislator* of the universal *Romani* is a debatable point. But when the medieval emperor saw himself as the successor of the Caesars,[3] it would seem that the descendants of the original Romans had a natural right to appoint him. Moreover, Louis pointed out, Rome, by virtue of its apostolicity, is the chosen city of Christ. Its inhabitants are a *gens electa*: they are the royal priesthood who stand for all priest-kings composing the

[1] *MGH, Const.*, II n. 424, pp. 559–65.

[2] See the encyclical issued by Castruccio Castrucani, 17 January 1328, which says that Louis and his empress 'per Romanum populum iuxta ritum antiquum in basilica beati Petri de Urbe cum miriffice venerationis et honorificentiae cultu imperiali sunt dyademate coronati': *MGH, Const.*, VI n. 383 p. 286. Chrism, symbolising the *rex-sacerdos* nature of the emperor, was used in the anointing: E. Dupré-Theseider, *Roma dal Comune di Populo alla Signoria Pontificia, 1252–1377* (Bologna, 1952), p. 467. It is interesting to notice that in January 1327, prior to the coronation of Edward III of England, Archbishop Reynolds preached on the text 'Vox populi, vox Dei'. The medal struck to commemorate the coronation bore the motto 'Populi dat iura voluntas': A. P. Stanley, *Historical Memorials of Westminster Abbey* (London, 1890), p. 57.

[3] William of Ockham, *Consultatio de causa matrimoniali*, p. 278; cf. Dante, *Ep.*, vii. 1, p. 89, 'tu, Caesaris et Augusti successor'; also Manfred, *loc. cit.*, p. 559, 'Nos itaque, os de osse ac caro de carne antiquissimae caesareae monarchiae'. This is reminiscent of Benzo of Alba's description of Henry IV and St. Bernard's characterisation of the papacy.

congregatio fidelium.[1] Rome therefore is the mother and root of empire, the nucleus of the Roman-Christian world,[2] and control of the city gives the emperor a universal dominion: in the words of Louis IV, 'Urbi et orbi Dei ac nostra potentia invincibili praesidemus'.[3]

Although the imperial coronation of 1328 represents the high water mark of the Roman idea of empire—indeed it is reported that Louis himself went far towards nullifying its effect by subsequently submitting to a second coronation by the anti-pope Nicholas V—it was within a few years to be expressly denied by another of Louis' ardent supporters, that very pro-German bishop, Lupold of Bamberg. According to Lupold the citizens of Rome have no more right to dispose of the empire than 'quicunque alius populus Romano imperio subiectus'. The expression *Romanus populus*, he urges, should not be understood as the 'populus urbis Romanae, sed totus populus Romano imperio subiectus'.[4] Later however he finds it necessary to qualify this, and the result is that for him the term comes in reality to have an even more specialised meaning, namely that of the German princes:

> Et sic intelligo populum Romani imperii connumeratis principibus electoribus ac etiam aliis principibus, comitibus et baronibus regni et imperii Romanorum. Nam appellatione populi continetur etiam patricii et senatores.[5]

[1] Baluze, iii. 426, 430: see above, p. 79 n. 2. Cf. *MGH, Const.*, VI n. 438 p. 362, 'ut sic populus electus et civitas sacerdotalis et imperialis'. So too Lucas da Penna called Rome the chosen city of Christ, 'sacerdotalis et regia, principatus omnium nationum et origo sanctitatis': Ullmann, *The Medieval Idea oj Law*, p. 75. This was in imitation of papal tactics: see Nicholas III's constitution *Fundamenta militantis Ecclesiae* of 1278, cited Dupré-Theseider, *op. cit.*, pp. 211–15.

[2] Louis IV, *MGH, Const.*, VI n. 438 p. 362, 'et Romanam praecipue urbem sacram quae antiquitus regum originem sortita est'; cf. Manfred, *MGH, Const.*, II n. 424 p. 563, 'Mater imperii urbs Roma . . . mundi caput . . . radix imperii'. For the idea of the emperor's 'marriage' to Rome with Dante and Petrarch see C. C. Bayley, 'Petrarch, Charles IV and the Renovatio Imperii', *Speculum*, xvii (1942), pp. 323–41 at p. 324.

[3] Baluze, iii. 426; cf. Ockham, *Allegationes de potestate imperiali*, p. 429, 'et hoc patet quia statim postquam electus est appellatur et vocatur rex Romanorum, et quia Roma est caput mundi, ideo cum statim ipse sit rex Romanorum per consequens est rex omnium membrorum, id est, totius orbis'.

[4] Lupold of Bebenburg, *De iure regni Romani*, ch. 12, p. 385.

[5] Lupold of Bebenburg, *De iure regni Romoni*, ch. 17, p. 406.

In his tract on the rights of the Roman empire Lupold declares that he is motivated by love for the *patria Germaniae*, and it is his aim to demonstrate the way in which the power of acting for the whole Roman world has passed into the hands of the German magnates alone. But whilst Lupold of Bebenburg is one of the first writers to emphasise the Germanic rather than the Roman nature of universal emperorship, his whole work is simply a restatement of the old imperial point of view which sought to explain how first the Franks, and then the Germans, had gained control of a universal empire. Since no one could doubt that the Roman empire had existed in the East until the time of Charlemagne, some form of the *translatio imperii* idea seemed inevitable. But several writers saw their way to using the translation theory in favour of the Germans, and at the same time linking it up with a view of the *Romani* as those having the right to dispose of the imperial crown. Accordingly they declared that the Roman empire had indeed been transferred to the Franks in 800, but that this had been done by the Roman people, not by the pope. Something of the sort had been hinted at by Jordan of Osnabruck; and with some of the French writers, notably John of Paris and Peter de la Palu, it is brought out as a statement of fact.[1] A few years later Ockham went beyond this and argued that the Roman people could still if necessary effect a further translation for the benefit of the general good.

> Illa translatio non fuit a papa sed a Romanis, quorum ab initio fuit imperium et a quibus imperator primo accepit imperium, quia omnem suam potestatem regendi propter bonum commune transtulerunt in imperatorem . . . nec a se abdicaverunt omnem potestatem casualiter disponendi de imperio.[2]

On the other hand, since it was fairly obvious, even in the four-

[1] Jordan of Osnabruck, *De praerogativa Romani imperii*, pp. 15–17; John of Paris, *De potestate regia et papali*, ch. 21, p. 244; Peter de la Palu, *De causa immediata ecclesiasticae potestatis*, iv. 2, fo. 48v, 'Nec est simile de translatione sedis imperialis cuius auctoritas est a populo Romano, qui ius suum et potestatem in imperatorem transtulit'. It has been pointed out by A. M. Stickler, 'Concerning the political theory of the medieval canonists', *Traditio*, vii (1949–51), pp. 450–63, that this idea is to be found with the French canonists c. 1180, and can be traced back to the ninth century.

[2] William of Ockham, *Octo quaestiones*, iv. 8, p. 152.

teenth century, that the pope had been the principal actor in the events of 800, a further refinement of this theory attempted to explain that it was after all the pope who had transferred the empire but that he had acted 'auctoritate et vice Romanorum'. The true act of transfer was the *consensus populi*, which the chronicles mentioned on the occasion of Charles' coronation; Leo III had merely declared and executed the will of the people; and in any case the whole coronation was an isolated event without further political significance.[1] But for the majority of the imperial writers this put far too much emphasis on the role of the pope and the Roman people. The German magnates favoured a much more romantic idea, which, being wildly unhistorical, had the advantage of not having to be subjected to any tests of accuracy. Picturing themselves as the descendants of Aeneas and his followers, they declared that not only the Romans, but equally the Franks and the Germans, were derived from the Trojans dispersed after the fall of Troy. It was pure invention, but was taken nonetheless seriously, and its plausibility enhanced by various apocryphal journals of the siege of Troy. Consequently Romans, Franks and Germans were all held to be one and the same people, and the Empire could be said to have passed naturally from one to the other in rotation.[2] This also had the

[1] William of Ockham, *Tractatus contra Benedictum XII*, vi. 13, p. 295, 'Dicitur ergo uno modo quod papa non transtulit dominium imperii de Graecis in Germanos auctoritate sibi data in Petro a Christo sed auctoritate Romanorum'; *Quoniam scriptura*, p. 77, 'Si autem dicatur quod papa transtulit Romanum imperium a Graecis in Germanos . . . respondetur quod nunquam papa ratione papatus vel alicuius auctoritatis vel potestatis sibi datae a Christo transtulit imperium vel quomodolibet de imperio ordinavit. . . Sic quicquid papa unquam fecit circa Romanum imperium auctoritate fecit illorum qui potestatem habuerunt de imperio disponendi et illam potestatem aliis committendi'; cf. Ugolinus de Celle's contention that no inferences can be drawn from the unique act of 800, *De electione regis Romanorum*, ch. 17, p. 78.

[2] Alexander of Roes, *De translatione imperii*, pp. 20–6; *Notitia saeculi*, p. 666; Jordan of Osnabruck, *De praerogativa Romani imperii*, p. 16; Lupold of Bebenburg, *De iure regni Romani*, ch. 1, p. 333; ch. 3, pp. 340–6; *De zelo catholicae fidei*, ch. 1, p. 412; cf. Marsilius of Padua, *De translatione imperii*, ch. 1, p. 148. A French version is in the *Quaestio in utramque partem*: see Leclercq, 'Un sermon prononcé pendant la guerre de Flandre', p. 170. The idea is in fact of Merovingian origin, but seems to have been popularised by Godfrey of Viterbo, who argued that the Germans descended on both sides from Priam, but the Romans on one side only. By the fifteenth century practically all the European nations,

merit of identifying Franks and Germans, which avoided the necessity for dealing with another translation from the Carolingians to the Saxons, and allowed every emperor to think of himself as a new Charlemagne.[1]

However much this theory owed to the idea of the ultimate right of all Roman Christians to appoint their own ruler, none of its adherents ever really conceived of popular action in the Aristotelian or modern sense. Even in the *Defensor pacis* it is not the Roman people (*legislator humanus*) which controls the prince, but only its *valentior pars*, which is a very different matter.[2] The *valentior pars*, says Marsilius, must be defined as that part which involves a consideration of both quantity and quality ('considerata quantitate personarum et qualitate'). These values are to be understood comparatively (*comparative*), and the single numerical quantity (*pluralitas*) appropriate to the mass of the citizens (*multitudo*) cannot apply here. On these lines *maioritas* will have a special interpretation of its own, and we may conclude that the greater the importance of the members of the *valentior pars*, the fewer they will need to be in number. Other factors support this assumption. Both the expression and its definition are, as Marsilius acknowledges, taken straight

as well as the Italian city-states, were boasting of their Trojan origin: A. Graf, *Roma nella memoria e nelle immaginazione del medio evo* (Turin, 1923), pp. 17–23; J. Seznec, *The Survival of the Pagan Gods* (New York, 1953), pp. 19–25.

[1] This was an idea which spread far outside the circle of imperial writers, and was lent support by Innocent III's loose wording in *Decretales*, I. vi. 34: e.g. Tholemy of Lucca, *De regimine principum*, iii. 20, p. 268, 'primus imperator Germanus Carolus Magnus'; cf. *Determinatio compendiosa*, ch. 13, p. 30. See also Alexander of Roes, *Notitia saeculi*, pp. 667, 672; Conrad of Megenberg, *De translatione Romani imperii*, ch. 5, pp. 260–1; Henry of Cremona, *De potestate papae*, pp. 465–6; Landulfus de Colonna, *De statu Romani imperii*, ch. 3, p. 91; ch. 6, p. 92; Lupold of Bebenburg, *De iure regni Romani*, ch. 7, pp. 360–1. For the idea of Charlemagne in medieval thought, see R. Folz, *Le souvenir et la légende de Charlemagne dans l'Empire germanique médiéval* (Paris, 1950).

[2] Although the citizens of Rome have the right to act on behalf of all in promulgating laws and electing the emperor, Marsilius does not seem to accept their identity with the *valentior pars*, but suggests that it is the latter which empowers them to act: *Defensor minor*, xii. 1, p. 35, 'Haec potestas sive auctoritas per universitatem provinciarum aut ipsorum valentiorem partem translata fuit in Romanum populum'. The imperial dukedoms were often regarded as the *propinquiores provinciae* of the empire as against the more distant *provinciae* of the other kingdoms.

from Aristotle's *Politics*[1]—Aristotle's 'prevalent part' being translated as *pars valentior* by William of Moerbecke, although Dante's term *praevalentes* is probably a better rendering. Aristotle had discussed whether quantity or quality was the better index of stability in the government of the community, and had quite definitely expressed his preference for the supremacy of a group compounded of both elements, which he refers to as a 'middle class'. There is every reason to suppose that Marsilius held the same opinion. But what Aristotle meant by a 'middle class' has not necessarily the same connotation as that which the phrase conveyed to Marsilius, or for that matter Dante or Ockham. Aristotle had thought in terms of a society which was little more than a city-state: his middle class stood in between the mass of the citizenry and the small numbers of the aristocratic oligarchy which governed it. But, as we have seen, Marsilius and the others were clearly thinking in terms of the universal Roman empire, and *in this context* the 'middle class' can refer only to those magnates who stand between the bulk of the population and the governing oligarchy of medieval society, the emperor and the other kings. Thus, although Marsilius still permits the whole community a consenting function,[2] it is the qualitative element which in fact tends to predominate, and the magnates who become the real power in the community. And when Marsilius adds that the nature of the *valentior pars* follows the honest custom of political societies,[3] we may reflect that, in the conditions prevailing in the fourteenth century, the magnates were indeed grasping the reins of power in most contemporary monarchies and, furthermore, were claiming to do so by customary right. This is certainly true of the Empire itself, whose situation Marsilius was most familiar with, and where the princes were already well on the way to establishing their ascendancy over the emperor. Consequently it seems that what Marsilius has in mind is simply the magnates, indeed in particular the seven electoral princes, who are unlikely to err[4] since they act by virtue of the authority of the human legislator

[1] Marsilius of Padua, *Defensor pacis*, I. xii. 3, p. 63, citing Aristotle's *Politics*, iv. 12; I. xii. 4, p. 65, citing *Politics*, vi. 3; I. xiv. 8, p. 93, citing *Politics*, iii. 15.

[2] Marsilius of Padua, *Defensor pacis*, I. viii. 3, pp. 37–8.

[3] Marsilius of Padua, *Defensor pacis*, I. xii. 4, pp. 64–5.

[4] Marsilius of Padua, *Defensor pacis*, II. xxvi. 9, p. 496, 'tres solempnes archie-

itself.[1] And in this respect Marsilius comes firmly into line with contemporary opinion.

This theory of government then, for all its suggestion of popular sovereignty, is thoroughly aristocratic: when the fourteenth century writer spoke of the *populus* he was thinking only of its *sanior pars*, the princes and magnates, who were held to represent the whole community.[2] Just as the election of the old Roman emperors had frequently been carried out by the army or the senate, so the election of the emperor was now to be carried out by their medieval equivalent, the German princes.[3] This becomes plainer when we appreciate that in the fourteenth century the prince-electors were held to comprise a corporation and were not simply a

piscopi christiani et quatuor fideles principes saeculares . . . Hos autem septem non est verisimile sic errare aut intentione perversa moveri . . .'; and note his remarks in favour of the few as the real legislators rather than the 'indocti et rudes' of the *communitas civium*, I. xiii. 1–8, pp. 69–77.

[1] Marsilius of Padua, *Defensor pacis*, II. xxvi. 5, p. 492, 'quibus idem legislator talem auctoritatem concesserit'; cf. III. ii. 10, p. 605. Note the implication in Dante that the seven electors are the *praevalentes*, *Monarchia*, iii. 14, p. 374; iii. 16, p. 376, who stand for the *communitas mortalium*. Cf. Lupold of Bebenburg, *De iure regni Romani*, ch. 5, p. 353, 'Et principes electores ratione iam dictae institutionis habent eligere regem seu imperatorem, repraesentantes in hoc omnes principes et populum Germaniae, Italiae et aliarum provinciarum et terrarum regni et imperii, quasi vice omnium eligendo'.

[2] Note the later scheme of Nicholas of Cues, *De concordantia catholica*, iii. 12 and 25, in which all the 'praesides et rectores' of the Empire are to govern on behalf of the 'totum imperium'. In 1380 Conrad of Gelnhausen described the members of a general council as the weightier part (*valentium aut potentium*) of the whole of Christianity: Martène et Durand, *Thesaurus novus anecdotorum*, ii. 1217–18.

[3] William of Ockham, *Allegationes de potestate imperiali*, p. 429, 'Et quod ille imperator qui eligitur ab electoribus imperii et verus et legitimus imperator et universalis dominus omnium temporalium: unde est in superius allegato XCIII *dist.* c. [24] *Legimus*, in textu dicitur, Exercitus facit imperatorem'. As Ockham says, the idea was well-known to the canonists: e.g. Johannes Teutonicus in the *glossa ordinaria* to this passage says that 'ex sola electione principum dico eum verum imperatorem antequam a papa confirmetur'. See also Anon., *Informatio de nullitate processuum papae*, p. 18; John of Paris, *De potestate regia et papali*, ch. 12, p. 222; Lupold of Bebenburg, *De iure regni Romani*, ch. 5, p. 353; Ugolinus de Celle, *De electione regis Romanorum*, ch. 1, p. 72. Louis of Bavaria is also reported to have used this by Conrad of Megenberg, *De translatione imperii*, ch. 23, pp. 322–7. The princes had claimed to be the heirs of the Roman senate during the thirteenth century, e.g. *MGH*, *Const.*, II n. 329 p. 440; and see Lupold of Bebenburg at p. 191 above.

body of individuals. This emerges from a discussion of the matter by Conrad of Megenberg. First he quotes the canonist Hostiensis as saying that the election of the emperor pertains to the princes as single people and not as a *collegium*: 'quod electio pertinet ad principes electores non tamquam ad collegium sed tamquam ad singulares personas'.[1] But against this he puts the opinion of Lupold of Bebenburg, who maintains that the princes have the right to elect in their corporate capacity, not as individuals, since they are acting 'vice et auctoritate universitatis principum et populi subiecti Romano imperio', who could themselves make the election if necessary. And it is Lupold's view that Conrad accepts: the electors form and function as a *universitas*, although in his view this corporate right stems from the pope rather than the Roman people. Also in this connection it may be noted that the increasing use of the majority principle to decide imperial elections was generally regarded by the lawyers as a mark of the electoral college's powers as a corporation.[2] To secure a majority of the votes was held to be legally equivalent to obtaining the unanimous consent of the whole *collegium*, unanimity in one form or another being felt to be necessary when the electors claimed to be guided in their choice by the Holy Spirit. It was on this basis that Louis IV described himself as having been elected *in concordia* in the disputed election of 1314; although Louis could not resist commenting that he would still have been the rightful emperor even if he had not secured a majority,[3] and it was not until Charles IV issued the Golden Bull of 1356 that the matter was settled and full imperial recognition was at last given to the right

[1] Conrad of Megenberg, *De translatione imperii*, ch. 15, pp. 301–2, referring to Hostiensis, *ad Decretales*, I. vi. 34, s.v. *Haec alternatio*.

[2] Gillet, *La personalité juridique en droit ecclésiastique*, pp. 74–5. For the development of the principle in the thirteenth century see Bayley, *The Formation of the German College of Electors*, p. 170. This is stressed by Lupold himself, *De iure regni Romani*, ch. 7, p. 358.

[3] Baluze, iii. 389, 'quia ille censetur in concordia electus ad imperium qui a maiore parte electorum, puta a quatuor, electus fuerit. Et tamen cum nos fuerimus non solum a maiore parte, immo a duabus partibus principum electorum electus. . .' Note the two parts argument suggestive of a papal election. For the details of this election see H. S. Offler, 'Empire and Papacy: the Last Struggle', *Transactions of the Royal Historical Society, Vth Series*, vi (1956), pp. 21–47 at pp. 28–31; H. S. Lucas, 'The Low Countries and the Disputed Imperial Election of 1314', *Speculum*, xxi (1946), pp. 72–114.

of the princes to act as a *communitas*.[1] In this way it is held that the corporate nature of the princes as representatives of the *Romani* mirrors the corporate nature of the whole society. They are not delegates of the members but an embodiment of the corporate will of the community. They do not act on behalf of the people in the sense of the mass of the subjects, although their benefit is presumed to follow, but on behalf of the *populus*, which every Roman lawyer knew to mean a corporation, a juridical entity distinct from the members who composed it. Thus, for example, Marsilius of Padua does not populate his Roman empire with individual *cives* but is careful to describe it as the *universitas civium*, the corporate body of citizens. The distinction is a fine one, but has far-reaching political consequences. The responsibility of the princes for their actions is to the abstract notion of the society rather than its individual members. Therefore the people themselves can claim no right to act of their own accord against the princes: they may act only as a *populus*, and a *populus* is represented by its magnates, who become responsible to virtually no one but themselves. The people can act only with and through the magnates, not against them. Similarly there is no need to view the princes as elected delegates of the people at large: they are not of the people but of the *populus*, and it is this corporate entity which provides them with their *raison d'être*. The *communitas imperii* therefore comes to mean nothing but the princes, forming an autonomous body which is the repository of all the rights and authority of the empire.[2] Thus the emperor becomes a nominee of the magnates, and is subject to their control. They create him and correspondingly they may, as Frederick II had admitted and the deposition of Adolf of Nassau in 1298 had demon-

[1] See the Golden Bull, *proem.*, p. 58: Altmann-Bernheim, *Ausgewählte Urkunden*, n. 38 pp. 56–85. The majority principle was stipulated at ch. 2. iv, p. 63, 'minor pars sequatur maiorem'; the princes were given practical autonomy within their own territories, with full rights of immunity (ch. 8, pp. 68–9; ch. 11, pp. 70–1); there was no appeal from their judgement (ch. 11, pp. 70–1); and it was high treason to plot or rebel against them.

[2] Note the corresponding development of the idea of the barons as the *communitas regni* in thirteenth-century England: e.g. the Twenty-five of Magna Carta, ch. 61, are equated with the *communa totius terrae*. The close link between Marsilius' *valentior pars* and the *communitas regni* has already been suggested by Ullmann, *Medieval Papalism*, p. 24 n. 4.

strated, deprive him of his power.[1] The *collegium* of the princes, acting as a court, has according to this theory in its fully developed form full power to correct and depose the emperor, even, according to the law books, to execute him. The president of the court was generally regarded as being the Count Palatine, and the basic right of the princes to dispose of the empire was shown by the view that its administration fell back into the hands of the Count Palatine during an imperial vacancy.[2] Total authority therefore comes to rest with an oligarchy acting as one man, and as far as the rest of the society is concerned there is little to choose between this and the traditional theory of absolutism. Princely liberty meant what it said: complete freedom of action for the princes and for nobody else, whilst popular movements come automatically under the heading of sedition and subversion.

[1] Frederick II, *MGH*, *Const.*, II n. 262 p. 365, 'nostrorum Germaniae principum, a quibus assumptio status et depressio nostra dependet'; cf. n. 116 p. 150, 'vocantibus nos principibus ex quorum electione nobis *corona imperii debebatur*'. On 23 June 1298, the prince electors had declared that Adolf of Nassau was *insufficiens*, *inutilis* and *indignus*, and that accordingly the princes, who had the 'regem in imperatorem postmodum promovendum ius et potestatem eligendi', had come together 'pro sanctae pacis reformatione, pro concordiae revocatione, pro reipublicae felici gubernatione, et pro totius regni salute' to deprive Adolf of his kingdom and absolve his subjects from obedience to him, Altmann-Bernheim, *Ausgewählte Urkunden*, n. 25 pp. 42–6. Similarly the Rhine electors declared Wenzel deposed in 1400 and elected the Count Palatine in his place. The principle of the electors' right to depose was vigorously contested by the papalists: e.g. Augustinus Triumphus, *Summa*, xlvi. 2 ad 1, p. 250; Peter de la Palu, *De causa immediata ecclesiasticae potestatis*, iv. 1, ff. 45–45v.

[2] The claim of the Count Palatine to decide a disputed imperial election appears in the *Sachsenspiegel*, *Landrecht*, iii. 52, and was voiced by the supporters of Richard of Cornwall, *MGH*, *Const.*, II n. 405 pp. 525–6, 'Et si . . . duo in discordia eligantur . . . ad praedictum comitem palatinum tamquam ad huius discordiae iudicem recursus habendus'. The view that by immemorable custom the 'ius administrandi iura imperii in partibus Alamanniae' devolves on the Count Palatine during an imperial vacancy appears in Anon., *Articuli de iuribus imperii*, ch. 7, p. 595; Anon., *Tractatus contra Iohannem XXII et Benedictum XII*, ch. 5, p. 602. By the Golden Bull the Count Palatine was permitted the right of administration *vacante imperio* in the south of the Empire, the Duke of Saxony in the north.

III. THE DEVELOPMENT OF LIMITED MONARCHY

ONE of the most remarkable features of fourteenth-century political thought is the regularity with which the publicists claim to have solved the eternal problem of the right relationship between pope and emperor, and to have done so in a manner which would prove acceptable to both parties. But before this could be done, an even more perplexing problem had faced the apostles of the *via media*. It has become clear that the papal and lay ideologies derived from two totally opposed conceptions of society and of the situation of ultimate authority within it. For the orthodox hierocrat the seat of power was the papacy, set up by God to govern the world and to act as the source from which all else flowed. For the lay writer it was useful, if not essential, to maintain that the original basis of authority was to be sought in the people. Consequently no adequate synthesis of the papal and lay points of view could be achieved unless the idea of power streaming from the head to the members could in some way be amalgamated with the reverse conception of power being delegated by the members to the head. This seemingly impossible task the publicists now set out to achieve, and it is this vitally important preliminary step in the construction of the synthesis that we must consider first.

The makers of the synthesis, who saw themselves as the followers of Thomas Aquinas, aimed to create an ideal constitution which could then be applied to the *Ecclesia-Imperium* on the grounds that this had *de iure* always been its rightful state, or to any other subsidiary community as required. Polemics could be avoided by discussing the matter as far as possible in abstract terms of the *communitas perfecta*. This was a thoroughly Aristotelian approach, and since Aristotle was in a large measure the means by which the synthesis was to be effected, the first move was to give the hierocratic and anti-hierocratic theories an Aristotelian classification. But whilst it was clearly appreciated that Aristotle had suggested various kinds of government in which any form of kingship was unnecessary,[1] the publicists were in the main so thoroughly imbued with the notion of monarchy that they never seriously considered any constitution which did not have a single ruler. In any case both the papal and the lay theories had a common assumption that there would be one head. Thus one after another the publicists pronounced themselves to be in favour of some sort of monarchy,[2] and restricted serious discussion of the matter to the type of kingship required. Here, using Aristotelian terminology, the hierocratic system is clearly seen to amount to a regal monarchy, in which the ruler draws his power from above, either from God direct (as in the case of the pope himself) or from the pope as vicar of God (in the case of any subordinate ruler). The king in this type of kingdom is, according to Tholemy of Lucca, a despot: he makes law for the whole society and is himself *legibus solutus*. Opposed to this is the politic kingship, in which the ruler derives his position and jurisdiction from the members of the community, and is therefore subject to them and the laws which they authorise. This type is exemplified by the *lex regia* theory of government.[3] Aegidius Romanus makes exactly the same distinction,

> Civitas autem quantum ad praesens spectat duplice regimine regi potest, politico scilicet et regali. Dicitur autem quis praeesse regali dominio cum praeest secundum arbitrium et secundum leges quas ipse instituit. Sed tunc praeest regimine politico cum non praeest secundum arbitrium

[1] Thomas Aquinas, *Summa theologica*, II. I. xcv. 4; *De regimine principum*, i. 1, p. 226; and in particular William of Ockham, *Dialogus*, III. I. ii. 8–17, 25, 30, pp. 796–803, 812–14, 818–19; III. II. i. 1–5, 9, 13, pp. 871–5, 877, 880; *Octo quaestiones*, iii. 3, 6–8, pp. 104–5, 111–13.

[2] Thomas Aquinas, *De regimine principum*, i. 5, p. 228, 'Magis igitur praeoptandum est unius regimen quam multorum;' *Summa theologica*, I. ciii. 3, 'Optima autem gubernatio est quae fit per unum'; William of Ockham, *Octo quaestiones*, iii. 5, p. 109, 'principatus regalis, quo una persona refulget, tam principatum aristocraticum quam politicum quorum utique praesident plures, superat et praeexcellit'. This attitude may be compared to later Stoic theory, which also emphasised the superiority of kingship as a form of government, but drew a sharp distinction between the king and the tyrant.

[3] Tholemy of Lucca, *De regimine principum*, ii. 5, p. 241; ii. 8–10, pp. 243–5; iii. 20, p. 268; iv. 1, p. 270.

nec secundum leges quas ipse instituit, sed secundum leges quas cives instituerunt.[1]

and there is an almost inexhaustible number of similar passages to be found in the work of other publicists. Throughout their manner remains impeccably polite. No favouritism is to be shown. One has just as much right to rule by virtue of the consent of the multitude, says James of Viterbo, as one has by divine institution.[2] But since the Thomists are determined to combine these two types, to marry the idea of power from God downwards to that of power from the people upwards, it also becomes necessary for them to assert the existence of a third type, the *dominium regale et politicum*, which preserves the main features of both. This 'mixed monarchy' is now declared to be the correct disposition of the universal community.[3] Here, at least, Aquinas had given a firm lead. On more than one occasion he had expressed himself in favour of a constitution which was a judicious admixture of monarchy, aristocracy and democracy. There should be one supremely virtuous ruler, but all were to participate in government: the virtuous monarchy was to be supported by an equally virtuous aristocracy, whilst the power of the people was to be demonstrated by their right to elect as ruler one out of themselves, with his attendant subordinate governors.

[1] Aegidius Romanus, *De regimine principum*, II. i. 14; also Alvarus Pelagius, *De planctu Ecclesiae*, ch. 62, pp. 191–2; Durandus de S. Porciano, *De iurisdictione ecclesiastica*, ch. 1, ff. 1v–2; Francis de Meyronnes, *Quaestio de subiectione*, ii. 2, p. 88; Hervaeus Natalis, *De potestate papae*, fo. 139v; William of Ockham, *Dialogus*, III. 1. ii. 6, pp. 794–5. Much of this seems to have been derived from a comparison of Thomas Aquinas, *Summa theologica*, II. 1. xcvii. 3 ad 3, and *Comm. in Polit.*, i. 1.

[2] James of Viterbo, *De regimine christiano*, ii. 10, p. 303, 'Recte quidem pervenit aliquis ad regimen quando vel ex condicto et communi consensu multitudinis perficitur, vel praeter hoc ex ipsius Dei speciali ordinatione . . . seu ex institutione illorum qui vicem Dei gerunt . . . verus rector efficitur vel per consensum subditorum vel per auctoritatem superioris'.

[3] Tholemy of Lucca, *De regimine principum*, iii. 12, p. 261, 'De imperiali vero post praedicta dominia congruum videtur esse dicendum, quia medium tenet inter politicum et regale, quamvis universalis'; iii. 20, p. 267, 'His habitis videnda est comparatio imperialis dominii ad regale et politicum, quia, ut ex dictis apparet, convenit cum utroque'; cf. Anon., *Somnium viridarii*, i. 147, p. 112. This later becomes the basis of Fortescue's political theory.

Unde optima ordinatio principum est in aliqua civitate vel regno in quo unus praeficitur secundum virtutem qui omnibus praesit; et sub ipso sunt aliqui principantes secundum virtutem; et tamen talis principatus ad omnes pertinet, tum quia ex omnibus eligi possunt, tum quia etiam ab omnibus eliguntur. Talis enim est optima politia bene commixta ex regno, in quantum unus praeest; ex aristocratia, in quantum multi principantur secundum virtutem; et ex democratia, id est, potestate populi, in quantum ex popularibus possunt eligi principes, et ad populum pertinet electio principum. Et hoc fuit institutum secundum legem divinam.

Divine approval for this particular form of constitution, he added, could be assumed from the fact that it had been instituted by Moses.[1] It was inevitable that this should now be applied to the *Ecclesia* itself, which was considered to be a greater continuation of the Jewish community. The best form of government for the Ecclesia, says John of Paris, is for there to be one pope, and under him the rulers of each of its provinces, whilst all can in some way or other share in the government of the society.

Et sic certe esset optimum regimen Ecclesiae si sub uno papa eligerentur plures ab omni provincia et de omni provincia ut sic in regimine Ecclesiae omnes aliquo modo haberent partem suam.[2]

But the most important feature of this ideal constitution is its double basis of power. All power is from God, but it is derived on earth through the media of both people and ruler. Consequently some form of balance has to be struck between the divine right authorities of king and subject: and whilst this balance may represent the normal state of affairs, the fact that power is derived from the king gives him an ultimate, overriding supremacy in certain cases; whilst in other cases the fact that the people are also a source of power permits them an absolute right to act over the head of the ruler in defence of their own interests.[3] Whether two such opposed ideas can

[1] Thomas Aquinas, *Summa theologica*, III. I. cv. I; II. I. xcv. 4, 'est etiam aliquod regimen ex istis [scil. ex regno, aristocratia, oligarchia, et democratia vel plebiscita] commixtum quod est optimum: et secundum hoc sumitur lex quam maiores natu simul cum plebibus sanxerunt'.

[2] John of Paris, *De potestate regia et papali*, ch. 19, pp. 236–7.

[3] For a good example of the double basis of power see the addition by Peter Bertrandus to the *De origine iurisdictionum* of Durandus de S. Porciano, ch. 4,

really be combined depends upon a clear delineation of the respective functions of people and ruler, and of the cases in which each may be presumed to have the power to act against the wishes of the other. It was this enormous task which, more than anything else, obsessed the minds of the publicists in the late thirteenth and early fourteenth centuries.

Needless to say, the evolution of this system bristled with difficulties. Whilst Aristotle had given the publicists the general idea of the mixed constitution, it was to the canon and Roman lawyers that they looked for guidance when the details of the system had to be worked out. Surprisingly enough the matter with which they encountered least trouble was over the question of whose will gave the law its force and validity. This was largely due to the development by the civilians of the idea that the whole community should at least consent to the laws devised by the ruler. If both subjects and ruler are seen as the source of law, legislation must now become a joint affair.[1] The law of the community, the common law, is a matter which affects all its members, and so they through their representatives must participate in its promulgation: 'Quod omnes tan-

fo. 99, 'Ad cuius declarationem est sciendum quod duplex est dominium: est enim quoddam dominium iure divino, quoddam aliud iure humano'. Of these the first comprises true divine right sovereignty: 'Divinum dominium est illud quod est apud Deum supra omnem creaturam . . . et est verum dominium simplex et absolutum'. This was held by Christ and then passed to his vicar: 'Huius autem regni et sacerdotii principatum perpetuum commisit Filius Dei Petro et successoribus eius'. On the other hand, 'Aliud est dominium quod secundum legistas vocatur legale dominium . . . secundum vero canonistas vocatur humanum. . . De isto legali vel humano dominio dicit Innoc. sic quod est ius quod ad aliquem spectat vel acquisitur de iure naturali, ut sunt dominia, obligationes et huiusmodi'. This is common to all men, not to the pope alone, and therefore they cannot be deprived of the rights which it gives them, except for a just cause: 'Videtur mihi quod dominium rerum legale vel humanum fuit a Deo collatum humanae creaturae. . . Et tale dominium non est apud papam, sed apud omnes qui iuste acquirunt et ex quo semel acquisitum est, non licet papae vel alicui alteri auferre vel occupare sine iusta causa, quod esset contra *ius naturale divinum*. . . Et hoc intelligo sine causa, quia ex iusta causa posset aliquis privari ab homine vel a iure tali dominio'.

[1] E.g. Anon., *De legibus*, fo. 17v; Aegidius Romanus, *De regimine principum*, III. ii. 3; Guilielmus Durantis, *De modo generalis concilii celebrandi*, i. 2, pp. 7–9; Anon., *Somnium viridarii*, ii. 293, p. 189; Alvarus Pelagius, *Speculum regum*, p. 522.

git, ab omnibus comprobetur'.[1] The approval of the people is as vital an element in the making of law as the authority of the ruler, and it is in this sense that his subjects are understood to be 'pars corporis sui'.[2] The moral duty to govern in consultation with his magnates, which most medieval writers assumed, is thus utilised and converted into a juristic obligation. The ruler is still held to represent the whole community, but since this is so, the whole community is to be associated with its head. It is still the ruler's authority which brings the representatives of the people together, but he cannot now refuse to call them: Estates and Parliaments have a right to be consulted, to assist in the framing of laws and the regulation of taxation, and in the long run to veto royal proceedings by the withholding of consent. As most rulers realised, this was in practice almost a necessity, but it is a hallmark of this theory that it seeks to make a virtue of that necessity, to rationalise what is basically only expediency, and to establish as a matter of right what had originated as a mere concession of the prince.

This characteristic becomes all the more apparent as the publicists proceed to tackle the far more formidable problem of the right relationship between law and ruler. Does the fact that he authorises the law exempt him from it, or can his subjects demand his adherence to it? Even the hierocratic writers emphasised that the king, in

[1] *Cod.*, V. lix. 5. On the earlier history of this phrase see the series of articles by Gaines Post, '*Plena potestas* and consent in medieval assemblies', *Traditio*, i (1943), pp. 355–408; 'Roman law and representation in Spain and Italy', *Speculum*, xviii (1943), pp. 211–32; 'A Romano-canonical maxim *quod omnes tangit* in Bracton', *Traditio*, iv (1946), pp. 197–251. In 1327 the English king swore to uphold the laws 'quas vulgus elegerit': see David, 'Le serment du sacre', pp. 246–9, although it may be suggested in opposition to David that this can only be election in the shape of consent, not that the *populus* is to initiate legislation.

[2] For the Roman law basis of this see for example John of Viterbo, *De regimine civitatum*, chs. 119–20, pp. 260–1. Having stated that all laws made by the *rector* must be approved by the elected representatives of the community on the basis of *quod omnes tangit*, he adduces the right of a representative council to assist the ruler in all legislation. It is noticeable that from this he sets out the idea that the ruler is bound by the laws so promulgated, except in cases where the public utility demands that they should be ignored: 'cum sit consilium pars corporis sui, quoniam caput potestas, illi vero membra sunt eius; et quod consilium decrevit, potestas observare tenetur... nisi ex causa, id est, si ad publicam utilitatem respiciat rescissio prioris decreti'.

this case the pope, ought to obey his own laws, but, they asked, how can he be forced to do so if he does not wish to? How can the ruler be put under the law without making the *populus* superior in the constitution? Whilst the hierocrats were neither able nor willing to provide an answer, the Thomists plunged with frantic zeal into the search for a solution. Again it was to the Roman jurists that they looked for a lead. However much the Roman law idea of the ruler had been instrumental in building up the hierocratic theory of sovereignty, the papalists had employed only what may be called the imperial tradition of Roman law, which, as we have said, was given prominence in the Codex. But Justinian's emphasis upon the autonomy of the imperial will had never quite eclipsed the older republican tradition in which the ruler was normally expected to observe the law enacted by himself and his predecessors. In this earlier tradition he was *legibus solutus* only in that he could dispense with certain specific private law restrictions. He had as it were two levels of power: on the lower level, within the sphere of *iurisdictio* which he generally exercised, he was subject to the law; but on the higher level he could occasionally make use of his *imperium* which overrode the normally existing law.[1] This idea had never quite vanished from view in the early Middle Ages—we might mention the importance of the *lex visigothorum* in this respect—and in the thirteenth century it was resurrected and worked up into a general principle by the Post-Glossators as a means of halting the advance of the absolute monarchs. The ruler was acknowledged to be absolute, but only in the sense that he could ignore the law in certain cases. 'Quod principi placuit' and 'Princeps legibus solutus' refer only to his dispensing power: something to be used in exceptional circumstances, a temporary instance of the necessity which knows no law. But in general the ruler is seen as the executive embodiment of the common customary law, operating only within the bounds permitted him by the *lex terrae*.[2] This conception had close

[1] Schulz, 'Bracton on Kingship', pp. 156–65; G. J. T. Miller, 'The Position of the King in Bracton and Beaumanoir', *Speculum*, xxxi (1956), pp. 263–96 at pp. 264–5; E. Lewis, *Medieval Political Ideas* (London, 1954), p. 351 n. 6; C. H. McIlwain, *Constitutionalism Ancient and Modern* (Ithaca, New York, 1947), p. 87; Wirszubski, *Libertas as a Political Idea*, especially pp. 61–4, 121–35.

[2] A. Esmein, 'La Maxime *Princeps legibus solutus est* dans l'ancien droit public

affinities with the feudal idea of kingship, and it was no accident that the doctrine was first elaborated by those lawyers like Bracton and Beaumanoir who were struggling to combine Roman law principles with local customary law. The king was the apex of the feudal triangle, but he was nevertheless bound in a mutual contract with his vassals to govern for the good of the community. As Bracton put it, he was under no man, but he was subject to the law in which this good was normally contained. And whilst his guardianship of the common good demanded that he should act as he saw fit in those matters to which the law did not run, his magnates were equally bound to fulfil their side of the contract by acting as his peers on such occasions: they could either accept his action and ratify it by their consent; or they could refuse to uphold either that act or in this case the authority of the ruler himself.[1] It was these commonly acknowledged but still vaguely defined theories of government which were taken over by writers like Aquinas and Ockham.[2] Convinced of the universal applicability of all legal formulae they had no hesitation in taking in all the elements of limited government in Aristotle, Roman law, canon law and feudal law and regurgitating them as a sovereign remedy for the cure of all forms of absolutism. And however much they failed to convince their opponents, although they were a good deal more successful in this than one might expect, they did succeed in developing the idea of a balanced constitution which the modern historian may perhaps regard as one of the greatest achievements of the Middle Ages.

Both hierocratic and Thomist writers agreed that the ruler had an absolute authority over the other members of the community, but

français', *Essays in Legal History* (ed. P. Vinogradoff, Oxford, 1913), pp. 201–14; F. Kern, *Kingship and Law in the Middle Ages* (Oxford, 1948), pp. 183–4; Lewis, *op. cit.*, pp. 266–7.

[1] Jolliffe, *Angevin Kingship*, p. 14; Lewis, *op. cit.*, pp. 241–7; Miller, *art. cit.*, pp. 265f.; M. David, *La souveraineté et les limites juridiques du pouvoir monarchique du IXe au XVe siècle* (Paris, 1954), especially pp. 240–7.

[2] The view that the supremacy of the law reached to the ruler himself was an important feature of Franciscan teaching in the thirteenth century: Jacob, *Essays in the Conciliar Epoch*, p. 93. For the close link between Bracton and Aquinas, and Ockham and the civilians generally see the remarks of Miller, *art. cit.*, pp. 271–2; Carlyle, *History of Medieval Political Theory*, vi. 50.

they held to two very different interpretations of its extent. Every publicist was forced to begin by asking himself the same question: does the ruler have an *imperium merum*, an absolute plenitude of power, so that he alone is the source of law, and can diminish at will the liberties and possessions of his subjects? Or does the subject have certain rights, guaranteed by equity and natural law, which the ruler may infringe only in cases of necessity when the common good or *status* of the community is at stake? In the latter case he will be referred to as having *merum et mixtum imperium*, an ability to act above the law in certain circumstances, but a normal or ordinary jurisdiction in which he must act with the consent of his subjects, and in such a manner as to keep within the law which protects their rights and liberties.[1] William Amidani of Cremona, for example,

[1] The Roman law separation of ownership into *dominium directum* and *dominium utile* can be found in Ulpian. This was quickly developed by the Glossators into a distinction between ownership by natural law (*dominium utile* or *possessio naturalis*) and ownership conferred by civil law deriving from the will of the emperor (*dominium directum* or *possessio civilis*), and further elaborated by Bartolus, Jacobus de Ravanis and Johannes Faber: E. Meynial, 'Notes sur la formation de la théorie du domaine divisé (domaine direct et domaine utile) du xiie au xive siècle dans les Romanistes: Étude de dogmatique juridique', *Mélanges Fitting* (Montpellier, 1908), ii. 409–61. The distinction between *imperium merum* and *imperium mixtum* is still, as Baldus said, 'sublime, diffuse and hitherto badly treated', notwithstanding that Jason de Mayno regarded it as 'the key and fundamental of the whole question of jurisdiction': but see the discussions of it in Woolf, *Bartolus of Sassoferrato*, ch. 2 and appendix C; M. P. Gilmore, *Argument from Roman Law in Political Thought* (Cambridge, Mass., 1941). In short it may be said that *merum imperium* (or *mera voluntas* or *regalia mera*) signifies arbitrary power. Thus Marsilius of Padua describes it as being claimed by the papacy, and interprets it as the power to do as the ruler pleases by virtue of his *plenitudo potestatis*, *Defensor pacis*, II. xxvi. 4, p. 490, whereas Marsilius argues that this should more properly be applied to the power of the *legislator Romanus*, II. iv. 12, p. 172; cf. Innocent IV, *App. ad Decretales*, II. xxii. 15, 'reges qui habent supremum et merum imperium'; Baldus, *Comm. in Cod.*, I. xiv. 4, 'suprema et absoluta potestas principis'. The term derives from *Dig.*, II. i. 3, 'Merum est imperium habere gladii potestatem ad animadvertendum facinorosos homines, quod etiam potestas appellatur': see T. Mommsen, *Romisches Staatsrecht* (2nd ed., Leipzig, 1876), i. 182–7; ii. 259–60; Pauly-Wissowa, *Realenzyklopädie* (Leipzig, 1894–1939), s.v. *merum imperium*. It was frequently used by medieval jurists to describe the ruler's power of life and death over his subjects. The absolutist view that the granting of rights and liberties to the subject is a mere *concessio principis* made *ex mera voluntate* appears in Magna Carta, ch. 1 of 1215. With the civilians Azo had interpreted *merum*

begins his attack on the notorious errors of his day with a discussion of the point. Most people accept the principle that the emperor has power over his subjects' goods, he says, but this can be taken in two ways: either in the absolute sense that 'omnia sunt imperatoris' because 'ius humanum residet apud imperatorem'; or in the limited sense that the emperor may use his subjects' possessions for the common good and utility, since it is his function to legislate for peace and security. But he has no right to use them for his own purposes as if they are his own possessions.

Bona subditorum liberorum sunt imperatoris dominio subiecta solum secundum potestatem et iurisdictionem in quantum potest ius condere et scribere et defendere et pacem servare communem; et solum talium bonorum habet potestatem in quantum ordinatur in bonum commune, non autem quantum ad aliquam proprietatem et propriam utilitatem.

William himself much prefers this second alternative: 'et ista opinio videtur mihi rationabilior'.[1] In fact the great majority of the publicists in the fourteenth century had little hesitation in choosing the limited definition, and it is with them that the idea of the casual jurisdiction of the ruler in cases of necessity is fully developed. The existence of this concept was first emphasised by C. H. McIlwain,[2] and in recent years it has been the subject of a large number of publications by American scholars.[3] It does not therefore require much

imperium as 'plenissima vel plena potestas'; but had then gone on to contrast it with *iurisdictio ordinaria*, which followed Ulpian in *Dig.*, II. i. 13, who said that *mixtum imperium* was that which contained both *imperium* and *iurisdictio* (absolute and ordinary power). The distinction was then associated with natural law. *Ius merum* describes law which does not take account of natural law, *ius mixtum* that which does.

[1] William Amidani, *Reprobatio errorum*, ch. 1, p. 21.

[2] McIlwain, *Constitutionalism Ancient and Modern*, especially pp. 67–95. The general lines of this idea had however been noted by Gierke-Maitland, *Political Theories of the Middle Age*, pp. 79–80: see also his remarks on the separation of public and private law. On the development of this, G. Chevrier, 'Remarques sur l'introduction et les vicissitudes de la distinction du *ius privatum* et du *ius publicum* dans les œuvres des anciens juristes français', *Archives de Philosophie du Droit* (1952), pp. 5–77.

[3] Amongst others P. Birdsall, '*Non obstante*: A Study of the Dispensing Power of the English Kings', *Essays in History and Political Theory in honor of C. H. McIlwain* (Cambridge, Mass., 1936), pp. 37–76; H. D. Hazeltine, 'The Early

elaboration here. But it may profitably be pointed out that this idea was not, as some historians have implied, standard medieval theory on the subject: it was an enormously popular idea, but from neither the hierocratic nor the anti-hierocratic point of view could it be called orthodox. Nor has any real attempt been made to demonstrate that at the bottom of this theory lay the principle that initially full power was in the possession of both ruler and people alike, or to determine the question of how one was to know the exact competence permitted to the ruler at each level. Far too little emphasis has been put upon the means employed to keep the ruler within the limits assigned to him. And, finally, it has never been adequately appreciated that the occasional right of the ruler to act against the liberties of the subject was counterbalanced by the casual right of the people to act over and against the ruler.

Fundamental to this theory is Aquinas' conception of natural law. To the publicists who followed him natural law is seen as the repository of *iustitia*, that is to say, of justice and equity, of goodness and virtue, of the right way of life for mankind. Whilst it is formally distinct from divine law, natural law tends to be taken together and equated with divine law by the publicists and for this there were firm canonistic precedents.[1] On the other hand a difference in emphasis can now be detected. For the hierocratic writers natural law was seen as a support for the tenets of divine law: papal supremacy, for example, being a matter of divine law, could automatically be held to be a matter of natural law—and therefore human law too. But, whilst the near-identification remained, the Thomists concentrated upon the natural rather than the divine aspect: the higher law is for them a divine natural law. If the papal-

History of English Equity', *Essays in Legal History* (ed. P. Vinogradoff, Oxford, 1913), pp. 261–85; Lewis, *op. cit.*, chs. 2, 3, 5; Gaines Post, '*Plena potestas* and consent', pp. 370–80; 'The theory of public law and the State in the thirteenth century', *Seminar*, vi (1948), pp. 42–59; 'Two Notes on Nationalism in the Middle Ages', *Traditio*, ix (1953), pp. 281–320 at pp. 282–8, 295; 'The Two Laws and the Statute of York', *Speculum*, xxix (1954), pp. 417–32; F. M. Powicke, 'Reflections on the Medieval State', *Ways of Medieval Life and Thought* (London, 1949), pp. 130–48; J. R. Strayer, 'Defense of the Realm and Royal Power in France', *Studi in onore di Gino Luzzatto* (Milan, 1949), i. 289–96; and now *KTB*, pp. 284–91.

[1] For the Decretists see Carlyle, *History of Medieval Political Theory*, ii. 102–13.

ist was intent upon the naturalisation of divine law, it is equally true that the Thomist was bent upon the divinification of natural law. The importance of this is apparent when it is appreciated that natural law to the Thomist was not a special ordinance of right living revealed to the ruler alone, but something which all men could comprehend. It is the divine reason transmuted into a form which all men may naturally understand by the exercise of their own reason. It is the link between the will of God and the comprehension of man. All valid human law is therefore something formed by the specifically human act of rationalising the natural law. Positive legal codes mirror the divine natural law: they are natural reason codified, and maintain their binding force only in so far as they reflect the principles of natural law. Human law therefore can normally be regarded as the embodiment of the divine natural law, and this is true not only of human law in general (*ius gentium*),[1] but of any specific legal code, whether it is universal like Roman law or merely a local collection of customary laws. All may be, and frequently were, described as written reason or as natural law itself.[2]

But whilst divine and natural law are immutable and eternally just, this is not necessarily true of human law. Aquinas found himself faced with a very common human dilemma. As a Christian he was perfectly convinced that there were absolute standards of right and wrong. But, like most people, he was uncomfortably aware that the rigid application of an arbitrary set of righteous principles sometimes produced results that were too awkward and inconvenient to be borne. They might even appear to assume the aspect of positive evils. His way out of this impasse was to develop the distinction between the divine and the human. Whereas the Augustinian frequently spoke as though human law, or at least papally

[1] E.g. Anon., *De legibus*, ff. 10–10v, 'Nam de iure gentium est illud quod ratio constituit inter omnes homines et vocatur ius gentium. . . Prima conclusio est quod iura gentium et iura naturalia non distinguuntur'.

[2] Anon., *De legibus*, fo. 17; cf. fo. 21v, 'ratio naturalis est lex quaedam tacita'; John of Paris, *De potestate regia et papali*, ch. 1, pp. 176–7; Thomas Aquinas, *Summa theologica*, II. I. xci. 1–3; II. I. xciv. 2; II. I. xcv. 4 and 4 ad 1; II. II. lvii. 3; William of Ockham, *Dialogus*, III. III. iii. 12, p. 942; Dante, *Convivio*, iv. 9, p. 438; also Anon., *Somnium viridarii*, ii. 313, p. 203; Johannes Branchazolus, *De principio imperatoris et papae*, i. 2, p. 45.

approved human law, was much the same as God's law, as would be appropriate in a society which was a reflection of heaven on earth, Aquinas was by no means disposed to permit a complete equation. Reflections are weaker than the original: human things must always therefore suffer by comparison. The ruler may be *imago Dei*, but he has not the unfailing rectitude of God himself. His law, human law, generally corresponds to divine and natural law, but not always. It is quite possible to draw a theoretical distinction between divine-natural law and human law, and occasionally the theory becomes fact. There must always be cases to which the positive law does not extend, or special circumstances in which it would be against the canons of *iustitia* to make a strict application of the law. If the good of the community, embodied in the divine 'rightness', is normally maintained by the application of human law, there are also cases, said Aquinas, when the law does not further the common good, and, being therefore out of accord with *iustitia*, cannot be considered binding.

Unde si emergat casus in quo observatio talis legis sit damnosa communi saluti, non est observanda.[1]

The exceptional event in which human law fails to conform to natural law becomes a period of emergency, a state of necessity in which all law ceases.[2] The divine-natural law may then be seen as

[1] Thomas Aquinas, *Summa theologica*, II. I. xcvi. 6; cf. Anon., *De legibus*, fo. 17v, 'Amplius videtur quod fuerit inutile propter impossibilitatem bene condendi leges, quia casus particulares qui possunt contingere sunt infiniti et quasi sub infinitis modis poterunt contingere'; fo. 21, 'quia contingit quod aliquid observare communi salute est utile ut in pluribus, quod tamen in aliquibus casibus est maxime nocivum... Si tamen emergat casus particularis in quo observatio ipsius legis communis sit nociva utilitate hominum, non est observanda'. There is a long discussion of this by Pierre Dubois, *De recuperatione Sanctae Terrae*, ch. 48, pp. 39–40; ch. 49, p. 42.

[2] William of Ockham, *Tractatus pro rege Angliae*, ch. 8, p. 259, 'Item in necessitate omne privilegium cessat, sicut dicunt canonicae sanctiones. Si enim leges non solum humanae *sed etiam divinae* in necessitate cessant et in eis excipitur necessitas, *Extra*, *De regulis iuris*, *Quod non est licitum* [V. xli. 4]; *distinctione 5 de consecr.*, *Discipulos* [D. 5 c. 26], quod ex verbis Christi accipitur *Matth.* xii [1f.], multo fortius privilegia humana in necessitate cessant et in eis necessitas excipi debent'. For Ockham and the theory of *epieikeia* see further B. Tierney, 'Ockham, the Conciliar Theory, and the Canonists', *Journal of the History of Ideas*, xv (1954), pp. 40–70.

existing on two levels: on the normal or lower level in which it is manifested in positive law, but occasionally on the higher level alone when this is not so. This then provides the justification for the ruler to act absolutely in certain cases. He is essentially *lex animata*, a personification of natural law.[1] He acts *loco Dei* because he is the point at which the divine will is translated into legal codes for the regulation of human conduct.[2] As the mediator between God and man it is his function to act as the mouthpiece of *iustitia*, to make the law which preserves the common good of the society. Just as natural law is the origin of all law, so the ruler as animated natural law is an initial source of authority in the community. All things are under his control, and his will has the force of law. But he is not regarded as having any independent personal role to play in this capacity. He merely seeks out the natural law and converts it into positive law: he is the *executor iustitiae*, a judge rather than a legislator.[3] Consequently he must always act in accordance with the precepts of natural law: 'Quod principi placuit' applies only in the sense that the will of the ruler is exercised for the common good.

[1] Anon., *De legibus*, fo. 17v, 'Praeterea ad iudicem confugiunt homines sicut ad iustitiam animatam. . . Iustitia animata melior est quam inanimata quae legibus continetur'; Anon., *Disquisitio iuridica*, ch. 9, p. 1391, 'Imperator igitur, qui est lex animata civilis in terris et vigor iustitiae sive iuris esse dicitur . . . iura talia [scil. naturalia vel gentium] tollere vel mutare non potest. . . Unde ipse imperator a tali lege non est solutus'; Aegidius Romanus, *De regimine principum*, III. ii. 29, 'Sciendum est regem et quemlibet principantem esse medium inter legem naturalem et positivam'; Thomas Aquinas, *Summa theologica*, II. II. lviii. 1 ad 5, 'iudex est iustum animatum et princeps est custos iusti'; *Comm. in Polit.*, *para.* 849, 'Et ideo recurrere ad regem est recurrere ad iustum animatum'. These generally refer to Aristotle, *Ethics*, v. 4 or *Politics*, iii. 10–11. See also Gilbert of Tournai, *Eruditio regum*, II. ii. 1–2, pp. 66–7.

[2] Thomas Aquinas, *De regimine principum*, i. 9, p. 233; i. 12, p. 235: see above p. 127 n. 2. Also Alvarus Pelagius, *De planctu Ecclesiae*, ch. 62, p. 199; Pseudo-Thomas, *De eruditione principum*, iii. 5, p, 418; cf. Aegidius Romanus, *De regimine principum*, II. ii. 8, 'rex quasi semideus'; III. ii. 32, 'princeps semideus'. The same idea is expressed by Gilbert of Tournai, *Eruditio regum*, III. 6, p. 89, 'Hanc igitur principes dum sectantur et amant, populum sibi subditum protegunt et gubernant. Ob hoc enim Christo coregnant, immo Christi regno humana dispensant'.

[3] Alvarus Pelagius, *Speculum regum*, p. 518, 'Principalis autem et praecipuus actus regiae potestatis est iudicare . . . leges componere . . . pacis unitatem in subiecta sibi multitudine procurare et facere'. Similarly Bracton had said that the duty of a king was *primo et principaliter* to judge, Woodbine, ii. 304.

His is the right to command, but only whilst he commands rightly.[1] The excellence of his function *quasi Deus* is all the more reason to expect him to act in the best possible manner: 'quare sic decet reges et principes esse quasi semideos et habere virtutes perfectas: decet eos habere omnes virtutes'.[2] Thus, for example, his authority over his subjects' goods is seen to mean protection, not possession.[3] Indeed the fact that he is *lex animata* means that he must conform with the common law of the community, even though he or his predecessors promulgated it, because that common law is, generally speaking, as much an embodiment of natural law as the ruler himself.[4] The law made, or custom approved, by one ruler is thus made binding upon his successors, and here again support could be derived from the Roman law doctrine that the heir to an inheritance is subject to the rulings of the original testator.[5] The whole conception of the ruler as *vicarius Dei* in the hands of the Thomists becomes a means of subjecting the ruler to law. As Aquinas himself had maintained, God's will is the source of law, but it is always a will prompted by reason, and it is this reason which God has set himself

[1] Thomas Aquinas, *Summa theologica*, II. 1. xc. 1 ad 3, 'ratio habet vim movendi a voluntate, ut supra dictum est; ex hoc enim quod aliquis vult finem, ratio imperat de his quae sunt ad finem. Sed voluntas de his quae imperantur, ad hoc quod legis rationem habeat, oportet quod sit aliqua ratione regulata. Et hoc modo intelligitur quod voluntas principis habet vigorem legis, alioquin voluntas principis magis esset iniquitas quam lex'.

[2] Aegidius Romanus, *De regimine principum*, I. ii. 31, p. 143; I. ii. 4, p. 57, 'Huiusmodi autem virtutem divinam, quae est quodammodo super virtus, maxime habere debent reges et principes qui, ut dictum est, semidii esse debent'; cf. Thomas Aquinas, *De regimine principum*, i. 9, p. 232.

[3] John of Paris, *De potestate regia et papali*, ch. 7, p. 190, 'habet princeps potestatem iudicandi et discernendi in bonis subditorum, licet non habeat dominium in re ipsa'. Cf. Andreas de Isernia, *Proem. super Const.*, 'Sed si intellexit hic glossa quod bona subditorum sunt regis . . . hic esset error magnus qui ab omnibus communiter reprobatur. Nam non sunt regis nisi quantum ad protectionem et iurisdictionem exercendam': F. Ercole, *Da Bartolo all'Althusio* (Florence, 1932), p. 205.

[4] Anon., *Disquisitio prior iuridica*, ch. 7, p. 1338, 'debet legibus stare contra se, maxime quae rationi naturali nitantur et canonibus approbantur, ut aequalitas observetur, quia non facias alii quod tibi non vis fieri'; Anon., *De legibus*, fo. 17v; Geoffrey of Fontaines, *Quodlibeta*, XI. 17 (v. 76–7); Guilielmus Durantis, *De modo generalis concilii celebrandi*, i. 3, pp. 9–10.

[5] 'Dicat enim testator, et lex erit': *Glossa ordinaria ad Cod.*, VI. xliii. 7; *Auth.*, IV. i. 2 (*Nov.*, xxii. 2).

to follow. How much more then should the ruler acting *loco Dei* ensure that his commands are tempered by reason and capable of being rationally comprehended, which in practice entails limitation by the law that is written reason.[1] As his vicar, he must adopt the example which Christ set by adhering to his own law.[2] It is this law which protects private rights and the liberties of the individual: such things are a matter of equity or *iustitia*, whose prime precept is that each shall be given his due.[3] Private rights are therefore enshrined in the divine natural law, and the ruler as *speculum iuris* must of necessity restrict his *voluntas*, his absolute power, so as to respect and preserve them.[4] No one disputed his right to confiscate his subjects' belongings as a penal measure, or to take a proportion of them in the form of taxation for the upkeep of government,[5] but the publicists insist that this must only be done in so far as the law permits. In spite of his original absolute power as a source of authority in the community, the ruler must make himself obey the *lex terrae*: he must bind himself to keep his own law—it is, so to speak, an enforced 'voluntary' act.[6] The civilians had been declaim-

[1] Thomas Aquinas, *Summa theologica*, I. xxxv. 3–5; II. I. xciii. I.

[2] This theme is common to most of the thirteenth-century law books, such as the *Assizes of Jerusalem*, the Norman law books, and the *Sachsenspiegel*. It is also in Bracton, Woodbine, ii. 33. See further Carlyle, *op. cit.*, iii. 39; Miller, *art. cit.*, pp. 272–3; and F. W. Maitland, 'Bracton and Azo', *Selden Society*, viii (London, 1895), p. 65.

[3] This derives from *Dig.*, I. i. 10. See for example Thomas Aquinas, *Summa theologica*, II. II. lxvi. 2; *De regimine principum*, i. 1, p. 225.

[4] Thomas Aquinas, *Summa theologica*, II. II. lxviii. 1 ad 5; *De regimine principum* i. 15, p. 238.

[5] E.g. Tholemy of Lucca, *De regimine principum*, iii. 11, pp. 260–1, 'Per quod habemus quod principes suis debent esse contenti *stipendiis* nec suos subditos gravare possunt in bonis eorum et rebus nisi in duobus casibus: videlicet ratione delicti et pro bono communi sui regiminis. Primo enim modo propter ingratitudinem suos privat feudo fideles, alios autem titulo iustitiae propter quam sunt concessa dominia... Item quod pro bono reipublicae possit exigere, sicut pro defensione regni vel pro quacunque alia causa pertinente rationabiliter ad bonum commune... Et ideo concludendum est quod isto casu possunt legitimae exactiones et talliae ac census sive tributa imponi, dummodo non transcendat necessitatis metas'. If he goes beyond these limits he must make compensation.

[6] This was generally inferred from *Cod.*, I. xiv. 4, but note also *Cod.*, VI. xxiii. 3; *Inst.*, II. xvii. 8. Commenting on this Aquinas had stressed the voluntary nature of the prince's abdication of absolute power: *Summa theologica*, II. I. xcvi. 5, 'Sed quantum ad vim directivam legis princeps subditur legi

ing for over a century that the ruler ought to obey his own law, and 'Patere legem quam ipse tuleris' was a phrase which everybody knew by heart,[1] but it was the writers of the late thirteenth and early fourteenth centuries who attempted to make this into something more than a pious assertion. For them the ruler's restriction of his own authority puts his power into the category of private right: and here he is on a par with his people and is therefore not only morally but also legally bound to observe the law. This voluntary abdication of absolute power thus comes to be seen as the first act of kingship. It serves in fact to explain the need for the coronation oath.[2] It is unnecessary for each king to make a separate restriction of his authority, since this is, as a result of the acts of his predecessors, already contained in the common law. It is merely necessary for him to reaffirm this. Just as he cannot become a true king without coronation, so that coronation comes to demonstrate his capacity as *rex sub lege* by making him swear to uphold the customs of the realm, to preserve the private rights of his subjects, and

propria voluntate . . . sed debet voluntarius non coactus leges implere'. With Cynus the obligatory aspect of this becomes more marked: *Comm. in Cod.*, I. xiv. 4, *rubr.* 14, 'Dico ergo quod imperator est solutus legibus de necessitate; tamen de honestate ipse vult ligari legibus quia honor reputatur vinculum sacri iuris'. Also Anon., *De legibus*, ff. 20v–21; Anon., *Disputatio inter clericum et militem*, p. 14; Anon., *Disquisitio prior iuridica*, ch. 7, p. 1338; Guilielmus Durantis, *De modo generalis concilii celebrandi*, i. 3, p. 15, deberent divinis et humanis legibus conformare et se per imitationem eis subiicere'. For the Germanic and feudal elements in this idea see G. L. Haskins, 'Executive Justice and the Rule of Law', *Speculum*, xxx (1955), pp. 531–2, 536–7; and Wirszubski, *op. cit.*, p. 168, for the idea of the self-limiting ruler in Roman thought.

[1] E.g. Anon., *De legibus*, fo. 21; Anon., *Disquisitio prior iuridica*, ch. 7, p. 1338; Thomas Aquinas, *Summa theologica*, II. I. xcvi. 5. This late Roman proverbial dictum, usually attributed to Cato, had always enjoyed considerable currency in the Middle Ages, chiefly as a result of its acceptance by Isidore, *Sententiae*, iii. 51 (*PL*, xvi. 1004). It was employed by Innocent III in *Decretales*, I. ii. 6. Note also the use of *Matthew*, vii. 12 in the introduction to Gratian's *Decretum* and by Celestine III in *Decretales*, II. iv. 2. A similar idea that the supreme wisdom of the prince is to obey his own laws was conspicuous in the very influential pseudo-Aristotelian *Secreta secretorum*.

[2] There is a significant passage in Thomas Aquinas, *De regimine principum*, i. 6, p. 229, 'Deinde sic disponenda est regni gubernatio ut regi iam instituto tyrannidis substrahatur occasio. Simul etiam sic eius temperetur potestas ut in tyrannidem de facili declinare non possit'. He promised to deal with this in more detail later, but was unable to complete the work.

to govern according to the law.[1] As Thomas Occleve put it at the beginning of the next century, the king's oath to observe the law is 'the lock and key of the public security'.[2]

There will, nevertheless, always remain cases which the existing law does not cover, or cases of emergency or special circumstances in which it would be detrimental to the common good, to the *status reipublicae*, to enforce the law as it stands. In these cases equity (which may be equated with *iustitia* or natural law) demands that the law should be ignored: it has temporarily ceased to conform to the standards of ultimate rightness which give it validity and force. A 'case of necessity' thus becomes seen as an occasion when natural-divine law, which transcends positive law, is directly involved.[3] Consequently it is a sacred duty for the ruler as animate divine natural law to override the provisions of the common law of the community.[4] In this limited sense he is absolute, *supra ius*, and can

[1] See for instance Anon., *Somnium viridarii*, ii. 293, p. 189; Alvarus Pelagius, *Speculum regum*, pp. 520, 522; Durandus de S. Porciano, *De iurisdictione ecclesiastica*, ch. 3, fo. 6; and in general Kern, *Kingship and Law*, pp. 75–8, 183; David, 'Le serment du sacre', *passim*. A good deal of English constitutional history centres round the perennial attempts of the magnates to force the king to take an oath by which he should promise not to act by will. Richard I gained his crown by an undertaking not to govern 'per voluntatem regis': Jolliffe, *Angevin Kingship*, p. 308. Note the demand for an oath in the early thirteenth-century *Leges Anglorum*, II. i. 6, on the grounds that 'voluntas et violentia et vis non est ius'. Magna Carta, ch. 39, may also be seen as an attempt to prohibit the acts of the king *per voluntatem* in favour of his adherence to the *lex terrae*. See also the view of Bracton that the coronation oath is a voluntary submission to the law, Woodbine, ii. 304. And it may be added that Richard II was deposed on the basis that his claim to act absolutely by will was a contravention of his coronation oath.

[2] Thomas Occleve, *De regimine principis*, ed. T. Wright (London, 1860), p. 100.

[3] Thomas Aquinas, *Summa theologica*, II. II. lxvi. 7. For the idea that 'necessity knows no law' in Aquinas, Ockham and the civilians see further C. C. Bayley, 'Pivotal Concepts in the Political Philosophy of William of Ockham', *Journal of the History of Ideas*, x (1949), pp. 199–218 at pp. 200–2.

[4] In times of crisis it was usual for the *podestà* of the Italian city states to be given *liberum arbitrium* or absolute power: for example full military power in time of war, or complete discretionary powers of punishment during a domestic crisis. Reggio in 1241 had given its *podestà* 'libertatem faciendo quicquid vellet'. It was understood that this was only a temporary measure, and the commune still regarded itself as able to depose the *podestà* if he infringed the general good, although during the fourteenth century this practice changed easily into tyrannical rule: M. V. Clarke, *The Medieval City-State* (London, 1926), pp. 115, 126–33.

do all things necessary for the preservation of the public safety.[1] If the community is threatened by invasion from without or by heresy or subversion from within, he, as the embodiment of the common good or *status* which resides in natural law, is free to do as he will. He acts in the name of the well-being of the community, *ratione status*. He can impose any taxation, confiscate his subjects' property, imprison without trial, condemn without warning. His powers are virtually limitless within the duration of the emergency. Although he has reduced himself from the upper level of absolute power to the lower level on which he *regulariter* acts within the law, a cardinal feature of this theory is the idea that he retains the right, *casualiter*, to revert to the upper level, to act beyond the law for the general welfare.[2] Normally possessed of an ordinary or self-ordained degree of authority in which his power is seen in terms of private right, he must avoid infringing the private rights of the rest of the community. Here public and private rights, like the common and the individual goods, are identical. It is only when the public need overrides private right, when private rights lose their usual protection from natural law, that the ruler is *legibus solutus*. Now the public good which he personifies stands superior to private goods,[3] and it is this belief in the supremacy of the common

[1] This is usually expressed in the phrase that the ruler is under divine natural law but above positive law: e.g. Aegidius Romanus, *De regimine principum*, III. ii. 29, 'Positiva lex est infra principantem sicut lex naturalis est supra'; William of Ockham, *Dialogus*, III. II. i. 16, p. 886, 'Ita imperator, qui est supra positiva iura, non est super aequitatem naturalem'.

[2] Instances of this are legion with the publicists and the Roman lawyers: e.g. Anon., *Somnium viridarii*, i. 141, pp. 111–12; Anon., *De legibus*, ff. 21, 23; Anon., *Disquisitio prior iuridica*, ch. 7, p. 1338; Gilbert of Tournai, *Eruditio regum*, I. ii. 1, p. 9; II. i. 5–6, pp. 48–9; Guido Terrenus, *Quodlibet*, IV. ii, pp. 319–20; Guilielmus Durantis, *De modo generalis concilii celebrandi*, i. 2, pp. 4–7; Thomas Aquinas, *Summa theologica*, II. II. lxvi. 7–8; lxxvii–lxxviii; William of Ockham, *Dialogus*, III. II. ii. 23, pp. 920–1; and in many other places. Even Marsilius could not resist dealing with it: *Defensor pacis*, I. xiv. 7, pp. 81–2; *Defensor minor*, i. 7, p. 3. Amongst the civilians I have noticed it in Baldus, Bartolus, Petrus Jacobus, Jacobus Butrigarius, John of Viterbo, and Lucas da Penna.

[3] E.g. Anon., *Disquisitio theologico-iuridica*, ii. 16, p. 1352; Aegidius Romanus, *De regimine principum*, I. i. 12; Guilielmus Durantis, *De modo generalis concilii celebrandi*, i. 3, p. 17. For a list of references to Aquinas' use of the idea that the common good is superior to private good see A. Darquennes, *De Juridische Structuur van de Kerk volgens Sint Thomas van Aquino* (Louvain, 1949), pp. 157–

good which goes far towards justifying and legalising what would otherwise be merely a matter of expediency.

What is rarely appreciated is the extent to which this doctrine corresponded to the radical Aristotelians' notion of the double truth, although the point was not lost upon the theologians who combined Thomistic and Averroistic theses in the condemnation of 1277. Aquinas' system was in fact far more comprehensive than some of his followers realised, and it was not until the sixteenth century that the debt of the *ratione status* principle to the double truth theory was clearly revealed. As we have seen, the theory of the double truth operated on the basis that there were two levels of truth or goodness, human and divine, which might well be contradictory. What was true or good on the human level might be untrue or bad on the divine level. What was bad seen in terms of purely positive considerations might be perfectly good, indeed more truly good, when divine factors were taken into account. Correspondingly what was normally good under human law was sometimes bad with reference to the absolute norms of divine righteousness; and an action generally considered bad might in fact be revealed as supremely right under special circumstances. Since the ruler was nothing other than the embodiment of truth and goodness, he was in effect required to utilise a double standard of morality. Normally, *ut Deus et homo*, he followed the standards of goodness as defined by human law, and could rest assured of his rightness in terms of divine and natural law. But in exceptional circumstances he was, *ut Deus* and in pursuit of overriding *iustitia*, forced to commit actions that the law of the community undoubtedly denounced as evil and therefore technically contrary to human standards of goodness. A normally bad action became occasionally good with reference to the supreme considerations of the divine will and the *status reipublicae*. In this way the theory of limited absolute power laid the foundations for the later doctrine of *raison d'état*. As preached in the early fourteenth century the notion

65; and in general I. T. Eschmann, 'A Thomistic Glossary on the Principle of the Preeminence of a Common Good', *Mediaeval Studies*, v (1943), pp. 123–65; 'Bonum commune melior est quam bonum unius', *ibid.*, vi (1944), pp. 62–120.

of casual power was lacking in none of the essentials of sixteenth-century casuistry. On both occasions it was agreed that the absolute power to do anything was to be understood *in casu*, in cases of necessity when the supreme good of preserving the 'state' was imperilled. The medieval publicist, it is true, did not revel in the use of private evil for public good as did Machiavelli. Nor was he prepared to accept the indefinite extension of cases which the Florentine permitted. But even Machiavelli was quite well aware that action *ratione status* was in normal terms an evil, and that it called for a distinction between, as he put it, absolute and ordained virtue. Where he differed was in his refusal to use the divine justification which inspired medieval writers, and thereby he laid himself open to the attacks of those who were in no way averse to the doctrine of *raison d'état* itself, but demanded that it should be justified according to Christian principles.

No less than the papalist, the Thomist was convinced that the supreme virtue was the preservation of society. Entrenched behind the doctrine of social necessity the ruler was to be permitted to do virtually as he pleased for the good of the community. But whilst both schools of thought agreed that the maintenance of society was the chief objective of political existence—an inescapable conclusion when that society was still held to be a church, the only instrument of salvation—the Thomist was not prepared to allow that this necessarily entailed blind adherence to the dictates of established authority. Although it was accepted that the ruler himself should have full discretion in deciding when a state of emergency existed and what measures should be taken to counteract it,[1] and this inevitably suggests that the theory imposes no real limitation upon his power, it would be unwise to assume that the publicists were not perfectly conscious of this danger themselves. Although the idea of casual jurisdiction dominates the political thought of the period, it must be remembered that it was employed here for the express purpose of suggesting that there was a balance between ruler and

[1] E.g. Anon., *De legibus*, fo. 21v, 'Sed tamen considerandum quod si observatio legis secundum verba non habeat nocumentum cui oporteat occurri non pertinet ad quemlibet ut interpretetur quid sit utile et quid non, sed solum ad principem'.

people in any rightly ordered society. The ability of the ruler to disregard the law in exceptional circumstances is therefore to be offset by the right of the whole community (or its representatives) to act extra-legally under similar conditions. Whilst the thirteenth-century publicists, faced with a situation in which absolute monarchy was becoming the normal state of affairs, had confined themselves to what may be called right-wing activities, the limitation of the ruler's sovereignty to casual jurisdiction, the publicists in the fourteenth century began to concentrate upon the left wing and gradually systematised the idea of the casual jurisdiction of the people over the too-powerful ruler.[1] This equally stems from the idea that both ruler and people initially possess a plenitude of power. If the ruler must limit his original absolute authority to leave untouched the fundamental private rights of his subjects, so the people, by consenting to the common law, are held to have voluntarily bound themselves to refrain from interference with the private rights (or ordinary jurisdiction) of the ruler. This consent, as Ockham repeatedly emphasised, might be either overtly or tacitly expressed. But just as the law of one ruler is considered to be binding upon successors, so the consent of the community is held to be valid for both its present and future members.[2] When the people themselves are a source of law they too in their collective capacity take on the character of a *lex animata*, restraining themselves from unwarranted excess. In other words the ruler in the normal course of his governmental duties is not to be subject to popular control beyond the necessity for gaining the community's consent to his legislative activity. Even Marsilius, although he permitted his *legislator mortalis* an authority closely akin to the hierocratic conception of papal

[1] Most of the Thomists acknowledge the right of the *populus* to depose its ruler: e.g. Anon., *De legibus*, fo. 13v; Geoffrey of Fontaines, *Quodlibeta*, XI. xvii (v. 76); John of Paris, *De potestate regia et papali*, ch. 14, p. 219; Thomas Aquinas, *Summa theologica*, II. I. xcvi. 4; II. II. xlii. 2 ad 3; II. II. civ. 5; *Commentum in Sententias*, II. xliv. ii. 2; *De regimine principum*, i. 1, p. 226; i. 3, pp. 227–8; William of Ockham, *Dialogus*, III. II. ii. 20, p. 918; *Octo quaestiones*, ii. 7, p. 82; viii. 5, p. 200.

[2] Anon., *De legibus*, fo. 17v, 'Et si [persona] habens auctoritatem publicam ex consensu populi faciat legem, ligat non solum praesentes homines sed et futuros. Verum est quod primi per suum consensum expressum ligantur, futuri per consensum praesumptum vel per consensum qui debet esse debito'.

power,[1] does not seem to have envisaged any unrestrained right on the part of the community to act over the head of the prince,[2] and none of the other medieval Aristotelians seriously considered that the people could take over the ruler's functions except *in certis causis*. They were well aware that Aristotle had regarded the tyranny of a democracy as the worst form of tyranny and practically irremediable.[3] On the other hand since both ruler and people were the legislative authorities, there was little room for doubt in the minds of the publicists that when necessary the people might act as absolutely as the ruler himself.[4] The right of the other parts of society to supplement the deficiency of the ruling part is now erected into a general principle.[5] As Aquinas had emphasised, if

[1] The power of the *legislator* is termed a *plenitudo potestatis, Defensor pacis*, III. ii. 13, p. 605. For Marsilius law is binding because it is the will of the legislator, not because it has any specific content of divine or natural law. On the legal positivism of Marsilius see Gewirth, *Marsilius of Padua*, i. 134–5, 256–9.

[2] The people have no right to withhold power from the ruler indefinitely, since the existence of a *pars principans* is essential to the normal conduct of government. Nor is a ruler to be deposed unless his offences are repeated and grave: *Defensor pacis*, I. xviii. 5–7, pp. 123–5.

[3] E.g. Alvarus Pelagius, *Speculum regum*, p. 519, 'inter iniusta igitur regimina intolerabilius est democratia, id est potestas populi, quando *totus populus est sicut unus tyrannus*'.

[4] This is very well brought out by the author of *Fleta* (ed. London, 1647), who says that what the prince wills has the force of law, but only provided that he wills in counsel with his magnates—it does not mean everything that he wills. Consequently it is the magnates who are responsible for holding him in check: 'verumtamen in populo regendo [rex] superiores habet ut legem, per quam factus est rex, et curiam suam, videlicet comites et barones . . . qui cum viderint regem sine fraeno, fraenum sibi apponere tenentur', i. 17, pp. 7–9. Bracton, or a later *additio* to Bracton, had said that if the king refused to implement *iustitia*, this should be done by the 'universitas regni et baronagium suum in curia': Carlyle, *op. cit.*, iii. 73. Aquinas remarked that the consent of the people to the observance of a custom was of more value than the authority of the ruler: *Summa theologica*, II. I. xcvii. 3 ad 3, 'plus est consensus totius multitudinis ad aliquid observandum quem consuetudo manifestat, quam auctoritas principis'.

[5] William of Ockham, *Octo quaestiones*, viii. 6, p. 204, 'sic in corpore mystico et in collegio seu universitate, uno deficiente, alius, si habet potestatem, supplet defectum eius'. The same idea had already been acknowledged by Philip the Fair: 'Et si brachium utrumque [scil. papa vel rex] deficiat, nonne caetera membra, pedes et alia, ut populi, ad defensionem assurgent propter necessitatem?', Boutaric, 'Notices et Extraits', p. 184.

the ruler was going to act above the law, it must be for a just cause.[1] Once he begins to act absolutely without a good reason for doing so, or if he continues when the state of emergency is past, he ceases to be the embodiment of the public good. He becomes in fact a tyrant, and the corresponding casual right of the people to act as the supreme power in the community comes into play. Thus Ockham permits the *Romani*, or their representatives, to depose an emperor who has in any way damaged the rights of the empire either by intention or by sheer negligence.[2] Even more explicit is the author of the *Somnium viridarii*. If the king imposes extraordinary taxation for some good reason, such as the defence of the community, and then fails to defend it to the best of his ability, or uses this revenue for his own personal benefit, he no longer deserves the right to collect taxes at all. That is to say, he denies justice to his people and ought to be deposed. No subject is bound to obey a ruler who does not function for the common well-being, and in this way his absolute power is limited by the needs of society.

Si enim princeps iustitiam denegaret subditis utpote . . . si sint inducti tales reditus extraordinarii de iusta causa, scilicet pro defensione patriae, nec eo modo defendatur quo possit et debet, nec reditus ad illum usum sed in alium convertatur, tunc tales reditus ordinarii iuste possent denegari, immo iure scripto super dictamine rectae rationis sundato merito a regimine tamquam indignus foret deponendus. Et si in regimine totius regni sic negligeret, omnino deponendus et liceret populo alium principem eligere; si in parte regni solum hoc negligeret, liceret populo illius loci alium sibi principem eligere. . . Exercitus enim ducem sibi elegit. . . Si autem illae talliae nullo modo sint ad utilitatem boni communis, nec rex nec princeps potest eas imponere, quod si imposuerit, subditi non tenentur obedire, quia potestatis suae limites excedit.[3]

[1] Thomas Aquinas, *Summa theologica*, II. I. xcvi. 5; II. I. xcvii. 4 and ad 1; II. II. lxxxviii. 12. See further J. Brys, *De dispensatione in Iure Canonico* (Bruges, 1925), pp. 262–9.

[2] William of Ockham, *Octo quaestiones*, ii. 8, p. 84, 'Et ideo si imperator committat crimen dilapidationis vel destructionis imperii aut damnabilis negligentiae. . . Romani, vel illi in quos suam potestatem Romani dederunt, debent ipsum deponere'. The whole of this theory drew heavily upon the feudal idea of the *diffidatio* or legalised rebellion against an unjust king.

[3] Anon., *Somnium viridarii*, i. 141, pp. 111–12. Note the feature suggestive of baronial rule in that those who have been wronged can exempt themselves

Behind all this lies the idea that the community, seen itself as animate natural law, is capable of measuring the acts of the ruler up against its own standards. If, the publicists argued, the provisions of natural law are eminently ascertainable by human reason, then the people as much as the ruler must be credited with the ability to recognise when and whether this law is being fulfilled. They too must be permitted equal discretion to decide when the *status reipublicae* is endangered, when, in fact, the ruler ceases to execute his function as *lex animata*. As the personification of natural law he is always bound by that law;[1] if he merely acts by will he is no true ruler.[2] To contravene natural law is not only a breach of his coronation oath, but also a denial of his capacity as the interpreter of God's purpose on earth. The very fact that he misuses his power, Durandus points out, surely proves that he is not a vicar of Christ.[3] The ruler acting against *iustitia* immediately ceases to be a ruler: he becomes a tyrant, and tyranny is the very antithesis of kingship.[4]

from the rest of the kingdom and set up their own community independent of the king.

[1] Anon., *De legibus*, fo. 12v, 'a legibus iuris naturalis imperator non est absolutus, quia illi non innituntur auctoritati suae'; fo. 15v, 'imperator condendo leges suas, si esset contrarius legi naturali, leges suae non essent tenendae'; cf. Anon., *Disquisitio iuridica*, ch. 9, pp. 1390–1.

[2] See the elaboration of the idea that he who acts *pro voluntate* is exercising a *potestas tyrannica* in Anon., *Disquisitio iuridica*, ch. 9, pp. 1390–1. This may be compared with Bracton's 'Non est enim rex ubi dominatur voluntas et non lex'. See also Geoffrey of Fontaines, *Quodlibeta*, XI. xvii (v. 78), 'In tali autem casu, scilicet cum princeps solo quo consilio privato contentus tale onus imponit nec vult quod alias causa vel necessitas propter quam imponitur innotescat, deberent subditi resistere si possent, quousque esset per praedictos prudentes sufficienter discussum; alioquin paulatim regnum in tyrannidem convertetur et subditi *liberi* redigerentur ad conditionem *servorum* subditorum . . . sicut tyrannus nititur principari secundum propriam voluntatem'; Gilbert of Tournai, *Eruditio regum*, iii. 3, p. 85, 'Haec enim inter regem et tyrannum est differentia quod tyrannus voluntate saevit et licentia effraenata, rex vero sola necessitate punit et causa'.

[3] Durandus de S. Porciano, *De iurisdictione ecclesiastica*, i. 1, ff. 1–IV.

[4] Gilbert of Tournai, *Eruditio regum*, II. i. 1, p. 44 '[rex] non recte regendo nomen regis amittat'; cf. Aegidius Romanus, *De regimine principum*, I. i. 12; Alvarus Pelagius, *De planctu Ecclesiae*, ch. 62, pp. 193–4. The test between king and tyrant is whether the ruler pursues the common good: e.g. Tholemy of Lucca, *De regimine principum*, iii. 11, pp. 259–60, 'ille legitimus rex est qui principaliter bonum subditorum intendit . . . quod si ad aliud faciunt, in seipsos commodum retorquendo, non sunt reges sed tyranni'; also John of Paris, *De*

Thereupon a state of emergency ensues. The *status* of the community is imperilled, and the doctrine of necessity operates. But in such a case the community has a free hand: necessity knows no law, neither animate nor inanimate: both the ruler and the common law of the society can be ignored. The normal subjection of people to ruler is converted into the casual authority of people over ruler.

Rex enim superior est *regulariter* toto regno suo, et tamen *in casu* est inferior regno, quia regnum *in casu necessitatis* potest regem suum deponere et in custodia detinere. Hoc enim habet ex iure naturali.[1]

Since there is now to all intents and purposes a vacancy in the headship of the community, and nature abhors a vacuum, the *populus* takes over all governmental functions. And, said Lupold of Bebenburg, this must apply in any case of a community *vacante imperio*: the people assumes control not only when the ruler has become a tyrant, but also when any normal vacancy occurs, either through the death of the ruler or if he is merely absent from the realm.[2] There is now slowly built up general agreement upon a number of situations in which a state of necessity is presumed to exist and abnormal authority may be exercised. In some the ruler may act over the heads of his subjects, in others the people become superior to their head. There should then prevail a system of checks and balances which may meet any occasion, and this has been achieved without the recognition of a single supreme authority.

The idea of the separation of powers, whose invention is sometimes attributed to Locke and Montesquieu, can therefore be said to be quite clearly envisaged in the political thought of the later Middle Ages. Sovereignty does not reside in any one part of the

potestate regia et papali, ch. 1, p. 177. For a historical survey see Schulz, 'Bracton on Kingship', pp. 151–3; J. Balogh, 'Rex a recte regendo', *Speculum*, iii (1928), pp. 580–2.

[1] William of Ockham, *Octo quaestiones*, ii. 8, p. 86; cf. iv. 8, pp. 152–3, 'Romani . . . qui, quamvis *regulariter* omnem potestatem regendi propter bonum commune transtulerunt in imperatorem, non tamen transtulerunt in ipsum potestatem dominandi seu regendi despotice, nec a se abdicaverunt omnem potestatem *casualiter* disponendi de imperio'; similarly Lupold of Bebenburg, *De iure regni Romani*, ch. 17, pp. 406–7.

[2] Lupold of Bebenburg, *De iure regni Romani*, ch. 12, p. 389.

political community, ruler or people, but is shared between them. Strictly speaking the term cannot be applied to either. In this sense the Thomist system represents a denial of sovereignty. But it would be inaccurate to suggest that sovereignty vanished altogether. Both ruler and people renounced their rights to absolute authority, but these rights did not disappear into a void. One can only renounce something to somebody. In this case the recipient was God. The absolute natural right of the people and the absolute divine right of the ruler were returned to God: when they were subsequently reactivated by ruler or people in emergency conditions they might then justifiably claim to be acting on behalf of God. Only God, as Aquinas emphasised, is sovereign in the constitution.[1] But the fact that God retains it means that sovereignty does not cease to exist. Using legal rather than theological phraseology, the thirteenth-century civilians had enunciated a very similar principle. Bracton, for example, speaks of the supreme Law which makes a king what he is, and of the duty of the king to make a return 'gift' to this Law. This gift is obedience to the law, or, in other words, a renunciation of the right to act absolutely.[2] Here also it may be suggested a foundation is being laid for the notion of State-sovereignty, of sovereignty vested in that abstract entity the State rather than in any of its human members. It may be pointed out that it was already customary for coronation oaths and charters of liberties etc., in which according to the publicists the renunciations of absolute rights were embodied, to be sworn *Deo et populo*. At a later date political writers would develop the notion of the social contract by which men renounced their natural rights to act absolutely and vested them in a corporation, the abstraction which today goes by the name of the State, but which for Hobbes was that

[1] Note Aquinas' description of Christ's kingship, *In Epistolam I ad Tim.*, 2 (Parma, xiii. 590–1), 'Dominium suum est maximum quia *solus* dominatur et habet *liberam* potestatem, *non secundum statuta ut polyticus*. Deus autem unus est dominus omnium'; also *Summa theologica*, II. 1. xiii and cix; *Commentum in Sententias*, II. xlix. 1–2; and Dante, *Monarchia*, i. 7–8, pp. 344–5. This emphasis on God and his law as superior to every earthly ruler is reminiscent of Bracton's famous statement that the king is 'sub Deo et lege'; cf. *Dig.*, I. iii. 2, 'Lex est omnium rex'.

[2] Schulz, 'Bracton on Kingship', pp. 141, 168–9.

artificial man and mortal God, Leviathan. In the sixteenth century Junius Brutus would speak of the *populus* as a mystical entity which combined possession of the community's natural rights and the ruler's divine rights. Something of the same sort is implied here. Absolute natural and divine rights are given up to God, the true Law. But since God can be seen as the mystical personality of the community, the *persona Ecclesiae*, this was tantamount to stating that absolute powers were granted to the society itself, the *Ecclesia* viewed as an abstract ever-righteous entity. Sovereignty, it may be said, is vested in the *Ecclesia* as opposed to any of its human parts. Law is an expression of the will of the sovereign *Ecclesia* issuing out of the joint mouthpiece of ruler and people acting together in unison on behalf of the *universitas*: if either acts absolutely *in certis causis* they do so in their official capacities as representatives of the corporation. As we shall see in due course, the more moderate conciliar thinkers were already at this time developing the view that the abstract rights of the community became actual in the hands of a general council acting in the name of God and the *Ecclesia* and empowered to preserve the *status* of the whole against a ruler who presumed to arrogate sovereignty to himself alone at the expense of the common good.

The basis for this conciliar development is not difficult to appreciate. On the Thomistic rendering of the right order in society the papacy, with its insistence upon absolute autonomy of action, and its authoritarian ideological outlook, began to appear as something like a monstrous despotism. It could not be denied that the hierocratic system was essentially paternalistic, particularly when the popes themselves were at such pains to stress the point.[1] On the other hand Aristotle had explicitly stated that the principles of domestic government could not be countenanced in the *polis*, and that men were to be free and equal, not slaves.[2] Hence Aquinas had no alternative but to assert that patriarchal principles savoured strongly of tyranny and denied the fundamental character of citi-

[1] E.g. Innocent III, *Consec. serm.*, ii (*PL*, ccxvii. 655), 'Ego namque sum servus ille quem Deus constituit super familiam suam'; (658), 'At omnes omnino qui sunt de familia Domini sub eius cura constituti sunt'.

[2] Aristotle, *Politics*, i. 7. The distinction between *liberi* and *servi* is maintained in Roman law: *Inst.*, i. 9; *Dig.*, I. v. 3.

zens as *liberi homines*.[1] And although it was some consolation to hear every pope emphasising that he was bound by the law of his own conscience and by his future need to render account to God,[2] it is not very surprising that it came to be questioned whether this was really a sufficient safeguard. Inevitably the avowed anti-hierocratic writers seized upon this new conception of authority as a stick with which to belabour the heads of their opponents. Whilst the majority of the followers of Aquinas, whatever their protestations to the contrary, had a distinctly pro-papal bias, and had accordingly elaborated their theory of a constitutional balance only in the most general terms and without mentioning names, Ockham, for one, was not prepared to be so non-commital. As might be expected the new theory made slow progress, and it was not until the early fourteenth century that the Thomist *rex sub lege* idea was linked up with the older conciliar theories of the canonists and deliberately woven into the publicists' discussions on the nature of papal power. And so whilst the theory of the limited lay ruler is a familiar feature of the thirteenth-century scene, the systematic application of this idea to the papacy has received remarkably little attention. Nevertheless Aquinas had stated quite explicitly that the natural law theory of lay power was equally true of ecclesiastical power,[3] and it was not long before the publicists began to ask why, if one could depose a lay ruler for exceeding his rights, the pope should not also be deposed for the same reason.[4] In the following

[1] Thomas Aquinas, *Comm. in Polit.*, i. 1; iii. 7; v. 2; *Comm. in Ethic.*, v. 8.

[2] E.g. John XXII, 'Licet enim super ius positi, simus a iure soluti, lege tamen astringimur conscientiae': A. Coulon, *Jean XXII (1316–34): Lettres secrètes et curiales relatives à la France extraits des registres du Vatican* (Paris, 1906), n. 72 c. 65; 'supra ius positi, simus a iure soluti, non ignoramus tamen eo magis nos observationi iustitiae apud Dominum obligatos, quo de maiore potestate percepta rationem reddere tenemur eidem': Rymer, *Foedera* (London, 1818–21), ii. 326.

[3] Thomas Aquinas, *Summa theologica*, III. II. cxlvii. 3, 'Sicut ad saeculares principes pertinet praecepta legalia iuris naturalis determinativa tradere de his quae pertinent ad utilitatem communem in temporalibus rebus, ita etiam ad praelatos ecclesiasticos pertinet ea statutis praecipere quae ad utilitatem communem pertinent in spiritualibus bonis.' Similarly Bartolus, *Comm. in Cod.*, I. ii. 10, maintained that both the emperor and the pope were in exactly the same position with regard to the law.

[4] Henry of Ghent, *Quodlibeta*, XIV. ix, 'Quod si non sit omnino spes cor-

chapters we shall see how the whole of this conception of government is steadily absorbed into hierocratic thought, and, as the assimilation takes effect, eventually leads into a complete denial of the traditional theory of papal monarchy.

rectionis in isto, debent subditi agere ad depositionem superioris. . . Nec video in hoc circa clericos aut laicos respectu suorum superiorum aliquam differentiam': de Lagarde, 'La philosophie sociale d'Henri de Gand', p. 115.

PART III
GOD AND CAESAR

I. THE STRUGGLE FOR INDEPENDENCE

If it remains true that during the central medieval period the lay ruler was almost constantly on the defensive against the encroachments of papal power, it must be remembered that the papal idea had itself originally been developed as a protection against the demands of the divine right monarch, and had only swung over to the offensive at the time of the Gregorian revolution. It succeeded in driving much of the theory of lay monarchy underground, but the hierocrats were never allowed to forget that a battle for absolute control of the Christian society was still in progress. As a rule the struggle was not conducted in the open, but under cover of subsidiary disputes such as the right of episcopal appointment, the competence of rival legal systems, or the right of the lay ruler to tax his clerical subjects. It was, so to speak, a subconscious conflict, the inbred hostility of opposing ideologies, punctuated by decrees of excommunication and deposition on the one side, and defiance on the other. It was only in the great controversies of the age, such as that between the Staufen and the papacy, or that between Philip the Fair and Boniface VIII, that the issue was openly acknowledged to be what it had always been, namely, whether pope or prince was to function as the supreme governor of the European community.

During the twelfth and thirteenth centuries the old imperial idea of the Roman emperor as the only *caput Ecclesiae* had been quietly laid aside in favour of a divided headship in which both pope and emperor were held to have their own clearly defined area of jurisdiction, and to respect the autonomy of the other within his own sphere. This dual vicariate of Christ remains the official lay doctrine throughout the fourteenth century. But the decline of the papacy which is now rapidly setting in inevitably tends to resurrect the whole tradition of lay supremacy. Whilst the papal writers of the period make their almost mechanical denunciations of the *dualitas* idea, they are aware that everything is once again at stake. The lay rulers are beginning to feel that the time for compromise is past, and their propagandists are set to work to elaborate a theory of lay omnicompetence that might have come straight out of the Saxon era. Moreover, as the French kingdom grows to parity with and surpasses the Empire, we find this idea as eagerly propounded by the Capetians as by the successors of the Staufen emperors from whom they had borrowed it.[1] As the anonymous author of the *Rex pacificus* pointed out, the pope is still to be permitted influence over the souls of men, but what this means, if it means anything at all, the author does not bother to say. The important point for him is that all jurisdictional power ought to be concentrated in the hands of the king.[2] The Goliath of Rome is at last to be confronted by a new David.[3] Holy Henry[4] and infallible Philip,[5] miraculously anointed,[6] the scourges of scrofula,[7] are to be the new gods on

[1] H. Wieruszowski, 'Vom Imperium zum Nationalen Königtum', *Historische Zeitschrift*, xxx (Munich and Berlin, 1933).

[2] Referring to I *Cor.*, ii. 15, the *Rex pacificus* comments, ch. 4, p. 680, 'apostolus non loquitur ibi de iudicio iurisdictionis, quod competit alicui per supremam impositionem, de quo intendimus ad praesens, sed loquitur de iudicio discretionis quod habetur per internam inspirationem'.

[3] With reference to the French king see Anon., *Somnium viridarii*, i. 144–5, p. 114, and as applied to the emperor, Dante, *Ep.*, vii. 8, p. 99. Augustinus Triumphus on the other hand suggests that Ben-hadad (I *Kings*, xx. 23–8) might be seen as a better example from the Old Testament, *Summa*, xlv. 2, p. 248.

[4] Dante, *Ep.*, v. 2, p. 49; vii. 8, p. 100, 'divus Henricus'. See further W. Ensslin, 'Gottkaiser und Kaiser von Gottes Gnaden', *SBAW* (1943), fasc. 6; *KTB*, p. 252.

[5] Nogaret (Holtzmann, p. 254), 'Vobiscum ergo est iudicium, O dominus rex, coram Deo et hominibus. Non habetis iudicem temporalem, habetis Deum, qui adest et falli non potest'; see also his use of 'Cor regis in manu Dei est et ubicunque voluerit, inclinabit illud' (*Prov.*, xxi. 1) to suggest this, Holtzmann, p. 273. The phrase was normally included in the imperial coronation order to imply that only a papally-created emperor could pursue *iustitia*.

[6] E.g. Anon., *Quaestio in utramque partem*, ch. 5, p. 102, 'Primo quidem possessionis huius iustum titulum probat unctio sacra, missa divinitus, qua reges Franciae semper opportunis temporibus inunguntur. Nonne regnum evidenter approbatur a Deo cuius reges divino munere consecrantur?' See also Peter Roger in Peter Bertrandus, *De iurisdictione ecclesiastica*, p. 1372b, where it is argued that the receipt of this gift from God is all the more reason for the French king to obey the pope as his vicar. Peter Roger later became Clement VI.

[7] On this see M. Bloch, *Les rois thaumaturges* (Strasbourg, 1924). According to the *Quaestio in utramque partem*, ch. 5, p. 102, this was handed down from

earth.[1] It is to them that the pope must look if he wishes to call himself the *vicarius Dei*. They are the only source of divine power in the Christian community, and it is from them that he must expect correction. According to Dante, the powers (*facultates*) of the priesthood come from the emperor, and if they are misused they must return to him.[2] The emperor is the judge ordinary of all men, and consequently of the pope:

Imperator fuit iudex ordinarius sancti Petri: ergo est iudex ordinarius papae, qui est Christi vicarius.[3]

Just as Christ was put to death by Pilate, the vicar of Caesar, so may the vicar of Christ be deposed by the successor of the Caesars.[4] There can be no doubt that this was exactly what the emperors themselves were thinking. As Louis IV subsequently put it, the function of the emperor is to declare the will of Christ, and it is by this authority that he pronounces John XXII to be a lapsed heretic, no longer capable of holding office in the Empire.

father to son: 'Secundo hoc idem probat aperta miracula... Sicut enim haereditario iure succedit patri filius in adoptionem regni, sic quasi haereditario iure succedendi, facultatem Deo tradente alter alteri in simile potestate miracula faciendi'. The current claim of the French and English kings to possess miraculous healing powers by hereditary right is discussed by Alvarus Pelagius, *Collirium*, p. 509, but denounced as heretical.

[1] See the attack by Alvarus Pelagius, *Speculum regum*, p. 524, on those kings who 'nec regem regum dominum timentes, dicentes saltem inter se, Deus sum'. For this idea in Roman law *KTB*, p. 92.

[2] Dante, *Monarchia*, ii. 12, p. 362; cf. Anon., *Somnium viridarii*, ii. 13, p. 151, 'Papa accepit potestatem ab imperatore'. This is attacked by Augustinus Triumphus at *Summa*, ii. 5–7, pp. 23–5; iii. 1, p. 27. Durandus de S. Porciano merely said that the imperial rights had now been abrogated, *De iurisdictione ecclesiastica*, ch. 3, fo. 6.

[3] Anon., *Somnium viridarii*, ii. 160, p. 173; Dante, *Monarchia*, ii. 13, p. 363, 'iudex ordinarius . . . supra totum humanum genus iurisdictionem habens'.

[4] Dante, *Monarchia*, ii. 13, p. 363; cf. *Ep.*, v. 10, p. 51. Dante's position on this is discussed by Davis, *Dante and the Idea of Rome*, pp. 57–63. See also Anon., *Somnium viridarii*, ii. 45, p. 155; John of Viterbo, *De regimine civitatum*, ch. 128, p. 266; Jordan of Osnabruck, *De praerogativa Romani imperii*, p. 14; Marsilius of Padua, *Defensor pacis*, II. iv. 12, pp. 173–4. The view that Pilate was not blameworthy for condemning Christ becomes a common feature of nominalist thought in the fourteenth century; Adam of Woodhouse, for example, sees Pilate's action as a mere instance of man carrying out God's will: Leff, *Bradwardine and the Pelagians*, p. 253.

. . . eo quod indigne gerit et gessit vicariatus officium ab eo tempore quo in alterum criminum praedictorum dignoscitur notorie lapsum fuisse, a Christo privatum esse et fuisse denunciamus nostraeque imperialis auctoritatis sententia episcopatu Romano et universali Ecclesia Dei seu papatu tenore praesentium privamus et ab eodem deponimus. . .[1]

This is not an act of personal animosity but a solemn duty enjoined upon him by his coronation oath: how else can he act as protector of the Roman church and defender of the Christian faith unless he exerts his control over them?[2] It is on the same grounds, the defence of the faith, that Pierre Dubois asserts the right of the French king in a universal capacity to seize, judge, punish and execute the pope,

Vous, noble roy, *fur tous autres princes* par herege defendeour de la foy, destruicur de bougres, pouez et devez et estes tenus requerre et procurer que ledit Boniface soit tenus et iugiez pour herege et punis en la maniere que l'en le pourra et devra et doit faire emprés sa mort,[3]

a claim which Philip the Fair presently endorses. The king in fact regards himself as having received full power from Christ to regulate every aspect of life in the society, and the Aragonese commentator who described Philip as behaving as though he was pope, emperor and king all rolled into one was not very wide of the mark.[4] In a highly significant passage the king tells us that he possesses the totality of care for the Christian community, whilst the bishops merely partake of a share in this power.

. . . ad defensionem, conservationem et exaltationem ipsius fidei ipse dominus rex collatam sibi recepit a Domino potestatem iidemque praelati sunt *in partem sollicitudinis* evocati.[5]

[1] Baluze, iii. 431.

[2] Baluze, iii. 391, 409. See also the discussions of this in Conrad of Megenberg, *Tractatus contra Wilhelmum Occam*, ch. 3, pp. 348–51.

[3] Pierre Dubois, *La supplication du pueuble de France*, p. 218. For Philip IV's approval see his letter, Dupuy, pp. 124–5, in which he declares that the French king and other princes have the right to intervene in all ecclesiastical affairs in defence of the faith; cf. pp. 102, 107. This attitude predates the Anagni incident. See further J. Rivière, *Le problème de l'Eglise et de l'Etat au temps de Philippe le Bel* (Louvain and Paris, 1926), pp. 113–16; '*In partem sollicitudinis*': évolution d'une formule pontificale', *Revue des sciences religieuses*, v (1925), pp. 210–31 at pp. 224–5.

[4] '. . . pus el es rey et papa et emperador': H. Finke, 'Zur Charakteristic Philipps des Schönen', *MIOG*, xxvi (1905), p. 209.

[5] Dupuy, p. 118.

At once the real intentions of the contemporary lay rulers are revealed. Not only are they to exercise supreme control over the clergy, but they are to do so in the very capacity hitherto claimed by the Roman church. It is the lay ruler who is now the *caput Ecclesiae*. As vicar of Christ he wields both royal and sacerdotal authority.[1] He indeed is the *verus papa*; and the long-awaited and much-publicised *reformatio totius orbis*[2] has no other interpretation than that of a political revolution which is to oust the pope from the headship of the Christian society and reinstate the lay monarch in his place.

By the fourteenth century both sides in the great papal–lay debate had equipped themselves with a vast arsenal of literary weapons, and the student of the period must contend with a paper warfare of alarming proportions and unparalleled ferocity. Each claim was immediately answered by an appropriate counter-argument, and these arguments become so familiar with regular usage as to suggest a game of chess played in terms of political theory. But amidst the interminable permutations of pro and con, the publicists never lost sight of the fact that they were debating the fundamental question of the origin of political authority. No one had or at that time was likely to have denied that it ultimately came from

[1] For the development of this idea in France see Kern, *Kingship and Law*, pp. 58f.; H. Kaempf, *Pierre Dubois und die Geistigen Grundlagen des Französischen Nationalbewusstseins um 1300* (Leipzig and Berlin, 1935), especially pp. 38–9; and in general *KTB*, pp. 44, 124–6. For its practical effect in the fourteenth century cf. G. Mollat, 'Le roi de France et la collation plénière, *pleno jure*, des bénéfices ecclésiastiques', *Academie des Inscriptions et Belles-Lettres*, xiv. 2 (Paris, 1951). It is pointed out by Riesenberg, *Inalienability of Sovereignty*, p. 31, that very much the same attitude can be found in the middle of the thirteenth century with the *Especulo* of Alfonso X. In England the coronation chair was used in the early fourteenth century as a sort of supra-episcopal *cathedra*: Stanley, *Memorials of Westminster Abbey*, p. 54.

[2] The idea of the *reformatio* is current in imperial thought from at least the time of Frederick I: see Ullmann, 'Cardinal Roland and Besancon', p. 109, n. 7; but is of Augustinian derivation. It is still in use with Louis IV but was already passing into the political vocabulary of the national kingdoms. See for example Pierre Dubois' demand for a 'reformatio status universalis Ecclesiae' to be effected by the French king through a general council at Toulouse, *De recuperatione Sanctae Terrae*, ch. 4, pp. 6–7; ch. 106, pp. 90–1; ch. 109, p. 97. There is little need to point out the relevance of this to the sixteenth-century 'Reformation'.

God, but in spite of a thousand years of argument, no one was nearer settlement of the question of whether its earthly orifice was the pope, the prince or the people. The anti-hierocratic writers indeed oscillated unhappily between the community seen as the body of God and the lay ruler as the vicar of God. For whilst their monarchs emphasised their direct grant of power from God, the lay writers were uncomfortably aware that this totally failed to answer the papal case. As Aegidius Romanus very pertinently queried, if the lay ruler really has been chosen by God, how is one to know this? On what evidence is this assertion based?[1] In face of the papal theory founded upon the rock of Biblical exegesis, it was hardly enough to maintain that alongside the Petrine commission there must have been a corresponding Caesarian commission which both Christ and the Evangelists had omitted to mention.[2] Whilst they held to the idea of divine right monarchy the lay rulers were in fact faced with an almost complete inability to demonstrate how they had become the powers that were ordained of God.

In view of this crippling weakness the Roman emperors had tended to look increasingly towards the *lex regia* theory of government as a justification for their universal rulership. As we have seen, most of the lay writers of the thirteenth and fourteenth centuries regarded the basis of imperial authority as being some sort of initial grant of power by the Roman people, and much as the emperors themselves might dislike the suggestion that their position stemmed from the German princes acting *vice omnium*, they were forced into a reliance upon this theory to counteract the hierocratic writers' emphasis upon papal coronation as the constitutive act of rulership. Aided by the growth of the idea of the natural origin of government, this justification of independent imperial

[1] Aegidius Romanus, *De ecclesiastica potestate*, ii. 5, p. 55, 'De hoc ergo est nostra quaestio qualiter Deus mandavit quod constitueretur rex super fidei populo'.

[2] Anon., *Somnium viridarii*, i. 42, p. 72, 'Christus enim commisit claves regni coelorum ligandi et solvendi quantum ad peccata Petro: ergo videbatur quantum ad temporalia *tacite* principibus temporalibus potestatem ligandi et absolvendi committere'. Tholemy of Lucca's suggestion, *De regimine principum*, iii. 13, p. 262, that Augustus had been the vicar of God without realising it was not very helpful either.

authority becomes more and more popular during the course of the thirteenth century, and receives full expression in the acrimonious dispute between Louis of Bavaria and John XXII.[1] Characteristically the matter was not discussed in abstract terms but as a question of practical politics, namely, does election by the German princes give the elect the exercise of imperial authority? This is not a mere formality, a question of whether there should be a proper time lag between election and coronation to accentuate the greater dignity of emperorship. It is a matter of vital importance since it involves the whole problem of the source of authority in the Empire. Does power come from below or above, from people or pope? Does it make the emperor virtually autonomous or a mere papal official? It is this which explains the concern expressed by both sides over the details of the disputed imperial election of 1314, and the prodigious length which publicists like Ockham went to in their discussions of it. The lay writers are fully appreciative of the fact that to accept the hierocratic contention that imperial authority comes only as a result of papal confirmation and coronation is to reduce the emperor to a creature of the Roman church. It means that his very existence depends upon papal approval, that failure to maintain absolute obedience to papal commands can result only in deposition. On the other hand to claim full imperial power from election implies, as Louis of Bavaria realised,[2] that the papacy is totally excluded from any real participation in the institution of the emperor. The imperial coronation becomes a meaningless formality, and the whole hierocratic argument that the pope is the only source of authority in the Empire is denied.

[1] The disputed election of 1314 between Louis of Bavaria and Frederick of Austria bears a close correspondence to that between Lothar of Saxony and Conrad in 1125–7 and that between Philip of Suabia and Otto of Brunswick in 1198. This is pointed out by Louis himself, Baluze, iii. 396; and cf. the comparison by Innocent III in *Decretales*, I. vi. 34. Louis' attitude is a conscious adaptation of the old Staufen theory of imperial election.

[2] Louis began to exercise imperial rights immediately after his coronation at Aix by ratifying imperial privileges on behalf of William of Hainault: these were to be respected 'on pain of imperial displeasure'. On 4 January 1315, he appointed John of Beaumont as vicar 'per totam Ytaliam' with full authority to transact any imperial business: *MGH*, *Const.*, V, pp. 130–1. For his use of imperial vicars in Italy in 1323 see n. 729, p. 568.

In the eyes of John XXII the right to examine the two candidates elected in 1314 belongs indisputably to the pope, and until this has been done and the pope has given his decision, the vacancy in the Empire following the death of Henry VII continues to exist. Imperial authority has returned whence it had come, and the right to administer the Empire belongs to the Roman church.[1] Louis' election is discounted on the grounds of discord amongst the electors,[2] and in spite of Louis' attempts at reconciliation with the pope in 1330–1 and 1334–7, the papacy was never prepared to recognise the validity of his election. The real reason for this refusal cannot be doubted, and has little to do with the question of which candidate was elected by the majority of the princes, or where he was crowned and by whom.[3] The insuperable obstacle to John's recognition of Louis is to be seen in the Bavarian's claim to have been elected 'in imperatorem promovendum'.[4] In this phrase is

[1] See the constitution *Si fratrum* of 1317, *Extravagantes Iohannis XXII*, v. 1; and his declaration of 1323 in *MHG*, *Const.*, V n. 792, pp. 616–19. This was repeated by Clement VI in 1343. See further Folz, *Le souvenir et la légende de Charlemagne*, pp. 407–10; Offler, 'Empire and Papacy', pp. 24–5.

[2] See his letter of 8 October, 1323, cited Offler, *art. cit.*, pp. 24–5.

[3] See Louis' enumeration of the points in his favour, Baluze, iii. 389–90. He points out that he was the first to be elected, that he was elected by a majority and in the right place (Frankfort), and that he was also crowned in the right place (Aix). Frederick on the other hand, iii. 395, was the second choice of the princes, or rather of a minority of them, and he was both elected and crowned at the wrong place (Bonn). He does not however mention that he was crowned by the wrong archbishop (Mainz), whilst Frederick was properly crowned by the archbishop of Cologne. The right of the archbishop of Cologne to crown the king was generally accepted, although not officially recognised until the Golden Bull: U. Stutz, *Der Erzbischof von Mainz und die deutsche Königswahl* (Weimar, 1910); A. Hofmeister, 'Zum Krönungsrechte des Mainzer Erzbischofs', *Historisches Vierteljahrbuch*, xv (1912), pp. 365f. The same points had been vigorously debated after the elections of 1198.

[4] Baluze, iii. 389–90, 'Item cum consuetudo imperii *approbata*, quae apud nos pro iure servatur, habeat manifeste quod electus in loco ad eligendum regem Romanorum *in imperatorem postmodum promovendum*, videlicet in oppido de Franckenfurt, ab omnibus electoribus sive a maiore parte ipsorum *sive etiam a minori* . . . huiusmodi electus est habendus tamquam *in vera concordia* electus, et sibi debet obediri ut regi a subditis et vassallis *imperii* et corona preberi sibi in Aquisgrani quandocunque voluerit, et si qui vassalli et fideles *imperii* eidem non obedierint, sunt ipso facto omnibus quae tenent *ab imperio* privandi'. Cf. Albericus de Rosate, *Comm. in Cod.*, VII. xxxvii. 3, where he refers to 'dominum Ludovicum de Bavaria electum in imperatorem': Ullmann, *The*

revealed the whole nature of the imperialist outlook: the part played by the pope in the making of emperors is to be completely excised. His predecessor had been even more explicit: in 1309 Henry VII's proctors told the pope that election was sufficient in itself, nothing else being needed, and it is not to be wondered at that Clement V's enthusiasm for Henry had suddenly waned.[1] So too the supporters of Louis of Bavaria now begin to stress that papal confirmation and coronation are mere formalities which the elected candidate has a right to expect. As John of Calvaruso declared, there are no grounds on which the pope can suspend the crowning of the emperor.[2] He is in duty bound to accept the electors' choice, and the only purpose of coronation by the pope is that it is a means of announcing their decision to all the world. But otherwise it is a solemn act without significance, having no constitutive character.[3] Lupold of Bebenburg, for example, pointed out that as the *electus* could do everything that the emperor could, the most that the coronation could be said to confer was the title of emperor alone.

Sed non plus importat haec promotio ad imperium quoad Italiam et alias provincias et terras regno et imperio subiectas nisi quadam intitu-

Medieval Idea of Law, p. 177. This corresponds to Philip of Suabia's claim to have been elected 'in imperaturam', cited by Innocent III, *R.N.I.* 14, p. 25. Philip had also referred to his control of the *imperium Romanum* from election: *R.N.I.* 61, p. 91; *MGH, Const.*, II. i p. 1 para 2.

[1] *MGH, Const.*, IV n. 294 p. 257, 'Nam promovendus in imperatorem debet esse rex Romanorum, et talis est sufficiens et non alius'; similarly n. 466, pp. 411–12.

[2] John of Calvaruso, *Quaestio an Romanus pontifex potuerit treugam inducere*, p. 1316, 'dico quod papa non potuit aliquibus conditionibus suspendere coronationem imperatoris'; cf. Frederick II, *MGH, Const.*, II n. 116, p. 150, '... principibus ex quorum electione nobis corona imperii *debebatur*'.

[3] Marsilius of Padua, *De translatione imperii*, ch. 12, p. 153, 'principes electores ... imperatorem eligunt ad solemnitatem, non quidem propter necessitatem aliquam, per Romanum episcopum coronandum'. The *Rex pacificus* cites the view that the imperial coronation is as declaratory as the papal one: ch. 4, p. 681, 'dicunt aliqui quod sicut cardinalis Hostiensis consecrat papam et tamen post consecrationem nullam iurisdictionem spiritualem habet super ipsum papam, ita papa confirmat imperatorem et etiam coronat, et tamen post confirmationem et coronationem nullam iurisdictionem temporalem super ipsum habet'. For similar opinions with the Roman and canon lawyers see Ullmann, *The Medieval Idea of Law*, pp. 176–8; *Medieval Papalism*, p. 143.

lationem et nominationem imperialem, cum *omnia possit* in his provinciis et terris quae potest imperator.[1]

Lupold was simply echoing the general consensus of opinion amongst the imperialists. The powerful symbolism of the papal coronation ceremony, even the oath, which for the hierocratic writers binds the emperor in obedience to the pope, is dismissed as of no account. In one very suggestive passage the author of the *Somnium viridarii* managed not only to convey the typical medieval ruler's distaste for the coronation oath—which he would apparently permit the king to repudiate—but also to give the impression that he himself fully appreciated that the imperial coronation was symbolically of a lower order than that of any other king. Thus he denies that the emperor is more subject to the pope than other rulers, arguing that since other kings are not bound by such oaths, then the emperor cannot be either.

In nullo est imperator magis subiectus papae quam alii reges; alii autem reges ad tale iuramentum minime obligantur, ergo nec imperator.[2]

So too we find that both John of Calvaruso and William of Ockham did their best to denigrate the oath. For them it is a purely voluntary matter, and although they allow that it might appear that the emperor is subjecting himself to the pope, they interpret this as nothing more than the formal courtesy paid by any layman to a priest.[3] It is understandable therefore that Ockham later says

[1] Lupold of Bebenburg, *De iure regni Romani*, ch. 11, p. 378. Similarly Ugolinus de Celle, *De electione regis Romanorum*, ch. 8, p. 74, 'Qui enim faciunt imperatorem nisi illi qui faciunt regem, videlicet, consensus principum et eorum electio? Non enim de novo eligitur cum inungatur et coronatur a papa. Ex eo enim tempore quo inter principes relatus est, *omnia potest* quae principi Romanorum sunt *concessa*, accepta ab ipsis principibus corona et insigniis *imperialibus*, quae sunt crux, lancea et spata, quae omnia suscepit antequam Romam proficiscatur, quando coronam recepit Aquisgrani. Et ideo cum ad ipsum Romanorum regem spectet *statim* quod electus est et coronatus Aquisgrani plena iurisdictio et administratio rerum temporalium'. In 1199 the German princes had declared 'nec dat ei inunctio imperialis nisi nomen': Bayley, *The Formation of the German College of Electors*, p. 150.

[2] Anon., *Somnium viridarii*, i. 163, p. 125. That the symbolism of the imperial coronation virtually demoted the emperor from royal rank is shown by Ullmann, *The Growth of Papal Government*, pp. 225–8, 253–61, 451 n. 1.

[3] William of Ockham, *Tractatus contra Benedictum XII*, vi. 13, p. 297, '... possitque sibi ob reverentiam Dei in multis reverentiam exhibere quemadmodum

outright that no coronation is necessary at all. Provided that the princes have legitimately chosen him, the pope cannot demand either to confirm or crown the elect, much less exact an oath of obedience. Indeed, he continues, their candidate becomes emperor even against the will of the pope and has full power over the Empire. This means that he may, like other kings, choose for himself whom he wishes to perform the coronation: 'imperator a quo voluerit poterit legitime coronari'; and the papal crowning of past emperors can be explained away as the result of imperial devotion or of sheer naivety. In any case the emperor submitted to the coronation of his own free will and there was no obligation involved: 'non ex necessitate sed ex spontanea voluntate'.[1]

In this way the imperialists were forced back upon the action of the electoral princes, which, taken on behalf of the whole Empire, must now be seen as the essence of imperial creation. As Ockham once again puts it, as soon as the election has taken place, the candidate is emperor in all but name.

> ... quantum ad id quod est de essentia imperatoris et quod pertinet ad verum esse, est imperator; sed quantum ad nominationem, famam et exteriorem apparentiam hominum, non est quia non sic appellatur.[2]

This, it need hardly be added, met with warm approval from Louis himself. Imperial election, he declares, embodies its own confirmation. No further ratification is required, and his supporters could not now fail to remark upon the similarity between the imperial and papal creative processes. 'Et eo ipso quod electus est a principibus', said Ugolinus de Celle, 'confirmatus est, sicut papa'.[3] In fact

reges et principes saepe ex devotione et humilitatis reverentiam magnam exhibent etiam simplicibus sacerdotibus propter Deum'; John of Calvaruso, *Quaestio an Romanus pontifex potuerit treugam inducere*, p. 1312, 'non est sacramentum subiectionis seu vassalagii nec enim illius per omnia formam habet, sed est sacramentum devotionis seu reverentiae ac humilitatis quam disciplina docuit christiana et eiusdam obsequii christianitatis'.

[1] William of Ockham, *Quoniam scriptura*, p. 77. John of Paris had already made the general observation that kings did not need to be anointed, *De potestate regia et papali*, ch. 18, p. 228.

[2] William of Ockham, *Allegationes de potestate imperiali*, p. 430. This passage is derived from Johannes Teutonicus.

[3] Ugolinus de Celle, *De electione regis Romanorum*, ch. 1, p. 72; cf. Louis of Bavaria, Baluze, iii. 429, 'unde eo ipso quod sumus electi, sumus etiam con-

Louis was never slow in asserting his full imperial stature: all imperial rights and authority are already in the hands of the *rex Romanorum*—'ipse electus administrare possit et omnia alia facere quae Romanorum principes facere visi sunt'[1]—even though his election is disputed.[2] There was, it is true, a certain amount of disagreement between Louis and his supporters over the matter of the Aix coronation. Louis himself seems to have regarded it as devoid of constitutional significance, whereas most of the princes tended to insist upon the coronation as a highly important factor in order to emphasise the royal coronation oath as a limiting feature. Certainly most of the publicists came round to adding that the imperial power which they had claimed for the candidate from election meant, of course, after the coronation at Aix.[3] Other writers tried to draw a distinction between the powers gained by election, and those that were reserved for the emperor until after his coronation at Rome. The main theory along these lines was that put forward by Lupold of Bebenburg, who appears, at times, to have been genuinely anxious to reach a settlement between the papal and imperial positions. Having in his more 'imperial' moments declared

firmati, nulla prorsus confirmatione fienda per hominem indigentes'. Louis' description of the process of election is closely modelled on the papal practice: the electors act by imperial authority (since their customary right to elect is only legally valid as a result of imperial confirmation); a two-thirds majority is required; the election embodies its own confirmation; it grants the emperor full power immediately; and the subsequent coronation is only declaratory in character. See below pp. 388f., 468.

[1] See Ugolinus de Celle, *De electione regis Romanorum, proem.*, p. 72, and Louis of Bavaria in Baluze, iii. 390; also Anon., *Articuli de iuribus imperii*, ch. 1, p. 593, 'Et quod ex sola electione ipsorum archiepiscoporum et principum electus efficitur verus rex Romanorum et *imperator*'. See also R. Most, 'Der Reichsgedanke des Lupold von Bebenburg', *Deutsches Archiv für Geschichte des Mittelalters*, iv (1941), pp. 444–85 at pp. 465–71. This was followed in the declaration of the princes at Rhense and Louis' bull *Licet iuris* in 1338, and in the Golden Bull of 1356: Altmann-Bernheim, *Ausgewählte Urkunden*, nn. 34, 36, 38, pp. 52–7.

[2] Baluze, iii. 396, 'Praeterea cum constet et notorium sit omnes reges Romanorum electos etiam in discordia, licet electio nostra haberi debeat omnino ex causis evidentibus pro concordi . . . tamen administraverunt semper *imperium* sicut et potuerunt *de iure*'.

[3] E.g. Johannes Branchazolus, *De principio imperatoris et papae*, ii. 6, p. 50; Ugolinus de Celle, *De electione regis Romanorum*, ch. 6, pp. 73–4; ch. 8, p. 74. Note that the anonymous *Articuli de iuribus imperii*, ch. 5, p. 595, also refers to the Aix crown as a 'corona regalis sive imperialis'.

that the empire is gained by election alone and that papal consent is unnecessary,[1] Lupold then develops a theory that election grants no more than the administration of those lands conquered by Charlemagne. The remainder of the imperial rights and the title itself do not follow until after coronation by the pope.[2] Lupold, like many of the contemporary imperialists, wavered hopelessly between a staunch laicism and an attempted accommodation with the hierocratic theory. But apart from their half-hearted essays at a compromise, the lay writers generally remembered for at least part of the time that their declared aim was the search for a source of imperial authority which completely ignored the papacy. And they came to appreciate, as we have said, that this new basis of power could ultimately be nothing else but the will of the people. The princes in making the election are, according to this view, giving voice to the wishes of the whole community, from whom the right to govern originally derives. Whilst this fact tends to be cloaked by the imperial insistence upon the rights of the electors as a matter of immemorable custom,[3] it is, as Ockham said, a natural law theory

[1] Lupold of Bebenburg, *De iure regni Romani*, ch. 5, p. 353; ch. 7, p. 358; ch. 8, p. 363; *Ritmaticum querulosum*, p. 481.

[2] Lupold of Bebenburg, *De iure regni Romani*, ch. 7, p. 361; ch. 8, p. 364; ch. 11, p. 378; ch. 13, p. 395; ch. 16, p. 404. This is also cited Anon., *Somnium viridarii*, i. 179, p. 133; Conrad of Megenberg, *De translatione Romani imperii*, ch. 18, p. 306. Lupold may have taken this particular idea from the distinction in the *Sachsenspiegel* between the royal power gained at Aix and the imperial authority gained at Rome: Bayley, *The Formation of the German College of Electors*, pp. 129–30. This follows the late twelfth-century jurist Benencasa of Arezzo, 'Solutio: ut rex habere potest gladii potestatem a principibus regni; sed ut imperator non potest habere potestatem gladii nisi iuret fidelitatem papae et eius auctoritate gladium accipiat': A. M. Stickler, 'Sacerdozio e regno nei Decretisti e Decretalisti', *MHP*, xviii (1954), pp. 1–26 at p. 9. For Dante's theory that kingship changed to emperorship with the entry into Italy see E. Jordan, 'Dante et la théorie romaine de l'empire', *Revue historique de droit français et étranger*, xlv (1921), pp. 353–96 at p. 356.

[3] Louis of Bavaria, Baluze, iii. 389, '. . . imperii consuetudinum quae apud nos pro iure indubitato servantur sunt ab antiquo . . . consuetudines imperii *approbatas* rationabiles et praescriptas et servatas in factis et processibus imperii ab eo tempore cuius memoria contrarii non existit': this is reproduced in the Rhense declaration of 1338, Altmann-Bernheim, *Ausgewählte Urkunden*, n. 34, pp. 52–3. Cf. the statement of Rudolf of Habsburg, *MGH*, *Const.*, III p. 389, 'De libero et expresso consensu imperii principum ius in electione regis Romani ex longa consuetudine tenentium. . .'.

of authority which lies behind the imperial idea.[1] Much as this conflicted with the emperors' own conception of their absolute divine right and their half-stifled desire for hereditary succession, the contest between papacy and empire had become for the political thinkers of the fourteenth century essentially a facet of the greater constitutional problem of whether true sovereignty was to be found in the head or the members of the Christian society.

The unalterable fact remained however that it was coronation by the pope in Rome which gave possession of the imperial crown, and it was this unpalatable but inescapable reality which vitiated the imperial ideology. No doubt it was this consideration which prompted Louis of Bavaria to undergo his second coronation of 1328 at the hands of the anti-pope. Writing some ten years later Lupold of Bebenburg finds himself totally unable to give a consistent account of the nature of emperorship. Having acknowledged the Germans as the successors of the Roman people, whose princes represent all when they elect and bestow full power upon the imperial candidate, having denied that papal consent is necessary in these proceedings, Lupold cannot but agree that it is the pope who is the real arbiter of imperial affairs. It is the pope who decides disputed elections and holds the empire during an imperial vacancy,[2] who may depose the emperor for misconduct,[3] who has translated the empire in the past,[4] and who may do so again.[5] In view of this,

[1] William of Ockham, *Tractatus contra Benedictum XII*, vi. 6, p. 281.

[2] Lupold of Bebenburg, *De iure regni Romani*, ch. 8, p. 365, 'papa succedit imperio vacante. Hoc enim est propter necessitatem facti, quia non est alius iudex superior, ideo recurri oportet ad papam, et idem esset si esset necessitas iuris, puta quia iudex dubius est quam sententiam de iure proferre debeat'; and cf. ch. 12, p. 380, where he says that the law of necessity makes a case for the papal intervention to settle a disputed election. He appears to see nothing strange in taking all this straight from the commentaries of Innocent IV and Hostiensis on the *Decretales*, II. ii. 10, s.v. *vacante*.

[3] Lupold of Bebenburg, *De iure regni Romani*, ch. 10, p. 372: he may be deposed 'propter crimen haeresis vel aliud gravius crimen notorium'.

[4] Lupold of Bebenburg, *De iure regni Romani*, ch. 3, pp. 340–6; ch. 13, p. 395, 'Et hoc secundo modo tenet imperium a papa virtute translationis imperii'; cf. *De zelo catholicae fidei*, ch. 15, p. 462. He refuses to give an opinion on the Donation of Constantine.

[5] Lupold of Bebenburg, *Ritmaticum querulosum*, p. 483: the symbolic figure of the Roman empire is made to say, 'Sed si praeceptis meis hiis nolunt obedire, Fac eos veraciter ex parte mea scire / Quod ad gentem aliam in brevi trans-

Lupold, no doubt wisely, decides that it is better not to enter into the matter of whether papal and imperial jurisdiction are after all really distinct from each other, and it is small wonder that he concludes by confessing his inability to discover the truth about the questions which he is discussing, and begs that those more qualified to deal with these matters may enlighten him.[1] This dichotomy in the work of Lupold underlines the character of the problem. The conflict over the right of election was not simply a dispute over means, but a clash between two ideological conceptions of society. The way in which the outlook of the papalists is fundamentally different from that of their opponents may be detected in the exasperated query of one hierocratic writer of where could the Roman people have gained the right to elect to power over Christ's kingdom?[2] They could not see farther than the logic of their own arguments. The view that all power came from Christ, the head of the community, so that the appointment of secular rulers must be in the hands of his earthly representative, seems to them such an elementary assumption that they could never bring themselves to believe that what the electors did was done without papal authority. Even the existence of the electors, it was felt, must have been due to some papal action in the past, and Augustinus Triumphus adopts the view that the electoral college had been instituted by Gregory V at the end of the tenth century.

Gregorius V tempore Otthonis imperatoris convocatis et requisitis principibus Alemaniae septem electores instituit officiales ipsius curiae imperialis: quattuor laicos, ut regem Bohemiae, ducem Saxoniae, comitem Palatinum, et marchionem Brandenburgensem, et tres clericos, archiepiscopum Maguntinensem, Coloniensem et Treverensem.

migrabo / Et sedem ubi Deo placuerit locabo. / Eos iuste deseram qui me deseruerunt, / Immo quae sim et qualis scire non curaverunt'.

[1] Lupold of Bebenburg, *De iure regni Romani*, ch. 12, p. 380, ch. 16, p. 405, 'Finaliter veritatem in hac materia, non obstantibus his quae dixi in hoc capitulo et supra in capitulo undecimo in secunda oppositione et in pluribus locis huius tractatus, ignorare me fateor et, huiusmodi dubii determinationem maioribus meis reservans, cupio in hac ardua materia discere non docere'. He is in fact one of the most muddled and contradictory writers of the period, and it is hard to understand the adulatory tone adopted by some recent historians.

[2] See the discussion of this by Opicinus de Canistris, *De praeeminentia spiritualis imperii*, pp. 93–6.

He adds that there were three reasons why Gregory chose the German princes: firstly because the Germans had protected the papacy from the Lombards; secondly because of their devotion to SS. Peter and Paul and the apostolic see; thirdly because Gregory was himself a German, being related to Otto himself.[1] The idea of Gregory's supposed institution did in fact enjoy a considerable popularity in papal circles during the later Middle Ages, and after a time the popes themselves came to believe it.[2] Consequently, when Louis of Bavaria declared that John XXII's claim to administer the Empire during an imperial vacancy was 'ad perpetuum gravamen et praeiudicium principum imperii electorum',[3] and other writers asserted the inalienable right of the princes to elect the emperor,[4] the immediate reaction of the papalists was one of sheer incredulity followed by a burning desire to correct this appalling ignorance. As Augustinus Triumphus repeatedly points out, the princes have the *ius et potestas eligendi* simply because the pope has given it to

[1] Augustinus Triumphus, *Summa*, xxxv. 2, p. 206; cf. xxxvii. 5, p. 222. These reasons appear to have been taken from Johannes Teutonicus: see Ullmann, *Medieval Papalism*, p. 172.

[2] It is stated by Clement VI, *MGH*, *Const.*, VIII n. 100 p. 156. For the canonists see Ullmann, *op. cit.*, pp. 174–6. It can also be found with Alvarus Pelagius, *De planctu Ecclesiae*, ch. 41, pp. 68–9. Augustinus Triumphus almost certainly copied his version from Tholemy of Lucca, *Determinatio compendiosa*, c. 13, p. 29; *De regimine principum*, iii. 18, p. 266; *De origine Romani imperii*, p. 72. According to other accounts this took place in the reign of Otto III, and the pope is not mentioned: Conrad of Megenberg, *De translatione Romani imperii*, ch. 7, p. 274; Landulfus de Colonna, *De statu Romani imperii*, ch. 9, pp. 94–5; Marsilius of Padua, *De translatione imperii*, ch. 11, p. 153. The source for all this seems to be the *Chronicon pontificum et imperatorum* of Martin of Troppau, *MGH*, *SS*, xii. 466. Another favourite suggestion deriving from the *Schwabenspiegel* is that the electors had been set up by Charlemagne: e.g. Alexander of Roes, *De translatione imperii*, p. 26; Jordan of Osnabruck, *De praerogativa Romani imperii*, pp. 16–17, 28; Anon., *Disquisitio iuridica*, ch. 1, p. 1379; Henry of Cremona, *De potestate papae*, p. 466. In reality the idea of the 'principes ad quos specialiter spectat regis Romani electio' only goes back to the late twelfth century, and many thirteenth-century writers refused to include the king of Bohemia.

[3] Baluze, iii. 389.

[4] See Augustinus Triumphus, *Summa*, xxxv. 1, pp. 205–6; xxxv. 4, p. 208. This may also be found in Jordan of Osnabruck, *De praerogativa Romani imperii*, pp. 16–17, and was put into the Golden Bull, Altmann-Bernheim, *Ausgewählte Urkunden*, n. 38 p. 58. Ockham said that it was heresy to injure the electoral rights of the princes, *Quoniam scriptura*, pp. 78–9.

them. He uses the princes as a means of nominating a suitable candidate, thereby avoiding all the uproar and distractions of competing claims usually associated with this business, but in reality it is he who, by means of his right of confirmation and coronation, has the final choice: 'papa elegit mediantibus electoribus'.[1] Election in itself has neither validity nor effect: the electors cannot be judges, he says, in their own cause.

Nullus in causa propria ponendus est iudex. Electores ergo non habent iudicare nec cognoscere de ipsa electione per eos facta.[2]

Since the emperor is created solely for the purpose of being used by the pope (*elegit in usum*) as a means of administering the more secular affairs of the community and maintaining order within it,[3] it is reasonable to assume that the pope is the best judge of the type of person required. He alone can decide whether the candidate will be suitable (*ydoneus*), that is to say, useful (*utilis*) in furthering the greater *utilitas* of the society. The princes, he remarks pointedly, are quite capable of electing men who are guilty of the worst possible crimes, and who cannot for a moment be considered:

Possent enim electores eligere hominem sacrilegum vel excommunicatum, haereticum, schismaticum vel paganum, tyrannum vel fatuum vel talem cuius progenitores fuissent persecutores ecclesiae, et in omnibus istis persona electa esset repellenda.[4]

Whoever is elected, it must be shown that he has the strength to act

[1] Augustinus Triumphus, *Summa*, xli. 2, p. 234, 'ad eum pertinet electionem aliquam examinare ad quem pertinet ius eligendi conferre et ordinare ac manus imponere et electionem confirmare. Sed planum est quod ad summum pontificem spectat immediate ius eligendi imperatorem conferre et ordinare imperium, quia cum sit minister eius in Ecclesiae defensione et temporalium administratione, potestas eligendi ipsum ab apostolica sede in ipsos electores est derivata'.

[2] Augustinus Triumphus, *Summa*, xli. 2 ad 2, p. 234.

[3] Augustinus Triumphus, *Summa*, xliii. 2, p. 238, 'et papa hanc eamdem immediatam administrationem *concedit* imperatori quem eligit in usum et in sui officii *stipendationem* pro defensione et pacifica gubernatione Ecclesiae'.

[4] Augustinus Triumphus, *Summa*, xli. 3 ad 3, p. 234. This follows Innocent III in *Decretales*, I. vi. 34. See also the list of qualifications given by Conrad of Megenberg, *De translatione Romani imperii*, ch. 12, pp. 288f., and by Clement V in Baluze, iii. 222–3.

as a universal protector, the uprightness of character to act as the guardian of faith and the right order, and the intelligence and education to know what he is doing: as Alvarus Pelagius reminds his readers, an illiterate king is a crowned ass.[1] And since the good or utility of the *Ecclesia* is represented by the pope, the predominant criterion of suitability must inevitably be whether he will carry out papal instructions. In fact it is papal confirmation which constitutes the real election: the actual election itself has no legal character unless it so happens that the pope decides to make the election himself, in which case confirmation becomes superflous: 'tunc papa immediate eligeret et in tali casu electio esset examinatio et confirmatio'.[2] Indeed the strength of the hierocratic idea is brought home to us when it is realised that Augustinus Triumphus regards the election of the princes as merely one of a number of ways in which the pope may select his chief officer. When the emperors resided in the East, he says, the pope allowed the Roman people, senate or army to appoint the emperor: in the West after Charlemagne he permitted the principle of hereditary succession to be used,[3] and this startling reinterpretation of history is justified on the grounds that if the popes had not approved of it they would have said so. As Francis de Meyronnes said, it follows from this that the German princes can always be deprived of their electoral rights, which the pope may give to whom he pleases: 'et auctoritatem eligendi dat summus pontifex et aufert, transferendo de gente in gentem'. Since Augustinus Triumphus found himself able to quote a similar passage from Innocent III he concluded that its orthodoxy was impeccable, and in point of fact Boniface VIII had more recently restated the principle.[4] As Augustinus says, it was never

[1] Augustinus Triumphus, *Summa*, xli. 3 ad 1, p. 234; Alvarus Pelagius, *Speculum regum*, p. 518 'rex illiteratus est quasi asinus coronatus'. This is quoted from John of Salisbury, *Policraticus*, iv. 6 (*PL*, cxcix. 524).

[2] Augustinus Triumphus, *Summa*, xli. 2, p. 234; also Francis Toti, *Tractatus contra Bavarum*, p. 80.

[3] Augustinus Triumphus, *Summa*, xxxv. 2 ad 1, p. 207; xxxvii. 5, p. 222. This again follows Tholemy of Lucca, *Determinatio compendiosa*, chs. 11–12, pp. 24–8; *De regimine principum*, iii. 18, p. 266.

[4] Francis de Meyronnes, *Quaestio de subiectione*, i. 12, p. 85; Augustinus Triumphus, *Summa*, xxxvii. 4, p. 222, quoting Innocent III, *Decretales*, I. vi. 34, 'Sicut ergo a sede apostolica potestas eligendi imperatorem electoribus est *con-*

maintained that the emperor had to be a German. Innocent III had expressly stated that the *imperium* was transferred 'in Germanos', which clearly related to the princes rather than the German ruler himself.[1] Why then need the electoral princes be Germans? Why for that matter need there be electoral princes at all? The pope always has the choice between acting through the princes and making a direct papal provision:

. . . tamen imperatorum electio planum est quod pertinet ad summum pontificem vel immediate per seipsum vel per electores quos ipse summus pontifex ordinavit.[2]

This was not unprecedented in practice. Although there had been no direct papal appointment in the full sense, there had been at least two occasions in the thirteenth century which might be said to have amounted to the same thing. In 1202 Innocent III had deliberately flown in the face of circumstances by recognising Otto of Brunswick as king, and in 1246 Innocent IV had directly instructed the princes to elect Henry Raspe as a replacement for Frederick II. Exactly a century later, in 1346, the process was completed when Clement VI chose a politically helpless candidate in Charles IV as emperor prior to any election by the princes themselves.[3] In each

cessa, ita a praedicta sede potest eis auferri'; Boniface VIII, *MGH*, *Const.*, IV. i n. 173 p. 140, 'Et attendant hic Germani quia, sicut translatum est imperium ab aliis in ipsos, sic Christi vicarius, successor Petri, habet potestatem transferendi imperium a Germanis in alios quoscunque, si vellet, et hoc sine iuris iniuria. . . Unde si subveniat iusta et legitima causa, iuste posset transferre et iuste faceret si eos privaret'. Cf. the report of Peter de Bosco, n. 245, p. 209.

[1] Augustinus Triumphus, *Summa*, xxxvii. 4, p. 222.

[2] Augustinus Triumphus, *Summa*, xxxvi. 4, p. 215; cf. William Amidani, *Reprobatio errorum*, pp. 24–5, 'Electores Alamaniae eligunt imperatorem: dicendum quod hoc ipsum habent a papa . . . qui cum possit eligere imperatorem per seipsum, tamen hoc communicat aliis ut eligere possint'.

[3] Innocent III, *R.N.I.* 62, p. 94, 'nos . . . Ottonem reputamus et *nominamus* regem'; Innocent IV, 'Cum imperio nunc vacante per imperatoris electionem *mandaverimus provideri*. . .': Bayley, *op. cit.*, p. 145; Clement VI, *MGH*, *Const.*, VIII n. 100 p. 163, 'eundem *nominamus*, denuntiamus, assumimus et declaramus regem Romanorum'. In 1273 Gregory X had ordered the electoral princes to bring the interregnum to an end by proceeding to an election within one month. This ultimatum was issued in the belief that the electors would be unable to reach agreement, in which case Gregory was determined to create the French king, Philip III, emperor. But contrary to expectations the princes

case there had been no sort of agreement amongst the princes, and, as Augustinus Triumphus pointed out, the pope is virtually forced to act himself if the electors cannot reach a unanimous decision.[1] Hence he was able to treat it as a general rule that the pope should always intervene when there was negligence on the part of the electors, or for any other good reason.

Est autem principaliter agentis eligere ministros et *instrumenta ad suum finem*. . . Unde puto quod papa, qui universos fideles in praesenti Ecclesia ad pacem habet ordinare et ad supernaturalem finem consequendum dirigere et destinare, iusta et rationabili causa existente, per seipsum possit imperatorem eligere, ut propter eligentium negligentiam et discordiam, aut propter electi bonitatem et condecentiam, vel propter populi christiani pacis providentiam, seu propter coercendum haereticorum, paganorum et schismaticorum potentiam et audaciam posse[t].[2]

Because the pope alone has the full understanding of the end towards which the *Ecclesia* is moving, he must be the final judge of its needs and of what constitutes its well-being. It can reach the goal, in which its ultimate good resides, only in and through him, since he is the earthly presentment of that end which is Christ himself. Seen in the context of this teleological conception of society the act

agreed upon Rudolf of Habsburg. See further W. Goez, *Translatio Imperii: ein Beitrag zur Geschichte des Geschichtsdenkens und der politische Theorien im Mittelalter und in der frühen Neuzeit* (Tübingen, 1958), pp. 178f.

[1] Augustinus Triumphus, *Summa*, xxxv. 5, p. 209, 'Si ergo contingat electores imperatores duos eligere, ad papam pertinet alteri parti in hoc favere ut unum illorum prae altero eligat quem magis cognoscit esse idoneum pro *advocatione* et defensione Ecclesiae, et cui fama, vita et iustitia magis suffragatur, vel quando altera pars vocata et expectata nollet eligeri vel ad eligendum convenire'; similarly Anon., *Disquisitio iuridica*, ch. 1, pp. 1379–80. This again follows Innocent III in *Decretales*, I. vi. 34; cf. Urban IV's reaffirmation of the papal right to choose between two candidates, even if his predecessor has already chosen one of them: C. Rodenberg, *Epistolae selectae saeculi XIII a regestis pontificum Romanorum* (Berlin, 1883–94), iii, n. 517 p. 481.

[2] Augustinus Triumphus, *Summa*, xxxv. 1, p. 206; xli. 2 ad 1, p. 234, 'quando electores admoniti et expectati nollent imperatorem eligere, cum congruum non sit Ecclesiam carere *advocato* et defensore, tunc papa immediate eligeret'. He adds that the pope has complete control over the manner in which the election should be made. Cf. Innocent IV, *App. ad Decretales*, I. vi. 34, 'Sed eis negligentibus eligere, imperatorem papa elegit', which was dutifully copied by Hostiensis.

of creating its officers, those who are to be used as the instruments by which the end is attained, must of necessity be regarded as an effluence of the *plenitudo potestatis*. For Augustinus Triumphus there can be no objection to the pope acting in his own cause, since 'the good' of the head, of Christ and his vicar, of the whole community and of the Christian faith, is one.

II. PAPA EST VERUS IMPERATOR

THE importance of the imperial coronation in the hierocratic system rests not only upon the fact that it is the means by which the inferiority of the emperor as a papal creature is demonstrated for all to see, but also in that it provides a vivid indication of the idea that the pope is in every sense the real ruler of the *imperium Christi*. It is the pope who is the *verus imperator* and has the exercise of full imperial rights and powers. How else, queried the papalists, can he claim to create the universal emperor unless he himself already possesses a plenitude of imperial power?[1] And since it is initially his, there can be no restriction of his use of it when and as he pleases. He is not only the source of imperial power and the overlord of the empire, says Augustinus Triumphus, but he also retains the right to be the emperor himself.

Plenum ius totius imperii est acquisitum summis pontificibus, non solum superioris dominationis verum etiam immediatae administrationis, ut ex ipsis tota dependeat imperialis iurisdictio.[2]

The accuracy of this point of view can, he argues, be tested by what happens during an imperial vacancy. When an emperor dies or is deposed, the power to administer the empire must return to its point of origin: and until he institutes another the pope is forced by the logic of the situation to act as his own emperor. Therefore, during a vacancy, all imperial rights are reserved to the apostolic see.

Papa confert imperatori temporalitatem et administrandi potestatem, cuius signum est quod vacante imperio immediata temporalium administratio et plena iurisdictio apostolicae sedi reservatur.[3]

[1] E.g. Henry of Cremona, *De potestate papae*, p. 466, 'Si ergo non haberet potestatem seu dominium imperii, ecclesia non potuisset transferre quod non data haberetur'. This is supported by the Roman law principle that no man may transfer a right which he does not possess himself already, *Dig.*, XLI. i. 20.

[2] Augustinus Triumphus, *Summa*, xxxviii. 1, p. 224.

[3] Augustinus Triumphus, *Summa*, xl. 1 ad 2, p. 230; cf. Francis Toti, *Tractatus*

No doubt this particular 'proof' was chosen for its topicality. In the elebrated decree *Si fratrum* of March 1317, John XXII had formally nnounced that a vacancy existed in the empire, and had claimed he right to administer it for the pope. Penalties were laid down for hose who infringed the papal right.[1] Augustinus Triumphus may iowever already have been familiar with the earlier assertion of this principle by Clement V, where the pope's imperial rights are made direct effluence of the divinely donated plenitude of power.[2] But nost writers of the time referred back to a judgement of Innocent II (*Decretales*, II. ii. 10) that the Roman church was, in default of ny other, the supreme court of appeal during an imperial vacancy. n their commentaries on this the canonists, especially Innocent IV nd Hostiensis, had elaborated Innocent's statement into an explicit leclaration that the pope 'succeeded' the emperor in a vacancy, and he publicists accept this as a matter of course. Their attitude is very ieatly summed up by the unknown author of the *Disquisitio iuridica*, who makes the pope the superior of a living emperor and the successor of a defunct one.[3] Nor was the matter allowed to rest there. Several writers went on to point out that since the empire was a iniversal organism, the same must apply to every lesser corpora-

ontra Bavarum, p. 78, 'apud illum residet regalis sive imperialis dignitatis plenitudo'; Anon., *Disquisitio theologico-iuridica*, ii. 1, p. 1342, '[Papa est] imperator et dominus super totum gregem fidelium et in omnimoda plenitudine egnat, imperat et dominatur sicut et Christus cuius est vicarius'. Note the eflection of the *laudes* in this: it is pointed out by Kantorowicz, *Laudes Regiae*, pp. 129–42, that during the twelfth century the papal coronation, acclamation and headwear had become thoroughly imperial in character. For the application of the term *imperialis maiestas* to the pope see David, *La souveraineté et les limites juridiques du pouvoir monarchique*, pp. 27–8, 198.

[1] *Extravagantes Iohannis XXII*, v. 1. For examples of John's activities in imperial matters, see F. Baethgen, 'Der Anspruch des Papsttums auf das Reichvikariat', *ZSSR*, *Kan. Abt.*, xli (1920), pp. 168–286 at pp. 247–63.

[2] *MGH*, *Const.*, IV n. 1166, 'Tam ex superioritate quam ad imperium non est dubium nos habere, quam ex potestate in qua vacante imperio imperatori succedimus, et nichilominus ex illius plenitudine potestatis quam Christus . . . nobis . . . concessit'. This was put into the *Clementines*, II. xi. 2.

[3] Anon., *Disquisitio iuridica*, ch. 1, pp. 1378–9, 'dominus papa imperio vacante imperatori succedit ac potestatem imperii, iurisdictionem iustitiamque imperialem exercet et potest exercere de iure, ut probatur *Extra*, *de foro comp. c. Licet* [II. ii. 10], et ibi not. Innoc. et Host. . . Cum igitur dominus papa sit imperatoris vacante imperio successor, et eo vivente superior. . .'.

tion within the all-embracing whole. The pope, says Hervaeus Natalis, takes over the government of any kingdom during the absence of its ruler: he is the real king in any kingdom.[1] Lay rulers are simply papal delegates. A pope will rule through them in some parts of the *Ecclesia*, but others he will keep for himself; even in those parts where lay rulers are normally permitted to function the pope will not always use them but will sometimes act immediately himself.

Sic et papa sua potestate spirituali aliqua temporalia et corporalia regit per seipsum, aliqua vero mediante potestate aliorum principum saecularium quorum potestas corporalis et temporalis est.[2]

He must of course moderate his exercise of royal power to conform to what he feels to be the best interests of the society: in practice one man cannot do everything all the time. But since all kingdoms are at his disposal, since they are merely administrative units of his universal community, there is nothing exempt from the dictates of his sovereign will.

[Papa]... est immediatus vicarius omnium, instituens aliquos sub se sive ordinarie sive delegate sicut sibi videtur expedire bono regimine Ecclesiae. Itaque quando unus exercet talem iurisdictionem per seipsum immediate in quemcunque de Ecclesia militante, et quando vult exercere eam mediante alio. Et ex hoc etiam sequitur quod potest committere potestatem suam et delegare cuicunque vult et cum quanto numero vult, ita quod arbitrio suo hoc subiacet, licet deceat ipsum hanc commissionem cum debito moderamine facere.[3]

What is, is so simply because the pope commands it. To attempt to place restrictions upon his governmental capacity is to deny the

[1] Hervaeus Natalis, *De potestate papae*, fo. 148, 'Papa se habet sicut vicarius generalis et ordinarius regis absentis'. Logically the pope becomes the head of any corporate body in the *Ecclesia*: Denifle pointed out that in 1283–4 the arts faculty at Paris stated that the pope was the real head of the University: see Powicke-Emden, *Rashdall's Medieval Universities*, i. 329 n. 3.

[2] Augustinus Triumphus, *Summa*, i. 6 ad 2, p. 10; cf. James of Viterbo, *De regimine christiano*, ii. 9, 'Potest enim agere et mediantibus aliis potestatibus et non mediantibus eis quando viderit expedire. Potest etiam agere et secundum leges quas ponit et praeter illas ubi opportunum esse iudicaverit'.

[3] Hervaeus Natalis, *De potestate papae*, fo. 148v

omnipotence of God upon earth. At this point many papal writers found it expedient to add a highly important caution. The theory of papal sovereignty, it is stressed over and over again, cannot be lifted out of the context of a thoroughly Christian community. The type of government simply conforms to the character of the society over which it is exercised, and can be understood only with reference to the nature of the political entity. The Clerk in the *Somnium viridarii*, for example, gives the pope total lordship of all temporal and spiritual things, and at once explains that this must follow from a proper understanding of what the empire is. It is no ordinary empire, but the whole terrestrial monarchy, nothing less than the kingdom of Christ himself, which the pope has now inherited.[1] It is the *Ecclesia universalis*, but for this reason it is also the *imperium Romanorum*. Its Romanity (*Romanitas*) denotes that it is both a universal and a Christian empire: it specifies its imperial and ecclesiastical character. Consequently the pope may equally well be held to act 'ratione Romani imperii'.[2] When the Universal Church is an empire, it must surely follow that its head is the universal emperor,[3] and is entitled to utilise all the distinguishing marks of emperorship.[4] The nature of papal power is complementary to the nature of

[1] Anon., *Somnium viridarii*, i. 61, p, 76, 'ipse [scil. Christus] enim fuit plenus dominus temporalium et spiritualium, utpote quia verus Deus et creator omnium, qui constituit sibi vicarium Petrum et eius successores . . . et sic in Petrum et successores suos translatum fuit imperium et monarchia terrestris, quae erat penes Salvatorem nostrum; sed illa erat plena et libera temporalium et spiritualium, cum ipsius veri Dei et factoris omnium sit plenitudo orbis terrae. . .'.

[2] Alvarus Pelagius, *De planctu Ecclesiae*, ch. 37, p. 45, 'Et ideo papa ratione imperii Romani quod obtinet. . .'. See also Guido Vernani's demonstration that the monarch of Dante's *Monarchia* must be the pope and not the Roman emperor, *De reprobatione Monarchiae*, ch. 1, pp. 128–9.

[3] Alexander de S. Elpidio, *De ecclesiastica potestate*, ii. 8, p. 26, 'Unde cum Ecclesia proprie possit dici regnum, ipse [papa] dicitur rex Ecclesiae ac totius regni Christi vicarius in terris'; Francis de Meyronnes, *De principatu temporali*, ch. 4, p. 62, 'sed princeps spiritualium praesidet principi temporalium; ergo praesidet eius principatui, qui est temporalis . . . quia imperator non praesidet imperio nisi per dignitatem imperialem; sed dignitatem imperialem habet in se virtualiter princeps spiritualium'.

[4] Cf. Gregory VII, *Dictatus papae*, c. 8, 'Quod solus possit uti imperialibus insigniis'; Innocent III, *De sacro altaris mysterio*, i. 32 (*PL*, ccxvii. 786), 'Per purpuram regiae dignitatis significatur pontificalis potestas'.

the society over which it is to be wielded, and an *Ecclesia-Imperium* can only be governed, from this standpoint, by one who is both *sacerdos et rex*.[1] Standing in line of descent from Melchisedech and Christ, the pope combines in his own person all the qualities of sacerdotal and royal authority.[2] In the anatomy of government Augustinus Triumphus refers to him as being both head and heart of the body politic.[3] The head directs the activities of the body, whilst the heart provides the life-force which enables these activities to be carried out. The pope is not only the motivating source of

[1] Augustinus Triumphus, *De duplici potestate*, p. 499, 'Unde ista de causa summus pontifex meretur dici rex et sacerdos. Nam dicitur rex propter potestatem regalem et temporalem, et dicitur sacerdos propter potestatem spiritualem'; he then quotes I *Peter*, ii. 9.

[2] Augustinus Triumphus, *Summa*, i. 7, p. 10, 'papa gerit vicem Christi, saltem quantum ad potestatem et iurisdictionem officii; in Christo autem planum est fuisse potestatem regalem et sacerdotalem'. For Melchisedech see ad 2, p. 11. Cf. Anon., *Disquisitio theologico-iuridica*, ii. 7, pp. 1347–8, 'Et iste Melchisedech, qui simul fuit rex et sacerdos, gerebat figuram tam Christi quam sui vicarii, qui simul est rex et sacerdos. . . Unde de Christo et eius vicario dicitur in *Psalmo* [cix. 4], Tu es sacerdos in aeternum secundum ordinem Melchisedech'. Innocent IV had said very much the same thing, Winkelmann, ii. 698, 'Dominus enim Iesus Christus, sicut verus homo verusque Deus, sic secundum ordinem Melchisedech verus rex ac verus sacerdos existens . . . in apostolica sede non solum pontificalem sed et regalem constituit monarchatum'. Cf. Innocent III, *Consec. serm.*, iii (*PL*, ccxvii. 665), 'In signum spiritualium contulit mihi mitram, in signum temporalium dedit mihi coronam; mitram pro sacerdotio, coronam pro regno; illius me constituens vicarium qui habet in vestimento et in femore suo scriptum, Rex regum et dominus dominantium [*Apoc.*, xix. 16], Sacerdos in aeternum secundum ordinem Melchisedech'. On Melchisedech see further G. Wuttke, *Melchisedech, der Priesterkönig von Salem* (Giessen, 1927); G. Bardy, 'Melchisédech dans la tradition patristique', *Revue biblique*, xxxv (1926), pp. 496–509; xxxvi (1927), pp. 25–45; J. Funkenstein, 'Malkizedek in der Staatslehre', *Archiv für Rechts- und Sozialphilosophie*, xli (1954), pp. 32–6; and in general G. Martini, 'Regale Sacerdotium', *Archivio della Società Romana di Storia Patria*, iv (1938), pp. 1–166.

[3] Augustinus Triumphus, *Summa*, xix. 2 ad 1, p. 118, 'Papa igitur est caput Ecclesiae propter similitudines superius dictas; potest tamen cor appellari propter alias conditiones'. This analogy is primarily a counter to the anti-hierocratic argument in which the king as heart is juxtaposed to the pope as head: Anon., *Somnium viridarii*, i. *proem.*, p. 60; i. 38, p. 71; Gilbert of Tournai, *Eruditio regum*, II. i. 2, p. 45; Anon., *Rex pacificus*, ch. 3, as in S. Bulaeius, *Historia Universitatis Parisiensis* (Paris, 1668), iv. 940–1. The idea of the pope as heart has specific reference to the *rex* function. Note Jacques de Cessoles, *De moribus hominum* (*c.* 1300), iv. 2, in which the lay prince is described as both head and heart: see Born, 'The Perfect Prince', p. 491.

all other jurisdictions,[1] but he himself can be seen as having a dual capacity. His is the ultimate responsibility for both issuing the orders and regulations by which the society is administered, and for ensuring that those orders are fulfilled. In his capacity as *caput Ecclesiae* he gains the knowledge of right living which is essential to a society existing for a specific purpose, whilst as emperor he must lend force to his words even to the extent of taking direct military action. The centuries-old distinction between the governor and the war leader is reunited in the hierocratic conception of the pope as *dux et caput*,[2] and with Augustinus Triumphus there is a constant emphasis upon the twin functions of the ecclesiastical monarch, upon his possession of two offices in the universal corporation. It is precisely because he has the duty of seeing that his rule is enforced that he comes to create lay rulers, to utilise those who may more easily manipulate the means of coercion. The idea of the pope's kingly priesthood is the kernel of the whole hierocratic theory of the relationship between papal and lay rulers. It emphasises the papal supremacy and at the same time underlines the exact nature of kingship in the *Ecclesia*. It demonstrates that he has a real plenitude of power in all spheres of government. His jurisdiction, says Augustinus Triumphus, is 'plena et totalis';[3] he can say and do as he pleases in any matter. There is no hint of a limit upon his authority

[1] William Amidani, *Reprobatio errorum*, ch. 2, p. 25, 'sic in potestate papali continetur omnis potestas sacerdotalis et regalis'.

[2] Augustinus Triumphus, *Summa*, vi. 6 ad 2, p. 62, 'Cum ergo totius Ecclesiae ordinis dux et caput sit ipse papa'; cf. 'dux et rector', ix. 3 ad 2, p. 74. This corresponds to the 'dux et pontifex' of Gregory VII: see Ullmann, *The Growth of Papal Government*, p. 306. The distinction between the (divine) head of the community and the *dux* is of Graeco-Germanic origin. It appears in Aristotle, *Politics*, iv. 8, as a distinction between warriors and judges. This is used by Marsilius, *Defensor pacis*, I. v, pp. 20f., who however allocates both functions to his ruler.

[3] Augustinus Triumphus, *Summa*, xlv. 2, p. 247. We may note Bellarmine's comment, *De potestate summi pontificis*, v. 1, 'Prima [sententia] est summum pontificem iure divino habere plenissimam potestatem in universum orbem terrarum, tum in rebus ecclesiasticis, tum in politicis. Ita docent Augustinus Triumphus . . . Alvarus Pelagius . . . et multi iureconsulti'. Cf. Anon., *Disquisitio theologico-iuridica*, ii. 7, p. 1347, 'in papa seu vicario Christi est plenitudo potestatis et penes ipsum residet in omni plenitudine utraque iurisdictio temporalium et spiritualium'.

or ability to act in secular affairs: 'summus pontifex habet omnem et omnimodam potestatem in temporalibus'.[1] The unrestrained power of the pope in temporals is something to be asserted without reservation, hesitation or even discussion. In orthodox hierocratic theory, that he is 'dominus simpliciter in terris',[2] is assumed as a matter of course. In the great *Summa* of Augustinus Triumphus the statement that the pope 'habet temporalium non solum universalem iurisdictionem verum etiam universalem administrationem' appears with the unfailing regularity of a punctuation mark.[3] And this brings us to the whole complex question of the respective duties of pope and lay ruler. What these writers are striving to express is the nature of the *rex* function in a Christian society, indeed the whole place of the temporal in something which is essentially the shadow of the heavens. In this conception the term 'temporal power' has a specialised and technical interpretation, and must not be seen as an equivalent category to 'spiritual power'. It will give an entirely erroneous impression if we simply interpret the popes' claim to be *rex et sacerdos* as meaning that they, in the words of the *Rex pacificus*, took 'both powers'. That the pope has the *rex* function, the so-called temporal power, merely means that he is able to carry out the directions which he himself has issued as *sacerdos*. He has not only universal jurisdiction, or legislative power, but also full right to administer or execute it:

> dominium temporale intelligitur . . . quantum ad immediatam administrationem, quam imperatores et reges et alii principes saeculares habent et habuerunt; aliter domini temporales non appellarentur nisi temporalium immediatam administrationem haberent.[4]

In other words the temporal power is the ability to exercise, act and enforce. It is repeated *ad nauseam* that the meaning of a king is one who does rightly—*rex a recte agendo*—and although attention has

[1] Aegidius Spiritalis, *Libellus contra infideles*, p. 112.

[2] William Amidani, *Reprobatio errorum*, c. 4, p. 27.

[3] E.g. Augustinus Triumphus, *Summa*, i. 1, p. 3; xxxvi. 1 ad 3, p. 213; xxxvi. 3, p. 214; xxxvi. 4 and ad 2, p. 216; xxxviii. 1, p. 224; xxxix. 1 ad 1, p. 228; xlv. 2, p. 248; xlv. 3 ad 2, p. 249; *Tractatus contra articulos*, i. 3, p. lxxiii; *De duplici potestate*, p. 497.

[4] Augustinus Triumphus, *Summa*, xxxvi. 3, p. 214.

been generally concentrated upon the rightness of his actions, it is equally important to stress that a king is essentially a doer, an *agens* or executive. To deny that the pope can carry out his own policy is to deny that he is priest *and king*.

The lay ruler in the hierocratic system is then simply a papal agent, an instrument or organ by which the pope implements the governmental programme which he has formulated and authorised.

Sed potestas spiritualis residet in ipso [scil. papa] quantum ad auctoritatem et ad executionem, sed temporalis quantum ad auctoritatem non autem quantum ad immediatam executionem, quia committit executionem talis potestatis saecularis regibus et principibus, qui debent esse *organa* et *instrumenta* eius.[1]

The pope has both swords,[2] but he gives the use of the temporal sword (not the temporal sword itself) to the lay ruler to exercise on his behalf.[3] We may remark here, however, that although practically every writer of the period talks about the two swords, there could hardly be a more inadequate analogy for expressing the papal point of view. Two swords immediately suggests two distinct powers, temporal and spiritual.[4] Yet any form of two power doc-

[1] Augustinus Triumphus, *De duplici potestate*, p. 500; also *Summa*, i. 7 ad 4, p. 11; Aegidius Romanus, *De ecclesiastica potestate*, ii. 4, pp. 49–53; ii. 5, p. 59; ii. 6, p. 69; iii. 4, p. 163; Alvarus Pelagius, *De planctu Ecclesiae*, ch. 41, p. 71; Tholemy of Lucca, *Determinatio compendiosa*, ch. 7, p. 18.

[2] Augustinus Triumphus, *Summa*, xl. 3, p. 232; Anon., *Determinatio compendiosa*, ch. 33, pp. 543–4; Aegidius Spiritalis, *Libellus contra infideles*, pp. 119–20; Alvarus Pelagius, *Collirium*, p. 505; Francis Toti, *Tractatus contra Bavarum*, p. 79; William Amidani, *Reprobatio errorum*, ch. 2, p. 25; and in most chapters of the *De ecclesiastica potestate* of Aegidius Romanus.

[3] Augustinus Triumphus, *Summa*, xxxvi. 6 ad 1, p. 218, 'cum gladium imperialem solum in ministerium Dei constat sibi esse datum'.

[4] Note also the use of the two keys in this sense, e.g. Anon., *Disquisitio theologico-iuridica*, ii. 7, p. 1346, 'Petrus et successores eius duas claves ad invicem connexas et a se invicem *inseparabiles* habere in manu dicitur, quia illae duae claves significant potestatem in temporalibus et spiritualibus. Non enim Petrus et successores eius unam solam clavem dicitur habere, sed duas quia non solum plenam habet potestatem spiritualium, sed simul spiritualium et temporalium. Duas enim claves et duos gladios Christus suo vicario commisit'; cf. Anon., *Rex pacificus*, c. 1, p. 666. One cannot avoid the conclusion that the hierocratic use of two swords, two keys or two powers was a major terminological blunder, and one can sympathise with John of Paris' stinging dismissal of all such allegories as mystical nonsense, *De potestate regia et papali*, ch. 19, p. 235.

trine, any real distinction between temporal and spiritual, is impossible in a society which is essentially *unum corpus*. At most it can only be a working distinction, and it is this fact which the lay writers, with their insistence upon a dualism of temporal and spiritual, never appreciated. The idea of temporal and spiritual is a necessary corollary to the conception of Church and State as two separate societies, but it has no place in a political society which is basically nothing else but an *Ecclesia*. The idea of Church and State is only possible when one presupposes the existence of two ends, natural and divine, to human life: in hierocratic theory there is only one end, and that a totally spiritual one, since it is God himself. There can be for the hierocrat no halfway house between grace and nature: the presence of one implies the absence of the other. He understands society to be a Church, all power to be essentially spiritual, and therefore located in the spiritual head who alone has a real right to exist. He could appreciate, even though he revolted from it, the Marsilian conception of society as a purely terrestrial polity in which all power is fundamentally temporal, and exercised only by lay rulers. But he was never really able to follow the Thomist view that grace and nature had come together to form a society which was almost equally Church and State, and which consequently demanded the relatively self-sufficient existence of both lay and ecclesiastical rulers and a conception of power in terms of temporal and spiritual as two distinct species of authority.[1] For Augustinus Triumphus everything exists for a spiritual purpose, otherwise it has no place in the *Ecclesia*. The lay ruler has a place in it only in so far as he furthers that purpose, and it is an essentially auxiliary position when his office is seen against the function of the spiritual man who governs all. In the words of Clement VI, the emperor has an *officium assistentiae*, and this can only be the case when, as Aegidius Spiritalis emphasises, the lay ruler and all temporal things function for the benefit of the spiritual end of the

[1] This can for example be seen creeping into Aegidius Romanus' otherwise rigidly orthodox description of papal power in the *De ecclesiastica potestate*, i. 4, p. 13, 'quia hic duo gladii [*Luke*, xxii. 38] sufficiunt in Ecclesia, oportet hos duos gladios, *has duas auctoritates et potestates*, a Deo esse quia, ut dictum est, non est potestas nisi a Deo [*Rom.*, xiii. 1]', although he attempts to retrieve the situation by adding that one is under the other and is derived from it.

society: 'temporalia omnia sunt propter spiritualia sicut propter finem: ergo princeps temporalium principi spiritualium debet subesse'.[1] The temporal is useful, and is to be used, because, for all its extra-terrestrial reality, the society is also an earthly one. But it is no more than useful. As Tholemy of Lucca put it, the lay ruler is needed in the same way that the soul needs a body during its earthly existence, but that body has no real importance.[2] Lay administration is as much an accessory to papal government as the body is to the soul.[3] A papal *maioritas*[4] is inevitable when secular jurisdiction has validity only when ordered towards a spiritual social purpose which the vicar of Christ alone is qualified to understand:

Ille enim qui rectam existimationem habet de fine, disponit et dirigit omnia in ordine ad ipsum . . . et isto modo tunc temporalia recte administrantur quando ordinantur ad consecutionem finis, cum sint quaedam instrumenta virtuose agendi et perveniendi ad finem.[5]

[1] Clement VI, *MGH, Const.*, VIII n. 100 p. 159; Aegidius Spiritalis, *Libellus contra infideles*, p. 126.

[2] Tholemy of Lucca, *Determinatio compendiosa*, ch. 7, p. 18, 'Manifestum est enim corporalia ex spiritualibus dependent sicut corpus ex anima, quia nec motum habet nec operationem nisi ex anima, unde corpus est *organum animae ad operandum*... Sed anima *utitur* corpore ut *instrumento*: ergo, cum summus pontifex ad imperatorem ratione sui officii sic se habeat sicut spirituale ad corporale . . . summus anthistes *utitur* imperatoris officio ut *instrumento* ad sui videlicet et Ecclesiae defensionem'. The theory of *organon* or *instrumentum* is of Aristotelian origin.

[3] Alvarus Pelagius, *De planctu Ecclesiae*, ch. 13, p. 30, 'Temporalia *accessoria* sunt ad spiritum'. See also Augustinus Triumphus, *De facto Templariorum*, p. 515, 'Nam sic comparatur princeps saecularis ad ecclesiam sicut corporale ad spirituale. Sed constat quod corporale propria virtute et auctoritate non habet potestatem super aliquid spirituale nisi quatenus est *instrumentum* superioris agentis . . . sed spirituale omne habet potestatem immediate super ipsum corporale'.

[4] Note again the connotation of majority with a minority, in this case one man who is *sanior* or knows better: see Augustinus Triumphus, *Summa*, xlvi. 3, p. 251. Other commonly used comparatives are *dignior*, *sublimior*, *excellentior* and *nobilior*. These all follow from the *propinquior Deo* position of the priesthood: xciii. 2, p. 457.

[5] Augustinus Triumphus, *Summa*, ci. 5 ad 1, p. 498; cf. i. 8 ad 2, p. 13, 'carnalia et corporalia bona per se sumpta non prosunt quidquam ad vitam sed ut ordinantur ad ipsa spiritualia tamquam organa et tamquam instrumenta . . . et ipsa facit invenire vitam aeternam. Et ad hunc finem papa habet potestatem ordinandi de ipsis corporalibus et temporalibus bonis'. The reverse view is of course impossible from this point of view, as Clement VI said, *MGH, Const.*,

From this it can be seen that temporal and spiritual have little or no meaning: ultimately everything is spiritual. Every crime is a sin, every matter is subject to papal jurisdiction *ratione peccati*,[1] every man has the pope as his *iudex ordinarius*.

Papa est immediate ordinarius cuiuslibet de Ecclesia in qualibet causa, iudex ordinarius immediatus in quocunque casu . . . papa sit immediatus ordinarius omnium de Ecclesia et in omni casu.[2]

There is only one spiritual power, that *potestas ecclesiastica* which belongs to the vicar of Christ as the personification of the *Ecclesia*.[3] Papal power cannot, for Augustinus Triumphus, be seen as a temporal power in our sense of the term any more than the infinite power of God can be judged by finite standards. Fundamentally there is no such thing as temporal power at all: all is embraced by the papal plenitude of spiritual power.

VIII n. 100 p. 156, '. . . aut ergo spiritualis [potestas] ordinatur ad temporalem, quod est impossibile, quia nobilius et dignius non ordinatur ad *ignobilius*, quia finis habet rationem non solum ultimi sed etiam optimi; aut temporalis ordinatur ad spiritualem, quod tenendum est'.

[1] Anon., *Disputatio inter clericum et militem*, p. 14, 'Si quid iniuste agitur, peccatum est'; Augustinus Triumphus, *Summa*, xxii. 2, p. 130; Boniface VIII, Dupuy, p. 76, 'tamen de omni temporali habet cognoscere summus pontifex et iudicare ratione peccati'. The phrase was popularised by Innocent III: see *Decretales*, II. i. 13.

[2] Hervaeus Natalis, *De potestate papae*, fo. 150. This is a common theme with both canonists and publicists. In 1312 the abbot of Cîteaux told Clement V that 'Summus pontifex . . . non solum est mediatus et generalis, sed etiam immediatus et proprius ordinarius cuiuslibet christiani': Raynaldus, *Annales ecclesiastici ad* 1312, n. 24 p. 105a. For other examples see Augustinus Triumphus, *Summa*, x. 4, p. 80, 'iudex universalis Ecclesiae'; Tholemy of Lucca, *Determinatio compendiosa*, ch. 9, p. 22, 'ipse est iudex omnium'; Anon., *Compendium maius*, p. 178, 'universalem iurisdictionem ordinariam'; Francis Toti, *Tractatus contra Bavarum*, p. 79, 'Ille simpliciter [est] praelatus omnium et monarcha ex cuius iudicio pendent omnes, vel qui pro omnibus est redditurus in divino examine rationem' (this last touch was a favourite hierocratic device and derives from Gelasius); Peter Olivi, *De renuntiatione papae*, p. 357, 'iudex proprius et ordinarius omnium christianorum'. This was another aspect of papal sovereignty attacked by Ockham as heretical, *Quoniam scriptura*, p. 79. Note also the use of I *Cor.*, ii. 15 in Augustinus Triumphus, *Summa*, vii. 1, p. 64; xli. 3 ad 1, p. 234; xlvi. 1, p. 250; Aegidius Romanus, *De ecclesiastica potestate*, i. 2, pp. 8–9.

[3] Augustinus Triumphus, *Summa*, lxi. 2, p. 322, 'omnis potestas spiritualis includitur in potestate clavium quae non nisi Petro est concessa'.

Papa ergo, qui vicem Dei gerit in terris, ex quo habet potestatem spiritualium, habebit similiter potestatem temporalium et corporalium.[1]

Everything temporal derives out of something spiritual: the administrative powers accorded to lay rulers are therefore simply derivations from and for the benefit of papal power:

... sicut materia est propter formam, ita corporale et temporale videtur esse propter spirituale. Dominium ergo imperiale derivatur et est propter ipsum dominium papale, non autem econverso.[2]

All lay rulership is then totally subject to the jurisdiction of the spiritual authority which contains it: if you judge angels, how much more temporal things?[3] In this way the hierocratic conception of the autonomous and solitary existence of the spiritual means that the lay power has no real right of its own to exist at all. The pope creates kings and emperors as he wishes and only because he wishes. He has, for Augustinus Triumphus, an intrinsic right to do as he pleases in secular affairs without reference to any other authority.[4] He is as absolute and unrestrained in the spiritual society as the Marsilian *legislator* is in a secular one, and indeed one

[1] Augustinus Triumphus, *Summa*, i. 6 ad 2, p. 10; also xx. 2, p. 122, 'Per potestate clavium, quae spiritualis est, papa praeest spiritualibus et temporalibus membris Ecclesiae', which he then explains, ad 3, p. 123, 'claves in Ecclesia sunt spirituales quantum ad suos principales et immediatos actus, sed quantum ad secundarios omnia corporalia et spiritualia sub potestate clavium includuntur'.

[2] Augustinus Triumphus, *Summa*, xxxvi. 2, p. 213; cf. Aegidius Romanus, *De ecclesiastica potestate*, ii. 13, pp. 113–15, 'Potestas ergo spiritualis est potestas generalis et extensa, cum non solum ad spiritualia sed ad corporalia se extendat ... Potestas itaque terrena est sub spirituali et instituta per spiritualem et agit ex institutione spiritualis potestatis. . . Habet ergo spiritualis gladius posse super utraque, tam super spiritualia quam super materialia.'

[3] I *Cor.*, vi. 3: see Innocent IV, Winkelmann, ii. 697; Alvarus Pelagius, *De planctu Ecclesiae*, ch. 29, p. 30; Anon., *Disquisitio theologico-iuridica*, ii. 7, pp. 1345–6; Henry of Cremona, *Non ponant laici*, p. 473; and Peter Roger in the *De iurisdictione ecclesiastica* of Peter Bertrandus, p. 1370.

[4] Augustinus Triumphus, *Summa*, xxxv. 2 ad 3, p. 207, 'quamvis imperium sit dominium temporale, ordinatum est tamen in ministerium et in obsequium dominii spiritualis. Est autem contra naturam rei temporalis in rem spiritualem agere sua propria virtute, sed spirituale supra temporale sua propria virtute actionem et iurisdictionem habere potest ut dicitur Apostolus I ad *Cor.* ii [14f.]'.

extreme or the other is vital to a doctrine of true sovereignty. As Hobbes sagely observed, a denial of sovereignty lies at the bottom of any attempt to distinguish between temporal and spiritual, State and Church,[1] and it was no mere coincidence that the publicists' success in separating them, in restricting the competence of pope and lay ruler to their respective spheres, was the prelude to the evolution of a complete system of limited government.

With Augustinus Triumphus this total *reductio ad unum*, the spiritual oneness of papal power, means that 'temporal' and 'spiritual' power used in conjunction with each other are merely descriptive terms for a functional distinction. There is one power but two ways in which it is utilised; not two swords but one sword with a double application[2]—or as pope Leo X subsequently put it, a two-edged sword.[3] With this one power the pope could do everything,[4] but the papacy (quite apart from the fact that it was usually physically incapable of it) had no wish to perform its own manual labour. It had always therefore insisted upon a distinction between the legislative and executive functions, a distinction which can be traced back in hierocratic writings to the famous Gelasian distinction between papal *auctoritas* and royal *potestas*.[5] According to this both pope and lay ruler operated with the same power, but they had different duties (*propria officia*) and used it in different ways.[6] There

[1] Hobbes, *Leviathan* (ed. M. Oakeshott, Oxford, 1946), iii. 39, p. 306, 'Temporal and spiritual government are but two names brought into the world to make men see double and mistake their lawful sovereign'.

[2] Augustinus Triumphus, *Summa*, i. 6 ad 3, p. 10, 'per duos gladios duae potestates intelliguntur, una tamen reducitur ad aliam'.

[3] 'Arripe ergo gladium divinae potestatis tibi traditum bis acutum', Labbé-Cossart, *Sacrosancta Concilia*, xix. 927. In 1171 William, archbishop of Sens, told Alexander III that he held a 'gladius anceps in manibus vestris' (*PL*, cc. 1430); cf. *Psal.*, cxlix. 6; *Apoc.*, xix. 15.

[4] See Peter Olivi's definition of the plenitude of power as 'tota Ecclesiae potestas et auctoritas', *Quaestio de infallibilitate*, p. 133.

[5] Gelasius, *Ep.*, xii. 2 (A. Thiel, *Epistolae pontificum Romanorum genuinae*, p. 351), 'Duo quippe sunt, imperator auguste, quibus principaliter *mundus* hic regitur, *auctoritas* sacrata pontificum et regalis *potestas*'. This was put into Gratian, D. 96 c. 10, and is quoted by Augustinus Triumphus, *Summa*, i. 3, p. 5; xxxvi. 5, p. 216. For the Roman basis of the distinction cf. Wirszubski, *op. cit.*, pp. 109f.

[6] Gelasius, *Tractatus*, iv. 2, p. 567, 'quoniam Christus, memor fragilitatis

was always the ideal of a functional separation (*discretio*) as the best means of fulfilling the final divine purpose of the Christian society. We may illustrate this by the letter in which Gregory X struggled to bring this very point home to Rudolf of Habsburg.

Sacerdotium et imperium non multo differe merito sapientia civilis asseruit. Si quidem illa tamquam maxima dona Dei a coelesti collata elementia principi coniungit idemptitas, ea velut auxiliis mutuis semper egentia suffragiis suis inter ipsa vicibus alternandi unit necessitas et ad perfectum mundi regimen instituta, ut alterum videlicet spiritualibus ministret, reliquum vero praesit humanis, una et eadem institutionis causa finalis ipsa inseparabiliter, licet sub ministeriorum diversitate coniuncta designat.[1]

The famous 'Render unto Caesar' text, the allegories of the two swords, or the sun and the moon, are for the papalists simply means of expressing this distinction of functions, but they do not deny the overriding papal right to exercise both himself.[2] Normally however the pope does not retain the executive power—otherwise there would be no real reason for having lay rulers. But he does not and must not shed his legislative function. His prime duty is a jurisdic-

humanae, quod suorum saluti congrueret, dispensatione magnifica temperavit, sic actionibus propriis dignitatibusque distinctis *officia* potestatis utriusque *discrevit*'. See Nicholas I in Gratian, D. 96 c. 6. This is cited by Augustinus Triumphus, *Summa*, cx. 6, p. 551; Aegidius Spiritalis, *Libellus contra infideles*, pp. 111–12; Tholemy of Lucca, *Determinatio compendiosa*, ch. 15, p. 33. See also St. Bernard. *Sermo XLIX in Cant.* (*PL*, clxxxii. 1018).

[1] *MGH*, *Const.*, III, p. 77. The 'sapientia civilis' refers to Justinian's *Novella*, vi. *proem.*, which Gregory is attempting to neutralise. For another example see Clement V's letter to Henry VII of 26 July, 1309, in Baluze, iii. 224–5.

[2] Commenting on the 'Render unto Caesar' text Tholemy of Lucca says, *Determinatio compendiosa*, ch. 16, p. 35, 'Non tamen excluditur quin iurisdictionis Caesaris ex iurisdictione papae dependeat, qui immediate ipsam habet a Christo, ex quo imperator minister Dei vocatur'. As Tholemy is pointing out, the text said nothing about the origin of Caesar's power. It could also be said, as with Francis Toti, *Tractatus contra Bavarum*, p. 79, that surely no one can maintain that there is anything belonging to Caesar which does not also belong to God, 'quae sunt Caesaris sunt etiam Dei', and therefore to the pope as his vicar. To say otherwise is to deny God's ownership of all things. Thus everything given to the emperor remains the pope's: 'sic dominatio imperatoris est papae suo modo'. It was also argued that as Caesar was a pagan at that time, no Christian owed him anything, and so the whole text was meaningless: Anon., *Compendium maius*, p. 179.

tional one, the direction and regulation of the right way of life in a Christian society. His position as pope makes him *lex animata*, the human legislator through which divine law is made applicable to earthly affairs. He inherits from Christ the task of promulgating binding rules of conduct which will enable the *Ecclesia* to achieve its aim, and as the *auctor* of rightness he must hold the supreme directive power, the *auctoritas Christi*. But for the most part he does not personally exercise the *potestas*: this is handed over to the emperor whom he creates for this purpose.[1] Augustinus Triumphus returns to the same point again and again. The emperor, or any lay ruler for that matter, is able to act simply because the pope has given him the *potestas executionis* to carry out papal mandates. Lay rulership is a purely executive function: 'Ecclesia dominium iustitiae exerceat per laicos'.[2] The pope does indeed possess the *rex* function initially, but this *potentia imperialis* is to be made actual by the lay prince,[3] and it is usually true to say that he retains immediate administration only in the papal states.[4] This brings out the full force

[1] Augustinus Triumphus, *Summa*, xliii. 2, p. 238; *De duplici potestate*, p. 500. This idea had been thoroughly developed by the canonists: see for example Rufinus, *Summa Decretorum ad* D. 22 [c. 1], ed. Singer, p. 47, 'ius aliud est auctoritatis, aliud administrationis'.

[2] Augustinus Triumphus, *Summa*, xxii. 2, p. 131.

[3] Augustinus Triumphus, *Summa*, xxi. 3, p. 128, 'quia per suos ministros sua *potentia* virtuali universum mundum debet visitare'; cf. Aegidius Spiritalis, *Libellus contra infideles*, p. 113, 'apud successorem Petri est omnis potestas spiritualis et temporalis, spiritualis *actu* et *habitu*, temporalis habitu licet non actu, sed ipsam temporalem transfert in laicum quia prohibetur clericis quod sanguinem effundant'. The use of this distinction derives from Innocent IV, Winkelmann, ii. 698, 'Huius siquidem materialis potestas gladii apud ecclesiam est *implicata*, sed per imperatorem, qui eam inde recipit, *explicatur*, et quae in sinu ecclesiae *potentialis* est solummodo et *inclusa* sit, cum transfertur in principem, *actualis*'.

[4] Augustinus Triumphus, *Summa*, xxi. 1, p. 127, 'cum praesit Romae papa et in partibus Italiae per immediatem administrationem temporalium et spiritualium'. In general lay rulers were to wield the bulk of executive power rather than the pope: i. 4, p. 7, 'Si vero loquamur de potestate iurisdictionis temporalis, similiter nullus est aequalis sibi in tali potestate quantum ad immediatem *auctoritatem* et universalem iurisdictionem, licet quantum ad immediatem *executionem* et administrationem imperator et alii reges et principes possint esse maiores eo'. It was also generally held at this time that the pope retained the *ius et proprietas* of all islands: L. Weckmann, *Las Bulas Alejandrinas de 1493 y la Teoria Política del Papado Medieval* (Mexico City, 1949).

of the hierocratic conception of kingship. The emperor is simply the arm which implements, and is controlled by, the wishes of the head. As Aegidius Romanus said, the will of the pope is expressed in words, but force, the Isidorian 'princely terror', is needed to compel obedience,[1] and it is for this reason that the lay ruler is given the sword. Fear must suffice where faith, as expressed in papal directives, is not enough. As a papal officer,[2] whose duty it is to preserve good order in the community, the emperor's function is essentially police action taken in its widest sense, the defence of the society against both internal and external disturbers of the *pax Ecclesiae*.[3] But, like a policeman, he has no power to alter or reject the law

[1] Aegidius Romanus, *De ecclesiastica potestate*, i. 3, p. 10, 'Ergo potestates spirituales requirunt quod mente et voluntate serviatur eis, sed potestates saeculares, si non servias eis voluntate et mente, cogant te per iudicium sanguinis et etiam per mortem, quae est finis omnium terribilium'; Augustinus Triumphus, *Summa*, xxxv. 4, p. 208, 'Dicit enim Isydo. in *de summo bono*, *lib.* 3, *cap.* 53 [*Sententiae*, III. li. 4 (*PL*, lxxxiii. 723)], quod potestates saeculares *intra Ecclesiam* necessariae non essent nisi quod non praevalet sacerdos efficere per doctrinae sermonem; potestas hoc imperit per *disciplinae terrorem*, quia saepe coeleste regnum per terrestre proficit, ut quando aliqui intra Ecclesiam positi contra fidem et disciplinam Ecclesiae agunt, *rigore principum* contulerantur'; cf. xxviii. 6, p. 172, 'militaris persecutio'. Although Augustinus Triumphus says that it is theoretically possible, he does not suggest that it is desirable for the pope to do without kings: xxxv. 6, p. 209, 'Ecclesia indiget imperatore tamquam advocato et defensore pro statu pacifico praesentis vitae'.

[2] Augustinus Triumphus, *Summa*, xxxvi. 6 ad 1, p. 218, 'cum gladium imperialem solum in ministerium Dei constet sibi esse datum'; cf. Gilbert of Tournai, *Eruditio regum*, I. i. 2, p. 7, 'Quod autem de manu ecclesiae princeps gladium accipit, eumdem ministrum ecclesiae ostendit'. Note also Aegidius Romanus, *De ecclesiastica potestate*, iii. 4, p. 163, 'potestas quidem terrena est quasi quoddam organum et quidam *martellus* potestatis ecclesiasticae'. See Augustinus Triumphus' comparison of lay rulers to those who fell trees to build a house, in this case the *domus Dei: De duplici potestate*, p. 498.

[3] Augustinus Triumphus, *Summa*, xxvi. 4 ad 2, p. 158, 'sed [papa et alii praelati] mediante potestate saeculari possunt et debent de tyrannis et de turbantibus pacem Ecclesiae iustitiam exercere'. See the very Augustinian passage in xxxvi. 1, p. 212, 'dominium regalis seu imperialis dupliciter intelligitur: primum est *permissum* in poenam dominantium et in poenam peccantium atque in correctionem malorum. Secundum est *consessum* in remedium peccati propter pacem iustorum'. It is the protective element which comes out most strongly in his descriptions of lay government: e.g. li. 5, p. 276, 'regibus et rectoribus quorum potentia protegimur et de rabie tyrannorum liberamur', and in the frequent use of such terms as *defensor*, *protector*, *tutor*, *adiutor* and *bracchium*.

which he is set to carry out. He is made responsible for preserving good government, but what good government means is not his to determine. He merely keeps the peace. His is a primarily negative function, utilising, but bounded by, death. It has not the positive quality of papal government, whose ultimate aim is one of life beyond death. With this final end in view papal government is by contrast essentially constructive government, the formulation of principles by which the end is to be achieved. Lay government on the other hand is essentially destructive. No doubt the use of the sword is necessary to maintain effective government at all, but it is not everything and cannot be enough.

The reason for the distinction between *auctoritas* and *potestas* underlines the essential difference between the papal and imperial functions. Nothing must be permitted to detract from the pope's legislative capacity, but this may happen if he becomes immersed in the cares of day to day administration: 'sollicitudo [temporalium] importat mentis distractionem'.[1] Indeed, as Augustinus Triumphus points out, it is virtually impossible for him to exercise a general watch over the whole *Ecclesia* and at the same time be responsible for all the minutiae of government. Nor, as St. Bernard had emphasised, is physical repression a fitting task for the priesthood, still less the vicar of Christ. He must avoid becoming embroiled in purely mundane matters which, in contrast with his celestial function, appear sordid and fit only for inferiors. Divine things are much more important in a society founded on faith: the end is more important than the means.[2] The pope should not there-

[1] Augustinus Triumphus, *Summa*, ci. 5, p. 498.

[2] Augustinus Triumphus, *Summa*, xliii. 2 ad 1, p. 228, 'Papa et alii ecclesiastici viri non recipiunt immediatam temporalium administrationem quantum ad personalem executionem . . . eo quod officium ipsorum proprium est vacare divinis et spiritualibus actibus et saluti animatum subditorum, sed solum quantum ad ministerialem commissionem: committitur enim temporalium administratio ministris et *oeconomis* quos quaelibet ecclesia tenetur habere'; xxvi. 4 ad 2, p. 158, 'papa et alii praelati non debent se immiscere in morte hominis per immediatam executionem ut propria manu pugnent vel interficiant, quia arma eorum militiae principaliter sunt spiritualia non carnalia, sed mediante potestate saeculari possunt. . .'. Most of this was, as he says, in accordance with Bernardine teaching: ci. 5 ad 3, p. 498, 'Bernardus non interdicit Eugenio temporalium administratione, sed inducit eum principaliter ad contemplationem per quam poterat de fine et de his quae erant ad finem recte disponere'.

fore exercise power except through the lay ruler.[1] But this is to give nothing away: as the anonymous *Disquisitio theologico-iuridica* stresses, the lay ruler still acts by virtue of papal authority and remains fully subject to the pope.

Sed ut praemisi, executionem temporalium papa committit imperatori, retenta tamen sibi super temporalibus plenitudine potestatis.[2]

His subjects can still appeal over his head direct to Rome,[3] but it is much more convenient if they only do it when absolutely necessary. The restriction upon the pope's exercise of power is thus seen to be nothing more than a matter of practical and administrative expediency, a point which it is of the utmost importance to stress in view of the modifications introduced by the followers of Aquinas. The hierocratic writers emphasised repeatedly that the pope could still wield all power himself if he so wished. The omnipotence of God is infrangible, and this fact remains unchanged even though he often prefers to work through human creatures:

. . . in hoc papa assimilatur Deo, qui, cum possit agere omnia per seipsum, tamen ut communicet bonitatem suam aliis creaturis, communicat potentiam agendi, sic et papa.[4]

In sum then, as Innocent III had said, the pope prefers to act *in certis*

[1] Similarly Aegidius Romanus, *De ecclesiastica potestate*, ii. 14, p. 135, 'Quod non est intelligendum quod nullo modo habeat executionem materialis gladii, sed quod non habeat eam vel non est decens quod habeat eam immediatem; habet enim eam per *vicarium* vel per *substitutum* vel per interpositam personam, ut sit persona interposita inter potestatem ecclesiasticam et iudicium sanguinis ad hoc quod cum decentia possit tale officium exerceri'.

[2] Anon., *Disquisitio theologico-iuridica*, ii. 7, p. 1346.

[3] Augustinus Triumphus, *Summa*, xlv. 3 ad 2, p. 249, 'Si ergo quis gravetur a domino temporali et ille dominum superiorem temporalem non habet, ad papam iuste potest recurrere, qui, etsi temporalium omnium administrationem non habet, habet tamen omnium universalem iurisdictionem'.

[4] William Amidani, *Reprobatio errorum*, pp. 24–5; cf. Opicinus de Canistris, *De praeeminentia spiritualis imperii*, p. 97, 'Licet autem summus pontifex utriusque gladii iurisdictionem habeat ac etiam executionem . . . ipse vero per se non agit, non ut in hoc eius potentia limitetur, sed hoc fit aliis rationibus'. This point had already been made by Gregory IX: see his letter of 23 October, 1236, A. Huillard-Breholles, *Historia Diplomatica Friderici II* (Paris, 1852–9), iv. 2, pp. 919–22, 'Sedes apostolica transferens in Germanos . . . nihil de substantia suae iurisdictionis imminuens, imperii tribunal supposuit et gladii potestatem in subsecuta coronatione concessit'.

causis only.[1] But that he should choose to lend the emperor a universal executive function does not in any way impinge upon his own right to exercise it at will:

Est enim ipse papa Dei Filii vicarius. Sicut ergo quod Deus facit mediantibus creaturis tamquam mediantibus secundis causis, sed totum potest facere immediate per seipsum, ita papa, saltem quantum ad potestatem iurisdictionis, sicut omnes fideles regit mediantibus ministris Ecclesiae, ita potest omnes immediate per seipsum regere.[2]

Normally however (*regulariter*) he will not do so unless the vital interests and general well-being of the society are seriously threatened. In the words of St. Paul, all things are lawful, but all things are not expedient. This, for Augustinus Triumphus, is the real meaning of Innocent's theory of casual jurisdiction, and the cases in which he thinks the pope should be prepared to act are those already specified by Innocent himself.[3] Even so, virtually nothing is excluded. The pope is to act, if he wishes, in all matters in which sin is involved, which, as we have said, covers all crimes. Secondly, he is to deal with all cases in which the *pax Ecclesiae* is liable to be disrupted. And as if this were not enough, all legal cases in which the law is ambiguous or difficult to interpret are to be referred to him.[4]

[1] Innocent III, *Decretales*, IV. xvii. 13, 'quod non solum in ecclesiae patrimonio, super quo plenam in temporalibus gerimus potestatem, verum etiam in aliis regionibus, *certis causis inspectis*, temporalem iurisdictionem *casualiter* exercemus'.

[2] Augustinus Triumphus, *Summa*, lxi. 1, p. 321. The existence of other rulers, he continues, is not to be taken as a mark of papal inability to govern directly, since these ministers only exist as a matter of grace: 'et si hoc non facit, non est ex defectu virtutis et potentiae, cum ministri non regant nisi ex virtute eius, sed magis hoc est ex communicatione eius bonitatis et clementiae'. This is comparable to Aquinas' description of Christ: 'Sed rex supernus, quia potens est per seipsum, servis suis potentiam tribuit', *In Ev. Ioh.*, 18 (Parma, x. 611).

[3] Augustinus Triumphus, *Summa*, i. 1 ad 3, p. 3, 'potestas iurisdictionis spiritualium convenit papae secundum immediatam institutionem et executionem, sed potestas iurisdictionis temporalium convenit sibi secundum institutionem et auctoritatem, non tamen secundum immediatam executionem nisi in quibusdam casibus, qui notantur *Extra*, *Qui sint legi.*, c. *Per venerabilem* [*Decretales*, IV. xvii. 13]'.

[4] See Augustinus Triumphus, *Summa*, x. 1 ad 2, p. 77, and xlv. 1, p. 247; the pope is to deal with anything 'difficile et ambiguum' which arises 'inter sanguinem et sanguinem, causam et causam, et lepram et lepram'. This closely follows Innocent III, and refers to *Deut.*, xvii. 8. Since Innocent had defined this as all criminal and civil, ecclesiastical and civil, and ecclesiastical and criminal

He must also take over the administration of the empire during an imperial vacancy and, of course, he retains the right to depose the emperor whenever he sees fit.[1] Not only is this no real restriction upon the papal plenitude of power, but it is not intended to be. It is all a matter of convenience. The whole theory falls into the category of exemption. Most people are in fact usually exempt from direct papal jurisdiction in that their immediate overlords are the local hierarchy of officials, but the existence of these officers can never free them from their overriding obedience to the pope.[2]

The purpose of all this is to deny the lay theory of autonomous monarchy, and to demonstrate that the emperor is essentially a papal representative, a *vicarius papae*.[3] His role as *protector Ecclesiae* does not give him any control over the pope, whom it is his supreme duty to protect, and this was brought out more strongly by coupling this term with that of *advocatus*, a word which embodies the whole hierocratic theory of emperorship. He is, says Augustinus Triumphus, 'vocatus per papam',[4] that is to say, one called into being by a commission of power from a superior authority. He does not function in his own right: but for this evocation he would

cases, the papalists were justified in interpreting this as all lay and clerical matters. Augustinus Triumphus himself adds, xlv. 3 ad 1, p. 249, 'Verum est a iudice saeculari non esse appellandum immediate ad papam indifferenter et in parvis negotiis; sed bene in negotiis arduis et necessitate urgente a quocunque iudice homo gravetur ad papam potest habere recursum tamquam ad universalem dominum'.

[1] Augustinus Triumphus, *Summa*, xxxvi. 4 ad 1, p. 216, 'Papa non debet sibi usurpare immediatam executionem vel administrationem temporalium ne propter talem immediatam executionem implicet se negotiis saecularibus. . . . Sed ex hoc non subtrahitur dominium temporalium ipsi papae, quin in delictis et violentiis non possit imperatores et reges corrigere et eos dominio temporalium privare si contingat eos forefacere'.

[2] Augustinus Triumphus, *Summa*, xxii. 2 ad 2, p. 131, 'nullus est exemptus a dominio papae mediate vel immediate, nam clerici immediate subduntur principatui ecclesiastico, laici vero subduntur ei mediante principatu laicali, qui in obsequium et ministerium est datus praesulatui spirituali'.

[3] Alvarus Pelagius, *De planctu Ecclesiae*, ch. 68, p. 247, 'Tum quia est imperator, vicarius papae est in temporalibus . . . quia a papa recipit imperium et tenet'.

[4] Augustinus Triumphus, *Summa*, xxxix. 2 ad 2, p. 229; for *advocatus* see ad 1, p. 228. Note Innocent III to Otto in 1202, *R.N.I.* 65, p. 104, 'Nos . . . ad coronam imperii te disponimus *evocare*'.

not even exist. To say that he holds his power from God, that emperorship is a divine office or that he is Christ's representative on earth, is meaningless unless it is understood that God in this context is the pope himself, the *Deus Pharaonis*.[1] It is quite true, says Augustinus Triumphus, that the emperor is subject to no one but God, but since God is (as far as human beings are concerned) to be found only in the pope, this merely brings us back to saying that imperial power is a delegation of the papal *rex* function. How else can one get power on earth from God except through the vicar of God?

... verum est potestatem imperialem esse a Deo, quia non est a papa ut est homo, sed est a papa ut gerit vicem Christi in terra, qui est verus Deus et verus homo.[2]

A few years later we find Clement VI making exactly the same point. The imperial power, he tells Charles IV, has no earthly provenance but is of divine origin. This is indisputable when St Paul has said that all power is from God (*Rom*., xiii. 1): and it is interesting to note that the pope follows this up with an appropriate passage from Gratian's *Decretum* (D. 96, c. 11). But, he concludes, this can only be true if that power is derived through the pope.[3] This clearly illustrates the prime function of the papal vicariate of Christ. It is the link through which the divine power of God is commuted

[1] Alvarus Pelagius, *De planctu Ecclesiae*, ch. 13, p. 29, '*Exod*., vii [1] ibi, Ecce te constitui Deum Pharaonis, et papa Deus est imperatoris'. This had always been an integral feature of the papal vicariate idea: see St. Bernard, *De consideratione*, IV. vii. 23 (*PL*, clxxxii. 788), and Innocent III, *Consec. serm*., ii (*PL*, ccxvii. 658).

[2] Augustinus Triumphus, *Summa*, i. 1 ad 2, p. 3; xxxviii. 4 ad 3, p. 227, 'Imperator nullum superiorem se recognoscit dominum temporalem et qui fungitur auctoritate puri hominis; sed bene debet recognoscere superiorem se vicarium illius qui est verus Deus et verus homo'; similarly xxxviii. 1 ad 1, p. 224; xlv. 1 ad 2, p. 247; Anon., *Disquisitio theologico-iuridica*, ii. 7, p. 1345; Alexander de S. Elpidio, *De ecclesiastica potestate*, ii. 8, p. 23; Henry of Cremona, *Non ponant laici*, p. 476. This appears to have been inspired by *Sextus*, I. vi. 17, and the gloss on it by Johannes Andreae, s.v. *homini*.

[3] *MGH*, *Const*., VIII n. 100 p. 151. He begins 'Dico secundo quod iste status [imperii Romani] est generose derivatur, quia a Deo, non de terra sed de coelo duxit originem'. Then follows a discussion of the two texts in question, and the conclusion is 'quod utique verum est, sed mediante pontificali'. Cf. Anon., *Determinatio compendiosa*, ch. 39, p. 548, 'Quid ergo habes, O homo christiane, quod ab ecclesia non accepisti?'

into earthly jurisdiction. The familiar assertion that one cannot go from high to low except through the middle is not a mere geometrical truism,[1] but an attempt to explain the idea that there is a 'point' in the universe at which the divine and the human connect with each other. This point is the pope as vicar of God, half human and half divine—*verus Deus et verus homo*. We cannot overestimate the importance of the mediatory role assigned to the pope in the religious and political thought of the Middle Ages. He becomes the bridge between heaven and earth, and this not only means that mankind cannot attain to God except through the medium of the pope, but equally that the divine wisdom as expressed in the Christian faith is obtainable only through the same channel. And since power exists *in causa fidei* this too must be derived through the same means.

> ... sit clarum et manifestum a Deo quod ... omnem potestatem, tam spiritualem quam temporalem, a Christo in praelatos et principes saeculares derivatam esse mediante Petro eius successore, cuius personam Romanus pontifex repraesentat.[2]

Consequently, declares Augustinus Triumphus, all who exercise power on earth by divine permission do so because they have received it from the pope.[3] Kings and emperors draw their very being from this divine-earthly orifice, which is to be found only in the papal vicariate. He sets them up and they are: he deposes them and

[1] Augustinus Triumphus, *Summa*, xliv. 1, p. 240, 'Illo ergo iure lex imperialis dependet ab auctoritate papae quo iure dependet a lege divina, cuius ipse papa est vicarius et minister, potissime cum secundum Dionysium lex divinitatis hoc habeat ut eius influentia non transeat ad inferiora nisi per media. Medius autem inter Deum et populum christianum est ipse papa, unde nulla lex populo christiano est danda nisi ipsius papae auctoritate'. The reference is to Dionysius the Pseudo-Areopagite, *De coelesti hierarchia*, iv. 3 (*PG*, iii. 181–2). Cf. Boniface VIII in the *Extravangantes communes*, I. viii. 1.

[2] Augustinus Triumphus, *De duplici potestate*, p. 486. The mediatory principle of papal government is constantly reiterated: e.g. *Summa*, xxii. 4, p. 132, '[papa] sit sequester et medius inter Deum et hominem seu totum populum christianum'.

[3] Augustinus Triumphus, *Summa*, xlv. 1 ad 3, p. 247, 'Potestas regibus temporalibus concessa est a Deo cum ordine quodam, puta mediantibus summis pontificis, quia quae a Deo sunt, ordinata sunt'; Alvarus Pelagius, *De planctu Ecclesiae*, ch. 17, p. 32, 'quia omnis iurisdictio ab eo, ipse autem immediate ipsam a Deo recipit'.

they vanish away.[1] He is the true king of kings and lord of lords,[2] the source of faith and righteousness, power and existence. He is the sun-king, the giver of life and light.[3] And as he gives, so he may take away again. Following closely the doctrine of Boniface VIII, Augustinus Triumphus calls him the maker and breaker of kingdoms,[4] the one by whom kings reign and princes decree justice.[5] Indeed the hierocratic writers can hardly restrain their enthusiasm as they seek to bring this point home to their adversaries. The pope becomes the *motor Caesaris*[6] which generates the emperor and gives

[1] Anon., *Disquisitio theologico-iuridica*, ii. 7, p. 1345, 'Et quia a summo et primo omnia alia oriuntur, idcirco a potestate vicarii Christi omnis potestas in terris oritur, sive sit regalis sive imperialis. . . Et hinc est quod potestas papae, Christi vicarius, habet instituere, destituere, corrigere, compescere, ligare et suspendere potestatem imperialem et regalem. . . Et hoc est quod dicitur Ieremias primo *cap.* [10], Constitui te super gentes et regna, ut evellas et destruas et disperdas et dissipes, et aedifices et plantes'. *Jer.*, i. 10, is one of the most often quoted texts in hierocratic thought, and passages similar to this will be found in nearly all papalist tracts.

[2] *Apoc.*, xix. 16. Again a favourite quotation: e.g. Alexander de S. Elpidio, *De ecclesiastica potestate*, ii. 9, p. 27, 'Rex ergo regum summus pontifex'; iii. 3, p. 34, 'Unus tamen, scilicet summus pontifex, proprissime dicitur rex regum, quia sibi soli commissa est plenitudo potestatis'.

[3] Conrad of Megenberg, *Oeconomica*, III. iii. 1 (Kaeppeli, p. 586 n. 1), 'papa, episcopus sive pontifex Romanus . . . sol coeli, servus servorum Dei'; Peter Olivi, *Quaestio de infallibilitate*, p. 334, 'unus sol mundi'. The pope also figures as the sun in the Cyprianic passage cited below p. 383, and of course in the famous sun and moon analogy, which most of the publicists derived from Innocent III in *Decretales*, I. xxxiii. 6. The pope is however compared to the sun from the time of Gregory I: S. Mochi Onory, *Fonti Canonistiche dell'Idea Moderna dello Stato* (Milan, 1951), p. 12 n. 1. The idea is of Indo-Persian origin and subsequently became a Byzantine imperial characteristic. It was copied by Frederick II. For further details see E. H. Kantorowicz, 'Dante's Two Suns', *Semitic and Oriental Studies presented to William Popper* (Berkeley and Los Angeles, 1951).

[4] Augustinus Triumphus, *Summa*, xlvi. 3, p. 251, 'Sicut ergo Deus est factor omnium regnorum et provisor, sic papa vice Dei est omnium regnorum provisor'; cf. Boniface VIII, Dupuy, p. 75, 'Rex deberet recognoscere regnum suum ab ecclesia propter Deum'.

[5] *Prov.*, viii. 15–16; cf. *Cod.*, I. i. 8: see Augustinus Triumphus, *Summa*, xxxvi. 1, p. 212; Alvarus Pelagius, *De planctu Ecclesiae*, ch. 41, p. 71; Boniface VIII, *MGH*, *Const.*, IV. i n. 105 p. 80.

[6] Conrad of Megenberg, *Oeconomica*, III. iii. 10 (Kaeppeli, p. 587, n. 1), 'motor Caesaris est summus pontifex, qui movet ipsum tam in fieri quam in facto esse. In fieri siquidem examinando iam electum an ydoneus sit et per papam approbandus, an non ydoneus et reprobandus per ipsum. Cumque approbatus fuerit, movet eum papa benedicando et coronando. . . Movet etiam

him *esse*;[1] and as Boniface VIII added, the same must logically apply to every other lay ruler in the Christian society. Just as all Christians draw their identity from Christ, so all powers must derive from the vicar of Christ. No other ruler may assert his individuality.[2] Each element is part of a whole and needs to take on the complexion of the whole, which is to be found in the pope representing all. This teaching is admirably summed up by Clement VI. Amid a wealth of quotations, he compares the standing of pope and emperor to that of God and his creatures. The papacy is the origin and effective cause of emperorship, and in the pope we see the beginning and the end of imperial power. Between these two terminals there can only be an emperor who is *imago papae*, whose actions correspond exactly with the directives which issue from his creator.[3]

Nevertheless, the pope continues, in return for complete obedience, the emperor may obtain substantial benefits. There is nothing degrading in the status of a papal vicar: indeed the pope himself is a vicar—of God—and thus becomes assimilable with the deity. In much the same way the papally instituted emperor virtually replaces the pope as the *active* ruler of the *Ecclesia*. 'Ipse regnabit pro me', says Clement, and he will sit on my throne—always provided of course that he remembers to be totally subject and inferior to me.

papa imperatorem in facto esse ipsius, scilicet dirigendo ipsum consiliis et pernotando facta eius an salubria sint Ecclesiae et felitia gregi dominico, an dampnifera mundo. Nam si imperando errando exercet gladium suum, papa corrigit ipsum et non emendabilem deponit'.

[1] Augustinus Triumphus, *Summa*, xxxix. 1, p. 228; xli. 1, p. 230; Conrad of Megenberg, *Oeconomica* III. iii. 10 (Kaeppeli, p. 604), 'imperator subditus est papae quantum ad *esse quod est*'.

[2] Boniface VIII, *MGH, Const.*, IV. i n. 173 p. 139, 'Sicut enim a Christo christiani dicuntur, sic a Christo et vicario Christi, successore Petri, *formantur* et defenduntur omnes dies, hoc est omnes potestates, et nemo in eis, quia non possunt dicere, Ego Pauli, ego sum Apollo [I *Cor.*, i. 12], sed omnes sunt a Christo et a nobis tamquam a vicario Ihesu Christi'.

[3] *MGH, Const.*, VIII n. 100 p. 154, 'Et videtur mihi quod ex istis tribus patet quod eminentia papalis habet in ordine ad excellentiam imperialem quasi triplex genus causalitatis, sicut Deus habet in ordine ad creaturam. Primo quidem originalem et effectivam, secundo exemplarem et directivam, tertio finalem et completivam. Potestas enim imperialis catholica et approbata a papa originatur, a papa exemplatur, ad papam terminatur'.

Like Solomon he will rule in place of God over the people of Israel. In this way the pope excuses himself from the charge that the hierocratic conception of emperorship greatly reduced the emperor's prestige.[1] However inferior with regard to the pope himself, the emperor will still appear to all the other members of the society as the supreme earthly head, governing in the name of, and for the benefit of, both head and members. This is a striking application of the hierocratic principle of society. When the whole community is *unum corpus* it will act as one man, and this means that every properly authorised action by the members is equivalent to an action by the head who represents this mystical man. Those who act by virtue of the power delegated to them by the pope are acting as if it is the pope himself, the human embodiment of the *persona Ecclesiae*, who acts. In a sense each delegate becomes, within the restricted scope of his function, a projection of the pope, a vicar of Christ at one remove. As Conrad of Megenberg explains, 'fidelis imperator est discipulus Christi, cum sit discipulus discipuli Christi in Ecclesia Dei',[2] and we have already had occasion to remark upon Innocent III's insistence that papal legates were legates of Christ rather than the pope. When all the members form the body of the pope, each authorised public activity will be an act on behalf of the whole society and its ruler, and of the corporate personality common to both. Each member in the performance of his function takes on the capacity of representing the mystical personality who is Christ. He becomes, in a very specialised and limited sense, the exemplar or image of God.

As we have seen, this role of acting on behalf of the real personality of the community is symbolically expressed by the idea that the human representative marries the *Ecclesia*. This can now be

[1] *MGH*, *Const.*, VIII n. 100 pp. 151–2, 'Sed additur in themate, et regnabit pro me, ut dicatur illud I *Par.* xxix [28], Regnabit Salomon filius eius pro eo. Sed quare dicit, pro me? Numquid dimittam sibi istam kathedram et istam sedem? Certe non intendo. Sed pro me regnabit quando pro honore meo et istius sedis regnabit; quando pro me regnabit quando suum regimen ad honorem Dei est istius sanctae sedis totaliter ordinabit . . . quia iunior est me . . . quia posterius me . . . quia sua [dignitas] mea inferior . . . quia sua originatur a mea . . . Regni enim solio eum praecedam, Gen. xli [40]'.

[2] Conrad of Megenberg, *De translatione Romani imperii*, ch. 24, p. 330.

taken a stage further. Each individual carrying out his duties on behalf of all may be said to be married to the community, and since he is thereby acting on behalf of the head, he may equally well be said to have married the head himself. The rightly acting member is wedded to the *Ecclesia* in all its forms: society, Christ and pope. This is particularly true of the emperor, the universal ruler under the head, who is the immediate recipient of power delegated by the pope. To establish this point Clement VI goes on to speak of the emperor's marriage to the pope and the society upon his appointment:

Unde ex electione non videtur nisi matrimonium nuntiatum; sed per confirmationem matrimonium videtur esse ratum et ratificatum et contractum: sed papa habet electum in imperatorem approbare; ergo potestas sua originatur a potestate papali.[1]

By his institution into the imperial dignity the emperor assumes the pope's function of acting for the whole society: he comes himself to personify the society seen as one man.[2] Clement is of course careful to insist that it is the pope who is responsible for all this. The emperor may replace the pope for practical purposes, but the pope still remains behind and above him, and is the real cause of the imperial position. It is, in this analogy, the pope who makes the political marriage effective. This point is also emphasised by Augustinus Triumphus. Like Clement, Augustinus speaks of the emperor's marriage and adopts the same comparison with Solomon. The imperial coronation becomes the emperor's wedding day, and he maintains that a ring should be bestowed upon the emperor by the pope to signify this.[3] At the same time however he cautions his readers against forgetting the necessary *interventio papae*. The pope cannot be excluded from the transaction. Solomon was crowned by his mother, and the *Ecclesia* is not only the bride but the mother

[1] *MGH*, *Const.*, VIII n. 100 p. 156.

[2] Innocent III, *Decretales*, I. vi. 34, had spoken of the empire being placed in the person of the emperor: 'quia Romanum imperium in personam magnifici Karoli a Graecis transtulit in Germanos'.

[3] Augustinus Triumphus, *Summa*, xxxviii. 3, p. 226. The whole coronation ceremony is expounded in the form of a commentary on the *Song of Solomon*, iii. 11. The phrase 'in die desponsationis illius' is made to refer to an 'anuli subarratio', the bestowal of a ring at a bethrothal.

of the emperor.[1] It is as the personification of the *Ecclesia* that the pope crowns the emperor, and since the mystical *persona Ecclesiae* is Christ himself, the emperor may indeed be acclaimed 'a Deo coronato'.[2]

Throughout, the papal identity with God is implicit. If we are to speak of the emperor as a projection of the pope, then it is equally necessary to regard the pope himself as a projection of God. The raising of the imperial status is accompanied by an even greater stepping up of the papacy itself. This did indeed confer a real benefit on the emperor. By his coronation he becomes the Lord's anointed, whom no man might touch. Only God can dissolve a spiritual marriage—or, to speak more plainly, only the pope may depose the emperor. As early as the ninth century the papacy had begun to speak of the emperor as the pope's 'special son', and of the *spiritualis coniunctio* which existed between them as a result of the imperial coronation. Later popes had continued to stress this unique relationship with the emperor, and had reserved the right to depose him to themselves.[3] Nevertheless there were moments when the papalists appear to have suffered from misgivings. The theory reached such a pitch of refinement that it might only too easily be misinterpreted: would the imperialists really understand the part played by the pope himself? Consequently the theory tended to fall out of favour during the great struggle with the Staufen, and it

[1] Augustinus Triumphus, *Summa*, xxxviii. 3, p. 226, 'Quo coronavit eum mater sua; mater enim imperatoris ecclesia est', which is then described as the 'interventio ipsius papae et eius auctoritatis'. The marriage of the earth-goddess who is both mother and daughter is a familiar figure in Greek mythology: see C. G. Jung and C. Kerényi, *Introduction to a Science of Mythology* (London, 1951), pp. 167f. The whole theory bears a striking similarity to the classical Indian idea of coronation. Here too the 'marriage' of the king to the priest, and hence to the community—the king being feminine to the priest but male to the community—makes the ruler into the 'sword of God' who acts under the direction of the priesthood. The coronation also symbolises the union of the divine and the human which translates the community into the *civitas Dei*: see further A. K. Coomaraswamy, *Spiritual Authority and Temporal Power in the Indian Theory of Government* (New Haven, 1942).

[2] Augustinus Triumphus, *Summa*, xxxviii. 3, p. 226: this cites the acclamation of Charlemagne in 800; cf. Ullmann, *The Growth of Papal Government*, pp. 97–8.

[3] Ullmann, *op. cit.*, pp. 152–3, 257–8.

became a matter of deliberate policy to denigrate the status of the emperor. Symptomatic of this was the omission of the ring from the coronation ceremony.[1] The popes were hard-headed men of affairs: they realised that emperors did not appreciate subtle distinctions. A beringed emperor would only assume that his claim to be bishop and true *caput Ecclesiae* had at last been recognised. The papal fears were in fact justified: the lay writers continued to speak of the emperor's marriage to the society without mentioning that the pope still stood between the emperor and God.[2] As Johannes Branchazolus maintained, the pope himself does nothing to cement the relationship between emperor and society: he merely declares the fact of the direct intervention of God. By crowning the emperor the pope does no more than voice the will of God. It is God who makes the union and grants the emperor his power: the pope has merely to give a visible demonstration of this—what Ockham termed an *exterior apparentia*[3]—lest it should otherwise be a purely invisible act. But the pope himself is no more the real author of the union than is the priest at any other marriage ceremony.

Et sic imperatoris potestati *substantialiter* papae coronatio nihil addit, sed demum ipsum a Deo recognoscere imperium *declaratur*, sicut est exemplum videre in benedictione matrimonii quam a sacerdote recipit desponsata, cum per ipsum nihil substantiae addatur, sed rite factum matrimonium *demonstratur*.[4]

For the imperialist no one stood between God and the emperor. The lay writer could not accept that the pope had any real capacity *vice Dei*, and it was this subtle difference in approach which alone

[1] The ring disappeared from the coronation order (*ordo D*) prepared for Otto IV by Innocent III in 1209. It had however already been omitted from the previous order (*ordo C*), in use since the early eleventh century, on the occasion of Frederick I's coronation by Adrian IV in 1158: W. Ullmann, 'The Pontificate of Adrian IV', *Cambridge Historical Journal*, xi (1953–5), pp. 233–52 at pp. 241–2. *Ordo D* was still in use for the coronation of Henry VII in 1311, and no ring is mentioned in the order of ceremony: see Clement V's letter of commission, 19 June, 1311, *MGH*, *Const.*, IV. i n. 644 pp. 609–13. There has since been no replacement of this order.

[2] For the lay theory of the prince as *sponsus reipublicae* see now *KTB*, pp. 212–23.

[3] William of Ockham, *Allegationes de potestate imperiali*, p. 430.

[4] Johannes Branchazolus, *De principio imperatoris et papae*, ii. 6, p. 50.

made the continued papal coronation bearable. To allow the pope any effective part in the ceremony was tantamount to equating him with God himself. Yet this was precisely what the hierocrats in their usual rather oblique manner were attempting to convey. The emperor takes the place of the pope as his vicar for the very reason that the pope has withdrawn himself from the personal administration of secular affairs into the solitude appropriate to a divine being. On this account the creation of the emperor is a matter of undoubted utility. He becomes the effective, if second-hand, head of the *Ecclesia* because the pope *qua Deus* prefers to remain remote from human affairs. And as it became once more desirable to bolster up the power of the emperor in face of the growing desire of other kings to be their own emperors, the theory again finds favour with the papal defenders. Augustinus Triumphus, for example, even goes so far as to express a wish for the old form of imperial unction with chrism on the head, now abolished, to be reinstated.[1] By the fourteenth century the papalists were almost eager to speak of the emperor as the *human* head of the society, provided that he recognised the existence of a superior *divine* head in the pope. For them the papal commission of power to the emperor parallels Christ's original commission of power to St. Peter, and just as Peter had acted *in persona Ecclesiae*, so now the emperor is turned into a personification of all the other members of the society. It comes to represent the transmission of divine power to the earthly community, the marriage of Christ to his Church, which is re-enacted at every imperial coronation when the pope bestows the crown upon the emperor. In that the emperor acts *loco papae* he becomes

[1] In spite of Innocent III's decree, *Decretales*, I. xv. 1, that only bishops should be permitted unction with chrism on the head, royal as opposed to imperial coronations had continued to include this type of unction. On this Augustinus Triumphus comments, *Summa*, xxxviii. 2 ad 1, p. 225, 'Tertium est oleum principalis chrismatis, quo inunguntur capita regum et pontificum: hac ergo unctione imperator debet ungi et consecrari'. He denies that this royal consecration gives episcopal power, civ. 3 ad 2, p. 514, which follows Thomas Aquinas, *Opusculum II, De perfectione vitae spiritualis*, ch. 26. This was a matter of widespread debate among the publicists, but the official viewpoint was summed up in John XXII's letter to Edward II of England in 1318, which emphasised the lack of sacramental value in the royal consecration by stating that it could be repeated any number of times: Kern, *Kingship and Law*, p. 55.

one with the pope in the same way that the society is one with its divine head. He becomes a projection of the *persona Ecclesiae* in order to actualise the will of the remote divinity of Rome.

But when the reverse side of the picture is borne in mind, it may be questioned whether the emperor really did receive any benefit at all from the suggestion that he was *imago papae*. After all the theologians had always insisted that any man was *imago Dei*, but they would have been shocked to have it thought that they were suggesting that he was God: likewise the hierocrat had no real intention of equating emperor and pope. The assimilation of the emperor to the status of a human *caput Ecclesiae* at one remove did no doubt seek to improve the emperor's position *vis-à-vis* the rest of society, but it did nothing to improve his standing against the pope himself. Rather it emphasised that the difference between them was one between the human and the divine, and made the unrestrained right of the pope to depose kings and princes an even more obvious corollary to the theory. For Augustinus Triumphus it follows as a matter of course. The pope, he declares, is the hammer of the tyrants,[1] and any ruler who fails to carry out the *rex* function falls into this category. Negligence or incapacity, as much as open disobedience, make the ruler *inutilis*, functionally disqualified from holding office in the *Ecclesia*.[2] But deposition is not the only remedy. It may be enough to render him temporarily incapable of governing by excommunicating him. In other cases, in which the pope does not wish to punish the ruler but the government of his kingdom is decaying, he may appoint caretakers to administer it in the king's name.[3] But it is disobedience to papal commands upon

[1] Augustinus Triumphus, *Summa*, ci. 4, p. 497, 'qui loco Christi positus est in malleum et tyrannorum flagellum'. This was borrowed from St. Bernard, *De consideratione*, iv. 7 (*PL*, clxxxii. 788). See also R. Arbesmann, 'The *Malleus* Metaphor in Medieval Characterisation', *Traditio*, iii (1945), pp. 389–92.

[2] Augustinus Triumphus, *Summa*, xlvi. 2, p. 250, 'Propter istum ergo duplicem defectum iustitiae papa potest reges deponere, vel propter defectum iustitiae particularis vel propter defectum vero iustitiae universalis'. As an example of the first he cites the case of Childeric (Gratian, C. 15 q. 6 c. 3), allegedly deposed by Zacharias because he was so feeble as to be *inutilis*; and to exemplify the second he refers to Innocent IV's deposition of Frederick II on the grounds of the emperor's *inobedientia*.

[3] The suggestion that a coadjutor should be appointed for a king like a bishop

which the hierocratic writers harp as being the crime worthy of the severest penalties. Since the ruler is bound by oath to obey the pope this constitutes a case of perjury, and William Amidani think it possible for the pope to inflict any additional punishment beyond deposition, such as imprisonment, short of a sentence of death.

Papa de iure potest punire imperatorem usque ad incarcerationem et sibi omnem poenam citra mortem inferre immediate ex propria auctoritate.[1]

If he can remove bishops from their sees, why not also lay rulers? asks Augustinus Triumphus, when a king is only the lay equivalent of a bishop in the hierarchy of ecclesiastical officers.[2] He is eager to stress that it is not only the emperor who is subject to the pope: every lay ruler must be subservient to one whose dominion extends over all kingdoms and empires,[3] who has the power to transfer them at will, who is in fact the owner of the whole earth.[4] They

is in Augustinus Triumphus, *Summa*, xlvi. 2 ad 2, p. 251; that only excommunication should be decreed, xl. 3 ad 2, p. 232.

[1] William Amidani, *Reprobatio errorum*, ch. 5, p. 28; cf. Augustinus Triumphus, *Summa*, xl. 2 ad 1, p. 231, 'Sed imperator ad multa alia tenetur quae in suo iuramento ponuntur, in quibus si negligens fuerit et contumax exstiterit deponendus est'. For the idea that this constitutes perjury see David, *op. cit.*, pp. 183–8, 201–2.

[2] Augustinus Triumphus, *Summa*, xlvi. 3, p. 251, 'papa potest in qualibet ecclesia praelatum ponere et deponere. . . Ergo potest in quolibet regno hoc facere, cum maius sit dominium spirituale quam temporale'. This may have been inspired by Huguccio: see Mochi Onory, *op. cit.*, p. 159.

[3] Augustinus Triumphus, *Summa*, xxxvii. 3 ad 1, p. 221, 'tamquam vicarius Dei Filii coelestis imperatoris iurisdictionem habet universalem super omnia regna et imperia'; Hervaeus Natalis, *De potestate papae*, fo. 144v, 'quia sicut dictum est ad talem potestatem pertinet tollere omne impedimentum tenendi in Deum in populo christiano et per consequens ad eum pertinet corrigere omnem abusum tam potestatis ecclesiasticae quam terrenae in quocunque existente de populo christiano'.

[4] Augustinus Triumphus, *Summa*, xxxv. 4, p. 208, 'papae est in omnibus regnis mutare et translationem facere tam in electo quam in electoribus propter duo. Primo quia vicarius est illius qui regnum a gente in gentem transfert propter iniustitias et iniurias et contumelias et diversos dolos, ut scribitur *Eccle.* x [8]. Secundo quia ipse solus habet considerare finem totius Ecclesiae et ad dictum finem omnes ordinare per debita media'; Conrad of Megenberg, *De translatione Romani imperii*, ch. 13, pp. 296–7, 'omnia regna christianae religionis per papam posse in alios quam in suos iam possessores transferri, quia cum papa

can all be deposed just as easily as they are appointed: 'unde sicut papa hanc potestatem confert omnibus, ita potest eam auferre'.[1] Indeed it really seems that he can rule the world all by himself if he so wishes. When the question of this is posed, Augustinus Triumphus curtly replies that God can do this—'Deus per seipsum posset imperare et regere universum orbem'—and his readers are left to draw their own conclusions whilst he goes on to illustrate the right of the pope to translate kingdoms without consulting anyone.[2] It becomes obvious that for the papal-hierocratic writers the pope is in no way compelled to create other kings, or once having created them, maintain them in being. As a contemporary puts it, he can decree that the power of the emperor shall not endure to the end of the year.[3] The existence of lay rulers depends solely upon his absolute pleasure, and nobody else is entitled to have any say in the matter.[4] In his relationships with kings the pope acts by will alone: he does not have to give reasons for what he does; indeed he does not need to have any discernible reason at all. As the Clerk in the *Somnium viridarii* has it, to say anything else would be an infringement of his God-like plenitude of power.

Amplius videtur indubiter tenendum quod omne regimen et imperium sit a papa, et taliter quod de plenitudine potestatis possit quandoque placuerit imperatorem seu regem instituere, et etiam pro libito voluntatis destituere ut placet absque causa et etiam sine culpa, et eidem alium subrogare, et sibiipsi imperium retinere sive regnum: aliter non haberet

iure divino transtulerit imperium, ita potest transferre alia regna, cum praecepta iuris divini omnes ligent'.

[1] Augustinus Triumphus, *De duplici potestate*, pp. 495–6. For other examples see Alvarus Pelagius, *De planctu Ecclesiae*, ch. 13, p. 30; ch. 44, p. 77; *Collirium*, p. 504; *Speculum regum*, p. 520; Anon., *Disquisitio iuridica*, ch. 1, p. 1380; Andreas de Perusio, *Tractatus contra edictum Bavari*, p. 70.

[2] Augustinus Triumphus, *Summa*, xxxvii. 1 ad 1, p. 220.

[3] Francis de Meyronnes, *Quaestio de subiectione*, i. 12, p. 85, 'et sic potest constituere quod eius imperium non duraret per annum'.

[4] Augustinus Triumphus, *Summa*, lxxi. 4 and ad 3, p. 374, 'Vicarius autem Christi in toto praesenti vita est ipse papa, ad quem de iure spectat omnes praelationes et omnia dominia in toto humano genere ordinare vice Christi quantum ad multos casus . . . Decimo quantum ad imperatorum et regum omnium et principum institutionem et destitutionem . . . quamvis in saeculari dominio multi praesint, eorum tamen institutio et destitutio iusta causa superveniente non nisi ad papam spectat'.

plenitudinem potestatis, sed haberet potestatem per iura alia quam divina limitatam.[1]

The creation of kings imposes no obligation upon the pope: kingship is a *beneficium*, a concessional gift received from above. It is no doubt, as Aegidius Romanus said, a divine gift, since all good things come from God, but this merely serves to emphasise that emperorship can only be gained from the vicar of God.[2] Because it is a concession it can always be withdrawn, and because it is a gift it is not something to be demanded as a right.[3] Rulership is a favour, held *ex gratia papae*, and cannot be taken for granted any more than the grace of God can be gained by man of his own volition.[4] The ruler has no self-sufficiency, no independence of action, no existence at all, except in so far as the pope wills it. He is not so much a son[5] in

[1] Anon., *Somnium viridarii*, i. 162, p. 121. It may however be noted that after this excellent description of the hierocratic view, the Clerk hastily adds that this is not his own personal opinion, and proceeds to put forward a much more moderate theory.

[2] Aegidius Romanus, *De ecclesiastica potestate*, iii. 2, p. 154; Augustinus Triumphus, *Summa*, xxxvii. 4, p. 222; xxxix. 1, p. 228; Henry of Cremona, *De potestate papae*, p. 467.

[3] Boniface VIII, Dupuy, p. 42, 'Nec Romanus pontifex in *concedendis gratiis* sic plenitudinem potestatis astringit quin posset eas cum decet et expedit *revocare* ac etiam immutare'; *MGH*, *Const.*, IV. i n. 105 p. 80, 'Quicquid honoris, praeeminentiae, dignitatis et status imperium seu regnum Romanum habet ab ipsius sedis *gratia*, *benignitate* et *concessione* manavit, a qua Romanorum imperatores et reges . . . receperunt gladii potestatem'.

[4] Conrad of Megenberg, *De translatione Romani imperii*, ch. 22, p. 318. See also Clement V's announcement at the conclusion of his examination of Henry VII's election, Baluze, iii. 222–3: the pope says, '. . . et personam ipsius approbantes pronunciamus et declaramus esse sufficientem, habilem et ydoneam ad promovendum in imperatorem . . . ex nunc *concedentes* eidem nostram et sanctae Romanae ecclesiae consuetos *gratiam et favorem*, praecipientes *ex nunc* omnibus subditis suis quod eidem tamquam regi Romanorum vero efficaciter pareant et intendant'. Much the same is repeated for Charles IV by Clement VI, *MGH*, *Const.*, VIII n. 100 p. 163, 'ei nostros *favorem et gratiam concedentes*.' The formula 'Rex Romanorum gratia papae vel sedis' was in standard use by the papacy: e.g. Innocent III to Otto, *R.N.I.* 3, p. 13—and subsequently adopted by Otto himself. Even Frederick II was induced to use it on one occasion, *MGH*, *Const.*, II p. 58. For the Gelasian roots of the *beneficium-favor-gratia* idea see Ullmann, 'Cardinal Roland and Besançon', pp. 111–18; 'The Pontificate of Adrian IV', pp. 243–4.

[5] Augustinus Triumphus, *Summa*, xl. 3, p. 231, 'papa imperatoris censetur esse pater et magister. . . Potest ergo imperatorem tamquam filium et disci-

the household of the *pater patrum* as a slave[1] over whom the head has powers of life and death. His subservient function places him amongst the 'contemptibiles et inferiores de Ecclesia'.[2] He has absolutely no rights of his own, and it is this which characterises the papal supremacy over the other members of the Christian society as true sovereignty.

pulum tali poena corrigere . . . imperator subest papae . . . filiali in spiritualium derivatione, derivantur enim *dona* spiritualia ab eo tamquam a fonte in imperatorem et in omnes filios Ecclesiae'.

[1] William Amidani, *Reprobatio errorum*, ch. 4, p. 27, 'sed papa est dominus simpliciter in terris . . . imperator vero est eius subditus et *servus*'; cf. Augustinus Triumphus, *Summa*, xxii. 2 ad 3, p. 131, 'laicis est maior servitus'. According to Matthew Paris (ed. London, 1640, p. 872), Innocent IV had referred to the English king as his *mancipium*: 'Nonne rex Anglorum noster est vasallus, et ut plus dicam, mancipium . . .?' This follows the Roman law principle that *dominatio* involves *servitus* on the part of those subject to it: F. Schulz, *Principles of Roman Law* (Oxford, 1936), pp. 140–4.

[2] Augustinus Triumphus, *Summa*, i. 4 ad 3, p. 7, 'sicut dicit Apostolus [1] ad *Cor*., i [28], ad iudicia et litigia determinanda contemptibiles de Ecclesia debent eligi. Per hoc enim quod imperatores et reges leges condunt per quas iudicia et litigia saecularium personarum terminantur, non habetur quod ipsi maiores sed potius contemptibiles et inferiores in Ecclesia, ut dicit Cyprianus et ponitur 10 *dist*., c. [8], *quoniam idem*'.

III. TO HAVE AND HAVE NOT

THE papal domination of the European monarchs was a logical extension of the theory of sovereignty which was built up round the *vicarius Christi* idea. This fact was fully appreciated at the time, and it was clearly understood by the anti-hierocratic writers that there was to be no freedom for the king or emperor until this *plenitudo potestatis* was either destroyed or effectively limited. The weapon with which this was to be achieved was provided, incongruously enough, by that group of publicists who set to work to elaborate the general principles propounded by Thomas Aquinas into a complete and comprehensive political system. And they, since they seek to satisfy all, ruled as well as ruler, have no taste for sovereignty. For them law, by which they mean divine-natural law, is to be regarded as the only true expression of sovereignty, and every legislator by his very nature as *lex animata* is held to be subject to it. It is by subjecting the pope to a law greater than himself that these writers see a means of carrying out the enormous task which they have assumed: namely, the complete amalgamation of the papal-hierocratic theory with the idea of the natural and popular institution of lay government resting upon Aristotelian and Roman law doctrines. For them the lay ruler is essentially a creature of the people, and the attempt to combine relative lay and papal autonomy is part of the greater aim of assimilating the papal monarchy into a community in which the individual members are seen as the ultimate source of political authority. The limitation of the *plenitudo potestatis in temporalibus* follows naturally from their ideal of limited government, and in those areas to which the papal power does not run there may be found room for the lay ruler to exist and act of his own accord and in his own right.

The great debating point amongst the political theorists of the fourteenth century therefore comes to be directly concerned with the nature of the *plenitudo potestatis*, and so fiercely does the contest rage that a later writer, reviewing the progress of the controversy, concludes that the extent of papal power is a matter of complete uncertainty.[1] But to a greater or lesser degree, most of the publicists came to agree with Ockham that the papal claim to the wrong sort of *plenitudo potestatis* was the root cause of all the trouble.[2] This is not, it must be noticed, an outright denial of the plenitude of power: the papal right to act in any matter with full discretionary powers when the well-being of the community is endangered is accepted. The dispute hinges on the question of whether he can use his absolute power (or, as a later generation would say, his prerogative) at will or only in certain specific cases. This distinction is not particularly new. It can be found in Gratian, and most of the Decretists had at one time or another disputed whether the pope ought to have an absolutely free use of the plenitude of power, or should be restricted, as Rufinus suggested, to employing it only *in certis causis*. Thus for example Huguccio, whose opinion was usually of decisive influence upon later writers, came to the conclusion that it should only be used in a 'necessitatis aut casualis eventus causa'.[3] It is difficult to estimate to what extent these views represented a well-established body of opinion, but the publicists certainly felt justified in taking up the scattered threads of Decretist thought and knitting them into a closely woven theory of limited power. And it is with these later writers that the first full-scale attack is launched

[1] Jacobus Almainus, *De auctoritate Ecclesiae*, ch. 3, 'Tanta est inter doctores controversia de plenitudine huius potestatis, et ad quae se extendat, ut pauca sint in ea materia secura': in Gerson, *Opera Omnia* (Antwerp, 1706), ii. 1013f.

[2] William of Ockham, *Tractatus contra Benedictum XII*, vi. 2, p. 273, 'Ista autem radix in quadam alia est fundata, quod scilicet papa habet a Christo plenitudinem potestatis tam in spiritualibus quam in temporalibus ut de potentia absoluta omnia possit quae non sunt contra legem divinam vel legem naturae, ita ut in omnibus talibus omnes christiani ei de necessitate salutis obedire firmiter teneantur. Quare istam radicem mortiferam, ex qua errores innumeri et infinita pericula et innumerabiles iniuriae oriuntur, ante omnia expedit exstirpare'.

[3] Gratian, C. 7 q. 1 c. 35, 'Scias frater dilectissime, aliud esse causam necessitatis et utilitatis, aliud praesumptionis ac propriae voluntatis': this is attributed to Pelagius II; Rufinus, *Summa Decretorum ad* C. 23 q. 1 (ed. Singer, p. 403); and for Huguccio see Brys, *De dispensatione in Iure Canonico*, p. 100. On the canonists' use of the distinction between direct and indirect power see further F. Gillmann, 'Von wem stammen die Ausdrücke *potestas directa* und *potestas indirecta papae in temporalia*?', *AKKR*, xcviii (1918), pp. 407f.

upon the hierocratic idea of unfettered absolutism. For them the pope, like any other king, must acknowledge that the law which protects the private rights and interests of his subjects is equally binding on himself. He is not the absolute owner of everything, but must permit others the normal right to control their own offices and possessions.[1] Otherwise, said Ockham, you will find that the pope is using the plenitude of power to turn the law of Christ into an instrument of servitude. To allow him to say and do as he pleases without reference to any positive law would permit him to convert kings into yokels, and to treat them like rustic slaves.[2] And whereas the Decretists had tended to regard this as a matter for academic speculation, the fourteenth-century publicist was far more ready to be convinced that the papal tyranny was already in existence. As early as 1331 Ockham was denouncing John XXII for political heresy in regard to the plenitude of power. The pope was claiming the right to divide and destroy kingdoms 'pro

[1] See for example Conrad of Megenberg's discussion of this in the *De translatione Romani imperii*, ch. 21, pp. 314–15: 'principis universi, qualis est summus pontifex aut etiam imperator, esse universale in sua potestate habere omnia, potest intelligi dupliciter'. The first is the absolute sense: 'uno modo immediate et usive, quod scilicet ipse immediate possideat omnia et singula atque ipsis utatur tamquam possessor proprius et immediatus, sicut ego meis utor in divitiis et possideo eas'. This however he rejects ('Hoc modo nec papae nec imperatoris sunt omnia sive iure divino sive humano') in favour of a remoter and less possessive interpretation: 'Secundo modo potest intelligi principis universi esse omnia directorie et regitive, quod scilicet omnibus de rebus suis habet facere iustitiam tamquam iudex *ultimus* ad quem recurritur *ultimate*. Et sic generalis principis omnia fore dicuntur'.

[2] William of Ockham, *Tractatus contra Benedictum XII*, iv. 12, p. 262, 'quia papa non habet talem plenitudinem potestatis ut aliquid possit contra scripturam sacram, sicut nec aliquid potest contra legem naturae; cum etiam non possit omnia quae nec sunt contra legem divinam nec contra legem naturae... Si autem papa omnia posset quae non sunt contra legem divinam et legem naturae, lex christiana esset maxime servitutis, quia per legem christianam omnes christiani essent facti in omnibus servi papae, ita ut de rebus et personis omnium regum et aliorum posset facere quicquid potest rex vel alius dominus facere de rebus et personis servorum suorum, et ita posset papa de plenitudine potestatis privare omnes reges christianos regnis suis et facere eos aratores, immo servos rusticorum suorum, et imponere eis quaecunque opera servilia quae potest aliquis dominus imponere servis suis'. Marsilius also complained that the papal plenitude of power reduced all other kings and peoples to 'total servitude': *Defensor pacis*, II. xxv. 14, p. 481; xxv. 17, p. 483; xxvi. 7, p. 493.

suo arbitrio voluntatis'; to appoint all lay officials and magnates, even against the wishes of the king concerned; to do as he pleased with all their worldly possessions; to deprive the German princes of their electoral rights; to revoke or annul any imperial decree; to cite any lay ruler to appear before the papal curia, and to permit inferior princes to appeal to it regardless of an imperial sentence. Seven years later another writer widened the scope of this declamation to include Benedict XII, and added the charges that the popes had wilfully misinterpreted the meaning of *Jeremiah*, i. 10; had arrogated to themselves the right to proclaim a vacancy in the empire; and were endeavouring to deprive the prince-electors of all their administrative powers during that vacancy. For all this both popes ought to have been deposed long ago.[1] Much of this is a commonplace of all contemporary imperial propaganda, but what gives it particular interest is the legalistic basis of the complaints. The pope is presumed to know that he must be subject to law, and the law in this sense is seen to embrace all matters affecting the proper relationship between lay rulers and the papacy. Moreover, apparently staunch supporters of the papacy were beginning to operate along the same lines, and this was made considerably easier for them by the fact that nobody, except extremists like Marsilius of Padua, openly professed a desire to do away with the pope's absolute power altogether, and so deprive him of all right to intervene in secular affairs. We must indeed, said Durandus of S. Porciano, give an immediate and affirmative answer to the question of whether the pope possesses temporal power. But he promptly added that it was quite another matter whether he had all of it all the time. And from here he was gradually able to work himself into the position in which he allowed the pope to wield the *rex* function in certain cases, but could otherwise assert that he had no ordinary jurisdiction in temporals and that a duality of powers must normally exist.[2]

[1] William of Ockham, *Quoniam scriptura*, pp. 78–9; Anon., *Tractatus contra Iohannem XXII et Benedictum XII*, ch. 2, pp. 599–600.

[2] Durandus de S. Porciano, *De iurisdictione ecclesiastica*, ch. 3, fo. 3v, 'Responsio: ista quaestio non est dubia quantum ad illud quod prima facie quaeritur. Sed aliqua argumenta statim facta arguendo ad quaestionem implicant unum quod

This view that the pope has only a casual or indirect jurisdiction in secular affairs was later to be elaborated by Cardinal Bellarmine, and is sufficiently well known to modern historians. For this reason it is surprising that little effort has been made to examine several fundamental questions relating to it. In the first place it is obvious that this theory had to take into account the nature of the Petrine commission. But why, when this commission to Peter was so clearly all-embracing, was his successor only to be permitted a casual exercise of his absolute power? Again, since it was believed that a duality generally held good, how were the boundaries between temporal and spiritual established and on what authority? And it may be added that remarkably little attention has been paid to the principle of reciprocity which underlay the theory. Yet by the first half of the fourteenth century it was being generally recognised that the casual power of the pope over the lay ruler must logically be counterbalanced by the casual right of the lay ruler to exercise jurisdiction over the pope. This is indeed an integral part of the whole idea, and without it the Thomists could never have hoped to make their compromise solution acceptable to the lay writers themselves. As it was, they were able to convince themselves that a *via media* had been found.[1] Some of them in fact professed to believe that there had never been any real grounds for dispute: as Bartolus said, 'I believe that both pope and emperor have exactly the same opinion on these matters'.[2] What he meant to say was that the so-

est dubium, viz., utrum potestas iurisdictionis ecclesiastica se extendit aliquomodo ad ea quae subsunt iurisdictioni saeculari'; cf. Anon., *Quaestio in utramque partem, proem.*, p. 96, 'Quaestio est utrum dignitas pontificalis et imperialis sive regalis sint duae potestates distinctae ad invicem. Et hoc est quaerere utrum summus pontifex *plenam iurisdictionem* et *ordinariam potestatem* habeat tam in temporalibus quam in spiritualibus, ita quod omnes principes temporales subsint ei quantum ad temporalia. Quod sint potestates distinctae et quod papa non habeat dominium *omnium* temporalium probatur. . .'

[1] E.g. Alvarus Pelagius, *De planctu Ecclesiae*, ch. 56, p. 152, 'Inter has duas opiniones accipio mediam quae probabilior esse videtur'; also James of Viterbo, *De regimine christiano*, ii. 7, p. 230; Francis de Meyronnes, *Quaestio de subiectione*, i. *proem.*, p. 76. Similarly John of Paris, *De potestate regia et papali, proem.*, pp. 173, 175, announces that he will show a mean between the error of the Waldenses, which denies the pope any temporal power, and the error of Herod, which allows the pope full power in temporals.

[2] Bartolus, *Comm. in Const. Ad Reprimendum*, 'Quare sic credo tenere eccle-

called papal extremists like James of Viterbo and Alvarus Pelagius had at last found common ground with their opponents. Close analysis shows that both sides were saying very much the same thing, and that divergencies were frequently only a matter of emphasis. For James himself the pope has a plenitude of power in temporals, but may only use it on certain occasions: for Ockham the pope has no temporal power—except on certain occasions. The reason for this was the influence exerted on both by the Thomist political synthesis: like Jack Sprat and his wife they licked the platter of political controversy clean. The difference between the hierocratic and the anti-hierocratic ideas was steadily being whittled away, and the whole question of papal power inevitably comes to be regarded as an arid discussion by pedantic scholastics over nothing in particular. The development of this trend during the fourteenth and fifteenth centuries could not fail to have a deleterious effect upon the medieval papacy, and it is this dilution of the hierocratic theme which becomes a potent factor in the movement towards the Reformation.

The effect of the Thomist solution was to make a virtue out of necessity. Since most rulers were in practice obliged to act by legal process, the idea of what they ought to do steadily hardened into the assertion that this was what they had to do. The hierocratic writers also stipulated that the pope ought to adhere to his own law, but they enthusiastically considered his not doing so. Although the division of functions suggested that he ought to leave most matters of secular administration to the lay ruler, this was not held to be a bar to his direct use of the *rex* function at will. But for the Thomists it is not only virtuous for him to restrict his activities: it is positively vicious to assert that he can do anything himself. As Cardinal Zabarella later said, the theory of 'papa omnia potest' puts the pope

siam, sic credo imperatorem sentire': see Woolf, *op. cit.* pp. 85–8. Note also Aegidius Romanus' claim that a papal plenitude of power in temporal things does not interfere with the rights of the secular prince: *De ecclesiastica potestate*, ii. 4, p. 48, 'Intendimus in hoc capitulo declarare quod omnia temporalia sub dominio et potestate ecclesiae collocantur. Nec per hoc intendimus potestati terrenae et saecularibus principibus sua iura subtrahere, sed potius conservare. Non enim praesentem tractatum suscepimus ut velimus quorumcunque iura solvere, sed potius adimplere'.

above God himself.[1] It was already frequently asserted in the fourteenth century—we may mention Ockham and Durandus of S. Porciano—that God had himself abdicated his right to act in an absolute manner as a matter of course. This was in direct contrast to the strict Augustinian or hierocratic view that God's power is omnicompetent and must remain so. God is all and man is nothing: at least he possesses nothing in his own right but is wholly dependent upon the gifts of divine grace. Even his existence depends entirely upon the sovereign pleasure of God, and nature has no ineradicable place in the world. Translated into political terms one arrives at the illimitable sovereignty of the pope as vicar of God. All other created beings, whether kings or subjects, have no power of their own: they can act only *ex gratia papae*, by virtue of the power which they receive from the pope. They have no inalienable right to it, and there is no restraint upon the pope to prevent him from exercising this power himself. But for the fourteenth-century Aristotelian God is held to have reduced his absolute power in order to grant nature a place in the universe. He still possesses a *potestas absoluta*, which is his from all eternity. This is omnipotence pure and simple, overriding all established temporal laws, a power in which the exercise of his will is untrammelled. But he does not use this except on the rare occasions on which direct divine intervention into terrestrial affairs is necessary. Normally he works through the institutions which he has created to act on his behalf: these he has established by his *potestas ordinata*. He has restricted himself to acting through others: his power is indirect, and only becomes directly active in special circumstances. We may say that he has limited his absolute power to a casual jurisdiction. One could, as Ockham did, still stress God's absolute power: indeed it can be even more heavily emphasised since observation teaches that it is unlikely that he will make much use of it. But we should not be

[1] Francis Zabarella, *Tractatus de schismate* (ed. Schardius, *De Iurisdictione Imperiali* (Basle, 1566), p. 560), 'Quae iura sunt notanda quia male considerata sunt per multos assentatores, qui voluerunt placere pontificibus, per multa retro tempora et usque ad hodierna suaserunt eis quod omnia possent; et sic quod facerent quicquid liberet, etiam illicita, et sic plus quam Deus.' Dietrich of Niem said that the papal claim to an illimitable plenitude of power was the real cause of the Great Schism.

dazzled by this sleight of hand: with Ockham the left takes away what the right one gives. He could afford to talk *ad nauseam* about the omnipotence of God (which was a useful counter to a charge of heresy) precisely because his empiricism taught him that it could in practice be largely ignored. This was a direct result of the theologians' acceptance of the distinction between God's absolute and ordained power. The *potestas absoluta* is God's power in the abstract, *potestas ordinata* that power as it is manifested to us through created things: it is the theory and practice of God's power.[1] Similarly his vicar is theoretically permitted an absolute *plenitudo potestatis* following upon the Petrine commission, but he is held to have ordained that certain ministers, kings and emperors shall exist for him to work through. His initial sovereignty remains indirect, and is only exercised *in certis causis* when his ministers become insufficient.[2] On these rather rare occasions he performs by his direct power what Aegidius Romanus calls the ecclesiastical equivalent of a miracle, for what else is the direct intervention of divine power into the world but an exceptional circumstance?[3] Otherwise he has limited his *plenitudo potestatis* and scaled it down to a *potestas ordinata*. This is in accordance with the dictates of natural law, and the same law grants the lay ruler a normal right to govern unmolested by papal interference. The reduction of papal power to casual jurisdiction is the political expression of the philosophical *medius status* between grace and nature. The existence of one does not compel the absence of the other. The lay ruler has a natural existence in his own right and is freed from constant dependence upon the pope. There is not

[1] Leff, *Bradwardine*, pp. 130–1, 232, 242–3.

[2] It is very noticeable that Ockham attacks John XXII on the grounds that he makes no distinction between the absolute and ordinary power of God: *Epistola ad Fratres Minores*, p. 14, 'Secund[us error] est quod Deus nihil potest facere de potentia absoluta nisi quod facit de potentia ordinata'. In other words his vicar can exercise his absolute power as a matter of course. For this John is denounced as a 'pseudo-papa haereticus'. John's views on the absolute power of God were broadcast in a sermon of 1330 significantly entitled 'Tulerunt iusta spolia impiorum', now in B.N., Paris, MS Lat. 3290. On this sermon see further G. Mollat, 'Jean XXII', *DTC*, viii. 634–42 at col. 639; H. S. Offler, *Guillelmi de Ockham Opera Politica*, iii. 20f.

[3] Aegidius Romanus, *De ecclesiastica potestate*, iii. 9, p. 191. The case in question is whether the pope can appoint a bishop other than through the normal means of canonical election.

to be dominion but coexistence. According to this view the pope is excluded from temporal affairs in the same way that God is *regulariter* remote from the world. It is the halfway stage to making God and man, pope and king, into two existent absolutes: both existing, both supreme in their own sphere, but exerting little or no interference into the affairs of the other.

We may now see how this attitude is reflected in the political theory of the publicists who regard themselves as the heirs of Aquinas. They believe that man has to a greater or lesser extent a natural self-sufficiency, that all Christian men, by virtue of the fact that they are men, are vicars of Christ. Both men and God have their place in the world, or expressed politically, both people and pope are repositories of God's power. One holds it by natural, the other by direct divine, right. Christ, it is said, explicitly recognised this by making the Petrine commission to Peter *in persona Ecclesiae*. In other words both pope and *congregatio fidelium* hold the plenitude of power. They do not share it between them: it exists in each, and consequently an arrangement has to be made so that one may not impede the other. Both therefore limit their original absolute power to a *potestas ordinata*. Of their initial *potentia absoluta* all that remains in practice is the casual right to exercise jurisdiction over one another *pro bono Ecclesiae*, although the superiority of the supernatural over the natural is reflected in the normal subjection of the members to the head. Neither however may as a rule infringe the private right exercise of ordinary jurisdiction or ordinary possession by the other. At the same time the twin basis of ecclesiastical power is demonstrated by the need for both pope and people to co-operate in the government of the society. The administration of the *Ecclesia* is therefore undertaken by the pope in conjunction with the people or their representatives, in this case the lay rulers, on a basis of mutual support. Equally the institution of these lay rulers, since they act on behalf of both pope and people, is a joint papal-popular act. Just as pope and people promulgate the law between them, so they create those who are responsible for the enforcement of that law. But whilst in the making of law the people merely approve of the pope's decisions, in this case the pope is merely required to approve the people's choice. Many of the Thomists were expert mathematicians and they tended to treat the problems of political theory like an algebraic equation. To them the right order consists simply in the symmetrical apportioning of power to both sides.[1] Here the election of the people is seen as the essential act in the appointment of a king or emperor: the pope has only to ratify the popular decision. This, according to James of Viterbo, is an excellent example of the way in which the divine power of God, deriving on earth by nature through the people and by grace through the pope, is reunited in a common action. Natural law gives any *populus* the right to appoint its governor: divine law requires that lay rulers should be instituted by the pope. But since there is no conflict between natural and divine law, both people and pope should act together in this matter, the people electing, the pope confirming.[2] Alternatively it may be suggested that the people create the royal office, whilst the pope nominates the holder.[3] There

[1] Similarly with Aristotle *iustitia* (or *aequitas*) is described as based upon arithmetical equality and geometrical apportionment, *Nichomachean Ethics*, v. 1–5.

[2] James of Viterbo, *De regimine christiano*, ii. 6, p. 225, 'Primo enim conveniunt haec duae potestates regiae secundum causam efficientem, quia utraque est a Deo, sed diversimode'. This is explained ii. 7, p. 233, 'Nam quod *homo* sit super homines ex iure *humano* est, quod a *natura* perficitur. Quod autem homo *fidelis* sit super homines fideles est ex iure *divino*, quod a *gratia* oritur. Gratia enim non natura fideles efficit, et quia ius divinum est apud Christi vicarium, ideo ad eum pertinet institutio fidelium regum et temporalis potestatis super fideles in quantum sunt fideles. Unde princeps temporalis *in Ecclesia* ex iure humano potestatem habet super homines, sed ex iure divino super fideles. Quia ergo fides naturam *format*, ideo temporalis potestas formando instituitur et instituendo formatur per spiritualem et per eam *approbatur* et *ratificatur*. Unde nec legitime uti debet temporalis potestas nisi per spiritualem fuerit approbatae'. Also Alvarus Pelagius, *De planctu Ecclesiae*, ch. 56, pp. 153–5; ch. 59, pp. 173–5; Durandus de S. Porciano, *De iurisdictione ecclesiastica*, ch. 3, fo. 8v. Bartolus also said that the emperor gained his power from the Roman people, but that it was necessary for his election to be approved by the pope: Ercole, *Da Bartolo all'Althusio*, pp. 53–6.

[3] E.g. William Amidani, *Reprobatio errorum*, ch. 2, p. 24, 'Sed licet status imperii sit a Deo, tamen quod iste vel ille sit imperator potest esse a voluntate humana habente auctoritatem, sicuti est voluntas supremi pontificis'. That the *imperium* is from God means from the Roman people is shown ch. 1, p. 21, where he says that the emperor has power 'ex voluntate populi ipsum eligentis, nec est verus princeps nisi de eorum voluntate tacita vel expressa. . . Sic etiam esset electus a Deo idem sequitur'. Hence it follows that papal deposition of a king affects the holder only, not the power of the office: e.g. James of Viterbo,

were in fact innumerable refinements of this idea, but all pointed to the Thomist belief that the people were the real source of secular power: papal institution was to be reduced to the mere approval of a person. This is because, Alexander of S. Elpidio explains, the papal ratification is only needed to perfect something that already exists imperfectly by the natural-human right of common consent.

Sic etiam ex simili dici potest quod temporalis potestas habet aliquid de veritate *potentiae*, cum sit ex iure humano quod a natura oritur, tamen *imperfecta* est et *informis* nisi *formetur* per spiritualem.

All the famous hierocratic texts which support the papal right of institution are to be conveniently reinterpreted in the light of this modification: 'per istam autem formationem nihil aliud convenientius intelligi potest quam ratificatio et approbatio'.[1] But basically lay government can, in true Aristotelian and Roman law style, be seen to originate in the natural will of the people, and the general attitude of the Thomists may be summed up aphoristically as 'Papa a Deo, rex a populo'.[2]

It follows from this that the lay ruler, as the representative of the people, comes to occupy the same position in regard to the pope as any community does in Thomist theory in relation to its ruler. Here, it will be recalled, the initial plenitude of power of the ruler as

De regimine christiano, ii. 7, p. 234, 'Quae destitutio non est ipsius potestatis ... sed est hominis male utentis potestate sibi data'.

[1] Alexander de S. Elpidio, *De ecclesiastica potestate*, ii. 9, p. 26, which follows James of Viterbo, *De regimine christiano*, ii. 7, p. 230. Both writers assert that this is the real meaning of the famous passage of Hugh of St. Victor according to which the spiritual power institutes the temporal. It is instructive to compare this with Bellarmine's opinion that 'primi qui temporalem potestatem summo pontifici ex Christi institutione tribuunt videntur esse Hugo de S. Victore et S. Bernardus', *De potestate summi pontificis*, v. 5.

[2] Alvarus Pelagius, *De planctu Ecclesiae*, ch. 59, p. 174, 'Item differt in hoc imperium a papatu quia imperator recipit iurisdictionem a populo, papa immediate a Deo'; Peter de la Palu, *De causa immediata ecclesiasticae potestatis*, iv. 1, fo. 47, 'Responsio non est simile quia imperator non habet potestatem nisi temporalem et mundanum quam populus *se ei subiiciendo* potest ei dare ... sed in spiritualibus nullorum hominum consensus facit iudicem... De sua ecclesia dicendum est quod a solo Deo primo et principaliter habuit principatum de iure'. Also Durandus de S. Porciano, *De iurisdictione ecclesiastica*, ch. 2, fo. 3; Francis de Meyronnes, *Quaestio de subiectione*, i. 9, p. 82; *De principatu temporali*, ch. 4, p. 64; Hervaeus Natalis, *De potestate papae*, fo. 150. For the use of this with the Decretists see Ullmann, *Medieval Papalism*, pp. 165–8. Cf. *John*, viii. 23.

a source of law and power is not denied: and the publicists are at pains to show that full sovereignty pre-exists in the pope by virtue of the Petrine commission.

Et propter hoc a Christo dicuntur esse concessa beato Petro iura coelesti imperii et terreni... Et quilibet eius successor in quo plenitudo spiritualis potestatis residet... *praehabet* potestatem temporalem.[1]

He has complete power over temporals *radicaliter*,[2] but this power is, and remains, only a latent or potential authority.[3] He is, says Alvarus Pelagius, a *rex et sacerdos* equal to Christ in potency, but not in actuality.[4] This distinction between potency and act was a prime principle of Thomistic philosophy,[5] and support for its application here could be derived from the use of similar terms by the popes themselves. As mentioned earlier, Innocent IV had used the idea of actual and potential papal power in 1245, when endeavouring to explain to Frederick II that the purpose of an emperor was to implement papal policy.[6] In true Gelasian style Innocent had recalled that the duty of the Roman bishop was primarily to concern himself with the divine mysteries of the Christian faith which no mere layman could be expected to understand. So important was this function that it became appropriate for the pope to create an executive instrument to handle purely temporal affairs. The promotion of the Christian religion was more likely to be hampered by continual reference to the daily cares of government which an inferior could be left to manage. Therefore emperors were useful. But In-

[1] Alvarus Pelagius, *De planctu Ecclesiae*, ch. 56, p. 153; cf. p. 156, 'potestas temporalis praeexistit in spirituali': this follows James of Viterbo, *De regimine christiano*, ii. 7, p. 236; ii. 9, p. 268.

[2] Anon., *Somnium viridarii*, i. 39, p. 71, 'Si ergo papa obtinet principatum, obtinet radicaliter in temporalibus'; Geoffrey of Fontaines, *Quodlibeta*, XIII. v, p. 228, 'quia primam et radicalem auctoritatem post Christum videtur habere ut rector principalis Ecclesiae et in temporalibus et in spiritualibus'; cf. Anon., *Commentarium in Unam sanctam*, ch. 3, p. 145, 'essentialiter'.

[3] Alexander de S. Elpidio, *De ecclesiastica potestate*, ii. 8, p. 26; ii. 13, p. 117; ii. 14, p. 132; Alvarus Pelagius, *De planctu Ecclesiae*, ch. 56, p. 157; ch. 58, p. 166.

[4] Alvarus Pelagius, *De planctu Ecclesiae*, ch. 58, pp. 165–7; also James of Viterbo, *De regimine christiano*, ii. 9, p. 272; William of Ockham, *Breviloquium*, ii. 8, p. 67; John of Paris, *De potestate regia et papali*, chs. 12–13, pp. 208–11.

[5] This derives from Aristotle, *De somno et vigilia*, ch. 1. For Aquinas and the idea of indirect power see M. Maccarrone, '*Potestas directa* e *potestas indirecta* nei teologi del XII e XIII secolo', *MHP*, xviii (Rome, 1954), pp. 27–47 at pp. 40–1.

[6] Winkelmann, ii. 698. See above p. 268 n. 3.

nocent had clearly not regarded them as essential. Because the pope found it expedient to act through an auxiliary organ it was not to say that he was bound to utilise one. To withdraw from secular affairs was preferable, but it was nothing which could be enforced: in the same document he refers to the papal power as one to which 'non solum quemcunque sed ne quid de rebus aut negotiis intelligeretur exceptum'. Nevertheless, in his efforts to convey the importance which Christ had attached to matters of faith, Innocent had spoken of a *divina prohibitio* upon his exercise of the *rex* function in order that he might better devote himself to superior things, and it was inevitable that later writers would seize upon this as one more example of the way in which a good pope denied himself the right to intervene in the sphere of lay government.[1]

As a result those publicists who were eager to hedge round the theoretical supremacy of the pope with practical limitations were quick to believe that the papacy itself had acknowledged its legal obligations to refrain from acting in matters best left in royal and imperial hands. The reason, they explained, why the pope does not have *in actu* the same power that he has *in potentia*, the reason why he is not allowed to exercise the *rex* function himself, is to be seen in the very fact that he is the vicar of Christ. As vicar he must follow the pattern laid down by Christ himself, and Christ, although lord of all temporal things, had not intended that either he or his vicar should be immediately concerned with anything but spiritual matters. In the normal course of events the papacy was not ordained to have direct access to temporal affairs.[2] Expressed in rather more

[1] E.g. Anon., *Somnium viridarii*, ii. 115, p. 167. Innocent's phraseology was adopted by Hostiensis in this modified sense in the belief that he was quoting Innocent's own view: there is a superficial similarity but real divergence of opinion between Innocent and Hostiensis. For earlier canonistic examples of the idea that the pope has been given all power but is subsequently denied the use of the *rex* function see Ullmann, *Medieval Papalism*, pp. 195–6.

[2] This appears to have been the teaching of Remigio de Girolami, himself a pupil of Aquinas, according to Maccarrone, *Vicarius Christi*, pp. 150–1. Remigio argued that 'Licet Christus fuerit dominus temporalium, tamen noluit vicario suo papae committere istud dominium, ut scilicet magis spiritualibus possit intendere,' and it could therefore be shown 'quod ecclesia non habet auctoritatem super temporalis *principaliter*', but 'quod iurisdictio ecclesiae *indirecte et in causa* ad temporalia se extendit'. Compare this with William of Ockham, *De*

legal terms, the Thomist insisted that the pope, like Christ, ought to regard himself as a living law, a *lex animata* bound by his own nature to act as the *speculum iuris*. In this instance it means that he must bind himself to keep his own law, in the same way that any other king is bound by his own oath to uphold the common law of the land.[1] The idea of canon law as the common law of the *Ecclesia* now takes on a new significance. The basic legal collections of the ancient customs of the realm, constantly being supplemented by royal statute law, are to this way of thinking analogous to the fixation of the 'old law' of the *Ecclesia* in Gratian's *Decretum* and its subsequent supplementation by papal decretals. And since every system of common law is held, as we have seen, to be a reflection of divine-natural law, the same may be said to be true of canon law. In practice, one writer explained, we can describe the positive legal codes of the universal community, civil and canon law, as natural law itself.[2] This was not to suggest that every canon automatically contained a precept of natural or divine law, and deciding which canons were reflections of divine-natural law and which were not provided a permanent subject for legal discussion. But the bulk of canon law concerning the structure and organisation of the universal community was seen to be a positive expression of the divine order in the universe on a lower level, and was therefore imbued with the authority of divine-natural law itself. Moreover, just as the pope is held to be bound by divine-natural law, as its personification on earth, so then must he logically be bound by the canon law which

imperatorum et pontificum potestate, ch. 1, pp. 5–6, 'Christus beatum Petrum constituens caput et principem universorum fidelium, non dedit ei talem in temporalibus et spiritualibus plenitudinem potestatis ut omnia de iure posset *regulariter* quae neque legi divinae neque legi naturae refragant. . . Perspiciendum est quod Christus, constituens beatum Petrum super omnes fideles, *certos fines* posuit quos ei transgredi non licebat'; cf. also Tholemy of Lucca, *De regimine principum*, iii. 19, pp. 266–7.

[1] Note the use of 'Patere legem quam ipse tuleris' to support this: Anon., *Informatio de nullitate processuum*, p. 19; and by Nicholas de Nonancourt as cited by Maier, *art. cit.*, p. 358, who adds, 'Legem quam tuleris *de iure* tenere teneris'. For canonistic teaching on the subject see Tierney, *Foundations of the Conciliar Theory*, pp. 48–53; Brys, *De dispensatione*, pp. 129–34, 163–253.

[2] E.g. Anon., *De legibus*, fo. 11v, 'Et illo modo etiam ius naturale vel ius civile dicitur vel ius canonicum'. They form the *lex terrae* in the fullest sense of *terra*.

contains it. One after another the Thomists pointed to the familiar maxim that the pope was above positive law but subject to divine and natural law. According to Henry of Ghent this means that the pope needs to distinguish between the canons which embodied divine-natural law, and were consequently binding upon him, and those which had no specific connection with the higher law and to which he could be superior.[1] Similarly Peter de la Palu argues that most people recognise the position of the pope as 'a legibus humanis solutus', but urges that it should not be forgotten that he is at the same time subject to that divine law which is 'consonum iuri naturali'. Therefore, he goes on, there is in reality a great deal in canon law to which the pope is subject. To illustrate, he points out that it is a precept of both divine and natural law that the pope shall be elected by the community: this has duly been put into canon law, so that the pope has now no power to change the means by which his successor is appointed. In the same way, for the pope to change his see from Rome would be a breach not only of canon law but also of divine-natural law.[2] The hierocratic conception of the pope's law as divine law is thus skilfully made to react as a limitation upon the papal position. Technically above human law, the pope is forced to make a 'voluntary' submission to its rulings in order to preserve his character as *lex animata* and *vicarius Christi*, the living expression of the higher law. This principle had indeed been stated quite unequivocally by Gratian himself, as so many of the publicists took the opportunity to point out:

Sic et summae sedis pontifices canonibus sive a se sive ab aliis sua auctoritate conditis reverentiam exhibent, et *eis se humiliando*, ipsos custodiunt ut aliis observandos exhibeant.[3]

In this way the pope becomes bound by his own acts and those of his predecessors, which together make up the law of the community. And if there were any doubts cast upon this assumption,

[1] Henry of Ghent, *Quodlibeta*, V. xxxvi.

[2] Peter de la Palu, *De causa immediata ecclesiasticae potestatis*, v. 2, fo. 58; v. 3, fo. 59v; vi, ff. 70v, 73v.

[3] Gratian, C. 25 q. 1 *post* c. 16. See further Brys, *op. cit.*, pp. 77–85, 119–20; B. Tierney, 'Grosseteste and the Theory of Papal Sovereignty', *Journal of Ecclesiastical History*, vi (1955), pp. 1–17 at pp. 7–8.

the publicists were quick to reveal that the great lawgivers had themselves expressly accepted this as an integral part of their official capacity as vicar of Christ.[1] Thus not only the *Decretum* but also the legal collections of the thirteenth and fourteenth centuries were raked through for passages which could be construed as self-binding papal laws. Perhaps the most expert at this pursuit was Ockham, whose attack on Benedict XII cites a most comprehensive list of canon law decrees which previous popes are said to have made binding upon themselves and their successors.[2] Here Ockham makes it clear that it is the 'good old law' which the pope codifies and thereby enforces upon future pontiffs, and in this way the general principle that the ruler is bound by the requirements of the common good is interpreted to mean simply that the pope must be subject to the laws of the community. For the pope to uphold the *status Ecclesiae* is only another way of saying that he is under the law.[3] As the absolute embodiment of the common well-being, the personification of the *status Ecclesiae*, he must adhere to that law in which this good is enshrined.

The relevance of this becomes clearer when we appreciate the extent to which these writers believed that Christ had expressly enjoined that the pope should not personally take part in secular activities. The dictum 'Render unto Caesar' is often quoted in this context. And the general principles laid down by Christ are

[1] E.g Innocent III, *Reg.*, I. ccclv (*PL*, ccxiv. 329), 'Unde nos, qui vices Christi, licet insufficientes, exercemus in terris, eius sequentes exemplum et praedecessorum nostrorum consuetudinem imitantes. . .' In point of fact Innocent was simply stating here that he had a customary obligation to impose peace upon warring princes.

[2] William of Ockham, *Tractatus contra Benedictum XII*, vi. 3–4, pp. 274–6. Note the Symmachian decree in Gratian, C. 12 q. 2 c. 20, which begins ominously 'Non liceat papae. . .' It is against the alienation of church goods, and contains the phrase 'Qua lege omnes custodes astringantur'. Naturally Ockham could not resist this, and his comment on it is interesting: 'Ubi Symmachus papa non intendit novam legem imponere successori suo, cum non habeat imperium par in parem, sed intendit exprimere legem cui quilibet papa est astrictus'.

[3] See for example Anon., *Libellus ad defensionem fidei*, p. 552; Hervaeus Natalis, *De potestate papae*, ff. 140v–1; J. & P. Colonna, *Memoranda*, iii, p. 521; John of Paris, *De potestate regia et papali*, ch. 24, p. 254; William of Ockham, *Tractatus pro rege Angliae*, ch. 2, p. 236.

thought to have been clarified and elaborated by succeeding popes Gelasius, for example, is constantly referred to. The pope, it is said retains the supreme direction of the *Ecclesia*—he possesses the Gelasian *auctoritas*—and this must be so when the natural end of government is still regarded as inferior to and ordered towards the supernatural purpose of the community. Papal direction is, according to Francis de Meyronnes, still to be seen as that essential ingredient in government needed to complete the unformed raw material of lay power.

Sicut virtutes politicae sunt *informes* nisi sint subiectae virtutibus theologicis, ita principatus temporalium est *informis* nisi principi spiritualium sit subiectus . . . sed totus ordo et facultas rerum temporalium est ordinatus ad facultatem et ordinem rerum spiritualium sicut ad finem.[1]

But at the same time it is equally important to emphasise that the pope must refuse to handle the *potestas* or executive function, at least in the normal course of affairs. No one is denying, argues James of Viterbo in his most persuasive manner, that the papal plenitude of power initially contains temporal as well as spiritual *potestas*. Admittedly the pope cannot be said to have this in quite the same way that the lay prince has it, but he reassures his readers that the fashion in which the pope holds this temporal power is a much superior one: it is to be used for commanding and directing the activities of the lay power towards a more noble end. But, with certain exceptions, the pope cannot be said to have temporal power in the sense that he can exercise it himself. And to leave no room for doubt on this point, James repeated himself twice.

[Summus pontifex] praehabet potestatem temporalem, non tamen secundum eundem modum secundum quem habetur a principe saeculari, sed modo superiori et digniori et praestantiori. Non enim sic habet eam ut exerceat eius opera immediate, *nisi aliquibus casibus*, sed agit opera eius nobiliori modo, scilicet imperando et dirigendo et ad suum

[1] Francis de Meyronnes, *De principatu temporali*, ch. 4, p. 65, which is largely based on Thomas Aquinas, *De regimine principum*, i. 14–15, pp. 236–8; *Summa theologica*, II. 1. cix. 2. Also Alexander de S. Elpidio, *De ecclesiastica potestate*, ii. 4, p. 18; Alvarus Pelagius, *De planctu Ecclesiae*, ch. 56, pp. 150–2; Durandus de S. Porciano, *De iurisdictione ecclesiastica*, ch. 3, fo. 5; James of Viterbo, *De regimine christiano*, ii. 7, pp. 235–6.

finem operibus eius utendo; et ideo temporalis potestas dicitur praeexistere in spirituali secundum primam et summam *auctoritatem*, non autem secundum immediatam *executionem* generaliter et regulariter.[1]

It is for this reason that the Gelasian principle has been intentionally inserted into canon law, and so remains binding upon all future popes.[2] Various parts of the *Decretum* which suggest a dualism are similarly emphasised, and, of course, great play is made with such later examples as Innocent III's 'non intendimus iudicare de feudo', which is held to be an explicit prohibition of the normal papal *rex* function.[3] In this way the Thomists convinced themselves (if not the papalists) that they were returning to the 'good old law' of the *Decretum*, that they were adhering to orthodox Gelasianism, which the thirteenth-century papacy and its supporters had overridden in their search for sovereignty. Indeed the enormity of the canon lawyers in this respect was enough to upset the poise and equanimity of Aquinas himself. The intrusion of the Decretalists into theological matters, he snapped, is both ridiculous and disagreeable.[4] This gave the signal for a series of attacks upon the Decretalists which reached a crescendo with Dante. The *Decretalistae* are denounced for having ignored the authentic doctrine of the Gospels, the Fathers and the 'traditional' papal decrees which the *Decretistae* had expounded. Gratian has his place in heaven (*Paradiso*, x. 103–5). But since then the *decretales*, with their aim of giving the pope a *libido dominandi*, their invasion of royal rights, and their 'monstrous conjunction of the crosier with the sword', have turned the

[1] James of Viterbo, *De regimine christiano*, ii. 7, p. 236; cf. Anon., *Commentarium in Unam sanctam*, ch. 3, p. 143.

[2] E.g. Alvarus Pelagius, *De planctu Ecclesiae*, ch. 52, p. 129; ch. 56, pp. 153–8. Again the best list of supposed self-binding papal prohibitions on the use of the *rex* function is in Ockham's tract against Benedict XII, vi. 5, pp. 279–80. This includes Gratian, D. 96 c. 6 ('nec pontifex nomen imperatoris usurpavit'), and the Gelasian passages in cc. 8 and 10; *Decretales*, II. i. 13 (see next note), and V. xxxiii. 2, 'Sicut in iudiciis laicorum privilegia turbare nolumus...' That the restriction of papal power in temporals is a logical extension of his subjection to natural-human law is made clear by Peter Bertrandus in a lengthy passage in the *De origine iurisdictionum*, ch. 4, fo. 99.

[3] *Decretales*, II. i. 13: see Durandus de S. Porciano, *De iurisdictione ecclesiastica*, ch. 3, fo. 5v; John of Paris, *De potestate regia et papali*, ch. 16, p. 223; Anon., *Somnium viridarii*, ii. 88–9, p. 162.

[4] Thomas Aquinas, *Contra retrahentes*, ch. 13; *Quodlibeta*, ix ad 1.

shepherds into ravening wolves and the *templum Dei* into a den thieves.[1]

Amid storms of reproach and the wagging of admonitory fingers the Gelasian division of functions, which for the papalist was simply a matter of utility and expediency, is now erected into a matter of immutable right. Through their vicariate the popes must maintain the precedents which Christ established. For although Christ had clearly had a complete plenitude of power in temporals, he had either refrained from using it or had deliberately shed it. God gave him power over all things, explained Aquinas, but all things were not subject to him *quantum ad executionem*,[2] and his followers were quick to take the hint: the same must apply to the pope. How do we account for this humble status when Christ was *dominus mundi*? asks Tholemy of Lucca, and answers that it is to point the difference between earthly rulers and one whose kingdom is not of this world. In spite of being the secular lord of the earth, the government of Christ was ordained to have direct and immediate reference to spiritualities only.[3] So too Durandus of S. Porciano vigorously

[1] Dante, *Monarchia*, iii. 3, pp. 364–5; and see further d'Entrèves, *Dante as a Political Thinker*, pp. 54–5, 69; M. Maccarrone, 'Teologia e diritto canonico nella *Monarchia*, iii. 3', *Rivista di storia della Chiesa in Italia*, v (1951), pp. 7–42. Note also Francis de Meyronnes, *De principatu temporali*, ch. 4, p. 62; and Louis IV of Bavaria's appeal to the Decretists for support, Baluze, iii. 429, 'Cui etiam decretistae assentiunt dicentes papam non habere utramque iurisdictionem, quoniam a Deo ex ipsa electione iurisdictionem et potestatem in temporalibus nos solus recipimus'. For examples of dualism with the Decretists see Ullmann, *Medieval Papalism*, pp. 143–5, 212; Mochi Onory, *Fonti Canonistiche*, *passim*. The papalists retaliated by attacks on the Decretists: e.g. Aegidius Spiritalis, *Libellus contra infideles*, p. 111, denounces Johannes Teutonicus and Huguccio for accepting the principles of dualism, and adds the name of Hostiensis for supporting the theory of casual jurisdiction: 'Sed maxime miror de domino Ostiensi, qui, nescio quo ductus iudicio rationis, dixit, Dico quod papa non habet se intromittere de temporalibus in alterius praeiudicium . . . nec regulariter nisi in casibus'.

[2] Thomas Aquinas, *Summa theologica*, III. lix. 4 ad 2, 'Christo sunt omnia subiecta quantum ad potestatem quam a Patre super omnia accepit . . . nondum tamen sunt omnia ei subiecta quantum ad executionem suae potestatis'.

[3] Tholemy of Lucca, *De regimine principum*, iii. 15, p. 263, 'Est et alia ratio quare Dominus noster statum humilem assumpsit, quamvis dominus mundi: ad insinuandam videlicet differentiam inter suum et aliorum principum dominium. Quamvis enim temporaliter esset dominus orbis, *directe* tamen ad spiritualem vitam suum *ordinavit* principatum iuxta illud *Iohannis* [x. 10], Ego

asserts that it would be contradictory to Biblical evidence to deny Christ's fullness of temporal power, since he is said to have all power in heaven and earth. But, he continues, it would be necessary to add that having got it, he did not use it himself, nor did he apply it to everything.

Sed bene contingit quod habens potestatem et auctoritatem iurisdictionis, non utitur ea in propria persona, nec decet quantum ad omnia.

So that whilst he gave Peter and his successors power to govern the *Ecclesia*, Christ's intention was that they should imitate him by using it mainly to convert others to the faith through preaching and the performance of miracles.[1] In short, the pope initially possesses a *potestas absoluta* which gives him full right to act in temporal affairs at will. But at the same time, as a true vicar of Christ, he must limit himself to those activities permitted by canon law and which include no regular use of secular jurisdiction.[2] Papal power, like that of any other ruler, is seen to exist on two levels. It can be described, as with Aegidius Romanus, as a *potestas duplex*, having its absolute and ordinary aspects. Although in the first instance the pope may be thought of as having an unbridled right to do as he pleases, this absolute power remains largely indirect and potential. In practice he restricts himself in order to observe the common law of the *Ecclesia*, and on this lower level of *potestas ordinata* he is normally concerned to use direct power in spiritual matters only. Papal supremacy is not infringed, since Aegidius is eager to stress that all the necessary restrictions are imposed on the pope by himself.

Distinguemus duplicem potestatem summi pontificis . . . unam absolutam et aliam regulatam. . . Si ergo summus pontifex secundum suum

veni ut vitam habeant et abundantis habeant. Hinc etiam verificatur suum verbum superius allegatum, Regnum meum non est de hoc mundo'.

[1] Durandus de S. Porciano, *De iurisdictione ecclesiastica*, ch. 3, ff. 7–7v. Also Anon., *Disputatio inter clericum et militem*, pp. 13–14; Anon., *Quaestio in utramque partem, proem.*, p. 97; ch. 3, p. 100; Anon., *Somnium viridarii*, ii. 67, p. 158; ii. 77, p. 160; ii. 81, p. 161.

[2] Anon., *Somnium viridarii*, ii. 18, p. 151, 'Dicendum est quod sibi communi lege non incumbunt [negotia saecularia] quoad executionem immediatam'; and for the identification of common law with canon law, ii. 122–3, p. 168.

posse absolutum est animal sine freno et sine capistro, ipse tamen debet sibi frenum et capistrum imponere *in seipso* observando leges et iura. Nam licet ipse sit supra iura, loquendo de iuribus positivis, ut tamen det suis iuribus et suis legibus firmitatem, decet eum secundum leges et iura commissam sibi Ecclesiam gubernare.[1]

This, it seems clear, is the real explanation of the famous 'mystery' passage in which Aquinas stipulates the existence of a division between temporal and spiritual power, but goes on to say that both powers are conjoined in the pope as *rex et sacerdos*, the apex of the two powers.[2] The same idea is in fact employed by many of the Thomists.[3] On the topmost level the pope enjoys his original possession of both powers, but as a result of his abdication of temporal power, his self-imposed reduction to ordinary power, temporal and spiritual divide on the lower level. Consequently, notwithstanding the unified source of all power, clerical and lay rulers have their own spheres of competence. In practice, as regards executive power, there are, as Peter Bertrandus says, two distinct

[1] Aegidius Romanus, *De ecclesiastica potestate*, iii. 7, p. 181. The self-binding element is brought out more forcibly with Guilielmus Durantis, *De modo generalis concilii celebrandi*, iii. 27, p. 278, 'Item quod [papa] legem sibiipsi imponeret, ne transgrederetur contenta in divinis et humanis legibus approbatis, quibus genus debet per eam et auctoritate imperiali et regali gubernari humanum'; iii. 31, p. 295, 'Iustum namque est sicut Isidorus, tertio libro, *de summo bono*, testatur principem legibus obtemperare suis. Tunc enim iura sua ab omnibus custodienda existimet quando et ipse illis reverentiam praebet. Principes legibus teneri suis, nec in se posse damnare iura quae in subditis constituuntur, iustum est'. Cf. Gratian, D. 9 c. 2.

[2] Thomas Aquinas, *Commentum in Sententias*, II. xliv. ii. 3 ad 4, 'potestas spiritualis et saecularis utraque deducitur a potestate divina: et ideo in tantum saecularis potestas est sub spirituali in quantum est ei a Deo supposita, scilicet in his quae ad salutem animae pertinent: et ideo in his magis est obediendum potestati spirituali quam saeculari. In his autem quae ad bonum civile pertinent est magis obediendum potestati saeculari quam spirituali secundum illud *Matth.*, xxii [21], Reddite quae sunt Caesaris Caesari. Nisi forte potestati spirituali etiam saecularis potestas coniungatur sicut in papa, qui utriusque potestatis apicem tenet, scilicet spiritualis et saecularis, hoc illo disponente qui est sacerdos et rex, ...'. For the most recent, but inconclusive, discussion of this passage see I. T. Eschmann, 'St. Thomas Aquinas and the Two Powers', *Mediaeval Studies*, xx (1958), pp. 177–205.

[3] Alvarus Pelagius, *De planctu Ecclesiae*, ch. 52, p. 126; ch. 56, p. 154; ch. 59, pp. 168–9; Durandus de S. Porciano, *De iurisdictione ecclesiastica*, ch. 3, fo. 3; Henry of Cremona, *De potestate papae*, p. 467.

swords.[1] There have always been effective limits to the powers of *regnum* and *sacerdotium*, which neither side may in the normal course of events overstep.[2]

The dualism which generally exists in practice and which is justified by this theory is most clearly revealed in a comparison between the activities of kings and bishops. Here there is a virtually complete separation of the two jurisdictions.[3] Unlike the lay power, episcopal power does not stem direct from the apex of the *plenitudo potestatis*, but derives immediately from the pope's *potestas ordinata*, or from what we may term his private right standing in which he is a mere *caput in spiritualibus*, a head of the *ecclesia* in the limited sense of the clerical order. Consequently no king need fear intervention from his bishops into the secular administration of his kingdom. The papal insistence that the pope is superior to the bishop by virtue of his plenitude of power is now given an entirely new significance. Episcopal power has no immediate connection with the pope's initial supremacy, but only with his ordained power in spirituals. Therefore the power of a bishop has no temporal affiliations. But behind the pope's own ordained power in spirituals there still stands his plenitude of power which comprehends all temporal things.[4] Hence there is no such absolute division between

[1] Peter Bertrandus, *De iurisdictione ecclesiastica*, pp. 1373b–4, 'Non obstat quod dicitur quod duo sunt gladii etc., et quod distinctum est sacerdotium ab imperio, quia verum est quod duo gladii sunt, istud dictum ecclesiae et verum est quod ius et potestas istorum duorum gladiorum est penes ecclesiam, licet executio gladii materialis sit penes temporales vel saeculares'; cf. *De origine iurisdictionum*, ch. 4, fo. 99.

[2] Durandus de S. Porciano, *De iurisdictione ecclesiastica*, ch. 3, fo. 7v, 'Et isti sunt veri termini iurisdictionis spiritualis et temporalis *a fundatione Ecclesiae* quos transgredi non licet'; also Francis de Meyronnes, *De principatu Siciliae*, ch. 1, p. 94; Anon., *Commentarium in Unam sanctam*, ch. 3, p. 145; Anon., *Somnium viridarii*, ii. 6, p. 150; Gilbert of Tournai, *Eruditio regum*, II. ii. 7, p. 75.

[3] Thomas Aquinas, *Summa theol.*, II. II. cxlvii. 3, 'sicut ad saeculares principes pertinet praecepta legalia iuris naturalis determinativa tradere de his quae pertinent ad utilitatem communem in temporalibus rebus, ita etiam ad praelatos ecclesiasticos pertinet ea status praecipere quae ad utilitatem communem fidelium pertinent in spiritualibus bonis'.

[4] Alexander de S. Elpidio, *De ecclesiastica potestate*, i. 7, p. 9, 'Christ[us] et eius vicari[us] quem sui loco praefecit in terris, propter quod b. Petro dicuntur esse concessa iura coelestis imperii et terreni, quia totius potestatis spiritualis et temporalis apicem tenet. Et si potestas temporalis a spirituali non solum

temporal and spiritual functions with the pope himself.[1] There is then a triangular arrangement by which each of the three categories of ruler—pope, bishop and lay prince—has his own distinctive capacity. Each claims to have the power of a *vicarius* Christi: this is so, but only in a particular sense and within a specialised sphere of activity which, generally speaking, prevents confusion between one category and another. There is a division of Christ's power. The proper duty of the pope is to act as *dux*, to formulate the guiding principles of the Christian faith by legislation, and to supervise the means of application. To this extent Aquinas would consider him a king, since he saw the imposition of law as a specifically royal function.[2] But this does not normally involve him in the lay ruler's main obligation actually to enforce and execute this legislation, in which the king needs to use his powers of coercion, his own legal codes appropriate to local needs, and other suitable measures. And since the task of the bishop is, by and large, to confine himself to his spiritual duties, the lay ruler is to all intents and purposes left with the effective administration of his kingdom. In spite of all the necessary qualifications, each type of ruler is in practice given quasi-independent charge of his own office, and may therefore be regarded as acting directly on behalf of Christ himself, who is alone legislator, priest and king at one and the same time:

quantum ad alios pertinet, alius est legislator, alius sacerdos, et alius rex: sed haec omnia concurrunt in Christo tamquam in fonte omnium gratiarum.[3]

iudicatur sed etiam instituitur et formatur, et specialiter a potestate plenaria cuiusmodi est potestas summi pontificis, quia aliter loquendum esset de potestate spirituali secundum partem qualis est in aliis praelatis ecclesiae, quae ad praesens dimittitur'; Alvarus Pelagius, *De planctu Ecclesiae*, ch. 56, p. 154, 'De aliis autem pontificibus secus est . . . quia non habent plenitudinem potestatis . . . unde in iis quae ad salutem animae pertinent, magis est eis obediendum quam principi. . . In iis autem quae ad bonum civile pertinent magis obediendum est principi'.

[1] Henry of Cremona, *Non ponant laici*, p. 476, 'Vel posset dici quod distinctio habet locum quantum ad alios pontifices, non quantum ad papam.

[2] Thomas Aquinas, *Summa theologica*, II. II. I. I ad 3, 'Philosophus denominat regnativam a principali actu regis, qui est leges ponere: quod *etsi conveniat aliis*, non convenit eis nisi secundum quod participant aliquid de regimine regis'.

[3] Thomas Aquinas, *Summa theologica*, III. xxii. I ad 3. For Christ as 'dux et rex et pontifex' see *Commentum in Sententias*, III. xiii. ii. I, *sol.* 7; and as king,

The earthly *Ecclesia* has its own trinity of command, united in the divine power of Christ; and it was felt that having due regard to the existing situation, only the recognition of this tripartite vicariate could solve the competing claims of temporal and spiritual powers on a realistic basis.

Although dualism emerges as the most characteristic and general feature of the system, and was nicely calculated to appeal to the lay writers, Aquinas still sought to preserve his orthodoxy by recognising an ultimate papal right to the exercise of temporal jurisdiction. The pope might, after all, take the secular sword into his own hands on certain occasions.[1] To appreciate how Aquinas arrived at this conclusion we must return to the basic principle governing the division of papal power into absolute and ordinary levels. According to this the pope is bound by divine-natural law; and since this is normally reflected in canon law, then the pope must act in accordance with the provisions of canon law as well. The only exceptions to the rule occur when a special situation arises in which the good or *status* of the community would be endangered by a rigid adherence to the letter of the law. This constitutes a case of emergency when the common law of the *Ecclesia* can no longer be said to mirror the precepts of the higher law,[2] and the pope as vicar of Christ, animated divine-natural law, has a positive duty to act extra-legally for the common good. In cases of necessity therefore he can resort once again to the use of his overriding *plenitudo potestatis*, which always stands behind his normal, limited and ordinary power.[3]

priest and prophet, *In Ev. Matth.*, I (Parma, x. 3 and 12). It was probably with this in mind that Augustinus Triumphus cites the same threefold capacity of Christ, but adds that all are now present in the pope, since Christ, 'nunc regnat mediante papa', *Summa*, i. 9, p. 13.

[1] Thomas Aquinas, *Summa theologica*, II. II. lx. 6 ad 3, 'Potestas spiritualis distinguitur a temporali, sed *quandoque* praelati habentes spiritualem potestatem intromittit se de his quae pertinent ad saecularem potestatem'.

[2] E.g. William of Ockham, *Dialogus*, I. vi. 62, p. 568, in reply to the view that 'ubi canon non excipit, nec nos debemus excipere', says that 'Respondetur quod illa regula est *regulariter* vera; fallit tamen ubi alius *casus* non excipit et ubi scriptura divina excipit vel etiam ubi ius naturale vel ratio evidens naturalis dictat excipiendum'.

[3] Anon., *De legibus*, fo. 17; Peter Olivi, *De renuntiatione papae*, p. 364, 'Prima est quod quamvis hoc semper possit de potestate absoluta, non tamen de potestate ordinata, id est licite et absque culpa non potest semper ...'.

Whereas normally private rights are protected by divine-natural law, and thereby gain equal protection from positive law, private rights are not admissible when the security of the *respublica* itself is at stake. No private right can stand against the overwhelming argument of equity and expediency invoked on behalf of the superior rights of the common utility. In this instance the private right possession of free action and existence, which canon law normally guarantees to the lay ruler,[1] may be ignored by the pope *in certis causis* in defence of the *status Ecclesiae*.[2] In other words there are certain occasions when he must be permitted to act absolutely and exercise the *rex* function himself. And this, as James of Viterbo triumphantly declared, ought to be a satisfactory solution to the two apparently contradictory positions.

Concludi potest quod spiritualis potestas temporalem iurisdictionem quam habet non debet exercere, immediate loquendo, regulariter et communiter . . . tamen potest et debet, causis necessariis exigentibus, immediate se de temporalibus intromittere. Et secundum hanc distinctionem solvatur contradictio aliqua quae in praedictis verbis esse videtur.[3]

[1] William of Ockham, *De imperatorum et pontificum potestate*, ch. 4, p. 9, 'Ex praemissis colligitur quod principatus papalis nequaquam ad iura et libertates aliorum *regulariter* se extendit, ut illa tollere valeat vel turbare, praesertim imperatorum, regum, principum et aliorum laicorum . . . quare papa non potest aliquos privare iuro suo'.

[2] William of Ockham, *Octo quaestiones*, viii. 6, p. 204, 'papa, quia ipse per ordinationem divinam est exclusus qua sanctitum est ne *regulariter* se de temporalibus negotiis intromittat . . . licet *casualiter*, aliis deficientibus, se possit huiusmodi negotiis implicare quando urgens necessitas vel evidens utilitas'. He is at great pains to point out that the pope must not use his casual power if anybody else can still be found to act instead: e.g. iv. 3, p. 132, 'Hoc etiam non potest quando per alium modum possunt pericula praecaveri et communis utilitas procurari'. See also *Tractatus pro rege Angliae*, ch. 6, p. 251; *Tractatus contra Benedictum XII*, vi. 13, pp. 296–7; *Dialogus*, III. I. i. 16, pp. 785–6; and Peter Bertrandus, *De origine iurisdictionum*, ch. 4, fo. 99; Anon., *Somnium viridarii*, i. 157, p. 119; i. 162, p. 121; i. 163, p. 124; i. 179, p. 134; ii. 6, p. 150.

[3] James of Viterbo, *De regimine christiano*, ii. 8, pp. 250–1. This would appear to be the solution to the contradiction noted in Bartolus by Woolf, *op. cit.*, pp. 94, 97–100. This may also be found with many writers on both sides: Durandus de S. Porciano, *De iurisdictione ecclesiastica*, ch. 3, ff. 5v, 7v, 8; Alvarus Pelagius, *De planctu Ecclesiae*, ch. 56, pp. 153, 158; Anon., *Disquisitio theologico-iuridica*, ii. 5, p. 1352; Anon., *Quaestio in utramque partem, proem.*, p. 98; ch. 3, p. 101; ch. 4, p. 101; Geoffrey of Fontaines, *Quodlibeta*, XIII. v (v. 228); Guiliel-

The occasions when a direct recourse to the higher law and absolute power is permitted have already, it is maintained, been carefully specified by the popes themselves, and are now embodied within the *corpus* of canon law. In the main they are those instances, previously mentioned, in which Innocent III had stressed the necessity for direct papal action *in temporalibus*.[1] It will be seen at once that the specified cases impose little real restriction upon the pope's exercise of power. Some of the publicists give enormous lists of cases in which the pope may act. Quite apart from cases which are on the borderline between temporal and spiritual, such as questions of matrimony, tithes, legitimacy, inheritance, usury, heresy, simony, sacrilege, and church goods,[2] all disputed cases and any dubious points of law can be referred to the pope.[3] Any matter involving a contract falls within his supreme right to deal with questions concerning an oath, and this leads on to his right to ratify or annul any peace treaty made between warring princes.[4] Rather

mus Durantis, *De modo generalis concilii celebrandi*, ii. 9, p. 72; Henry of Cremona, *Non ponant laici*, pp. 476–8.

[1] Aegidius Romanus, *De ecclesiastica potestate*, iii. 4, pp. 161–3; cf. iii. 7, p. 181, 'Quod ergo dictum est quod summus pontifex *casualiter* exercet temporalem iurisdictionem, ut patet ex illo capitulo *Per venerabilem* [*Decretales*, IV. xvii. 13], istud *casuale* vel istud quod exercet *in certis casibus* est longe amplius quam sit istud regulare quod habet dominus saecularis. Nam istud casuale quasi universale est, cum omnis quaestio et omne litigium habeat hoc casuale annexum, quod potest deferri cum denuntiatione criminis. . . Sic distinguere possumus duplicem eius iurisdictionem in temporalibus rebus: unam directam et regularem, et haec est, ut diximus, iurisdictio superior et primaria, quam habet ipse in omnibus tam super potestates terrenas quam super temporalia, ratione cuius ex culpa vel ex causa potest animadvertere in potestates terrenas. Aliam quidem iurisdictionem habet summus pontifex super temporalibus rebus quae non est directa et regularis, sed est *certis causis* inspectis et *casualis*, et haec iurisdictio non solum est superior et primaria, sed est *immediata* et *executoria*'.

[2] Aegidius Romanus, *De ecclesiastica potestate*, iii. 4–7, pp. 161–85; Alvarus Pelagius, *De planctu Ecclesiae*, ch. 56, pp. 159–60; Henry of Cremona, *Non ponant laici*, pp. 478–9; Anon., *Quaestio in utramque partem*, ch. 4, p. 101.

[3] E.g. Durandus de S. Porciano, *De iurisdictione ecclesiastica*, ch. 3, fo. 5, 'Et hoc est quod expresse dicitur in canone xi q. 1 c. [7] *Quaecunque*, ubi dicit quaecunque contentiones inter christianos orte fuerint ad ecclesiam deferantur et ab ecclesiasticis viris terminentur'.

[4] E.g. Aegidius Romanus, *De ecclesiastica potestate*, iii. 6, p. 178, 'Viso quomodo ecclesia debet se praecipue de temporalibus intromittere ut inter suos filios valeat pacis foedera reformare, videre restat quando postremo debet hoc facere quando talia foedera sunt iuramento firmata. Dicemus enim quod fractio

more surprisingly, it is often suggested that this right also extends to feudal matters, since a contract is the essence of the feudal relationship. Even the rabidly anti-papal author of the *Quaestio in utramque partem* was disposed to argue in favour of this view. Although he regards feudal rights as essentially lay matters ('causae mere temporales sunt causae feudales'), and could appeal to Innocent III as his authority on this point, he is aware that Innocent had promptly evaded this conclusion by declaring feudal rights to be his own concern since sin would be involved by the breach of a feudal oath. Therefore, concluded the Frenchman, feudal matters are after all semi-spiritual ones, and may be regarded as subject to the pope's casual jurisdiction.[1] Indeed it became extremely difficult to find any matter which did not have some sort of spiritual connotation, however remote, and there were few aspects of lay government which did not therefore become subject to papal jurisdiction one way or another. The pope is acknowledged to have the right to take over the administration of the empire during a vacancy,[2] to trans-

iuramenti dicitur esse crimen ecclesiasticum, quia ad iudicem ecclesiasticum spectat iudicare de periurio sive de fractione iuramenti'. This was developed by the canonists out of the dispensing power of the pope in matters concerning vows: Brys, *De dispensatione*, pp. 204–21; Ullmann, *Medieval Papalism*, pp. 66–75.

[1] Anon., *Quaestio in utramque partem*, ch. 4, p. 101, 'Causae mixtae sunt causae temporales quae connexionem quandam habent cum spiritualibus, sicut causa feudalis, quae est de se temporalis, connexionem potest habere cum iuramento vel pacto, sicut patet de dissensione mota inter reges Franciae et Angliae super comitatu Pictaviensi [cf. *Decretales*, II. i. 13]. Papa, qui non poterat *directe* cognoscere de causa feudali, *indirecte* ratione iuramenti vel pacti intromisit se de illa'.

[2] E.g. Anon., *Somnium viridarii*, i. 151, p. 117; note the influence of the idea that when one side fails the other may step in, which Ockham had emphasised: 'nequaquam igitur ex hoc quod papa est iudex in spiritualibus sequitur quod habeat *regulariter* saecularia iudicare. Ex hoc tamen concludi potest quod *in casu*, cum non est alius inferioris gradus qui ex officio possit et velit saecularia negotia iudicare, papa potest se huiusmodi iudicio immiscere quemadmodum unum membrum corporis naturalis officium alterius membri ipso deficiente vel non valente actum suum exercere, si potest, assumit. Qui enim non potest pedibus ambulare, manibus reptare conatur, et qui non potest manibus percutere, dentibus mordere molitur'. It is significant that two pages later the author is applying the same principle to the relationship between an unsatisfactory pope and a general council acting on behalf of the *congregatio fidelium*. Cf. Bartolus, cited Ercole, *op. cit.*, p. 55, 'istae iurisdictiones sunt distinctae: nec papa in temporalibus nec imperator in spiritualibus potest se immiscere, nisi

ate the imperial power from one ruler to another if this should be necessary for the furtherance of good government, and to depose a prince if he is negligent, becomes a heretic, or in any other way lays himself open to deposition for a just cause.[1] We are probably justified in thinking that it was never likely that the papacy would wish to act imperially to any greater extent than this. Indeed, since the publicists also emphasised the right of the pope to act in any matter *ratione peccati*, there was, as they themselves pointed out, virtually nothing to which the pope's casual jurisdiction could not extend.

Dicendum est quod de se et iure suo extenditur ad cognoscendum et iudicandum de omnibus peccatis, non solum de illis quae sunt contra articulos fidei et sacramenta, in quibus principaliter fundatur religio christiana, sed etiam de omnibus peccatis mortalibus . . . ad ecclesiam pertinet iudicare de peccato quocunque.[2]

They positively glow with self-satisfaction at being able to point out that the pope has only spiritual jurisdiction, but yet is able to exercise a very full measure of temporal power. Since the pope is also acknowledged to have full discretion as to when a case of necessity exists,[3] all the hierocratic debating points may be said to

vacante imperio'. This developed out of the idea that a feudal superior could take over a vacant fief, and again illustrates the Thomistic 'feudalisation' of the papal-imperial relationship: Baethgen, *art. cit.*, pp. 172–83.

[1] Aegidius Romanus, *De ecclesiastica potestate*, iii. 11, p. 204, 'ex culpa vel ex causa potest ecclesia privare Caesarem sive potestatem terrenam suo dominio et suis temporalibus bonis'; William of Ockham, *Allegationes de potestate imperiali*, p. 428, 'ipsa translatio non fuit facta ex eo quod papa tamquam dominus in temporalibus posset imperium transferre a Graecis in Germanos, sed facta fuit propter crimen in ecclesiam Romanam commissam, cuius criminis tamquam ecclesiastici punitio ad papam pertinebat ratione iurisdictionis quam habet in spiritualibus'. See also Durandus de S. Porciano, *De iurisdictione ecclesiastica*, ch. 3, ff. 6v–7, 8v; Anon., *Quaestio in utramque partem*, ch. 5, p. 106.

[2] Durandus de S. Porciano, *De iurisdictione ecclesiastica*, ch. 3, ff. 4v–5; also Aegidius Romanus, *De ecclesiastica potestate*, iii. 5, pp. 171–2; iii. 7, p. 181; James of Viterbo, *De regimine christiano*, ii. 7, p. 234; John of Paris, *De potestate regia et papali*, ch. 16, pp. 223–4; Anon., *Somnium viridarii*, i. 50, p. 74; and note also Ugolinus de Celle, *De electione regis Romanorum*, ch. 9, p. 75; ch. 15, p. 77.

[3] Peter de Lutra, *Tractatus contra Michaelem de Cesena*, ch. 2, p. 35, 'pro fidelium necessitate Ecclesiae pontifex, si oporteat et sibi bonum visum fuerit'; Anon., *De legibus*, fo. 17; Peter Olivi, *De renuntiatione papae*, p. 364. See further Brys, *De dispensatione*, pp. 204–21; Lewis, *Medieval Political Ideas*, pp. 29–30.

hold good provided that the pope acts on the basis of casual right and does not regard his exercise of secular authority as something due to him as a matter of course.[1] Provided that there is a just cause, that his action will benefit the whole society, he can do anything. Tholemy of Lucca for example mentions his right to tax all Christian people, and to destroy any town or city,[2] whilst even Ockham goes to a great deal of trouble to show that there is ultimately little that the pope cannot do.

Papa iure divino regulariter vel casualiter omnia potest quae sunt necessaria regimini et gubernationi fidelium, quamvis eius potestati ordinarie et regulariter sint certi termini constituti quos regulariter transgredi sibi non licet.[3]

All is possible to him as supreme ruler of the community so long as it is clearly understood that this is an emergency action undertaken *ratione status Ecclesiae*, and that he is only temporarily permitted to overstep the bounds which normally circumscribe his field of action.

[1] E.g. Anon., *Somnium viridarii*, i. 149, p. 116, 'et ideo si dictum est pontifici veteris legis, Ecce constitui te super gentes et regna, hoc est ut *casualiter* etiam in temporalibus super gentes et super regna iurisdictionem assumens non in praeiudicium regum et principum sua *legitimi* utentium potestate. Et haec fuit intentio sua quam colligunt ex verbis dicti Innocen. quem sequitur, relinquitur ergo Romanum pontificem saltem casualiter exercere etc. Quibus verbis innuitur quod non nisi casualiter, ex quo sequitur quod papa non habet *regulariter* praedictam plenitudinem potestatis'; and see the following note.

[2] Tholemy of Lucca, *De regimine principum*, iii. 19, p. 267, 'Simile contingit in principe totius regni, quia pro conservatione regiminis super subditos ampliatur eius potestas imponendo talias, destruendo civitates et castra pro conservatione totius regni. Multo igitur magis hoc conveniet summo et supremo principi, id est papae, ad bonum totius christianitatis . . . per quam ostenditur et concluditur summum pontificem in dicto *casu* plenitudinem potestatis habere. In duobus igitur *casibus* ampliatur eius potestas ut supra patet, vel ratione delicti vel ad bonum totius fidei, quod eleganter nobis ostendit propheta Ieremias cui in persona vicarii Christi dicitur, Ecce, inquit, constitui te super gentes et regna etc., quod ad rationem delicti referimus . . . [et] pro bono universalis Ecclesiae'.

[3] William of Ockham, *De imperatorum et pontificum potestate*, ch. 13, p. 27; cf. ch. 12, p. 26, 'Sic licet non omnes fideles sint immediate subiecti in omnibus papae, nec papa in multis casibus sit iudex ipsorum, tamen quia in omni causa necessario definienda per iudicium regulariter vel casualiter iure divino potest esse iudex, immo concedendum est quod papa sub Christo est caput et iudex summus omnium fidelium'.

On the other hand we must not allow ourselves to be misled by appearances. Whilst not yet perhaps very serious, the Thomist theory was a deliberate attempt to break down the hierocratic notion of sovereignty. Under the blanket of the natural law and natural rights doctrine the idea of the real papal *plenitudo potestatis*, of true sovereignty, quietly disappears, and is replaced by the view that society itself, seen as an abstract entity, is the sole possessor of supreme power. This is brought about by the renunciation of absolute powers on the part of both pope and people, these powers now becoming invested in the fictitious personality of the *Ecclesia*. Although the pope is still permitted to act as the human representative of this 'person'—and so intervene in temporal affairs—it is emphasised that he does so only under special circumstances when he alone is in a position to act on behalf of the community. As Ockham put it, the power to judge secular things now applies 'non ... pro praelatis spiritualibus tantummodo, nec praecipue pro summo pontifice *nisi in casu*, sed ... *in persona communitatis* fidelium'.[1] Therefore the pope taken by himself is not the only embodiment of the society. Permanent and absolute sovereignty rests with the immaterial *Ecclesia*, not with any of its individual parts, with Christ, not with any one of his vicars: it cannot be completely activated by any one human representative in isolation for more than a short space of time. Consequently the Thomists can still grant the pope a *plenitudo potestatis*, but it becomes apparent that this is now only a relative term. To say that the pope has the fullness of power simply means that his power is temporarily fuller than that of anybody else.[2] It does not mean that his power is so full that there is none left for others, and the hierocratic assumption that if the pope has all nobody else can have anything fades away. Since the term *plenitudo potestatis* had to be retained, this was bound to lead to considerable problems of exposition. No reader can be altogether happy at

[1] William of Ockham, *Octo quaestiones*, i. 11, p. 46.

[2] Anon., *Disquisitio theologico-iuridica*, ii. 1, p. 1342, the pope as vicar of Christ is 'in maiori plenitudine quam mortalis aliquis alius homo'; Anon., *Somnium viridarii*, i. 162, p. 121, 'papa habet quandam aliam plenitudinem potestatis'. Alvarus Pelagius, *De planctu Ecclesiae*, ch. 59, p. 171, describes the pope as having a 'potestas regia tota et perfecta et plena' which is however simply 'modo excellentiori' than that of any other ruler.

being confronted with Alvarus Pelagius' conclusion that 'the pope, who has all power, does not have total power'.[1] Yet Alvarus is merely trying to point out that the papal *plenitudo potestatis*, as used by the hierocratic writers, is to be bereft of its sovereign content. It still retains its absolute element—for occasional use—but is now nothing more than a very great power. In fact by the fourteenth century the term has already become so diluted that it can be applied to any ruler.[2] Fundamentally this theory involves a denial of the whole hierocratic ideology. It is still maintained that the temporal derives out of the spiritual, but there is never any complete assimilation of one to the other as in the papal one power doctrine.[3] Correspondingly the king is still in a sense a papal vicar, deriving his right to act from papal authorisation, but the Thomists have come round to accepting the lay assumption that a king has a natural right to his position and powers. If the pope must normally reduce himself to spiritual jurisdiction only, the existence of other rulers becomes essential: as Alvarus Pelagius goes on to say, they are not superfluous.[4] They cannot be done away with, 'quia sic tolleretur

[1] Alvarus Pelagius, *De planctu Ecclesiae*, ch. 59, p. 179, 'dato quod nomine vicarii non importetur plenitudo potestatis, non propter hoc dicendum est quod papa, qui est vicarius, non habeat plenitudinem potestatis'.

[2] E.g. Alexander de S. Elpidio, *De ecclesiastica potestate*, iii. 1, p. 31, 'sicut videmus quod in regimine alicuius regni tota plenitudo potestatis est in rege'. Here again Aquinas appears to have set a precedent by remarking that a plenitude of power was an indispensable element of kingship—'si aliquid defuerit non dicitur rex'—which meant the right to make his own laws, rather than accept the laws imposed on him by another: 'Secundo rex importat plenitudinem potestatis. Qui principaretur non cum plenitudine potestatis, sed secundum leges impositas, non diceretur rex, sed consul vel potestas [podesta?]', *Sermo in prima dominica adventus*, 2, a Parisian sermon of *c.* 1270 attributed to him by J. Leclercq, 'Un sermon inédit de Saint Thomas sur la royauté du Christ', *Revue Thomiste*, xlvi (1946), pp. 152–66. For another version see T. Kaeppeli, 'Una raccolta di prediche attribuite a san Tommaso d'Aquino', *Archivum Fratrum Praedicatorum*, xiii (1943), pp. 60–4.

[3] E.g. Alvarus Pelagius, *De planctu Ecclesiae*, ch. 44, p. 77, 'Ad haec potestas papalis dignissima et utilissima est omnium potestatum, quia composita et media et communis et quia *mixta* de spiritualis et temporalis dependentis ab *eisdem* et *utraque* regens et dirigens. Nam sicut Filius Dei est una persona in duobus naturis, divina et humana . . . sic eius vicarius papa in sua una dignitate papali duplicem iurisdictionem sibi vendicat quae sunt *diversae naturae*, spiritualem et temporalem'.

[4] Alvarus Pelagius, *De planctu Ecclesiae*, ch. 56, pp. 157–8, 'licet ille qui habet

ordo potestatum'.[1] Therefore the pope has no right to withhold the imperial crown from an elected candidate: by natural law there must be an emperor.[2] This is reflected in the steady acceptance of the imperial right to govern from election. Tholemy of Lucca, for example, permits the *electus* to administer the German kingdom by right of long established custom and the consent of the princes. Half a century later Alvarus Pelagius has extended this capacity to the whole empire, and the position is rapidly being reached where the pope has merely to give formal approval to what God has granted the lay ruler by natural-human right: or, as Dante put it, 'Cui Deus concedit, benedicat et Petrus'.[3] Alvarus in fact went so far as to acknowledge that the pope was in practice forced to accept the choice of the German princes,[4] and although many writers still stipulated some sort of theoretical papal right to ignore the prince-electors, it was now generally held that their election had become to a large extent a matter of necessity.[5] Thus the reduction of papal

potestatem spiritualem *praehabet* in illa etiam temporalem, non tamen est superfluum esse in Ecclesia principem temporalem tantum potestatem habentem'. This is followed by six reasons to show why the pope may not handle secular affairs, 'per quas ostensum est quod non superfluit potestas principum temporalem in Ecclesia, licet spiritualis potestas praehabet temporalem, concludi potest quod spiritualis temporalem iurisdictionem quam habet non debet exercere immediate loquendo regulariter et communiter'; cf. Anon., *De legibus*, fo. 17, 'Indiget ergo populus regibus pro temporalibus regendis et pontificibus pro spiritualibus . . . et ista ratio innuitur in decretis distinctione x [c. 8], Reges pontificibus propter aeterna, et pontifices regibus indigent pro temporalibus'.

[1] James of Viterbo, *De regimine christiano*, ii. 7, p. 234.

[2] E.g. Alexander de S. Elpidio, *De ecclesiastica potestate*, ii. 10, p. 28; Alvarus Pelagius, *De planctu Ecclesiae*, ch. 56, p. 152. Again this was found to fit in well with the feudal idea that a fief must not be left vacant for more than a year and a day: Bayley, *The Formation of the German College of Electors*, pp. 171–2.

[3] Tholemy of Lucca, *Determinatio compendiosa*, ch. 10, p. 23; Alvarus Pelagius, *De planctu Ecclesiae*, ch. 40, p. 67; Dante, *Monarchia*, ii. 9, p. 358.

[4] Alvarus Pelagius, *De planctu Ecclesiae*, ch. 41, p. 68, discusses a proposition of Johannes Andreae that the pope cannot deprive the princes of their electoral rights: 'Papa non posset privare electores iure eligendi'. Alvarus rejects this in theory: 'Contra crederem, cum ab ecclesia hanc habeant potestatem', but accepts it in practice: 'sed propter periculum et scandalum non est faciendum'.

[5] Conrad of Megenberg, *Oeconomica*, II. ii. 7 (Kaeppeli, p. 580 n. 3), allows the pope to disregard the electors' rights by the use of his casual power: 'Sed *potestate ordinaria* et communicata papa non potest eligere imperatorem imperio vacante, posito quod principes eligere velint et possint. . . Mihi autem videtur altius dicendum videlicet quod papa ex *potestate absoluta* posset principes

institution to a formalised approval gives the lay power a capacity to exist and act in its own right—again we may refer to Dante:

Sic ergo dico quod regnum temporale non recipit *esse* a spirituali nec virtutem quae est eius auctoritas, nec etiam *operationem simpliciter*; sed bene ab eo recipit ut virtuosius operetur per lucem gratiae, quam in coelo et in terra benedictio summi pontificis infundit illi[1]

—and to deny this is seen as a usurpation of the lay ruler's just authority. Secular government may still be inferior to that of the pope, but it is rapidly assuming a positive quality and is no longer to be regarded as a mere *organum papae*: it is an essential part of the body politic in the same way that for Aquinas the body was an essential part of man, whose autonomous existence does not place any real obstacle before the ultimate purpose of life. The civil power, as Alvarus Pelagius says, is something with its own inherent value. It has its own divine justification, and is not to be denied.[2] And this, coupled with the acceptance of the lay ruler's general right to act independently of the pope, put the Thomist halfway towards breaching the unity of Church and State which was so vital a feature of hierocratic thought. He did not go so far as to deny the inclusion of kings within the Universal Church, or the desirability of their acting with papal authority and approval. But he was eager to allow them the capacity to act without constant intervention from above. Church and State, we may say, were still ultimately joined in theory, but normally they were not to be confused in practice. The *Ecclesia* was coming to be seen as a universal spiritual entity, a *communitas christianorum*, which could generally speaking be seen as something other than the secular institution, the *communitas humanorum*. It stood, *regulariter*, as a unity of faith along-

electione privare et ipse eligere vacante imperio, posito etiam quod principes eligere velint et possint canonice concordare'. But this is then followed by a chapter designed to show 'Qualiter electio principum electorum sit *necessaria* ad creationem imperatoris', in which he says, II. ii. 9, 'Videtur itaque mihi quod electio principum electorum sit dispositio *necessaria* praeambula ad confirmationem imperatoris per papam fiendam'.

[1] Dante, *Monarchia*, iii. 4, p. 367.

[2] Alvarus Pelagius, *De planctu Ecclesiae*, ch. 59, p. 168, 'Dicendum est quod potestas regalis secundum se bona est, et ad utilitatem humanae societatis ordinata a Deo'.

ide the kingdom existing as a body politic rooted in nature and ınder the direction of the lay prince. Hence for the Thomist the ight relationship between pope and emperor, or any other king or that matter, was one between two near-equals. If the emperor emains under an obligation to obey the pope, he still possesses ights which are to be respected,[1] and this relationship is closely anaogous to that existing under feudal law. Consequently the imperial coronation oath may be interpreted as a specifically feudal one, not that of a subordinate officer to his superior.[2] Lay rulers are subject to the pope, but it is the subjection of vassallage, which implies rights and duties on both sides.[3] The empire is held from the pope as a fief: the pope deposes its tenant and takes over its administration not by absolute right but in accordance with feudal custom.[4] Thus the right order between them is essentially a contractual one and the way is laid open for the development of a com-

[1] Cf. Conrad of Megenberg, *Oeconomica* (Struve, p. 87), 'et si imperatorem papae obedire magistro, papam tamen iniuriari augusto non commendo'.

[2] Anon., *Disquisitio theologico-iuridica*, v, pp. 1356–7, 'Secundum istam rationem videretur aliquibus quod sicut imperator est astrictus domino papae ratione imperii quod tenet ab eo vinculo fidelitatis, ut sic se habeat ad dominum papam sicut fidelis subditus se debet habere ad suum dominum, sic vice versa dominus papa sit astrictus vinculo cuiusdam fidelitatis ad ipsum imperatorem, sicut dominus debet esse fidelis servo vel subdito vel vassallo': the writer accepts this himself, p. 1361; also Anon., *Disquisitio prior iuridica*, ch. 1, pp. 1320–1, 'contractus'; Anon., *Disquisitio iuridica*, ch. 1, p. 1380; Conrad of Megenberg, *De translatione Romani imperii*, ch. 19, p. 310, 'iuramentum quod imperator praestat domino papae et ecclesiae Romanae . . . est iuramentum fidelitatis, id est homagii quod feudatarius praestat domino suo. Et hanc conclusionem probo sic. Imperator tenet iurisdictionem temporalem quam exercere habet per universum orbem a manibus domini papae: ergo ratione imperii est feudatarius papae'; also ch. 21, p. 317; John of Paris, *De potestate regia et papali*, ch. 15, p. 221. This was also the opinion of Hostiensis. It was generally believed that Albert of Hapsburg had agreed to take a feudal oath to Boniface VIII in 1303, and later to Clement V: F. Baethgen, 'Die *Promissio* Albrechts I für Bonifaz VIII', *Aus Politik und Geschichte: Gedächtnisschrift für Georg von Below* (Berlin, 1928), pp. 75–90.

[3] Alvarus Pelagius, *De planctu Ecclesiae*, ch. 68, p. 247, 'Tum quia imperator imperium tenet ab ecclesia sicut vassallus fidelis'; also *Collirium*, p. 513; Conrad of Megenberg, *De translatione Romani imperii*, ch. 22, p. 319; Thomas Aquinas, *Quaest. Quodlib.*, XII. xiii. 19 ad 2, 'reges sunt ergo vassales ecclesiae'.

[4] Tholemy of Lucca, *Determinatio compendiosa*, ch. 30, p. 60, 'probatum est superius imperator sit verus minister ecclesiae, quam administrationem ab ipsa recipit sub iureiurando sicut fidelis ecclesiae sub titulo feudi, et inde est ratio quod ecclesia facilius procedit ad eius depositionem quam aliorum principum'.

promise arrangement between Church and State as two separate and semi-independent societies.

The effects of this were slow to appear, but the Thomist theory had more immediate and devastating consequences for the papal monarchy. We shall have occasion to deal with this aspect later, but it is necessary to point out that the logical corollary to the idea of casual papal jurisdiction over the lay ruler was the right of the lay ruler to exercise casual jurisdiction over the pope. By the first half of the fourteenth century this idea was already well developed. It is stressed that the pope's use of his plenitude of power can only be temporary: it is subject to the doctrine of economy and may not be used without cause, that is to say, only in a case of necessity when nothing else suffices. It must not be utilised a moment longer than necessary.[1] If the pope goes beyond these limits he has begun to use his power arbitrarily, to govern by will. As soon as this happens he ceases to be a true pope: he becomes a tyrant, and there is to all intents and purposes a vacancy in the papal office.[2] Immediately the latent plenitude of power which resides in the people comes into play. Their jurisdiction too is divided into absolute and ordinary levels. For normal purposes the members of the society have limited their competence by submitting to the ruler: it is this, the publicists suggested, which is meant by the Roman law theory that the people have handed over their power to the prince. Corres-

[1] Guilielmus Durantis, *De modo generalis concilii celebrandi*, iii. 31, p. 296, 'Si quid autem pro remedio aut pro necessitate temporis statuatur, cessante necessitate, cessare debet pariter quod urgebat, cum alius sit ordo legitimus, alius usurpatio, prout Gelasius attestatur'. One of his main complaints about the contemporary papacy is that it has been dispensing with, exempting from and overriding the law 'absque evidenti necessitate vel utilitate', iii. 47, p. 329. Also Anon., *Somnium viridarii*, ii. 313, p. 203; Guido Terrenus, *Quodlibeta*, IV. ii, pp. 319–20; William of Ockham, *Dialogus*, III. II. iii. 12; *Octo quaestiones*, i. 15, p. 59; iii. 9, p. 114.

[2] Tholemy of Lucca, *De regimine principum*, iii. 10, p. 259, 'Quamvis in omnibus istis summi pontifices non extenderunt manum nisi ratione delicti, quia ad hoc ordinatur eorum potestas et cuiuslibet domini ut prosint gregi; unde merito pastores vocantur, quibus vigilantia incumbit ad subditorum utilitatem. Alias non sunt legitime domini sed tyranni, ut probat Philosophus et dictum est supra. Unde Dominus utitur in Iohanne quadam importuna interrogatione, ter quaerens a suo successore beato Petro quod si ipsum diligit, gregem pascat. . . Hoc ergo supposito quod pro utilitate gregis agat sicut Christus intendit'.

pondingly the ruler limits his own plenitude of power over them. But just as he has the right to act absolutely *in certis causis*, so there may be certain occasions when the popular prerogative is to be used. The negligence, error or virtual absence of the ecclesiastical ruler constitutes such an occasion.[1] And since, as we have seen, the lay ruler is for the Thomists the representative of the popular will, it is the duty of the emperor and the other European kings to judge a delinquent pope on behalf of all and in defence of the *status Ecclesiae*.[2] The dualism which normally exists between pope and lay ruler may in cases of necessity be replaced by the casual right of the king to correct and depose the pope,[3] just as in other cases it is replaced by the casual right of the pope to depose a king.

> [Iudices saeculares] etiam super crimina mere spiritualia potestatem [habuerunt] coactivam qualem etiam potestatem coactivam habuit beatus Petrus et habent successores ipsius casualiter super crimina saecularia.[4]

In its turn the community, acting through its representatives, becomes temporarily the sole embodiment of the sovereignty vested in the society as an abstract entity. It is the counterbalance to the papal right to act *ratione peccati*. Thus Petrarch, for example, was to speak of the emperor's duty to correct an erring pontiff, if necessary by force of arms, whilst at the same time asserting the supremacy of the golden mean as a political principle: 'aurea medio-

[1] William of Ockham, *Consultatio de causa matrimoniali*, pp. 283–4, 'Imperator, in quem populus suam transtulit potestatem, causa huiusmodi ad se revocare potest, praesertim propter culpam clericorum et ex causa'.

[2] William of Ockham, *Tractatus contra Benedictum XII*, vii. 12, p. 318: if the pope becomes dangerous to the *Ecclesia* he is to be expelled from the apostolic see 'per imperatorem et Romanos, quorum est quodammodo episcopus proprius, de consilio et assensu, si necesse esset, concilii generalis. Hoc enim habet ius gentium quod praeter naturale dominium videtur communius et antiquius quod praepositus alicui communitati, praesertim quae superiorem non habet, per ipsam communitatem est, quando expedit, corrigendus vel poenitus amovendus'; also vii. 14, p. 320. In 1328 Louis of Bavaria claimed to depose the pope for the preservation of the 'universalem statum Ecclesiae sanctae Dei ac sacri imperii', Baluze, iii. 429.

[3] William of Ockham, *Tractatus contra Benedictum XII*, vii. 9, p. 316, 'principes et laici *in casibus pluribus* habent potestatem super clericos et super papam haereticum *absque constitutione Ecclesiae*', and he once again (p. 315) resorts to the analogy of one part of the natural body replacing a defective part.

[4] William of Ockham, *Tractatus pro rege Angliae*, ch. 4, p. 245.

critas est in omni fortuna'.[1] Understandably the supporters of the papacy amongst the Thomists were much slower to elaborate this aspect of the system than the lay writers. Henry of Cremona, for instance, at the time of the conflict between Boniface VIII and Philip the Fair, contented himself with the general comment that the laity had certain rights over ecclesiastical matters to correspond with the clerical rights over secular affairs.[2] But his opponents had no such hesitation. The *Rex pacificus* agreed that each power should keep to its own sphere, but argued that they were mutually obliged to defend each other when necessary, and therefore one power was dependent upon the other when its executive abused it.[3] Similarly John of Paris maintains that the lay ruler has jurisdiction in ecclesiastical matters for a pious cause, namely, 'pro utilitate terrae si necessitas immineat vel utilitas exposcat'; and it is therefore false to regard a king as a purely civil ruler denied the care of men's souls. He is as much concerned with the upholding of the common good of the community and its pursuit of virtue as any cleric.[4] When we come to Ockham this principle of reciprocal rights is fully recognised and is being adapted for any purpose which suits the convenience of the lay prince. To take one example, Louis of Bavaria's appropriation in 1342 of the manifestly papal prerogative to dispense for marriages within the prohibited degrees—so that he

[1] Bayley, 'Petrarch, Charles IV and the *Renovatio Imperii*', pp. 338–40.

[2] Henry of Cremona, *Non ponant laici*, pp. 480–4. Given the necessary degree of misinterpretation, it was possible to cite Augustine as an authority for this reciprocal arrangement: *Enarrationes in Psalmos*, vi. 8 (*PL*, xxxvi. 735), 'Et aliquando ipsa commixtio temporalis facit ut quidam pertinentes ad civitatem Babyloniam administrent res pertinentes ad Ierusalem; et rursum quidam pertinentes ad Ierusalem administrent res pertinentes ad Babyloniam'.

[3] Anon., *Rex pacificus*, ch. 4, p. 681, 'Nam et iurisdictio spiritualis quam habet papa, et iurisdictio temporalis quam habet rex in regno suo, omnino distinctae sunt, et distinctae ita quod sicut rex non habet se intromittere de iurisdictione spirituali quod est penes papam, ita nec papa habet se intromittere de iurisdictione temporali quae residet penes regem. Unde non est inter duas istas iurisdictiones mutua dependentia nisi quantum ad mutuam defensionem, quam sibi mutuo tenentur exhibere cum necesse fuerit'.

[4] John of Paris, *De potestate regia et papali*, ch. 17, pp. 224–5, 'quia supponit quod potestas regalis sit corporalis et non spiritualis, et quod habeat curam corporum et non animarum, quod falsum est . . . cum ordinetur ad bonum commune civium non quodcunque, sed quod est vivere secundum virtutem'.

might solve the Tyrolean question by marrying his son to Margaret of Tyrol—was warmly applauded by Ockham on the grounds that this was an action undertaken for the *status reipublicae*. Whilst he allowed that no emperor has a general right to handle a matter so closely associated with the Christian faith, and therefore forbidden him under canon law, this law was of human origin and could not therefore be expected to conform in every case to the demands of absolute rightness (*epieikia*). Consequently the emperor has a casual right to act absolutely in such cases, which are of obvious utility and urgent necessity, even to the extent of assuming the power of the pope himself. Indeed he becomes superior to the pope, since the pope on this occasion was clearly obstructing the emperor and endangering the well-being of the community.[1] It was now an easy matter to assert the position of the lay ruler as guardian of the popular welfare when it came to dealing with an heretical or otherwise undesirable pope. Here too the prince should revert to the indirect absolute power contained in himself as representative of the *populus* and intervene in a situation which struck at the very roots of the Christian faith and was of the utmost concern to all the faithful. It is obviously desirable, added Ockham, that the emperor should himself be a Christian,[2] but the canon law prohibi-

[1] William of Ockham, *Consultatio de causa matrimoniali*, pp. 280–1, 'Esto autem absque praeiudicio quod causa matrimonialis etiam quantum ad illa de quibus in sacram scripturam serie nil reperitur expressum ad imperatorem *regulariter* minime pertinet; ambigere tamen non deberet quin ad causam huiusmodi *in multis casibus* sua licite valeret extendere potestatem, etiam quantum ad gradus consanguinitatis. Nec leges ecclesiasticae etiamsi ipsis esset arctatus, ipsum prohibere valerent, quin *pro urgenti necessitate* ac etiam *evidenti utilitate* venire posset *casualiter* contra ipsas, Romano episcopo, etiamsi in temporalibus inferior esset eodem, minime requisito. Leges enim humanae et potissime ecclesiasticae, quae non minori inniti debent *aequitate* quam leges aliae, sic instituti debent et intelligi quod illis quos tangunt prosint, et nemine praesertim notabile afferant nocumentum. . . Quare leges suae in eo casu nullatenus sunt servandae in quo non prodessent sed in detrimentum praesertim reipublicae redundarent. Quamvis igitur legibus summorum pontificum de matrimonio esset astrictus, tamen quia ipsas agnosceret aperte, si servarentur, in damnum vel impedimentum reipublicae redundare, utendo *epieikia* iuxta sententiam sapientis contra ipsas licite venire valeret, etiam summo pontifice irrequisito'.

[2] William of Ockham, *De imperatorum et pontificum potestate*, ch. 12, p. 26, 'quia imperator *in quantum imperator*, cum multi *veri* imperatores fuerunt infideles, non debet se etiam casualiter spiritualibus immiscere, licet si est fidelis,

tions which *regulariter* keep the lay ruler out of spiritual affairs are no longer binding when the common good is imperilled. The needs of ultimate justice as contained in natural law demand that the king shall override the positive law and exercise jurisdiction *in spiritualibus*.[1] And whilst the lay ruler acts *casualiter* above the law, the pope is still bound by the common canon law and may be deposed for heresy. An unjust pope may be deemed to have created a vacancy in the papal office, and the emperor may take over the papacy in a papal vacancy in the same way that the pope may take over the empire in an imperial vacancy.[2] The public right of the lay ruler acting *vice omnium* now stands superior to the private right of the individual pope. This brings out the full force of the contractual relationship which the Thomist thinks to exist between pope and lay ruler: they have, as Michael of Cesena said, a mutual obligation to depose each other.[3] Indeed, according to Ockham, the pope as vicar of Christ is obliged to make a voluntary submission to the emperor when he is accused of heresy, since he is bound by the precedent of Christ submitting himself to the judgement of Pilate.[4] He must recognise that just as he by his divine(-natural) right as vicar of God

in quantum fidelis de multis casibus se intromittere teneatur, et praecipue de fidei causa quae ad omnes omnino pertinet christianos.'

[1] Cf. Nogaret, Dupuy, pp. 243–4, 'in casu manifeste tam necessario ubi non erat locus alii remedio, moraque etiam brevis temporis grave ac irreparabilis periculum allatura fuisset, maxime schismatis, ut est dictum, ad occurrendum et resistendum . . . debuit et potuit assurgere quilibet catholicus christianus, potissime miles et maxime dicti regni cuius specialiter intererat, etiam privatus quilibet in ecclesiasticae et saecularis potestatis defectum auctoritate legis divinae et humanae, et si nulla lex hoc exprimeret, satis hoc ratio naturalis ostendit'. See further Baethgen, *art. cit.*, pp. 169–70.

[2] This view is cited by Alvarus Pelagius, *De planctu Ecclesiae*, ch. 64, pp. 248–9, and *Collirium*, p. 514: 'Item si imperator succederet in papatu, ergo in iure papatus' in the same way that 'papa succedit imperio'; although Alvarus himself rejects this.

[3] Michael of Cesena, *Litterae deprecatoriae, proem.*, p. 1346.

[4] William of Ockham, *Dialogus*, III. II. iii. 23 *additio*, p. 392; cf. Alvarus Pelagius, *De planctu Ecclesiae*, ch. 68, p. 247. The theory behind this was that Christ became the representative of sinful man and was condemned by the Roman emperor, acting through Pilate, as the representative of God. It could now therefore be argued that a sinful pope, i.e. as a man, should be condemned by the emperor acting with the absolute power which he wielded (*casualiter*) as *vicarius Dei*. The divine aspect of Christ and the papal office respectively were not involved.

has the power to decide when his casual power may be used, so all men, as represented by the lay ruler, may by their natural(-divine) right as men decide when the people's casual authority becomes actual. And it is by this extreme but very logical extension of the Thomist theory of checks and balances that Ockham unwittingly underlines the point at which the great synthesis begins to fall apart. What was to happen when both pope and lay ruler declared at the same time that a situation existed in which absolute power might be used? If each was to be placed on terms of equality in this matter there was no solution to the impasse. If taken far enough the whole system ultimately forced one back to the old conflict between two absolute monarchies as at least preferable to the anarchy which follows upon everybody having power over everybody else. In the long run the Thomist system could never be satisfactorily operated because it gave no clear-cut answer to the problem of sovereignty, a problem which can only be ultimately settled by the acceptance of one extreme view or the other.

PART IV
VICARIUS CHRISTI

I. THE PROBLEM OF EPISCOPAL GOVERNMENT

To judge from the volumes of refutation and counter-refutation which materialised under the busy pens of the publicists it was not the lay attacks upon sacerdotal supremacy which were regarded as presenting the gravest threat to the papal monarchy in the fourteenth century. Rather it was from within the ranks of the priesthood itself that a potentially greater danger seemed to menace the papal-hierocratic idea. The refusal of many bishops to obey papal instructions, their defiance under correction, and the support given to them by excommunicate or deposed rulers are all common features of medieval political history, and the repeated stress laid upon the primacy of the Roman church bears witness to the constant need of the papacy to assert its control over the ecclesiastical as much as the lay princes of Europe. Whilst the most Christian kings strove to reduce the pope to a mere *caput sacerdotii*, the priests in question were hard at work to deny papal headship altogether. In this, it hardly needs to be added, they were ably aided and abetted by the kings themselves, who saw in the breaking of the link between bishop and Rome a means of asserting total control over the episcopate within their own territories. The royal claim that the lay monarch represented the source of the medieval bishop's regalian rights[1]

[1] See for example the *Rex pacificus*, ch. 3, p. 676, in which the author extols the services of the French monarchy to the papacy, and adds that by reason of this 'ius plenum habet rex Franciae accipiendi regalia, id est reditus episcopales, dum vacant episcopatus in aliquibus ecclesiis Franciae et conferendi ecclesiastica beneficia quorum collatio ad ipsos episcopos, dum viverent, pertinebat'; cf. Anon., *Somnium viridarii*, i. 78, p. 85, 'nec [papae] quoad temporalia [rex] subest in aliquo, immo econtra ecclesia Gallicana subest regi Franciae quoad temporalia'; Nogaret, 'Item certum, notorium et indubitatum existit quod dictus dominus rex habet iura regalia universa in regno suo': cited Wieruszowski, *op. cit.*, p. 205. It was of course denied by hierocratic writers that the bishops and clergy were in any way subject to the lay ruler: e.g. Augustinus Triumphus, *Summa*, xxii. 2 ad 3, p. 131, 'clerici vero a principatu laicali sunt exempti, quia coram iudice seculari conveniri non possunt'.

provided the spark for innumerable contests with the papacy, and most of the great political struggles of the Middle Ages were marked by a trail of disputed episcopal elections. The emergence of Gallicanism as an important factor in the ecclesiastical politics of the later medieval period was largely due to the deliberate encouragement given by the crown to the French bishops in their periodic revolts against papal domination. The reason for this is not difficult to determine, particularly when the importance of the medieval bishop to the administrative system of his day is borne in mind. It is still true in the fourteenth century that the episcopacy is to a large extent the normal channel of government: its members are the administrators, the civil service without which there can be no effective government. They are, says Augustinus Triumphus, 'duces et rectores totius Ecclesiae',[1] appointed for the government and instruction of all the pope's subjects: and accordingly he favours the appointment of the nobility, as members of the ruling classes, to bishoprics.[2] With Alexander of S. Elpidio they are the real kings, and the only reason why they do not use the name of king is to avoid the sin of pride and to set an example of humility. Thus Christ had never spoken of them as kings or princes, but they are more entitled to be called this than anybody else.[3] Similarly the lower clergy is to carry out the functions of local government officials: Peter de la Palu describes them as acting on behalf of the pope in the same way that prefects, castellans, seneschals and bailiffs maintain

[1] Augustinus Triumphus, *Summa*, i. 9 ad 2, p. 74.

[2] Augustinus Triumphus, *Summa*, xlvii. 4, p. 255, 'nunc pro eiusdem utilitate Ecclesiae possunt nobiles et potentes ad ecclesiastica beneficia vocari ... potestas et nobilitas non est honoranda in praelatura ecclesiastica secundum se, sed in ordine ad utilitatem Ecclesiae ipsius promotionis beneficio'. This was in fact common contemporary practice: for English examples see W. A. Pantin, *The English Church in the Fourteenth Century* (Cambridge, 1955), pp. 22–3; J. R. L. Highfield, 'The English Hierarchy in the Reign of Edward III', *Transactions of the Royal Historical Society, Vth series*, vi (1956), pp. 115–38 at pp. 120–1.

[3] Alexander de S. Elpidio, *De ecclesiastica potestate*, iii. 3, p. 34, 'Ex quo habetur quod pastores Ecclesiae bene et proprie possunt dici reges; communiter autem a fidelibus reges non appellantur, nec principes nec duces, sed magis pastores, episcopi et pontifices ad evitandam superbiam et imitandum humilitatis exemplum. Unde nec Christus eos tali nomine insignivit, licet res nominis propriissime conveniat eis'.

the royal government in France.[1] The priesthood, in particular the bishops, were in fact the sinews of government, and when the majority of the bishops in any particular kingdom were prepared to acknowledge the supremacy of either royal or papal authority, so correspondingly that kingdom passed under effective royal or papal government. The lay writers indeed, provided that the bishops recognised the king as their real superior, were only too willing to stress the importance of the episcopal governmental function,[2] and the marked increase in the process of centralisation by both the papal and lay monarchies between the eleventh and fourteenth centuries is adequate testimony to the recognized importance of the medieval bishop in the processes of government. Indeed for the papacy, so often in practice excluded from control of the lay monarchs, a firm hold over the episcopacy was vital if the papal domination of Europe was ever to become a reality.

According to the papal ideology the bulk of the work of shaping the Christian society fell into the hands of what was in a sense an intellectual aristocracy. In the methodical minds of the hierocratic writers every king has his bishop who stands as an *alter ego* behind the throne.[3] The kings are to be left to deal with the minutiae of day-

[1] Peter de la Palu, *De causa immediata ecclesiasticae potestatis*, ii. 8, f. 38; cf. Augustinus Triumphus, *Summa*, xciii. 3 ad 2, p. 458, 'Episcopis enim committitur cura principaliter in diocesi non solum super laicos, immo etiam super ipsos presbyteros et diaconos. Habent enim sub episcopo aliquos subministrationes et sunt quasi balivi et officiales eius'.

[2] E.g. Anon., *Rex pacificus*, ch. 3, p. 672; John of Paris, *De potestate regia et papali, proem.*, p. 175.

[3] Conrad of Megenberg, *Tractatus contra Wilhelmum Occam*, ch. 7, p. 367, 'Et dicuntur clerici, id est sorte electi, ipsos enim Deus in suos elegit. Hii namque sunt reges, id est se aliosque virtutibus regentes et ita in Deo regnum habent. Et hoc designat corona in capite: hanc coronam habent ab institutione Romanae ecclesiae in signum regni quod in Christo expectatur'. Note the statement of William of St. Botolph, steward to the bishopric of Durham in 1302: 'Duos in Anglia esse reges, videlicet dominum regem Angliae gerentem coronam in signum regalitatis, et dominum episcopum Dunelmensem gerentem mitram in loco coronae in signum suae regalitatis in diocesa Dunelmensi'. There appears to have been some attempt to uphold this claim in practice. Not only did the bishop claim to have a royal prerogative in the prosecution of the Scottish wars, but he also argued that the king's writ did not run in his diocese without his consent: C. M. Fraser, 'Edward I of England and the Regalian Franchise of Durham', *Speculum*, xxxi (1956), pp. 329–42.

to-day administration, but they are to do so under the direction of a corps of mitred grey eminences. Just as the whole *Ecclesia* is composed of a hierarchy of lesser ecclesiastical corporations ranging from the village to the *regnum*, so at the head of each community is to be found an appropriate clerical governor ranking from the local priest to the primatial archbishop. In this grand design for the sacerdotal government of the world it is the bishop who is the *caput communitatis*,[1] one of the princes who, according to Alexander of S. Elpidio, the pope has set up over all the earth.[2] The universal political organism is essentially a Church, an earthly manifestation of the spiritual kingdom, and correspondingly each constituent part, each kingdom, is itself a local church. There is no divorce between the *regnum* and the 'national' *ecclesia*. Accordingly it is the ecclesiastical superior who guides and directs it, who by virtue of his all-embracing spiritual power has full right to exercise all temporal jurisdiction himself: 'unde in praelatis ecclesiae, et praecipue in summo praelato, est potestas regia tota et perfecta et plena'.[3] This point is brought out by Peter Roger, archibishop of Rouen, in his speech to the council of the French clergy held at Vincennes in 1329. Although chancellor of the kingdom, Roger stood firmly against royal control of the clergy (and was later to become pope himself as Clement VI). When the royal advocate, Peter de Cugneriis, complained that the clergy had been encroaching on the king's jurisdiction,[4] Roger replies that de Cugneriis is making a totally unwarranted separation between temporal and spiritual power, so that he may deny that the bishop has any real right to temporal power at all.

[1] Augustinus Triumphus, *De potestate collegii*, p. 505, 'rector civitatis'; cf. Thomas Aquinas, *Commentum in Sententias*, IV. xx. i. 4, 33, 'iudex civitatis'. For the canonistic view that the bishop was the true *dominus loci* see Ullmann, *Medieval Papalism*, pp. 190–1, and note the assimilation of the metropolitan and his suffragans to the king and his dukes within a kingdom and its provinces in Gratian, C. 6 q. 3 c. 2.

[2] Alexander de S. Elpidio, *De ecclesiastica potestate*, i. 10, p. 12, 'sed etiam consecuti sunt principatum et praelationem iuxta illud *Psalmi* [xliv. 17], constitues eos principes super omnem terram, et nimis honorati sunt amici tui Deus, nimis confortatus est principatus eorum; super quo verbo dicit glossa quod facti sunt duces et pastores Ecclesiae'; cf. Augustinus Triumphus, *Summa*, i. 4 ad 1, p. 7, 'primates mundi'.

[3] James of Viterbo, *De regimine christiano*, ii. 7, p. 236.

[4] As reported by Peter Bertrandus, *De iurisdictione ecclesiastica*, pp. 1362–5.

Otherwise, de Cugneriis had argued, there would be no distinction between kings and bishops. But this, declares Roger, is exactly what I wish to demonstrate: both temporal and spiritual jurisdictions are to be found in the same person, above all in clerics.[1] The power of the bishop, the hierocratic writers maintained, must be strictly analogous to that of the pope. In the same way that the pope is the *verus imperator*, the universal *rex et sacerdos*, so it must follow that the principle applies to each bishop in his diocese or kingdom. Although he regards the whole idea as nonsense on the grounds that the pope does not have temporal power, even the Knight in the *Disputatio inter clericum et militem* is constrained to admit the logic of this argument. If, he says, the pope really was the lord of the world, then I should find that my real local overlord was the bishop.

Si enim cum creatur papa creatus sit dominus omnium, simili ratione creare episcopum erit creare illius patriae dominum, et sacerdos meus erit dominus castri mei et dominus meus, quia sicut potestas papae est in toto, ita potestas istorum est in illa parte cui praeest.[2]

The comparison is to be found with a number of other writers,[3] and this suggests that the idea was widely held. In fact no less a person than Aquinas deals with the matter in some detail, and on this occasion seems to forget his customary qualified dualism altogether. Just as the pope's plenitude of power, he says, makes him king in his kingdom, so the bishop must be seen as the head of each lesser community.[4] He is like a prince in his see (*quasi princeps in ecclesia*), and

[1] 'Et quia dominus Petrus pridie per iurisdictionis distinctionem, scilicet temporalis et spiritualis, conabatur probare quod habens iurisdictionem spiritualem non debebat habere temporalem, alioquin non esset distinctio sed potius confusio iurisdictionum, idcirco volo probare oppositum, quod istae iurisdictiones compatabiles sunt in eadem persona et maxime in ecclesiasticis': see Peter Bertrandus, *De iurisdictione ecclesiastica*, p. 1368. This is followed by a list of the more familiar hierocratic texts used in favour of the bishops.

[2] Anon., *Disputatio inter clericum et militem*, p. 15.

[3] E.g. Anon., *Somnium viridarii*, i. 166, p. 126; i. 170, p. 127; Alvarus Pelagius, *Speculum regum*, pp. 518–19; Alexander de S. Elpidio, *De ecclesiastica potestate*, ii. 5, p. 19, 'Licet alii quicunque praelati Ecclesiae possint dici capita suorum subditorum, summus tamen pontifex caput universale est...'.

[4] Thomas Aquinas, *Commentum in Sententias*, IV. xx. iv. 3 ad 3, 'Papa habet plenitudinem potestatis pontificalis quasi rex in regno; episcopi vero assumuntur in partem sollicitudinis quasi iudices singulares civitatibus praepositi';

may judge any member of his diocese *ratione peccati*.[1] Even kings, it would appear, come into the category of episcopal subjects: 'in lege Christi reges debent sacerdotibus esse subiecti'.[2] And from this it is clear that the bishop may truly be said to be a king himself. In the same way that the lay ruler has his crown and sceptre, so the bishop has mitre, crosier and ring, all the marks of royal power, to denote that his is the chief government in the kingdom.[3] Following Aquinas, Augustinus Triumphus is able to describe episcopal power as both *principalis et regalis*,[4] thereby underlining the traditional conception of the legislative and executive functions of the priesthood. This is not to imply that the hierocrats ignored the equally traditional division of functions. As Alvarus Pelagius points out, there must be a distinction between the duties of the two types of kings, and this functional distinction is reflected in the different names which each use, a *discretio in nominibus*. Bishops should not be termed *reges* but 'pastores, episcopi, pontifices et praesules', although, he hastily adds, they have the power if not the name of 'rectores, iudices et duces'. And from this he concludes that there

Summa contra Gentiles, iv. 76, 'Sicut igitur in uno speciali populo unius ecclesiae requiritur unus episcopus, qui sit totius populi caput, ita in toto populo christiano requiritur quod unus sit totius Ecclesiae caput . . . manifestum est quod summa potestas regiminis fidelis populi ad episcopalem pertinet dignitatem'.

[1] Thomas Aquinas, *Summa theologica*, III. lxv. 3 ad 2; *Comment. in Ep. I ad Tim.*, iii. 1, 'quasi superintendens'. See further Darquennes, *De Juridische Structuur van de Kerk*, pp. 79–90.

[2] Thomas Aquinas, *De regimine principum*, i. 14, p. 237. Gregory VII had said that the lowest cleric, the exorcist, was superior to any lay ruler—see Gratian, C. 8 q. 1 c. 21—which is cited by Augustinus Triumphus, *Summa*, xciii. 2, p. 457; Anon., *Somnium viridarii*, i. 59, p. 78; cf. Alvarus Pelagius, *De planctu Ecclesiae*, ch. 37, p. 47, 'quilibet princeps et imperator nedum papae subest sed etiam aliis episcopis et suo etiam simplici sacerdoti, qui ipsum solvit et ligat et iudicat'.

[3] Thomas Aquinas, *Commentum in Sententias*, IV. iv. i. 2, 'Cum qualibet potestate exterius datur aliquod visibile signum illius potestatis, sicut regi in signum regiae potestatis datur corona et sceptrum, et pontifici mitra et baculus et anulus'. According to Augustinus Triumphus, *Summa*, ciii. 1, p. 506, the episcopal crosier is a rod of governmental power, deriving from Christ's injunction to the apostles to carry a staff, *Mark*, vi. 8.

[4] Augustinus Triumphus, *Summa*, xciii. 1 *ad arg.*; Alexander de S. Elpidio, *De ecclesiastica potestate*, ii. 8, p. 24, '*Quilibet* sacerdos in nova lege dicatur sacerdos secundum ordinem Melchisedech'. For Innocent III's application of the term *regale sacerdotium* (I *Peter*, ii. 9) to the episcopacy see *Decretales*, I. xv. 1.

cannot be a true separation of the regal from the sacerdotal, since bishops are as royal as kings:

Et propter hoc est sciendum quod ad rei veritatem et nominis proprietatem potestas principum saecularium et spiritualium non debet sic distingui ut una dicatur regalis et alia sacerdotalis, cum regalis vere conveniat praelatis ecclesiae . . . immo utraque vere potest dici regalis.[1]

Equally definite on this point is Augustinus Triumphus. Although it is desirable for most of the government of the kingdom to be carried on by the king rather than the bishop, who may the better concern himself with those spiritual duties which he alone is qualified to carry out, it is the bishops who are the ultimate superiors of the lay kingdoms. Their supereminence may be attributed to four things: their priority of institution, the quality of their acts, the dignity of their office, and above all to the extent of their jurisdictional power. For whereas kings have power in secular matters only, the jurisdiction of the priest extends equally to temporal and spiritual.

In iurisdictionis etiam potestate planum est quod eis praeferuntur, cum iurisdictio regum solum sit super temporalia, sacerdotum vero potestas ad temporalia et spiritualia se extendit.[2]

In this way both Augustinus Triumphus and Alvarus Pelagius concur, at least on this occasion, in stipulating the inferiority of kings to bishops. It is not for the bishop to obey the king: rather the lay ruler exists as an auxiliary organ of episcopal government, acting in obedience to episcopal directives. The penalty for rebellion, adds Alvarus, is excommunication, and Augustinus agrees with him. The catholic king must obey his spiritual father.[3] Moreover this

[1] Alvarus Pelagius, *De planctu Ecclesiae*, ch. 52, pp. 128–9. He appears to be quite unaware of the extent to which this conflicts with his other statements of episcopal power.

[2] Augustinus Triumphus, *Summa*, civ. 3, pp. 513–14; and note his argument in xlvi. 3, p. 251, that the pope must be able to depose kings because he can depose bishops, who are superior to kings.

[3] Augustinus Triumphus, *Summa*, lxxv. 3 ad 1, p. 389, 'cum clerici ponuntur conservatores, si per seipsos non possent eis commissos a manifestis iuris defendere, bracchium saeculare super hoc possent invocare et eos per sententiam excommunicationis compellere ad praebendum auxilium'; Alvarus Pelagius, *Collirium*, p. 504, 'Et reges ab episcopis excommunicari possunt si contumaces

royal inferiority, it is stressed, is denoted by the fact that kings are anointed on the arm, which demonstrates their executive capacity, whereas the jurisdictional supremacy of the bishop is symbolised by his unction with chrism on the head.[1] And this superiority extends not only over the king of the bishop's own kingdom, but equally over all secular princes, as may be seen from their duty to make and break peace treaties and agreements between the kings themselves.[2]

Whilst this enhancement of episcopal power was a firmly rooted feature of the hierocratic system, from the papal point of view it gave rise to problems no less serious than those with which it had to contend when dealing with the lay monarchies. Many medieval bishops, delighted with the conception of their own supremacy, at once began to exhibit all the tendencies towards independence to which other kings were prone. Moreover they were able to provide a far stronger theoretical basis for their aspirations. The idea that every bishop was pope in his own diocese could be, and frequently was, interpreted to mean that he owed allegiance to no-

fuerint et *rebelles* . . . et reges et principes habent episcopis obedire, non econverso'; *Speculum regum*, p. 517, 'Sacerdotium autem est officium necessarium in qualibet politia regni et dignissimum omnium aliorum officiorum regni. Summo autem sacerdoti, id est papae . . . et aliis episcopis quilibet rex catholicus obedire debet sicut patri spirituali'. It may however be mentioned that true to form Alvarus promptly contradicts all this: 'Non nego tamen quod episcopi tenentes regalia suis regibus manus debeant osculari, quia pro temporalibus subsunt eis', although he later denies that any king can exercise jurisdiction over clerics: *Speculum regum*, p. 520; *Collirium*, p. 505.

[1] Alvarus Pelagius, *De planctu Ecclesiae*, ch. 37, p. 57, 'ad quod significandum inungitur pontifex in capite, rex in bracchio'; Hostiensis, *Summa ad Decretales*, IV. xvii. 13, 'Inde est quod caput episcopi chrismate et rex oleo, ut scias quod episcopus est vicarius capitis nostri, id est Christi . . . et ut ostendatur quanta sit differentia inter *auctoritatem* pontificis et principis *potestatem*'; Thomas Aquinas, *Opusc. II, De perfectione vitae spiritualis*, ch. 26, 'in regno Ecclesiae episcopus ungitur tamquam principaliter habens curam regiminis . . . et quasi regalem'; also Peter Bertrandus, *De origine iurisdictionum*, ch. 4, fo. 99. This is based on Innocent III's ruling in *Decretales*, I. xv. 1. For the development of royal unction and acclamation for the bishops see Kantorowicz, *Laudes Regiae*, pp. 63–4, 87–8, 93–4, 112–25.

[2] Anon., *Disquisitio prior iuridica*, ch. 2, p. 1324, 'Praelati singularum provinciarum possunt indicere treugas inter principes et alios christianos. . . Ergo multo fortius hoc potest facere dominus papa . . . in quo est plenitudo potestatis, licet alii in partem sollicitudinis sint vocati'.

body but God. He became a true monarch, and the jurisdiction of the Roman pontiff was correspondingly confined to the see of Rome itself.

Sicut dicimus quod aliquis episcopus est dominus temporalis et spiritualis in sua civitate, et sic est ibi monarcha utrumque obtinens principatum, sic ergo concedimus quod papa habet monarchiam utriusque potestatis in Urbe, non tamen in orbe.[1]

Christ's commission of power to St. Peter was not denied, but it was denied that it had been made to him alone, and great play was made with the fact that the words by which the power of binding and loosing was granted to him in *Matthew*, xvi. 19, were subsequently repeated to the other apostles in *Matthew*, xviii. 18. This contention had a long history, and had been given full expression in the writings of Cyprian and other Church Fathers.[2] It reappeared in the *Decretum* statement that 'Ceteri apostoli cum eodem [scil. Petro] pari consortio honorem et potestatem acceperunt',[3] and by the beginning of the fourteenth century several clearly defined 'episcopalist' theories had been formulated. These were mainly variations on the theme that all bishops are the heirs of Christ by virtue of their succession to the apostles, all of whom had been the beneficiaries of the Petrine commission. As *vicarii Christi*[4] they have

[1] Anon., *Quaestio in utramque partem*, ch. 2, p. 1067. On this view Augustinus Triumphus comments, *Summa*, xix. 5, p. 121, 'Eodem modo absurdum est dicere quod papa non possit solvere et ligare in diocesi cuiuslibet episcopi et parochia cuiuslibet presbyteri vel absolutionem et ligationem committere quibus placet'. He also cites the view that the pope has no authority in another bishop's diocese without the bishop's permission, xix. 3 *prop*. 3.

[2] Cyprian, *De unitate Ecclesiae*, ch. 4 (*CSEL*, iii. 209f.); *Epp*., lxxv, lxxxi; Ambrose, *Comm. in I Cor*., ii; Jerome, *Ep*., lxxxv.

[3] Gratian, D. 21 c. 2.

[4] E.g. Alvarus Pelagius, *De planctu Ecclesiae*, ch. 52, p. 129, 'Quia episcopus sub vicario Christi universali Romano pontifice et ipse Dei vicarius est in parte suae sollicitudinis et personam Christi habet'; cf. p. 127, 'Potestas autem regia spiritualis . . . in novo autem testamento communicata est et tradita a Christo apostolis et eorum successoribus'; Hostiensis, *Comm. ad Decretales*, II. i. 12, 'Et etiam episcopus vicarius Dei est'. Reference could also be made to Gratian, D. 3 c. 35; C. 33 q. 5 c. 19. Marsilius insisted upon the essential equality of all priests and bishops, *Defensor pacis*, II. xv. 4, pp. 328–9; hence all the apostles/bishops together are superior to Peter/pope in a faith (II. xvii. 6, p. 360) and authority (II. xvi. 6, pp. 342–3) by a simple numerical majority.

equal power with the pope, at least in their own dioceses, and are thus free from all external interference. This remarkable claim is discussed by the French Dominican, Peter de la Palu, titular Patriarch of Jerusalem. In a most interesting passage he refers to those who claim to hold power direct from God, to whom they alone are subject since they recognise no other superior.[1] In this category he puts first those kings and barons who maintain that hereditary right puts them beyond the jurisdiction of any superior, but also those prelates who reject the pope's plenitude of power by denying that they hold any authority from him. This Peter castigates as the error of the Greeks.

Illi ergo praelati qui dicunt se non tenere a papa auctoritatem et potestatem suam sed a solo Deo, eo ipso negant se subesse papae in illa, et si negant papam primatem in Ecclesia, qui est error Graecorum ... negant papae plenitudinem potestatis.

Whilst Peter does not specify who these prelates are, the description could be applied to many of the Gallican bishops, and he probably had in mind the position taken up by his great antagonist, John de Pouilli, who in 1313 was accused of saying that the other members of the clergy had immediate power from Christ equally with the pope. John also appears to have denied the pope any right to make a direct grant of privileges to the lower clergy on the grounds that this would by-pass the episcopacy, and so upset the 'essentialis ordo et obligatio iuris divini et naturalis' which not even the Universal Church itself could change.[2] Elsewhere we are told that some bishops were pointing to their episcopal unction as evidence of their direct vicariate of Christ,[3] and it becomes plain that for

[1] Peter de la Palu, *De causa immediata ecclesiasticae potestatis*, v. 2, fo. 56, 'Unde in franco allodio quod dicunt se a nullo tenere nisi a Deo, dicunt se non subdi nisi Deo, nec in illo recognoscunt superiorem nisi Deum'.

[2] 'Primo dixit quod episcopi, qui succedunt apostolis, et curati discipulis succedentes, totam auctoritatem et potestatem suam aeque et immediate habent a Christo sicut et dominus papa pro eo quod apostoli et lxxii discipuli auctoritatem et potestatem suam aeque et immediate a Christo susceperunt': J. Koch, 'Der Prozess gegen den Magister Johannes de Polliaco und seine Vorgeschichte', *Recherches de théologie ancienne et médiévale*, v (1933), pp. 391–422 at pp. 394–5; see further J. G. Sikes, 'John de Pouilli and Peter de la Palu', *EHR*, xlix (1934), pp. 219–40.

[3] Peter Bertrandus, *De origine iurisdictionum*, ch. 4, fo. 99.

many the pope is no more than the bishop of Rome, a bishop amongst bishops. It is acknowledged that he may be a *primus inter pares*, and many writers endeavour to account for this by saying that the bishops are 'vocati in partem sollicitudinis', that is to say, that they have been given power only in their own dioceses, whilst the papal plenitude of power enables him to act throughout the world.[1] But if both are equal within the diocese, what is to happen when papal and episcopal commandments conflict? It is clear that the use of the *in partem sollicitudinis* formula in this context is in reality designed to deny the pope any concern with the government of the diocese without the bishop's consent, and that the pope is intended to restrict himself to the Roman province. Did not James, the first bishop of Jerusalem, it is argued, demonstrate his superiority in his own see by giving judgement although Peter himself was present?[2] The right order then in the *ordo episcopalis* is a horizontal rather than a vertical one. All belong to the brotherhood

[1] E.g. John of Paris, *De potestate regia et papali*, ch. 10, p. 197; ch. 12, pp. 208–10; Aegidius Spiritalis, *Libellus contra infideles*, p. 107, 'Et licet largo modo quilibet episcopus quoad quaedam sit vicarius Christi . . . tamen papa solus est vicarius Christi propter plenitudinem potestatis ad quam vocatus est; alii in partem sollicitudinis sunt vocati'. For a full exposition of this view see Augustinus Triumphus' denunciation of it in the *De duplici potestate*, pp. 489–90. The history of this expression is traced by J. Rivière, '*In partem sollicitudinis*: évolution d'une formule pontificale', *Revue des sciences religieuses*, v (1925), pp. 210–31, although this mainly concerns the papal use of the formula. For its use by the Decretists in the episcopalist sense see Tierney, *Foundations of the Conciliar Theory*, pp. 145–6, 168, who points out that the acceptance of the papal plenitude of power in this context merely cloaks a real limitation of papal authority.

[2] The argument is quoted by Augustinus Triumphus, *Summa*, xix. 5 *prop.* 3, p. 120, 'Praeterea scribitur *Act.*, xv [13–21] quod Iacobus episcopus Hierosolymitanus, praesente Petro, dedit sententiam in sua diocesi de observatione legalium . . . quod non fecisset si Petrus potuisset in sua diocesi quod ipse poterat'; also *De duplici potestate*, p. 487; Peter de la Palu, *De causa immediata ecclesiasticae potestatis*, i. 1 ad 3, fo. 24. Alternatively it was suggested that the true pope ought to be the bishop of Jerusalem not Rome, since the former was the real see of Christ: this is also noted by Augustinus Triumphus, xix. 4 *prop.* 2, p. 119, 'sed Christus fuit episcopus singulariter Hierosolymitanus non Romanus, ergo etc.' In fact the Clerk in the *Somnium viridarii*, ii. 365, p. 225, says that the pope is bishop of Jerusalem: 'Unde Christus videtur fuisse episcopus Hierosolymitanus . . . et sic quia papa est eius vicarius, Hierosolymitanus episcopus per excellentiam dici debet'. Marsilius of Padua, *Defensor Pacis*, II. xvi. 15–18, pp. 350–4, maliciously championed the church of Antioch, St. Peter's first bishopric, as the primatial see.

of bishops, and there is no authority amongst brothers. The apostolic succession of all bishops places them on a level footing with the successors of Peter. Once appointed they exist in their own right, the recipients of directly given divine power. No pope can depose them, and they are all at full liberty to refuse obedience to the Roman church.

The upsurge of conciliar theories of government in the late thirteenth century opened up even more glorious vistas for the rebellious bishops, and it is a characteristic of fourteenth-century episcopalism that it is no longer on the defensive against papal supremacy but has begun an outright attack upon the immunity of the Roman church. The main objective appears to be not so much the preservation of the bishop's unfettered control of his diocese as the assertion of the right of the bishops to act as judges and superiors over the popes themselves. The old Cyprianic view that heresy in one bishop was to be rooted out by the others[1] is revived to support the right of an episcopal synod to depose a heretical pope, heresy in this case being given its widest possible interpretation. The basis of this view is the idea that the Petrine commission was made to the whole *Ecclesia* in the person of the apostles, not to Peter himself.[2] It accepts the familiar conciliar view that the pope is merely an elected agent of the *congregatio fidelium*, but orientates this theory in favour of the bishops alone. Just as the apostles received the initial grant of Christ's power on behalf of all, so now the bishops as their

[1] Cyprian, *Ep.*, lxvii, 'Idcirco enim, frater carissime, copiosum corpus est sacerdotum, concordiae mutuae glutino atque unitatis vinculo copulatum, ut siquis ex collegio nostro haeresim facere, et gregem Christi lacerare et vastare tentaverit, subveniant caeteri et quasi pastores utiles et misericordes oves Domini in gregem colligant'. At the beginning of the thirteenth century Johannes Teutonicus in his *glossa ordinaria* on the *Decretum*, *ad* D. 19 c. 6, had suggested that a council of bishops was superior to the pope in matters of faith: 'Videtur ergo quod papa teneatur requirere concilium episcoporum quod verum est ubi de fide agitur, et tunc synodus maior est papa': Tierney, *op. cit.*, p. 50.

[2] Guilielmus Durantis, *De modo generalis concilii celebrandi*, i. 5, p. 26, 'Concordat ad praemissa Augustinus exponens illud *Ioan.* 22 et *Matth.* 16, Quodcunque ligaveris etc., quia dicit quod super hoc non est dictum tantum Petro sed Ecclesiae'; Anon., *Commentarium in Unam sanctam*, ch. 3, p. 142, 'Apostoli locum tenebant Ecclesiae'. For examples from Augustine see S. J. Grabowski, 'St. Augustine and the Primacy of the Roman Bishops', *Traditio*, iv (1946), pp. 89–113 at pp. 97–9.

successors are the only permissible representatives of the Universal Church. They have the right to elect the pope, and consequently do themselves possess the papal *plenitudo potestatis*.[1] A pope who lays down his power resigns it into the hands of the bishops,[2] and from here it is but a short step to the elaboration of a complete theory of episcopal supremacy. Ockham indeed, as individualistic as ever, would permit any bishop the power to depose a heretical pope resident in his diocese,[3] but the main trend of episcopal opinion was towards combined action. Perhaps the best contemporary example of this is to be found with Conrad of Megenberg, a canon of St. Ulric of Regensburg, in a tract which was in fact specifically designed to reject the doctrines of Ockham. The thought of Conrad is dominated by the functional qualification of the priesthood as the governing force in the *Ecclesia*, and it is this emphasis upon the superior knowledge of the faith contained in the ordained members of the society which predisposes him in favour of the right of the bishops to condemn a pope for heresy. Pre-eminent even

[1] The view that the pope should be elected by the bishops is quoted by Augustinus Triumphus, *Summa*, iii. 1 *prop*. 3, p. 27. It rests on the idea that Peter's primacy derived from the choice of the other apostles after the Ascension, as mentioned in Gratian, D. 21 c. 2, 'ipsumque principem eorum esse voluerunt'. In the fifteenth century Nicholas of Cues worked this up into a complete theory of the bishops as representatives of the *Ecclesia*, having the same power as the pope: *De concordantia catholica*, ii. 13, 'Scimus quod Petrus nihil plus potestatis a Christo recepit aliis apostolis. Nihil enim dictum est ad Petrum quod etiam aliis dictum non est. . . Ideo recte dicimus omnes apostolos in potestate esse cum Petro aequales'. Having quoted a similar argument, Hevaeus Natalis, *De potestate papae*, fo. 151v, replied that the *voluntas apostolorum* had no causal effect, and was nothing more than a demonstration of the apostles' acceptance of what had already been determined by Christ: 'ipsis habentibus complacientiam in praesidentia Petri'. The same reply is made by Peter de la Palu, *De causa immediata ecclesiasticae potestatis*, i. 2 ad 2, fo. 25.

[2] This view is cited by Aegidius Romanus, *De renuntiatione papae*, iii, p. 4.

[3] William of Ockham, *Tractatus contra Benedictum XII*, vii. 8–9, pp. 311–13: dealing with the question of what is to be done when the pope becomes a heretic, he says, 'si episcopus, in cuius diocesi [papa haereticus] commoratur, est catholicus et super expurganda de sua diocesi haeretica pravitate sollicitus atque potens, ipse de consilio fratrum suorum, vel si expediret de consilio vicinorum episcoporum si essent catholici, invocato auxilio bracchii saecularis, papam haereticum de haeresi iudicare posset et deberet'. If the said bishop refuses to do this, then it should be done by the primate or metropolitan of the province, or failing this by a 'concilium praelatorum aliorum'.

amongst bishops, however, for their knowledge of the right way of life are the cardinals, and it is the cardinals rather than the bishops who are to make the first move. As soon as they have reason to think that the pope has strayed from the true faith, the cardinals are to attempt to show him the error of his ways. If this fails, they are to accuse him before a *concilium ecclesiae*.[1] Whilst there is a great similarity between the conciliar theories of both the bishops and the college of cardinals, as this particular theory demonstrates, for Conrad the cardinals have only the role of accusers. The actual judgement and deposition of the pope is a matter for the 'council of the church',

Si papa super manifesta vel convicta haeresi corrigi non vult, tunc omni auctoritate et potestate est privandus . . . per concilium ecclesiae,[2]

and this, it is clear, is not a general council but a convocation of the *ecclesia* understood in the sense of the priesthood. It is the clergy, particularly their prelates, who alone can have true knowledge of the faith. The laity, being unordained, are ignorant and not worth consulting.[3] It is the bishops who are the salt of the earth and the light of the world, and it is quite impossible that when the clergy are called together they should err in matters of faith.

Dico quod est impossibile omnes praelatos ecclesiae et totum clerum errare in fide. . . Clerici namque et praelati ecclesiae in locum aposto-

[1] Conrad of Megenberg, *Tractatus contra Wilhelmum Occam*, ch. 9, p. 377, 'dicendum quod hoc verum est si deviat a fide devio manifeste super quo a cardinalibus aut ceteris ecclesiae praelatis adiunctis cardinalibus ammonitus corrigi non vult nec emendari; tunc enim per concilium condempnandus est praelatorum ecclesiae, et per consequens ab imperatore et ab omnibus christianis detestandus tamquam omnium auctoritate et potestate privatus. . . Si vero occulta est eius haeresis super illa occulte est ammonendus, qua si se occulte coram cardinalibus non expurgaverit, aut si de illa convictus corrigi non curaverit, concilio utique est accusandus et condempnandus'; ch. 8, pp. 371–2, 'Sed in causa haeresis submittitur universitatis sive concilii iudicio, sicut patet 40 di. [c. 6], *Si papa*. Illud tamen intelligendum est cum non vult corrigi, quia si paratus esset corrigi non posset concilio accusari: tunc enim papa potest accusari seu condempnari de haeresi cum pertinax fuerit, alias non, ut dicit Huguccio et post eum Guido archidiaconus super c. [7] *Nunc autem*, d. 21'.

[2] Conrad of Megenberg, *Tractatus contra Wilhelmum Occam*, ch. 9, p. 377.

[3] Conrad of Megenberg, *Tractatus contra Wilhelmum Occam*, ch. 7, p. 367. 'Genus autem clericorum sapientiam scripturarum possedit, sed genus laycorum ignorantiam retinuit'.

lorum successerunt, quibus Dominus ait, Vos estis sal terrae, quod si evanuerit, in quo salietur? *Matth.*, v [13], quasi diceret, in nullo. Et iterum, Vos estis lux mundi [*Matth.*, v. 14].[1]

Indeed Conrad is so convinced of the exalted nature of priesthood that the severest sentence of the council is one of degradation, which is appropriately enough to be performed by the cardinal-bishops who had originally anointed and consecrated the pope.[2] It is only after this that the now 'worthless body' of the degraded is left to the forcible removal, sentence and punishment of the secular arm.[3] But it is essentially the bishops who create and destroy the popes.[4]

The attempts of the medieval bishops to secure autonomous status for themselves in their own kingdoms is clearly of the utmost importance as a factor in the ultimate development of national churches. And whilst little attention has hitherto been paid to the growth of the episcopal threat to the papal monarchy, still less interest has been attached to the means by which the episcopal idea became widely disseminated in the later Middle Ages. It was un-

[1] Conrad of Megenberg, *Tractatus contra Wilhelmum Occam*, ch. 9, p. 378.

[2] Conrad of Megenberg, *Tractatus contra Wilhelmum Occam*, ch. 8, p. 373, 'Sed diceres, per quem vel quos papa haereticus vel pertinax est degradandus? Estimo quod per dominum Hostiensem, Portuensem et Albanensem episcopos, per quos inungitur et benedicitur sicut in pontificali continetur, ipso tamen prius per concilium praelatorum et *doctorum* ecclesiae condempnato et iudicato'.

[3] Conrad of Megenberg, *Tractatus contra Wilhelmum Occam*, ch. 8, p. 373, 'Hostiensis clare patet quod iudicium condempnatio et degradatio clerici super crimen haeresis ad forum ecclesiasticum pertinet, non ad forum saeculare. Sed cadaver corporis degradati et clericalibus insigniis privati spiculatoribus committitur per iudicium saeculare'; p. 372, 'Sed ipse [imperator] auscultare habet sententiam praelatorum cleri christiani, si vocatur ad tale officium et eam exequi prolatam. . .'; ch. 9, p. 378, 'immo si tanta ingrueret necessitas, concilium praelatorum ecclesiae auxilium imperatoris invocaret atque aliorum principum saecularium iuvamen'.

[4] It is interesting to note the use of the *in partem sollicitudinis* formula by Philip the Fair in his attempt to induce the French bishops to form a council to sit in judgement over Boniface VIII: Dupuy, p. 107, 'Vos archiepiscopos, episcopos et praelatos alios hic praesentes, tamquam Ecclesiae filios et *columnas fidei*, ad exaltationem, augmentum et conservationem ipsius fidei *a Domino* in partem sollicitudinis evocatos, instanter requirimus et obsecramus. . .' Note the idea of direct divine right implied here, although it may be added that the king had little doubt that his own vicariate of Christ qualified him to act as the immediate source of episcopal jurisdiction in this case: see for example his insistence that he possesses the power of Christ, pp. 107, 124–5.

doubtedly the assimilation of the episcopal theory into the comprehensive system built up by the followers of Aquinas, the insistence that the aims of the bishops were not at variance with the principles laid down by the Angelic Doctor, that secured a large measure of intellectual support for the idea of local ecclesiastical autonomy. Foremost amongst the publicists responsible for propounding this doctrine were those Thomists who were also bishops or of similar standing—James of Viterbo,[1] Alexander of S. Elpidio,[2] Alvarus Pelagius,[3] Guilielmus Durantis the Younger,[4] and John de Pouilly[5]—although much of the preliminary work had already been achieved in the cross-talk of that inimitable pair of thirteenth-century Belgian writers, Henry of Ghent and Geoffrey of Fontaines. Faced with the crucial question of deciding whether Christ's commission of power had been made to Peter alone or to all the apostles, they see no other solution than the acceptance of the now familiar Thomistic idea that it had been made direct to both parties.[6] The

[1] Archbishop of Benevento, then of Naples, 1302: see the introduction to H. X. Arquillière, *Le plus ancien traité de l'église, Jacques de Viterbo, De Regimine Christiano* (Paris, 1926).

[2] Prior General of the Augustinian Order, and Bishop of Melfi, 1326: U. Mariani, *Chiesa e Stato nei teologi agostiniani del secolo xiv* (Rome, 1957), pp. 97–103.

[3] Bishop of Coron (Greece), 1332–3, and of Silves (Portugal), 1333–50: N. Iung, *Un Franciscain, théologien du pouvoir pontifical au xive siècle, Alvaro Pelayo, évêque et pénitencier de Jean XXII* (Paris, 1931), pp. 17–18.

[4] Bishop of Mende, 1296–1330. On the episcopalist theories of Durantis see the excellent account by Tierney, *Foundations of the Conciliar Theory*, pp. 190–7.

[5] The spokesman of the French secular clergy: see N. Valois, *Histoire littéraire de la France*, xxxiv. 220–81; P. Glorieux, *La littérature quodlibétique de 1260 à 1320* (Kain, 1925), pp. 223–8; and p. 340 n. 2 above.

[6] Guilielmus Durantis, *De modo generalis concilii celebrandi*, i. 5, pp. 24–5, 'Et ligandi atque solvendi potestatem tam Petrus quam apostoli a Christo receperunt. Primo tamen Petrus, sicut Anacletus papa ait, hanc ligandi et solvendi supra terram potestatem accepit a Domino . . . Caeteri vero apostoli cum eodem Petro pari consortio honorem et potestatem acceperunt a Christo. . . Ipsis vero apostolis decedentibus, in loco eorum successerunt episcopi, quos . . . qui autem spernit, Deum a quo missi sunt et cuius funguntur legatione spernit. . . Loquitur Dominus ad Petrum, Ego dico tibi quod tu es Petrus etc., . . . et quamvis apostolis omnibus post resurrectionem suam parem potestatem tribuat et dicat, Sicut misit me Pater, et ego mitto vos, accipite Spiritum sanctum [*John*, xx. 22]'. Similarly Alexander de S. Elpidio, *De ecclesiastica potestate*, i. 4, p. 5, declares that 'summus pontifex habeat universalem potestatem immediate a Christo', but adds, i. 5, p. 6, 'Quod *etiam* sancti apostoli et discipuli habuerunt potestatem iurisdictionis immediate a Christo probari potest' by reference to *Luke*, vi. 13, and *Mark*, xvi. 15–20.

bishops are therefore justified in entitling themselves vicars of Christ,[1] because they derive Christ's powers through the apostles.[2] But it is also emphasised that the apostles had received their power *vice omnium*, so that the bishops may now act only in the capacity of representatives of the *congregatio fidelium*.

Unde *Matth.* xvi [18], dixit Dominus Petro, super hanc petram, id est me petram, aedificabo Ecclesiam meam; sed praelati Ecclesiae, scilicet episcopi et curati, qui sunt principaliores in Ecclesia, sunt Ecclesia prout hic sumitur Ecclesia: ergo Christus episcopis et curatis dedit potestatem.[3]

The relationship between pope and bishops is now turned into another aspect of the basic relationship between any community and its ruler.[4] Every papal action which concerns the well-being of the *Ecclesia* must be subject to the principle of 'quod omnes tangit', although the approval of all in this case, it is implied, can be ascertained by gaining an episcopal vote of confidence.[5] The making of

[1] Alexander de S. Elpidio, *De ecclesiastica potestate*, ii. 5, p. 19, 'licet enim alii rectores Ecclesiae qui succedunt aliis apostolis Christi vicarii dicantur'; Alvarus Pelagius, *De planctu Ecclesiae*, ch. 70, p. 260, 'Episcopus enim vicarius Christi est': this refers to the *auctoritas episcopi*; Thomas Aquinas, *Summa theologica*, III. lxiv. 2 ad 3, 'Apostoli et eorum successores sunt vicarii Dei quantum ad regimen Ecclesiae'.

[2] Alexander de S. Elpidio, *De ecclesiastica potestate*, i. 6, pp. 7–8, 'Sed successores apostolorum non possunt esse nisi episcopi, cum apostoli episcopi fuerint, nec successores discipulorum possunt esse nisi sacerdotes curati, qui sunt sacerdotes secundi ordinis'; i. 10, p. 12, 'omnes ergo sacerdotes maiores ponendi sunt successores apostolorum'; James of Viterbo, *De regimine christiano*, ii. 3, p. 180, 'Potestas autem regia spiritualis . . . in novo autem testamento communicata est et tradita a Christo apostolis et eorum successoribus, tunc scilicet quando dictum est eis [*Matthew*, xviii. 18], Quaecunque ligaveritis super terram ligata erunt et in coelo. Potestas enim ligandi et solvendi est potestas iudicaria'; Geoffrey of Fontaines, *Quodlibeta*, XII. iii (v. 95), 'Quia licet episcopi habent potestatem suam et iurisdictionem immediate a Deo, prout dicitur in distinctione vigesima prima, capitulo [2] *In novo testamento*, caeteri apostoli, quibus succedunt episcopi, cum beato Petro pari consortio honorem et potestatem acceperunt'.

[3] Alexander de S. Elpidio, *De ecclesiastica potestate*, i. 6, p. 8; cf. Alvarus Pelagius, *De planctu Ecclesiae*, ch. 54, p. 139. For the same view with John de Pouilli see Sikes, *art. cit.*, pp. 227–30.

[4] Geoffrey of Fontaines, *Quodlibeta*, XII. iii (v. 93) and iv (v. 96); William of Ockham, *Dialogus*, III. I. iv. 11 and 23, pp. 855, 865–6.

[5] E.g. Guilielmus Durantis, *De modo generalis concilii celebrandi*, i. 3, pp. 16–17; Geoffrey of Fontaines, *Quodlibeta*, XI. xvii (v. 77); and John de Pouilli in Sikes, *art. cit.*, pp. 239–40.

law is a joint act between the pope and a council of bishops and others convened for that purpose, and whilst this legislative activity is basically a papal act with episcopal consent added, the balance is redressed in the creation of a bishop, which is essentially an act of the episcopal chapter acting *vice omnium*, to which the pope merely gives his consent. Accordingly the resignation of a bishop is a matter affecting the whole community and cannot be legitimately undertaken without the consent of another superior bishop who represents it.[1] Even the election of the pope himself demonstrates a neat division of divine and human authority. The power of the papal office comes from God by virtue of the Petrine commission, but its potency can only be activated by human exercise through a person who is the choice of the whole community. And whilst the community normally acts through the cardinals in its election of this individual, it may always resort to the use of the bishops as a means of recording its decision if the cardinals are unable to make a speedy election.

Item quod si dicta Romana ecclesia vacaret ultra tres menses, quod ex tunc cardinales essent eligendi potestate illa vice [omnium] privati, et quod ad aliquos archiepiscopos et episcopos et alios de quibus videretur expediens illa vice [omnium] devolveretur eligendi potestas.[2]

In fact the election of the bishops would more accurately represent the Biblical tradition. For whilst Christ had directly instituted the power of the other apostles and of the Petrine office, Peter himself had required the consent of the apostles acting on behalf of the whole *congregatio fidelium*.[3]

[1] Geoffrey of Fontaines, *Quodlibeta*, XII. iv (v. 96), 'Immo cum totus populus ius habeat in isto ad hoc quod praelatus legitime cedat, consensus populi vel alterius praelati superioris a quo iste praelatus inferior curam populi suscepit vice ipsius populi est merito requirendus'.

[2] Guilielmus Durantis, *De modo generalis concilii celebrandi*, iii. 27, p. 282.

[3] Alexander de S. Elpidio, *De ecclesiastica potestate*, i. 5, pp. 6–7, 'Ipsi etiam sancti apostoli quantumcunque essent a Christo immediate vocati et instituti, communi tamen approbatione recognoverunt Petrum ipsorum caput, principem et magistrum totius Ecclesiae . . . omnes alii apostoli et discipuli, licet a Christo immediate potestatem habuerunt, Petrum tamen semper recognoverunt in dominium et magistrum'; cf. Alvarus Pelagius, *De planctu Ecclesiae*, ch. 59, p. 179; Geoffrey of Fontaines, *Quodlibeta*, XII. iii (v. 95); Guilielmus Durantis, *De modo generalis concilii celebrandi*, i. 5, p. 25.

The same pattern of divided authority emerges from the further elaboration of this theory. Since the bishops are on the same level as kings, their status with regard to the papacy is protected in a similar manner to that of the lay rulers in the Thomist scheme. It is acknowledged that the pope initially possesses a plenitude of power over the episcopacy by virtue of his succession from Peter, but this is what Geoffrey of Fontaines calls an *auctoritas radicalis*:[1] it does not appear in its entirety but remains partly buried. By this absolute power, as Peter de la Palu shows, the pope would theoretically be able to remove bishops and upset the normal ordering of the *Ecclesia* at will:

> ... de *potentia* absoluta ... episcopus vel curatus et quicunque alius in dignitate ecclesiastica constitutus ab ea per papam potest deponi sine causa rationabile et iuris ordine non servata, et ita tenet sententia.

The reason why this should not happen however lies in the fact that this *potestas absoluta* is not so much power as potency: normally it only becomes actual in the form of a *potestas ordinaria* by which the pope is not permitted to depose bishops.

> Si intelligunt de *potestate* ordinaria verum est quod nec episcopus curatum nec papa episcopum debet deponere, nisi ex causa rationabile, alias peccant.[2]

[1] Geoffrey of Fontaines, *Quodlibeta*, XIII. v (v. 228), 'quia primam et radicalem auctoritatem post Christum videtur habere ut rector principalis Ecclesiae'. Another version of this can be found with Henry of Ghent, *Quodlibetae*, VII. xxiv, IX. xxii, XI. xxvii–xxviii, and XII. xxix: see de Lagarde, 'La philosophie sociale', pp. 134–7.

[2] Peter de la Palu, *De causa immediata ecclesiasticae potestatis*, vi. fo. 70; cf. fo. 72. Note also the *Articulus circa materia confessionum*, ff. 82v, 85v, where he distinguished between the 'common law' ruling that a man must confess to his parish priest, and the capacity of the *potentia absoluta* to permit confession to a friar. It is curious to note that Peter thus ends up by accepting exactly the same distinction as his adversary, John de Pouilli: 'Aliter est loquendum de potestate plenaria sive de plenitudine potestatis domini papae, et de sua potestate ordinata'. By the former the pope can exercise complete jurisdiction over all, but by the ordained power he has authority only over those immediately subject to him: 'Si autem nos loquamur de plenaria potestate eius, sic ipsa est universalissima et immediatissima, ut dictum est, quia per ipsam dominus papa potest immediate *omnem actum* ierarchicum exercere in omnes de universo. Si autem loquamur de eius potestate ordinata ... aliqui [sunt] super quos dominus habet

This, it will be noted, does not altogether deny the pope's right to punish bishops, but when he does so this is specifically an exercise of his superior absolute power, and his use of this is restricted in that it may only be used *casualiter*, in certain cases and for a just cause:

... sic quod modo supradicto in casibus et ex causis potest dominus papa iurisdictionem eorum [scil. episcoporum] restringere vel suspendere.[1]

Underlying this distinction is the motivating belief in a general good which overrides all personal and individual considerations. The pope has been given power specifically for the preservation of the corporate well-being: 'non est sibi data potestas in destructione sed in aedificatione';[2] and he utilises this by promulgating laws which embody the *status Ecclesiae* in concrete form. But a necessary corollary to this conception of the papal office is that the pope himself is bound by these laws in spite of the fact that they originate from him. As the reflector and example of the right order,[3] the pope cannot avoid the obligation to adhere to the common (canon) law of the community which is the mainstay of this order.[4] He is forced to make a 'voluntary' submission to the law by reason of his very nature as legislator, and this he, or rather his predecessors, have done by deliberately renouncing any general papal right to interfere with the bishops in the administration of their own dioceses. It is enough for the present pope to obey the provisions of canon law, which preserve the normal independence of the episcopacy from

iurisdictionem et subsunt ei soli, et ita illorum est immediatus ierarcha vel princeps; alii vero sunt super quos ipse solus non habet iurisdictionem sed alius, et illi non dicuntur ei subesse immediate': see Sikes, *art. cit.*, p. 37. This is a good example of the way in which the Thomist system made common ground between opponents.

[1] Geoffrey of Fontaines, *Quodlibeta*, XII. iii (v. 95).

[2] Peter de la Palu, *De causa immediata ecclesiasticae potestatis*, vi, fo. 73. Cf. II *Cor.*, x. 8, xiii. 10.

[3] Guilielmus Durantis, *De modo generalis concilii celebrandi*, iii. 1, p. 240, 'sacrosancta Romana ecclesia quae ... est omnibus posita in speculum et exemplum'.

[4] Guilielmus Durantis, *De modo generalis concilii celebrandi*, iii. 31, p. 295, 'Et si ad humanas leges contentas in conciliis et in sacri canonibus consideratio habeatur, ad eorum observationem secundum Gelasium et Zosimum prima sedes prae ceteris obligatur'. For the remainder of this passage and the principle that the ruler must make himself obey his own laws, see above p. 308, n. 1.

papal control.[1] In practice the other bishops are real vicars of Christ, and the pope may not disturb them in the possession of their sees nor wield regular jurisdiction over them.

Item cum episcopi sint in locum apostolorum, qui parem cum Petro honorem et potestatem acceperunt a Deo. . . Item quod potestatem et iurisdictionem praedictis praelatis et curatis competentem et attributam a Deo apostolis, conciliis, Romanis pontificibus et universali Ecclesiae in locis et plebibus eisdem commissis, dicta Romana ecclesia non turbaret nec usurparet in causarum et appellationem cognitionibus . . . cum ex contrario totus ordo ecclesiasticus confundatur.[2]

As the younger Durantis emphasises, canon law expressly denies the pope the title of universal bishop.[3] The fact that the bishops are called *in partem sollicitudinis* gives local churches certain privileges and private right immunity which no pope can transgress at pleasure. Bishops have a real right of their own to exist, and are not mere creatures of the papal will. As Alvarus Pelagius says, even if the *Ecclesia* could do without its kings (which he elsewhere denies), it may not be left without its bishops.[4] Only when an emergency situation arises is the pope able to exercise his plenitude of power over other churches. In such cases public necessity overrides private right, and full papal jurisdiction comes temporarily into play.

[1] Geoffrey of Fontaines, *Quodlibeta*, XII. iii (v. 94), 'quae autem a Deo sunt, ordinata sunt: ideo praelati a Deo ordinatam potestatem debent sic ordinate conservare quod unus per alium non impediatur, sed potius adiuvetur. Habens ergo potestatem superiorem quantum ad id quod inferiori *de iure communi* competit nihil habet *regulariter* immutare'. This is supported by a list of *Decretum* passages in which earlier popes were supposed to have bound themselves to observe episcopal privileges.

[2] Guilielmus Durantis, *De modo generalis concilii celebrandi*, iii. 27, pp. 278–9. He may not for example tax them or translate them without their consent: ii. 7, p. 70; ii. 23, p. 114.

[3] Guilielmus Durantis, *De modo generalis concilii celebrandi*, ii. 7, p. 68, 'Et, ne detrahatur honori ceterorum praelatorum, *inhibeat se* universalem papam vocari'; also ii. 34, pp. 130–1; iii. 27, p. 282. This refers to Gratian, D. 99 c. 5. Augustinus Triumphus, *Summa*, xxix. 1 ad 3, p. 176, dismisses this as mere humility.

[4] Alvarus Pelagius, *De planctu Ecclesiae*, ch. 54, p. 136, 'Necessitas enim Ecclesiae requirit pluralitatem rectorum: dux ad regimen totius ecclesiasticae multitudinis unus non sufficit per seipsum'; and see also Peter de la Palu on this point in Sikes, *art. cit.*, p. 233.

The existing law no longer reflects the *status Ecclesiae*, and the normal order may be overturned.[1] The pope as the *speculum iustitiae*, as the personification of that which is right and good for the society, has a positive duty to ignore the existing law and intervene in the dioceses, deposing the bishops where he deems it necessary, to the extent required for the preservation of the general security.

Per haec patet quid dicendum sit ad quaestionem qua quaeritur utrum superior possit auferre ab inferiori illud quod sibi secundum suam dignitatem et iurisdictionem de iure competit. Et est dicendum quod *non regulariter* sed *in casu* potest . . . propter bonum commune.[2]

But as Aquinas had himself emphasised, the papal plenitude of power in operation is essentially a casual jurisdiction, a dispensing power above the law for use only when the common good is imperilled.[3] In this way the Thomist theory of casual power is utilised to impose severe restrictions upon papal control of the episcopacy. Even more it denies the immunity of the pope himself. As Geoffrey of Fontaines and Guilielmus Durantis explained, an overgreat use of his absolute power, a retention of it beyond the strictest necessity, renders the pope liable to immediate charges of tyranny, of putting his own private gain before the welfare of the whole community.[4]

[1] William of Ockham, *Octo quaestiones*, vii. 4, p. 176, 'Si igitur ecclesiae abutuntur privilegiis sibi concessis, ipsa merentur amittere . . . licet non debite quod nec ecclesia nec persona propter *favorem* alterius debeat *regulariter* privari iuribus et privilegiis suis, tamen *casualiter* privari debet'; cf. *Dialogus*, III. I. iv. 11, p. 855; Guilielmus Durantis, *De modo generalis concilii celebrandi*, ii. 3–5, pp. 61–3; ii. 7, p. 65.

[2] Geoffrey of Fontaines, *Quodlibeta*, XII. iii (v. 94).

[3] Thomas Aquinas, *Quodlibeta*, iv. 13, 'Papa habet plenitudinem potestatis in Ecclesia, ita scilicet quod quaecunque sunt instituta per Ecclesiam vel Ecclesiae praelatos sunt dispensabilia a papa'; *Summa theologica*, II. II. lxxxix. 9 ad 3, '. . . non videtur habere locum dispensatio vel commutatio nisi aliquid melius occurrat ad communem utilitatem faciendum, quod maxime videtur pertinere ad potestatem papae, qui habet curam universalis Ecclesiae'. Cf. Geoffrey of Fontaines, *Quodlibeta*, XII. iii (v. 93), 'Responsio: dicendum quod principes et praelati quibus incumbit cura subditorum principaliter intendere ad bonum communitatis debeant et quaecunque agunt ad hoc dirigere debent, quia finis per se et principalis politicae prudentiae quae est propria principi est bonum commune'.

[4] Guilielmus Durantis, *De modo generalis concilii celebrandi*, i. 4, p. 19; iii. 47, p. 329; Geoffrey of Fontaines, *Quodlibeta*, XII. iii (v. 94).

And once the bishops smell a suspicion of tyranny in the air it is time for them to carry further their duties of representing the Universal Church. Any vicious action on the part of the pope is tantamount to heresy,[1] and the threat of an heretical head creates the greatest possible emergency. The plenitude of power possessed by the congregation of the faithful—equal to that of the pope but hitherto remaining latent—is at once brought into action if the bishops and cardinals cannot make him acknowledge the error of his ways. Had not Christ himself (*Matthew*, xviii. 15–17) prefaced his commission of power to the bishops with precise instructions that a brother who failed to submit to fraternal correction should be dealt with by the *Ecclesia* itself? In cases of necessity the whole community may act through its bishops to preserve the *status Ecclesiae*.[2] The logical counterpart to the idea of the pope's exercise of casual jurisdiction over the bishops can be nothing else but the stipulation that the bishops acting *vice omnium* may exercise casual jurisdiction over him. As yet it was too early for this further refinement of the Thomist synthesis to receive full expression, and certainly none of the writers whom we have been discussing here ventured to do more than hint at it. But it was now inevitable that the more episcopally minded amongst the later conciliar writers would find this concept a valuable and welcome addition to their armoury.[3]

[1] Geoffrey of Fontaines, *Quodlibeta*, XII. iv (v. 98).

[2] We may note the very vague statement in Alexander de S. Elpidio, *De ecclesiastica potestate*, i. 10, p. 13, '. . . sed defectu iurisdictionis a domino papa non acceptae, non potest reduci in actum nisi in casu necessitatis, quando Ecclesia omnibus peccatoribus per omnes presbyteros tamquam curatos seu animarum curatores succurrere fideliter et pie intendit'.

[3] The conciliar theory of both Gerson and d'Ailly contains many elements of Thomist-episcopalism. For them a general council was essentially one composed of bishops, and the laity had only a consultative function: see Gerson, *Opera Omnia*, ii. 250f. and i. 661f. respectively. For episcopalism in another Thomist, Cardinal Zabarella, see Tierney, *Foundations of the Conciliar Theory*, pp. 232–3; W. Ullmann, *The Origins of the Great Schism* (London, 1948), p. 212. Later in the fifteenth century Panormitanus, *ad Decretales*, I. xxxiii. 17, regarded a general council as a convocation of bishops: 'praelati totius orbis conveniunt et faciunt unum corpus repraesentantes Ecclesiam universalem'.

II. THE SUPREME GOVERNOR

THE idea of the pope as *vicarius Christi* was designed and initiall used to refute the validity of the episcopal claims. However usefu the conception was in furthering the papal claim to imperial power the real value of the papal vicariate of Christ lay in its use agains the bishops, and it is interesting to notice how frequently Innocen III, the first pope to put particular emphasis upon it, had used the idea alongside arguments intended to rebuff the advances of episcopalism. Nevertheless the fact that it did not receive full expression until the time when the papal hegemony in Europe hac reached its peak does not mean that the *vicarius Christi* theory wa. an unheard of novelty before the middle of the twelfth century.[1] The conception of the papacy as a visible vicariate of Christ hac been inherent in the hierocratic system ever since the *congregati fidelium* came to be seen as a political entity. Its roots, as with most of the hierocratic ideology, lay deep in the Pauline doctrine of the one body of Christ and the Augustinian conception of the kingdom of God on earth. Its premise was the belief that the community of the faithful forms one being in Christ: the corporate body of Christians is the earthly counterpart of that celestial perfection in which Christ and the faithful are united as one. In essence there is no real distinction between Christ and his Church: the latter forms one body or person, and that person is Christ. He is, as St. Augustine had said, the *una persona Ecclesiae*: the *Ecclesia* is the *unum corpus Christi*. The important point to notice in this conception is that the personality of the community is non-terrestrial and non-material. Christ is the perfect pattern of human existence but, like Plato's *Republic*, which also represented the ultimate 'good', is situated in heaven. The personality is spiritual, mystical, invisible, and cannot in itself be equated with any living member of the society any more than the juristic personality of a corporation is

[1] The general development of the theory is outlined by M. Maccarrone, *Vicarius Christi* (Rome, 1952).

immediately identifiable with any of the individuals who form it. It is Real in the Platonic sense that it is the intangible which is perfect. On the other hand, however much the *Ecclesia* is a reflection of divine Reality, it remains nonetheless a terrestrial society. And as a civil community it requires a visible representation of its personality to act on its behalf, just as any corporation, although legally defined as one person, still requires the presence of some individual to represent it in a court of law. There must in fact be a physical personification of the community to act in its place and for its benefit on the physical plane of existence. This, according to the hierocratic idea, has been explicitly demonstrated by Christ's own assumption of human form. And although Christ is no longer physically present, his function on earth remains. It would be absurd to think, said Innocent IV, that Christ had departed from the earth without leaving a vicar, a corporeal manifestation of himself, behind.[1] The human personification of the mystical personality of the *Ecclesia*, who is Christ, is to be found in the visible vicariate which he set up in Peter and his successors before his corporeal presence was withdrawn.

Nam quia suam corporalem praesentiam subtracturus erat a suis fidelibus, expediens erat ut alicui uni committeret Ecclesiae universale regimen qui Ecclesiam regeret loco et vice sui. Hic autem fuit Petrus et in Petro commissum est regimen omnibus successoribus.[2]

The holder of this vicariate is the living embodiment of the immaterial *persona Ecclesiae*. Where the pope is, says Augustinus Triumphus, there is the human representation of Christ: 'ubi repraesentatus est Christus, ibi repraesentatus est papa, qui est vicarius

[1] Innocent IV, 'Eadem ratione et vicarius eius potest hoc: nam non videretur discretus Dominus fuisse, ut cum reverentia eius loquar, nisi unicum post se talem vicarium reliquisset qui haec omnia posset: fuit autem iste vicarius Petrus, *Matth.*, 16, ultra medium, et idem dicendum est de successoribus Petri, cum eadem absurditas sequeretur si post mortem Petri humanam naturam a se creatam sine regimine unius personae reliquisset': Maccarrone, *op. cit.*, p. 128.

[2] Alexander de S. Elpidio, *De ecclesiastica potestate*, ii. 1, p. 14. The same idea is expressed by Augustinus Triumphus, *Summa*, xix. 2 ad 1, p. 118, 'ideo licet cordi possit comparari Christus principaliter vel papa *instrumentaliter* secundum quod *invisibiliter* vivificat Ecclesiam, magis tamen comparatur capiti secundum *visibilem* naturam qua homo homini praefertur'.

Christi'.[1] He is at the same time the image of God and of the earthly society, which is the one body of God. The pope, Christ, and the *Ecclesia* are all fundamentally one and the same thing. As the vicariate of Christ the papacy is Christ and the *Ecclesia*, the head and the whole, on earth.[2] It holds the power, the *potestas Dei et papae*, the ecclesiastical power, which is common to both.

This conception of the visible vicariate of Christ had existed in embryo ever since Augustine had linked the idea of the *unum corpus Christi* to the earthly *civitas Dei*. During all the great periods of expansion in the hierocratic idea it was on the verge of breaking out into a fully fledged theory, but as a matter of historical fact it required nearly nine centuries of gestation before it was brought forth as a result of the great reawakening and reworking of hierocratic ideas which began in the middle of the eleventh century and culminated in the Bernardine 'papacy' of the mid-twelfth century.[3] Innocent III, as we have said, was largely responsible for making it a major item in the papal repertoire, and during the course of the thirteenth century it was systematically developed and extended. By the early fourteenth century it was due for complete exposition, and much of the importance of Augustinus Triumphus' political thought may justly be attributed to the fact that it was in his hands

[1] Augustinus Triumphus, *Summa*, viii. 1, p. 67; cf. ix. 4, p. 75, 'sed longe melius Deus repraesentatur per papam'; *De duplici potestate*, p. 488, 'papa est caput ipsius Ecclesiae, cum repraesentat personam Christi'; also James of Viterbo, *De regimine christiano*, ii. 9, pp. 308–9, 'dicendum quod Christus et eius vicarius non dicuntur duo capita sed unum, quia papa non dicitur caput nisi in quantum gerit vicem Christi et eius personam repraesentat'.

[2] Aegidius Romanus, *De ecclesiastica potestate*, ii. 4, pp. 50–1, 'pro petra significetur Christus iuxta illud apostoli, Petra autem erat Christus [I *Cor.*, x. 4], ut sit sensus quod dicat Christus, Ego sum petra et tu es Petrus dictus ab hac petra, et super hanc petram, id est super meipsum, aedificabo Ecclesiam meam. Tu igitur Petrus, qui a me petra nomen accepisti, totam Ecclesiam super me fundatam reges et gubernabis. . . Tu es Petrus qui dicitur a petra, id est a Christo, super quem Ecclesia est fundata'; Alvarus Pelagius, *De planctu Ecclesiae*, ch. 55, pp. 141, 143, 'Petra erat Christus. . . Petrus autem a petra; petra vero Ecclesia; ergo in Petri nomine figurata est Ecclesia'.

[3] For its use by St. Bernard see *Ep.*, ccli (*PL*, clxxxii. 451); *De consideratione*, II. viii. 16 and IV. vii. 23 (*PL*, clxxxii. 752, 788); *De moribus*, viii and ix (*PL*, clxxxii. 829, 832). The term was used by his pupil Eugenius III according to the curial officer's report in *MGH, SS*, xx. 543, and was brought into general use by Adrian IV: Ullmann, 'The Pontificate of Adrian IV', pp. 238–9.

that the concept was thoroughly analysed and given its most mature expression. Although, as we shall see, the papal vicariate idea in its final form represented a tremendous advance in the hierocratic theory, it rested upon the same Biblical foundation, the twin texts of *Matthew*, xvi. 18 and 19, which had always been the main support of the Roman primacy. *Matthew*, xvi. 19 was indeed particularly valuable in this respect. Not only did its famous 'Quodcunque' denote the universality and all-embracing nature of papal power, but the text as a whole illustrated the half-earthly and half-divine character of the *vicarius Christi*. By virtue of his vicariate the pope has the 'iura terreni *simul et coelestis* imperii':[1] that which he binds on earth is also bound in heaven. His earthly actions predetermine the judgement of heaven, so that what is done in heaven is in a sense dependent upon what is done on earth. For this reason the pope may have attributed to him a *coeleste arbitrium*,[2] the power to act in both aspects of the *Ecclesia, militans et triumphans*. Just as the earthly society is a reflection of heaven and intimately connected with it, so the cosmological unity of the universe is portrayed in Augustinus Triumphus' conception of the pope as ruler in heaven, earth and hell.

[1] Augustinus Triumphus, *De duplici potestate*, p. 488. This very popular phrase was used by Peter Damian and was included in Gratian, D. 22 c. 1, where it is attributed to Nicholas II. See further J. Rivière, *Le problème de l'Église et de l'État au temps de Philippe le Bel* (Louvain and Paris, 1926), Appendix I, pp. 387–93; B. Tierney, 'Some Recent Work on the Political Theories of the Medieval Canonists', *Traditio*, x (1954), pp. 594–625 at pp. 600–1. The phrase was sometimes interpreted in a weaker sense as meaning that the pope had both 'temporal and spiritual power'.

[2] Aegidius Spiritalis, *Libellus contra infideles*, p. 108, which was probably taken from Johannes Andreae on the *Decretales*, *ad* I. vii. 3. Cf. Tholemy of Lucca, *De regimine principum*, iii. 10, p. 259, 'Dominii vero amplitudo ostenditur cum subiungit Dominus, Et tibi dabo claves regni coelorum. In hoc enim insinuatur nobis potestas Petri et successorum suorum, quae se extendit ad totam Ecclesiam, scilicet militantem et triumphantem, quae per regnum coelorum designantur et quae clauduntur clavibus Petri. Sed dominii plenitudo ostenditur cum ultimo dicitur, Et quodcunque . . . et in coelis'; and the constitution *Ab exordio* of John Peckham, 'Quippe quos legum suarum Petrus ligat vinculis in summi et coelestis imperatoris palatio sunt ligati': cited Maitland, *Roman Canon Law*, p. 28 n. 3. Note also Gregory VII, *Reg.*, vii. 14a, p. 487, '. . . ut omnis mundus intellegat et cognoscat, quia, si potestis in coelo ligare et solvere, potestis in terra . . .'. Innocent IV had contented himself with a 'potentia iudicii' in heaven: Winkelmann, ii, n. 1035 p. 698.

Quamvis Dei Filius humani generis naturam assumens infirma mundi elegerit ut fortia quaeque confunderet, ecclesiasticae tamen potestatis altitudinem suos fideles latere noluit: quinimmo tamquam supra petram fundatam, ipsam esse supra omnem principatum et potestatem ut ei genua cuncta curventur coelestium, terrestrium et infernorum, verbis apertissimis declaravit.[1]

Not only does the power of the keys enable him to exclude the living from the earthly paradise,[2] but, declares Augustinus Triumphus, he can control their destiny after death through his manipulation of the spiritual treasury of the Church.[3] All souls in purgatory are *de foro papae*, and he may at any moment remove them from their awful abode.[4] He is the judge of the quick and the dead—'papa sit iudex vice Christi vivorum et mortuorum'[5]—to whom has been committed all power in heaven and earth.[6] It will therefore occasion no surprise when we learn that he is not only superior

[1] Augustinus Triumphus, *Summa*, *Dedicatio*; cf. Thomas Aquinas, *In symb. apost.*, ch. 9, 'sciendum est quod Ecclesia est catholica, id est universalis, primo quantum ad locum, quia est per totum mundum. . . Habet autem tres partes: una est in terra, alia est in coelo, tertia est in purgatorio'.

[2] Augustinus Triumphus, *Summa*, xx. 4, p. 124, 'Clavis Ecclesiae est potestas solvendi et ligandi et scientia, qua dignos debet recipere et indignos excludere a regno ecclesiasticus iudex'. This is taken from distinction 18 of the *Sentences* of Peter Lombard.

[3] Augustinus Triumphus, *Summa*, xviii. 1 ad 2, p. 113, 'papae committitur cura et custodia omnium universaliter, et hoc non solum dum vivunt, sicut committitur angelis, sed etiam post mortem per communicationem suffragiorum Ecclesiae'. See also Alvarus Pelagius, *De planctu Ecclesiae*, ch. 55, p. 143, who rather hesitantly acknowledges that the pope has the power to bind the dead as well as the living, taking Augustine as his authority.

[4] All this is discussed in *Summa*, xxix. 4, pp. 177–8, and xxxii. 1–4, pp. 190–6. His power appears to stop short at Limbo, xxxiii. 3–4, pp. 198–9. For a fuller account see Rivière, 'Une première "Somme"', pp. 169–70. Aegidius Romanus had considered the matter, but eventually decided against the pope's possession of this power: *De ecclesiastica potestate*, ii. 5, p. 58; iii. 9, p. 193; iii. 10, p. 196. This was still a matter for debate in the Augustinian Order throughout the remainder of the fourteenth and fifteenth centuries, and was a common canonistic principle: see for example Augustinus Favaroni and Petrus de Monte in Maccarrone, *op. cit.*, p. 266.

[5] Augustinus Triumphus, *Summa*, xlvi. 1, p. 249. This derives from Acts, x. 42, and had been used in this sense by Innocent III in *Decretales*, IV. xvii. 13, and Boniface VIII in *Extravagantes communes*, I. viii. 1.

[6] Matthew, xxviii. 18, 'Data est mihi omnis potestas in coelo et in terra': used by Augustinus Triumphus, *Summa*, i. 7, p. 11; xxxiii. 1, p. 136; *De duplici potestate*, p. 500, and by most of the other papalists.

to the angels,[1] but that he may, if he wishes, kick away his earthly footstool and govern the world from a celestial throne.[2]

All this would seem totally implausible if we failed to appreciate what Augustinus Triumphus is trying to say. When he describes the pope's earthly actions as binding heaven, when he pronounces the pope predestined, he is not suggesting that the power of God itself is thereby limited in any way. He is merely voicing his urgent desire to portray the divine nature and origin of papal power. Fundamentally the pope exists in God, that is to say, draws his being and power from Christ and acts by virtue of Christ's authority: 'in ipso enim vivimus et movemur et sumus'.[3] When the pope acts it is really Christ himself who is acting: the visible vicariate is essentially an *instrumentum Dei*,[4] a means by which God may antedate in time

[1] Augustinus Triumphus, *Summa*, xix. 2, p. 118, 'Christus principaliter et papa, qui est vicarius eius, *instrumentaliter* convenit esse caput Ecclesiae. Primo quidem quia in situ habet eminentiam. Tenet enim supremum gradum non solum super homines sed etiam super angelos. Unde ad *Ephes.* i [22–3], statim cum dixit apostolus, Omnia subiecit sub pedibus eius, subiunxit, Ipsum dedit caput super omnem Ecclesiam quae est corpus eius'; ix. 4 ad 3, p. 75, 'Christus . . . est dominus et caput hominum et angelorum, cuius vicarius papa existit'; xviii. 1, p. 113, 'Maior est iurisdictio papae quam cuiuslibet angeli. . . Nulli ergo angelo commissa est iurisdictio et cura totius orbis, sed papae totius mundi iurisdictio et cura commissa est, non solum ut nomine mundi importetur terra, sed *etiam* ut nomine mundi importetur *coelum*, quia super coelum et terram iurisdictionem accepit'. Alvarus Pelagius on the other hand was careful to emphasise that the papal vicariate was more limited: *De planctu Ecclesiae*, ch. 58, p. 165, it does not extend 'nec ad omnes huiusmodi creaturas, quia non ad angelos sed solum ad homines, nec ad hos omnes sed solum ad viatores.' The question of papal jurisdiction over angels was still being hotly disputed by the Augustinians in the fifteenth century: Maccarrone, *op. cit.*, p. 266. For relevant literature on the idea of the ruler as a *character angelicus* see *KTB*, p. 8.

[2] Augustinus Triumphus, *Summa*, xxi. 1, p. 126, 'Papa non necessitatur residere in aliquo determinato loco, quia vicarius est illius cuius sedes coelum est et terra scabellum eius pedum, ut scribitur *Isaiae*, lxvi [6]. Implet enim coelum et terram sua potestate et iurisdictione, ut scribitur *Hiere.*, xxiii [24]'. This may have been intended as a rebuff for Dante, *Monarchia*, iii. 7, p. 368, who had denied the pope's equality to Christ on this basis. There were however Byzantine and Ottonian precedents for this description of the ruler as elevated to heaven: see *KTB*, pp. 62–73, who suggests Augustine's commentary on *Psalm* xc as the immediate source of this idea.

[3] *Acts*, xvii. 28: Augustinus Triumphus, *Summa*, xxxvi. 6, p. 217. For its use by Clement V see above p. 167 n. 3.

[4] Augustinus Triumphus, *Summa*, xix. 2 ad 1, p. 118. The idea of the pope as instrument and agent of Christ as principal is basically Leonine: H. M. Klinkenberg, 'Papsttum und Reichskirche', *ZSSR, Kan. Abt.*, xxxviii (1952), pp. 37f.

the judgements which he will give in heaven. The *vicarius Christi* is simply a projection of God, who is spirit, on to the earthly plane. For all practical purposes, and as far as mankind is concerned, the pope is Christ himself. What can be said of one, as Alexander of S. Elpidio points out, may logically be said of the other, since they are essentially one and the same thing.

Hoc est nomen quod vocabunt eum: Dominus iustus noster, *Hier.*, xxiii [6]. Verba ista, quae dicta sunt de Domino nostro Iesu Christo, convenienter exponi possunt de quolibet ipsius generali vicario, qui sic suas vices expresse gerit in terris ut plerumque quod de ipso scribitur convenienter de ipsius vicario possit exponi.[1]

The pope then is God in human form, a reincarnation of Christ. Yet the fact that he is incarnate emphasises that he is also a man, and for Augustinus Triumphus this is an equally necessary part of the *vicarius Christi* idea. The incorporeal may rule the corporeal, but it may do so only through the medium of the latter. The divine ruler must also be a human being.

Tertio hoc patet ex parte Christi cuius auctoritate papa super fideles *fungitur*. Nam qui constituitur aliorum caput et rector debet esse eiusdem naturae cum eis et eiusdem conversationis in vita.[2]

Moreover this unique character of the pope as a mixture of the human and the divine denotes his function as the mediator between

This concept of the pope as *organon*, the earthly *instrumentum divinitatis*, emerges much more clearly however in the thirteenth century when the Aristotelian roots of the idea were combined with a similar Byzantine idea deriving through John of Damascus: E. H. Kantorowicz, 'Mysteries of State: An Absolutist Concept and its Late Medieval Origins', *Harvard Theological Review*, xlviii (1955), pp. 65–91 at p. 89.

[1] Alexander de S. Elpidio, *De ecclesiastica potestate*, *proem.*, p. 2. The same is often implied by the use of a singular verb for the pope and Christ taken together: e.g. Anon., *Disquisitio theologico-iuridica*, ii. 11, p. 1348, 'Christus et eius vicarius *est* in medio totius populi christiani sicut medi*us* perfectissim*us*'; cf. Augustinus Triumphus, *Summa*, ix. 1, p. 72, 'Una est potestas Christi secundum quod Deus et papae'. One of the accusations made against John XXII was 'quod Lucibel voluit esse similis Deo et iste papa voluit esse similis Iesu Christo; item quod Lucibel voluit esse similis Deo in sua potestate seu potentia, et iste papa voluit esse similis Deo in sua sapientia vel scientia': W. H. May, 'The Confession of Prous Boneta, Heretic and Heresiarch', *Essays in Medieval Life and Thought* (ed. Mundy, Emery and Nelson, New York, 1955), pp. 3–30 at p. 13.

[2] Augustinus Triumphus, *Summa*, ii. 1, p. 18.

God and man. The knowledge of God's will, of the right way of life, is, since it is divine knowledge, existent on another plane of Reality: it can only reach and operate on the terrestrial level through an earthly agent.[1] This agency is the vicariate of Christ, the link between the material and spiritual spheres, situated at the point at which they meet. The symbolic representation of St. Peter's power as keys, the *claves scientiae et potentiae*, serves to emphasise the papal guardianship of this connection: as the vicar of Christ the pope is the keeper of the gateway which joins heaven and earth.[2] And it is for this reason that the vicar of Christ must appear in hierocratic thought as both God and man,[3] or, more accurately, as a divine power united to a human being. In the same way that Christ himself on earth had been a spiritual essence which took to itself a human form, so now the papal vicariate must be seen in terms of a distinction between the vicariate itself and the man who possesses it. As Augustinus Triumphus himself puts it, 'potest ab ipsa persona vel illa separari papatus'.[4] Indeed a clear conception of the difference between the power and the man is fundamental to

[1] Augustinus Triumphus, *Summa*, ix. 1, p. 72, 'Convenit ergo creatori et creaturae potestas et dominio et multa alia, ut bonitas, scientia et iustitia, quae attribuuntur Deo tamen conveniunt creaturae, Deo quidam *essentialiter*, creaturae vero participative et *ministerialiter* et *instrumentaliter*'.

[2] Augustinus Triumphus, *Summa*, iii. 8, p. 36, 'Christus post resurrectionem non est executus talem potestatem nisi mediante papa; licet enim ipse sit ostium, Petrum tamen et successores eius constituit ostiarios mediantibus quibus aperitur et clauditur ianua intrandi ad ipsum'; xx. 1, p. 122, 'iuxta illud *Ioan.*, x [9], Ego sum ostium; si quis per me introierit salvabitur. Clavigerum autem Petrum et omnes successores eius ordinavit . . . qui beato Petro aeternae vitae clavigero terreni simul et coelestis imperii iura commisit. Praeest ergo papa Ecclesiae per potestatem clavium'; also Conrad of Megenberg, *Oeconomica*, III. iii. 1 (Kaeppeli, p. 586), 'papa . . . portarius sive ianitor coeli'. Cf. *Luke*, xi. 52.

[3] Augustinus Triumphus, *Summa*, i. 1 ad 2, p. 3, 'verum est potestatem imperialem esse a Deo, quia non est a papa ut est homo, sed est a papa ut gerit vicem Christi in terra, qui est verus Deus et verus homo'; Anon., *Disquisitio theologico-iuridica*, ii. 7, p. 1345, 'Christi autem vicarius habet naturam principis secundum naturam principatus Christi, qui tam ratione *deitatis* quam ratione unite *humanitatis* princeps est generalissimus omnium temporalium et spiritualium'. Cf. Boniface VIII, *MGH*, *Const.*, IV, i. n. 173 p. 140, 'Christus homini et Christi vicario dedit potestatem'.

[4] Augustinus Triumphus, *Summa*, iv. 3, p. 42; cf. Peter Olivi, *De renuntiatione papae*, p. 359, 'potestas papae potest considerari vel secundum se . . . vel potest considerari per respectum ad personam in qua est'.

the vicariate idea, and it was the development of a distinction between the office and the holder which did much to make possible the elaboration of the *vicarius Christi* theory. By the second half of the twelfth century lay writers were beginning to express this idea in the form of a division between the *persona regis* and the *corona regni*, and during the thirteenth century it was firmly established in political thought that kingship was an office. Aquinas, for example, repeatedly refers to the *officium regis* rather than the king himself,[1] and both he and other writers had been greatly assisted by the old Roman law separation of the public and private capacities of the ruler.[2] All this had however been long foreshadowed in the recognition of a difference between the pope and the Roman church. It was the Petrine see which, in earlier hierocratic theory, had been the recipient of Christ's commission of power,[3] and it was by his spiritual marriage to the Roman church that each individual pope was able to gain possession of it. Consequently it had been common practice to draw a distinction between the *sedens* and his

[1] See for example the *De regimine principum*, i. 7–13, pp. 230–6. For the distinction between the king and his crown see further F. Hartung, 'Die Krone als Symbol der monarchischen Herrschaft im ausgehenden Mittelalter', *Abhandlungen der Preussischen Akademie der Wissenschaften, Phil.-hist. Kl., Jahr* 1940 (Berlin, 1941), xi; Riesenberg, *Inalienability of Sovereignty*, pp. 95–104; for further examples and literature *KTB*, pp. 336–83, and for the classical background pp. 496–505.

[2] E.g. Thomas Aquinas, *Summa theologica*, II. II. lxvii. 2; Tholemy of Lucca, *De regimine principum*, ii. 6, p. 250, 'princeps etiam sicut privata persona . . . amplius autem in quantum dominus;' and note the distinction in Aegidius Romanus, *De ecclesiastica potestate*, i. 2, pp. 6–8, between a personal condition and one 'secundum statum qui consistit in iurisdictione et in plenitudine potentiae'; also the use of *persona publica* and *persona privata* by Augustinus Triumphus, e.g. *Summa*, lx. 3 ad 2, p. 315. In 1298 it had been suggested that Boniface VIII should act in a private capacity, not as pope, to arbitrate between the French and English kings: Rivière, *Le problème de l'Église et de l'État*, p. 102.

[3] Innocent IV, Winkelmann, ii. 697, 'Dominus enim Iesus Christus . . . *in apostolica sede* non solum pontificalem sed et regalem constituit monarchatum'; Boniface VIII, Dupuy, p. 182, 'Super *Petri* solio excelso *throno* divina dispositione *sedentes*, illius vices gerimus cui per patrem dicitur, Filius meus es tu, et ego hodie genui te, postula a me, et dabo tibi gentes haereditatem tuam et possessionem tuam terminos terrae. . . Sed licet tanta potestate sit praedita *Petri sedes*, tantaque polleat dignitate'. Cf. Peter Olivi, *Quaestio de infallibilitate*, p. 337, 'unde potius verba [of the Petrine commission] videntur referri ad *officium* et ad auctoritatem et *sedem* ipsius'.

sedes as far back as the tenth and eleventh centuries, if not earlier.[1] When the Petrine power came to be seen as constituting nothing less than a visible vicariate of Christ, when the pope was no longer the vicar of a man but of God,[2] there was a natural transition from this old distinction between the sitter and the see[3] into the new one between the *papatus* or vicariate of Christ and the individual pope.

The medieval notion that legislation must be the act of someone holding public office in the community thus finds full expression in the papal-hierocratic conception of the vicariate of Christ. The Bernardine view that the pope is God by virtue of his office rather than his personal qualifications[4] is reflected in the repeated emphasis laid by the fourteenth-century publicists on the fact that the pope does not possess his power by personal right but through the office of the vicariate in which the power resides. As Augustinus Triumphus says, 'Papa . . . non vice sua sed vice Dei universalem iurisdictionem habet in toto orbe'.[5] It is this office which, according

[1] See for example Auxilius at the beginning of the tenth century: *Infensor et defensor*, ch. 18 (*PL*, cxxix. 1089), and *De ordinationibus papae Formosi*, ch. 35 (*PL*, cxxix. 1073), 'Aliud sunt pontificales sedes, aliud praesidentes'. The schismatic cardinals of 1084 has also referred to the difference between the *sedes* and the *sedens*, *MGH*, *Lib. de Lit.*, ii 418. Similarly Huguccio, *ad* D. 19 c. 2, 'Hoc non fit ratione papae sed propter auctoritatem sedis unde caute dixit apostolicae sedis et non dixit apostolici': Tierney, *Foundations of the Conciliar Theory*, p. 79; and for a later example Zabarella, *ad Sext.*, I. iii. 5, 'Aliud autem papa, aliud sedes apostolica': Ullmann, *Origins of the Great Schism*, p. 200.

[2] E.g. Innocent III, *Reg.*, I. cccxxvi (*PL*, ccxiv. 292), 'non homo quia non vicarius hominis, sed Deus quia vicarius Dei'; Guilielmus Durantis, *Speculum iuris*, I. i. 51, 'Ipse est successor Petri et vicarius Iesu Christi, vicem non puri hominis sed veri Dei gerens in terris'.

[3] This distinction is however still common in the fourteenth century: e.g. Peter de la Palu, *De causa immediata ecclesiasticae potestatis*, iv. 2, fo. 49, 'Sed potestas papae . . . non acquiritur per *personalem* consecrationem, sed eo ipso quo aliquis est *in sede* acquirit et habet illam potestatem, et eo ipso *sedem* perdit, potestatem perdit quae semper remanet *in ipsa sede* quae non moritur'.

[4] St. Bernard, Mansi, xxi. 468–9, 'Praeter Deum non est similis ei nec in coelo nec in terra. . . Secundum officium dico, non secundum meritum'. This itself follows Augustine, *Quaestiones ex Veteri Testamento*, ch. 11 (*PL*, xxxv. 2223), 'quia officii dignitas est, non hominis meritum quam Dei sequitur benedictio'.

[5] Augustinus Triumphus, *Summa*, xlv. 2 ad 3, p. 248; cf. John of Naples, 'potestas imperialis dicitur esse concessa a Deo quia est concessa a papa non in quantum est homo sed in quantum est vicarius Dei in terris': Maccarrone, *op. cit.*, p. 178.

to Peter de la Palu, is 'that by which the pope is pope',[1] and consequently, adds Alexander of S. Elpidio, it is the office which is holy, not the man himself.[2] Augustinus Triumphus is particularly careful to stress that, although the same honour should be paid to the pope as to God and his saints, this honour is not to be paid to the pope personally but as a participator in the power which is common to both God and his office.[3] Conversely, since it is the office which is the essence of the papal position, the function of *vicarius Christi* which is all-important, personal considerations are of little concern to him. As vicar the pope assumes the perfect nature and power of Christ: with the change from his personal to his papal name, as Lambertus Guerrici de Hoyo says, the office makes a new man of him.

Ipse dominus papa, quando fuit elevatus dispositione divina ad apicem omnium Ecclesiae dignitatum, fuerit quasi in alium hominem, quod denotari credo per mutationem nominis, commutatus.[4]

[1] Peter de la Palu, *De causa immediata ecclesiasticae potestatis*, iv. 1, fo. 46v, 'Papa, in eo quo papa, habet plenitudinem potestatis'; cf. Alexander de S. Elpidio, *De ecclesiastica potestate*, iii. 7, p. 37, 'Sed potestas papalis non debetur personae sed debetur statui'. The distinction is frequently seen in terms of the philosophical separation of matter (person) and form (office): e.g. Aegidius Spiritalis, *Libellus contra infideles*, p. 125, 'cum forma principatus sit virtus per quam praesidet princeps': on the further use of this see below pp. 374, 493f.

[2] Alexander de S. Elpidio, *De ecclesiastica potestate*, i. 10, p. 11, 'Nam etsi persona possit esse non sancta, semper tamen sanctissimus appellabitur ratione status quem tenet, a quo omnis sanctitas in Ecclesia derivatur'.

[3] Augustinus Triumphus, *Summa*, ix. 1, p. 72, 'quia honor debetur potestati', and it would be idolatry to pay this honour to the pope personally, ix. 2, p. 73. This was by no means a new idea: it can for example be found with the Anglo-Norman Anonymous, *Tractatus Eboracenses*, iv (*MGH, Lib. de Lit.*, iii. 671), 'Reddite potestati, non personae. Persona enim iniqua, sed iusta potestas'; and see further examples in *KTB*, pp. 55–8.

[4] Lambertus Guerrici de Hoyo, *Liber de commendatione*, ch. 12, p. 164. In 1206 Innocent III had stated that the pope changed his name to symbolise his acceptance of the 'officium apostolicae servitutis' and became 'quasi mutatum in virum alterum': *Reg.*, IX. cxxxvi (*PL*, ccxv. 955). The idea of a rebirth by coronation had also been used by the Anglo-Norman Anonymous, *MGH, Lib. de Lit.*, iii. 664–5; and in the fourteenth century was applied to Charles V of France by Jean Golein: Bloch, *Les rois thaumaturges*, p. 483; and to the emperor Charles IV by Petrarch: Bayley, 'Petrarch, Charles IV and the *Renovatio Imperii*', p. 333. The idea is of Byzantine origin: Bloch, *op. cit.*, pp. 198, 476.

The mystical union of God with his church which takes place with the election of the pope can, as *Luke*, i. 35 proclaims, produce nothing but a holy thing. When there is a new occupant of the papal office, it either receives a saint or, so it must be believed, makes him one: 'papa enim aut sanctus est, aut sanctus praesumendus est'.[1] However bad the man himself, his power is and must remain unpolluted, so that the pope in his official capacity can do no wrong.[2] By comparison with his great function his personal characteristics and deeds are irrelevant. This point is very well illustrated by Augustinus Triumphus. So long as the papal candidate will make a good governor for the Christian society it does not really matter what he is like.[3] He can perfectly well commit simony or fornication, in fact any mortal sin except heresy, without thereby becoming any the less a true pope. For these are private actions, not the actions of a pope in his official role as vicar of Christ.[4] Logically, he points

[1] Alvarus Pelagius, *De planctu Ecclesiae*, ch. 35, p. 37; cf. ch. 54, p. 139, 'Nam etsi persona quae praeest possit non esse sancta . . . locus et status est sanctus'; Aegidius Romanus, *De ecclesiastica potestate*, i. 2, p. 9, 'Ideo dicimus de illa sede quod vel sanctum recipit vel sanctum facit'. Note also Gregory VII, *Dictatus papae*, c. 23, 'Quod Romanus pontifex, si canonice fuerit ordinatus, meritis beati Petri indubitanter efficitur sanctus'; cf. Gratian, D. 40 cc. 1–2. Augustine had maintained that a man's previous sins became irrelevant when he assumed the headship of the *Ecclesia: Contra Faustum*, xxii. 70 (*PL*, xlii. 455; *CSEL*, xxv. 667–8), 'Quid ergo incongruum si Petrus post hoc peccatum factus est pastor Ecclesiae, sicut Moyses post percussum Aegyptium factus est rector illius synagogae?'

[2] The same principle had been expressed by John of Viterbo, *De regimine civitatum*, ch. 128, p. 266, 'Unde etsi pollutus est sacerdos, sibi pollutus est: officium autem pollui non potest, quia a Deo est'; cf. Alvarus Pelagius, *De planctu Ecclesiae*, ch. 8, p. 28, 'Quod dignitas vel iurisdictio vel potestas non peccat, etsi iudex vel praelatus *in ea residens* sicut homo peccare valeat. Et hoc ideo quia omnis iurisdictio et dignitas de se bona est et a Deo est': to illustrate this he quotes the example of a bad priest whose sacraments do not lose their validity for this reason, ch. 9, p. 28. The view that sacraments given by a bad priest lose their validity was a common Joachist contention: for its application to John XXII see May, *art. cit.*, p. 15.

[3] Augustinus Triumphus, *Summa*, iii. 4, p. 31, merely stipulates that he should be 'sufficiens', but adds, iii. 6, p. 34, that the choice may very well fall upon one of the cardinals because 'Assumptum enim de collegio plenius novit consuetum usum et consuetam iurisdictionem potestatis clavium'.

[4] Augustinus Triumphus, *Summa*, xxix. 3, p. 177. Cf. Innocent III, *Consec. serm.*, iv (*PL*, ccxvii. 670), 'Verum aliud est evanescere in agendis, et aliud est evanescere in credendis'.

out, the distinction should make it possible for the pope to wipe ou
the stain of a bad personal action by granting indulgences to him
self, granting as pope, receiving as man:

Papa potest dare indulgentiam sibiipsi . . . sed ut est membrum Ecclesia
recipit et ut est caput dat.[1]

But, be that as it may, the important thing is his performance of hi
public, governmental function, and in that function there should b
little to choose between one pope and another, since it is the sam
for all. For this reason personalities become almost incidental t
what is essentially the history of the papacy. By virtue of assumin
the same office all popes have an identical policy, which individual
simply implement to a greater or lesser degree.

By the fourteenth century the concept of office is acknowledge
to be fundamental to the theory of the papacy. It is in his office, or
perhaps we should say, by possession of the power contained in hi
office, that the ruler becomes equated with God. The hierocrati
writers are also insistent, if not always consistent, in maintainin
that the office absorbs the individual and for legal purposes obliter
ates his personal character. The divinity of the pope's officia
capacity smothers his human personality: the presence of grace, th
Augustinian repeated, must deny the importance of nature. Theo
retically it remains possible to consider the pope as having a dua
personality, official and individual, but to all intents and purposes h
is to be regarded as one with his see or office. As the papalist phrase
it, the spiritual marriage of the pope to the Roman church is indis
soluble: hence the distinction does not have practical significanc
and cannot detract from the papal position. We may at a later dat
query the wisdom of overrationalising, or even of rationalising a
all, something that was essentially a divine mystery, but it is eviden
that the contemporary publicist was only too pleased to have formulated a theory which would explain how a human being becam
divine. Once the pope was totally identifiable with his functio

[1] Augustinus Triumphus, *Summa*, xxix. 2, p. 176. The Colonna family seem
to have made a point of denying this: Aegidius Romanus, *De renuntiatione papae*
xiv, p. 39; James and Peter Colonna, *Memorandum*, i. 511; but there wer
Roman and Byzantine precedents for this in the emperor who gave and receive
sacrifices as Pontifex Maximus: *KTB*, pp. 61, 501.

there could be no reason for seeing him as anything but God incarnate. He becomes transformed into a completely different being, and this belief is reflected in the care with which the papalists chose their words. He is not simply this pope or that, but the *vicarius* or *apostolicus*, signifying that he bears the supreme official position in the community. This position is covered by a wide range of terms —*officium*, *papatus*, *dignitas*, *status*, *apostolatus*, *vicariatus* and so forth —but each is intended to convey the idea of office: the papal *nomen* or title is as much a symbol of office as his *regalia* or *corona*. Moreover these symbols are applicable to both the office itself and to the whole society. We have already mentioned that for Henry of Cremona the papal tiara 'designates' both papal power and the ordering of the community at large, just as the term 'crown' with the lay writers was coming to represent the corporate character of the kingdom itself.[1] Since it is through his office that the pope becomes the earthly Christ, that he becomes the human embodiment of the mystical *persona Ecclesiae*, the papal office comes to stand for the whole *congregatio fidelium* itself. The juridical personality of the community is located in the office of the head, so that a common terminology may be employed to represent either the papal office or the *Ecclesia universalis*. Hence the *status* of the pope, meaning his office, is a term which comes in course of time to apply to the whole political organism. Other examples are not wanting. It is a commonplace with the publicists that the phrase *ecclesia Romana*, which initially applies to the papal *sedes* or office, may also be used of the whole body of Christians. When a hierocratic writer speaks of the Roman church it is often extremely difficult to know whether he is using the expression in a universal or capital sense, and most of them appreciated the difficulty enough to give explanations. Following Innocent III's classic definition of 1199,[2] Hermannus de Schildiz points out that the *nomen* of the Roman church can refer equally to the entire corporation or its headship alone:

. . . est considerandum quod nomine Romanae et apostolicae ecclesiae consueverunt sancti patres et doctores uti dupliciter: uno modo ut distinguitur contra omnem haereticorum vel scismaticorum congregation-

[1] See above p. 34.   [2] Innocent III, *Reg.*, II. ccix (*PL*, ccxiv. 763).

em, et sic includit omnes ecclesias et omnes fideles. . . Alio modo accipitur Romana et apostolica ecclesia ut distinguitur contra omnem ecclesiam cui non immediate praesidet pontifex Romanus, et sic includit solum ea quae pertinent ad rationem capitis.[1]

The pope, by becoming the physical manifestation of the abstract corporate personality, acts *in nomine Ecclesiae*, a situation which is portrayed by the use of the name of his office for the whole community. Conversely the descriptive terms applied to the society in general may be used with reference to the papal office alone. A case in point is that of the *corpus mysticum*, a term generally used to refer to the whole *Ecclesia* as it forms a single juristic entity identifiable with Christ. But since the *vicarius Christi* represents this mystical entity and therefore the whole body of Christians, the mystical body may be used with reference to him alone. In his official capacity the pope becomes the only living embodiment of the *corpus mysticum*, and in this way all Christians are *pars corporis sui*, part of the body of the pope. But once again it is emphasised that it is only in his official capacity that the pope possesses the *corpus mysticum*. As various writers during the early part of the thirteenth century had been at pains to demonstrate, the expression was not to be used even of Christ himself without discrimination. Christ is man as well as God: in addition to his divine, mystical nature he also possessed a natural, human aspect. In other words he had a double body, a *corpus duplex*, one side of which referred to him as an individual—his personal or natural body—and the other to his corporate nature, that mystical body formed by all the faithful in Christ.[2] As a human person he had merely a *corpus naturale*: but in that he represents all Christians on the heavenly level he has also a *corpus mysticum*, an official capacity as *caput Ecclesiae*. It is this latter capacity which is now exercised by his vicar on earth. In respect to the Christian society both the pope and Christ wield the same func-

[1] Hermannus de Schildiz, *Contra haereticos*, ch. 7, p. 134; also Hervaeus Natalis, *De potestate papae*, fo. 150, 'omnis gradus in Ecclesia instituit ecclesia Romana, non prout ecclesia Romana accipitur pro universali Ecclesia . . . sed accipitur specialiter pro sede [Petri]'.

[2] Lubac, *Corpus Mysticum*, pp. 116–29, 185; and for its later development in lay thought F. W. Maitland, 'The Crown as Corporation', *Selected Essays*, pp. 103–27; and now *KTB*, *passim*. For the Pauline basis see I *Cor.*, xv. 35–50.

tion, and accordingly both may be seen as having a dual capacity or a double body: they are God and man, officer and individual.

Whilst the theologians of the years around 1200 had limited themselves to speaking of Christ alone in this context, a century later the publicists were taking it for granted that any description of Christ could be applied to his vicar. This reflects the growing confidence in the pope's divinity engendered by the assimilation of the *vicarius Christi* theory. Indeed Augustinus Triumphus uses the difference between the pope as vicar of Peter and the pope now seen as vicar of Christ to give weight to his assertion that he becomes a direct replacement of God on earth. If we choose to regard the pope as a man, he argues, then he will appear as no more than the most recent of a long line of human individuals, beginning with St. Peter, who have held the papal office. In this personal and individual sense the pope is only a successor of Peter. But in his official capacity he has taken over the function of Christ himself, and may be accounted as no less than his direct successor.

Papa succedit Petro in personali administratione... Christo autem succedit in officio et in universali iurisdictione, quia Petrus in persona omnium summorum pontificum recepit universalem iurisdictionem a Christo.[1]

It is this similarity of functions which the publicists—and most of them now spoke of the pope as *successor Christi*—wished to convey. Christ, explains Alexander of S. Elpidio, is not only the founder of the Church but also its governor, and it is Christ 'qui eam etiam continuo regit et dirigit per successores suos'.[2] The pope in office, according to Aegidius Romanus, is simply a substitute for his departed original: Christ still rules 'per vicarium vel per substitutum vel per interpositam personam'.[3] Nor was the introduction of this particular phrase a complete innovation at the time. As far back as 1133 Arnold of Lisieux had referred to the pope as the successor of Christ,[4] and by the end of the twelfth century it was becoming a

[1] Augustinus Triumphus, *Summa*, xix. 4, pp. 119–20; cf. Alvarus Pelagius, *De planctu Ecclesiae*, ch. 68, p. 247, 'Unde nec in hoc [scil. ut homo] papa Christo succedit; succedit enim in potentia'.

[2] Alexander de S. Elpidio, *De ecclesiastica potestate*, ii. 1, p. 14.

[3] Aegidius Romanus, *De ecclesiastica potestate*, ii. 14, p. 135.

[4] Maccarrone, *op. cit.*, p. 94.

familiar expression with the canonists. Huguccio, for example, had pointed out that the vicariate of Christ made the pope a substitute for Christ, and his pupil, Innocent III, had followed suit.[1] But it was Innocent IV who seems to have been the first to make the equation of vicar and successor into official doctrine. As he told Frederick II, imperial power derives 'a Christi vicario, successore videlicet Christi',[2] and the emperor could hardly dissent from the principle when Roman law emphasised the identity of predecessor and successor in office and equated the power of a vicar with his prototype. As Tholemy of Lucca acknowledged, the first book of the Justinian Code specifically states that he who acts in place of another must be able to do the same as the one whom he represents. If the pope is the vicar of Christ, then he must have the power which Christ himself had possessed, namely, full power over the whole human race.[3] Tholemy, it must be admitted, seems to have been trying to convince himself as much as anybody else, and he was by no means always so certain on this point. For although the idea of the pope as *successor Christi* becomes traditional hierocratic theory, the papal attempt to argue that a vicar was equal to his originator fell far short of gaining universal approval. Whereas for Augustinus

[1] Huguccio, 'Item a vice vicarius . . . vel per vices succedens, vel vicem domini vel alterius agens'; Innocent III, 'quia [Petrum] in officio vicarium sibi substituit Dominus': Maccarrone, *op. cit.*, pp. 118, 110.

[2] Winkelmann, ii. 697. This was of course followed by Hostiensis, *Summa ad* IV. xvii. 13, 'Nec mirum quia Christus reliquit ipsum successorem seu vicarium' and becomes a very familiar expression in the fourteenth and fifteenth centuries: e.g. Turrecremata, *Summa de Ecclesia*, ii. 40 (Venice, 1561, fo. 154v), 'Vicarius, id est successor illius, vel vicarius, id est vicariam potestatem quam ipse Petrus gessit tenens sive exercens'. The general principle that a vicar has the same power as his original is constantly stated: e.g. Alvarus Pelagius, *De planctu Ecclesiae*, ch. 59, p. 179, 'cum aliquis dicitur alicuius vicarius in officio seu potestate insinuatur potestas in eo non diminuta sed aequalis'; cf. Boniface VIII in *Sextus, De reg. iur.*, c. 43.

[3] Tholemy of Lucca, *Determinatio compendiosa*, ch. 25, pp. 47–8, 'De natura vero vicarii ordinarii, qui per electionem constituitur, quam lex ponit c. *De officio eius* [*Cod.*, I. l. 2], qui alterius gerit vices est quod idem possit quod ille cuius vices gerit. . . Ex hoc ergo argumento concluditur quod si papa est vicarius Christi, quod nullus nisi desipians contradicit, cum Christus . . . plenam habeat potestatem super totum genus humanum, manifestum est eius vicarium, scilicet summum pontificem, eandem potestatem habere'. On the Roman law theory of the vicar see further Maccarrone, *op. cit.*, pp. 122–3; Ercole, *Da Bartolo all' Althusio*, p. 157.

Triumphus the vicar was less than Christ only in that his office was limited in time, and would become superfluous when Christ once again took over the reins of government in person,[1] the whole idea of the absolute equality of the pope with Christ raises a chorus of horrified protests not only, as might be expected, from the lay writers,[2] but also from the followers of Aquinas.[3] Can the pope really work miracles? If so, why does he not show us a few examples?[4] He cannot read the thoughts of one's own conscience,[5]

[1] Augustinus Triumphus, *Summa*, i. 9, pp. 13–14; cf. Alexander de S. Elpidio, *De ecclesiastica potestate*, ii. 1, p. 14, 'quia talis potestas similis et aequalis in successoribus continuata est et continuabitur per Dei gratiam usque *in diem iudicii* . . . ut secundum hoc congrue verbum Christi *ad universalem Ecclesiam*, Et vobiscum sum omnibus diebus usque ad consumationem saeculi [*Matthew*, xxviii. 20], exponi possit pro successoribus suis, quia qui per alium facit, per seipsum facere videtur. Quilibet enim successor, licet non sit idem secundum *personam*, potest tamen dici idem secundum *potentiam*'. Note the Thomistic assumption in this passage that Christ's words apply equally to the pope and to the whole *congregatio fidelium* through the apostolic succession of the bishops.

[2] The most common argument is that as Peter was granted no temporal power, no vicar can be considered equal to Christ: e.g. William of Ockham, *Consultatio de causa matrimoniali*, p. 284, 'Dicitur itaque quod quamvis Romanus episcopus sit vicarius Christi, non successor proprie, et ideo Christo in potestate sit inaequalis, cum potestas vicarii potestate illius cuius vices gerit non debet adaequari'; *Tractatus pro rege Angliae*, ch. 4, p. 243, 'papa non habet potestatem tantam quantam habuit Christus, licet papa est vicarius Christi'; also Dante, *Monarchia*, iii. 3, p. 364. This debate certainly extends back to the mid-thirteenth century: Maccarrone, *op. cit.*, pp. 143–4, 152–3.

[3] Most of the Thomists accept the equation in one (hierocratic) breath and deny it with the (Thomist) other: e.g. Aegidius Romanus, *De ecclesiastica potestate*, iii. 9, p. 193; *De renuntiatione papae*, xxi, p. 52; Tholemy of Lucca, *De regimine principum*, iii. 15, p. 264; James of Viterbo, *De regimine christiano*, ii. 9, pp. 269–70, 310.

[4] Dante, *Monarchia*, iii. 7, p. 368; Anon., *Rex pacificus*, ch. 4, p. 676. According to Tierney, *Foundations of the Conciliar Theory*, p. 200, the canonist Guilielmus de Monte Lauduno denied that the pope could turn black into white, but against this some canonists expressly claimed that the pope could work miracles: e.g. Johannes Andreae, *ad Decretales*, I. vii. 3, 'et ideo naturam rerum immutat, substantia unius rei applicando alii . . . et de nullo potest aliquid facere'; and further examples in Ullmann, *Medieval Papalism*, pp. 50–2. James of Viterbo, *De regimine christiano*, ii. 1–3, pp. 163, 168, 172, and Alvarus Pelagius, *De planctu Ecclesiae*, ch. 51, p. 124, said that the power to work miracles had been granted to Peter and his successors in the Early Church, but that it had now been abandoned as unnecessary.

[5] Zabarella, *Lect. super primo Decret.*, 'Septimo nota quod papa non gerit vicem Dei in cognoscendo conscientiam': Maccarrone, *op. cit.*, p. 239.

and surely he is unable to grant sacramental grace without the use of the sacraments, or revoke the indelible character of sacramental power?[1] As Alvarus Pelagius said, even the Bible does not tell us everything, but only those things necessary for us to achieve salvation. Nor then does the pope as a living evangelical oracle need to have the complete power of Christ himself.[2] Underlying these qualifications is a very different attitude towards the papacy from that assumed by the orthodox papalist. Both hierocrat and moderate regarded the pope as the *instrumentum Christi*, and were able to describe him as such in almost identical language. But there is a subtle differentiation which reveals a very wide difference of approach towards the matter. For the hierocrat the instrument becomes the reality in its earthly form: it is nothing more than a corporeal mask for the Deity, and may for all practical purposes be made identical with God himself. Applied to the papal office the theory of instrumentality means simply that the vicariate of Christ becomes the earthly divinity: the reality swamps the instrumentality. But for many of the publicists an instrument is essentially something used by another without necessarily gaining identity with the user: the instrument and its operator may not be the same thing. Thus the papal office remains the *instrumentum Dei*, the link with God, but it does not contain God himself, however much his power operates through it. Papal acts continue to have a divine effect, but without thereby implying the divinity of the papacy itself. To claim more was running counter to the philosophic trend of the times. Whilst extreme realism applied to the sacraments required the actual manifestation, the real presence of Christ, in the mass, so in the later Middle Ages moderate realism was reacting in favour of the sacraments as *instrumenta deitatis*, things through which God operated without requiring that God should himself be actually present on the altar. Similarly the idea of the Church as an instrument of salvation was changing its meaning: it no longer suggested that the society of the faithful was actually heaven on

[1] Anon., *Rex pacificus*, ch. 4, p. 676; Aegidius Romanus, *De renuntiatione papae*, x. 7, p. 30; xiv, pp. 38–9; Alexander de S. Elpidio, *De ecclesiastica potestate*, i. 4, p. 6.

[2] Alvarus Pelagius, *De planctu Ecclesiae*, ch. 58, pp. 164–6.

earth, but merely a means by which heaven could be attained. And since there is the closest possible relationship between sacramental, ecclesiastical and papal theory—the sacraments, the *Ecclesia* and the pope could all, for example, be covered by the term *corpus Christi*—it is understandable that there was a considerable amount of interaction between them. The net result was to confine God to heaven without completely breaking his connection with earthly things, and in this respect the critics of the papal theory stood midway between the Augustinian attitude, which sought to emphasise the identity between the material and spiritual world, and the Averro-Aristotelian who demanded their total separation. Since however the moderates continued to regard the *Ecclesia*, the sacraments and the pope as earthly sources of grace, their deviation from what had gone before passed largely unnoticed.

Nevertheless, in one respect at least, the moderates can be said to have performed a useful service to the hierocratic idea. By cutting away a good deal of verbiage about the mystical power of the pope, they highlighted the main function of the papacy. It was made clear that the papal identity with Christ was essentially in regard to governmental power. The main reason for the assimilation of papal power to that of Christ was that it provided the only logical and possible justification for the hierocratic theory of sovereignty, and, as Torquemada pointed out a century later, the underlying motive for most of the attacks on the papal identity with Christ was the destruction of the papal claim to be the *dominus legis*, a sovereign legislator.[1] The papacy required the identification to be recognised primarily in support of this, not merely to bolster up superstitious awe amongst the masses of the population. The popes argued that they possessed a plenitude of power because they were the legates of God—'pro legatione Christi fungimur'[2]—and a legate has the full

[1] Turrecremata, *De decreto Irritanti*, Mansi, xxx. 585, 'Si dicatur quod non est simile, quia, cum Christus sit Dominus, est super omnem ordinem et dominus legis, papa autem non: hoc nihil est, tunc quia papa, licet non sit Dominus simpliciter, est locum habens Domini in ecclesiastica hierarchia'. The phrase *dominus legis* is used by Gratian, C. 25 q. 1 *post* c. 16.

[2] II *Cor.*, v. 20: Augustinus Triumphus, *Summa*, cii. 5, p. 505; cf. Innocent IV, Winkelmann, ii. 697, 'Generali namque legatione in terris fungimur regis regum'.

jurisdiction of his principal:[1] but this was above everything else a governmental conception. It is, as Augustinus Triumphus expressly said, only in jurisdictional power that all popes are necessarily one with Christ:

> . . . omnes papae non sunt nisi unus papa, puta Christus, quia omnes recipiunt iurisdictionem et potestatem administrandi immediate ab eo.[2]

Aegidius Romanus presents the same idea in a much more picturesque fashion. In the course of a very lengthy account he announces that there is still the same pope in office as there was at the time of St. Peter himself, just as today the Roman *populus* is the same as it was a thousand years before, and the Roman river that same Tiber that it has always been. The material changes but the form is unalterable: 'Sic semper est idem summus pontifex, licet non sit idem *homo* in huiusmodi *officio* constitutus'.[3] Every pope is the same pope, namely Christ, because all possess the same supreme func-

[1] Augustinus Triumphus, *Summa*, xlv. 2, p. 247, 'Idem est dominium Dei et papae sicut eadem est iurisdictio delegantis et delegati; et quando delegatio est plena et totalis, nulla reservatione facta'; cf. Anon., *Disputatio inter clericum et militem*, p. 13, 'Tenet enim fides nostra Petrum apostolum pro se et suis successoribus institutum esse plenum vicarium Iesu Christi, et certe plenus vicarius idem potest quod et dominus eius cum nulla exceptione, nulla potestatis diminutione est vicarius institutus'.

[2] Augustinus Triumphus, *Summa*, iii. 8 ad 2, p. 36; similarly iii. 7, p. 35, 'omnes papae qui fuerunt a principio et erunt usque in finem mundi non sunt nisi unus papa, quia habent omnes illud idem *officium*'. Cf. Bernardus Parmensis, *Glossa ordinaria ad Decretales*, I. iii. 36, fo. 23v, s.v. *viveret*, 'finguntur una persona antecessor et successor', which follows Roman law: *Inst.*, III. i. 33; *Dig.*, XXVIII. ii. 11.

[3] Aegidius Romanus, *De ecclesiastica potestate*, ii. 4, p. 51, 'Idem est enim nunc papa et idem summus pontifex qui fuit a tempore Petri, sicut idem est populus Romanus nunc qui fuit iam sunt plus quam mille anni, et etiam idem est Tiberis et idem Romanus fluvius qui fuit a principio. Homines enim sunt alii et alii, quia hii fluunt et refluunt, qui constituunt Romanum populum; sic alia et alia aqua quae fluit et refluit, quae constituit Romanum fluvium; semper tamen est idem Romanus fluvius quia semper est idem *formaliter*, licet non sit idem *materialiter*. . . Sic semper est idem summus pontifex, licet non semper sit idem *homo* in huiusmodi *officio* constitutus'. This extract is enough to show that the idea is basically an expression of realism in politics: Christ's power, which constitutes the papal office, is the universal essence common to all individual holders of the office. Cf. Aristotle, *Politics*, iii. 3.

tion, all share the same power of administering the society.[1] The identity with Christ is above all else an indication of the papal possession of an office, an undying office which reflects the undying nature of the mystical personality of the corporation which the pope assumes in his official character.

Correspondingly, when Augustinus Triumphus at the same time acknowledges the identity of all priests and bishops with one another and with Christ, it is noticeable that this identification does not rest upon their participation in the same governmental or jurisdictional power, but in their common use of the same sacramental power, the *potestas ordinis*:

> . . . ordines episcoporum sunt plures non propter plures potestates ordinis, cum in tali potestate, ut dictum est, omnes episcopi non sint nisi unus episcopus et omnes sacerdotes unus sacerdos.[2]

This emphasises the second and more important distinction upon which the vicariate of Christ theory depends: the separation of *potestas iurisdictionis* and *potestas ordinis*, or, as we should say, between office and order. Without it an effective papal vicariate theory would have been impossible, and it is significant that the papal vicariate of Christ did not emerge until the Decretists had begun to weave together the threads of older theological and legal

[1] Aegidius Spiritalis, *Libellus contra infideles*, p. 117, 'Unde papa in quantum Christi mortui vices agens omnia potest circa administratione quae Christus'.

[2] Augustinus Triumphus, *Summa*, i. 6 ad 1, p. 10; cf. iii. 8 ad 2, p. 36, 'Sed sacerdotium Christi aeternum est quantum ad illud quod *formale* est in Christo. Quia sicut omnes sacerdotes non sunt nisi unus sacerdos, puta Christus, quantum ad potestatem conficiendi, quia omnes conficiunt in persona eius, sic omnes pontifices non sunt nisi unus pontifex'; xix. 1 ad 2, p. 117, 'Unde Christus, papa, episcopus et sacerdos non dicuntur nisi unus sponsus Ecclesiae'; also xx. 4, p. 124; lxxxviii. 1, p. 439; Aegidius Romanus, *De renuntiatione papae*, xviii, p. 47; xix, p. 49; xxi, pp. 51–3; xxii, p. 53; xxii, p. 55; John XXII, Raynaldus, *Annales ecclesiastici ad 1327*, xxiv. 327, 'unus et idem est sacerdos interior, videlicet Christus . . . unus et idem auctor'. For a thirteenth-century example see Grosseteste in E. Brown, *Fasciculus rerum expetendarum et fugiendarum* (London, 1690), ii. 251. The idea is however of Patristic origin: e.g. Cyprian, *Ep.*, 52, 'Episcopatus unus, episcoporum multorum concordi numerositate diffusus'; *De unitate Ecclesiae*, p. 195, 'Episcopatus unus est, cuius a singulis in solidum pars tenetur'; Symmachus, *Ep.*, 1, Mansi, viii. 208, 'Ad Trinitatis instar, cuius una est atque individua potestas, unum sit per diversos antistites sacerdotium'; Augustine, *In Iohannis evangelium tractatus*, XLVII. 5. x (*PL*, xxxv. 1730).

distinctions to produce this clearly defined separation.[1] Thus for convenience we may speak of the separation of office and order as a second distinction whose development in the late twelfth century paralleled the growth of that between the office and the man. But it should be pointed out that the publicists, and the canonists before them, regarded this second distinction as simply an extension of the first. We have already mentioned how Christ's dual nature as God and man was expressed in terms of his *corpus duplex*, one aspect of which is mystical, the other natural and personal. It is Christ's own natural body which is now also described as the *corpus verum*, from which sacramental power originates, whilst his *corpus mysticum* or 'political' capacity represents the Universal Church. This extension is clearly displayed in Innocent III's tract on the sacraments, probably written in the last decade of the twelfth century. Here Christ's mystical body is seen as the *Ecclesia*, of which all Christians are members, but his natural body, born of the Virgin and crucified, is automatically equated with the true body from which the sacraments flow.

Dupliciter enim corpus Christi comeditur, quia dupliciter intelligitur: verum, quod de Virgine traxit et in cruce pendit, et mysticum, quod est Ecclesia Christi spiritu vegetata. De vero corpore Dominus ait, Hoc est corpus meum quod pro vobis tradetur [*Luke*, xxii. 19]; de mystico dixit Apostolus, Unus panis et unum corpus multi sumus [I *Cor*., x. 17]. Verum corpus Christi comeditur sacramentaliter . . . mysticum autem comeditur spiritualiter.[2]

In other words it is the human and personal side of Christ which is connected with the *potestas ordinis*, and this has a profound significance for the future. It suggests that the priesthood, whose main function is to confer sacraments, relates to Christ's human nature, whilst the possession of governmental power, *potestas iurisdictionis*, refers to the divine or spiritual aspect of Christ. As there could be no question about the superiority of Christ's divine nature over his humanity, the obvious implication was that Christ as a governor

[1] See further the discussion of this in my '*Papa est Nomen Iurisdictionis*,' I, *Journal of Theological Studies*, viii (1957), at pp. 74–80.

[2] Innocent III, *De sacro altaris mysterio*, iv. 14 (*PL*, ccxvii. 866). For other canonistic sources see Lubac, *op. cit*., pp. 123–6, 185.

was much superior to Christ as a priest. A century later the publicists did in fact reach the point of acknowledging this. James of Viterbo for example openly recognises the supremacy of the regal over the sacerdotal function in Christ:

Est enim sacerdos in quantum homo, rex autem est et in quantum Deus et in quantum homo ... et sic maior dignitas importatur ex eo quod rex dicitur quam ex eo quod sacerdos.

Consequently, when it was appreciated that the pope was in every respect vicar of Christ, it could be said that as a priest he was vicar of Christ the man, whereas the pope seen simply as a legislator was vicar of Christ as God: 'una est potestas Christi secundum quod Deus et papae'.[1] Already the emphasis is turning upon the governmental function of the pope to the detriment of his sacerdotal as-aspect. James of Viterbo realised that this was the case himself: 'Quare et in praelatis Ecclesiae', he concludes, 'superior est potestas regalis quae dicitur iurisdictionis, quam sacerdotalis quae dicitur ordinis'. The same conclusion is reached by Alvarus Pelagius.[2] But already the process had been taken much farther by Augustinus Triumphus, and we shall now see how, step by step, he pursues the logical consequences of this principle until he emerges with a pope who is in every respect the Pontifex Maximus of Roman emperorship but in no way a bishop.

Augustinus Triumphus does not give the impression that this

[1] Augustinus Triumphus, *Summa*, ix. 1, p. 72.

[2] James of Viterbo, *De regimine christiano*, ii. 4, p. 199; Alvarus Pelagius, *De planctu Ecclesiae*, ch. 53, p. 134, 'Christus enim simul constitutus est rex et sacerdos... De comparatione autem secundum prioritatem dignitatis considerandum est quod potestas regia spiritualis superior et dignior est quam sacerdotalis ... unde et Christus dignior est et superior in quantum rex quam in quantum sacerdos; est enim sacerdos in quantum homo, rex autem in quantum Deus et in quantum homo'. This, curiously enough, had been the central thesis of the Anglo-Norman Anonymous: see G. H. Williams, *The Norman Anonymous of 1100 A.D.* (Cambridge, Mass., 1951); Ullmann, *The Growth of Papal Government*, pp. 394–403; *KTB*, pp. 42–61; N. F. Cantor, *Church, Kingship and Lay Investiture in England*, 1089–1135 (Princeton, 1958), pp. 174–97. The Anonymous gives one of the best examples of the episcopalist case prior to Gratian. It is also interesting to note that nearly all the writers who deal with the distinction between jurisdictional and sacerdotal powers were either Frenchmen or products of the Parisian schools.

was his original intention. His immediate aim is to demonstrate the right relationship which he believes should exist between the papacy and the episcopacy. But his starting point is this same theory of the *duplex corpus Christi* which the canonists had used, and he operates with exactly the same division of power developed in Decretist literature. Broadly speaking, he says, Christ's powers may be divided into those of order and jurisdiction, thereby reflecting the dual nature of his body: the true body (or sacramental aspect of his power) and the jurisdictional embodiment of his person in the *Ecclesia*, which is designated his mystical body. Both powers are possessed by the pope as his vicar.

In papa est duplex potestas, una respectu corporis Christi veri, et ista vocatur potestas ordinis . . . alia respectu corporis Christi mystici, et ista vocatur potestas iurisdictionis vel administrationis.[1]

The *potestas ordinis*, deriving from the true body of Christ, is present in all priests and bishops, thereby enabling them to confer the sacraments.[2] The degree to which this is imprinted on a member of the *sacerdotium* determines the distinctive nature or character of his priesthood—whether he should be simply a priest, or a bishop, the perfect priest,[3] who has power to create other priests and bishops.[4]

[1] Augustinus Triumphus, *Summa*, i. 6, p. 9; also Aegidius Romanus, *De renuntiatione papae*, x. 8, p. 32; Alexander de S. Elpidio, *De ecclesiastica potestate*, i. 4, p. 5; Alvarus Pelagius, *De planctu Ecclesiae*, ch. 70, p. 261; and cf. John of Paris, *De potestate regia et papali*, ch. 13, pp. 211–14.

[2] Augustinus Triumphus, *Summa*, xx. 5, p. 125, 'potestas ordinis data est sacramento'.

[3] Aegidius Romanus, *De renuntiatione papae*, x. 1, p. 22, 'nec videtur differentia inter sacerdotem et episcopum nisi illa quae est hominem puerum et hominem virum, quia homo vir est homo magnus et est homo perfectus, homo puer non est magnus nec est homo usquequaque perfectus'; Alexander de S. Elpidio, *De ecclesiastica potestate*, i. 1, p. 3, 'Sacerdotium maius est sacerdotium episcoporum, tum quia in ipsis est ordo sacerdotalis secundum quamdam perfectionem, quia perfectum unumquodque dicitur cum potest aliud sibi simile producere'.

[4] Augustinus Triumphus, *De duplici potestate*, pp. 490–1, 'potest tamen dici potestas ordinis non solum character, qui ut dictum est imprimitur in quolibet ordine, verum etiam perfectio characteris potest spiritualis potestas appellari, quae non imprimitur nisi in ordine episcopali, qui, licet non sit ordo distinctus ab aliis vii, est tamen perfectio ordinum, unde et episcopus potest omnes ordines conferre quod non potest simplex sacerdos. Nam licet sit eadem potestas

Once received it cannot be taken away again: 'potestas ordinis est incorruptibilis et immutabilis'. It has an indelible nature, and this explains the meaning of the phrase 'Once a priest, always a priest'.[1] But *potestas iurisdictionis* (or *administrationis*) on the other hand is 'mobilis et transitoria', since its holder can at any time forfeit it, either by resigning or by being deposed from his office.[2] We may define it as governmental power, and as such it is to be found in anyone who has an administrative capacity. This includes not only members of the clergy but equally kings, princes and all other lesser officials. It is only by obtaining this power that a person can exercise a governmental function in the community. But from here, still following the example of the Decretists, Augustinus Triumphus goes on to draw a further distinction within the category of *potestas iurisdictionis*. It comprises not only governmental power properly speaking, *potestas administrationis*, possessed by all officers of the ecclesiastical corporation, but also that power which

ordinis in sacerdote et episcopo, in sacerdote tamen est talis potestas modo imperfecto et modo parvo, sed in episcopo est modo excellenti et magno'. The usual definition of character, 'character est signaculum quoddam', follows that of Peter Lombard in the *Sentences*, IV. xxiv, but the whole conception is basically Augustinian: N. M. Haring, 'St Augustine's use of the word *character*', *Mediaeval Studies*, xiv (1952), pp. 79–97; S. McCormack, 'The Configuration of the Sacramental Character', *Thomist*, vii (1944), pp. 458–91; F. Brommer, *Die Lehre von sakramentalen Charakter in der Scholastik bis Thomas von Aquino inklusive* (Paderborn, 1908). According to Augustinus Triumphus, bishops, priests and deacons derived from the apostles and the 72 disciples, but the other four orders were added later by papal decree.

[1] E.g. Augustinus Triumphus, *Summa*, ci. 8 ad 2, p. 500, 'puta cum sacri ordinis susceptione, et ista semper manet, quia sacerdos semper manet sacerdos et episcopus semper manet episcopus'; iv. 1, p. 40, 'omnia illa quae pertinent ad potestatem ordinis vel ad ordinis perfectionem non possunt tolli nec auferri quocunque modo vel per cessionem vel per depositionem. Sed illa quae pertinent ad potestatem iurisdictionis possunt tolli et auferri'. Although he stresses that *potestas ordinis* cannot be given to a layman, xxii. 2, p. 131; xciii. 4 ad 3 p. 459, it was common royal practice in the fourteenth century for the king to regard himself as a 'persona mixta, laica et clerica' whose priestly kingship was indelible: for Richard II of England see H. G. Wright, 'The Protestation of Richard II in the Tower in September, 1399', *Bulletin of the John Rylands Library*, xxiii (1939), pp. 151–65 at pp. 152–3, 157. It may be added that Edward I had been buried as king and priest: P. E. Schramm, *Archiv für Urkundenforschung*, xv (1938), p. 355.

[2] Augustinus Triumphus, *Summa*, iv. 1 ad 2, p. 41, 'potestas autem iurisdictionis tolli potest aut per voluntariam cessionem aut per depositionem'.

authorises a bishop or priest to use his sacramental power.[1] This latter, *potestas executionis*, permits the use of *potestas ordinis* in a given area and for a specified period, normally until translation or death.[2] It gives the bishop the right (as opposed to the ability) to confer the sacraments, and determines his ranking within the broad division of the episcopal order.[3] As a recipient of the episcopal degree of *potestas ordinis* he becomes a bishop: but his office in the sense of executive power marks him out as a bishop, an archbishop, a primate or a patriarch.[4] In short, episcopal power is not only divisible into *potestas ordinis* and *potestas iurisdictionis*, but this jurisdictional power can itself be subdivided into *potestas administrationis*, the power of a government official, and *potestas executionis* by which the bishop is permitted to use his sacramental gifts.[5]

The importance of this can be seen in that for Augustinus Triumphus the episcopal vicariate of Christ is purely and simply a matter of *potestas ordinis*. Whilst his main object is to demonstrate the inferiority of the episcopacy, he does not hesitate to affirm that all bishops have a sacramental vicariate equal to that of the pope.[6] All

[1] Augustinus Triumphus, *Summa*, lxii. 3, p. 329, '. . . in absolutione sacramentali, ad quam requiritur . . . potestas ordinis ex ipsius ordine susceptione, ordinis executio ex superioris iurisdictione'.

[2] Augustinus Triumphus, *Summa*, lxiv. 2, p. 338, 'Sed quantum ad officii executionem, quia hoc requirit iurisdictionem super determinatam diocesim et super determinatam parochiam'.

[3] Conversely the divisions of order distinguished between the members of the office of cardinal, which office was greatly superior to that of a bishop, although any priest was superior in *potestas ordinis* to a cardinal-deacon: Augustinus Triumphus, *Summa*, cii. 2–3, pp. 502–4; Alexander de S. Elpidio, *De ecclesiastica potestate*, i. 10, p. 12; Dante, *Ep.*, viii. 4, p. 130.

[4] Augustinus Triumphus, *De duplici potestate*, p. 491, 'Sed potestas iurisdictionis est illa per quam aliquis potest exequi vel executioni mandare primam potestatem, quae est ordinis, in tali vel in tanta materia, secundum quod sua iurisdictio est magis vel minus, universalis vel particularis'; Nicholas de Nonancour, 'Et ista potestas diversificatur secundum diversitatem congregationum in ecclesiis, quia archiepiscopalis dignitas est super aliquos episcopos et eorum subditos; modo tamen iure posito, patriarchalis super aliquos archiepiscopos': Maier, *art. cit.*, p. 359.

[5] Augustinus Triumphus, *Summa*, lxxxiv. 1, pp. 422–3, 'In praelatione autem eorum tria possumus considerare: primo potestatis iurisdictionem quae confertur in electione. Secundo spiritualem consecrationem quae confertur in ordinatione. Tertio executionem . . .'.

[6] Whilst Augustinus Triumphus makes no direct reference to the bishops as vicars of Christ, he indirectly accepts it by agreeing to the *propositiones* in *Summa*

the apostles had received sacramental power by a *sufflatio sancti Spiritus* at the same time, that is, after the Resurrection; and so now all bishops possess their *potestas ordinis* immediately from Christ by right of their succession to the apostles.

Omnes apostoli simul cum Petro aequaliter receperunt potestatem ordinis a Christo, *Ioannis*, xx [22–3], quando dictum est eis, Accipite spiritum sanctum: quorum remiseritis peccata, remittuntur eis; nec talis potestas ordinis singularius fuit data Petro quam aliis discipulis, quia non est dictum sibi *Accipias* sed *Accipite*; sed personas apostolorum repraesentant episcopi sicut papa gerit vicem beati Petri. Ergo omnes episcopi sunt aequales papae in potestate ordinis sicut omnes apostoli fuerunt Petro in praedicta potestate.[1]

In this respect Peter had been no greater than the others, and the pope now, considered simply as a bishop, is not superior to any other bishop. Every bishop possesses the power of the keys in their sacramental aspect, and this symbolism again demonstrates his mediatory position between God and man and his identity with the one mediator, Jesus Christ.[2] It is clearly not the possession of *potestas ordinis* which had made Peter the *princeps apostolorum*, or which now makes the pope *caput Ecclesiae*. It is here that the separation of the mediatory power of the keys into *potestas ordinis* and *potestas iurisdictionis* comes into play: 'distinguitur clavis potestatis ordinis et potestatis iurisdictionis'.[3] In their jurisdictional aspect

lxi. 2, p. 322 and lxxxviii. 1, p. 438. He does however accord this title to the apostles, xvi. 4 ad 3, p. 108. Cf. Innocent III, *De sacris altaris mysterio*, i. 9 (*PL*, ccxvii. 779–80), 'Verumtamen et maiores et minores sacerdotes communiter in quibusdam vices gerunt summi pontificis, id est Christi, dum pro peccatis obsecrant et peccatores per poenitentiam reconciliant'; John XXII, Raynaldus, xxiv. 325, 'dicendum quod immo ipsi quidem pontifices vicarii, licet differenter, sunt Christi'.

[1] Augustinus Triumphus, *Summa*, i. 4, pp. 6–7; cf. Aegidius Romanus, *De renuntiatione papae*, x. 8, pp. 31–2; Alexander de S. Elpidio, *De ecclesiastica potestate*, iii. 3, p. 34. For the controversy over the question of the occasions on which Christ gave power to the apostles see Appendix I.

[2] Augustinus Triumphus, *Summa*, xciii. 2, p. 457, 'sunt enim ipsi quasi medii inter Deum et populum'; cf. Alexander de S. Elpidio, *De ecclesiastica potestate*, i. 1, p. 3; Peter de la Palu, *Articulus circa confessionem*, fo. 95v.

[3] Augustinus Triumphus, *Summa*, xxvii. 1 ad 2, p. 160; also lxxiv. 3 ad 3, p. 385; Alexander de S. Elpidio, *De ecclesiastica potestate*, i. 2, p. 24; Peter de la Palu, *De causa immediata ecclesiasticae potestatis*, ii. 8, fo. 36; *Articulus circa confessionem*, fo. 86.

only Peter had been granted possession of the keys,[1] and so there i now for Augustinus Triumphus only one vicar of Christ in *potestas iurisdictionis*, namely, the pope: 'potestas iurisdictionis reside solum in papa'.[2] He is convinced that since all jurisdictional powe in the world, temporal and spiritual without exception, belongec to Christ, then it must now pass to the pope as his vicar.

... quantum ad universalem et totalem iurisdictionem, totalis enim e universalis dominus spiritualium et temporalium est ipse Christus e vicarius eius summus pontifex.[3]

He is the *fons et origo*,[4] the source of all governmental power exercised in the community, and consequently the bishops may act a governors only in so far as this *potestas iurisdictionis* is derived in them from the pope.[5] Augustinus Triumphus graphically describes this power as flowing down to the bishops from the pope

[1] Augustinus Triumphus, *Summa*, iv. 1 ad 2, p. 41, 'potestas clavium est potestas ligandi et solvendi et potestas discernendi quae, cum respiciat corpus Christi mysticum, importat potestatem iurisdictionis, unde ideo singulariter fuit data Petro'.

[2] Augustinus Triumphus, *Summa*, i. 1, p. 2.

[3] Augustinus Triumphus, *Summa*, xxxvi. 3, p. 214; cf. Alexander de S. Elpidio, *De ecclesiastica potestate*, ii. 8, p. 26, 'Et pro tanto sine hesitatione asserendum esse videtur quod omnis potestas et iurisdictio tam temporalis quam spiritualis quae a Christo est communicata et tradita hominibus residet apud summum pontificem'.

[4] Augustinus Triumphus, *Summa*, lxviii. 3 ad 2, p. 359, 'potestas iurisdictionis tamquam in fonte residet in papa, et ab eo tribuitur et restringitur in aliis'; Alvarus Pelagius, *De planctu Ecclesiae*, ch. 68, p. 248, 'Item cum a papa tamquam a primo fonte descendat omnis iurisdictio et episcoporum et presbyterorum'. Note also Bonaventure, *Breviloquium*, vi. 12, 'Christi vicarius, fons, origo et regula omnium principatuum ecclesiasticorum, a quo tamquam a summo derivatur ordinata potestas usque ad infirma Ecclesiae membra'.

[5] Alvarus Pelagius, *De planctu Ecclesiae*, ch. 54, p. 136, 'Ita ab illo uno cui primum et maxime convenit spiritualis regiminis potestas derivatur ad alios haec potestas partialiter et secundum gradus quosdam. . . Et ab hoc uno dependent omnes qui sunt quocunque modo participes spiritualis regiminis'; Peter de la Palu, *De causa immediata ecclesiasticae potestatis*, iv. 3, fo. 53; Thomas Aquinas, *Commentum in Sententias*, IV. xliv. ii, 'Sicut se habet potestas Dei ad omnem potestatem createm, et sicut etiam se habet potestas imperatoris ad potestatem proconsulis, sic etiam se habet potestas papae ad omnem potestatem spiritualem in Ecclesia, quia ab ipso papa gradus dignitatis diversi in Ecclesia et disponuntur et ordinantur'. The same ground is covered by Hervaeus Natalis, *De potestate papae*, ff. 145–52, who adds that it is heresy to believe the contrary.

like rivers radiating from a source, or rays from the sun, or like roots spreading out from beneath a tree.

... potestas episcoporum et praelatorum iurisdictionis temporalium et spiritualium est derivata et non immediata. Derivata enim est in eis a Christo *mediante* papa, quod patet tali ratione sicut se habent rivuli ad fontem, et radii ad solem, rami ad arborem, sic se habet potestas episcoporum ad potestatem papae.[1]

The idea of papal headship, of the pope as Cephas, is essentially a jurisdictional expression.[2] Whilst by the power of their order the bishops are direct links between God and the other members of the *congregatio fidelium*, in *potestas iurisdictionis* only the pope stands next to God, and the bishops become no more than secondary mediums through whom the pope governs the universal society.[3] Even this is a statement of fact rather than of right. For since the pope may exercise immediate control over the people of any diocese at will,[4] it logically follows, according to Augustinus Triumphus, that he may do without bishops altogether and rule the whole world by himself. He does not of course suggest that the pope is likely to do this, or that he ought to do it. If this should happen, he says, then the pope would be the bishop of every diocese and there would be no more bishops: 'sic cessarent omnium aliorum pontificum potestates'. This is certainly undesirable, and it seems that the pope

[1] Augustinus Triumphus, *Summa*, i. 1, p. 2. This analogy may also be found with Peter Olivi, *Quaestio de infallibilitate*, pp. 322, 334. It derives by way of Gratian, C. 24 q. 1 c. 18 from Cyprian, *De unitate Ecclesiae*, ch. 4.

[2] For the description of the pope as 'Cephas et caput' see e.g. Augustinus Triumphus, *Summa*, viii. 3, p. 50; xxxvi. 7 ad 3, p. 218; *De duplici potestate*, p. 493. Cf. Conrad of Megenberg, *Oeconomica*, III. iii. 1 (Kaeppeli, p. 586), 'cephas, id est caput mundi'. This favourite expression derives from *John*, i. 42 and I *Corinthians*, iii. 22.

[3] Augustinus Triumphus, *Summa*, iii. 5, p. 32, 'papa . . . debet esse medius inter Deum et alios pastores et praelatos Ecclesiae'; lxi. 4 ad 3, p. 324, 'verum esse praelatos esse medios inter summum pontificem et inferiores subditos'.

[4] Augustinus Triumphus, *Summa*, xix. 5, p. 121, 'Potest etiam in provinciis et parochiis eis deputatis omnia facere per seipsum'; cf. lxiv. 5, p. 341, 'non minoris auctoritatis est papa in tota Ecclesia quam quilibet episcopus in sua propria diocesi, immo maioris, cum in propria diocesi episcopus iurisdictionem non exerceat nisi auctoritate papae'; Alvarus Pelagius, *De planctu Ecclesiae*, ch. 54, p. 137, 'qui, licet aliis *mediantibus* pastoribus gubernet diversas ecclesias speciales, tamen immediatum regimen exercere potest super ecclesiam quamlibet'.

must appreciate this since he refrains from doing it. On the other hand one must not forget that the magnitude of papal power makes an obliteration of the episcopacy possible: 'quamvis possit totum orbem immediate per seipsum gubernare'.[1] But whether the pope chooses to do this or not, it is certainly true that the continued existence of any individual bishop is always a matter of uncertainty. He is created, like any other ecclesiastical officer, by an act of sovereign will, and remains in being only at the pope's pleasure. The episcopal office is conferred by divine papal grace, and the conferment of grace is a gift, not a right.[2] No bishop has any rights of his own over his see at all. The existing organisation of the priesthood mirrors the pattern of the *mundus*: by reason of the absolute will of God and his vicar, what is may always be different. The pope wields an unfettered control over the institution, deposition, translation and resignation of bishops. He may exempt whom he pleases from their jurisdiction. Their sees may be broken up, merged together, or completely abolished. And he can create new dioceses whenever and wherever he sees fit.

Vicarius autem Christi in tota praesenti vita est ipse papa, ad quem de iure spectat omnes praelationes . . . ordinare vice Christi quantum ad multos casus:

primo quantum ad eorum translationem;
secundo quantum ad eorum depositionem;
tertio quantum ad ipsorum renunciationem;
quarto quantum ad eorum confirmationem;
quinto quantum ad exemptionem;

[1] Augustinus Triumphus, *Summa*, xix. 3, p. 119; also Hervaeus Natalis, *De potestate papae*, fo. 148; Peter de la Palu, *De causa immediata ecclesiasticae potestatis*, ii. 2, fo. 27.

[2] This is brought out when he discusses whether bishops and cardinals can create other ecclesiastical officers during a papal vacancy: *De potestate collegii*, pp. 506–7, 'Sed . . . Christus dixit apostolis, *Ioh.*, xv [5], Sine me nihil facere potestis. . . Intellexit Christus ergo apostolos sine ipso nil posse facere quantum ad operationem gratuitam et meritoriam, quia *dona gratuita non debentur alicui ex debita vel ex sua natura*, sed ex morali legalitate Christi. Voluit ergo Christus dicere, Sine me et sine *gratia* mea, quae ex mea *liberalitate* procedit, nihil potest-[is] facere quod valeat ad meritoriam et gratuitam operationem: et quia facere cardinales, episcopos et archiepiscopos [et?] dispensare beneficia ecclesiastica *ex mera voluntate* papae procedit . . . ideo mortuo papa collegium non potest talia facere sine ipso'.

sexto quantum ad depositorum restitutionem;
septimo quantum ad novorum constructionem: potest enim episcopatum ordinare ubi prius non erat, et *revocare* ubi prius erat;
octavo quantum ad duorum in unum unionem, quia potest plures in unum unire et unum per plures dividere;
nono quantum ad dignitatum *non vacantium* collationem.[1]

It goes without saying that if the bishops have no say in these matters, still less have the chapters who nominate them: the pope can ignore whatever the chapters decide and make direct provision to any vacant sees.[2] Although he may be generous enough to address his bishops as brothers, there is no room for Cyprian's fraternity of bishops in this view: the pope is their father, the *pater et caput episcoporum*[3] and to him the obedience owed to a father is due.

Perhaps one of the chief merits of this interpretation is its integration of the papal supremacy with the old-established view that all priests and bishops are vicars of Christ. The bishops may still term themselves *vicarii Christi*, as long as this is understood to refer to sacramental power only, whilst the monarchical status of the papacy is left unimpaired. Moreover the nature of the papal vicariate means that the pope has a double check upon the power of the episcopacy, and it is here that the distinction between *potestas administrationis* and *potestas executionis* is so useful. Not only may the pope deprive a bishop of his governmental function by withdraw-

[1] Augustinus Triumphus, *Summa*, lxxi. 4, p. 374; also Anon., *Rationes quod Bonifacius legitime ingredi non potuit*, p. 453; Aegidius Romanus, *De renuntiatione papae*, vi, p. 13; viii, p. 17; Alexander de S. Elpidio, *De ecclesiastica potestate*, iii. 9, p. 40. These examples were probably inspired by Innocent III in *Decretales*, I. vii. 1.

[2] Augustinus Triumphus, *Summa*, xlv. 3 ad 3, p. 249, 'illa ratio non habet locum in papa . . . quia si ad capitulum istius ecclesiae spectat praelatum eligere, potest sine electione capituli illius ecclesiae de praelato providere': this supported, ii. 2, p. 19, by a reference to Gratian, C. 7 q. 1 c. 17. Similarly he can depose a bishop without reference to the chapter, xlvi. 3, p. 251, 'papa potest in qualibet ecclesia praelatum ponere et deponere absque aliorum requisitione et consensu', whilst the chapter itself cannot proceed to deposition without papal authorisation: lxxi. 4 ad 4, p. 374, 'sicut electores secundum ordinem a papa institutum praelatos eligunt, sic praelatos confirmare vel deponere non nisi ad papae ordinationem spectat'.

[3] Augustinus Triumphus, *Summa*, i. 4 ad 1; cf. iii. 5, p. 32, 'Nam papa idem sonat quod pater patrum'.

ing his administrative power, but he may also effectively preven his performance of sacramental duties. For although the *potesta ordinis* is held from Christ, it may only be used if coupled wit *potestas executionis* which, being a jurisdictional power, derives onl from the pope.[1] The bishop's executive power may be withhel where his *potestas ordinis* cannot.[2] Consequently a bishop threatened with loss of office also faces the legal nullification of his sacramental powers. In practice both *potestas iurisdictionis* and *potesta ordinis* are dependent upon the pope, and this explains why fourteenth-century writers sometimes suggest that *both* powers derive from the pope himself.[3] At the same time the use of the idea of *potestas executionis*, which specifies each bishop's diocese, serves to emphasise another aspect of the papal superiority. The pope as a bishop, says Augustinus Triumphus, may not seem to be very different from any other bishop, but in reality he is far greater in that there are virtually no limits to the exercise of his episcopal function.[4]

[1] Augustinus Triumphus, *Summa*, lxiv. 2, p. 338, 'sicut dioceses et parochias determinare spectat immediate ad papam, sic executio praedicationis et sacramentorum administrationis ex officio recepto non convenit episcopo vel prebytero sine auctoritate papae'.

[2] Augustinus Triumphus, *Summa*, lxx. 3 ad 2, p. 369, 'perfectio characteris semper manet in episcopo nec illa potest umquam privari, sed executio potest impediri propter aliqua impedimenta supervenientia'; Alexander de S. Elpidio, *De ecclesiastica potestate*, iii. 4, p. 35, 'Potest ergo sacerdos sive episcopus executionem suorum ordinum renuntiare et possunt etiam talium ordinum executionis ab aliis privari, characteris vero indelibiliter impressi nec ab eis nec ab aliis tolli possunt'.

[3] E.g. Augustinus Triumphus, *Summa*, xxii. 2, p. 131, 'papa praeest clericis potestate ordinis et potestate iurisdictionis, quia utraque potestas derivatur ab eo in clericos'; Peter de la Palu, *De causa immediata ecclesiasticae potestatis*, v. 1, fo. 53v, 'quia ab ipso [scil. Petro] processerunt omnes alii episcopi etiam quoad potestatem ordinis'; cf. Anon., *Rationes quod Bonifacius legitime ingredi non potuit*, p. 455, 'Unde certissimum est quod plenitudo potestatis non solum consistit in iurisdictione, sed in ordine principaliter faciendo maxime relationem ordinis ad corpus Christi mysticum . . . et sic certum est quod plenitudo potestatis quae penes summum hierarcham est, et in ordine et in iurisdictione consistit'.

[4] Augustinus Triumphus, *Summa*, iv. 2 ad 3, p. 42, 'quantum ad potestatem ordinis, *dato quod papa sit episcopus*, non est magis summus sacerdos quam unus alius episcopus. Vel potest dicere dictae potestatis executionem, et sic solus papa est summus sacerdos, quia solus ipse potest ipsam exequi et executioni mandare indefinite et universaliter'; xx. 5, p. 124, 'nec in tali potestate clavium papa differt a quolibet episcopo vel sacerdote nisi solum quantum ad usum et ad-

His is an essentially universal power of binding and loosing, so that no *fidelis* can be exempt from his total and overall jurisdiction.

Iurisdictio autem universaliter super totam Ecclesiam et omnes fideles residet solum in papa; unde sicut ad eum spectat universaliter ligare, sic ad eum spectat universaliter absolvere.[1]

It is with the nature of executive power in mind that the papal use of the *in partem sollicitudinis* formula is to be understood. Many of the popes themselves had pointed out that it was precisely because they derived executive power from the pope that the bishops were permitted a share in the care of the Universal Church.[2] And as Augustinus Triumphus succinctly remarks, it removes a lot of trouble from the pope to have bishops, but it does not remove the bishops from the pope.[3] The fact that the bishops are granted power in no way detracts from the pope's retention of the plenitude of power. This point had been made by Innocent III—'alios vocavit in partem sollicitudinis, retenta sibi plenitudine potestatis'—and many of Augustinus Triumphus' contemporaries followed suit.[4] He

ministrationem: quia papa posset uti administrationi sacramentorum universaliter in tota Ecclesia, episcopi vero vel sacerdotes non nisi in diocesibus et parochiis per papam deputatis'.

[1] Augustinus Triumphus, *Summa*, xxvii. 5, p. 163; cf. xxvii. 1, p. 160, 'Secundo quia universalior; extendit enim se eius iurisdictio supra omnes praelatos Ecclesiae et supra subditos ipsorum praelatorum'; lxv. 1 ad 3, p. 343, 'papa autem in omnes christianos immediatam iurisdictionem habet'.

[2] Boniface VIII, Dupuy, p. 75, 'certe auctoritate summi pontificis et *derivatur* in omnes ab eo episcopi, etiam archiepiscopi, habent determinatam provinciam, et sunt assumpti in partem sollicitudinis, unde habent certam potestatem, summus pontifex habet plenissimam, *nullus est qui possit eam limitare*'; John XXII, Raynaldus, xxiv. 325, 'quia papa universalis, velut vocatus in potestatis plenitudinem, alii vero particulares, velut illi qui in partem sollicitudinis sunt vocati, unde a Deo videntur iudicari quia ab eo iudicantur . . . cum ille cuius auctoritate fit, illud facere videatur'. For its repeated use by Innocent III see Rivière, '*In partem sollicitudinis*', pp. 119–21. Cf. Augustinus Triumphus, *Summa*, i. 4, p. 7; xxix. 6, p. 179; lxiv. 2 ad 1, p. 338; ci. 1 ad 3, p. 494.

[3] Augustinus Triumphus, *Summa*, xix. 5 ad 1, p. 121, 'per auxilium exvitur a periculo et oneratione, sed non a potestate et iurisdictione'.

[4] Innocent III, *Reg.*, II. ccii (*PL*, ccxiv. 750); also Opicinus de Canistris *De praeeminentia spiritualis imperii*, p. 94, '. . . ut spiritualis [iurisdictio] quam praelatis inferioribus *concedit* in partem, plenitudinem sibi potestatis *retineat*'; Alvarus Pelagius, *De planctu Ecclesiae*, ch. 54, p. 137, 'Si autem habent alii partem sollicitudinis, nihil huic deperit de plenitudine potestatis'.

who, in the words of St. Paul (II *Corinthians*, xi. 28), has the care of all the churches daily, remains the real bishop in any diocese. Just as the *Ecclesia* is an essentially universal entity, so the pope's spiritual marriage to it,[1] his representation of the whole ecclesiastical corporation, underlines that the whole world is his see.

In this way it comes to be seen that the real basis for the papal supremacy over the other bishops was the belief that Christ's commission of governmental authority was made to St. Peter alone,[2] and Gratian's text stating that the other apostles 'cum eodem pari consortio honorem et potestatem acceperunt' is taken by the hierocratic writers to refer to *potestas ordinis* only. In the words of Alvarus Pelagius,

> Petrus fuit maior apostolis in dignitate seu officio, sed in apostolatu seu ordine episcopali par fuit et aequalis.[3]

With Augustinus Triumphus it is made abundantly clear that it is solely by his office that the pope becomes *caput Ecclesiae*. The headship of the universal society is a purely governmental matter: 'papatus est nomen iurisdictionis et non ordinis'.[4] To be a pope it is only necessary to obtain the jurisdictional vicariate of Christ,[5] in

[1] Augustinus Triumphus, xix. 1, p. 117, 'ipse solus est universaliter sponsus Ecclesiae'; xxix. 5 ad 1, p. 178, 'papa, qui in tota Ecclesia obtinet universalis sponsi auctoritatem'.

[2] E.g. Anon., *Compendium maius*, p. 171, 'In quibus omnibus continetur palam dictae potestatis et vicariatus firma commissio ipsi soli Petro facta'; cf. Alvarus Pelagius, *Collirium*, p. 514, 'Nam et Petro data est potestas pro se et prae aliis apostolis quibus succedunt episcopi'.

[3] Alvarus Pelagius, *De planctu Ecclesiae*, ch. 68, p. 248. There are many similar passages in papal writings: e.g. Peter de la Palu, *De causa immediata ecclesiasticae potestatis*, i. 1 ad 1, fo. 24, quotes the Gratian text and adds, 'Solutio: verum est de potestate ordinis. . . Sed non est verum de potestate iurisdictionis'. For the canonists' use of this distinction see Tierney, *Foundations of the Conciliar Theory*, p. 33. It is used by Innocent III, *Reg.*, I. ccliv (*PL*, ccxiv. 328).

[4] Augustinus Triumphus, *Summa*, iv. 2, p. 42; cf. Alexander de S. Elpidio, *De ecclesiastica potestate*, iii. 3, p. 35, 'Est etiam diligenter considerandum quod papatus non est nomen ordinis, sed est nomen dignitatis et officium'; Peter de la Palu, *De causa immediata ecclesiasticae potestatis*, v. 1, fo. 54, 'Sed papa est nomen dignitatis sicut curatus, decanatus et archidiaconus et huiusmodi'; cf. John of Paris, *De potestate regia et papali*, ch. 25, p. 258, 'ex nomine iurisdictionis'.

[5] Alvarus Pelagius, *De planctu Ecclesiae*, ch. 59, p. 179, 'Vicarius enim dicitur a vice, quo nomine opus et *officium* insinuatur'; cf. Boniface VIII, Dupuy, p. 53, 'Ante promotionem nostram ad summi apostolatus *officium*'.

which the plenitude of power appropriate to a *caput Ecclesiae* is situated.[1] Moreover since it is a generally accepted principle that *potestas iurisdictionis* is obtained by election, nothing beyond election is necessary in order to enable the pope to gain possession of his office: 'papa eligitur in caput totius Ecclesiae'.[2] It is the office which for Augustinus Triumphus is the essence of the papacy, and consequently election is all that matters. Whatever the time lag between the pope's election and his subsequent consecration (if he is not already a bishop), he is able to act at once in all matters which concern the determination of the faith and the government of the *Ecclesia*. This doctrine had a long history in hierocratic thought, and may be traced back to at least the papal election decree of 1059.[3] It subsequently became a familiar canonistic principle,[4] and the whole idea was inherited from the Decretists and greatly elaborated by the publicists in the early fourteenth century.[5] Its basis was the idea that

[1] Augustinus Triumphus, *Summa*, xx. 4, p. 125, 'Potestas vero iurisdictionis data est officio, ita ut tantum papa possit mediante papali officio quantam potestatem Christus dedit officio'; cf. lxi. 2, p. 322, 'mediante capitis Ecclesiae officio'; also Alexander de S. Elpidio, *De ecclesiastica potestate*, *proem.*, p. 2, 'dici potest Dominus ratione plenitudinis potestatis, quia loco illius caput est'; James of Viterbo, *De regimine christiano*, ii. 11, p. 309, 'quia papa non dicitur caput nisi in quantum gerit vicem Christi et eius personam repraesentat'.

[2] Augustinus Triumphus, *Summa*, v. 1, p. 50; cf. Anon., *Determinatio compendiosa*, ch. 33, p. 544, 'et ipse papa per sacrum collegium cardinalium canonice electus est verus et legitimus successor beati Petri et Iesu Christi unicus vicarius'.

[3] Nicholas II, *MGH*, *Const.*, I. p. 538, c. 8, 'electus tamen sicut papa auctoritatem obtineat regendi sanctam Romanam ecclesiam et disponendi omnes facultates illius, quod beatum Gregorium ante consecrationem suam fecisse cognoscimus'. This was repeated in the decree of 1179. See F. Wasner, 'De consecratione, inthronizatione, coronatione Summi Pontificis', *Apollinaris*, viii (1935), pp. 86–125, 248–81, 428–39, at pp. 118–21, 256–7, 269–71; E. Eichmann, 'Die Weihe und Krönung des Papstes im Mittelalter', *Münchener Theologische Studien*, i (1951), pp. 34–5, 48. This was again repeated by Innocent III, *Consec. serm.*, iii (*PL*, ccxvii. 663), and Innocent himself provides an excellent example of this. Although still only a cardinal-deacon at his election on 8 January, 1198, he exercised full papal jurisdiction between then and the episcopal consecration which preceded his coronation on 22 February. Augustinus Triumphus' theory does in fact follow the main lines of Innocent's justification of his position in *Consec. serm.*, iv (*PL*, ccxvii. 663–6).

[4] The idea that the elected pope is *verus papa et caput Ecclesiae* without further delay may be found with Huguccio, *ad* D. 79 c. 9, and the Gloss 'Ecce vivet Leo', *ad* D. 79 c. 2: Tierney, *Foundations of the Conciliar Theory*, pp. 28, 144.

[5] E.g. Alexander de S. Elpidio, *De ecclesiastica potestate*, iii. 3, p. 35, 'unde

any bishop could exercise his jurisdictional capacity from the time that his election by the chapter was confirmed,[1] although this itself owed much to the earlier Roman law theory of corporations.[2] Nevertheless the essentially episcopal nature of the theory impeded any major advance on the position already taken up in the eleventh century: until the fourteenth century this principle was applicable to the pope for the very reason that as pope he was bishop of the Roman church, and might be treated in the same way as any other bishop in this respect. The orthodox view was that he gained governmental power from election precisely because he was then *electus episcopus*.[3]

siquis aliquis eligatur in papam, verus papa est ante consecrationem episcopalem'; also Alvarus Pelagius, *De planctu Ecclesiae*, ch. 18, p. 32; Hervaeus Natalis, *De potestate papae*, fo. 147; William of Ockham, *Octo quaestiones*, iv. 8, p. 147.

[1] On the canonistic development of this see Tierney, *op. cit.*, pp. 126, 129, 144, with special reference to Rufinus and Huguccio. See also Innocent IV, *App. ad Decretales*, I. vi. 15, s.v. *confirmationem*, 'nota quod electus quam cito est confirmatus sine alia possessione vel investitura vel stallatione statim potest administrare res ecclesiae suae in temporalibus et spiritualibus tam in colligendis fructibus quam in actionibus intentandis nomine ecclesiae suae'. Note also the Fourth Lateran Council decree, iv. 26 (Mansi, xxii. 1014), which permitted non-Italian bishops canonically elected in concord to dispense in temporals and spirituals for the necessity and utility of their churches, that is, to use their *regalian* or official rights. For an example of this with the publicists see Aegidius Romanus, *De renuntiatione papae*, xvi. 2, pp. 42–3. The transposition of this from the episcopal to the papal level is reflected in Aegidius' point that the pope has no jurisdictional power from the election itself, but from its confirmation, although he adds that this is provided by the pope's consent to his own election: x. 1, p. 21; xvi. 2, p. 43; similarly Tholemy of Lucca, *Determinatio compendiosa*, ch. 29, p. 59.

[2] The right of a rector to exercise jurisdiction from election is a common feature of corporation law: Gillet, *La personalité juridique*, pp. 131–2.

[3] Peter de la Palu, *De causa immediata ecclesiasticae potestatis*, v. 1, fo. 54, 'Sic papa potest omnia quae pertinent ad plenitudinem potestatis sive talem statum. Inde est quod papa est verus papa ante consecrationem, quamvis electus et confirmatus in episcopum non sit verus episcopus ante consecrationem, quia episcopus principaliter est *nomen ordinis*, sed papa est *nomen dignitatis*... Ita est verus papa et *essentialiter* ex quo rite assensit antequam consecretur in episcopum, potens omnia quae potest papa *ut papa*, id est, quae sunt iurisdictionis'; Peter Olivi, *Epistola*, p. 367, 'Constat enim quod cum papa vel episcopus est in papam vel episcopum canonice electus et confirmatus et eidem electioni assensum liberum praebens, confestim habet iurisdictionem papalem vel episcopalem, quamvis nondum sit sacerdos vel in episcopum consecratus'; Alvarus Pelagius, *De planctu Ecclesiae*, ch. 54, p. 136, 'ita et in Ecclesia *succedit* vice Christi *pontifex* per electionem'. The diplomatic formula used between the election and con-

But for Augustinus Triumphus there was nothing specifically jurisdictional about the attainment of episcopal status. Just as he regards the papacy as nothing more than an office, so he sees the essence of a bishop to be the possession of order or sacramental power. The office is not enough to make a man a bishop. Indeed a layman can perform all the jurisdictional duties of a bishop, but this does not make him one—he remains a *non-episcopus*.[1] Just as the vital act in the creation of a pope is election, not consecration, so the real creative act for a bishop is consecration and not election:

Papa enim, *ut papa est*, non potest nisi per electionem. Inquantum vero est sacerdos vel episcopus potest esse per consecrationem.[2]

Until the elected candidate has been consecrated he cannot be a bishop. But he can be a pope. And this can, to Augustinus Triumphus' way of thinking, only lead to the conclusion that the papacy in itself has little or nothing to do with any sacramental vicariate of Christ, or, in other words, that there is nothing episcopal about the papacy.

Whilst this was for Augustinus Triumphus a thoroughly logical step to take, it was one which his contemporaries viewed with the greatest hesitation. In his earlier tracts Augustinus Triumphus himself, although nearly approximating to his later theory, still appears to regard *potestas ordinis* as an essential ingredient of papal power.[3]

secration of a non-ordained pope was 'N., episcopus electus, servus servorum Dei'.

[1] Augustinus Triumphus, *De potestate collegii*, p. 502, 'Similiter dicimus potestatem episcopi esse potestatem ordinis, quae est characteris perfectio; sed potestas iurisdictionis sacerdotis aliquando potest esse et potest remanere in non-sacerdote, et potestas iurisdictionis episcopi esse potest et remanere in non-episcopo'. For this reason he rejects Huguccio's opinion, *ad* D. 95 c. 1, that the pope could grant episcopal powers to a priest without episcopal consecration: *Summa*, lxxiv. 2, p. 384. Cf. Aegidius Romanus, *De renuntiatione papae*, x. 3, p. 24, 'Potest ergo concedi quod episcopus sit nomen ordinis'.

[2] Augustinus Triumphus, *Summa*, lxxiv. 1, p. 383; cf. xxv. 3, pp. 151–2, 'duplex potestas dignoscitur esse in Ecclesia, una ordinis et consecrationis, alia iurisdictionis et executionis. Prima datur in consecratione ordinis sacramenti vel in perfectione ordinis quae quidem tanta est, quanta potestas data est sacramento, unde in tali potestate papa non excedit alios sacerdotes nec alios episcopos. Secunda vero datur magis in electione quae tanta est quanta potestas data in officio'.

[3] Augustinus Triumphus, *De duplici potestate*, p. 495, 'Nam dicemus quod nomen episcopatus, archiepiscopatus et papatus est nomen potestatis iurisdic-

The explanation for this would seem to be that at this time he was still strongly influenced by the work of Aegidius Romanus; and Aegidius, although occasionally coming to the very verge of denying the episcopal or sacerdotal content of papal power, always draws back and eventually concedes that the papacy is only a superior type or order of the episcopacy:

Quattuor ergo sunt ordines episcoporum, quia in infimo gradu sunt episcopi, supra quos sunt metropolitani seu archiepiscopi, supra quos sunt primates seu patriarchae, super omnes quidem est Romanus pontifex.[1]

For him papal power is essentially a *potestas mixta*:[2] the pope is first and foremost a bishop with the papal plenitude of jurisdictional power superimposed upon his order.[3] Twenty years later Alexander of S. Elpidio can still be found propounding the Aegidian doctrine, but by this time Augustinus Triumphus was himself ready to take the decisive step forward. *Potestas iurisdictionis* can be completely separated from *potestas ordinis*, and so, to become pope, the pope does not need to be ordained at all. A layman elected to the papal office is immediately in all respects a true pope,

tionis et potestatis ordinis'; cf. *De potestate collegii*, p. 501, 'Potestas papalis est potestas iurisdictionis: nihil videtur *addere* potestas papae *supra* potestatem simplicis sacerdotis vel simplicis episcopi nisi iurisdictionem tantum'. The first passage is taken straight from Aegidius Romanus, *De renuntiatione papae*, x. 5, p. 26. Cf. Peter de la Palu, *De causa immediata ecclesiasticae potestatis*, ii. 8, fo. 37v, 'Unde quando sacerdos sit papa, non augetur in eo potestas ordinis, sed augetur ei obiectum seu materia per additionem potestatis iurisdictionis'.

[1] Aegidius Romanus, *De renuntiatione papae*, x. 4, p. 25.

[2] Aegidius Romanus, *De renuntiatione papae*, xii, p. 37, 'Nam cum papatus non solum dicat ea quae sunt ordinis, sed etiam quae sunt iurisdictionis. . .'; Alexander de S. Elpidio, *De ecclesiastica potestate*, iii. 3, p. 35, 'Quae omnia bene ostendunt quod talia ad potestatem mixtam pertinent'; and note the same attitude in the anonymous Colonna tract of 1310, *Rationes quod Bonifacius legitimi ingredi non potuit*, p. 452.

[3] Aegidius Romanus, *De renuntiatione papae*, xxiv. 1, p. 59, 'Sufficienter autem patere potest per habita quod papa *ultra simplicem pontificem* non dicit ea quae sunt ordinis, sed ea quae sunt iurisdictionis'; Alexander de S. Elpidio, *De ecclesiastica potestate*, i. 1, p. 3, 'Sacerdotium maximum est *sacerdotium* summi pontificis, qui est vicarius Christi et successor Petri, quia *praeter* potestatem ordinis habet universalem et plenam potestatem iurisdictionis'; also John of Paris, *De potestate regia et papali*, ch. 25, pp. 258–9.

Puto quod supposito quod esset laicus et non esset constitutus [in] sacris, electus in papam esset verus papa et haberet omnem potestatem iurisdictionis papalis,[1]

and has immediate use of all the powers of the papal office: 'statim habet omnem papalem iurisdictionem'.[2] Although this would mean that the pope would be unable to create other bishops himself, at least as far as *potestas ordinis* is concerned,[3] this only emphasises the governmental nature of the papal position. And, what is more important, since *potestas ordinis* and *potestas iurisdictionis* can be

[1] Augustinus Triumphus, *Summa*, iv. 2 ad 1, p. 42; also iv. 1, p. 40; xx. 5, p. 125; lxxiv. 2 ad 1, p. 384. An indication of how close other writers came to this can be seen in Aegidius Romanus, *De renuntiatione papae*, x. 5, p. 26, 'dicemus quod si electus in papam *non sit nec sacerdos nec episcopus*, non poterit conficere corpus Christi nec poterit conferre ordines; poterit tamen ea quae sunt iurisdictionis, ut poterit conferre praebendas, dignitates et alia huiusmodi facere', cf. xii, p. 36, 'Nam electus in papam, si assentiat electionem, data quod *non sit sacerdos* et dato quod non habeat characterem sacerdotalem nec perfectionem illius characteris, plenam iurisdictionem habebit'; Peter Olivi, *De renuntiatione papae*, p. 357, 'sciendum quod potestas papalis *integratur* ex sacramentali potestate ordinis sacerdotalis et episcopalis, sine qua non posset missam celebrare nec ordines conferre, et ex potestate iurisdictionis per quam est praelatus et iudex proprius et ordinarius omnium christianorum. . . Haec autem secunda *non est essentialiter aut inseparabiliter* colligata primae, nec prima isti, quia si aliquis *nondum* sacerdos sit in papam electus, eo ipso habet totam papalem iurisdictionem, et tamen non habet ordinem sacerdotalem nec episcopalem'. Both writers however go on to declare that an elected layman must subsequently be consecrated as bishop of Rome. It may be noted that Stephen III had decreed in the Roman synod of 769 that, following the scandalous elevation of the layman Constantine as anti-pope in 767, not only were laymen barred from becoming pope, but the pope had also to be chosen from amongst the Roman clergy: S. Kuttner, '*Cardinalis*: the history of a canonical concept', *Traditio*, iii (1945), pp. 129–214 at p. 149. But the election of a layman as pope followed with Leo VIII in 963. According to modern canon law it is still possible for a layman to be elected: see the constitution *Vacante sede apostolica* of Pius X, 25 December, 1904, and note that this is upheld in the new *codex* for the *ecclesia orientalia* in canon 185, para. 2: *Acta Apostolicae Sedis*, September, 1957.

[2] Augustinus Triumphus, *Summa*, iv. 5, p. 46.

[3] Augustinus Triumphus, *Summa*, xxv. 3, p. 151, 'Et [potestas ordinis] indelibiliter permanet in quolibet sacerdote vel episcopo nec per papam conferri *ut est papa* nec tolli, quia si papa *non esset sacerdos vel episcopus*, non potest aliquem in sacerdotem consecrare nec in episcopum ordinare'. This is regarded as a prohibitive consideration by Alexander de S. Elpidio, *De ecclesiastica potestate*, iii. 3, p. 35.

considered in isolation, a divorce is now pending between the pope and the Roman bishopric.[1]

As might be expected, this theory was given a very mixed reception. A century later a nearly apoplectic Gerson declares that if a layman could be pope, then there would be nothing—awful thought—to prevent the *Ecclesia* being governed by a woman.[2] Ockham, on the other hand, seizes upon the idea with glee: by all means let the pope be a layman, and then there will be no question about his subjection to the emperor, whom God has acknowledged to be the head of all laymen.[3] Here however we must confine ourselves to calculating the effect of this idea upon traditional hierocratic thought. As we have just said, the idea that the pope considered *ut papa* is something other than the pope *ut episcopus* amounts to no less than a complete separation of the papacy from the Roman church. Whatever else the Roman church might be, it was unquestionably an episcopal see. Yet if the pope, *qua* pope, has no need to be a bishop, it follows that he does not necessarily have to be bishop of Rome, and that consequently the Roman church

[1] Cf. Aegidius Romanus, *De renuntiatione papae*, x. 5, p. 26, '*Distincta* ergo sunt ea quae sunt ordinis, quae respiciunt characterem vel perfectionem characteris, quae potest simplex *episcopus*, et ea quae sunt iurisdictionis cuius plenitudinem habet *papa in papatu*'. It has been pointed out by Tierney that the canonists had already developed a distinction between the pope *ut papa et caput* and the pope as bishop of Rome: *Foundations of the Conciliar Theory*, p. 39, n. 2. See for example the *Summa Parisiensis, ad* D. 65 c. 6, 'Dominus papa Romanus pontifex est *patriarcha* illius provinciae, et est *apostolicus* totius orbis': ed. T. P. McLaughlin (Toronto, 1952), p. 57; and the *Summa Imperatoriae Maiestatis, ad* D. 21 c. 7: Tierney, 'Pope and Council: Some New Decretist Texts', *Mediaeval Studies*, xix (1957), pp. 197–218 at p. 214.

[2] Gerson, *De potestate ecclesiastica, Opera Omnia*, ii. 239, 'Et quamvis ex electione possit aliquid iurisdictionis habere, non tamen habet ante consecrationem in episcopum plenitudinem ecclesiasticae potestatis tam ordinis quam iurisdictionis utriusque; quod perspicuum est ex terminis. Hic autem consurgit aequivocatio non modica propter dominos iuristas, qui loquentes de plenitudine potestatis papalis solum loqui videntur de potestate iurisdictionis, ex qua locutione videtur haec absurditas sequi quod pure laicus immo et femina posset esse papa et habere plenitudinem ecclesiasticae potestatis'.

[3] William of Ockham, *Dialogus*, III. II. iii. 23 *Additio*, p. 395, 'purus servus imperatoris, etiam si tonsuram clericalem non haberet, possit elegi in papam, et ita cum imperator non debeat privari iure suo per ecclesiam, papa talis remaneret subiectus imperatori, et per consequens papa ratione papatus non est exemptus a iurisdictione imperatoris'.

has ceased to be an essential constituent of the papacy. Even more telling is Augustinus Triumphus' implicit acceptance of the logical extension of this separation, namely, that the pope and the bishop of Rome might be two different people.[1] As he points out, the jurisdictional vicariate of Christ had been separated from the sacramental in Old Testament times. Moses had held the governorship of God's chosen people in the pre-Christian *Ecclesia*, whilst his brother Aaron had assumed the sacerdotal function.

Moyses repraesentabat Christum cuius vicem papa gerit in terris. . . Similiter Aaron Christum repraesentabat. . . Aliter tamen Moyses et aliter Aaron Christum significabant, quia Moyses significabat Christum ut legislator, Aaron vero ut summus sacerdos.[2]

Augustinus Triumphus thus takes over and reshapes the old French doctrine, most recently given expression by the *Rex pacificus* and Peter Dubois, but stretching back to the Anglo-Norman Anonymous of the early twelfth century, in which the separation of Christ's kingship from his priesthood is made to support the absolute independence of the legislative and sacerdotal functions in the Christian society. Although designed to emphasise the imperial nature of the fourteenth-century papacy at the expense of its episcopal character, Augustinus Triumphus' theory indirectly lent weight to the long-standing contention of the anti-hierocratic writers that lay government in the *Ecclesia* could operate without reference to the Roman church. Moreover the further development of this distinction could only serve to pave the way for a more radical laicalisation of the papacy. It was not, we may perhaps suggest, entirely unrelated to this that two centuries later the king of England was able to effect a political revolution in favour of his own

[1] In his *Liber de ecclesiastica potestate* of 1438–40, Laurentius Aretinus spoke of a bishop in the papal see who was a vicar of the Roman bishop rather than a papal vicar: 'Illud autem verum est quod papa habet suum specialem et certum episcopatum praeter generalem in urbe Romana, scil. certam diocesim in qua suum facit vicarium, qui est vicarius episcopi Romani, non papae': K. Eckermann, *Studien zur Geschichte des monarchischen Gedankens im 15. Jahrhundert* (Berlin, 1933), p. 121. Laurentius was certainly familiar with the *Summa* of Augustinus Triumphus: Eckermann, p. 163.

[2] Augustinus Triumphus, *Summa*, i. 3 ad 1, p. 6; cf. Anon., *Rex pacificus*, ch. 3, p. 671; Pierre Dubois, *La supplication du pueuble de France*, pp. 215–16.

jurisdictional headship and vicariate of Christ, whilst at the same time maintaining that the apostolic succession of the English episcopacy remained unbroken.[1]

Just how great a revolution this was in hierocratic theory itself requires some explanation. We must return for a moment to a point which we have already mentioned, namely, that in the old papal theory the Roman church was held to be the quintessence of the papal position. According to the traditional doctrine the pope becomes vicar of Christ because he succeeds to Peter[2]—hence the usual papal formula, 'nos sumus successores Petri et vicarii Christi'.[3] But the pope only becomes the successor of Peter by gaining the Petrine see, the Roman church.[4] Only by obtaining the *sedes Petri* can he exercise the power of Peter which Christ had constituted as his vicariate.[5] The papal-Petrine powers are embodied in the Roman church, and it is by becoming bishop of Rome, by his spiritual marriage to the church in which his office consists, that

[1] Mention might also be made of the scheme put forward by the emperor Maximilian I in 1511 according to which, being a widower, he was to be elected pope: *The New Cambridge Modern History* (Cambridge, 1958f.), i. 215. Marsilius of Padua had suggested that the emperor could become pope by succession in a papal vacancy, but since he denied the pope any jurisdictional power he was forced to emphasise the episcopal character of the papacy: *Defensor pacis*, II. iii. 2–4, pp. 152–3.

[2] Tholemy of Lucca, *De regimine principum*, iii. 10, p. 258, 'totum dominium inter fideles *ex Petro* dependeat in eius successores'; cf. the papal argument cited by the *Rex pacificus*, ch. 1, p. 665, 'Ergo Christus Petro, et eius successoribus *in ipso*, dedit imperium non solum spirituale sed etiam temporale'.

[3] This is clearly illustrated by Pierre Dubois' use of the formula: *De recuperatione Sanctae Terrae*, ch. 29, p. 22, 'Si ergo summus apostolicus, mundi totius speculum, beati Petri principis apostolorum locum tenens et *sedem*, vicarius Domini nostri Ihesu Christi ...'; and for a fifteenth-century example, Stephen de Palec, *Tractatus de Ecclesia*, 'Ideo non vicarius Petri, cum sit secum aequalis dignitatis et potestatis in officio ecclesiastico, sed *successor eius in potestate et sede*, et Iesu Christi est vicarius appellandus': Maccarrone, *op. cit.*, p. 244. Cf. Innocent III, *Reg.*, II. cxcvii (*PL*, ccxiv. 746).

[4] E.g. Peter de la Palu, *De causa immediata ecclesiasticae potestatis*, iv. 2, fo. 47v, 'Romana ... debet dici sedes Petri. Unde qui in sede Romana legitime constituitur, successor Petri efficitur, et per consequens plenus et perfectius vicarius Christi'.

[5] Aegidius Spiritalis, *Libellus contra infideles*, p. 107, 'sedet in sede illa quam Dominus sibi in personam beati Petri specialiter elegit ... *Ideoque* summus pontifex appellatur'; Alexander de S. Elpidio, *De ecclesiastica potestate*, i. 10, p. 11, 'Dicitur etiam singulariter apostolus, *quia* vertici apostolorum succedit et toti Ecclesiae praesidet, et in sede sedet quae apostolica nuncupatur'.

each succeeding pope acquires them.[1] Although these powers had since the twelfth century been held to constitute a direct vicariate of Christ, there is here little change from the time when the papacy claimed no more than a vicariate of Peter.[2] The Roman church remains the basis of the papal vicariate of Christ: the pope is still primarily the bishop of Rome. It is essential that the pope should become a bishop,[3] since a pope who is not a bishop can hardly occupy the *cathedra Petri*, nor therefore assume the *primatus Petri* contained within it. For this reason the papal election is essentially an episcopal one: the process is not complete until consecration has taken place. Only then can the elected person be declared pope by the formal act of coronation. Papal power is indissolubly bound up with the Roman see: it is headship of the Roman church which makes the pope *caput Ecclesiae*. Indeed, since it contains the papal power,[4] it is the Roman church which signifies the papal office and is itself the real head of the Christian society: the vicariate of Christ

[1] E.g. Clement VI, Baluze, iv. 8, 'In sacra Petri sede, cuius sumus licet immeriti successores, in plenitudinem potestatis assumpti, tunc potestate ipsa laudabiliter utimur'. This is still modern doctrine: see the constitution *Pastor aeternus*, c. 2, of Pius IX, 18 July, 1870, 'Unde quicunque in hac cathedra Petri succedit, is secundum Christi ipsius institutionem primatum Petri in universam Ecclesiam obtinet'.

[2] Ullmann, *The Growth of Papal Government*, pp. 2–9.

[3] Aegidius Romanus, *De renuntiatione papae*, x. 1, p. 21, 'si aliquis sit in papam electus antequam ordinetur in episcopum, habebit plenam iurisdictionem summi pontificis, non tamen erit summus pontifex nisi sit pontifex'; Alvarus Pelagius, *Collirium*, p. 514, 'Item omnis papa est episcopus consecratus'; Peter de la Palu, *De causa immediata ecclesiasticae potestatis*, i. 5, fo. 26, 'nullus habet claves ligandi et solvendi nisi sacerdos . . . quia potestas clavium in illo foro quo respicit corpus Christi mysticum fundatur super potestate quae habetur super corpus Christi verum'. The alternative is to imply that a layman can hold an episcopal see, which would be in direct contravention of canon law: this was however hinted at by Alexander de S. Elpidio, *De ecclesiastica potestate*, iii. 7, p. 37, 'potestas papalis . . . non acquiritur per papalem consecrationem, sed eo ipso quod aliquis est in sede'.

[4] Alexander de S. Elpidio, *De ecclesiastica potestate*, ii. 2, pp. 15–16, 'Et secundum hanc acceptionem ecclesia Romana est . . . universalis ecclesia prima, videlicet, et praecipua, quia *in ea* plenitudo potestatis existit. . . Et sicut *eius episcopus* pater est et pastor omnium pastorum, ita Romana ecclesia mater et caput est omnium ecclesiarum'; cf. Alvarus Pelagius, *De planctu Ecclesiae*, ch. 54, p. 138, 'ecclesia Romana . . . prima videlicet et praecipua velut caput in corpore, quoniam *in ea* plenitudo potestatis existit'.

is held by the Roman church rather than the pope himself.[1] It is thi office, the *ecclesia Romana*, from which all the power in the *Ecclesi* descends,[2] and to which all members of the Christian community owe allegiance.[3]

Now, however, with Augustinus Triumphus, the vicariate o Christ is regarded as an entity quite distinct from the Romar bishopric. The pope becomes pope simply by election to an office—'papa eligitur in caput totius Ecclesiae'—and it is from this vicariate, not from the Roman church, that all other powers draw their being. It still remains true that the pope is the successor of Peter, but, as Hervaeus Natalis says, he succeeds Peter in office rather than as a bishop.

Petrus autem, cui succedit papa *non sicut simplici episcopo sed sicut generali vicario* Christi, super totam Ecclesiam factus est expresse a Christo vicarius generalis.[4]

Moreover, as we have seen, in this office he is essentially the successor of Christ himself rather than of Peter. Indeed Innocent III had been positively indignant at the suggestion that he owed his official capacity to a man.[5] The papal position, which has hitherto owed so

[1] Anon., *Compendium maius*, p. 171, 'quia in dicta sede pleno vicariatu Christi ... [papa] solus seu praecipuus praesidet'.

[2] Opicinus de Canistris, *De praeeminentia spiritualis imperii*, p. 103, 'a sola Petri sede necesse est omnem ecclesiasticum gradum et dignitatem descendere'; Peter de la Palu, *De causa immediata ecclesiasticae potestatis*, iv. 3, fo. 49v, 'Omnis potestas iurisdictionis ecclesiasticae et praelatio in Ecclesia procedit, derivatur et originatur a papa vel a sede papali, id est, ab ecclesia Romana'. Cf. a dualistic version of this in Engelbert of Admont, *De ortu imperii Romani*, ch. 21, p. 771, 'quia stante adhuc capite Ecclesiae in spiritualibus, scilicet apostolica sede, et capite in temporalibus, scilicet imperio Romano'. Thus the emperor too gains power by obtaining the imperial office: e.g. Francis de Meyronnes, *Tractatus de principatu temporali*, ch. 4, p. 62, 'quia imperator non praesidet imperio nisi per dignitatem imperialem'.

[3] For this reason the episcopal oath was not made to the pope personally but to the 'papatus Romanus et regalia sancti Petri'. This compares with current lay practice, which demanded that the episcopal oath should be to the *corona regni* or the *regnum*.

[4] Hervaeus Natalis, *De potestate papae*, fo. 142.

[5] Innocent III, *Reg.*, I. cccxxvi (*PL*, ccxiv. 292); cf. Johannes Andreae, *Glossa ordinaria ad Clem.*, II. vii. 1, 'Si alicubi invenitur quod est Petri vicarius, illa est impropria locutio'. In the fifteenth century there are traces of a conscious return to a vicariate of Peter: note the argument quoted by Turrecremata, *Summa de*

much to the descent from St. Peter through the medium of the Roman church, is now for Augustinus Triumphus an immediate successorship to Christ. And since Christ had held the government of the whole world in his hands, the pope likewise becomes a truly universal ruler. Christ had had no ties with Rome or the Roman church, so therefore the pope, as pope, has no necessary connection with them either. He gains the *plenitudo potestatis* regardless of whether he holds the Roman see or not. It is merely appropriate for him to identify himself with the Roman church by virtue of his personal succession from Peter. The connection between the pope and the Roman church (or Rome) is the essentially personal one between himself and Peter, not the official one between himself and Christ.

> ... sicut Christus passus est pro omnibus, ita papa vice Christi in omnes christianos iurisdictionem episcopalem habet; quia tamen personaliter succedit Petro, ideo illius ecclesiae [scil. Romanae] singularem administrationem habet.[1]

A complete cleavage can now be seen between the governmental, official nature of the pope as vicar of Christ and his personal, episcopal character which links him to the Roman church. Since only the former is essential to his position as pope, tenure of the Roman see has become quite superfluous.

However novel this theory, it was a matter of the greatest practical significance for much of the fourteenth century. The removal of the papal court to Avignon by Clement V had immediately raised

Ecclesia, ch. 40 ad 2, 'Romanus pontifex dicitur vicarius beati Petri ut in c. *Ego Ludovicus, dist.* 63: ergo videtur quod non a Christo immediate sed a beato Petro potestatem acceperit'.

[1] Augustinus Triumphus, *Summa*, xix. 4 ad 2, p. 120; also ad 1, p. 120, 'Non quaelibet ecclesia tali praerogativa honorata est praesentia beati Petri, cuius successor papa est in vita et in morte, sicut Romana ecclesia: et ideo nec papa quamlibet ecclesiam debet praesentiali administratione in curam assumere sicut civitatem Rom[an]am'. We may note here how he emphasises that the Roman connection is a personal one with the pope as successor to Peter: a dead pope remains a *successor Petri*, but he ceases upon death to be vicar of Christ because he then relinquishes possession of the papal office, viii. 3, p. 70. A dead pope could be condemned for heresy because he would be tried in a personal capacity, not as vicar of Christ, v. 7, p. 55. Hervaeus Natalis, *De potestate papae*, also emphasises that the pope as a bishop is essentially a (personal) successor to Peter: e.g. fo. 149v, 'papa est successor Petri antistes [i.e. episcopus] totius mundi'.

the question of whether the papacy could exist without any real contact with Rome itself, and a solution to this problem was a matter of some urgency in view of Louis of Bavaria's deposition of John XXII on the very grounds that, because he no longer resided in Rome, he could not be considered a true pope. For Louis Rome is the *urbs regia*, the source of government. The Roman church has been divinely instituted as the head of the Christian world, and for a pope to separate himself deliberately from this holy place can only mean that he has deposed himself.[1] And although Louis was merely eager to make political capital out of this, there were still many ardent supporters of the papacy who were profoundly disturbed by the move to Avignon. Not only did they feel this to be an unpardonable wrench with tradition, but they were also uncomfortably aware of its constitutional implications. They felt that the pope was bound by the express wish of Christ for, as Innocent III had said, Rome was the 'locus quem elegit Dominus'.[2]

[1] Louis of Bavaria, *MGH*, *Const.*, VI. 1, n. 438, p. 362: Rome is a holy city, the fount of kings, whose people are a chosen race, the royal priesthood. Consequently the see of Peter was divinely instituted there, and 'per sacram beati Petri sedem caput totius orbis vocaretur effectu'. A papal absence from Rome constitutes a danger to the whole *Ecclesia*, and so the pope must reside there and not leave it except with the consent of the clergy and people. Thus if the pope does not return to Rome, he may be presumed to have deliberately deposed himself: 'quod talis huiusmodi summus pontifex in urbe Romana continuam residentiam facere teneatur, nec extra urbem praedictam seu per duas vulgares dictas longe ab ipsa urbe, absque cleri et populi Romani petita licentia et obtenta, se absentare valeat ullo modo. . . Si vero talis summus pontifex contra praescriptam formam se absentare praesumpserit, et a clero populoque Romano tertio monitus, infra terminum eidem per dictum clerum et populum moderandum ad urbem Romanam celeriter non redierit, ibidem ut praemittitur continue moraturus, *ipso iure* pontificatus sui honore et dignitate praesentis constitutionis auctoritate volumus fore privatum, decernentes ad alterius summi pontificis electionem procedi debere acsi per mortem ipsius naturalem de alio electionem fieri immineret'. Cf. Baluze, iii. 430, 'hanc sacratissimam gentem et urbem Romanam . . . sua personali praesentia tota sui vicariatus duratione privavit contra expressam Christi prohibitionem'. For Dante's disgust with the move to Avignon and his assertion that it created a vacancy in the papacy see Davis, *Dante and the Idea of Rome*, pp. 196–7.

[2] Innocent III, *Decretales*, IV. xvii. 13. Cf. Alvarus Pelagius, *De planctu Ecclesiae*, ch. 32, p. 35, 'Fateor tamen quod non posset mutari sedes apostolica et papalis ab urbe Romana in aliam civitatem propter verbum istud praed. cap. *Rogamus*, ibi, Iubente Domino, quia non est discipulus super magistrum'; also

In fact a clear appreciation of the constitutional importance of the Roman church to the papal position had already sparked off a controversy on the need for papal residence at Rome long before the move to Avignon actually took place.[1] As Nicholas de Nonancourt said—and he was simply echoing a commonly expressed opinion of the time—it is only by becoming bishop of Rome, the *caput mundi*, that he becomes a universal ruler. Putting his words into the mouth of Boniface VIII, he makes the pope declare that he is bishop of any place on earth solely because he holds the Roman church which epitomises the whole society.[2] The pope is essentially a ruler *urbis et orbis*.[3] The pope might be the *verus imperator*, but as

Alexander de S. Elpidio, *De ecclesiastica potestate*, iii. 10, p. 340; Anon., *Somnium viridarii*, ii. 366, p. 227. For a discussion of Alvarus Pelagius' completely contradictory attitude to this question see Iung, *Alvaro Pelayo*, pp. 110–12. Alexander de S. Elpidio, from whom Alvarus frequently borrowed, is equally uncertain.

[1] For Hostiensis on this see Tierney, 'A Conciliar Theory of the Thirteenth Century', pp. 428, 433. Cf. Peter Olivi, *Quaestio de infallibilitate*, p. 336, 'In hoc enim Christus multum magnificavit se et Ecclesiam suam, quia dominam mundi [scil. Romam] sic subiugavit sibi et sic ad se traxit quod ibi sedem principalem *fixit*'; p. 338, 'constat autem quod in nulla alia sede successorem universalem habuit nisi Romae, satis eo ipso licet quod ibi fuerit et sit principalis sedes eius'. The controversy may have begun with Innocent IV's protracted refuge in Lyons during 1244–51, although most of the thirteenth-century popes had found it advisable to leave Rome for various periods, and there were many precedents for this. The first to suggest a permanent curia away from Rome (in Lombardy) is reported to have been Benedict XI: G. Mollat, *Les Papes d'Avignon* (Paris, 1930), pp. 9–13. The argument was still going on in the early seventeenth century with Bellarmine: see the *De potestate summi pontificis*, ii. 1; ii. 12; iv. 4.

[2] Nicholas de Nonancour, 'ecclesiam Romanam, quae est vinea mea, quia ibi sum pontifex *proprius*, quam rego per me sine medio pontifice aliquo. Et ideo dicar pontifex Romanus; et *in eo quod pontifex Romanus*, pontifex summus omnibus aliis pontificibus superior et *ita* summus, et *ex hoc* pater summus et *ita* papa sine determinatione loci debeo dici': Maier, *art. cit.*, p. 353. Cf. Francis de Meyronnes, *De principatu Siciliae*, ch. 3, p. 105, '*quia* ecclesia Romana est magistra aliarum ecclesiarum et mater, *ideo* princeps Romanae ecclesiae convincitur esse pater et magister aliarum ecclesiarum'.

[3] Aegidius Romanus, *De ecclesiastica potestate*, iii. 1, p. 143, 'summi pontificis, qui est dominus urbis et orbis'; Alexander de S. Elpidio, *De ecclesiastica potestate*, i. 1, p. 3, 'Qui licet appropriate dicatur pontifex Romanus, quoniam Romana ecclesia mater et caput est omnium ecclesiarum, universaliter tamen est pontifex omnium christianum, unde et dicitur episcopus urbis et orbis'; iii. 10, p. 40, 'quia etsi dominus papa praesideat omnibus ecclesiis universaliter, nihilominus tamen alicui, videlicet Romanae, specialiter ut vere et proprie dicatur episcopus non solum orbis sed etiam urbis'.

Francis Petrarch enquired, where is the Roman empire if not at Rome?[1] To this question Augustinus Triumphus and the more progressive papal writers had but one answer: Rome and the Roman church are where the pope is. The position of the vicar of Christ is no longer dependent upon the Roman church. Rather the preeminence of the Roman church depends upon its being the see of the pope.[2] It is only because the pope is *caput Ecclesiae* that his see may also be similarly described.[3] As Alvarus Pelagius said, the place does not sanctify the man: it is the pope who sanctifies Rome and its church by his presence. Christ gave his power to a man, not to an inanimate collection of buildings.

Alia haeresis est quae dicit papa suam perdit iurisdictionem quando Romae non stat. Quod est contra sacram scripturam, quia ubicunque est papa, ibi est ecclesia Romana et sedes apostolica et caput Ecclesiae ... et papa a Roma[na] civitate vel sede iurisdictionem non recipit sed a Deo ... et locus non sanctificat hominem nec Roma papam, sed homo locum et papa urbem Romanam. Etenim Christus non dedit iurisdictionem suam et potestatem loco vel Romae, quae res inanimata est, sed Petro et successoribus eius.[4]

[1] Francis Petrarch, *Ep.*, viii, p. 1355, 'Si imperium Romanum Romae non est, ubi quaero est? Nempe si alibi est, iam Romanorum imperium non est ...'.

[2] This change in emphasis can be seen in Sybert of Beek, *Reprobatio sex errorum*, ch. 3, p. 12, 'dico quod negantes Petrum et eius successores esse Christi vicarios et caput Ecclesiae post Christum, et *per consequens* Romanam ecclesiam esse caput, matrem et magistram omnium Christi ecclesiarum per mundum, scismatici sunt censendi'. It may be mentioned that during the course of the twelfth century the episcopal *laudes* rendered to the pope were replaced by a specifically imperial type of acclamation which omitted all reference to the pope's episcopal see: Kantorowicz, *Laudes Regiae*, pp. 129–35.

[3] Alvarus Pelagius, *De planctu Ecclesiae*, ch. 54, p. 137, '[Papa] est rex omnium spiritualium regum, pastor pastorum, pater patrum, caput omnium fidelium et omnium qui fidelibus praesunt, *unde* et ecclesia cui praesidet, scilicet Romana, mater et caput est omnium ecclesiarum'; cf. ch. 31, p. 35, 'Item ecclesia Romana fundata est in Petro, non econverso'.

[4] Alvarus Pelagius, *Collirium*, p. 506; cf. Zenzellinus de Cassanis, *Glossa ordinaria ad Extravagantes Iohannis XXII*, iii. 1, fo. 22, sv. *Romana ecclesia*, 'Certum est enim quod Deus non in loco sed in persona sancti Petri suam Ecclesiam fundavit, dicens, Tu es Petrus'. The same may be found with Pierre Dubois, who had of course a vested interest in a French papacy: *De recuperatione Terrae Sanctae*, ch. 57, p. 46; ch. 108, p. 94. This is again reminiscent of the Anglo-Norman Anonymous: *KTB*, pp. 56–7, 82–3. Cf. II *Maccab.*, v. 19. 'Verum non propter locum gentem, sed propter gentem locum Deus elegit.'

The pope may be chosen from any place on earth, argues Augustinus Triumphus, so why should he not choose to make anywhere in the world his see?[1] If he can change the see of any other bishop, why not his own?[2] Had not Peter himself changed his see on no less than three occasions?[3] However convenient it may be for him to reside in Rome, he is as free as the air to live where he pleases[4]—and there will be found Rome and the Roman church: 'ubicunque est papa, ibi est Roma et ecclesia Romana'.[5] Underlying this is the typical hierocratic emphasis upon the sovereign will of the pope. According to Lambertus Guerrici de Hoyo there is no more obligation upon the pope to remain in one place than there is upon God himself. The earth belongs to him, and he is free to go where he pleases, since no residential obligations were written into the terms of the Petrine commission which outlines the scope of his vicariate. The other members of the *congregatio fidelium* are bound to follow him to wherever he chooses to summon them.

Sicut enim Deus nullo artatur loco, quin ubique *voluerit*, possit esse, sic nec eius in terris vicarium artat aliquis terrae locus, an ad alium *ad libitum* ire possit et ibi commorari. Quin enim sibi dixit. . . Quodcunque

[1] Augustinus Triumphus, *Summa*, ii. 5 ad 3, p. 23. This even applied to a 'terra interdicta vel quae esset in rebellione contra Romanam ecclesiam'. Note his comments on the demand for a non-Italian pope which caused the election of Clement V: *Tractatus contra articulos*, iii. 3, pp. lxxxviii–lxxxix. This point was underlined by the French cardinals throughout the fourteenth century, and was subsequently used by Nicholas of Cues to advocate the choice of the archbishop of Triers as pope: *De concordantia catholica*, ii. 34, p. 774.

[2] Alexander de S. Elpidio, *De ecclesiastica potestate*, iii. 10, p. 40.

[3] Alvarus Pelagius, *De planctu Ecclesiae*, ch. 32, p. 35, 'Quod papa non cogitur stare Romae nec a Romana civitate. . . Item *sedes papalis* primo fuit Antiochiae ubi Petrus primo sedit . . . et postea iubente Domino translata est sedes Roma; . . . sicut ergo verus papa fuit Petrus in Antiochia a Domino constitutus . . . sic est ubicunque est'; cf. Peter Olivi, *De renuntiatione papae*, pp. 356–7, 360.

[4] Augustinus Triumphus, *Summa*, xxi. 1, p. 126, 'Papa non necessitatur residere in aliquo determinato loco', although he adds that it is more convenient for him to be at Rome. Cf. Conrad of Megenberg, *Oeconomica*, III. iii. 20 (Kaeppeli, p. 588), 'Ex cuius conclusione iam dicta lucide patet quod in quacunque civitate orbis papa potuerit licite residere'.

[5] The expression derives from the Roman formula, 'Roma illic est ubi imperator est': for details and examples of its application to the medieval emperors see now *KTB*, pp. 204–5. It was applied to the papacy by Peter the Venerable in the 1130s: Baluze, i. xii–xiii.

ligaveris super terram: non dixit, super Romam, nec ibi fuit data papalis potestas. . . Restet ergo, cum tota terra sit ipsius domini nostri papae Iohannis regimine dedita, et tota Ecclesia sua sedes, quod ubique *voluerit* et expeditius viderit possit esse et ibi, cum ubi sit papa ibi Roma, curiam Romanam tenere, ac praelatos ac ceteros christianos saeculares et ecclesiasticos *iuxta velle* ad sui praesentiam evocare.[1]

Conversely the *Somnium viridarii* suggests that the pope has a positive duty not to remain in Rome, since he can only fulfil his function of universal care by visiting as many parts of the *Ecclesia* as possible.[2] But even the Thomists found this a clear case for the exercise of the pope's casual right to do anything under the appropriate conditions,[3] and a feverish search for precedents began.[4] Old Rome has ceased to have any governmental importance, and so the papacy may follow the imperial example and create a New Rome on Frankish soil.[5]

[1] Lambertus Guerrici, *Liber de commendatione*, ch. 9, p. 162; cf. Opicinus de Canistris, *De praeeminentia spiritualis imperii*, p. 97, 'eo quod beatus Petrus in urbe Romana cursum vitae consumans suis successoribus illic claves vitae reliquit, quas, ut puto, possent alibi, si expediret, relinquere vel transferre'.

[2] Anon., *Somnium viridarii*, ii. 365, pp. 225–6, 'Et ubicunque papa suam eligeret mansionem, ibi Roma erit, cum sit universalis totius Ecclesiae episcopus, maxime quia orbis maior est urbe. . . Praeterea papa est episcopus Ecclesiae universalis: ergo universalem Ecclesiam tenetur visitare'.

[3] For a detailed exposition of the pope's casual right to move from Rome, provided that this is due to a case of necessity and that he makes the change with the consent of the cardinals acting *vice omnium*, see Peter de la Palu, *De causa immediata ecclesiasticae potestatis*, iv. 2, fo. 48v; Peter Olivi, *De renuntiatione papae*, pp. 356–7. The former adds however that although the pope may change his see, he must not be without one, v. 3, fo. 59v. Both state that the pope must also be directed by God to make the change, which is later interpreted by Antonio Roselli to mean that God must signify his will through a miracle: Eckermann, *op. cit.*, p. 122.

[4] The two most popular ones were Stephen II's refuge in France in the mid-eighth century, e.g. Anon., *Somnium viridarii*, ii. 365, pp. 225–6, and Christ's flight into Egypt, e.g. Anon., *Determinatio compendiosa*, ch. 39, p. 548.

[5] Avignon is described as *Nova Roma* by Opicinus de Canistris on his map of Europe: R. G. Salomon, 'A Newly Discovered Manuscript of Opicinus de Canistris', *Journal of the Warburg and Courtauld Institutes*, xvi (1953), pp. 45–57 at p. 57. This raises the question of whether Avignon was regarded as the papal see during the fourteenth century. It is so described (*sedes papalis* or *sedes pontificum*) by Francis Petrarch, *Ep.* x–xiv, pp. 1458–63: e.g. x, p. 1458, 'De tertia Babylone et quinto Labyrintho, id est, Avinione in Gallia, ubi sedes papalis'. Note also the reputed statement of Ockham that with Clement V 'Roma in Galliam migravit':

This theoretical separation of papacy and Roman church represents the last stage in the erection of the papal monarchy into a truly universal power. In the early medieval period the local connection between the papacy and Rome was of incalculable importance to the papal-hierocratic theory. Indeed it was largely by the capture of Rome that Christianity had itself become a universal force, and the universality of papal power came to rest upon the assured eminence of Rome and the Roman church. Because the pope governed from Rome, because he held the apostolic see which embodied the all-embracing power committed to St. Peter, his rule reached to the ends of the earth. The strength of the papacy lay in its having the closest possible link with Rome, and a divorce between the pope and the Roman bishopric could only have been a source of weakness when the papacy was still seeking to establish itself in a hostile world. But by the thirteenth century it had become firmly established as the dominant force in Europe, and the tie with Rome was coming to lose some of its usefulness. As Rome became more of an Italian as opposed to a universal city, so the Roman connection began to be a possible hindrance instead of a positive support to the papal universality of rule. It tended to localise the papacy; and much the same could be said of the Roman church. Indeed, with the aspirations of the cardinals mounting steadily higher, the union of pope and Roman church presented a very definite threat to papal independence of action. Rome and the Roman church had in fact

Wenck, *op. cit.*, p. 99. At a later date Alphonsus Ciaconius, *Vitae et res gestae pontificum Romanorum*, with additions by Andreas Victorellus (Rome, 1677), ii. 368, speaks of Clement V as 'episcopus Romanus Avenione'. But in general the Avignon papacy continued to refer to the Roman see as if it were itself still in Rome. It may be noted however that John XXII was still technically bishop of Avignon when he became pope, since his successor in the see (Jacobus de Via) was never consecrated. John did not in fact permit a bishop of Avignon to be created, reserving the see to himself and delegating its administration to papal vicars. Benedict XII created a bishop of Avignon in 1336, having built a separate episcopal palace there, but this bishop was immediately translated elsewhere by his successor, and the see was reserved to the pope throughout the pontificates of Clement VI and Innocent VI. After 1362 there appears to have been no definite papal policy with regard to the Avignon bishopric, and there is a confused alternation of bishops and papal administrators: Baluze, *passim*; P. P. B. Gams, *Series Episcoporum Ecclesiae Catholicae* (Ratisbon, 1873), p. 504; C. Eubel, *Hierarchia Catholica Medii Aevi* (Monasterium, 1913), i. 123–4.

served their purpose, and, as Augustinus Triumphus saw, might now with advantage be discarded. He realised that they had ceased to be vital to the papal position, and he had no hesitation in thrusting them into the background. But if the Petrine see was to diminish in importance, so too must the corresponding link with St. Peter himself. The vicariate of Christ reduced Peter to no more than another pope: it was the papal link with Christ which became all-important. Christ's office, not Peter's see, was now held to be the basis of papal power, because a direct successorship to Christ alone could emancipate the papacy from the Petrine heritage with all its local Roman ties. With the development of papal sovereignty the papal identification with Christ had to be emphasised at the expense of the successorship to Peter, and this could not be done whilst papal power was dependent upon the Roman church. Above all others Augustinus Triumphus saw how the vicariate of Christ could be made to achieve this result. But he also realised that in order to free the pope from the Roman bishopric it was necessary to rid him of his episcopacy altogether. Only a lay pope could not be bound to Rome through the connection with the Roman church. Even a trace of sacerdotal character could be dangerous to the supreme governor. And so the emphasis passed from the episcopal to the royal, from the theocratic to the bureaucratic. The hitherto vital principle that the priesthood alone was functionally qualified to govern a Christian society could safely be put aside in favour of the monarchical status of the pope as the divine head of the community. The pope was essentially a man of government, and all his necessary attributes were shaped by the needs of government. When this attitude was sufficiently marked, the need for ordination came to appear as something less of a desirable qualification and more of a possible barrier between the elected pope and the assumption of the supreme jurisdictional power which provided his *raison d'être*. To this way of thinking a fundamentally theological requirement could not be allowed to impose any restraint upon the jurisdictional omnipotence of the vicar of God. The stress upon the value of ordination, so useful a weapon for the hierocrat against the claims of the lay princes, was no longer needed when the papal supremacy could be demonstrated by the much simpler concept of the vicariate of Christ, and was almost unwelcome when ordination began to appear as a brake upon the absolute independence of the pope in the sphere of government.[1] In fact all these former supports to papal power, the association with Rome, the identification with the apostolic see, the succession from Peter, and the headship of the *sacerdotium*, were becoming liabilities rather than assets, and were largely dispensed with by the papal-hierocratic theory in its maturity. They had served to raise up the papacy as it struggled to assert itself in the early medieval world, but they had outlasted their utility and might now prove burdensome. Their rejection naturally denied much that had been part and parcel of the hierocratic system since birth, but it would give the papacy the complete freedom of action for which it sought. In this sense the move to Avignon could be seen as a vindication of the new orientation of papalist thought. It demonstrated that the papacy had snapped the links which bound it to a definite place and a specific local church. More than anything else it denoted that the papacy had become a truly universal monarchy. The 'Babylonish captivity', often regarded as being in fact the nadir of the medieval papacy, was in theory its crowning triumph.

[1] This is justified by an ingenious reversal of the traditional argument. According to Augustinus Triumphus the pope does not hold power because he has the knowledge of the right way of life in the community, but he has this knowledge or *scientia* for the very reason that he has this power. The granting of the keys to St. Peter was not only a commission of power but also of the knowledge of how to use it: the keys are both *potestas* and *scientia*, *Summa*, i. 10, p. 15; iv. 1 ad 2, p. 41; xx. 4, p. 124; xxx. 5, p. 185. The important point here is the suggestion that power is not given by God without the knowledge of how to use it: e.g. xx. 2 ad 2, p. 122, 'Sed immediata iurisdictione omne rectum iudicium quod sit in Ecclesia datur clavium potestate'. See also Pierre Dubois, *De recuperatione Terrae Sanctae*, ch. 97, p. 79. This follows the teaching of Abelard: A. Landgraf, 'Some Unknown Writings of the Early Scholastic Period', *The New Scholasticism*, iv (1930), p. 12; F. Courtney, *Cardinal Robert Pullen: An English Theologian of the Twelfth Century* (Rome, 1954), pp. 237–8. For the development of the idea of the keys as power and knowledge with the Decretists, see Tierney, *Foundations of the Conciliar Theory*, pp. 31–2; although the distinction was derived by them from Bede, *Homilia in natale beatorum apostolorum Petri et Pauli* (*PL*, xciv. 222). The fourteenth-century theory reflects the current trend in Augustinian theology by which the knowledge of what is to be done and the power to do it are both present together in the will of God.

PART V

CHANGING CONCEPTIONS OF UNIVERSAL AUTHORITY

I. THE NEW WORLD ORDER

ONE of the most interesting aspects of later medieval thought is the way in which contemporary views on society were influenced by the expansion of Europe in the twelfth and thirteenth centuries. Although early medieval writers had been well aware of the existence of barbaric *terrae incognitae* beyond the horizon of contemporary geographical knowledge, it had still been possible to consider the world as a predominantly Christian and Roman entity. There was only one society, the *congregatio fidelium* or *imperium Romanorum*, and the lost tribes of Israel, waiting menacingly beyond Alexander's Gate, could be, and were, tacitly ignored. One of the effects of the crusading movement, however, was to bring this society into abrupt and violent contact with a vast non-Christian civilisation, beyond which, it was dimly perceived, other civilisations stretched away into the Abyss. In face of this the universal nature of the Christian society was immediately called into question, and became for many writers the occasion of a retreat into the Augustinian formula by which the *Ecclesia* was universal, not in that it covered the world, but was diffused throughout it.[1] For popes and emperors on the other hand, accustomed through long usage to the title of *dominus mundi*, the steady rolling back of the ends of the earth simply permitted the forward movement of their own claims to universal domination. This was not without practical significance: the Crusades had already posed the problem of the status of pagan communities *vis-à-vis* the Christian society. Were they to be accepted as existing in their own right, or could they be seen as mere usurpations, the *latrocinia* of the *De civitate Dei*, fit only for

[1] 'Catholica Ecclesia per totum orbem longe lateque diffusa': see Gratian, D. 11 c. 8, where it is incorrectly attributed to Augustine's *De christiana fide*: it is actually *De vera religione*, 6 (*PL*, xxxiv. 127); cf. *Enarrationes in Psalmos*, lvi. 1 (*PL*, xxxvi. 662). Augustine himself however probably intended the expression to cover all men: e.g. *Sermo CCLXX*, 6 (*PL*, xxxviii. 1243), 'Congregatur enim unitas corporis Christi ex omnibus linguis, per omnes scilicet gentes toto terrarum orbe diffusas'; and see above p. 21 n. 4.

conquest and expropriation? Since it was necessary to destroy the Saracen kingdoms for the recovery of the Holy Land, the latter view tended to gain greater acceptance, and hand in hand with this went the theoretical extension of papal and imperial power to embrace the whole human race as a means of justifying attacks on non-Christian rulers. The relatively restrained programme laid out for Henry IV by Benzo of Alba, which had included the emperor's reception of the *corona mundi* at Jerusalem,[1] blossomed out in the following century with the flamboyant assertion of Frederick I that 'super omnes mortales constituti sumus',[2] and the initial attempts of Henry VI to set in train the movement for world conquest. It is true that at this point the imperial schemes ground to a halt, but already the defenders of the papal supremacy had been encouraged to follow suit, and St. Bernard's teaching that Christ had left Peter the government of the whole human race[3] becomes a familiar feature of hierocratic thought in the thirteenth and fourteenth centuries.

[1] On Benzo see Ullmann, *The Growth of Papal Government*, pp. 387–93; A. Fliche, *DHGE*, viii. 298–9. This and similar ideas were linked up with the notion of Charlemagne's crusade and the Emperor of the Last Days: Folz, *Le souvenir et la légende de Charlemagne*, pp. 134–41; N. Cohn, *The Pursuit of the Millennium* (London, 1957).

[2] *MGH*, *Const.*, I n. 191, p. 276; cf. Frederick II, *Const.*, II p. 224, referring to the German people: 'Nostrum nobis defendatis imperium, per quod invidiam omnium nationum, dignitatum omnium et mundi monarchiam obtinetis'. The usual sources quoted for universal emperorship were *Dig.*, XIV. ii. 9 and Gratian, D. 63 c. 22; D. 8 c. 1; C. 7 q. 1 c. 41; and C. 11 q. 1 c. 37. Damian had said, *Ep.*, ii. 2, that 'humanum genus veri imperatoris Christi valeant legibus subiugare' and had urged the emperor to subjugate the 'cunctae gentes', a reference to *Cod.*, I. i. 1. For publicistic examples see Anon., *Determinatio compendiosa*, ch. 37, p. 547; John of Viterbo, *De regimine civitatum*, ch. 128, p. 166; Ugolinus de Celle, *De electione regis Romanorum*, ch. 9, p. 74 and c. 11, p. 76. Note also Louis IV in Altmann-Bernheim, *Ausgewahlte Urkunden*, n. 36 p. 54.

[3] Bernard, *De consideratione*, II. ii. 8 (*PL*, clxxxii. 752), 'Nempe signum singularis pontificii Petri, per quod non navem unam, ut caeteri quique suam, sed *saeculum* ipsum susceperit gubernandum. Mare enim saeculum est, naves ecclesiae'; which was adopted by Innocent III, *Reg.*, II. ccix (*PL*, ccxiv. 759), 'Petro non solum universam *Ecclesiam* sed totum reliquit *saeculum* gubernandum . . . per hoc quod Petrus se misit in mare, privilegium expressit pontificii singularis per quod universum orbem susceperat gubernandum; caeteris apostolis ut vehiculo navis contentis, cum nulli eorum universus fuerit orbis commissus, sed singulis singulae provinciae vel ecclesiae potius deputatae'. Cf.

In spite of a *prima facie* incongruity, the extension of ecclesiastical jurisdiction to non-Christian communities had become essential as soon as a similar authority was asserted on the imperial side. Not to have done so could only have lent weight to the anti-hierocratic view that the domain of *imperium* and *ecclesia* were separated, and would ultimately have suggested that the *Ecclesia* could no longer be equated with the Roman empire and had consequently lost its identity as a political organism.[1] By the mid-thirteenth century the Staufen claims had been met by a very comprehensive statement of the papal position at the hands of the canonist, Sinibaldus Fiescus, later to become better known as Innocent IV, and this we find adopted almost word for word by Augustinus Triumphus. Underlying it is the belief that there is only one right way of life for mankind, and that the papal monopoly of this knowledge makes obedience to the pope the only means of salvation: 'Papa loco Christi habet toti humano generi consulere quid expediat ad salutem'.[2] Pagans have a right to salvation even though they them-

Augustinus Triumphus, *Summa*, xix. 4, p. 120, 'Christo autem [papa] succedit in officio et universale iurisdictione . . . non in uno loco, nec in una gente singulariter, sed universaliter in toto orbe'; ci. 1, p. 494, 'cum sit sibi commissa cura non unius ecclesiae nec unius plebis sed totius mundi'; Anon., *Determinatio compendiosa, proem.*, p. 542, 'Denique navicula Petri, cui Deus tradidit omnia regna mundi, verissime non peribit'. Note also Innocent III's justification of the crusade on the grounds that the *regnum Christi* extended 'a mari usque ad mare, et a flumine usque ad terminos orbis terrae [*Zach.*, ix. 10]', *Reg.*, XIV. lxviii (*PL*, ccxvi. 433).

[1] See Woolf, *Bartolus of Sassoferrato*, pp. 106–7, who cites an example from Albericus de Rosate, *Comm. in Cod.*, I. iv. 3, 'Ergo Iudaei subsunt Romano imperio et legibus, sed Romanae ecclesiae non': such a statement is fundamentally incompatible with the idea of a single universal Christian society. But most of the imperialists continued to assume the identity of *Ecclesia* and *Imperium*: e.g. Ubertus de Lampugnano, *Utrum omnes christiani subsunt Romano imperio*, pp. 250–1, 'Imperium mundi translatum est ad Theutonicos, nam ipsi habent regnum mundi et ecclesiae Romanae . . . quia extra Ecclesiam non est imperium [Gratian, C. 24 q. 1 c. 39]'; Alexander of Roes, *De translatione imperii*, p. 18, 'Germani . . . regnum totius Ecclesiae gubernabunt'; Anon., *Disquisitio iuridica*, ch. 1, p. 1379, 'idcirco summus pontifex regnum suum seu imperium et Ecclesiam . . . transtulit in Germanos'.

[2] Augustinus Triumphus, *Summa*, xlix. 3 ad 2, p. 266; cf. xlix. 2, p. 264, 'administratio papalis includit . . . totius reipublicae utilitatem: habet enim providere utilitati non solum unius hominis vel unius populi, immo totius mundi. Est enim vicarius Christi, qui . . . non solum uni homini sed etiam toti humano

selves disclaim it: they are to be saved in spite of themselves, and so must be subject to the power of the keys whether they recognise it or not.[1] The papalists had no fear of appearing unduly sanctimonious: they had nothing to lose and everything to gain. The subjection of pagan communities to Christian rulers is portrayed as being in the real interest of the pagans themselves, and the hierocrat might even have been shocked if it was suggested that this theory, or the crusades which were to effect it, cloaked thoroughly imperialistic aspirations. At the same time however it is made clear that logically the government of non-Christian rulers does not possess a shadow of legality. Had not Christ's kingdom embraced the whole earth, and do not those who deny it usurp the inheritance of his vicar? Did not St. Augustine, asks Aegidius Romanus, specifically state the principle that the only true *respublica* is one in which *iustitia* is to be found, and how can this refer to any community other than the Christian society? Therefore, unless pagans have been regenerated by conversion to the faith, it is safe to assume that they are not justified in possessing anything, and may be deprived of all that they hold. There cannot be any dominion worthy of the name amongst the infidels.

Dicemus enim cum Augustino, ii *De civitate Dei*, *cap*. 22 [ii.21.4: *PL*, xli.68], quod vera iustitia non est nisi in ea republica cuius conditor rectorque Christus . . . sed quicunque non est regeneratus per Ecclesiam non est sub Christo domino suo; digne igitur privatus est omni dominio suo, ut nullius rei iuste dominus esse possit.[2]

generi consulit *quid agendum*'. Note also *Decretales*, I. i. 1; and *Extravagantes communes*, I. viii. 1. For Innocent IV's teaching see Ullmann, *Medieval Papalism*, pp. 121–36.

[1] Augustinus Triumphus, *Summa*, xxiii. 1 ad 1, p. 136, 'Pagani et infideles potestate clavium ligati sunt et iudicati, quia qui non credunt iam iudicati sunt'; cf. Zenzellinus de Cassanis, *Glossa ordinaria ad Extravagantes Iohannis XXII*, v. 1, fo. 40, sv. *Commisit*, 'Sed an istam commissionem Christus fecisse videatur nedum super catholicos et fideles, an etiam super non-catholicos et infideles, dicas quod sic'.

[2] Aegidius Romanus, *De ecclesiastica potestate*, ii. 7, pp. 73–4; cf. iii. 11, p. 201, 'Immo apud infideles non solum non sunt regna neque imperia, cum apud eos regna et imperia sint *latrocinia*, immo etiam apud eos non sunt aliqua iusta dominia, ut non sit aliquis infidelis iustus dominus sive iustus possessor'; also Guido Vernani, *De reprobatione Monarchiae*, ch. 1, p. 128, 'in infidelibus numquam fuit vera respublica nec aliquis v rus imperator'; and note Augustinus

A rigid adherence to Augustinian principles could lead to no other conclusion. But on the whole most of the fourteenth century writers were prepared to temper their theories with practice. It is acknowledged that the papal supremacy over pagans is a *de iure*, not a *de facto* one, and, indeed, many of them went further and recognised the right of pagan communities to exist by natural law. Even Augustinus Triumphus says that it is better to have a ruler, albeit a pagan one, than no ruler at all, and since the sun shines on the just and the unjust without distinction, it is not to be supposed that pagan government is devoid of all value.[1] Pagan rulers may even perhaps be said to have a divine right existence of their own which exempts them from automatic conquest by Christian princes.[2] But if natural law justifies this, then a breach of natural law by a pagan ruler would equally justify the right of the pope to intervene:

> . . . pagani non sunt subiecti de facto sed de iure, quia de iure nulla rationis creatura potest se de eius dominio subtrahere sicut nec a dominio Dei. Unde cum transgressores legis naturae devolvuntur ad iudicium papae, iuste potest eos punire.[3]

Triumphus, *Summa*, xxxvi. 1, p. 212, where he contrasts the 'dominium usurpatum et tyrannicum' with 'omnes qui iusto titulo dominio naturali et politico sumpserunt dominium ad reipublicae defensionem et Ecclesiae Dei tuitionem vere per summos sacerdotes ordinati sunt'.

[1] Augustinus Triumphus, *Summa*, xxiii. 3, p. 138, 'dominium unius super alterum inter beneficia naturalia computatur... Ordo ergo principandi, cum sit beneficium naturae, omni humanae creaturae concessum, nec per papam nec per alios reges christianorum ab infidelibus subtrahendum est, cum Deus, cuius iudicium Ecclesia imitatur, talia beneficia naturae omnibus bonis et malis largiatur, quia solem suum oriri facit super bonos et malos, et pluit super iustos et iniustos, ut dicit *Matt.*, v [45]; cf. Thomas Aquinas, *Summa theologica*, II. II. xii. 2, 'Infidelitas secundum seipsam non repugnat dominio'. Papal power over pagans was denied altogether by Alexander de S. Elpidio, *De ecclesiastica potestate*, i. 4, p. 6; Durandus de S. Porciano, *De iurisdictione ecclesiastica*, ch. 3, fo. 4; Anon., *Somnium viridarii*, ii. 35, p. 154: but Augustinus Triumphus castigates this as the teaching of *pseudo-doctores*, *Summa*, xxii. 7, p. 135.

[2] Augustinus Triumphus, *Summa*, xxiii. 2, p. 137, 'Si vero dicti pagani vel barbari non subsunt regibus vel principibus christianis sed reguntur per reges vel soldanos eorum, tunc probabiliter videtur dicendum quod illis subdantur quorum sub potestate consistunt, quia omnis potestas a Deo est'; cf. xxiii. 5 ad 3, p. 140, 'Si vero dicti pagani existant sub soldano vel sub aliquo alio principe infideli debent vivere secundum ritus et observantias ac statuta illorum'.

[3] Augustinus Triumphus, *Summa*, xxiii. 4 ad 2, p. 139. The only pagans fully subject to papal control are those living within the territories of Christian kings,

In this case the pope may depose pagan rulers,[1] and he is at full liberty to levy war against them if they infringe the rights of any Christian subjects resident in their territories.[2] But there is to be no forceful conversion of non-believers to Christianity,[3] and Augustinus Triumphus' whole attitude to the pagan question is that papal action is to be considered as a special circumstance rather than a conformance with normal practice. There is no outright denial of pagan rule: once again the acceptance of the natural law theory covers a multitude of sins.

However reasonable it might appear, this use of the Thomist natural law idea to limit papal freedom of action was a falling away from the hierocratic viewpoint in its most orthodox form, and we may mark it as the point at which Augustinus Triumphus begins to succumb to the undeniable attractions of the Thomist synthesis. In practice the theoretical universality of papal authority is severely curtailed. Yet what Aquinas took away with one hand, he gave with another. Since the universality of papal government now becomes a largely theoretical matter, there need be no limits to its development, and it is Aquinas who is responsible for the extension of

as for example in Spain: xxiii. 2, p. 137. A similar *de iure—de facto* distinction is used by Alvarus Pelagius, Aegidius Spiritalis, Francis Toti de Perusio, Hermannus de Schildiz and Peter Bertrandus.

[1] Augustinus Triumphus, *Summa*, xxiii. 3 ad 3, p. 138, 'Ecclesia persequitur infideles christianos impugnantes vel iura ecclesiastica et iura nostra tyrannica rabie occupantes et multa turbulenta contra christianos attentantes; *in talibus casibus* iuste papa potest ab eis dominia et iurisdictiones auferre et licitum bellum eis indicare'. In general this follows Thomas Aquinas, *Summa theologica*, II. II. x. 10–11.

[2] Augustinus Triumphus, *Summa*, xxii. 7, p. 135, 'Sciendum est tamen quod propter tria papa potest christianos a dominio infidelium iuste subtrahere: primo propter iniustam dominii adeptionem. Unde si infideles violenter acceperunt dominium supra fideles, iuste papa posset fideles a dominio eorum subtrahere. Secundo propter iniustum usum, ut si non iuste uterentur eorum dominio, praecipiendo eis illicita contra mandata Dei et virtuosos mores, vel insolita imponendo onera gravia et importabilia. Tertio propter indecentem statum'. Like Innocent IV Augustinus Triumphus asserts complete papal control over Christians subject to pagan rulers: one could not escape papal jurisdiction by moving to non-Christian territories: xxvi. 3 ad 3, p. 157; xlvi. 2, p. 250; similarly Thomas Aquinas, *Summa theologica*, II. II. xii. 2.

[3] Augustinus Triumphus, *Summa*, xxiv. 2, p. 142; also Thomas Aquinas, *Summa theologica*, II. II. x. 8.

the *Ecclesia* itself, as opposed simply to papal power, beyond the bounds of Christianity. Admittedly this might be regarded as no more than a logical expansion of Augustinian theory, and so it was made to appear. If the only political society in the world which has a real right to exist is a Christian one, it could be argued that the whole world must therefore automatically become a Christian society. This was no doubt a very praiseworthy ideal, but in the long run it meant a dilution of the concept of the Universal Church. Ultimately the inclusion of pagans within an essentially Christian society makes nonsense of the whole idea. But since Aquinas saw the *Ecclesia* as no more than a superimposition upon a number of naturally existing, not specifically Christian, communities, it was for him logically perfectly possible, and the attractions of the idea to those who sought to bring every human being under papal control were well nigh irresistible. Moreover it seemed to offer an answer to the extreme lay position: the Universal Church may now be seen as a real *communitas mortalium*.[1] The point is laboured by Guido Vernani in his answer to Dante. The universal monarchy, which Dante had described as the *universitas* of mortals, is none other than the monarchy of Christ, and Dante's emperor is the pope, the 'monarcha totius humani generis'.[2] But be this as it may, the universal society inevitably takes several steps towards the secularisation which comes out so strongly in the *Defensor pacis*.

In moments of unwonted sobriety the fourteenth-century publicist sometimes managed to recall the fact that the *Ecclesia* was in reality nothing more than a *populus christianus*,[3] and special credit is

[1] Thomas Aquinas, *Commentum in Sententias*, III. xxix. 6, 'omnes homines communicant in uno corpore Ecclesiae vel *actu* vel *potentia*'; *De potentia*, v. 6 ad 3, 'Homo naturaliter non solum de seipso sollicitatur sed etiam de statu communitatis . . . etiam totius orbis'; and see his description of the *communitas humana sub Deo* in which all should live by faith in *Summa theologica*, II. 1. c. 5.

[2] Guido Vernani, *De reprobatione Monarchiae*, ch. 1, p. 128; cf. Hervaeus Natalis, *De potestate papae*, fo. 142, 'communitas christiana sit communitas humana'. Similarly Aegidius Spiritalis, *Libellus contra infideles*, p. 122, describes the *Ecclesia* as the 'universitas humani generis' or 'politia humana': therefore the pope is ruler 'in toto universo'.

[3] Note for example Alvarus Pelagius' careful distinction, *De planctu Ecclesiae*, ch. 60, p. 187, 'Sed aliter dicitur regnum Christi omnis creatura, aliter Ecclesia . . . Regnum enim Christi dicitur omnis creatura secundum potestatem divinitatis, Ecclesia vero dicitur regnum Christi secundum proprietatem fidei quae de

due to Augustinus Triumphus as one of the very few hierocratic writers who remembered to acknowledge the existence of the Greek schism.[1] But in general the exponents of the papal claims were only too delighted to assert that all the earth was, or rather ought to be, a gigantic Christian community. There are many governments, says Augustinus Triumphus, which *de facto* do not acknowledge the pope, but this does not alter the even more important fact that these *praelationes apud Gentiles* ought to obey him.[2] If the emperor is to hold sway 'ad omnes fines terrae', then, declares Tholemy of Lucca, how much more this must apply to the true vicar of God.[3] Imbued with a deep sense of ultimate reality, to the

illo est et per quam regnat in ipsis fidelibus'; cf. Augustinus Triumphus, *Summa*, xxiii. 1 ad 3, p. 137, 'secundo, imitatione et voluntate, et sic solum fideles et boni sunt de Ecclesia'. Alexander of Roes, *Notitia saeculi*, p. 662, had referred to the *mundus* as including Africa, Asia and Europe, but decided to speak only of 'de terminis Europae et de populo christiano'; cf. p. 668, 'Verum respublica Ecclesiae Romanae residet in Europa'.

[1] Augustinus Triumphus would seem to be about the only contemporary publicist to deal with the status of the Greeks at any length. He emphasises that they are technically part of the Ecclesia (*Summa*, viii. 2, p. 69) and argues that this is shown by the fact that a Greek submitting to the Roman church does not require a second baptism (xxv. 6, p. 153): on the whole question of this see the excellent historical survey by L. Saltet, *Les réordinations* (Paris, 1907). Nevertheless he sees serious theological difficulties in the way of accepting the Greeks wholeheartedly, as for example the *Filioque* affair (xxv. 5, p. 153: the matter is discussed at length in his *Theoremata*; see Ministeri, *De vita et operibus*, pp. 150–1) and it is undeniable that they are in a state of schism. Whilst he agrees with the general opinion of the time that schism is tantamount to heresy, he decides that the Greek heresy is still indefinite (*inchoatum*) and that therefore they are more properly only schismatics: the door is not closed to their return to the fold. It is interesting to notice that he maintains that the Greeks seceded out of pique at the unwillingness of the popes to grant them high office in the *Ecclesia*, cii. 4, p. 504. For a contemporary scheme to reunite the Greek and Roman churches see C. Giannelli, 'Un progetto di Barlaam Calabro per l'unione delle Chiese', *Miscellanea Giovanni Mercati* (Vatican City, 1946), iii. 157–208; also M. Jugis, *DHGE*, vi. 817–34.

[2] Augustinus Triumphus, *Summa*, lxxi. 4 ad 2, p. 374, 'apud Gentiles sunt praelationes quas licet non recognoscant [papam] *de facto*, recognoscere tamen tenentur *de iure*, illo scilicet iure quo omnes tenentur subiici Christo'.

[3] Tholemy of Lucca, *Determinatio compendiosa*, ch. 15, p. 33: thus, he concludes, 'apparet ex plenitudine potestatis pontificalis omnia dependere, in cuius manu sunt omnes fines terrae, ut propheta dicit, tamquam vicem Dei gerentis'. Note also Dante, *Ep.*, vii. 3, p. 92, where the empire is described as reaching to the ocean encircling the earth. Cf. *Psal.*, xciv. 4.

papalist what is factually realised is of much less significance than what ought to be according to the divine pattern of society. True reality, the basis for procedure, is what is known to be right, not the inadequacy of the existing situation. As Conrad of Megenberg urges, the whole world is the *Ecclesia* even though the whole world refuses it.[1] All men are for Augustinus Triumphus the sheep of Christ whether they wish it or not. They are created by God, their only chance of salvation lies in God, and so *iure creationis et iure redemptoris* they are subject to his vicar.[2] And since salvation is impossible outside the Church, they must be regarded as members of the *communitas fidelium*.[3] In this sense both pagans and Christians are part of the *Ecclesia*.

Esse de Ecclesia potest intelligi tripliciter: primo iudicaria potestate, et sic omnes sunt de Ecclesia, boni et mali, fideles et infideles. Quia sicut omnes habent unum Deum, sic omnes de iure debent habere unum pastorem qui vicem eius gerat.[4]

[1] Conrad of Megenberg, *Oeconomica* (Struve, p. 87), 'Totus enim mundus est in Ecclesia, quamvis totus mundus Ecclesiam odiat'.

[2] Augustinus Triumphus, *Summa*, xxiii. 1 ad 2, p. 136: this follows St. Bernard, *De consideratione*, iii. 1 (*PL*, clxxxii. 758). Cf. Aegidius Spiritalis, *Libellus contra infideles*, p. 110, 'Et notandum quod summus pontifex non solum super christianos et fideles, verum etiam super Saracenos et infideles et scismaticos in spiritualibus et temporalibus obtinet iurisdictionem plenariam et plenitudinem potestatis. Nam ipse Deus dicendo, Pasces oves meas, non distincxit has vel illas, et ipsi infideles et scismatici sunt oves Christi per creationem, licet non sint de ovili . . . bene sequitur quod papa super omnes infideles et scismaticos habet iurisdictionem et potestatem *de iure*, licet non *de facto*. . . Nam in adventu Christi omnis honor et omnis principatus et omnium dominium ut iurisdictio de iure ex causa iusta . . . omni infideli subtracta fuerunt et ad fideles translata'. This last sentence is taken from Hostiensis, *ad Decretales*, III. xxxiv. 8.

[3] Augustinus Triumphus, *Summa*, i. 6 ad 1, p. 10, 'Sed in quinta communitate [scil. in communitate totius orbis] praeest summus pontifex, quia quantum est de iure omnes qui sunt in toto orbe debent subiici summo pontifici, sicut enim de iure legis divinae nullus potest salvari nisi sit de corpore Ecclesiae, quia extra Ecclesiam non est salus, ita de iure est quod omnes qui sunt in toto orbe sint sub potestate papae'; cf. Aegidius Romanus, *De renuntiatione papae*, x. 4, p. 25, 'Sed nostra Ecclesia est catholica et universalis, ut extra eam non possit esse salus; ergo de iure Ecclesia occupat totum mundum, quia de iure omnes deberent obedire Evangelio, omnes deberent subesse summo pontifice. . . Sic ergo est de iure quod Ecclesia totum contineat'.

[4] Augustinus Triumphus, *Summa*, xxiii. 1 ad 3, p. 137. Cf. Thomas Aquinas, *Summa theologica*, III. viii. 3 ad 1, 'Dicendum quod illi qui sunt infideles, etsi *actu* non sint de Ecclesia, sunt tamen de Ecclesia in *potentia*', which follows on the

This theory is indicative of the whole papal ideology. Convinced of its supreme duty of furthering God's purpose on earth, it becomes equally certain that all things exist for this end, and may be used accordingly. Augustinus Triumphus brings this out very well indeed. Pagan nations are to be regarded as part of the *Ecclesia* because they can be utilised for Christian purposes,

tertio occasionaliter fructuosa utilitate, et sic omnes pagani infideles possunt dici de Ecclesia,[1]

and he tends to assume that any 'right thinking' pagan would permit himself to become an *instrumentum Ecclesiae*. Had not the great Augustine declared that even the enemies of the faith recognised its universality? And so, although clearly very inferior members of the society, pagans might still have their 'fruitful purposes'. It might even be permissible to make alliances with the infidels in order to correct by pressure from without those unruly Christians who disturbed the right order in Europe.[2] The pagan has only colonial status in the ecclesiastical empire, but colonies are useful and possess nominal membership. Indeed the roots of much of the imperial outlook of post-Reformation history, with its combination of missionary activity and territorial conquest, lie deep in the hierocratic conception of a Christian empire on which the sun—in this analogy the pope himself—never sets.

statement that 'Christus est caput eorum qui in *potentia* sibi sunt uniti, quae numquam reducetur ad *actum*'. Note the general equation of act and potency with *de facto* and *de iure* respectively. The whole Thomist theory of casual jurisdiction is now in fact being applied to the relationship between the pope and pagan rulers.

[1] Augustinus Triumphus, *Summa*, xxiii. 1 ad 3, p. 137. This is supported by a quotation from Augustine, *De vera religione*, ch. 6 (*PL*, xxxiv. 127), 'Catholica Ecclesia . . . omnibus utitur ad profectos suos. Nam utitur paganis et Gentilibus ad materiam operationis suae'. The passage continues, 'Tenenda est nobis christiana religio et eius Ecclesiae communicatio quae catholica est, et catholica nominatur non solum a suis verum etiam ab omnibus inimicis'.

[2] The general principle that enemies of the society may be used to punish its rebellious elements is stated by Augustinus Triumphus, *Summa*, xlviii. 1 ad 2, p. 260, 'rebelles fidei per eos tamquam per inimicos reipublicae corrigere'. The actual question under discussion is whether the pope may make use of magicians. One may call to mind the long series of alliances with the Turks made by Christian rulers, notably the papacy and the French, from the fifteenth century onwards.

Following however the short Indian summer after the collapse of the Staufen in 1250, when even Alexander of Roes came to regard the papacy as the centre of a truly universal monarchy,[1] the papal sun, as Dante said, had gone rapidly into eclipse, and by its move to Avignon had given itself as hostage to a ruler who was totally opposed to all forms of universal domination other than his own.[2] The aspirations of the French monarchy towards autonomy were by this time a far more realistic approach to the problem of the right order than the unattainable idealism of universal government. Yet the dream of universal power was never in any danger of dying out, and even in the fourteenth century must be regarded as the orthodox attitude of both papalists and imperialists. It almost seemed that for once the great antagonists really had reached a measure of agreement. Whatever their views on the right distribution of authority within the community, both were united in the belief that the community ought to be universal, and that all lesser rulers should be subject to a universal head. Viewed against the contemporary situation, Augustinus Triumphus' repeated assertion that 'papa habet universalem iurisdictionem in toto orbe',[3] Henry VII's claim that only the *pax Romana* can regulate the world,[4] and the joint papal-imperial emphasis upon universality of care[5]—to take only a few examples—seem like echoes from an age

[1] Alexander of Roes, *Notitia saeculi*, p. 665: these were the years after the deposition of Frederick II when 'ad pedes Romani pontificis non solum populus christianus et praelati ecclesiastici, sed etiam reges mundi, Iudaei, Graeci et Tartari convenientes, recognoverunt Romano sacerdotio mundi monarchiam'.

[2] Dante, *Ep.*, viii. 10, p. 138, 'erubescendum esse vobis, dolendum quis dubitet, qui tantum insolitae sui vel solis eclipsis causa fuistis?'

[3] Augustinus Triumphus, *Summa*, xxxviii. 4, p. 227; also iii. 6, p. 34; xlv. 2 ad 3, p. 248; cf. xix. 3, p. 119, 'regit totum mundum'; lxxxviii. 1 ad 1, p. 439, 'caput omnium populorum'.

[4] *MGH, Const.*, IV. 2 pp. 965–6, 'Romanum imperium in cuius tranquillitate totius orbis regularitas requiescit'. Dante, *Ep.*, vi. 6, p. 75, said that the movement of the world became irregular during an imperial vacancy.

[5] Augustinus Triumphus, *Summa*, xviii. 1 ad 2, p. 113, 'papae committitur cura et custodia omnium universaliter'; lxi. 5, p. 325, 'Et ideo per papam cui cura debet esse de omnibus'; lxv. 6 ad 3, p. 348, 'qui de omnibus curam habet'; Conrad of Megenberg, *Oeconomica*, III. iii. 19 (Kaeppeli, p. 604), 'De sollicitudine papae circa orbem'; Louis IV, Baluze, iii. 240, 'omnem totius reipublicae curam gerens'.

already assuming the character of a mythology. Nevertheless the old universalism retains a quite remarkable degree of currency in thirteenth- and fourteenth-century thought. Popes and emperors still figure as the *dominus mundi* of the Roman law books,[1] kings of kings and lords of lords;[2] kingdoms are still only provinces of the universal empire, their rulers only papal-imperial governors;[3] Rome is still the *caput mundi*, the common fatherland of all believers;[4] and Roman law is still common to all the world.[5] Even the grossly ineffective Louis of Bavaria did not find it outrageous to suggest that God had made him capable of creating and destroying all other kingdoms.[6]

Whilst papal writers in the fourteenth century naturally tended to concentrate more upon the universal monarchy of the pope and less upon the universality of imperial jurisdiction, remarkably little attention was paid to suggestions that the imperial office should be

[1] E.g. Conrad of Megenberg, *De translatione Romani imperii*, ch. 1, pp. 252–3; Alvarus Pelagius, *De planctu Ecclesiae*, ch. 37, p. 46; John of Calvaruso, *Quaestio an Romanus pontifex potuerit treugam inducere*, p. 1309; cf. p. 1315, 'Totus enim mundus imperatoris est'.

[2] Jordan of Osnabruck, *De praerogativa Romani imperii*, p. 14, 'Ostendit enim potestatem Caesaris aliis potestatibus mundanis praeeminere et ipsas sub eo *contineri*. Quid est enim potestatem dari desuper nisi dari ab eo cuius supereminet potestas et alias potestates mundanas tamquam inferiores et minores sub se *continet* et *includit*'; Augustinus Triumphus, *Summa*, xlvi. 2 ad 3, p. 251, 'ad papam spectat correctio regum et aliorum . . . propter universalem iurisdictionem quam vice Christi habet in toto orbe super reges et super omnes alios principes'; Anon., *Somnium viridarii*, i. 35, p. 67, 'cum omnes reges et principes debeant subesse imperatori in temporalibus quoad administrationem et executionem; mundi enim dominus est . . . sub imperatore enim subsunt omnes nationes . . . totius orbis obtinet monarchiam'.

[3] E.g. Johannes Branchazolus, *De principio imperatoris et papae*, ii. 1, p. 49; Alexander of Roes, *De translatione imperii*, p. 19; Augustinus Triumphus, *Summa*, i. 6 ad 1, p. 10.

[4] Anon., *Disquisitio prior iuridica*, ch. 4, p. 1330, 'Roma communis patria'; also Francis Petrarch, *Ep.*, viii, p. 1357; cf. Bartolus, *ad Dig.*, I. xxxiii. 2, 'Quaero ad quid dicitur communis patria Roma? Respondeo quia quilibet potest ibi convenire. . . Praeterea quilibet de imperio Romano est ibi civis': Ercole, *Da Bartolo all'Althusio*, p. 50.

[5] Louis IV, Baluze, iii. 395; Bartolus, *ad Cod.*, I. xii. 6, 'Regulariter autem lex communis est omnibus civitatibus et locis'; *Quaestio*, i. 20, 'iura communia civitatis Romanae seu Romani imperii': Ercole, *op. cit.*, pp. 96, 99; and see further Ullmann, *The Medieval Idea of Law*, pp. xxxiii, 72f.

[6] See for example his adaptation of *Jeremiah*, i. 10, in Baluze, iii. 426.

abolished altogether. In many ways it seemed as if the papalists were only just beginning to discover how useful an emperor was, and since the middle of the thirteenth century, since ironically enough the Empire became moribund, there was an increased emphasis upon the exalted status of the emperor as against other rulers. As Augustinus Triumphus says, he is personally elected and crowned by the pope, and this is something which cannot be said for any other ruler:

... non est simile quia papa confert imperatori immediatam administrationem et est minister ecclesiae in administratione temporalium, quam non confert aliis; constitutio aliorum regum vel principum vadit per successionem, non autem sic institutio imperatoris; quicquid agitur circa imperium, tam eius electio quam eius confirmatio, totum est ex institutione ecclesiae, quod non contingit de aliis.[1]

Yet this emphasis merely served to add weight to a problem already posed by the author of the *Rex pacificus*. It is all very well, he argues, for the pope to claim to be the source of all royal jurisdiction, but since no king, certainly no king of France, is ever crowned by the pope, how can this really be said to be the case?[2] The Frenchman had scored a telling point, and it is very noticeable how all the

[1] Augustinus Triumphus, *Summa*, xxxix. 1 ad 2, p. 228; also xli. 2 ad 3, p. 234; Conrad of Megenberg, *De translatione Romani imperii*, ch. 13, p. 295; Lambertus Guerrici de Hoyo, *Liber de commendatione*, ch. 2, p. 159. This is taken from Innocent IV: see Winkelmann, ii. 699; and cf. his *App. ad Decretales*, II. ii. 10, sv. *vacante*, 'Nam specialis coniunctio est inter papam et imperatorem, quia papa eum consecrat et examinat, et est imperator eius advocatus, et iurat ei, et ab eo imperium tenet', which was followed by Hostiensis.

[2] Anon., *Rex pacificus*, ch. 2, p. 667, 'Sed multi sunt reges et domini temporales qui nec in personis suis nec praedecessorum suorum unquam in regnis suis receperunt aliquam investituram a papa'. By contrast Aegidius Spiritalis, *Libellus contra infideles*, p. 106, refers to the emperor 'et aliis regibus et principibus qui ab eo recipiunt *immediate* gladii potestatem': as an example he quotes (p. 110) Innocent III's coronation of Peter of Aragon. This was in fact the first example he could have quoted since Frankish times, and the curial state of unpreparedness for crowning kings is apparent in the lack of a royal coronation order: a royal *ordo* had to be hastily prepared for the coronation of Charles of Anjou in 1289, and it was not until Robert of Naples required crowning in 1309 that an official order was drawn up: W. Ullmann, 'The Curial Exequies for Edward I and Edward III', *Journal of Ecclesiastical History*, vi (1955), pp. 26–36 at p. 28.

hierocratic writers of the next few decades give their earnest attention to the matter. The more conservative publicists immediately fell back on the traditional canonistic explanation that royal authority was derived from the pope through the emperor: it is the emperor's task to subdelegate authority to other rulers. He is, Augustinus Triumphus explains, the medium through which papal jurisdiction passes on to all lesser lay officials, a 'quasi quoddam medium inter alios reges et papam',[1] a sort of ecclesiastical sundog.[2] The imperial coronation is to be considered as the act of institution for all other princes, whose own coronations validate the appointment of their own lower officers.

> ... innuendo ut cum imperialis dignitas omnium sub ecclesia temporalium dignitatum ... sit principosa, domina et magistra, caeterorum regum fidelium coronationes ... semper per summum pontificem commode celebrari in imperatoris coronatione, ut membra in capite et subditi in domino repetantur. De caeteris autem christianis principibus, ducibus, comitibus, baronibus, militibus et aliis nobilibus sub regibus constitutis, et per eos in suis dignitatibus, dominationibus et iurisdictionibus approbatis, potest dici quod in regum coronationibus, ut reges in imperatoris ... confirmantur.[3]

Thus the imperial coronation oath covers all subsidiary offices. For example a bailiff's oath to the king is, through the king's oath at his coronation, and the emperor's oath at the imperial coronation, in

[1] Augustinus Triumphus, *Summa*, xlv. 3 ad 3, p. 249; cf. xliv. 1 ad 2, p. 241, 'imperator medius est et sequester inter sibi subditos vel populum et papam quantum ad curam temporalem'. It may be noted however that he carefully avoids answering the question of whether a royal election should be subject to imperial approval: xli. 2 *prop.* 3, p. 233. See also Opicinus de Canistris, *De praeeminentia spiritualis imperii*, p. 94, 'et temporalem [potestatem] imperatori terreno relinquat, inferioribus regibus et ducibus dispensandum per ipsum imperatorem'; p. 97, 'sed potius alii tradere, videlicet imperatori saeculari in plenitudinem saecularis potestatis, qui ministerium illius in partem aliis *subcommittit*'. For the canonistic view see Ullmann, *Medieval Papalism*, pp. 145, 195. Examples of imperial creation of kings are fairly numerous compared to the number of papal creations.

[2] Boniface VIII told the legates of Albert I in 1303 that the pope was like the sun compared to the emperor, but added that otherwise the emperor 'est sol sicut monarcha, qui habet omnes illuminare': *MGH*, *Const.*, IV. 1 p. 133.

[3] Lambertus Guerrici de Hoyo, *Liber de commendatione*, ch. 2, pp. 159–60.

reality an oath to the pope.[1] On the other hand nearly every papal writer is constrained to admit that most kings were enjoying hereditary succession, and so it was painfully obvious that the emperor had nothing to do with the creation of other European rulers. And with the confused state of affairs which arose from the current demand of so many kings to be free of imperial jurisdiction, an alternative solution quickly gains acceptance. We have already had occasion to refer to the hierocratic scheme of things in which the primate of any kingdom becomes the real head *loco papae*, and this is now taken a stage further. The king's coronation by his archbishop is held to be exactly analogous to the papal coronation of the emperor.

Item est notandum quod rex recepit coronam et gladium ab ecclesia sicut imperator, ut sit defensor fidei et ecclesiae et conservator iurium ecclesiae, unde videtur se habere ad papam sicut manus ad caput in defendendo et ministrando. . . Unde quilibet rex ab episcopo aliquo regni sui *nomine ecclesiae dantis* recipit gladium, intelligendo quod in gladio recipit curam et regimen totius regni.[2]

Hence the king's election or succession is seen to be nothing more than a nomination. The coronation is the real constitutive event, and is brought about by the pope acting through the archbishop in his capacity as a papal vicar:[3] and in this way the direct papal appointment of lay rulers can be said to be maintained.

[1] Augustinus Triumphus, *Summa*, xl. 4, p. 232; Aegidius Romanus, *De ecclesiastica potestate*, ii. 5, p. 59; Peter Bertrandus, *De iurisdictione ecclesiastica*, p. 1373b.

[2] Alvarus Pelagius, *Speculum regum*, pp. 518–19; cf. Anon., *Somnium viridarii*, i. 166, p. 126, 'Rursum dico quod rex accipit aliquam potestatem super temporalia a persona ecclesiastica ex eo quod a persona ecclesiastica inungitur: exemplum in rege Franciae, qui inungitur ab archiepiscopo Remensi': the author points out that this has special reference to kings succeeding to the throne by hereditary right, i. 170, p. 127; i. 172, p. 128. It is significant that the bulk of the opposition to this idea comes from imperial sources: e.g. John of Calvaruso, *Quaestio an Romanus pontifex potuerit treugam inducere*, p. 1311; Lupold of Bebenburg, *De iure regni Romani*, ch. 8, p. 365; William of Ockham, *Tractatus contra Benedictum XII*, vi. 13, p. 296; *Octo quaestiones*, v *passim*; Ugolinus de Celle, *De electione regis Romanorum*, ch. 13, p. 77.

[3] There is a long statement to this effect in Aegidius Romanus, *De ecclesiastica potestate*, iii. 2, p. 154. Alexander de S. Elpidio, *De ecclesiastica potestate*, ii. 3, p. 17, makes the point that on this basis no king should be permitted to govern

Such expedients were ingenious, but they were hardly likely to influence the lay monarchs whose minds were obsessed by the desire for national autonomy and freedom from all external interference in the affairs of their own kingdoms. The growth of the national sovereign state has already been the subject of much discussion, which does not require repetition here: we wish now merely to underline certain aspects of the form which the idea was taking in the publicistic writings of the early fourteenth century. It goes without saying that the aim of the French monarchy, for example, was to throw off all legal subjection to the emperor. What however is not generally made clear is the fact that French independence of the emperor was, for all the appeals to the famous statement of Innocent III,[1] just as much an oblique attack upon papal supremacy. 'Qui vos spernit, me spernit': and the constant clamour of the French tracts that 'rex non habet superiorem sed Deum' and 'rex in regno suo est imperator' was received on the papal side as a direct insult to the Roman church. As Boniface VIII said, the Frenchman lie in asserting royal independence of the Empire, which by right (*de iure*) they should acknowledge lest the rights of the papal monarchy should thereby be infringed.[2] The jurisdiction

before coronation. This may be the influence of Innocent IV's statement that the imperial candidate could act as king after coronation by the archbishop of Cologne at Aix, although here Innocent had intended only to show why Otto [IV] should have been preferred to Philip of Suabia by the German people in 1198: Bayley, *The Formation of the German College of Electors*, p. 145. In the modern *Pontificale Romanum* a king is still referred to as *futurus rex* until after his anointing by the archbishop.

[1] E.g. Anon., *Rex pacificus*, ch. 2, p. 667; Pierre Dubois, *La supplication du pueuble de France*, p. 215. Innocent had remarked 'Insuper cum rex superiorem in temporalibus minime recognoscat . . .', *Decretales*, IV. xvii. 13. Elsewhere, however, Innocent had made it clear that a king with no lay superior had a superior in the person of the pope as vicar of God; see his long discussion of this, *Comm. in Psal.*, 4 (*PL*, ccxvii. 1055–6).

[2] Boniface VIII, *MGH*, *Const.*, IV. 1 n. 175, p. 136, 'Nec insurgat hic superbia Gallicana quae dicit quod non recognoscit imperium. Mentiuntur, quia de iure sunt et esse debent sub rege Romano et imperatore . . . *quia* constat quod christiani subditi fuerunt monarchis ecclesiae Romanae et esse debent'. Cf. Augustinus Triumphus, *Tractatus contra articulos*, iii. 2, p. lxxxvi, 'reges moderni gentis Francorum, suorum praedecessorum vestigia non sequentes, in tantum sunt in superbia elati quod, quasi ad modum Nabuchodonosor regis, nolunt *aliquem* super se recognoscere'.

of a papal official was being called into question, and this could only cast a reflection upon the papacy itself. In fact during the fiercest stages of the conflict between Philip the Fair and Boniface, the French king and his supporters had abandoned all pretence and turned the attack upon imperial authority into an outright denial of papal supremacy. As Philip told the papal legates in 1297, in governmental affairs the French crown is subject to nobody, and nobody means nobody.[1] The French monarchy holds a prescriptive right against the Roman church which, according to Pierre Dubois, has been in force for a thousand years,[2] and the papalists must understand that what is said of the emperor is intended to apply to his master. The very fact that the French kingdom is not part of the Roman empire, says the *Rex pacificus*, must indicate that the pope is not the overlord of its king.

Quantum ergo ad illa regna quae non subsunt Romano imperio, non est papa dominus superior in temporalibus. Regnum autem Franciae non subest Romano imperio: immo sunt certi limites et fuerunt a tempore ex quo non extat memoria per quos regnum et imperium dividuntur. *Ergo* papa in regno Franciae non est dominus nec superior in temporalibus.[3]

Somewhat illogically most of the French writers agreed that the emperor was subject to papal authority, as this contrasted all the

[1] According to the report of the legates, 20 April 1297, the king told them 'Regimen temporalitatis regni sui ad ipsum regem solum et neminem alium pertinere, seque in eo neminem superiorem recognoscere nec habere, nec se intendere supponere vel subicere modo quocunque viventi alicui super rebus pertinentibus ad temporale regimen regni': Dupuy, p. 28.

[2] Pierre Dubois, *Deliberatio super agendis*, p. 46; *La supplication du pueuble de France*, p. 218; also Anon., *Rex pacificus*, ch. 3, p. 675; Anon., *Quaestio in utramque partem*, ch. 5, p. 102. The figure varies from a hundred to a thousand.

[3] Anon., *Rex pacificus*, ch. 3, p. 675: the time to which memory did not run was usually regarded as a century, the requisite period for the establishment of a prescriptive right. See also Anon., *Somnium viridarii*, i. 36, p. 70, 'rex Franciae non recognoscit superiorem . . . nec de facto nec de iure. . . Ex quibus clare concluditur regem Franciae in *nullo* subesse imperatori et *per consequens* nec Romanae ecclesiae in temporalibus saltem ex illo capite quia imperator subest papae'; Anon., *Quaestio in utramque partem, proem.*, p. 98, 'Omnia enim quae pro imperatore faciunt, valent nihilominus pro rege Franciae, qui imperator est in regno suo. Specialiter ostendo quod rex Franciae non subsit papae in temporalibus'.

more unfavourably with the independence of other kingdoms,[1] but they were at pains to show that either the Roman empire had never had any legal right to include France,[2] or that from the time of Charlemagne, from whom the French kings are said to descend, the Empire and France have been split apart.[3]

The French claim to descent from Charlemagne, which was emphatically denounced by Augustinus Triumphus,[4] leads on to other considerations and provides an apt illustration of the way in which the French writers of the period were ultimately incapable of forgoing all ideas of a universal community. The French denial of imperial authority comes in fact to be seen as not so much an attempt to create a nation state, as to gain the universal primacy of the imperial title for themselves. It would be fair to add that in the thirteenth century the French monarchy not only became great, but tended to have greatness thrust upon it. The steady reorientation of curial policy towards France as a counterbalance to the Staufen menace, the papal emphasis upon the possibility of a new translation of the Empire to more deserving hands, and the eventual residence of the papacy on French soil, all went to suggest that a new empire was about to appear. Consequently throughout the fourteenth century French nationalism is inextricably bound up with the desire for European domination, and the contest between the Roman and a national idea of emperorship went unsolved.

[1] E.g. Anon., *Rex pacificus*, ch. 4, p. 681, 'Ego dico quod quicquid sit de imperatore numquam tamen super regem Franciae habet papa vel habuit aliquam temporalem iurisdictionem. . . Quia aliquae causae sunt in imperatore quare subditus sit papae in temporalibus, quae non inveniuntur in aliquibus regibus'.

[2] Anon., *Somnium viridarii*, i. 36, p. 70, 'Nam ibi dicitur quod princeps Romanus, qui totius mundi monarchiam tenebat, et hoc non negatur quin tenuerit, sed negatur quod iuste tenuerit'.

[3] Anon., *Disputatio inter clericum et militem*, p. 17; Anon., *Quaestio in utramque partem, proem.*, p. 97: on this see further Berges, *Die Fürstenspiegel*, pp. 75–8.

[4] Augustinus Triumphus, *Summa*, xxxvi. 4 ad 1, p. 222, 'tempore Caroli Magni imperium non erat divisum, sed ipse imperabat Germanis et Francis. Sed postmodum deficiente genere Caroli, Hugo, dux Aurelianensis, regnum Franciae sibi usurpavit . . . unde de dicto Hugone descenderunt omnes reges Franciae usque ad ista tempore, non de Carolo Magno'; also Tholemy of Lucca, *Determinatio compendiosa*, ch. 12, p. 27; ch. 14, p. 32, who adds that the French kingdom was subsequently legitimised after an appeal by the barons to the pope.

Quite apart from the audacious proposals of Dubois in which not only the Empire itself but also Byzantium, Egypt, Africa and the Eastern regions were to become French provinces:

Expediret totum mundum subiectum esse regno Francorum;[1]

the sporadic attempts already made by the French to create a Mediterranean empire during the course of the thirteenth century—the establishment of French influence in *Nova Francia* (Constantinople) in 1204, the occupation of Italy and Sicily under Charles of Anjou, the ill-fated African 'crusades' of Louis IX, the even more disastrous attempt by Philip III to conquer Aragon in 1285; and the laborious but vain steps which the French kings took to gain the imperial crown for themselves or their families[2]—a study of the French pamphleteers in the fourteenth century reveals an almost total adoption of the imperial ideology. The most Christian King becomes a new species of the *rex Romanorum*,[3] his lands, the

[1] Pierre Dubois, *Summaria brevis*: see the *De recuperatione Sanctae Terrae*, p. 129 n. 1. According to this scheme the French king was to force obedience from all European rulers to a French pope, surrounded by French cardinals (*De recuperatione*, ch. 112, p. 102; ch. 116, pp. 105–6). The pope was to give Central Italy to the French king to be governed by one of his relatives, and the same with Germany itself. Charles of Valois was to have the Eastern Empire. Metropolitan France was to be extended to the Rhine so as to include Cologne, the seat of empire (ch. 116, pp. 104–5): this was in fact an important item in French policy in the first half of the fourteenth century—see for example the terms of the treaties of Fontainebleau and Frankfort, 1332–3. Northern Italy was also to become part of the French kingdom. Further afield Jerusalem, Acre, Egypt, Cyprus and 'Babylon' were to be made subject to the jurisdiction of the French king (*De recuperatione*, *Appendix*, ch. 6, pp. 134–6; ch. 10, p. 138), and the heirs to these kingdoms were to be brought up in France. The king of Egypt was to assist a French army to conquer Africa and the East (*Appendix*, ch. 10, p. 139). Note also the Knight in the *Somnium viridarii*, i. 52, p. 74, who says that if superiority gave a right to possession, France would own Spain.

[2] G. Zeller, 'Les rois de France candidats à l'empire', *Revue Historique*, clxxiii (1934), pp. 273f.; and for Philip the Fair's attempts to put up French candidates in the imperial elections of 1308 and 1314, Lucas, *art. cit.*, p. 74.

[3] E.g. Augustinus Triumphus, *Tractatus contra articulos*, iii. 2, p. lxxxvi, refers to the French kings of the thirteenth century as having been 'caput christianorum'; cf. Durandus de S. Porciano, *De iurisdictione ecclesiastica*, ch. 3, fo. 5v, 'regnum Franciae christianissimum'. On the use of the *rex christianissimus* idea to suggest a right to the imperial title see Kämpf, *Pierre Dubois*, pp. 27–33; Berges, *op. cit.*, pp. 74–5.

sacred soil of France, a revised version of the *sacrum imperium*.[1] The French have become God's chosen race, the *populus praeelectus Christi*; their king is the guardian of the earthly treasury.[2] He is *pater patriae*,[3] his capital a holier Rome, the common fatherland of all Christians,[4] and it is Philip IV not Henry VII in whose peace the world is now to be regulated.[5] Indeed, in face of all this, it is not so

[1] For examples see Kämpf, *op. cit.*, p. 111; E. H. Kantorowicz, '*Pro Patria Mori* in Medieval Political Thought', *American Historical Review*, lvi (1950–1), pp. 472–92 at pp. 478–9, and note p. 483 the use of the term *sancti reges francorum* to correspond with the title of Holy Roman Emperor.

[2] E.g. Anon., *Somnium viridarii*, ii. 365, p. 224, speaks of the 'thesaurus Domini in terra, cuius thesauri Christus cum suis angelis et christianissimus rex Franciae custos existit specialis': note the use of the singular to denote the identity of king and Christ. He continues, 'Patet igitur qualiter christianissimus rex Francorum cum suo populo et terra divino thesauro est munitus, et a Deo in conservatione tam preciosarum reliquiarum et iocalium nostrae fidei nostraeque redemptionis et *totius Ecclesiae* typum gerentium a Deo nunc est *praeelectus*, et per consequens ipsum suumque populum et suam terram *praeeligere* vel saltem eidem adhaerere prae caeteris regibus et nationibus Romanus pontifex *obligatur*'. For another example of France as the kingdom of Christ see now *KTB*, p. 255 n. 191. This reflects Clement V's description of France as 'regnum Franciae in peculiarem populum electum a Domino . . . insignitur': Kämpf, *op. cit.*, p. 99. The *Somnium viridarii* also bolsters up its case here by referring to France as the home of the priesthood, since the Druids had lived there: this particular hare seems to have been started up by Aquinas, *De regimine principum*, i. 14, p. 237.

[3] Kantorowicz, '*Pro Patria Mori*', pp. 476–7; Gaines Post, 'Two Notes on Nationalism', pp. 291–2; Berges, *op. cit.*, p. 127. This old imperial title was borrowed direct from the medieval emperors: e.g. Frederick I, *MGH*, *Const.*, I n. 137, p. 191; cf. John of Viterbo, *De regimine civitatum*, ch. 125, p. 264. Note also Thomas Aquinas, *De regimine principum*, i. 1, p. 226, 'Habet tamen aliquam similitudinem regis, propter quam aliquando reges populorum patres vocantur'.

[4] The idea of Paris as a new Rome combines the idea of each kingdom as an *imperium* with the more universalistic notions of the French monarchy: e.g. Anon., *Somnium viridarii*, ii. 365, p. 223, 'locus Franciae sit sanctior Urbs'. Note also Guilielmus de Cuneo, 'In regno Franciae potest sic aequipari praepositus Parisiensis, quia sicut erat in Roma princeps, ita rex in Francia. . . Et idem in aliis regibus qui de facto non recognoscunt superiorem'; Bertrand de Deucio, 'sicut praefectus Urbis erat in capiti imperii . . . sic et ille praepositus est in civitate quae est caput regni Franciae': Ercole, *Da Bartolo all'Althusio*, pp. 190–2. Cf. the remark of Geoffrey of Paris, 'Si firent de Paris leur Romme/Où saint Pierre onques ne sist': Rivière, *Le problème de l'Église et de l'État*, p. 108. For the idea that Paris is a common *patria* superior to Rome see Gaines Post, *art. cit.*, pp. 290–1.

[5] The French sermon of 1302 refers significantly to 'quomodo reges Franciae dederunt pacem Ecclesiae non solum in regno suo sed in omnibus aliis regnis': Leclercq, 'Un sermon prononcé pendant la guerre de Flandre', p. 170.

surprising that the supposed collaborator of Marsilius, John of Jandun, regarded the French king as a much better choice for the world monarch than his patron Louis of Bavaria.[1]

Much of the French monarchy's search for autonomy was due to historical circumstances rather than any new theoretical developments. Yet it would be idle to deny that by the fourteenth century the contemporary outlook was already conditioned to receive such ideas. The corrosive influence of Aristotle on the traditional Christian concept of society as a single universal political entity only becomes apparent by degrees and does not fully manifest itself before the sixteenth century. Nevertheless signs of a totally different view of the right order in Europe are unmistakable by the end of the thirteenth century. For Aristotle the *polis* had been the perfect community, and the usual equation of this with the medieval *civitas* or *regnum* made inevitable the development of the idea of the national kingdom as a self-sufficient entity. This movement was slowed down by the application of the terms *civitas*, *regnum* and *polis* to the *Ecclesia* at large, but a growth of a conception of the kingdom as *unum corpus*, complete in itself, is inexorable, and is adequately reflected in the French outlook at the beginning of the fourteenth century.[2] The idea of political society as the *corpus Christi* moves steadily if imperceptibly down from a universal to a national level. The world is no longer composed of *unum corpus*, but of a great number of singular bodies. On the other hand the *Ecclesia* cannot be anything other than catholic and universal, and accordingly can no longer be permitted the character of a true political organism. This, we may recall, had been brought out most strongly in the thoroughly Aristotelian theories of John of Paris.

[1] John of Jandun, *Tractatus de laudibus Parisius*, ii. 8, 'illustrissimis et praecellentissimis Franciae regibus monarchicum totius orbis dominium, saltem ex native pronitatis ad melius iure, debetur': ed. Le Roux de Lincy and L. M. Tisserand, *Paris et ses historiens* (Paris, 1867), p. 58. For this and other discrepancies between the views of Marsilius and John see A. Gewirth, 'John of Jandun and the *Defensor Pacis*', *Speculum*, xxiii (1948), pp. 267–72.

[2] Philip IV, 'omnes et singuli, clerici et laici, regni nostri tamquam membra simul in uno corpore vere viventia': Strayer, 'Defense of the Realm', pp. 289–90. The parallelism of this with the idea of the *Ecclesia* as *unum corpus* is of course deliberate. For other examples see Leclercq, *art. cit.*, p. 169; Kantorowicz, 'Mysteries of State', pp. 77–82, 90; and now *KTB*, especially pp. 219f., 448f.

For John the *Ecclesia* is essentially the *totus populus christianus*,[1] but it becomes impossible to equate this universal society with any specific political community. The Roman empire is only *pars Europae*: how can it be otherwise when it includes neither France nor the Greek empire?[2] This denial of the universal nature of the Roman empire has a devastating effect upon the medieval world order. Political society is not one: there are now many political societies. The *Ecclesia*, which is by definition essentially one, must therefore be something other than a political organism. It is, said John, a *unitas fidei*, a purely spiritual union of believers existing outside the political field.[3] The way is now clear for a full separation of Church and State. The hierocrat, on the other hand, could not for a moment afford to consider the possibility that the Roman empire was not universal. It was only by preserving the existence of a universal political community, which could then be identified with the Universal Church, that it was possible to maintain the nature of the *Ecclesia* as a political society, and of the papacy as a jurisdictional institution. But here the papacy comes to be seen as a mere oracle, a dispensary of pious propaganda, devoid of any real governmental function. Political society is centred in the national states. The right order in Europe has become an atomistic one: society is a collection of states large and small, a multitude of greater and lesser powers, each in its own view sovereign and independent, and with nothing more than its own interests to guide its way of life and course of action.

[1] John of Paris, *De potestate regia et papali*, ch. 3, p. 180: see above pp. 104, 146.
[2] John of Paris, *De potestate regia et papali*, ch. 21, pp. 243–6.
[3] John of Paris, *De potestate regia et papali*, ch. 3, pp. 180–1.

II. THE UNIVERSAL CARETAKER

By the beginning of the fourteenth century a clear choice was emerging between two quite different conceptions of the universal order, between a world community under papal and imperial direction and 'Europe', a collection of sovereign kingdoms whose rulers recognised no superior. The former was fully justifiable and desirable in theory: in practice the latter conception was already gaining the upper hand. However, as we have seen, the formulation of distinctions between theory and practice had become the breath of life to the followers of Aquinas. They appreciated that to all intents and purposes there was little difference between a pagan and a Christian state which denied papal supremacy, and they had no hesitation in applying the same principles to this problem as to that of the status of non-Christian societies. The *de facto* independence of the national kingdoms could, in their view, be perfectly well combined with the *de iure* universality of papal-imperial government. And since the separatist tendencies of the local kingdoms had become so pronounced that they could no longer be ignored, practically every writer of the period who adhered to the idea of a universal society was forced to make use of this device. Even Augustinus Triumphus, the champion *par excellence* of the *communitas totius orbis*, is constrained to admit the *de facto* independence of the national monarchies.

The origins of this distinction have been traced to the legal commentaries of the canonists and civilians of the twelfth and early thirteenth centuries, and it has been shown that they were sufficiently familiar with the 'rex in regno suo est imperator' and 'rex non recognoscit superiorem' ideas.[1] The precise interpretation of these

[1] For a discussion of the relevant literature see B. Tierney, 'Some Recent Works on the Political Theories of the Medieval Canonists', *Traditio*, x (1954), pp. 594–625 at pp. 612–19; and also Gaines Post, 'Two Notes on Nationalism in the Middle Ages', *Traditio*, ix (1953), pp. 281–320; 'Blessed Lady Spain', *Speculum*, xxix (1954), pp. 198–209; W. Ullmann, 'The Development of the

phrases with the earlier commentators has in recent years been the subject of much heated discussion, although it is not our purpose to enter into the controversy here. It may however be pointed out that neither the canonists nor the imperial lawyers were people likely to favour the idea of national independence. This is not to deny that the idea of local sovereignty existed, but to suggest that the *commentaria* and *glossae* are not the best places in which to look for it. A study of the publicistic contribution on the other hand leads to the conclusion that the main purpose of these earlier writers, from whom so many of the publicists' theories were derived, was to develop a distinction between the overall public right of the universal ruler and the private right possession of independence by the local ruler. The idea that the king is emperor, a ruler with no superior, *in* his own kingdom—which to the French lawyers for example meant fully-fledged sovereignty—is here seen to be nothing more than a statement of private right. It does not conflict with the public right beyond the kingdom of the Roman emperor or the pope as the ultimate *dominus mundi*: and this, it is submitted, explains the perplexing tendency of so many writers to describe the emperor as a world ruler in one sentence and the king as his own emperor in the next.

The need for some such solution is not only a matter of principle, an example of the overpowering desire of so many publicists to fit all views however contradictory into a great synthesis, but is for Augustinus Triumphus an urgent necessity. Every day, he writes, we experience the effects of the mass of conflicts into which the

Medieval Idea of Sovereignty', *EHR*, lxiv (1949), pp. 1–33. The view that the early use of the 'rex in regno suo est imperator' idea was basically a statement of private right was originally suggested by O. von Gierke, *Das Deutsche Genossenschaftsrecht* (Berlin, 1868–1913), iii. 198–210, 350–60, 381–90, and has been followed to a greater or lesser extent by Woolf, *Bartolus of Sassoferrato*, chapter 3 and pp. 369–83; F. Calasso, *I Glossatori e la Teoria della Sovranità* (Milan, 1951); and David, *La souveraineté et les limites juridiques du pouvoir monarchique*, pp. 68–72. Against this Ercole, *Da Bartolo all'Althusio*; Mochi Onory, *Fonti Canonistiche dell'Idea Moderna dello Stato*; and Riesenberg, *Inalienability of Sovereignty*, pp. 81–8, take it to be an unqualified assertion of national sovereignty, although it has been pointed out by E. M. Meiers, *Revue historique du droit*, xx (1952), pp. 113–25, that this is taking the matter much too far.

Empire has now dissolved.[1] Under the impact of the royal attempts to gain independence from the emperor and the lust for power (or 'princely liberty') of the German magnates, the fourteenth-century Empire was rapidly approaching the condition in which, some three hundred years later, it came to be described by Samuel Pufendorf as 'an irregular formation resembling a monster'. And if the emperor cannot control his curia, how, asks Conrad of Megenberg, can he expect to control the world?[2] Various writers were in fact even then discussing the possibility of abolishing the Empire, and splitting it up into several separate kingdoms,[3] although, as Augustinus Triumphus remarks, this will soon be unnecessary: the process has already begun. Nor does there seem to be any hope of improvement in the situation.

Cum ergo *iam* Romanum imperium in multas partes sit divisum, magis est speranda eius desolatio quam eius reintegratio.[4]

Schisms amongst the faithful have let loose Gog and Magog in the house of God:[5] the day of Antichrist is at hand. The Christian world will divide into ten kingdoms, the ten-horned beast of Daniel, and since the Empire is a Universal Church, the split will be not only a political but equally a religious one. The growth of independent kingdoms means the creation of national churches in opposition to the Roman see: 'erit separatio multarum ecclesiarum

[1] Augustinus Triumphus, *Summa*, xxxv. 7, p. 210, since the death of Henry VII 'plura bella et praelia et litigia insurgere percipit in suis fidelibus et plerumque ipsamet ecclesia a suis vasallis parvipenditur et impugnatur sicut experimentaliter omni die videmus'.

[2] Conrad of Megenberg, *Oeconomica* (Struve, p. 89): cf. II. ii. 2 (Kaeppeli, p. 579 n. 3) '... ut imperator, quem eligunt, potius angustus sit quam augustus, plus imperatus quam imperans, plus Caesar ab hostibus caesus quam Caesar caedens inimicos, advocatus ecclesiae non ut patrocinetur ei, sed potius ut misericordiam non distribuens possessiones singulis proprias, sed perdens imperialia iura'.

[3] For details Offler, 'Empire and Papacy', p. 21; Woolf, *Bartolus of Sassoferrato*, pp. 220–6, 312–15; Folz, *Le souvenir et la légende de Charlemagne*, p. 407.

[4] Augustinus Triumphus, *Summa*, xlii. 2, p. 236: he continues, 'manente causa, effectus removeri non potest. Causa autem divisionis in membris Ecclesiae est divinae voluntatis repugnatio. Et quia ista causa manebit usque ad finem saeculi . . . idcirco usque ad finem saeculi non est speranda Romani imperii reintegratio, sed potius amplior divisio'.

[5] Augustinus Triumphus, *Summa*, xlii. 1, p. 235.

a Romano pontifice'.[1] Such prophetic outbursts were by this time becoming increasingly common, although it was usual to employ them as a means of urging the preservation of the Empire a little longer:[2] a somewhat contradictory attitude in view of the fact that most writers considered the reign of Antichrist as a necessary prelude to the *renovatio mundi* and the reappearance of Christ to govern his kingdom on earth.[3] However Augustinus Triumphus immediately consoles his readers with the information that in reality the universal community will not die after all. The soul survives when the body rots: the ultimate reality of righteousness will prevail when the lesser reality of fact is destroyed. The Empire may be split apart, its rulers may find it impossible to govern it and keep their subjects under control, but their right to govern, their jurisdiction, although paralysed, will never fail: and in this sense the Empire will last till the end of the world.[4]

[1] Augustinus Triumphus, *Summa*, xxi. 4, p. 129; and note also the *Tractatus contra articulos*, iii. 3, pp. lxxxviii–lxxxix, where he says that the 'Gallici ac omnes ultramontani' are determined to 'Ecclesiam per se facere sicut Graeci'. See also Engelbert of Admont, *De ortu imperii Romani*, ch. 18, p. 768; Peter Olivi, *De renuntiatione papae*, p. 361; and for its use by the Roman lawyers to support the theme that 'Imperium semper est': *KTB*, pp. 292–4. The immediate source for this was Aquinas, *Expos. in II Thess.*, ii. 1–8, 'Sed quomodo est hoc? Quia iamdiu gentes recesserunt a Romano imperio et tamen necdum venit Antichristus? Dicendum est quod nondum cessavit, sed est commutatum de temporali in spirituale. . . Et ideo dicendum est quod discessio a Romano imperio debet intelligi non solum a temporali sed a spirituali, scilicet a fide catholica Romanae ecclesiae': this was probably not written by Aquinas himself, but is a copy of his lecture notes made by Reginald of Piperno: M. Grabmann, 'Die Werke des hl. Thomas von Aquin', *Beiträge zur Geschichte des Philosophie und Theologie des Mittelalters*, xxii (1931), pp. 255f. The idea goes back however to at least the *De civitate Dei* (xx. 19) and was a common feature of medieval milleniary speculation: Graf, *Roma nella memoria e nelle immaginazioni del medio evo*, pp. 49, 726–53.

[2] Alexander of Roes, *Notitia saeculi*, pp. 672–3, 'Et apostolus dicit quod nullatenus Antichristus veniet nisi Romanum imperium poenitus sit ablatum. Igitur advertendum est'; also Engelbert of Admont, *De ortu imperii Romani*, ch. 5, p. 756; Lupold of Bebenburg, *Ritmaticum querulosum*, p. 482.

[3] E.g. Augustinus Triumphus, *Summa*, xxi. 4, p. 129; Tholemy of Lucca, *De regimine principum*, iii. 13, p. 262; Alexander of Roes, *Notitia saeculi*, p. 674.

[4] Augustinus Triumphus, *Summa*, xlii. 1 ad 3, p. 236, 'Romanum imperium . . . usque ad finem saeculi durabit quantum ad iurisdictionem, sed non quantum ad integrationem et actualem administrationem vel quantum ad ipsorum subditorum subiectionem'.

Augustinus Triumphus' use of the distinction between rightful jurisdiction and actual administration heralds his acceptance of the contrast between *de iure* and *de facto* government. Although, he says, it is customary to refer to the Roman emperorship as a universal entity, this is only a general way of speaking and tacitly ignores the fact that many are not subject to it:

... omnia regna sunt sub potestate imperatoris quantum ad protectionem et illorum dumtaxat qui eis iurisdictioni subduntur. Quandoque enim in generali sermone quaedam tacite excipiuntur.[1]

To understand this it is necessary to realise that the term *Romanum imperium* has two interpretations. It is a universal empire in that its ruler has authority over the whole world, as is denoted by his control of the Roman province, the epitome of the Roman empire. But he only exercises personal control over certain provinces which the pope has specifically given him to govern.[2] These are of course Germany and Italy, and various other areas which Augustinus Triumphus, in common with other contemporary publicists, studiously left vague and undefined.[3] Consequently *Imperium* has both an authoritative and a territorial connotation: there is an empire within an empire.

... imperator praeest omnibus provinciis suae iurisdictioni subiectis, vel potest dici omnibus provinciis praeesse, quia specialiter praeest Italiae, quae propter praeeminentiam potestatis et dignitatis potest dici domina provinciarum, ratione cuius imperator dominus mundi esse describitur eo quod Romanorum rex nuncupatur et Roma caput mundi appellatur.[4]

[1] Augustinus Triumphus, *Summa*, xxiii. 2 ad 2, p. 137.

[2] Augustinus Triumphus, *Summa*, xxxvi. 7 ad 3, p. 218, 'Non enim imperator vel rex accipit potestatem gladii super bonos et malos universaliter, sed solum super eos qui sunt eorum potestati commissi'; and see also xxiii. 2 ad 1, p. 137, where, in reference to Gratian, C. 11 q. 1 c. 37, he is said to hold only those provinces 'qui specialiter nominantur'.

[3] Augustinus Triumphus, *Summa*, xxiii. 2, p. 137, 'in Italia et in partibus illis in quibus imperator dominatur'; Conrad of Megenberg, *De translatione imperii*, ch. 14, p. 297, 'regni et imperii in Ytalia et aliis provinciis eiusdem regni et imperii'; Lupold of Bebenburg, *De iure regni Romani*, ch. 11, p. 378, 'imperium quoad Italiam et alias provincias et terras regno et imperio subiectas'.

[4] Augustinus Triumphus, *Summa*, xxiii. 2 ad 3, p. 137. For the idea that *imperium* means simply universal authority see further Riesenberg, *Inalienability of Sovereignty*, pp. 5, 15, 22; le Bras, 'Le droit romain', p. 389: '*Imperium*

This distinction now merges into the one between the emperor's *de iure* universal and *de facto* limited possession. Conrad of Megenberg for example distinguishes between on the one hand a universal empire which is *formale, mentale seu conceptuale* and is described as an *imperium de iure*, and on the other hand a territorially limited empire which is *materiale* and *reale*, an *imperium de facto*.[1] But even more explicit is a passage in Bartolus' commentary on the first chapter of the Code in which universal directive power is seen as something pertaining to the empire *de iure*, whilst the area which he personally governs is held to be the empire *de facto*.

Aut verbum 'regit' hic positum intelligitur prout de iure est, et tunc de iure regit omnes populos... Aut vis intelligere prout de facto est: et tunc quia quidam de facto non obediunt, et sic talis qualitas non competit omnibus de genere, tunc relativum ponitur restrictive.[2]

How has this distinction come about? Augustinus Triumphus obligingly explains. Just as the pope possesses a universal *auctoritas*, but does not choose to exercise power himself, so it is to be appreciated that the emperor also possesses the ability to administer the world, but does not choose to hold—or rather the pope has not chosen that he shall hold—executive power beyond specific territorial limits.[3] To begin with, of course, the Empire was a truly uni-

signifie l'universel pouvoir de commander'. For example Thomas Aquinas, *De regimine principum*, i. 15, p. 237, 'dirigere suo imperio'. The distinction derives from the old Roman law division between *imperium* and *potestas*, later used by Gelasius. Cf. *Jude*, 25.

[1] Conrad of Megenberg, *De translatione imperii*, ch. 9, pp. 277–8.

[2] Bartolus, *Comm. in Cod.*, I. i. 1: Woolf, *op. cit.*, p. 22.

[3] The papacy always made it plain that the emperor was not permitted to exercise jurisdiction over specific areas, such as the papal states: e.g. Gregory IX, 'Patrimonium beati Petri . . . inter caetera imperii iura quae saeculari principi tamquam defensori sacrosancta commisit ecclesia ditioni suae in signum universalis dominii reservavit': A. Huillard-Bréholles, *Historia Diplomatica Friderici II* (Paris, 1852–9), v. 2, p. 177. Boniface VIII had declared in 1300 that the pope could always reserve any part of the Empire 'ad ius et proprietatem ecclesiae': Jordan, 'Dante et la théorie romaine de l'empire', i. 373; Folz, *L'idée d'empire en occident du Ve au XIVe siècle* (Paris, 1953), pp. 409–10. And in 1346 Clement VI told Charles IV that although the Roman law books spoke of the emperor as *dominus mundi* with unlimited powers over the world, 'hodie secundum iura canonica principatus suus limitatus est', and referred to Clement V's refusal to grant Henry VII authority over the kingdom of Naples in *Clem.*,

versal monarchy. At the time of Constantine for example the Empire was still in a completely whole state. But since then it has steadily disintegrated, and the pope has decided that the cause of peace can be served only by reducing the amount of territory allotted to the emperor. By now, he admits, this has been reduced to little more than certain parts of Italy, a fact which, to use his own words, prudently conceals the real and effective government of other faithful princes.[1] The same question is raised on another occasion. Why does the pope only administer some parts of Italy through the emperor? Because, he replies, he wishes to bring peace and unity to a divided empire. But this does not imply a diminution of ultimate authority.[2] Augustinus Triumphus is compelled to acknowledge that this expedient move is somewhat forced, but this does obscure that it is, as he sees it, a deliberate self-restrictive act.

The suggestion that the pope is made 'voluntarily' to limit the effective jurisdiction of his agent has a familiar ring. We have seen that in dealing with the problem of non-Christian kingdoms Augustinus Triumphus had been forced to couple his *de iure – de facto* distinction with the idea of natural law. Natural law had accounted for the pope's inability to depose pagan rulers at will: it is now the underlying principle which restricts imperial jurisdiction over the *rex in regno suo*. And whilst Augustinus Triumphus himself can

II. xi. 2: *MGH*, *Const.*, VIII n. 100 p. 151. But whereas the publicists allow the emperor to administer only a few permitted areas, the papacy seems to assume that the emperor can administer anywhere not specifically forbidden to him.

[1] Augustinus Triumphus, *Summa*, xxxix. 3 ad 2, p. 229, 'tempore Constantini Romanum imperium erat totum integrum, sed postmodum tyrannice et usurpative tam imperium orientale quam occidentale fuit et est multipliciter divisum. Et ideo ecclesia propter pacem servandam solum circa partes Italiae temporalium *administrationem* committit imperatori cum solemnitate confirmationis et coronationis. In aliis autem partibus non exequitur *iurisdictionem* quam habet, sed prudenter dissimulat suorum fidelium principum dominationem'.

[2] Augustinus Triumphus, *Summa*, xlv. 2, p. 248, 'Quare autem ecclesia non utitur temporalium administratione nisi in partibus Italiae mediante quem elegit, et non in aliis regnis quae sunt in occidentali imperio? Hoc est non propter carentiam *auctoritatis*, sed propter nutriendum in suis filiis vinculum pacis et unitatis, quia ex quo imperium fuit divisum et a diversis partibus diversimode et tyrannice usurpatum, ecclesia propter vitandum scandalum et schisma temporalium *administrationem* in regnis illis dimisit'.

hardly be said to make this clear, the appearance of the same idea in the vast majority of contemporary papal and imperial tracts is a reasonably certain indication of the influence to which he had succumbed. Basically it is nothing more than an application to the emperor (or the pope in place of the emperor) of the well-worn Thomist notion of the ruler as *lex animata*. Initially possessed of an absolute power which gives him *de iure* possession of the universal empire in its entirety[1]—as for example the pre-Christian empire was truly universal[2]—the emperor as a Christian ruler must conform to the dictates of the divine-natural law which recognises the existence of private rights. Although therefore it may still be possible to consider the emperor as a source of royal power, the need to preserve the private right rulership of each king in his kingdom forces the emperor as the embodiment of natural law to promulgate laws and decrees which exempt the kings from his ordinary jurisdiction. Each succeeding emperor must follow suit by observing the normal independence of the local monarchs: he is bound by his own law.[3] The existence of *de facto* independent rulers is essentially the result of imperial acts of exemption,[4] although the

[1] E.g. Alvarus Pelagius, *De planctu Ecclesiae*, ch. 37, p. 50; Conrad of Megenberg, *De translatione imperii*, ch. 1, p. 254; Engelbert of Admont, *De ortu imperii Romani*, cc. 17–18, p. 767; Henry of Cremona, *Non ponant laicis*, p. 478; Landulfus de Colonna, *De statu Romani imperii*, ch. 1, p. 89.

[2] Augustinus Triumphus, *Summa*, xciv. 4, p. 463 '... Romanos ideo victores fuisse et monarchiam renuisse in toto orbe'. Hence Constantine had been able to hand over to the pope the 'plenum ius totius imperii ... non solum superioris dominationis, verum etiam immediatae administrationis', xxxviii. 1, p. 224.

[3] Anon., *Disquisitio prior iuridica*, ch. 7, pp. 1338–9, which gives a list of the supposed passages in Roman law by which the emperors have limited their own authority.

[4] Lupold of Bebenburg, *De iure regni Romani*, ch. 11, p. 378, 'Cum ergo ad subiectionem et obedientiam imperatoris teneantur, nisi se ostendant se esse exemptos'; Ugolinus de Celle, *De electione regis Romanorum*, ch. 11, p. 76, 'ipse imperator est dominus mundi ... quod et decretistae fatentur quod et in Francia et in Ispania et in omnibus provinciis est dominus. Est enim unus solus imperator ... nisi probarent se exemptos ab imperatore'; Landulfus de Colonna, *De statu Romani imperii*, ch. 10, p. 95, 'Imperator siquidem iste Romanus super omnes reges est ... his regibus exceptis dumtaxat qui per privilegia et consuetudinem sunt exempti'. Alexander of Roes believed that French exemption had been granted by Charlemagne, *De translatione imperii*, pp. 26–7.

papalists allow that the pope, as the source of imperial jurisdiction, must be equally competent to make such exemptions from imperial power. Into this category comes the Innocentian statement that the French king 'superiorem in temporalibus minime recognoscit'.[1] As we have already had occasion to remark, the distinction between the *potestas absoluta* and the *potestas ordinaria* is one between the theory and practice of the ruler's power: here it becomes identical with the distinction between the *de iure* universality of imperial authority and the *de facto* limitation of his exercise of that power in other kingdoms. In this conception the description of the emperor as *dominus mundi* no longer clashes with the substantial independence demanded by other lay rulers.

In the normal course of events the executive power of the emperor is confined to his own immediate territories: to all intents and purposes he has reduced himself to the private status of any other king.[2] The general situation, as the publicists point out, shows a considerable similarity to that existent within any kingdom, where the royal power exists primarily for the external defence of what is little more than a federation of semi-autonomous communities.[3]

[1] E.g. Tholemy of Lucca, *Determinatio compendiosa*, ch. 14, p. 32, 'Quid de aliis principatum apicibus seu dignitatibus dominorum cuiuscunque generis sive gradus? Ab ipso summo pontifice invenimus ex causa subtracta propriis dominis extraneisque collata. De quibus omnibus copiosissime diffinitum habemus ab Innocentio III, scribente singulis praelatis per Galliam constitutis, *Extra*, *de iuditiis*, c. *Novit* [II. i. 13], et *de maior. et obed.*, c. *Solite* [I. xxxiii. 6], quod et *de facto* satis apparet a L annis et circa in partibus Europae et praecipue in regionibus Galliae et Yspaniae et in maiori Brithaniae, in quibus per summum pontificem a gente in gentem dominia translata conspeximus prout exigebant merita dominorum et status incolumnis regionis'. Reference is also made to Gregory VII's apparent exemption of Hungary from imperial jurisdiction (*PL*, cxlviii. 414) and above all to the papal claim that Sicily pertains to the Roman church alone. But it is evident that there is no unanimity of opinion amongst the publicists over which kingdoms were exempted, when and by whom.

[2] Augustinus Triumphus, *Summa*, xxxix. 3 ad 3, p. 229, 'administrat in regno Alemaniae magis ut rex quam ut imperator'.

[3] Having defined the sufficiency of the *civitas* for most human needs, Aegidius Romanus continues, *De regimine principum*, III. i. 5, p. 412, 'Cum ergo regnum sit quasi quaedam *confederatio* plurium civitatum eo quod uniantur sub uno rege, cuius est quamlibet partem regni defendere et ordinare civilem potentiam aliarum civitatum ad defensionem cuiuslibet civitatis regni'.

The king's government does not deprive the magnates of the realm of all power: generally each local lord is supreme upon his own estates: 'dux, comes vel baro potest dici princeps in sua iurisdictione et suo territorio'. At the same time the overall government of the king is not in dispute, and so it is with the emperor.[1] The administrative freedom of the national ruler does not deny the authority of the emperor over the world: the two can exist together,[2] since the emperor always retains certain inalienable rights over other kingdoms.[3] A national monarch, as Augustinus Triumphus stresses, is 'imperator *in* regno suo', that is to say, *within* his own kingdom,

> rex non recognoscit superiorem *in* suo regno quoad dominium temporale, seu non habet *in* regno suo dominum temporalem maiorem ipso,[4]

but this does not preclude the existence of a superior *outside* it. The emperor does not lose his right to deal with some, at least, of the external affairs of the local ruler any more than the king can lose his right to control matters affecting the well-being of the whole king-

[1] Philip of Leyden, cited Berges, *Die Fürstenspiegel*, p. 124. The same can be found in John de Pouilli according to Sikes, 'John de Pouilli and Peter de la Palu', p. 233; also in Beaumanoir, *Coutumes de Beauvaisis*, ch. 34, sect. 1043.

[2] William of Ockham, *Dialogus*, III. II. i. 15, p. 884, 'Quia enim imperator in imperio mundi *et* rex in regno suo solutus est legibus nec tenetur de necessitate iudicare secundum leges'; Bartolus, *Comm. in Dig. Vet.*, VI. i. 1, 'Ego dico quod imperator est dominus mundi vere. Nec obstat quod alii sunt domini particulariter, quia mundus est universitas quaedam; unde potest quis habere dictam universitatem, licet singulae res non sint suae': Woolf, *op. cit.*, p. 22 n. 3.

[3] William of Ockham, *Dialogus*, III. II. ii. 7, p. 908, 'Licet imperator possit multas libertates concedere regi Franciae et aliis, tamen nullo modo potest regnum Franciae vel aliud totaliter ab imperio separare ut nullo modo subsit imperio. Quia hoc esset destruere imperium, quod non potest imperator'. Note also Bartolus' emphasis upon the retention of the French and English kingdoms within the Roman empire, although exempted from obedience to the emperor and imperial law: Woolf, *op. cit.*, pp. 25–7.

[4] Augustinus Triumphus, *Summa*, xlv. 1 ad 2, p. 247; cf. Anon., *Disputatio inter clericum et militem*, p. 17, 'Et ideo sicut omnia quae *infra* terminos imperii sunt subiecta esse noscuntur imperio, sic quae *infra* terminos regni regno'. See further Woolf, *op. cit.*, p. 154; Kämpf, *Pierre Dubois*, p. 15, '*infra* fines regni vel de regno Franciae'.

dom. He still possesses a certain (temporal) plenitude of power over and above other kings,[1] and this also follows logically from his function as *lex animata*. Dante, for instance, emphasises that there are certain occasions on which the normal order, the possession *regulariter* of private rights and property, becomes itself a contravention of the ultimate order of *iustitia* or righteousness. In these circumstances the emperor has a casual public right to act absolutely, or rather to make effective his potential or *de iure* universal power in defence of the general good of the whole society.[2]

The restriction of imperial government to a certain casual jurisdiction over other kings is not meant by Augustinus Triumphus to be in any way a limitation upon papal authority. The dilution of imperial power only serves to emphasise the need for royal subjection to papal lordship:

rex non recognoscit superiorem in suo regno quoad dominium temporale. . . Sed sicut nullus sanae mentis potest dicere se non habere

[1] Restauro Castaldi, *De imperatore et eius iurisdictione*, ch. 54, 'licet multi iura imperialia habeant in eorum territoriis . . . sciendum tamen . . . non habeant [reges] tantam plenitudinem potestatis et praeeminentiae quantam habet imperator': *Tract. Univ. Iuris*, xvi. 1, p. 20.

[2] Engelbert of Admont, *De ortu imperii Romani*, ch. 18, p. 768, 'In quo *casu* et *causa* nullum regnum christianum a subiectione et obedientia imperii credimus esse liberum vel exemptum. Nec ideo quia aliqua regna sunt libera et exempta ab imperio utile esset vel iustum alia omnia esse exempta vel libera in futurum'; Dante, *Monarchia*, i. 14, p. 349, 'cum dicitur humanum genus potest regi per unum supremum principem, non sic intelligendum est ut nimia iudicia cuiuscunque municipii ab illo uno immediate prodire possint; cum etiam leges municipales *quandoque* deficiant, et opus habeant directivo, ut patet per Philosophum in quinto ad Nicomachum, *epiichiam* commendantem. Habent namque nationes, regna et civitates inter se *proprietates*, quas legibus differentibus regulari oportet. . . Sed sic intelligendum est ut humanum genus secundum sua communia, quae omnibus competunt, ab eo regatur, et communi regula gubernetur ad pacem. Quae quidem regulam sive legem particulares principes ab eo recipere debent. . . Et hoc non solum possibile est uni, sed necesse est ab uno procedere ut omnis confusio de principiis universalibus auferatur. Hoc etiam factum fuisse *per ipsum ipse* Moyses *in lege* conscribit, qui adsumptis primatibus de tribubus filiorum Israel, eis inferiora iudicia relinquebat, superiora et communiora sibi soli reservans'. The presence of a conception of the emperor as exercising only an indirect, regulating oversight of the community, leaving the normal course of affairs to the national rulers, was first pointed out by Ercole, *Da Bartolo all'Althusio*, pp. 125–6, with regard to Engelbert, Dante and Bartolus: see here for a full list of the relevant passages.

Deum supra se, ita nullus potest dicere vicarium eius, qui eius auctoritate dominatus, supra se dominium non habere.[1]

On the other hand most of his contemporaries had already accepted the Thomist principle that the pope only held a casual power over lay rulers, and the application of this idea to the emperor is primarily intended to serve as the complement to the papal case. Thus although Augustinus Triumphus holds out in favour of the absolute and unhampered power of the papacy, it must be recognised that he has compromised by accepting a new conception of universal authority, and one which steadily increases in favour during the fourteenth and fifteenth centuries. Its origin may be sought in the old-established idea of the *causae maiores*, the view that there are certain matters reserved to the cognisance of the universal ruler, which the canonists had elaborated in favour of the pope, and the civilians on behalf of the emperor. But in the period under discussion the *causae maiores* are by a piece of skilful political engineering assimilated into those occasions on which the absolute *de iure* power is allowed to operate.[2] Thus the old idea that only the emperor or his delegate could legitimise, annul infamy, or create notaries, reappears as an example of the casual jurisdiction of pope and emperor over other rulers.

[1] Augustinus Triumphus, *Summa*, xlv. 1 ad 2, p. 247; and also Alexander de S. Elpidio, *De ecclesiastica potestate*, i. 7, p. 9, where he tells 'illi qui putant nulli se esse subiectos' that 'serviatis domino omnium, id est Christo et eius vicario'. Cf. Conrad of Megenberg, *De translatione Romani imperii*, ch. 13, p. 297, 'Si vero tales reges ostendant se exemptos ab imperatore forsitan per privilegia imperatoris, tunc mox papa succedit imperatori de iure in dominio temporali super eos'. This follows Innocent IV, *App. ad Decretales*, IV. xvii. 13, sv. *recognoscat*, 'De facto, nam de iure subest imperatori Romano ut quidam dicunt: nos contra, immo papae'.

[2] Lupold of Bebenberg, *De iure regni Romani*, ch. 7, p. 359, 'Quaedam vero est alia potestas exercendi actus reservatos de iure, quae consistit in legitimandis illegitimis quoad temporalia, in restituendis infamibus ad famam, in creandis tabellionibus, et in similis'; William of Ockham, *Octo quaestiones*, iv. 3, p. 133, 'inter actus reservatos imperatori'; Anon., *Somnium viridarii*, i. 179, p. 133, 'potestatem imperialem seu actus imperatori reservatos exercendi in aliis provinciis ac terris quae de facto non subsunt regno et imperio Romanorum'; Conrad of Megenberg, *De translatione Romani imperii*, ch. 21, p. 316, 'imperator in regnis regum christianorum habet iura solis imperatoribus reservata'. See further David, *La souveraineté*, pp. 58–60; Riesenberg, *Inalienability of Sovereignty*, pp. 7–8; Ullmann, 'The Development of the Medieval Idea of Sovereignty', p. 3.

... sicut de iure papa et imperator praesunt toti reipublicae et cuilibet communitati, ita de iure solum illis personis et communitatibus convenit notarios facere quibus per sedem apostolicam vel per imperatorem est concessum.[1]

On these particular points there was however little unanimity of opinion, and in any case it is difficult to see how such a common function as the institution of notaries—essential to the drawing up of all legal documents—could be described as an instance of necessity, in which the *de iure* powers were alone theoretically permitted exercise. Of far more significance here was the view that a just war could only be declared 'auctoritate papae et imperatoris',[2] since it could always be argued that war was an exceptional circumstance undertaken in defence of the universal good. The modern paradox that wars are waged to preserve peace has its medieval counterpart,[3] and it is the pope as *princeps pacis*[4] who is the supreme warlord. He

[1] Augustinus Triumphus, *Summa*, cx. 1 ad 2, p. 548; also p. 547, 'notarius est persona publica habens officium scribendi instrumenta super contractibus aut super aliis negotiis ad faciendam fidem super eisdem. Illius ergo auctoritate notarii instituendi sunt qui totius reipublicae curam habet, vel per universalem iurisdictionem sicut papa vel per immediatam administrationem sicut imperator. Et ideo solum papa et imperator possunt notarios publicos facere vel illi quibus auctoritate papae vel imperatoris est concessum'; also Conrad of Megenberg, *De translatione Romani imperii*, ch. 18, pp. 305–6; Alvarus Pelagius, *Speculum regum*, p. 526.

[2] Augustinus Triumphus, *Summa*, lxxiii. 2, p. 379; also *De facto Templariorum*, p. 512, 'Quin immo non erat licitum regibus et principibus saecularibus iustum bellum committere sine licentia domini... Et si iustum bellum licitum non erat regibus et principibus committere sine licentia domini et auctoritate summi pontificis qui pro illo tempore erat...': he cites the example of David seeking Saul's permission to fight Goliath. Cf. Thomas Aquinas, *Summa theologica*, II. II. xl. 1; and see also Anon., *Disquisitio prior iuridica*, ch. 2, p. 1326; Anon., *Disquisitio theologico-iuridica*, ii. 7, p. 1347; John of Calvaruso, *Quaestio an Romanus pontifex potuerit treugam inducere*, p. 1309; Lupold of Bebenburg, *De iure regni Romani*, ch. 18, pp. 407–9. For secondary literature see Ullmann, *The Growth of Papal Government*, p. 308 n. 1.

[3] Augustinus Triumphus, *Summa*, xxxvii. 6, p. 223, 'finis imperialis militiae pax est': this derives from Augustine.

[4] Augustinus Triumphus, *Summa*, ii. 8 ad 3, p. 26; cf. *Isaiah*, ix. 6. See also John XXII, 'regis pacifici, qui auctor pacis et operum eius amator cuiusque in ortu per angelos pax fuit bonae voluntatis hominibus nuntiata ... beneplacitis, cuius licet immeriti vicem exercemus in terris': Baethgen, 'Der Anspruch des Papsttums', p. 248. This is a favourite term for the pope with Pierre Dubois,

or the emperor is responsible for initiating all corporate action against the enemies of the Christian society, whether external or internal.[1] However not only public wars but private conflicts come within their jurisdiction, and accordingly they act in a regulating capacity over all wars waged by one national kingdom against another. Further, this entails ratifying or annulling all peace treaties between rulers, and even the right to impose them on warring princes against the wishes of the princes themselves.[2] Anything connected with peace comes within the compass of their authority. The papal and imperial curiae thus come to be seen as semi-international tribunals whose prime function is to put an end to disputes between other rulers and arrange them in their right relationship with each other.[3] This is perhaps best seen in the proposals of Dante and Pierre Dubois in the early years of the fourteenth century. Both in the *Convivio* and the *Monarchia* Dante appeals to the necessity for some authority to prevent wars between kingdoms as one of the principal arguments in favour of a universal monarchy: whilst Dubois suggests that a permanent general council, acting in conjunction with the pope, and superior to all kings, should be set up to deal with all disputes between princes and exercise a general care for the peace of the world. Either the pope or the council would be permitted to excommunicate offenders and take up arms

but he cannot forbear to add that if the pope is the prince of peace he ought to have nothing to do with war, just or unjust: *De recuperatione Sanctae Terrae*, ch. 40, p. 33, 'Sic papa, qui totius pacis auctor et promotor debet esse, guerras non movebit'.

[1] See Augustinus Triumphus, *Summa*, xxiii. 3 ad 3, p. 138, for the right of the pope to declare a *licitum bellum* against the *Saraceni et infideles*, and against heretics, *De facto Templariorum*, p. 512. A very similar idea is propounded by Engelbert of Admont, *De ortu imperii Romani*, ch. 18, p. 768, and is subsequently developed by Bartolus, Woolf, *op. cit.*, pp. 198f.

[2] Francis de Meyronnes, *De principatu temporali*, ch. 3, p. 61, argues in favour of a *caput in temporalibus* who shall be *concilians et regulans* between kings. See further Baethgen, *art. cit.*, pp. 203f.

[3] Anon., *Disquisitio prior iuridica*, ch. 2, p. 1324, 'Sed pacem facere et servari facere inter principes et alios christianos ad ecclesiam pertinet et de foro eius est . . . Ergo et treugae indictio, quae ordinantur ad pacem, immo est pars pacis et pax temporalis . . . ad ecclesiam pertinebit'. In 1312 Clement V declared that to prevent discord all treaties between kings should be submitted to the apostolic see on pain of excommunication: Winkelmann, ii. 151. Cf. the general statement of Boniface VIII, *MGH, Const.*, IV. 2 n. 1159.

against disturbers of the peace. Likewise they are to be responsible for confirming all peace treaties.[1] But there were many other suggestions put forward, and most of the publicists had some contribution to make. Thus Lupold of Bebenburg holds that anyone can appeal to the emperor, although this is not normally permitted, in the case of a royal dereliction of duty:[2] and if a king is found to be incompetent it is, according to Alvarus Pelagius, the emperor's duty to appoint guardians or coadjutors for his kingdom.[3] With Ockham the emperor still retains a casual right to depose subordinate rulers in the interests of the common good when they become deficient,

> dummodo deficientibus aliis sive per malitiam sive per impotentiam sive per negligentiam dampnabilem, saltem *casualiter*, per supremum puniri valeant principantem, quia hoc bono communi non derogat. . . Cum igitur princeps, maiorem habens quam doctor et monitor potestatem, sit principalissime institutus ad corrigendum et puniendum legitime delinquentes. . .[4]

and to appoint kings over newly created provinces.[5] And we may notice that in his list of the cases in which the pope may act universally against warring kingdoms, one author makes him responsible for securing the freedom of the seas.

[1] Dante, *Convivio*, iv. 4, p. 416, 'discordie e guerre conviene surgere tra regno e regno. . . Il perchè, a queste guerre e alle loro cagioni torre via, conveniene di necessità . . . uno solo principato e uno principe avere, il quale . . . li re tenga contenti nelli termini delli regni, sicchè pace intra loro sia . . .'; *Monarchia*, i. 10, p. 345. Pierre Dubois, *De recuperatione Sanctae Terrae*, ch. 5, p. 8; ch. 12, p. 11; ch. 99, p. 81; ch. 101, p. 82.

[2] Lupold of Bebenburg, *De iure regni Romani*, ch. 15, pp. 399–400, 'imperator in eisdem regnis nullam omnino iurisdictionem in causis meri et mixti imperii exercere possit, nec in casu appellationis a regibus ad eum interponendae, nisi *in casu* negligentiae ipsorum regum vel quando denegaverint facere iustitiam'.

[3] Alvarus Pelagius, *Speculum regum*, p. 522.

[4] William of Ockham, *Octo quaestiones*, iii. 10, p. 115; cf. viii. 4, p. 199, 'Sed de terris mediate et non immediate subiectis imperatori, quae habent dominos alios immediatos, non posset hoc facere imperator nisi pro culpa vel ex causa rationabili et patenti propter bonum commune posset privare dominos huiusmodi terris suis'.

[5] William of Ockham, *Octo quaestiones*, v. 6, p. 162, 'imperator enim potest facere novos reges in provinciis quae non habent reges'

Et omnes homines subsunt papae ratione peccati... Unde nulli venire debet in dubium quod si dominus papa videat aliquos paratos ad contentiones et guerras, ex quibus pericula animarum et corporum et scandala imminet et turbatio Ecclesiae et totius christianitatis et ultramarinum passagium impeditur, ut notorium est concurrere *in hoc casu*, quin se possit interponere et treugas indicere ex officio, etiam renitentibus et invitis.[1]

It is still then far too early to speak of the myth of universal government: on the other hand there is already a widespread acceptance of the idea that the universal head is no longer a *dominus mundi* in the old sense of a *possessor totius orbis*, and this indicates a growing belief in the idea that the *curator* of a corporation must safeguard its well-being without being permitted ownership of the corporation itself.[2] The universal ruler now stands behind the ordinary structure of administration, and his influence is becoming indirect and remote from the normal course of events.[3] He is no longer a sovereign head of the world, but rather, as Dante terms him, a universal caretaker, concerned only with the more general promotion of the society's welfare.[4] It is true that relationships between the national kingdoms are still seen as coming within the category of private law, whilst the pope and the emperor represent the public law of a universal society. Nevertheless the basis is being laid for the idea of a properly international authority into which the theory of *de iure* power will slowly merge as the conception of the sovereign national state becomes fully developed.

[1] Anon., *Disquisitio prior iuridica*, ch. 2, p. 1324.

[2] William of Ockham, *Octo quaestiones*, viii. 4, p. 199, 'quia quamvis omnia sint imperatoris tamquam supremi domini, non tamen omnia sunt imperatoris illo scilicet modo quo bona servi sunt domini, quia subiecti imperatoris non sunt servi imperatoris sed sunt liberi, propter quorum utilitatem et commodum est principatus imperialis, si vere est regalis, principaliter institutus'. See also Bartolus, *Comm. in Cod.*, *Ad Reprimendum*, no. 8, where the emperor is spoken of as the *regulator orbis* but not its *possessor*.

[3] Conrad of Megenberg, *De translatione Romani imperii*, ch. 21, pp. 314–15, 'principis universi, qualis est summus pontifex aut etiam imperator esse universale in sua potestate habere omnia, potest intelligi... principis universi esse omnia directorie et regitive... tamquam iudex *ultimus* ad quem recurritur *ultimate*'.

[4] Dante, *Monarchia*, iii. 16, p. 376, 'curator orbis, qui dicitur Romanus princeps'; cf. Pierre Dubois, *De recuperatione Sanctae Terrae*, ch. 106, p. 91, 'summus salutis reipublicae curatus in terris'; chs. 108–9, pp. 93–4, 'curatus omnium'.

The idea was not without its hidden drawbacks, and Ockham could, as usual, be trusted to show up its deficiencies by an over-zealous application of it. He emphasises that the levying of a just war by the emperor is as much a means of protection against internal enemies as external ones. Consequently into the category of a just war comes the right of the emperor to attack any pope who acts against the well-being of the society. This he uses to justify Louis of Bavaria's opposition to Benedict XII,[1] and he urges that even if Benedict is still legally a true pope, the emperor should seize control of Rome, confiscate all papal possessions, and instal a new pontiff.[2] And it is not without significance that, as we shall see, Augustinus Triumphus also regards it as part of the function of the emperor as universal custodian to summon a general council for the purpose of deposing a heretical pope. However, much as Louis undoubtedly welcomed the suggestion, the result of Ockham's further exploration of the idea cannot have sounded so pleasant to imperial ears. For Ockham never loses sight of the main reason why the publicists had adopted the distinction between absolute and ordinary power. Above all else it is a means of providing a workable accommodation between the members and the head of a community who are in equal possession of an initial plenitude of power. And whilst it remains true that the normal conception of the right order between head and members means the due subjection of the community to its ruler, the occasional acts of prerogative by the ruler against the rights of the members are always to be counterbalanced by the stipulation that in cases of necessity the community has a casual supremacy over its head.[3] Natural law always preserves the rights of the members of the Roman empire to ultimate action through their representatives in certain cases and

[1] William of Ockham, *Tractatus contra Benedictum XII*, vii. 13, p. 319, 'Quare imperator potest iustum bellum habere contra istum nomine Benedictum XII occupantem iura imperii, etiam si esset verus apostolus; qua etiam, quamvis esset verus papa, deponendus esset si esset incorrigibilis et de eo scandalizaretur Ecclesia'.

[2] William of Ockham, *Tractatus contra Benedictum XII*, vii. 7, pp. 309–10.

[3] William of Ockham, *Octo quaestiones*, ii. 8, p. 86, 'Rex enim superior est toto regno; et tamen in casu est inferior regno, quia in casu necessitatis potest regem deponere . . . hoc enim habetur ex iure naturali'. This follows the general scheme outlined above pp. 223f.

under conditions of necessity against the emperor.[1] They have not altogether lost the power of transferring the care of the society to another: 'nec a se abdicaverunt omnem potestatem *casualiter* disponendi de imperio'.[2] And who else in the universal society can be regarded as the representatives of the whole Roman people but the princes inside Germany and the national monarchs without? The *de iure* powers of the emperor over other kings exemplify any ruler's prerogative right over his community or its representatives. Correspondingly the European kings must be accorded equal rights to act against the emperor in defence of the society's interests. Just as in the local kingdom so in the universal community subordinate authorities must themselves intervene *casualiter* when the *principalissimus institutus* abuses its powers, and may be regarded as capable of deposing and punishing a tyrannical emperor.

> . . . sicut non derogat optimae ordinationi communitatis generalis vel specialis quod supremus in eodem communitate sit *exemptus regulariter* a potestate totius communitatis, et tamen quod *in casu necessitatis* sit eidem communitate subiectus.[3]

The emperor is merely as exempt from the power of the kings in the normal course of events as they are exempt from his jurisdiction. But this can no longer apply, on either side, in a state of emergency when the common good is imperilled. As yet there were only isolated suggestions of anti-imperial conciliarism in the fourteenth century, and the publicists did not advance far beyond the enunciation of the general rules. It was two hundred years before the French king accused Charles V of *tyrannis*, of striving after absolute monarchy, and went to war in defence of the rights of the national states. By this time however the ability of the subjects of any community to act against their head had been thoroughly worked out in the anti-papal conciliar idea. But it is clear that the principle of casual authority was a potent factor in the development

[1] William of Ockham, *Octo quaestiones*, ii. 9, p. 87, 'Et ideo si imperator committat crimen dilapidationis vel destructionis imperii aut damnabilis negligentiae. . . Romani, vel illi in quos suam potestatem Romani dederunt, debent ipsum deponere'.

[2] William of Ockham, *Octo quaestiones*, iv. 9, p. 153.

[3] William of Ockham, *Octo quaestiones*, iii. 3, p. 105.

of conciliar theories of government, and it is to this aspect of medieval thought in the thirteenth and fourteenth centuries that we must now turn our attention.

PART VI

THE CONCILIAR THEORY

I. PAPA A NEMINE IUDICATUR

THE tacit deposition of Urban VI, on which the election of the Avignonese Clement VII set the seal in the late summer of 1378,[1] not only plunged the ecclesiastical organisation of the Christian Church into half a century of disruption and chaos, but also brought to a head the whole question of what was to be done with a pope who was manifestly unsuitable for the role of universal governor. It was a question which had been exercising the minds of the publicists for some eighty years before the Great Schism began, and one which no political theorist of the early fourteenth century could avoid asking himself.[2] Moreover, once the problem had been posed, the ever-probing scholastic thinkers were constitutionally incapable of resting content until they had produced a vast and bewildering complex of 'solutions' which left the great writers of the conciliar epoch bedazzled not so much by the novelty of the situation as by the *embarras des riches* which a study of their predecessors' works revealed to them. Indeed the publicists themselves were in something of a similar position. As has been recently emphasised,[3] the roots of the conciliar idea must be sought well back in the glosses of the twelfth-century Decretists, and the republication of their views in Guido de Baysio's *Rosarium* of 1300 greatly assisted

[1] The idea that a second election by the cardinals invalidated the first had been suggested by Hostiensis: B. Tierney, 'A Conciliar Theory of the Thirteenth Century', *Catholic Historical Review*, xxxvi (1951), pp. 415–40. See also Francis Toti, *Tractatus contra Bavarum*, p. 81, 'Si autem nollet [papa] corrigi, sed pertinaciter defendere sententiam et erroneam, credo quod potest ab eis [scil. cardinalibus] iudicaliter deponi, vel directe contra ipsum sententiam proferendo, vel saltem indirecte *alium eligendo*, cum ipso iure incorrigibilis sit privatus'. On the part played by the cardinals in the outbreak of the Schism see W. Ullmann, *The Origins of the Great Schism* (London, 1948).

[2] E.g. Alexander de S. Elpidio, *De ecclesiastica potestate*, iii. 8, p. 38, 'Sed quid facit collegium vel universalis Ecclesia si papa sit ita malus quod sua mala conversatione et suis pravis operationibus videatur destruere et inficere Ecclesiam Dei?'

[3] B. Tierney, *The Foundations of the Conciliar Theory* (Cambridge, 1955).

the expansion of the conciliar idea in the first half of the fourteenth century. The zealous pursuit of papal sovereignty by the canonists, even if it tended to get somewhat out of hand during the thirteenth century, had not blinded contemporaries to all the disadvantages attendant upon the acceptance of absolute rule. Already by the time of Innocent III two diametrically opposed conceptions of the right relationship of power between the pope and the *congregatio fidelium* had come into existence, and were to be found side by side in the work of both the canonists and other commentators. This paradoxical situation amply demonstrates the effect of the application of Roman law corporation concepts to the organisation of the Christian society, and when these streams of corporation thought were swollen many times over by the onrush of Aristotelian notions of tyranny and the natural right of men to regulate their own government, it is little wonder that the writings of the publicists exhibited the same dichotomy to a much more marked degree. Here we shall attempt to illustrate how even the staunchest defenders of the papal supremacy came to accept totally antagonistic ideas of the origin of political power. At the same time however we shall seek to emphasise that neither the harsh abrasive action of Marsilian Aristotelianism nor the pathological outpourings of the younger Durantis adequately represent the conciliar idea as it manifested itself in the early fourteenth century. The decline and fall of the monarchic ideal was due in a far greater degree to the poison of sweet reasonableness which characterises the Thomist synthesis, and the insidious working of the idea of the Great Compromise was the lure which drew even Augustinus Triumphus into the labyrinths of conciliar thought and makes the *Summa* a work of outstanding importance in the development of the conciliar idea.

The events of 1378 were set in motion by a problem which, whilst closely allied to the conciliar idea, is worthy of separate consideration. By the fourteenth century the nature and composition of the Roman church, the apportionment of power between pope and cardinals, was already a matter of fierce debate, and no useful solution to the conciliar problem could afford to neglect a rigorous definition of the status of the cardinalate. The cardinals' struggle for power was indeed older than the conciliar movement, and had been in full swing ever since the position of the College was stabilised in the papal election decree of 1059.[1] During the twelfth and thirteenth centuries the cardinals had come to assume an ever-increasing share in the government of the *Ecclesia*, and their position was greatly advanced by the papal custom of discussing weighty decisions in consistory, a custom which in course of time took on all the appearance of a prescriptive right. Moreover the steady devolution of administrative matters into the hands of the cardinals, particularly during the Avignon papacy, seemed to make it clear that the cardinalate was an integral part of the headship of the *Ecclesia*.[2] In this the cardinals were able to seek support from that very ambiguous term, the *ecclesia Romana*. Whilst it is indisputable that the papacy was accustomed to use the expression in the sense of the popes themselves, the acceptance of the idea that papal power rested in the apostolic see, the 'caput et *cardo* omnium ecclesiarum',[3] rather than any particular individual, could only suggest that the pope and the Roman church were not necessarily the same thing. Indeed it could hardly be denied that the cardinals were equally members of the Roman church, and it logically followed that by virtue of this membership they could be considered as *pars corporis papae*.[4] Although this was an expression which could have a much

[1] For the early history of this problem and the rise of the cardinals from the ranks of the Roman clergy see S. Kuttner, '*Cardinalis*: the history of a canonical concept', *Traditio*, iii (1945), pp. 129–214; J. B. Sägmüller, *Die Thätigkeit und Stellung der Kardinäle bis Papst Bonifaz VIII* (Freiburg, 1896); Tierney, *op. cit.* especially pp. 68f., 179f.; W. Ullmann, 'Cardinal Humbert and the *ecclesia Romana*', *Studi Gregoriani*, iv (Rome, 1952), pp. 111–27; 'The Legal Validity of the Papal Electoral Pacts', *Ephemerides Iuris Canonici*, xii (1956).

[2] Of particular importance in this respect was the act of Nicholas IV by which he assigned a considerable portion of the papal revenues to the College: see the bull *Coelestis altitudo* of 18 July, 1289 (Potthast, n. 23010); and in general J. Lulvès, 'Die Machtbestrebungen des Kardinalats bis zur Aufstellung der ersten päpstlichen Wahlkapitulationen', *Quellen und Forschungen aus italienischen Archiven und Bibliotheken*, xiii (1910), pp. 73–102, especially pp. 84f.; G. Mollat, 'Contribution à l'histoire du sacré collège de Clément V à Eugene IV', *Revue d'histoire ecclésiastique*, xlvi (1951), pp. 22–112, 566–94; F. Merzbacher, 'Wandlungen des Kirchenbegriffs im Spätmittelalter', *ZSSR, Kan. Abt.*, xxxix (1953), pp. 274–361, especially pp. 346–51.

[3] Gratian, D. 22 c. 2.

[4] For examples see Tierney, *op. cit.*, pp. 95, 149, 204, 211, 233–4. Note also Urban IV, 'ut tamquam membra in unum corpus convenientia summo pontifici velut proprio capiti deservirent, et existentes eiusdem ecclesiae *columnae* praecipue ipsius onera supportent': Sägmüller, *op. cit.*, p. 214.

more general application, it was considered particularly appropriate to the cardinals, and its Roman law antecedents[1] furnished proof that this was the correct designation of the Roman senate, which the College claimed to succeed. Thus it was used repeatedly during the latter half of the thirteenth century to suggest a complete assimilation of the cardinalate with the papacy, and its participation in the plenitude of power.[2] When at the turn of the century the Colonna faction in the College came out into open opposition to Boniface VIII the whole of this theory was exploited to raise the status of the cardinals to virtual supremacy over the government of the *Ecclesia universalis*. From now on they are to be *coniudicatores* and *coadiutores* with the pope,[3] and the Roman church rapidly comes to be given the structure of a cathedral chapter in which, according to contemporary canonistic theory, the bishop can act only with the advice and consent of the chapter itself.[4] According

[1] *Cod.*, IX. viii. 5, where it is applied to the Senate; cf. XII. i. 8. Also John of Viterbo, *De regimine civitatum*, ch. 120, p. 261, 'cum sit consilium pars corporis sui, quoniam caput potestas, illi vero membra sunt eius; et quod consilium decrevit, potestas observare tenetur'. The position of the imperial electors as *pars corporis imperatoris* was recognised by Frederick II in his summons to the council of Verona in 1244: *MGH*, *Const.*, II. n. 244, p. 333, 'Porro cum imperii principes *nobilia* membra sint corporis nostri, in quibus imperialis sedis iungitur potestas'; and is also to be found in the Golden Bull of 1356.

[2] Hostiensis, *Lect. ad Decretales*, V. vi. 17, 'summum et excellens collegium super omnia alia unitum a Deo cum papa, quod cum ipso unum et idem est'; *ad* IV. xvii. 13, 'Multo fortius ergo decet papam consilia fratrum suorum requirere . . . non solum papa sed et cardinales includerentur in expressione plenitudinis potestatis'. Charles of Anjou had spoken to the cardinals as 'Vos inquam convenio, patres patrum, vos adloquar, principes sacerdotum, qui sacris tribunalibus assidentes latus summi principis decoratis et sic tamquam pars eius corporis vocati videmini non tam in partem sollicitudinis quam in plenitudinem potestatis'.

[3] See for example the anonymous Colonna memorandum to Philip IV, p. 226, 'Item cardinales sunt coniudices Romani pontificis et sunt membra non tantum corporis Ecclesiae sed capitis. Quomodo ergo poterunt privari coniudices sine causa? Certe nullo modo'. The Colonna group remained a potential storm centre throughout the pontificate of Clement V: for literature Tierney, *op. cit.*, pp. 158–9. The term *coadiutor* was apparently introduced by Nicholas II and was used by St. Bernard; cf. Innocent III, *Decretales*, IV. xvii. 13.

[4] On this see Tierney, *op. cit.*, pp. 106f. For publicistic examples see Augustinus Triumphus, *Summa*, iii. 9 ad 2, p. 37; Peter de la Palu, *De causa immediata ecclesiasticae potestatis*, i. 1, fo. 24; iv. 1, ff. 45, 46; v. 2, fo. 55v; Peter Olivi, De *renuntiatione papae*, p. 354.

to the Colonna it is a positive act of tyranny for the pope to govern by himself,[1] and the principle that he should act *de consilio fratrum* is elevated into a binding rule for the papal conduct of affairs.[2] Indeed from this point of view the relationship of pope and cardinals is not one of head and members at all. The cardinals have full equality with the pope: as Opicinus de Canistris says, all are brothers in the Roman church.[3] This parity gives the cardinals an inalienable right to exist, and the Colonna, for whom this was a matter of personal concern, are prepared to go to any lengths to show that the pope cannot dismiss them at will, or in any other way infringe the *status cardinalium*.[4] The idea that this *status* is perpetual only serves to emphasise the corporate character of the Roman church as an entity which never dies and never errs[5] and, in a word, exists over and above any individual holder of the papal office. In fact the Roman church comes to be identified solely with the college of cardinals,[6] and the distinction between the pope and the Roman church is accentuated and utilised as a means of suggesting that the pope is in every way subject to the jurisdiction of the College.[7] The attitude

[1] See the complaint of James and Peter Colonna against Boniface VIII, *Memoranda*, iii. 521, 'Porro cum in quibuslibet arduis peragendis maxime in alienationibus rerum ecclesiae, etiam verus pontifex cardinalium consilia petere et sequi consensus nichilominus consueverit et etiam teneatur, iste pseudo-praefectus nec ipsorum concilia dignatus est petere, nedum etiam exspectare consensus . . . ac glorians omnia per se solum posse pro libito de plenitudine potestatis'.

[2] For examples and the earlier use of this phrase see Sägmüller, *op. cit.*, pp. 214–18; Tierney, *op. cit.*, pp. 222–5; *art. cit.*, pp. 423–5, 433–4; Ullmann, *op. cit.*, pp. 206–9.

[3] Opicinus de Canistris, *De praeeminentia spiritualis imperii*, pp. 96–7, 'Cardinales quoque in consilio papae vel consistorio, quamvis pauci sint inter eos episcopi, papa fratres appellat eo quod in omnibus agendis eorum utitur consilio tamquam fratrum'.

[4] Anon., *Colonna memorandum to Philip IV*, p. 226, 'status cardinalis est perpetuus'; also James and Peter Colonna, *Memoranda*, iii. 521–2.

[5] E.g. Peter de la Palu, *De causa immediata ecclesiasticae potestatis*, iv. 3, fo. 50; vi, fo. 72v. Cf. Gratian, C. 21 q. 1 cc. 9–18.

[6] Peter Olivi, *De renuntiatione papae*, p. 353, and *Ep.*, pp. 369–70, seeks to justify his refusal to obey Boniface VIII on the grounds that his oath as a Franciscan binds him 'non solum papae et successoribus eius sed etiam sanctae Romanae ecclesiae, per quam, sicut alibi probari, intelligitur ibi collegium cardinalium'.

[7] Peter Olivi, *De renuntiatione papae*, p. 359, 'potestas papae potest considerari

of the cardinals now takes on much the same complexion as the episcopalist opposition. Starting from the same claim to parity and to an autonomous right to exist, there is a comparable development into a demand to be competent to exercise full authority over the pope. The origins of the Sacred College are pushed further and further back into the misty regions of the Primitive Church[1] until it emerges that the cardinals as members of the *apostolic* see are, more than the bishops, the real successors of the apostles,[2] and that through this succession they are true vicars of Christ. The traditional hierocratic theory that the pope only becomes *vicarius Christi* through the medium of the Roman church is given a drastic re-interpretation to demonstrate that papal power is from God only because it derives from the cardinals.[3] In setting up the pope the cardinals are the instruments of God,

vel secundum se, et sic est maior sede papali tamquam imperans et praesidens ei, vel potest considerari per respectum ad personam in qua est, et sic quoad diuturnitatem perdurandi non est maior sua sede, quia persona papae potest facilius corrumpi aut ad regimen ecclesiarum inutilis reddi quam sedes Romana'; Anon., *Libellus ad defensionem fidei catholicae*, p. 557, 'quando quaestio pertinens ad finem dubia est et de tali quaestione diversae sunt opiniones inter catholicos tractatores, tunc talis quaestionis cognitio et determinando solummodo ad papam catholicam pertinet sive ad sedem apostolicam aut ad concilium generale'.

[1] According to Peter de la Palu, *De causa immediata ecclesiasticae potestatis*, iv. 1, fo. 44v, the cardinals were first called by this name by Silvester I, but had in reality existed before this. Alvarus Pelagius said that they had been set up by Marcellinus in 304.

[2] E.g. Alexander de S. Elpidio, *De ecclesiastica potestate*, i. 10, p. 12; Peter Olivi, *Ep.*, p. 369. The expression becomes common in the middle of the thirteenth century, being used by Frederick II and Grosseteste: Huillard-Bréholles, *Historia Diplomatica*, v. 1, p. 282; Brown, *Fasciculus rerum expetendarum*, ii. 251. The cardinal bishops appear to have used the expression first in their capacity as bishops, but as the distinction between the cardinal bishops and the other cardinals diminished, it was applied to all. In 1412 the Parisian doctors urged that the College should be reduced to twelve to compare with the apostles, and the same suggestion was made at the council of Constance: Mollat, *art. cit.*, p. 107.

[3] Peter Olivi, *De renuntiatione papae*, p. 359, 'Quod etiam ibi numeri dicitur papalem potestatem et sedem esse a Deo, non sic intelligendum quin in successoribus Petri sit per intermediam electionem cardinalium, quamvis ex hoc non sit minus a Deo nec minus divina'; *Ep.*, p. 369, 'Nec dubitet quisquam quin electores papae, qui hodie communiter cardinales vocantur, maximam et *divinissimam* quoad hoc habeant potestatem'.

Deus ergo per cardinales tamquam per organum suum Romanum pontificem constituit sibi vicarium suum,[1]

the means by which the divine will is transmuted into a form of speech audible to human ears, and their mediatory role between God and man can be symbolically expressed by depicting them as the columns which connect the terrestrial society with the celestial paradise.[2] Not so much assisting the pope as directing him, they are the only permanent guardians of the Christian faith.[3] The whole government of the *Ecclesia* is in their hands, and this always suffices to give them control of the popes themselves. The power of Christ remains with the College during a papal vacancy, and it must logically follow that they have full right to revoke this power when necessary. As the Colonna repeatedly asserted, it was their duty to resist and repel an unsuitable pope, and although for this purpose it might be regarded as expedient to have recourse to the emperor, or to the French king, or to a general council,[4] it is sufficiently clear

[1] Anon., *Somnium viridarii*, ii. 161, p. 174: this continues significantly, 'Nec obstat quod ab homine propter haeresim deponitur. Nam non est vera depositio, quae sit tunc ab homine, sed est quaedam declaratio depositionis factae ab ipso Deo'.

[2] This was also applied to the cardinals by Frederick II. For the idea that the earthly and heavenly parts of the *Ecclesia* are connected by columns see Greenhill, 'The Child in the Tree', p. 367.

[3] Anon., *Colonna memorandum to Philip IV*, p. 227, 'Item cardinales positi sunt ut excubent et observent quicquid ad cultum pertinet multitudinis Ecclesiae, et constituti sunt ut custodiunt cultum sacerdotii religione perpetua'; James and Peter Colonna, *Memoranda*, iii. 522, 'sanctae Romanae ecclesiae cardinales, qui ab *exordio* nascentis Ecclesiae instituti leguntur, potissime ad *dirigendos* Romanos pontifices et consulendum eisdem, non ut consiliarii voluntarii sed *necessarii* potius ad considendum et *coniudicandum*, et ad *resistendum* eisdem cum reprehensibiles essent et *opponendum* se murum pro domo Domini et veritate tuenda.'

[4] This point is made by Opicinus de Canistris, *De praeeminentia spiritualis imperii*, pp. 94–5: discussing the question of whether the emperor has the power to depose the pope, he says that if some emperors are seen to have had this in the past, then they must have derived it either from the popes themselves 'vel ab hiis in quibus vacante sede *remanet* auctoritas clavium supernorum, qui sunt procul dubio hii quos papa statuerit post suum decessum ipsarum clavium auctoritatem obtinere et per consequens tradere successori'. Cf. Anon., *Colonna memorandum to Philip IV*, p. 226, 'Item cardinales instituti sunt ad resistendum in facie Romano pontifici cum reprehensibilis, sicut Paulus resistit Petro, sicut ipse dicit, In faciem ei restiti qui reprehensibilis erat. Quomodo aliquis cardinalis audebit in faciem resistere Romano pontifici si sine causa possit eos expellere et privare'. Note that this applies to each cardinal individually.

that the cardinals have come to regard themselves as the real universal rulers.

Although the pretensions of the cardinals were considerably strengthened by the growth of conciliar notions, there was little or nothing in this conception of the Roman church which was intended to favour the emergence of a more representative system of government. The opposition of the College to the papacy was a thoroughly aristocratic movement. Certainly this theory embodied elements which were capable of a much more radical interpretation, but individual rights in this context meant the rights of individual cardinals, not of individuals in general. The frequently repeated statement that the cardinals form *pars corporis papae* is a case in point. According to hierocratic doctrine all Christians were technically part of the *corpus papae* as members of the *Ecclesia*, and this was used as a basis for asserting that the acts of the head were automatically binding upon the members. The subject is assumed to accept the will of the head simply by virtue of his membership of the body: he retains his status as *fidelis* only by identifying himself with the commands of the pope. Needless to say, this version of the *caput-corpus* identification did not go unchallenged: there were few papal formulae which were not sooner or later reorientated in favour of the community at large, and this was no exception. It was not difficult to invert the whole process and argue that all the members automatically participated in the government of the head, at least by consent, thereby becoming collectively far superior to the individual ruler himself. Consequently no action taken by the ruler is valid for others if made without the consent of all: the members are an equally vital part with the head in the composition of the mystical body. Taken to extreme lengths it could be argued that every individual must consent to a governmental ruling for it to be binding upon him. But in the thirteenth and fourteenth centuries it is comparatively rare to find this principle applied to anybody but the cardinals, the *valentior pars corporis papae*. Time and time again it is the College which insists that its membership of the head qualifies it to approve or veto papal rulings. And on more than one occasion a minority of the cardinals sought to suggest that this meant the consent of every member. As we have seen, the Colonna group often protested that papal actions taken against themselves were void without the agreement of the members concerned, and this came dangerously close to implying that every individual member of the Roman church needed to accept a papal decree for it to be binding upon him. At the same time this insistence upon the individual rights of the cardinals was upheld at the expense of the remaining members of the community. The deposition of the pope is a matter which can be undertaken without necessary reference to the *congregatio fidelium* or a general council, and it was on this basis that the cardinals proceeded in 1378. Similarly it is urged that the right to elect the pope rests with the cardinals however small the College should become. According to Alvarus Pelagius the electoral rights of the College can devolve upon a single individual before it would become necessary to seek an alternative electing body.[1] Accordingly, although the cardinals protested throughout that their actions were undertaken on behalf of the whole *Ecclesia*, the notion developed that this meant not so much the individual members as the mystical personality of the corporation itself. The responsibility of the college of cardinals to act for the good of the whole community does not imply responsibility to all the faithful *ut singuli*, but to that abstract entity, the *Ecclesia* seen as Christ himself. Since the cardinals alone claim the capacity of being able to interpret the divine will of the *Ecclesia* in this sense, they become in practice responsible to no one but themselves.

This theory, with its skilful combination of episcopal and corporation ideas, produces a formidable argument in favour of the unrestrained right of the cardinals to do as they pleased, and it was only by meeting the cardinals on their own ground that Augustinus Triumphus felt it possible to combat this potent threat to the papal monarchy. He fully appreciated that the mainstay of the cardinals' case was the conception of the Roman church as an episcopal see which was also the repository of the plenitude of power. But, as we have seen, for Augustinus Triumphus the pope can be seen either as pope or as bishop of the Roman church. His membership of the Roman church no longer has for him any essential connection with

[1] Alvarus Pelagius, *De planctu Ecclesiae*, ch. 1, p. 26, 'Et si unus cardinalis remaneret, solus ille papam posset eligere'.

his popedom, which is a purely jurisdictional office. The Roman church concerns the pope only in so far as he is a bishop, and it is quite unnecessary for him to be a bishop to become pope. The papacy is therefore something quite apart from the apostolic see, and by inference, from the cardinals, who, as they themselves were at pains to point out, were very much the chapter of the Roman bishopric. Hence he argues that the link between the pope and the cardinals is fundamentally a personal and episcopal one, not an official and jurisdictional one. In fact the cardinals can be treated in exactly the same way as the bishops, and it is to emphasise this similarity that Augustinus Triumphus makes use of the cardinals' conception of themselves as *successores apostolorum*. The twin functions of the apostles in the early days of the Christian Church, those of personally assisting Christ and of governing the local churches after his ascension, have now been divided between cardinals and bishops respectively,[1] but otherwise there is no difference between them. Thus Augustinus Triumphus proceeds to make the same careful distinction between the official and priestly capacities of the members of the College. Just as the pope is on the one hand vicar of Christ and universal governor and on the other hand Roman bishop, so the cardinals have both a jurisdictional capacity as papal officers, electors and advisers, and a clerical function as members of the Roman church.

Sicut papa, non obstante quod sit universalis Ecclesiae pastor, est tamen singulariter praetitulatus episcopus et Romanus pontifex . . . sic cardinales, non obstantes quod sint iudices et principes totius mundi iuxta illud *Psal.*, xliv [17], Constitues eos principes super omnem terram, praetitulantur in titulis ecclesiarum Romae et in districtu Romanae urbis existentium, unde clerici Romanae ecclesiae appellati sunt.[2]

[1] Augustinus Triumphus, *Summa*, iii. 1, pp. 27–8, 'Quamvis enim episcopi repraesentant personas apostolorum, non tamen repraesentant personas eorum ut Christo vel ipsi papae vicem eius gerenti praesentialiter astiterunt vel assistunt; sed magis ut ipsi diffusi in orbem terrarum quilibet aliquam partem mundi in forte praedicationis acceperunt. Cardinales vero personas apostolorum repraesentant ut Christo et papae vicem eius gerenti praesentialiter astiterunt vel assistunt, et ideo convenientius electio summi pontificis sit per eos quam per episcopos vel alios praelatos Ecclesiae'; also viii. 4 ad 2, p. 71; *De potestate collegii*, p. 505; *Tractatus contra articulos*, iii. 11, p. xciv; Aegidius Romanus, *De renuntiatione papae*, xi, p. 33.

[2] Augustinus Triumphus, *Summa*, iii. 1 ad 2, p. 28.

He is still prepared to acknowledge that in their capacity as papal officers the cardinals are *coadiutores*, *consiliarii* and *iudices orbis terrae*,[1] but since *potestas iurisdictionis* can be derived only from the vicar of Christ, they are also the pope's *servientes*. They have a universal function, but, like the Roman church itself, this universal quality depends entirely upon their connection with the pope.[2] Consequently they have no shadow of a right to limit papal authority in any way:[3] the pope is neither bound to ask for their advice, nor, having received it, to accept it. He has the absolute legislative freedom of Christ himself:

. . . non est de ratione papae *ut papa* determinare vel ordinare negotia Ecclesiae de consilio cardinalium: potest enim sine eorum consilio talia expedire et determinare. Quia Christus, cuius vicem gerit, non legimus quod aliqua de consilio apostolorum egerit vel determinaverit.[4]

The cardinals are called into being by the papal will and so can be removed at his pleasure.[5] Accordingly, as another writer pointed

[1] Augustinus Triumphus, *Summa*, cii. 3, p. 503.

[2] Augustinus Triumphus, *Summa*, vi. 5, p. 60, 'cardinales assistunt papae sicut consiliarii et sicut famulantes et *servientes* sibi: . . . Unde cardinales a cardine dicti sunt, quia sicut in cardine vertitur totum ostium, sic inter eos vertuntur negotia consiliabilia totius mundi'. Their universal character is also emphasised by the fact that they can be taken from any country in the world, although he adds that it would be definitely unwise to choose Germans in case they were forced to divulge secret information to the emperor: cii. 4 ad 2, p. 505. In point of fact no German cardinals were created in the fourteenth century up to 1375: Mollat, *art. cit.*, p. 23.

[3] Augustinus Triumphus, *Summa*, xiv. 3, p. 97, '*potestas papae non limitatur in aliquo* nec dependet a collegio, sed potius econverso. Non enim collegium assistit papae per modum determinationis seu limitationis eius potestatem, sed magis per modum ministerii et consilii ut debito modo huiusmodi potestatem exequatur'.

[4] Augustinus Triumphus, *Summa*, vi. 5 ad 2, p. 61; cf. vi. 5, p. 60, 'ostendunt enim ipsi papae diversas vias super negotiis propositis super quibus consilium vult accipere, et ad ipsum postmodum spectat eligere et terminare quod magis expediens Ecclesiae esse videtur'; also Lambertus Guerrici de Hoyo, *Liber de commendatione*, ch. 5, p. 161; cf. Zenzellinus de Cassanis, *Glossa ordinaria ad Extravagantes Iohannis XXII*, iii. 1, sv. *De ipsorum consilio*, fo. 25, 'Scilicet cardinalium quorum consilio papa utitur quia vult ut hic vides; non autem ad hoc de necessitate tenetur . . . vocatus enim est in plenitudinem potestatis . . . nec potest ei dici, Domine, cur ita facis?'

[5] Augustinus Triumphus, *Summa*, cii. 3, p. 503. Vincent of Beauvais, *Speculum doctrinale*, vii. 61, p. 602, had compared the cardinals to a royal

out, there is really no need for cardinals to exist at all. However much they may be regarded as members of the *corpus papae* through their various useful functions, Christ had expressly enjoined that members should be plucked out when they became offensive:

> . . . quamvis cardinales sint oculi papae quoad consilia, manus papae quoad praecepta exequenda, pedes papae quoad portanda mandata, tamen si oculus, manus vel pes scandalizaverint eum et Ecclesiam, eruendi sunt et proiciendi.[1]

This denial of what the cardinals had come to regard as immutable rights extends even to the question of the papal election. Since the election provided the College with its best opportunity for asserting its mediatory position between God and the pope, Augustinus Triumphus' treatment of this subject is of special importance. The recurrent necessity for a papal election was the weakest joint in the hierocratic structure, yet it was difficult to see how this could be obviated. To an age which took for granted the status of the ruler as the direct choice of God, the question of deciding on whom God's choice had actually fallen represented a tremendous problem. And whilst election had become the accepted means of determining this, and was stipulated as the correct mode of procedure in canon law, election inevitably brought in an element of human choice which was highly dangerous to a divine right ruler. As Augustinus Triumphus asked himself, could not the pope be said to have been chosen by purely human means, 'ab industria et sagacitate hominum'? Undoubtedly it was to be inferred that the authentic voice of God was speaking in the election, but, he goes on to remark, the divine voice cannot always be heard, and it is simply assumed that God has chosen the pontiff. Moreover this automatically presupposes the divinely ordained capacity of the electors, and it is almost impossible to explain this without implying that the community has the right to appoint its own ruler: 'illum vocari a Deo

council in this: 'Dominus enim papa in foro ecclesiastico solus iura condit, et cum dico solus, consilium cardinalium non excludo nec consilia quae quandoque facta sunt, ipsius tamen auctoritate . . . Quod autem in domino papa dixi, in imperatore intellige in suo imperio et in rege in regno'.

[1] Nicholas of Nonancour: Maier, *art. cit.*, p. 353. Cf. *Matthew*, v. 29–30; xviii. 8–9; *Mark*, ix. 43–7.

quem elegit communitas Ecclesiae'.[1] In this respect the lay rulers were in a much better position than the papacy. With the growth of the hereditary principle contemporary princes were able to eradicate this weakness, and in consequence demonstrate their own divine sanction, since it was obvious that only God could create an heir.[2] It is perhaps surprising that the popes did not make more of an effort to emulate the lay princes in this respect. They could hardly of course produce a natural heir, but one might have expected a more positive attempt to adopt the Roman example by developing the right of one pope to appoint his successor. True, Innocent III had described all popes as the sons of St. Peter, and had cited the example of Peter's own choice of Clement as his successor,[3] but the matter is not elaborated. With Augustinus Triumphus on the other hand we find an outright assertion of the pope's right to choose his own successor. This would, he admits, run counter to a previous ruling (Gratian, C.8 q.1 c.1), but this may be ignored on the grounds that one pope cannot bind a future pope: 'par in parem

[1] Augustinus Triumphus, *Summa*, i. 2 ad 2, p. 5, 'ille vocatur a Deo non quod vox divina semper ibi audiatur, sed ab illis qui boni sunt tamquam si Deus diceret, Veni, quia dignus es: vel vocatur quis a Deo eo ipso quod vocatus voce eligentium qui a Deo ordinati sunt'.

[2] J. N. Figgis, *The Divine Right of Kings* (Cambridge, 1934), p. 36.

[3] Innocent III, *Reg.*, II. ccix (*PL*, ccxiv. 761), '[Petrus] primatum *cathedrae* successori reliquit, totam *in eo* transferens plenitudinem potestatis. Pro patre siquidem nati sunt ei filii, quos Dominus principes super omnem terram constituit'. The example of Peter and Clement is also cited by Augustinus Triumphus, *Summa*, iv. 8, p. 48. For the attempt to provide the papacy with a provable title-deed of inheritance from Peter to Clement I see the remarks of W. Ullmann on the significance of the *Epistola Clementis* in his forthcoming paper in the *Journal of Theological Studies*, xi (1960). There were in fact isolated instances of a pope designating his own successor. According to the *Liber Pontificalis* (ed. L. Duchesne, 2nd ed.: Paris, 1955), i. 68–9, 153, the first occasion was Lucius' appointment of Stephen I in 254: it is possible that Stephen himself subsequently appointed Xystus II (cf. i. 154). But the most important example of this was Felix IV's designation of Boniface II: see the decree of 530, i. 282 n. 4; cf. E. Eichmann, *Lehrbuch des Kirchenrechts*, sect. 58 pt. 5 n. 1 (7th ed.: Munich, 1954). Boniface is said to have attempted to regularise this and to appoint Vigilius, but later rescinded the decree, i. 108, 281. And in 1045 Benedict IX appointed his godfather to succeed him as Gregory VI, ii. 270; for discussion and further literature, iii. 133. Note the practice of making the heir appointed by the Roman emperor into his adopted son: Wirszubski, *op. cit.*, pp. 154–8.

non habet imperium'.[1] It seems clear that on this occasion Augustinus Triumphus was merely outlining a papal right, and he does not favour this method as a general rule. But at the same time he stresses that the college of cardinals has no fundamental right to elect the pope, who may always authorise some other body or person to make the appointment.[2] In any case he seeks to prove that the cardinals have little or nothing to do with the effective appointment of the pope even when they do make the election. This is essentially an act of God. The cardinal's election is a mere nomination for which they have already been authorised by the pope when they were appointed as cardinals.[3] This nomination is then confirmed by the new pope himself after his election, and consequently in his capacity as vicar of Christ, when he consents to his own choice.[4] As the whole process is in this way sanctioned by one pope or another, each acting in his official capacity, it is really Christ himself, rather than the cardinals, who has made the appointment.[5] The need for God to speak through a human mouthpiece has not been eliminated, but that mouthpiece now becomes—technically at any rate—

[1] Augustinus Triumphus, *Summa*, ii. 3, p. 21. Peter Olivi, *De renuntiatione papae*, p. 353, said that the pope could do this with the consent of a general council: 'Nam et papa cum Ecclesia posset ordinare quod ille post mortem papae succederet quem papa ante mortem praeelegisset'. This point was also discussed by Peter de la Palu, *De causa immediata ecclesiasticae potestatis*, v. 2, fo. 58, although he himself rejects it.

[2] To emphasise this Augustinus Triumphus declared that at one time the *ius eligendi* had been granted by the pope to the Roman people and at another time to the emperor: *Summa*, iii. 1, p. 27. This right was always revocable: xxxvi. 2 ad 2, p. 214.

[3] Augustinus Triumphus, *Summa*, iii. 7, p. 35, 'Cardinales possunt papa mortuo eligere et terminare personam hanc vel illam ita ut fungatur *auctoritate papatus* super universalem Ecclesiam, et hoc non nisi auctoritate papae, quia quod ipsi cardinales sint deputati ut possint eligere et terminare personam hanc vel illam ad papatum non nisi auctoritate papae hoc faciunt'; also vi. 5 ad 1, p. 61.

[4] Augustinus Triumphus, *Summa*, iv. 5, p. 46, 'papa seipsum confirmat suae electioni consentiendo'; also ii. 6 ad 1, p. 24; xxxix. 1, p. 228.

[5] Augustinus Triumphus, *Summa*, iii. 7 ad 3, p. 35, 'Sed collegium sic elegit papam quod tamen papatus non est a collegio quantum ad auctoritatem et officium, quod est quid *formale* in papatu. Isto enim modo omnis papa est a Christo immediate'; also ad 4, p. 35. See also Aegidius Romanus, *De renuntiatione papae*, vi, p. 13; xvi. 2, pp. 43–4; xxiv. 1, p. 58; Alexander de S. Elpidio, *De ecclesiastica potestate*, iii. 7, pp. 37–8; Anon., *Rationes ex quibus probatur quod Bonifacius legitime ingredi non potuit*, p. 451.

the ruler himself. At all events it cannot be said that the election gives the cardinals any legal basis for claiming to judge and depose the pope. It is, he concludes, a *magna dementia* to imagine that anyone can appeal to the cardinals against him. The College has no control whatsoever over him in his official capacity as vicar of Christ.[1]

The underlying reason for this is to be seen in the character of the papacy as the embodiment of a juridical personality,[2] the nature of the vicar of Christ as the human representative of the *una persona Ecclesiae* who is Christ. The pope in his office constitutes a corporation portraying the universal *corpus Ecclesiae* which forms one being. The Roman church in its old sense of the papal office consists therefore of the pope alone: 'in Romana ecclesia, id est in solo papa, est plenitudo potestatis'—the papacy is a corporation sole.[3] Its holders may come and go, but the office goes on for ever,[4] and since a corporation can do no wrong, the pope in possession of the papal office is infallible. The faith of the vicar of Christ, writes Augustinus Triumphus, has been *permansive* affirmed by Christ himself, and it is in this context that we may understand the old formula that the Roman church cannot err.[5] Only in the infallibility of the papacy can be seen the guarantee that the *Ecclesia* itself shall not fail: God's

[1] Augustinus Triumphus, *Summa*, vi. 5, p. 60. The phrase *magna dementia* is a favourite expression with Aegidius Romanus.

[2] This is emphasised by the separation of the papacy into formal and material elements: Gillet, *La personalité juridique*, pp. 208–15.

[3] Alexander de S. Elpidio, *De ecclesiastica potestate*, iii. 9, p. 39; also Peter de la Palu, *De causa immediata ecclesiasticae potestatis*, iv. 1, ff. 46v, 49v; Anon., *Compendium maius*, pp. 171, 179; Aegidius Spiritalis, *Libellus contra infideles*, p. 107. Cf. Clement V, 'et summus pontifex seu Romana ecclesia . . . et ipse summus pontifex vel ecclesia . . . quod ipse pontifex vel Romana ecclesia': Baluze, iii. 133. See further Maitland, 'The Corporation Sole', *Selected Essays*, pp. 73f.

[4] E.g. Peter Olivi, *De renuntiatione papae*, p. 360, 'Tertia est quod aut potestas papalis non est aliud quam potestas Dei, ut sic papae commissa et data, ac si esset sibi *formaliter* impressa, et tunc papa moriente vel renuntiante, ipsa non periit, sed in *personam* sequentis papae transit, nulla reali mutatione in se facta'.

[5] Augustinus Triumphus, *Summa*, ci. 1, p. 494; cf. xvii. 3, p. 110. This had been laid down by Gregory VII, *Dictatus papae*, c. 22. For the principle that a corporation cannot err see Gillet, *op. cit.*, pp. 121–6; W. Ullmann, 'The Delictal Responsibility of Medieval Corporations', *Law Quarterly Review*, lxiv (1948), pp. 77–96; R. Feenstra, 'L'histoire des fondations à propos de quelques études récentes', *Revue d'histoire du droit*, xxiv (1957), pp. 381–448.

care of the world is manifested through his special care of its head.[1] It is a contradiction in terms to doubt the unfailing rightness of the pope:[2] by his very function he is predestined to righteousness and cannot be damned: 'summus pontifex dampnari non potest'.[3] This is no mere pious assertion: it is the necessary complement to his proclamation of the pope's legislative sovereignty. An assumption of the permanent rectitude of the ruler is the only possible justification for a theory of sovereignty, and a belief in papal infallibility must accompany any complete expression of the hierocratic system of government.

In this setting the *Decretum* statement that a pope *could* deviate from the faith[4] strikes a jarring and discordant note. By all rights it should, from the papal-hierocratic point of view, never have been there. And although this text, notably through its acceptance by Innocent III, had gained an established position in thirteenth-century thought,[5] the further development of papal sovereignty in the

[1] Augustinus Triumphus, *Summa*, xxi. 4 *prop.* 3, p. 129, 'Ecclesia, de qua cura est Deo et cuius pastor papa est, deficere non potest, quia dictum est Petro, cuius papa successor est, *Luc.*, xxii [32], Ego pro te rogavi, Petre, ut non deficiat fides tua': similarly Aegidius Romanus, *De ecclesiastica potestate*, ii. 5, p. 59; Alvarus Pelagius, *De planctu Ecclesiae*, ch. 55, p. 144. See also Augustinus Triumphus, *Summa*, i. 5, p. 8, 'Potestas papae sit singularius a Deo quam potestas aliorum . . . quamvis enim Deus habeat curam generalem de gubernatione omnium rerum, singulari tamen modo habet curam de potestate summi pontificis regentis et gubernantis suam Ecclesiam. . . Deus habet specialem curam de potestate papae, mediante qua regit Ecclesiam, quam non habet de potestate aliorum'.

[2] The pope as vicar of Christ cannot be anything else: Augustinus Triumphus, *Summa*, ci. 7 ad 1, p. 500, 'Sicut enim papa non potest negare se vicem Christi non tenere, sic non potest negare se rerum dominium non habere'; cf. lxi. 2, p. 322, 'Sicut ergo papa non posset negare se non habere potestatem clavium . . . ita non posset aliqua membra de Ecclesia eximere a seipso'. Commenting on the phrase 'Dominus iustus noster' of *Jer.*, xxiii. 6, Alexander de S. Elpidio emphasises that the nature of his saintly office makes it impossible for the pope to be unjust: *De ecclesiastica potestate*, *proem.*, p. 2, 'Sed *iustus* dicitur ratione praecipue sanctitatis, unde et pater sanctissimus appellatur *ratione status quem tenet*, qui est totius sanctitatis principium'.

[3] Augustinus Triumphus, *Tractatus contra articulos*, i. 2, p. lxxiii. This is attributed to Boniface VIII. See above pp. 160f.

[4] Gratian, D. 40 c. 6, '[papa] a nemine est iudicandus, nisi deprehendatur a fide devius'. This provision derives from Humbert.

[5] Innocent III, *Consec. serm.*, ii (*PL*, ccxvii. 656), iii (665), iv (669–70).

early fourteenth century tended to diminish its importance. As Augustinus Triumphus said, one pope may not bind 'pro futuro tempore in quo ipse non esset iudex',[1] and so it surely follows that any succeeding pope can annul the *Decretum* passage. Indeed it might appear that Boniface VIII had already done this when he declared that he was not to be judged by man at all.[2] Certainly the papal supporters seem to have accepted it in this light, and the blunt statement that *papa a nemine iudicatur* becomes one of the most overworked phrases in publicistic writings.[3] There can be no deposition of the vicar of Christ since, being a reflection of God himself, only God can judge him.[4] He has no superior on earth: 'He who judges me is the Lord'.[5] And consequently, says Aegidius Romanus, he is perfectly free to do just as he pleases.

Sed cum papa nullum superiorem habeat, totum est in potestate sua, nullo enim iure ligatur.[6]

[1] Augustinus Triumphus, *Summa*, ii. 3, p. 21; also xliii. 3 *prop*. 2, p. 239; Aegidius Romanus, *De ecclesiastica potestate*, iii. 1, p. 143, 'Dicemus igitur quod si . . . papa quicunque qui fuerit pro tempore aliqua protulit contra iurisdictionem ecclesiasticam vel contra ecclesiae potestatem in nullo suo praeiudicavit vel praeiudicare potuit successori'; iii. 4, p. 165; iii. 11, p. 205, 'Et posset hoc successor revocare quia par in parem non habet imperium'; Alexander de S. Elpidio, *De ecclesiastica potestate*, iii. 9, p. 40, 'antecessor et successor sunt pares in officio'.

[2] Boniface VIII, *Extravagantes communes*, I. viii. 1, 'sed si deviat spiritualis minor a suo superiori, si vero suprema a solo Deo non ab homine, poterit iudicari, testante apostolo [I *Cor*., ii. 15], Spiritualis homo iudicat omnia, ipse autem a nemine iudicatur'. Huguccio had suggested that the pope might revoke Gratian, D. 40 c. 6: Ullmann, *Medieval Papalism*, p. 156.

[3] E.g. Augustinus Triumphus, *Summa*, i. 3, p. 5; i. 7 ad 2, p. 11; v. 1 *prop*. 3, p. 50; v. 4, p. 52; vii. 1, p. 64; xli. 3, p. 234; xlvi. 1, p. 250; also Anon., *Determinatio compendiosa, proem*., p. 542; Aegidius Romanus, *De ecclesiastica potestate*, i. 2, p. 8; Aegidius Spiritalis, *Libellus contra infideles*, p. 108. For the later use of this maxim by lay writers see Kantorowicz, 'Mysteries of State', pp. 74–6.

[4] Alvarus Pelagius, *De planctu Ecclesiae*, ch. 5, p. 27, 'Nemo iudicabit primam sedem, causam enim domini papae suo iudicio Christus reservat'; Henry of Cremona, *Non ponant laici*, p. 476, 'Item non est sub saeculo qui possit dicere se solius Dei iudicio reservatum nisi Dei vicarius, scil. papa, cui quicquid fidelium ubique submittitur, cum totius corporis caput designatur'.

[5] I *Cor*., iv. 4: Augustinus Triumphus, *Summa*, ii. 6, p. 24; v. 3, p. 51; xxxix. 1, p. 228; Aegidius Romanus, *De ecclesiastica potestate*, i. 2, p. 8; Anon., *Rationes quod Bonifacius legitime ingredi non potuit*, p. 456; Tholemy of Lucca, *De regimine principum*, iii. 19, p. 267.

[6] Aegidius Romanus, *De renuntiatione papae*, vi, p. 13.

It was certainly useless, in the considered opinion of the publicists, to attempt to bind the pope by any sort of pre-election or coronation oath. How can a people, especially a Christian people, it was argued, depose its *sponsus*, the ruler, any more than a woman can divorce her husband for failure to live up to his marriage vows. It offends against the whole Christian doctrine of marriage. Augustinus Triumphus refuses even to discuss the idea that the pope can voluntarily submit himself to the judgement of others. To preserve the perfect sovereignty of the vicar of Christ he must be free of all restraint, even self-imposed.[1] He is in fact quite prepared to accept that the pope should be an out and out tyrant, and that there is absolutely nothing to be done about it. Indeed, he remarks complacently, it would probably be very good for the *Ecclesia* if there was a really vicious pope who might scourge its depraved clergy.[2] Even if the pope orders something out of sheer malevolence, no matter how bad it is, his commands are still to be fulfilled.

> ... livor autem mandantis et si redundat in malum praecipientis, non tamen absolvit subditum ab impletione praecepti.[3]

In a theory of absolute government there can logically be no remedy for tyranny. The ruler must be obeyed, and the subject is beyond human aid: all that he can do is to pray to God for mercy.[4]

[1] Aquinas had suggested that the pope might submit to the emperor of his own free will, since Christ had done the same: *Summa theologica*, II. II. lxvii. 1 ad 2; cf. II. I. xciv. 5 ad 3. This is denied by Alvarus Pelagius, *De planctu Ecclesiae*, ch. 34, p. 36. On the question of voluntary submission see W. Ullmann, '*Nos si aliquid incompetenter*', *Ephemerides Iuris Canonici*, ix (1953), pp. 279–87.

[2] Augustinus Triumphus, *Tractatus contra articulos*, iii. 1, p. lxxxv, 'in quo ostenditur quae sit causa quod Deus permittit quandoque papam suum vicarium esse malum et prave uti ecclesiastica dignitate ... Primo propter Ecclesiae utilitatem, secundo propter clericorum penalitatem, et tertio propter subditorum pravitatem; cf. Tholemy of Luca, *De regimine principum*, iii. 7, pp. 255–6 'tyranni sunt instrumentum divinae iustitiae ad puniendum delicta hominum'.

[3] Augustinus Triumphus, *Summa*, xl. 2 ad 2, p. 231. On the desirability of obeying a tyrant see also Aegidius Romanus, *De regimine principum*, III. ii. 34; Innocent IV, *App. ad Decretales*, V. xxxix. 44. This attitude was basically Augustinian: see the *De civitate Dei*, v. 19–21.

[4] Alvarus Pelagius, *Speculum regum*, p. 518, 'deficiente omni humano auxilio, recurrendum est ad Deum'; similarly Thomas Aquinas, *De regimine principum*, i. 6, p. 230. Cf. Peter de la Palu, *De causa immediata ecclesiasticae potestatis*, iv. 1,

When faced with an unsuitable pope, the extreme papalist's only answer was to leave him to heaven.

Even this suggestion that there should be a 'recurrendum ad Deum' is too much for Augustinus Triumphus. Since the pope is God on earth, to appeal to God is nothing more than an appeal to the pope against himself: 'sententia papae et sententia Dei una sententia est'. The whole notion of appeal to this way of thinking is a waste of time: 'est ridiculum et frivolum'.[1] For all practical purposes it may be assumed that God himself will do nothing about the pope. Still less then should any man dare to touch him. There is no room for a conciliar theory at all,[2] and Augustinus Triumphus strongly rebuts any suggestion that the *Ecclesia* as a whole may act over the head of the pope through the medium of a general council. As he points out, canon law expressly forbids the convocation of a general council without papal authority. Nor are any actions of a council valid without this authority. Again the whole matter is laughable.

Et similiter alia ratio quare a papa ad concilium appellari non potest. Quia ordinem rerum naturalium in regimine naturali nullus potest mutare nisi Deus, et in regimine morali ordinem iudiciarium nemo potest mutare nisi papa qui vicem Dei gerit in terra. Sed ordo iudiciarius

fo. 46, 'Secundum remedium est exemplo b. Hylarii, qui contra Leonem papam praevalit orando, quia orandum esset pro ipso a tota Ecclesia quod Deus ipsum corrigeret'; Alexander de S. Elpidio, *De ecclesiastica potestate*, iii. 8, p. 38, 'Cum illa quam papa praeeminentiam habet regere universum populum christianum non sit ex statuto concilii nec etiam universalis Ecclesiae sive totius mundi, ideo totus mundus illam immutare non posset nec etiam papam a papatu deponere... Sicut ergo Ecclesia tollere non potest statum papalem quem Christus ordinavit, sic etiam nec aliquem amovere a statu papali quem Christus confirmavit'.

[1] Augustinus Triumphus, *Summa*, vi. 3, p. 59; also vi. 1 and 1 ad 2, p. 57. Cf. Tholemy of Lucca, *De regimine principum*, iii. 19, p. 267, 'Item non licet appellare ab eius sententia. Item ipse est qui superiorem non habet. Item ipse est qui vices Dei gerit in terris'. Note Augustinus Triumphus' distinction that one can pray to God, but that appeals may be addressed only to his vicar: 'per modum appellationis recurratur ad hominem, potissime ad vicarium Iesu Christi, et per modum orationis et supplicationis recurratur ad Deum', *Summa*, vi. 2 ad 3, p. 58.

[2] See also Anon., *Somnium viridarii*, i. 157, pp. 119–20, 'Papa enim est maior concilio generali'; similarly Alexander de S. Elpidio, *De ecclesiastica potestate*, iii. 8–9, pp. 38–9; Hervaeus Natalis, *De potestate papae*, fo. 144; Peter de la Palu, *De causa immediata ecclesiasticae potestatis*, iv. *proem.*, fo. 44; iv. 1, fo. 44v.

qui vertitur inter homines praesupponit auctoritatem papae ad concilium convocando et auctoritatem tribuendo et modum appellationis unius ad alterum ordinando. Ridiculosa ergo est appellatio a papa ad concilium, cum ordinem iudiciarium in regimine Ecclesiae concilium mutare non possit absque auctoritate papae.[1]

Nothing can be inferred from the corporate nature of the Christian society. Indeed the very fact that the *Ecclesia* is a corporation is used to justify this attitude. Since the corporation forms a single juristic entity, a being on another plane of reality, there is no real contact between the head, who represents this person, and the corporation itself. As *vicarius Christi* the pope dwells on the supernatural, mystical level of being, over and beyond the purely human members of the society. It is this disparity between head and members which Augustinus Triumphus is struggling to express when he compares the pope to heaven and the colleges of the cardinals and the Universal Church to the earth.

Papa vero comparatur ad cardinales sicut coelum comparatur ad terram... Sicut ergo coelum generat et corrumpit ista inferiora, alterat et variat ipsa, nihil tamen istorum inferiorum insurgit contra eum vel appellatur contra ipsum, sed patienter tolerat quicquid coelum operatur in eis...[2]

Neither may rise up against him, but must patiently endure all that he wishes to do with true Christian humility. To endure is in reality a greater good than to rebel. Indeed the common good of the community, the *status Ecclesiae*, cannot be divorced from the head, a personification of the good which is Christ. It is the good of the pope which is at all times the paramount consideration, and in such a climate of thought there can be no freedom for the members of

[1] Augustinus Triumphus, *Summa*, vi. 6, pp. 61–2. This rests upon Gratian, D. 17 cc. 1–6. Cf. Boniface VIII, 'Numquid ergo supra praedictis contra nos petatur a nobis, sine quo congregari non potest concilium generale', Dupuy, p. 167.

[2] Augustinus Triumphus, *Summa*, vi. 5, pp. 60–1. The general principle of this had been stated by Innocent IV, *App. ad Decretales*, I. ii. 8, 'Et est notandum quod rectores assumpti ab universitatibus habent iurisdictionem et non ipsae universitates . . . aliqui tamen dicunt quod ipsae universitates, deficientibus rectoribus, possunt exercere iurisdictionem sicut rectores, quod non credo'; cf. Alvarus Pelagius, *De planctu Ecclesiae*, ch. 31, p. 35, 'Papa etiam successor est Christi, non Ecclesia . . . unde nec vacante papatu succedit sibi Ecclesia'.

the society to act of their own volition.[1] They have *libertas* only in that they shall be free to obey, free to do right, whilst the pope has complete immunity from all redress of wrongs, because it cannot and must not be believed that he can commit a wrong.

The papal solution to the conciliar problem was no solution at all: strictly speaking the problem should not even exist. Yet however admirable this might be in theory, the publicists fully appreciated that in practice a pope might turn out to be totally unsuitable for his office. A heretical pope, causing untold harm in a society based upon faith, was, for all its difficulty of acceptance in principle, a very real danger. Few, if any, of the publicists felt able to rest content with the doctrine of infallibility or the belief that there was no remedy against the depredations of a tyrannical pope. Moreover they were always subject to pressure from the small but very vocal group of anti-papal writers who had no intention of allowing the claim to infallibility or the identity with Christ to remain a moment longer than necessary.[2] But the papal idea died hard, and many generally ardent supporters of the hierocratic thesis could only be induced to accept a theory of passive disobedience. An evil pope, they said rather hesitantly, might be 'reverently resisted', that is to say, his unjust commands could be ignored,[3] but he did not lose his

[1] Anon., *Rationes quod Bonifacius legitime ingredi non potuit*, p. 455, 'ubicunque sunt multa ordinantia in uno oportet esse aliquod universale regimen super particularia regimina, quia in omnibus virtutibus et actibus, ut dicitur I *Ethicorum*, est ordo secundum ordinem suum. Bonum autem commune est divinius quam speciale . . . et oportet quod ad hoc quod ista unitas debet conservari . . . et huiusmodi est potestas summi hierarchiae, Romani pontificis, quae *indissolubiliter* ei inest, et a solo Deo est, nec per ullum hominem tolli potest'.

[2] See also Peter Olivi, *Ep.*, p. 368, 'Unde autem sequitur quod quia papa vel episcopus est quoad aliquid Christi ymago, ergo quoad omnia est Christi ymago? Dicant ergo quod est increatus et immensus et impeccabilis et infallibilis et omnium praescius sicut Christus, quod nullus dicet vel sapiet nisi demens'.

[3] Alexander de S. Elpidio, *De ecclesiastica potestate*, iii. 8, p. 38, 'Duplex potest esse remedium. Unus est quod abstinendum est a culpa et insistendum est mundis orationibus ut talis malus praelatus tollatur de medio ab illo qui regere facit hypocritam propter peccata populi. Et pie credendum est quod in tali casu Deus orationes fidelium exaudiret nec suam Ecclesiam periclitari permitteret. Esset etiam in tali casu a cardinalibus et ab universali Ecclesia cum sobrietate et debita reverentia resistendum, exemplo b. Pauli qui b. Petro, quantumcunque gereret Christi vices, in faciem resistit, quia reprehensibilis erat, ut scribitur *Galat.*, ii [11]'; also William Amidani, *Reprobatio errorum*, ch. 2, pp. 24–5.

office, and he could not be deposed.[1] By the fourteenth century however this milk and water attitude no longer attracted general respect, and most of the writers of the time would have agreed with Henry of Ghent that it was better to depose the culprit than merely to disobey him.[2] Ockham, with his customary somewhat cynical air of assumed piety, declared that it would be wrong to bother God with things that men could just as well do for themselves.[3] Indeed as Aristotelian theories of the self-sufficiency of man ate their way deeper into the political consciousness of the publicists, the view that man, that the members of the Christian society, were capable of solving their own problems flourished with a startling rapidity. Aristotle's emphasis upon the human basis of society, the growth of governmental institutions from the natural desire of all men to live in community with each other, and the worthiness of satisfying human needs, breathed new life into the doctrines of popular sovereignty engendered by the study of Roman law. In the long run these might well in themselves have proved fatal to the hierocratic theory without the added stimulus of Aristotelian thought. Sooner or later the identification of the *Ecclesia* with the Roman empire was bound to lead to an adoption of the Roman conception of society, with its emphasis upon the nature of the community as a

[1] Hervaeus Natalis, *De potestate papae*, ff. 140v–141, 'nec tamen, si papa ut singulis persona sententiat errorem, teneat vel sequitur quod auctoritas eius obliget ad illam sententia tenenda, nec etiam quod auctoritas illa sibi erranti subtrahatur, sed quod auctoritas sua non habet locum obligandi in tali casu'.

[2] Henry of Ghent, *Quodlibeta*, XIV. ix, 'Quod si non sit omnino spes correctionis in isto, debent subditi agere ad depositionem superioris potius quam tolerare ipsum et non obedire. Nec video in hoc circa clericos aut laicos respectu suorum superiorem aliquam differentiam': de Lagarde, 'La philosophie sociale', p. 115.

[3] William of Ockham, *Dialogus*, I. vi. 62, p. 568, 'ubi fideles possunt humanum auxilium invenire, non debent ad potentiam divinam recurrere; hoc enim esset Deum tentare, quare si aliquod membrum apparet incurabile, debet humanitus amputari'. Note the list of alternatives given by Guido Terrenus, *Quaestio de magisterio*, p. 26, 'Ergo multo fortius, si esset papa haereticus, propter immutabilem veritatem Dei et fidei datam a Deo benedictionem toti Ecclesiae et populo christiano, non permitteret Deus eum determinare haeresim aut aliquid contra fidem; sed prohiberet eum Deus aut per mortem, aut per aliorum fidelium resistentiam, aut per aliorum instructionem, aut per internam inspirationem, aut aliis modis secundum quos Deus Ecclesiae sanctae et fidei veritati multipliciter providere potest'.

res populi, a concern of the people based upon a unity of common consent.[1] And since Roman law taught that the structure of authority in such a community rested upon the popular will as expressed in the *lex regia*, it was equally certain that a similar principle would be applied to a pope who regarded himself as the true heir of the Caesars. It cannot be denied, argues the Clerk in the *Somnium viridarii*, that the pope is now the real holder of the Roman empire. But unless the papal power in this respect is to be based upon prescriptive right, it must follow that that power derives from the voluntary consent of the Roman people, who are known to be the source of imperial authority.[2] Hence the conjunction of Roman law and Aristotelian teachings here brought pagan and Christian principles into open opposition to each other. Moreover, what seemed to be the universal validity of the new learning secured its application to every aspect of political thought. The end of the thirteenth century sees the steady transposition of the Aristotelian-Roman law conceptions of government from the lay to the clerical hierarchies. If the laity can depose their superior, asks Henry of Ghent, why not the clergy theirs? And the cry was taken up by writer after writer. The same form and manner, writes Marsilius of Padua, ought to be used in ecclesiastical as much as civil government.[3] It was no accident that the *Defensor pacis*, a supreme example

[1] E.g. Alvarus Pelagius, *De planctu Ecclesiae*, ch. 63, p. 208, 'Ecclesia . . . potest dici respublica . . . Nam respublica est res populi. Populus autem est multitudinis coetus iuris consensu et utilitatis communione sociatus'. This derives from Cicero, *De republica*, i. 25, by way of Augustine, *De civitate Dei*, ii. 21 (*PL*, xli. 67), Isidore, *Etymologia*, ix. 4, and Vincent of Beauvais, *Speculum doctrinale*, vii. 7, p. 561.

[2] Anon., *Somnium viridarii*, i. 162, p. 121, 'Hic tamen advertendum quod si imperium vel omne regnum iure divino sit a papa secundum quod est dictum, quod non debet negari: si negaretur tamen, hoc non potest negari quin iure humano, scilicet ex voluntaria concessione Romanorum, imperium sit a papa, qui omnem potestatem quam habuerunt super imperium Romano pontifici concesserunt, vel ex praescriptione legitima, quam summus pontifex ius et potestatem seu imperium acquisivit'.

[3] Marsilius of Padua, *Defensor pacis*, II. xxiv. 12, p. 460, 'Quam siquidem formam et modum in ecclesiastico necnon et civili quolibet regimine oportet attendere'. John of Paris had already pointed to a close link between the right of the people to depose their king and their right to depose the pope: *De potestate regia et papali*, ch. 13, p. 214.

of the union of Roman law and Aristotelian ideas, contained a thorough-going theory of popular sovereignty over the Roman emperor and at the same time gave expression to a conciliar doctrine of the most radical type.

II. ROOT AND BRANCH CONCILIARISM

THE conciliar theory of the *Defensor pacis* is sufficiently familiar not to require restatement. It is in many ways simply a means by which Marsilius advocates imperial intervention into papal affairs and asserts the emperor's control of the Roman church.[1] What is perhaps most significant about it is that the final authority in the Marsilian general council, even in matters of faith, rests not with the bishops and clergy but with the lay *valentior pars*, which we have already seen generally means the secular princes.[2] Consequently, however significant for the future, this intense laical orientation tended to rob Marsilius' theory of much of its immediate influence, and the real factor in the development of what we may call the radical conciliar idea in the early fourteenth century was its adaptation by the college of cardinals. In this 'cardinal conciliarism' there is to be found the same blend between the direct divine right by apostolic succession of the members of the council and their authority as representatives of the whole community which is a prominent feature of the Marsilian idea,[3] but it is the

[1] Marsilius' general council is to be convoked by the 'humanus fidelis legislator superiore carens' (*Defensor pacis*, II. xviii. 8, p. 382; II. xxi. 1, p. 402), which body is also the source of authority for its decisions (II. xxi. 4, p. 405), and on behalf of which the council elects, controls and deposes the pope (II. xxii. 9, p. 428; II. xxii. 11, p. 430; II. xxii. 6, p. 425). This legislator is however essentially an imperial one, the 'supremus imperii Romani humanus legislator' (II. xxx. 8, p. 601). Ockham too had argued that by natural law any community has the right to remove its governor, and he therefore advocates that a heretical pope should be expelled from the apostolic see 'per imperatorem et Romanos, quorum est quodammodo episcopus proprius, de consilio et assensu, si necesse esset, concilii generalis': *Tractatus contra Benedictum XII*, vii. 12, p. 318.

[2] Marsilius of Padua, *Defensor pacis*, II. xx. 5, p. 396, 'Unde sacerdotibus invicem dissidentibus de credendis ad salutem aeternam, de ipsorum saniori parte fidelium pars valentior habet iudicare'. In support of this he points out that in the early councils of the Church 'aderant imperatores et imperatrices fideles cum suis officialibus'.

[3] The council not only derives its authority from representing the *universitas*

ecclesiastical princes, the cardinals, who, as the Colonna asserted, fulfil the function of the *valentior pars*.[1] Most of the extreme conciliar theories of the period were in fact biased in favour of the ultimate supremacy of the cardinalate, and some confirmation of this is to be found in one of the minor works of no less a person than Augustinus Triumphus himself. In stark contrast with all that has gone before, we find in his *De potestate collegii* an advocacy of the complete supremacy of the College over the pope. His treatment of this is sketchy, but the main outline is clear and is in full agreement with contemporary 'cardinal conciliar' opinion. The mainstay of this is the belief that it was the universal *Ecclesia*, the *congregatio fidelium*, which had been the real recipient of the Petrine commission and is accordingly the repository of all ecclesiastical power. It is the *unum corpus Ecclesiae* which is the physical representation of Christ on earth and is therefore in possession of his vicariate.[2] From this point there is no serious obstacle to a full scale application of the legal doctrine that members of a corporation may appoint and remove their head to the relationship between the pope and the *Ecclesia*.[3] Thus the pope draws his authority from the community at large, and is to be seen as representing the *Ecclesia* only in the sense that he is its executive minister.[4] His *plenitudo*

fidelium, which comprises 'omnes mundi provinciae seu communitates notabiles' (*Defensor pacis*, II. xx. 2, p. 393), but is also the immediate recipient of the Holy Spirit, which gives it infallibility, by virtue of the succession from and representation of the apostles and elders of the Early Church by its members (II. xix. 2, pp. 384–5). In the decree *Sacrosancta* of 6 April, 1415, the council of Constance declared that 'concilium generale faciens et Ecclesiam catholicam repraesentans potestatem a Christo immediate habet': Mansi, xxvii. 585.

[1] James and Peter Colonna, *Memorandum*, i. 513, 'cardinales tamquam principalia membra et Ecclesiae cardines'.

[2] In the early sixteenth century Cajetan attacks the view that 'non papa sed Ecclesia esset proxima et immediata Christi vicaria': Maccarrone, *Vicarius Christi*, p. 276.

[3] Tierney, *Foundations of the Conciliar Theory*, pp. 132f.

[4] This is developed by John of Paris, *De potestate regia et papali*, ch. 6, pp. 186–8, with regard to the goods and possessions of the society. The society itself is the real possessor of its own property: 'sola communitas universalis Ecclesiae est domina et proprietaria omnium bonorum generaliter', whilst the pope simply acts on its behalf as the 'universalis dispositor et dispensator bonorum'. It is significant that this leads John straight on to a consideration of papal deposition: 'si apparet quod papa bona ecclesiarum infideliter detraheret non ad

potestatis is assimilated to the *plena potestas* of a proctor, who acts on behalf of and in the best interests of the universal ecclesiastical corporation, but is not permitted to diminish or impair the rights of his principal.[1] And from here the ability of the community to revoke papal jurisdiction follows as a matter of course.

The clarification of this idea was mainly due to the growth of a new conception of the college of cardinals as intermediaries between the *Ecclesia* and the pope. This itself owed much to contemporary parliamentary development, and in fact the College had long been referred to as the papal senate.[2] But the claim of the cardinals to act *vice omnium* is more generally advanced on the basis of their apostolic succession.[3] As Peter Olivi explains, when St. Peter received power from Christ he did not do so on his own behalf, but for all the apostles—who are significantly termed co-apostles and co-disciples. Moreover these apostles and disciples held this power not in their own right but as representatives of the whole *Ecclesia*.[4]

bonum commune cui superintendere tenetur, cum sit summus episcopus, deponi posset . . . licet secundum aliquos per solum concilium generale'. John himself however favours the joint action of the cardinals and emperor taken on behalf of the people: ch. 13, p. 214, 'si papa esset criminosus et scandalizaret Ecclesiam et incorrigibilis esset, posset princeps ipsum excommunicare indirecte et deponere ipsum per accidens, monendo ipsum scilicet per se vel per cardinales . . . et posset aliquid facere in populo unde compellaretur cedere vel deponetur a populo, quia posset imperator . . . inhibere omnibus et singulis ut nullus ei obediret vel serviret ut papae'.

[1] Gaines Post, '*Plena potestas* and consent', pp. 355–65. For publicistic examples see Guilielmus Durantis, *De modo generalis concilii celebrandi*, ii. 3–5, pp. 61–3; Peter de la Palu, *De causa immediata ecclesiasticae potestatis*, iv. 1, fo. 46; v. 3, fo. 59v.

[2] E.g. Tholemy of Lucca, *Determinatio compendiosa*, ch. 31, p. 64, who refers to the application of this term to the Roman clergy in the Donation of Constantine: see also his *De origine Romani imperii*, p. 67, and Peter de la Palu, *De causa immediata ecclesiasticae potestatis*, v. 2, fo. 58. For the widespread use of this and similar expressions such as *patres conscripti* and *patricii* see Sägmüller, *op. cit.*, pp. 41, 160–1, 213; Tierney, *op. cit.*, pp. 176–7, 184; and in general the comparison between the cardinals and the imperial electors as representatives of the whole community in Gierke-Maitland, *Political Theories of the Middle Age*, pp. 66–7. The view that the senate acts *vice populi* is in Roman law at *Inst.*, I. ii. 5.

[3] Augustinus Triumphus, *De potestate collegii*, p. 505; *Tractatus contra articulos*, p. xciv.

[4] Peter Olivi, *De renuntiatione papae*, p. 350, 'Et etiam ex hoc quod ubique in

They were simply the agents through which the community gained its authority. Correspondingly it is the cardinals who now act as the agents and representatives of the *congregatio fidelium*, and transfer its power into the hands of the pope: their voice in the papal election is the voice of all Christian people.[1] The Roman church epitomises the whole community: its constitution exactly mirrors the structure of authority existing within the universal body. Since power is now seen to flow, through the cardinals, from the members to the head, so the cardinals themselves become the effective superiors of the pope. Thus their consent to papal actions is necessary to mark the approval of the whole Church.[2] And it is in accordance with this that during a papal vacancy the *potestas papalis* reverts to the College, and through it to its source, the *congregatio fidelium*. The *Ecclesia*, says Augustinus Triumphus, may be compared to a tree, whose life-power is derived from its roots. There is the *radix propinqua* of the college of cardinals,[3] and below this the *radix remota* of the whole body of the faithful. Both retain papal power when the blossom and fruit, in this analogy the pope himself, wither away.

tantum praefertur caeteris coapostolis et condiscipulis quod in ipso [scil. Petro] omnes intelliguntur tamquam gerente personam totius Ecclesiae, ut *Mat.*, xvii [26], ubi Christus dicit ei, Aperte ore piscis, invenies staterem, et da eis pro me et te, id est, pro me et omnibus discipulis meis. . . . etiam dicit in persona omnium . . . sibi pro omnibus dicit Christus. . .'; cf. *Quaestio de infallibilitate*, p. 338, 'Cum igitur constet quod Christus auctoritatem hanc in stabilitatem potius dederit sibi pro universali Ecclesia quam pro se, et sic per consequens ita successoribus suis sicut et sibi'.

[1] Peter Olivi, *De renuntiatione papae*, pp. 355–6, 'Quod vero si in electione papae plebis assensus necessario praeexigeretur, multa pericula et incommoda possunt contingere; ideo congrue ordinatum est quod *vicem omnium* in hoc gererent aliqui praecipui, qui nunc communiter cardinales vocantur'; cf. John of Paris, *De potestate regia et papali*, ch. 24, p. 254, 'collegium cardinalium, quia ex quo consensus eorum facit papam loco Ecclesiae'.

[2] Peter Olivi, *De renuntiatione papae*, pp. 358–9, 'cardinales gerunt *vicem superioris* in eligendo papam et in praeceptorie cogendo ipsum consentire electioni et in ipsum consecrando et in eius renuntiationem acceptando. Si autem papam propter aliquod crimen deponerent. . .'; cf. p. 356, 'qua ratione collegium cardinalium quoad quid participat *vim superioris* in substituendo papam, eadem ratione debet eam consimiliter participere in acceptando renuntiationem papae'.

[3] The electoral princes are described as the 'propinquiora membra sacri imperii' in the Golden Bull of 1356, ii. 4, ed. Zeumer, p. 15.

... sicut potestas rami quae flores et fructum producit *remanet* in radice ipso ramo destructo, sic ut videtur potestas papalis *remanet* in collegio vel in Ecclesia ipso papa mortuo. Imaginamur enim quod sicut in Ecclesia primitiva fundata per Christum apostoli Christo praesentaliter astiterunt et per universas mundi provincias et civitates rectores et praelati constituti fuerunt, sic in moderna Ecclesia ab illa derivata cardinales repraesentant personas apostolorum ut Christo praesentaliter astiterunt, alii vero episcopi et archiepiscopi, quorum nomine Ecclesia intelligi potest, repraesentant personas apostolorum ut in diversis provinciis mundi et civitatibus rectores et praelati constituti fuerunt. Collegium ergo cardinalium potest dici *radix propinqua*, sed congregatio omnium praelatorum aliorum et fidelium, quorum nomine Ecclesia designari potest, *radix remota* potest appellari.[1]

This fundamental role of the *congregatio fidelium*, and more especially of the college of cardinals, naturally comes into play not only when the pope dies, but also when he wishes to resign or is thought worthy of being deposed.[2] Without any hesitation the publicists in their more radical moments assert that the pope can only resign with the permission of the cardinals, and that it is the College which is to be responsible for bringing about his deposition. Just as we have said that the *Ecclesia* receives from Christ the power to create and elect the pope, argues Peter Olivi, so we are bound to say that the community has the necessary authority to depose him when he becomes heretical. He acknowledges that the pope has the right to decide the manner in which he is elected, and therefore he must be allowed the ability to resign. But since it is the *Ecclesia*, and in particular the cardinal-electors, who are most closely affected, their

[1] Augustinus Triumphus, *De potestate collegii*, p. 505, and repeated in the *Summa*, iii. 8, p. 36. Note the same implication in the *Tractatus contra articulos*, iii. 11, p. xciv, that the *praelati* are the *valentior pars Ecclesiae*. For the idea that the essence of the branch derives from the roots see his *Destructio arboris Porphyri*, *proem.*, as cited by Ministeri, *De vita et operibus*, p. 66. The same idea was later used by Nicholas of Cues, but the comparison of the *Ecclesia* to a tree has always been common in Christian thought: Greenhill, 'The Child in the Tree', *passim*; *KTB*, p. 200 n. 20. See *Ezech.*, xvii. 22–4 and *Daniel*, iv. 7–14. Note also Gregory I, *Moralium*, xix. 1 (*PL*, lxxvi. 97), who also identifies it with Christ. The representation of Christ as the *flos et fructus* is in Bonaventure, *Opera Omnia*, viii. 68–9; and the view that the roots have a special importance as the seat of the virtues can be found in Damian, *Ep.*, xxii (*PL.*, cxliv. 405–6).

[2] Augustinus Triumphus, *De potestate collegii*, p. 503.

approval must be obtained.[1] It is this same concern with the welfare of the community which motivates the theory of John of Paris. The pope, he points out, is only elected in the first place for the common good of the Church, and so, whenever he is in any way found to be unfit to fulfil his duties, he ought to seek permission to withdraw from his high position. This may be given by the cardinals on behalf of all Christians. But when it comes to deposing the pope, John feels that it may be more appropriate for the *congregatio fidelium* itself to act. On the other hand he is quick to add that in his view there is nothing to prevent the cardinals from acting by themselves. After all, he argues, they created him by conceding him power in the first place, and so it is not to be supposed that they cannot withdraw it when they deem this to be desirable. It is hardly necessary to mention that in this case the pope has no say in the matter.

. . . non eligitur aliquis in papam nisi propter bonum commune Ecclesiae. . . Si ergo, postquam fuerit in papatum, invenerit se vel inventus fuerit ineptus totaliter et inutilis vel superveniat impedimentum vel insania vel aliquid consimile, debet petere cessionem a populo vel a coetu cardinalium, qui in tali casu est loco totius cleri et totius populi, et, licentia obtenta vel non, cedere tenetur . . . ad renuntiationem sufficit quod causam alleget coram collegio cardinalium, quod est in hoc casu loco totius Ecclesiae. Sed ad deponendum decet quod fiat per concilium generale. . . Credo tamen quod simpliciter sufficeret ad depositionem huiusmodi collegium cardinalium, quia ex quo consensus eorum facit papam loco Ecclesiae, videtur similiter quod possit eum deponere.[2]

In a similar manner the Knight in the *Somnium viridarii* argues persuasively in favour of the competence of the cardinals on the grounds of convenience. The College can assemble more easily

[1] Peter Olivi, *Ep.*, p. 369, 'Dicendum quod sicut Ecclesia accepit a Christo auctoritatem eligendi et creandi papam, et papa accepit a Christo auctoritatem ordinandi formam eligendi suum successorem, sic eadem ratione et eodem iure accepit Ecclesia auctoritatem deponendi papam haereticum et approbandi renuntiationem vel cessionem papae renuntiantis, et papa ipse accepit potestatem renuntiandi, Ecclesia et praecipue electorum seu eligentium, quorum maxime interest, hoc approbante'.

[2] John of Paris, *De potestate regia et papali*, ch. 24, p. 254; cf. ch. 25, p. 257, 'Ergo a simili collegium cardinalium vice totius Ecclesiae poterit papam invitum deponere'.

than any other body. In this respect then the College may be regarded as the whole community itself: he speaks of the 'Ecclesia, id est congregatio cardinalium, qui possunt facilius convenire ad iudicandum'.[1] Certainly the Colonna did not feel that they had any need to refer to others when it came to deposing the pope. One of their pamphlets, written to the French king in 1304, has quite a prophetic touch. It warns the king that if the pope is allowed to abuse the plenitude of power allotted to him, then a general schism of the whole Church may easily result. To illustrate this the writer takes the case of an unwise pope who would use his powers to deprive other princes of their rights, and he draws a horrifying picture of a pope who might depose all the good cardinals and replace them with heretics. The dangers which would accrue from this, he solemnly declares, would be infinite, and it would be absolutely essential for the cardinals to revoke their original commission of power to him.[2] But the general consensus of opinion was that this was far too grave a matter to be left entirely to the College. Peter Olivi, for example, maintains that as the cardinals are acting on behalf of all, this deposition must be regarded as a joint move between the College and the *Ecclesia*. The latter is to be represented in this case by a general council, summoned by the cardinals by virtue of their possession of ecclesiastical power.[3] The deposition of the pope is a matter which concerns all, and the majority of the publicists feel that a general council is needed as an additional support for the action of the cardinals.

Whilst it is clear that the conciliar idea is being used here simply to further the claims of the College, the development of this theory

[1] Anon., *Somnium viridarii*, i. 171, p. 120.

[2] Anon., *Colonna memorandum to Philip IV*, p. 227, 'Item ex abusu plenitudinis potestatis de facili sequeretur generale schisma Ecclesiae: quid si unus papa forte minus sapiens vellet privare de plenitudo potestatis tantum reges; quid si unus papa forte haereticus vellet privare omnes cardinales catholicos et haereticos ordinare. Infinita sunt igitur pericula quae evenirent, ad quae vitanda omnino necessarium est per viam *revocationis* et restitutionis procedere'.

[3] Peter Olivi, *Ep.*, pp. 368–9, 'Et certe, si Petrus in haeresim publicam laberetur, fuisset utique per apostolos et per Christi Ecclesiam deponendus'; *De renuntiatione papae*, p. 353, 'potestatem habet super hoc Ecclesia Dei, et specialiter illud collegium quod elegit papam'. See also Francis Toti, *Tractatus contra Bavarum*, p. 81.

opens up the way for the full exposition of conciliar supremacy as it was to be elaborated in the early fifteenth century. Already it is acknowledged that in cases where the cardinals themselves prove insufficient, the basis of authority in the *Ecclesia* permits the use of a general council to settle all matters. It is quite possible, according to Augustinus Triumphus, for the members of the society to act without regard to their head,[1] and if need be take over the functions of the cardinalate:

> . . . secundum quem modum potestas papalis mortuo papa videtur remanere in collegio cardinalium tamquam in radice propinqua, sed in Christi Ecclesia remanet tamquam in radice remota, quia deficiente tali collegio, illud posset Ecclesia quod collegium potest.[2]

The full government of the society can be maintained either by the cardinals or by the council, and whilst it may be presumed that this will be exercised only until such time as a new pope is elected,[3] the question is unavoidably posed of whether it is really necessary to have a pope at all. Is not the continuing headship of Christ sufficient to maintain the quasi-monarchic character of the society?[4] The question is discussed by Augustinus Triumphus, but he hesitates to take the final step,[5] and eventually uses the rather weak argument

[1] Augustinus Triumphus, *De potestate collegii*, p. 504, 'Sed membris corporis mystici convenit aliqua virtus et aliqua actio sine virtute capitis'. This is in direct contravention of *Summa*, vi. 5 ad 1, p. 61.

[2] Augustinus Triumphus, *De potestate collegii*, p. 505.

[3] Augustinus Triumphus, *De potestate collegii*, pp. 505–6: on the death of the pope the college of cardinals has power not only to elect a new pope ('in ramum producere, quia potest eligere papam'), but also to take over the whole government of the society: 'ac omnia facere quae faciunt ad Ecclesiae gubernationem'. Similarly Peter Olivi, *Ep.*, p. 370, 'Et certe mortuo papa et necdum altero substituto, residet apud eos [scil. cardinales] praecipua auctoritas totius Ecclesiae gubernandae'.

[4] Augustinus Triumphus, *De potestate collegii*, p. 504, 'Nam caput Ecclesiae simpliciter est ipse Christus. . . Moritur tamen hoc caput Ecclesiae vel illud, quia moritur iste papa vel ille. Sed caput Ecclesiae simpliciter est immortale . . . et per consequens potestas papae est perpetua simpliciter loquendo, quia semper remanet in collegio vel Ecclesia quae est simpliciter ipsius Christi capitis incorruptibilis et permanentis'. Cf. Marsilius of Padua, *Defensor pacis*, II. xxii. 5, p. 423. This argument was later used by Conrad of Gelnhausen and Gerson: Jacob, *Essays in the Conciliar Epoch*, pp. 10–11, 13–14; but it had already been used by Johannes Andreae and Guido de Baysio: Tierney, *op. cit.*, pp. 209–11.

[5] Augustinus Triumphus, *De potestate collegii*, p. 506, 'Sed an possit collegium

that as only a pope can create cardinals, popes are after all necessary.[1] Since Augustinus Triumphus is putting forward this scheme mainly for the benefit of the cardinals, this demur is perhaps understandable. But Ockham, who was considerably less well disposed towards the College, was quite prepared to suggest that the *Ecclesia* could do without the Roman church altogether.[2] At this stage the point is a highly theoretical one, but it amply demonstrates how dangerous the conciliar idea was to the papal monarchy. Not only did it deny the ultimate supremacy of the Roman church, but threatened its very existence. One can appreciate the fears of the fifteenth-century papacy that the much publicised movement for reform of the head might mean a total decapitation.

sine papa quidquid potest cum papa, vel an possit collegium mortuo papa quidquid potest papa vivens . . . forte est dubium. Quia tunc non esset necessarium quod collegium papam eligeret ex quo simpliciter posset facere mortuo papa quidquid potest facere papa vivens vel eo vivente'. Cf. *Summa*, ii. 3 ad 4, p. 21, where he says that it is better to be without a pope for a long time rather than have a wolf in the fold, although he is probably referring here to the prolonged vacancy after the death of Clement V. The point had already been raised by Hostiensis and Guido de Baysio: Tierney, *op. cit.*, pp. 208–9; *art. cit.*, p. 433.

[1] Augustinus Triumphus, *De potestate collegii*, pp. 506–7: nor can they appoint to other offices in the *Ecclesia* or revoke previous papal rulings without a pope being present. This follows Johannes Andreae, *ad Clem.*, I. iii. 2, p. 15, s.v. *potestatis*.

[2] William of Ockham, *Dialogus*, I. v. 24, p. 494, 'et ideo quamvis Romana ecclesia post papam sit membrum principale Ecclesiae, sine ipsa tamen potest Ecclesia esse'.

III. ECCLESIA IN PAPA, PAPA IN ECCLESIA

SINCE many of Augustinus Triumphus' views in the *De potestate collegii* are reproduced in the *Summa*, the reader of this latter work is sometimes confronted with two utterly contradictory conceptions of the relationship between the pope and the *congregatio fidelium*. Could they be reconciled? The answer which Augustinus Triumphus returns to this question is important, not only because it exemplifies the way in which the great majority of hierocratic writers of the time came to terms with the problem, but also because it indicates a trend in later medieval political thought which was influential far beyond its relevance to the development of conciliar theory. The conflict between the papacy and the conciliar thinkers was fundamentally one between the defenders of the idea of sovereignty in the ruler and those who sited it in the community at large, and it was this issue which was eventually fought out in the fifteenth century. Nevertheless a concentration upon fifteenth-century conciliarism tends to ignore a separate stream of conciliar thought which was developed towards the end of the thirteenth century and gained almost universal acceptance during the fourteenth century. This idea, which we may describe as a moderate conciliar solution, was simply the transference of the whole idea of limited rulership, elaborated and expounded by the followers of Aquinas as a matter of general principle, into the realms of concilar thought.

The basic contention of the Thomists was that since they were faced with one party which claimed that full authority was held by the pope, and another which claimed to see it in the *congregatio fidelium*, then the only reasonable explanation must be that both pope and *Ecclesia* possess a similar plenitude of power.[1] The over-

[1] Compare Thomas Aquinas, *Summa theologica*, II. II. lxxxviii. 12 ad 3, 'quia summus pontifex gerit plenarie vicem Christi in tota Ecclesia, ipse habet pleni-

great use of it by one side is prevented by its possession by the other, and in this way all tyranny can be averted. This novel conception of the right order was greatly assisted by the contemporary identification of head and whole, of pope and *Ecclesia*. Buttressed by feudal notions of reciprocal rights and fortified by copious doses of Aristotelian logic, the mathematical minds of the publicists argued for a complete equation of the powers of each. If the pope is the *Ecclesia*, then may it not be equally well said that the *Ecclesia* is pope? As Cyprian had put it, the bishop is in the church and the church is in the bishop.[1] Both have the same power, and consequently the supreme knowledge of the faith, and if a deficiency is suspected in one, it may be measured up against the other. Neither St. Augustine's statement that Peter received Christ's power *in persona Ecclesiae*,[2] nor Gratian's recognition of the comparable status of papal and conciliar decrees,[3] need be regarded as favouring one side or the other. Taken together both monarchists and radicals are right: the pope *and* the *Ecclesia* hold the *potestas Christi*, and may be put upon a level footing. Two centuries later this view was given full expression when John Major wrote that alongside the Petrine commission 'auctoritas communicata est Ecclesiae a Christo sicut summus pontificatus, et auctoritas illa non dependet ab auctoritate summi ponti-

tudinem potestatis', with *Comm. in Ep. ad Ephes. I, lect.* 8, 'quia Ecclesia est instituta propter Christum, dicitur quod Ecclesia est plenitudo eius, scilicet Christi'.

[1] Cyprian, *Ep.*, lxvi. 8, as in Gratian, C. 7 q. 1 c. 7, 'Scire debes episcopum in ecclesia esse, et ecclesiam in episcopo'. Cf. Lucas da Penna, 'Princeps est in respublica et respublica in principe': Kantorowicz, 'Mysteries of State', pp. 79–80.

[2] Augustine, *Ep.*, liii (*PL*, xxxiii. 196), 'Cui [scil. Petri] totius Ecclesiae figuram gerenti Dominus ait, Super hanc petram etc.'. Cf. Alvarus Pelagius, *De planctu Ecclesiae*, ch. 55, p. 144, 'Et ei solus Iesus respondit in persona omnium de Ecclesia, quorum futurus erat caput . . .'; ch. 55, p. 149, 'Petrus tamquam caput pro toto corpore apostolico et Ecclesia'. As Peter de la Palu said, this could be interpreted in two ways (and in his case both at once): 'Solutio. Ecclesia est fundata super Petrum dupliciter. Uno modo quia super fidem Petri, quia *pro omnibus* respondit, Tu es Christus, Filius Dei vivi . . . Secundo modo fundata est Ecclesia super Petrum . . . quia tota potestas Ecclesiae fuit collata Petro, nec habet Ecclesia aliquam potestatem iurisdictionis nisi a Petro', *De causa immediata ecclesiasticae potestatis*, iv. 3, fo. 53.

[3] Gratian, D. 20 *ante* c. 1, 'Decretales itaque epistolae canonibus conciliorum pari iure exequantur'.

ficis sed immediate a Deo',[1] but the roots of this doctrine may easily be traced back to the contention of the fourteenth-century publicists that the power was given 'papae *et* Ecclesiae'. An acceptance of this idea, we suggest, accounts for the apparent dichotomy in the works of so many writers of the period, and underlies Augustinus Triumphus' statement that 'per Ecclesiam potest intelligi praelatus *vel* ipsa congregatio fidelium'.[2] The preponderance of conciliar ideas in the fourteenth century rests upon an assumption of the double plenitude of power.

This theory enables the publicists to take full advantage of the canonistic distinction between the acts of the head of a corporation on behalf of its members, the right of the members to act on their own initiative in defence of their own interests, and the normal action taken with the common consent of both head and members.[3] The view that all decisions affecting the common good of the society should generally be the result of joint action does in fact illustrate the way in which a working arrangement between the two supremacies is made possible. Once again the principle of the self-limiting ruler is applied: it is a matter of equity or natural law that what touches all should be approved by all, and accordingly the pope as *vicarius Christi*, the human embodiment of divine-natural law, must voluntarily submit to this limitation on his freedom of action. To act with the consent of all is, for the publicists, part of the fundamental *lex Ecclesiae*. They were able to point out that practically every other ecclesiastical institution, bishoprics, the religious orders, and the like, were administered by regular series of chapters and councils, and that this machinery always derived from papal edicts. Was it to be supposed that the papacy itself should be denied what was granted to others? Even Innocent III had been

[1] John Major, *De auctoritate concilii super pontificem maximum*: Gerson, *Opera Omnia*, i. 886. Cf. i. 889–90, where he speaks of the possession of power by both the people of a kingdom and the king, so that there are 'duae potestates realiter'.

[2] Augustinus Triumphus, *Summa*, vii. 3 ad 1, p. 66.

[3] It was common in corporation law theory to suggest that the members could act by themselves during a vacancy in the rectorship: Gillet, *La personnalité juridique*, pp. 129–30; Gaines Post, 'The Two Laws', p. 425, n. 35; Tierney, *Foundations of the Conciliar Theory*, pp. 106–31.

constrained to admit that Christ had only promised to be present when two or three were gathered together: clearly too much was at stake to risk reliance upon the unsupported decisions of one man—there is safety in numbers.[1] Understandably the publicists were rather vague as to which particular canons decreed this, although the younger Durantis had little difficulty in compiling a formidable list of *Decretum* references,[2] and the situation was much improved when Boniface VIII inserted the maxim *quod omnes tangit* into the *Sextus*.[3] They were even vaguer, in default of a papal coronation oath, about the occasion of the pope's renunciation of his absolute power, although John of Paris went so far as to assert that the pope took an oath to 'se gerere curam universalis Ecclesiae' for the tenure of his office like any civil rector,[4] and sporadic attempts were made during the course of the next century to induce popes to limit their future actions by means of election capitulations.[5] The movement culminated in the attempt of the council of Constance, in its celebrated decree *Frequens* of 1417, to oblige every newly elected pope to make a *professio fidei* binding himself to observe the decrees of all general councils.[6] But with these reservations, it was generally

[1] Innocent III, *Reg.*, X. xxxii (*PL*, ccxv. 1128), 'Ubi multa consilia, ibi salus'. Cf. *Prov.*, xi. 14.

[2] Guilielmus Durantis, *De modo generalis concilii celebrandi*, i. 2, pp. 4–9.

[3] *Sextus, De regulis iuris*, xxix. It may be noted that in 1262 Urban IV had set aside Alexander IV's recognition of Richard of Cornwall as *rex Romanorum* on the grounds that his predecessor's approval had not been given 'omnium consensu': C. Rodenburg, *Epistolae selectae saeculi xiii e regestris pontificum Romanorum* (Berlin, 1883–94), iii n. 560 p. 546.

[4] John of Paris, *De potestate regia et papali*, ch. 23, p. 252; ch. 25, p. 259.

[5] For the election capitulation at the election of Innocent VI in 1352 see Raynaldus, *Annales ecclesiastici ad 1352*, xxv. 540; and the discussion in Mollat, 'Contribution à l'histoire du sacré collège', pp. 100f.; and in general W. Ullmann, 'The Legal Validity of the Papal Electoral Pacts', *Ephemerides Iuris Canonici*, xii (1956), pp. 3–35.

[6] *Acta Concilii Constantiensis*, ed. Finke, Heimpel and Hollnsteiner (Münster, 1896–1928), ii. 616f.; and see in general H. Jedin, *A History of the Council of Trent* (London, 1957f.), i. 14–15. The formula for this oath was based upon a supposed *professio* of Boniface VIII, and contained the phrase 'cum quorum [scil. cardinalium] consilio, consensu, directione et rememoratione ministerium meum geram et peragam': Baluze-Mansi, *Miscellanea novo ordine digesta* (Lucca, 1761–4), iii. 418. This *professio* was however only drawn up in 1407: J. Lulvès, *MIOG*, xxxi (1910), pp. 375–91.

accepted that government by consent was part of the old custom of the Church and was legally enforceable upon every holder of the papal office.

An interesting feature of this theory is the way in which it incorporates the claims of the cardinals. It does not advocate a permanent general council: that is only necessary in certain specific and important cases. It is enough for most matters that the consent of the College should be obtained, since the cardinals, by virtue of their succession from the apostles, represent the whole community. Support for this view could be gleaned from the fact that the popes of the early fourteenth century often sought to excuse themselves from taking unpalatable measures on the grounds that the cardinals had not been consulted. Clement V had even gone so far as to affirm that 'pontifex non sit solitus facere absque concilio sacri collegii', although the popes usually made it clear enough that they were not bound to seek or accept the views of the cardinals, and that consultation was not to be confused with consent.[1] Most of the publicists however had no hesitation in brushing this important distinction aside. The consent of the College, they repeated, is essential in all matters affecting the *status Ecclesiae*, in particular matters of faith, the deposition of the pope, his resignation and election. As Peter de la Palu said, taking the example of resignation, this consent is necessary to maintain the proper relationship between the rights of the pope himself and the rights of the whole community which he is bound to respect.

Unus est ius suum quod ei acquiritur. Aliud est ius Ecclesiae cui obligatur. . . igitur papa papatui ex parte quidem sua renunciare potest, sed quia semel *se obligavit* Ecclesiae, ex illa parte renunciare non potest nisi de assensu cardinalium, qui in omnibus quae ad papam spectant vicem Ecclesiae repraesentant.[2]

[1] Mollat, *art. cit.*, pp. 98–100.

[2] Peter de la Palu, *De causa immediata ecclesiasticae potestatis*, iv. 2, fo. 49; cf. Alexander de S. Elpidio, *De ecclesiastica potestate*, iii. 6, p. 37, 'papa renuntiare potest quantum est ex parte sua, sed quia *se obligavit* Ecclesiae et cardinales totam Ecclesiam repraesentant, non videtur tenere talis renuntiatio nisi cardinales acceptent, quia etsi papa renuntiare potest, non tamen se potest excutere a iugo *nisi sponsa consentiente*. Sed summus pontifex nascitur sive creatur per electionem cardinalium et ipsius consensum; ergo per contrarium per sui dis-

Or again, since one pope has decreed that the cardinals shall elect the pope, and this is now enshrined in canon law, no succeeding pope can alter this or designate his own successor.[1] As far as the pope is concerned, the rights of the College are fixed for all time. And indeed the election of the pope by the cardinals *vice omnium* is an important example of the way in which divine power descending through the papal vicariate links up with the authority deriving from the *congregatio fidelium*. The power which constitutes the papal office is direct from God, but the person who exercises it is chosen by the cardinals on behalf of the universal society.[2] The creation of a pope is a joint act between God and man, and reflects the nature of the papacy itself.

At once we are on familiar ground, namely, Augustinus Triumphus' distinction between the formal and material elements of the papacy, and it is through this idea that Augustinus Triumphus edges his way into such a position that he is able to accept the main tenets of the moderate conciliar idea. The growth of the distinction between the office and the man, which was on the one hand so useful in conveying to the pope the attributes of God, could however be elaborated into a theory which was a virtual denial of this idea altogether. In the long run the process of rationalisation that the papal

sensum *in certis casibus* sicut dictum est, cum acceptatione cardinalium, renuntiare potest et papatui cedere'. Amongst many other examples of this see in particular Geoffrey of Fontaines, *Quodlibeta*, XII. iv (v. 96–8).

[1] Peter de la Palu, *De causa immediata ecclesiasticae potestatis*, v. 2, fo. 58, 'nec potest ad libitum mutare modum constituendi papam, sed est in constitutionem papae aliquid de iure divino quod ipse mutare non potest. De iure enim divino est quod successor Petri sit per electionem et consensu Ecclesiae, et hoc est consonum iuri naturali . . . Sed est de iure naturali et divino quod ex electione universalis Ecclesiae vel illorum ad quos de consensu universalis Ecclesiae translatum est ius eligendi sicut sunt hodie cardinales'.

[2] Peter de la Palu, *De causa immediata ecclesiasticae potestatis*, iv. 2, fo. 49v, 'Unde potestas principalis prout est *in sede Romana* habet fundamentum divinum non humanum. Et ideo numquam destruitur. Sed prout est *in persona* quae est in sede solis, per consensum humanum habet fundamentum humanum'; John of Paris, *De potestate regia et papali*, ch. 25, p. 255, 'Licet igitur *papatus* sit in se a solo Deo, tamen in hac *persona* vel illa est per cooperationem humanam, scilicet per consensu electi et eligentium, et secundum hoc per consensum humanum potest desinere esse in isto vel in illo'; similarly Aegidius Romanus, *De renuntiatione papae*, vi, p. 11; Alvarus Pelagius, *De planctu Ecclesiae*, ch. 55, p. 150; Hervaeus Natalis, *De potestate papae*, ff. 142, 143.

position underwent at the hands of the canonists and publicists was a serious source of weakness. From the hierocratic point of view distinctions were dangerous, and the papal monarchy would have been much safer if left cloaked in the mystery appropriate to a divine institution. A god does not become more clearly revealed by dispelling the cloud of unknowing, nor a symbol become more real by assessing its positive value: and the pope was above all a divine symbol. In a society which sees its true ruler as the heavenly Christ the source of government is essentially an abstraction; and whilst the pope as *vicarius Christi* exists to give human shape to that abstraction, he himself as far as possible takes on its abstract qualities. In his office he is a symbol of an invisible power, and his symbolic character swallows up his personal capacity. The individual becomes a symbol of the ideal ruler, Christ, in much the same way that his *regalia* also symbolises the divine majesty: the pope and his crown are no more than animate and inanimate representations of Christ's kingship. And from this it followed that the pope could no more act out of character than his crown could walk and talk of its own accord. He has ceased to be a human being and become a *vir alius*, a living image of Christ. His natural personality is obliterated by the divine grace of his function, the man totally absorbed by his office. There is a mystical marriage between the pope and his office, and by marriage two entities become one. As Conrad of Megenberg put it, the pope becomes a single divine thing, a oneness compounded of two natures on the model of Christ himself.[1] To continue to discuss the pope in terms of office and man can therefore be nothing more than an intellectual pursuit for the extreme hierocrat. But whilst the Thomist continued to accept the notion of the mystical ever-righteous abstraction, he insisted on combining fact with fiction. He could not ignore the fact that the

[1] Conrad of Megenberg, *De translatione Romani imperii*, ch. 25, p. 344, 'Et si quaerens utrum habuerit dominium praesentium rerum ut Deus vel ut homo, dico quod tamquam Christus *unus ex utroque*; sicut enim anima rationalis et caro unus est homo, ita Deus et homo unus est Christus. Similiter papa dominium talium habet non ut homo sed ut vicechristus aut tamquam vicedeus'. Similarly the Tudor lawyers emphasised the indivisibility of the king and his crown, and stressed that a distinction did not involve the question of a separation: *KTB*, pp. 9, 365.

living symbol of Christ still appeared to be a man, that he exercised something that looked remarkably similar to free will, and that he still seemed to be subject to purely human emotions and desires. Reason began to replace faith, and in the harsh light of reason the total depersonalisation of the ruler was impossible. Consequently the Thomists insisted on considering the pope *ut persona*. They insisted on measuring the individual up against the perfect ideal. They insisted on making comparisons between the pope and Christ. And they found, as might be expected, that comparisons were odious. Indeed the more they compared, the less the pope looked like an earthly Christ, and they were correspondingly strengthened in their resolve to divorce the practice of the man from the theory of his office.

In this way the notion of the instrumental character of the papacy underwent a transformation at the hands of the publicists. The hierocratic insistence on the nature of the pope as *instrumentum Christi* was calculated to assert the inability of the pope to do other than as Christ desired. An instrument, it was argued, can function only in the hands of its manipulator: hence there can be no papal action which is not an act of Christ himself. To all intents and purposes therefore, Christ and his vicar become identical. The Thomist on the other hand viewed the matter from a rather different angle. Whatever the instrument did, he maintained, it still remains obvious that an instrument is something utilised by somebody else. It can perform divine actions, but it does not thereby become itself divine. The result, said Aquinas, must not be attributed to the instrument but to its principal agent: 'effectus non assimilatur instrumento sed principali agenti'.[1] Thus there cannot be any proper identification of the instrument with its prime mover. They are two different things, and, provided that it is not inanimate, the instrument must be regarded as having some sort of capacity to act of its own accord apart from the agent that uses it.[2] Aquinas, it is true,

[1] Thomas Aquinas, *Summa theologica*, III. lxii. 1. Cf. *KTB*, pp. 441f.

[2] Thomas Aquinas, *Summa theologica*, III. lxii. 1 ad 2, 'instrumentum habet duas actiones: unam instrumentalem secundum quam operatur non in virtute propria sed in virtute principalis agentis; aliam autem habet actionem propriam quae competit ei secundum propriam formam'.

did not admit to having the pope in mind here: he was discussing the sacraments on one occasion, the humanity of Christ on the other. But his disciples immediately appreciated that there was a close similarity between these matters and the status of the papacy. General principles applied in one case could equally well be applied elsewhere. They had already used this idea to affirm that the lay ruler, although *organon papae*, had a semi-autonomous function. And they saw that it would also suggest that the pope, although a divine instrument, could still act of his own volition apart from Christ. Papal actions did not therefore necessarily have the same standard of perfection as divine actions: no complete identification of God and his vicar is possible.[1] In other words the human personality of the pope, although normally instrumental to the papal office, might still do things which had no connection with his official capacity. The twin natures of the pope, human and divine, although conjoined in the same person, remain to some extent independent of each other and may be treated in isolation: 'cum unitate personae remanet distinctio naturae'.[2] Consequently what has hitherto been a purely theoretical distinction between person and papacy now becomes a very practical matter, and has the gravest political consequences. We can watch this development in Augustinus Triumphus. Already we find him prepared to agree that the pope may resign, and this is presented as a human action taken independently of his divine power.

Sed ex hoc non arguitur quod papa non renunciare possit, quia potestas iurisdictionis, per quam papa est summus sacerdos, potest tolli et auferri opere humano sicut opere humano conferri potest.[3]

[1] E.g. Alvarus Pelagius, *De planctu Ecclesiae*, ch. 58, p. 184, 'Item Christi vicarius agit non excellenter ut Christus, sed ministerialiter'.

[2] Thomas Aquinas, *Summa theologica*, III. vii. 1 ad 1.

[3] Augustinus Triumphus, *Summa*, iv. 6, p. 46; cf. iv. 3, p. 43, 'Similiter ergo modo, non obstante quod *papatus* singulariter sit a Deo, tamen quia non est a Deo in isto *homine* vel in illo nisi cooperante eius consensu et eius volitione, ideo potest ab eo tolli cooperante eius dissensu et volitione'. This human consent could however equally well be interpreted as being that of the cardinals, whose approval thereby becomes necessary for the pope's resignation: Alexander de S. Elpidio, *De ecclesiastica potestate*, iii. 6, p. 37; Peter de la Palu, *De causa immediata ecclesiasticae potestatis*, iv. 2, fo. 49; Peter Olivi, *De renuntiatione papae*, p. 364; and see p. 493 n. 2 above.

Indeed the papal office is made dependent upon human consent. Certainly, at this stage, Augustinus Triumphus affirms that the human consent is that of the pope himself, and he emphasises that this is a matter for his own decision alone.[1] But the very suggestion that a pope may be incapable of carrying out his function means that a crack has appeared in the apparently solid edifice of the papal supremacy.[2] In fact Augustinus Triumphus now slips almost imperceptibly towards a very different conception of the vicariate of Christ than we have hitherto found with him. Because the pope is *vicarius Christi* he can do no wrong. But this no longer means that he is infallible and omnipotent; rather that he cannot really be a true pope if he does falter in his direction of the society. The difference is a subtle one, but explosive in its effect. To appreciate this we must remember that in orthodox hierocratic eyes the pope personifies divine wisdom: he is *lex animata*, righteousness in human form. It is therefore logically impossible for him to be a heretic,

[1] Augustinus Triumphus, *Summa*, iv. 5, p. 46, 'Papa inter homines superiorem se non habet. Ideo sicut consentire electioni de se factae est confirmatio, quia statim habet omnem papalem iurisdictionem, ita renunciare et dissentire eius iurisdictioni est eius *depositio* . . . sicut papa seipsum confirmat suae electioni consentiendo, ita *seipsum deponit* suae iurisdictioni renunciando'. See also the opinion of Peter of Auvergne as given by J. Leclercq, 'La renonciation de Célestine V et l'opinion théologique en France du vivant de Boniface VIII', *Revue d'histoire de l'Église de France*, xxv (1939), pp. 183–92 at pp. 186–8. This is in accordance with modern canon law (Canon 221).

[2] The question of resignation arose from the dispute over the validity of Celestine V's abdication in favour of Boniface VIII in 1295. For a survey of contemporary opinion see W. Ullmann, 'Medieval Views concerning Papal Abdication', *Irish Ecclesiastical Review*, lxxi (1949), pp. 125–33. The outcry against Celestine's resignation was largely a propaganda weapon in the contest between the Colonna and Boniface VIII, but it served to bring up for discussion the whole nature of the papal office, and its very great importance may be gauged from the close relationship between renunciation and deposition in the eyes of the publicists—as Aegidius Romanus says of resignation, 'ipse tamen debet hoc facere et debet *seipsum deponere*', *De renuntiatione papae*, ix, p. 21. To acknowledge that the pope can resign is half way towards admitting that he can be deposed, and the most curious feature of the dispute is that the situation required both sides to argue against their own position. The supporters of Boniface had to argue that he could resign, but could not be deposed; whilst the Colonna were forced to use the traditional hierocratic idea of the indissoluble marriage of the pope to his office, and yet at the same time allow that he could be deposed, at least by the cardinals.

and the question of deposition does not arise. Anything else would denigrate the nature of God, and suggest that Christ himself could conceivably have been heretical. The idea of an unsuitable pope verges on blasphemy. Yet this is what Augustinus Triumphus now admits: had not Christ himself made the mistake of choosing Judas?[1] And we now hear that a pope may be ignorant, impotent, incapable or demented, and that his continuance in office would be 'contra commune bonum totius Ecclesiae'.[2] Does not canon law expressly state that he can be 'a fide devius'?[3] It is the voice of a real Thomist that we can hear. The infallibility of the vicar of Christ is retained, but this only leads to the conclusion that a deviating pope is not the *vicarius Christi*, and has put himself outside his office.[4]

The conception that the pope can do no wrong now comes to be seen as a limitation of papal sovereignty, a denial of the 'papa omnia potest' idea. Just as God can commit no sin, so the power of his vicar stops short at the point at which it would contradict itself:[5] otherwise it would be a denial of his essential nature as 'the good'. The pope, whose function it is to act as the projection of this 'good' on earth, can act only in the best interests of the society: he has power for its edification, not its destruction.[6] The purpose of the

[1] Augustinus Triumphus, *Summa*, ii. 1 ad 2, p. 18.

[2] Augustinus Triumphus, *Summa*, iv. 5, p. 45; cf. ci. 1 ad 1, p. 494, 'ratione ignorantiae aut infirmitatis'; iv. 4 and 4 ad 1, p. 44, 'demens, impotens vel insufficiens ad regimen Ecclesiae'.

[3] Augustinus Triumphus, *Summa*, v. 1, p. 50; vii. 1, p. 64. John of Paris remarks that in view of the *Decretum* statement the doctrine of infallibility is unintelligible: 'illud non intelligo', *De potestate regia et papali*, ch. 25, p. 257.

[4] As Guilielmus Durantis put it, a 'rector catholicus non iudicatur a quoquam', but this does not apply to merely any rector: *De modo generalis concilii celebrandi*, iii. 1, p. 241.

[5] The position was summed up by the fifteenth-century canonist Andreas de Barbatia, 'et sic papa omnia potest ut Deus excepto peccato': Ullmann, 'The Legal Validity of the Papal Electoral Pacts', p. 16. Cf. William of Ockham, *Dialogus*, III. ii. iii. 23, *additio*, p. 393, 'Papa ergo, cum sit solummodo vicarius Christi, servare tenetur ea quae Christus verbo et exemplo docuit servanda'.

[6] Peter de la Palu, *De causa immediata ecclesiasticae potestatis*, vi. fo. 73, 'non est sibi data potestas in destructione sed in aedificatione'; Peter Olivi, *De renuntiatione papae*, p. 353, 'Nam secundum Apostolum, II *Cor.*, x [8], potestas apostolica non est data in destructione Ecclesiae sed in communitionem'. Cf. Tholemy of Lucca, *De regimine principum*, iii. 10, p. 259, 'unde merito pastores vocantur, quibus vigilantia incumbit ad subditorum utilitatem. Alias non sunt

papal office is the promulgation of the right way of life in a Christian society, and, consequently, if he orders or teaches anything contrary to this ideal, he must be presumed to be acting outside his office, to have shed his papal status and to have reduced himself to the level of an ordinary person. As such there is no need to obey him.

Praeceptum vero papae numquam ligat nisi ad bonum, quia ad malum praeceptum papae non esset tenendum, immo omnino spernendum.[1]

This must not be taken too far. Augustinus Triumphus continues to grant the pope a wide personal immunity. As St. Augustine had taught, there was a great deal of difference between the acts of an individual which concerned only his personal chances of salvation, and the acts of the ruler in his official capacity ordering the lives of others, so that the salvation of all was involved.[2] In the same way Augustinus Triumphus insists that no crime committed by the pope detracts from his legal position as pope: he does not lose his office simply because he personally falls into a state of mortal sin. This only comes about when his personal actions tend to influence others, when, for example, he orders others to follow suit, or seeks

legitime domini sed tyranni, ut probat Philosophus'. To exemplify this he takes Christ's admonition to Peter to care for his sheep (*John*, xxi. 17) adding, 'Hoc ergo supposito quod pro utilitate gregis agat, sicut Christus intendit'; also Hervaeus Natalis, *De potestate papae*, ff. 139–139v. This follows the corporation law theory that an officeholder has no right to injure the corporation: e.g. Engelbert of Admont, *De officiis*, pp. 112–13, 'Officium est debitum obligans officiatum ad proprium uniuscuiusque rei et personae negotium utiliter peragendum. Quod unusquisque commissit sibi negotium faciens recte, utitur suo officio; sed hoc negligens aut contrarium faciens suo officio non utitur sed abutitur. Est autem abusio a sua rectitudine distortus actus et usus officii uniuscuiusque'; and see further Tierney, 'A Conciliar Theory', pp. 425–7.

[1] Augustinus Triumphus, *Summa*, lxiii. 2, p. 335; cf. xxii. 1, p. 130, 'Si [illa quae papa praecipit] clauduntur sub iure divino, non est obediendum papae si mandaret aliquid contra illa . . . sibi non esset obediendum, immo fortius resistendum. Si aut clauduntur sub iure naturali et papa mandaret aliquid contra illa fieri, ut fornicati, furari, vel innocentem occidere, vel quod homo non comederet, vel quod matrimonium non contraheret, similiter in talibus sibi non obediendum est'.

[2] Augustine, *Ep.*, clxxxv. 5 (*PL*, xxxiii. 801), 'Aliter enim servit [Deum] quia homo est; aliter quia etiam rex est: quia *homo* est, ei servit *vivendo* fideliter; quia vero etiam *rex* est, servit leges iustas *praecipientes* et contrarias *prohibentes* convenienti vigore sanciendo': also Gratian, C. 23 q. 4 c. 42.

to justify his actions so that others are led to believe that they too may commit these crimes. For then he would be failing in his function of defining the right way of life in a Christian society.

. . . papam esse incorrigibilem potest intelligi dupliciter. Primo per ipsius criminis vel peccati continuationem, puta quod monitus non propter hoc desistat a peccato fornicationis vel alio accusationis digno. Secundo per ipsius criminis pertinacem *defensionem* ut quod *defendat* et *dicat* tale crimen habens circumvolutam malitiam non esse peccatum, ita quod crimina prohibita iure divino *laudaret* et *defenderet tamquam licita*. Prima igitur incorrectio et contumacia non facit papam desinere esse papam. Sed secunda puto quod sic, quia talis incorrectio et contumacia aequipollent haeresim.[1]

Thus any command contrary to the right order automatically comes within the classification of heresy, for which, according to Gratian D.40 c.6, the pope can alone be deposed, and puts him beyond the immunity which he normally enjoys in his capacity as vicar of Christ. The infallible officer and the fallible man, he writes, are two very different things,

praeceptum papae *personaliter* et *instrumentaliter* mutabile est et fallibile; sed *auctoritative* et *principaliter* immutabile est et infallibile, quia auctoritas divina cui innititur immutabilis est et infallibilis,[2]

and the distinction can now be given a very practical significance. Immediately the pope acts contrary to his function, he declares, the man and his office fall apart. The pope who becomes a heretic is no longer a true pope but a tyrant, and usurps his position if he continues to occupy it.[3]

[1] Augustinus Triumphus, *Summa*, v. 4 ad 3, p. 53.

[2] Augustinus Triumphus, *Summa*, lxiii. 1 ad 1, p. 333; cf. xx. 6, p. 126, 'Quia cum talis potestas sit sibi a Deo collata, non potest in ipsa excedere vel errare vel ea male uti *per se* et *formaliter*, quia omnis usus clavis potentiae rectus et iustus est, cum ab illo sit derivata qui iustus est et rectum iudicium eius. Similiter omnis usus clavis scientiae verus et rationabilis est, cum sit derivata ab illo qui est via, veritas et vita [*John*, xiv. 6]. Sed *per accidens* et *materialiter* papa et in clave potentiae potest excedere et in clave scientiae potest errare'; also Alvarus Pelagius, *De planctu Ecclesiae*, ch. 68, p. 245, 'Intueamur ergo oculo fidei unam ecclesiam, sedem eius, dignitatem eius, quae non peccat; peccare potest qui stat in ea, quia homo est'.

[3] The medieval tradition of the tyrant as a usurper derives through Aquinas: e.g. *Summa theologica*, II. II. civ. 6 ad 3, 'Et ideo si non habeant iustum princi-

The development of the idea that a ruler could be removed from his office without process of deposition owed much to the Aristotelian distinction between a king and a tyrant, and had been made abundant use of by Augustinus Triumphus in his discussion of the instrumental nature of kingship in the *Ecclesia*. Although anxious to emphasise the papal role as the 'hammer of the tyrants', he nevertheless declares that the pope does not actually need to depose an unsuitable ruler. The man had already done this himself by his own misdeeds: 'iam non esset rex sed tyrannus'.[1] The function of a true emperor is to support the pope in his government of the society and an emperor who fails to do this cannot be emperor. A heretical emperor, for example, is a contradiction in terms:

> [Imperator] enim papae fulci[men] debet esse veritate, iustitia et aequitate; non enim potest adversus veritatem sed pro veritate, ut dicit Apostolus ad II *Cor.* [xiii.8].[2]

He is *ipso facto* deposed by his own act, and his subjects are automatically released from obedience to him.[3] No formal act of de-

patum, sed usurpatum . . . non tenentur eis subditi obedire'; cf. *Commentum in Sententias*, II. xliv. ii. 2 ad 4, 'qui per violentiam praelationem accipiunt non sunt veri praelati; unde nec eis obedire tenentur subditi'.

[1] Augustinus Triumphus, *Summa*, xxxv. 6 ad 2, p. 209; and note his use of *Hosea*, viii. 4, in i. 2, p. 4.

[2] Augustinus Triumphus, *Summa*, xxxv. 1, p. 206; cf. Alvarus Pelagius, *De planctu Ecclesiae*, ch. 37, p. 44, 'Non debet dici verus imperator qui catholicus non est'.

[3] Augustinus Triumphus, *Summa*, xl. 4, p. 232, 'Si ergo [imperator] fidelitatem quam iurat, recusat observare, *ipso facto* eis subditi sunt a iuramento eius fidelitatis absoluti'; cf. xliv. 3 ad 1, p. 242, 'Ideo cum princeps contra iustitiam gravamina infert subditis per violentias et leges iniquas, in talibus homo non obligatur ut obediat talibus legibus si sine scandalo vel maiori detrimento resistere possit. . . Homo tenetur parere legi sui superioris dummodo iusta sit. . . Ideo nulli legi contra mandata Dei est parendum, sed pro viribus resistendum'. This follows Thomas Aquinas, *Summa theologica*, II. II. xii. 2, 'Et ideo quam cito aliquis per sententiam denuntiatur excommunicatus propter apostasiam a fide, *ipso facto* eius subditi sunt absoluti a dominio eius et iuramento fidelitatis quo ei tenebantur'. The use of the failing officer but unfailing office device was necessary for Aquinas so that it could be argued that the pope might depose the emperor without destroying the imperial power. Note however Bernardus Parmensis, *Glossa ordinaria ad Decretales*, V. vii. 16, fo. 459, sv. *Absolutos*, 'Absolutus *ipso iure* ex quo manifeste lapsi sunt . . . et est arg. quod papa potest absolvere laicum a iuramento fidelitatis . . . quia ad ipsum spectat interpretatio iuramenti'.

position is required, merely the papal declaration of his unsuitability. The basis of this is the conception of emperorship as an office, and since for Augustinus Triumphus this is essentially true of the papacy, he sees no reason to distinguish between the pope and any other ecclesiastical officer.

Ecclesia punit haereticos . . . depositione, quia sive sit clericus sive laicus, cuiuscunque *dignitatis* existat, sive papa sive imperator, ab omni *dignitate* debet deponi, immo *ipso facto* est depositus.[1]

The pope who acts contrary to his function can no longer be regarded as a *verus papa*,[2] and has from that moment divorced himself from his office. He is always to be measured up against an idealised picture of the good pope, the individual pontiff against Christ himself: the man is to be set against the fictitious personality expressive of the good of the community, which his office represents. And if he is found wanting, it is manifest that he has put himself beyond his office. But a pope apart from the papal office is no pope at all,[3] so that he too may be said to be *ipso facto* deposed by his own act,[4] or, as Alvarus Pelagius puts it, condemned out of his own

[1] Augustinus Triumphus, *Summa*, xxviii. 6, p. 172; cf. Anon., *Somnium viridarii*, i. 177, p. 132, 'Et etiam quilibet sive sit clericus sive sit laicus, cuiuscunque fuerit status, etiam papa, propter haeresim est a dignitate sua deponendus'. This is probably inspired by a similar passage in Gratian, D. 20 c. 1.

[2] Augustinus Triumphus, *Summa*, lxvii. 1 ad 3, p. 353, 'Non enim potest papa contra veritatem sed pro veritate'; similarly James and Peter Colonna, *Memoranda*, i. 509, 512; ii. 515; iii. 519–23. John XXII was frequently accused of being no true pope for his teaching on the beatific vision: e.g. William of Ockham, *Epistola ad Fratres Minores*, pp. 10, 15–16; Michael of Cesena, *Litterae ad omnes fratres*, p. 1340. This led to the assertion that John was Anti-Christ: Maccarrone, *Vicarius Christi*, p. 201. For a short account of John's teaching see Offler in Ockham, *Opera Politica*, iii. 20f.

[3] Augustinus Triumphus, *Summa*, v. 7 ad 3, p. 55, 'ex tali crimine *statim* desistit esse papa, nec amplius habet iurisdictionem in Ecclesia'; cf. v. 2, p. 50, 'Papa ergo, si Christum negat, negandum est quod sit papa'.

[4] Augustinus Triumphus, *Summa*, v. 1, p. 50, 'sicut homo mortuus non est homo, its papa deprehensus in haeresi non est papa, propter quod ipso facto est depositus'. Also James and Peter Colonna, *Memoranda*, iii. 520; Nogaret, Dupuy, pp. 58, 265; William of Ockham, *Dialogus*, I. vi. 90, pp. 607–8; *Epistola ad Fratres Minores*, p. 15; *Allegationes de potestate imperiali*, p. 431; *Tractatus contra Iohannem XXII*, ch. 3, p. 42; *Tractatus contra Benedictum XII*, vii. 1, p. 303; vii. 3, p. 306; vii. 4, p. 307; vii. 5, p. 308; vii. 8, p. 312. For the development of this idea by the Decretists see Tierney, *Foundations of the Conciliar Theory*, pp. 9, 62–3, 214–16.

mouth.[1] He does not need to be judged, because he has judged himself by the very fact of becoming a heretic: 'seipsum iudicaret, quia qui non recte credit iam iudicatus'.[2] There is accordingly no need for anyone else to pass sentence of deposition upon him:[3] he has ceased to be head of the *Ecclesia* and to all intents and purposes a vacancy ensues.

We may give Augustinus Triumphus full credit for his ingenious (if not particularly original) explanation of how a pope might become a heretic and be deposed without contravening the maxim that *papa a nemine iudicatur*. He was not judged by any man, but by the Truth, by a fictitious picture of himself.[4] It was perfectly true

[1] Alvarus Pelagius, *De planctu Ecclesiae*, ch. 6, p. 27, 'Quod synodus etiam universalis in eum corrigibilem praesertim iurisdictionem non habet, nec in eum sententiam depositionis profert etiam in haeresi; sed dicit ei, Ore tuo iudica causam tuam . . . ex ore tuo condemnaberis'.

[2] Augustinus Triumphus, *Summa*, xxii. 1 ad 2, p. 130; also v. 4, p. 52. Cf. *John*, iii. 18; I *Cor*., v. 3; and note its use by Innocent III in his consecration sermons (*PL*, ccxvii. 656, 664, 670). This was also employed by Aegidius Romanus, *De renuntiatione papae*, ix. p. 20; John of Paris, *De potestate regia et papali*, ch. 22, p. 248; and note the following passage with its typically Thomistic distinction between a *de iure* and a *de facto* deposition: Peter de la Palu, *De causa immediata ecclesiasticae potestatis*, iv. 1, fo. 46, 'Ad secundum dicendum quod papa in nullo casu quamdiu est papa propter quodcunque crimen potest nec a consilio nec a tota Ecclesia nec a toto mundo deponi, non solum quia est superior, sed quia est a Deo. . . Sed quando labitur in haeresim tunc *eo ipso* praecisus est *ab Ecclesia* et desinit esse caput, et tunc deponitur *de facto*, non *de iure*. Quia qui non credit, iam iudicatus est, de iure scilicet. . . Unde haereticus non potest manere nec esse papa'.

[3] Anon., *Libellus ad defensionem fidei catholicae*, p. 554, 'si papa aliter sentiat seu dogmatizat de fide quam docet sancta Ecclesia catholica aut faveat aut communicet haeretico, est ab ipsius obedientia et communione recedendum, *nec expectari debet quod per concilium condempnetur*, cum iam sit *ipso iure et facto* dampnatus'; Alexander de S. Elpidio, *De ecclesiastica potestate*, iii. 8, p. 38, 'Et si opponatur de papa qui labitur in haeresim, dicendum est quod tunc *non deponitur, sed sua depositio manifestatur*, quia, *eo ipso* quod haereticus est, est praecisus ab Ecclesia et desinit esse caput Ecclesiae a qua praecisus est . . .; sed propter haeresim sit caput aridum, immo omnino sic desinit esse caput ut nullum omnino influxum possit habere in membra'.

[4] Augustine, *De vera religione*, ch. 31 (*PL*, xxxiv. 148), 'licet spiritualis iudicet omnia, tamen iudicatur ab ipsa veritate'. This is cited by Thomas Aquinas, *Summa theologica*, III. lix. 6 ad 2, who also uses Augustine's definition of a fiction as a *figura veritatis:* Augustine, *De quaest. evang*., ii. 51 (*PL*, xxxv. 1362)= Aquinas, *Summa theologica*, III. lv. 4 ad 1. For a similar idea with Dante see now *KTB*, pp. 459f.

that *the* pope, the *vicarius Christi*, could not err; but *a* pope, any pope taken as an individual, was as liable to falter in matters of faith and government as any other man. As Peter Olivi said, we must always distinguish carefully between the pope who is pope and the one who only appears to be pope.[1] But for all its ingenuity, this theory gave no guide as to when or how it should be known that the pope had ceased to be; and it merely served to underline the need for some other body capable of acting as guardian of the common good. It is at this point that the Thomist double plenitude idea comes into play. We have seen that in order to provide an accommodation between the two absolute powers, both pope and *congregatio fidelium* were held to have renounced their initial authority in conformity with divine-natural law, and to have bound themselves to accept the provisions of canon law.[2] Sovereignty does not entirely disappear: it remains vested in the abstract personality of the society—in the *Ecclesia* as a juridical entity, or, in other words, in Christ himself as *persona Ecclesiae*. But total possession of this sovereignty is denied to any person or group within the community. Both pope and *congregatio fidelium* have handed over their initial absolute rights to this divine or abstract personification of the whole, and now function on its behalf. In this capacity they are limited by the law which they promulgate *vice Christi*, as the joint earthly representatives of the mystical personality which is the supreme good of the community. But in the interests of this common good the pope may still rise above his normal adherence to the law, and retains the right to act absolutely *in certis causis*: tempor-

[1] Peter Olivi, *Quaestio de infallibilitate*, p. 340, 'Secunda distinctio est de ipsa sede et eius praesule. Est enim sedes secundum nomen seu secundum solam apparentiam, et est sedes Romana secundum rem et existentiam aut secundum utrumque. Et idem potest dici de papa'.

[2] It may be noted that this prevents the pope from repealing or annulling the provisions of Gratian, D. 40 c. 6: this is contained in the list of decrees made by earlier popes which are binding on all future popes as given by William of Ockham, *Tractatus contra Benedictum XII*, vi. 3, p. 274. On this he comments, 'papa non potest statuere ut non valeat de haeresi accusari'. This had however already been said by Augustinus Triumphus, *Summa*, v. 5 ad 2, p. 53, 'Stat[ut]um prohibens ne papa posset incusari de haeresi esset in praeiudicium totius Ecclesiae, periclitaretur enim universitas fidelium sub regimine eius'. Similarly Michael of Cesena, *Tractatus contra errores*, p. 1335; *Litterae ad omnes fratres*, p. 1344; cf. Guido Terrenus, *Quaestio de magisterio infallibilis Romani pontificis*, p. 18.

arily and within strict limits he becomes the sole representative of the immaterial *Ecclesia* and exercises its plenitude of power. The same, according to this theory, must also be true of the *congregatio fidelium*. Under normal conditions the members of the community rest subject to the pope in accordance with canon law and their own best ordering. They maintain the right to participate with the pope in legislating for the whole community, but their independent use of the plenitude of power remains indirect and merely potential. Nevertheless, in certain circumstances, when the good of the society is at stake, above all in cases where the true faith is threatened by the depravations of a heretical pope, the potential power of the community can, Augustinus Triumphus explains, be put to active use through the medium of a general council.

. . . ergo est dicendum quod maioritas dicta de potestate ut residet in Ecclesia *et* in papa non accipitur secundum univocam rationem, quia ut est in Ecclesia vel in concilio est *radicaliter* et *habitualiter*, quia deficiente papa et collegio cardinalium posset sibi de Romano pontifice providere. Sed in papa huiusmodi *potentia* est *actualiter*, et quia quod est in actu potest agere, quod vero est in habitu et in potentia non agit. Ergo potestas Ecclesiae maioritate potentiali vel habituali maior est in concilio et in tota congregatione fidelium quam in papa, quia in concilio fidelium talis potestas numquam moritur, in papa vero isto vel illo moritur. Sed maioritate actuali maior est potestas Ecclesiae in papa quam in concilio, quia concilium per illam potentiam non potest agere, papa vero potest agere quando vult.[1]

The justification for this view, as Augustinus Triumphus makes clear, is the idea that supreme power rests 'in Ecclesia *et* in papa'. Consequently neither the papacy nor the Universal Church can fail: but since any individual pope can, then for all practical purposes the *Ecclesia* alone remains as the undying source of the true faith,[2] and can exercise a casual jurisdiction *ratione indeviabilitatis*

[1] Augustinus Triumphus, *Summa*, vi. 6 ad 1, p. 62; cf. vii. 1, p. 64, 'inferior sit superior cum agatur causa Dei'; Alvarus Pelagius, *De planctu Ecclesiae*, ch. 6, p. 27, 'Quod si totus mundus sentiret in aliquo negotio contra papam, quod sententia papae standum esset, quod verum intellige nisi esset causa fidei'; John of Paris, *De potestate regia et papali*, ch. 22, p. 250, 'puto quod *in hoc casu* Ecclesia contra papam deberet movere et agere in ipsum'.

[2] E.g. Aegidius Romanus, *De renuntiatione papae*, xi, p. 34, 'Sic etiam dice-

over any occupant of the papal office. A general council may therefore be considered the lawful body capable of distinguishing between a true pope and one who merely presumes to be pope, but is in fact already a self-deposed heretic.[1]

This is a direct transference to the universal society of the right of any community to act *in casu necessitatis* against its head.[2] Basically it is an attempt to put the Aristotelian view of the natural, human source of authority alongside the traditional medieval idea of the divinely empowered ruler. Here the hierocratic identification of pope and *Ecclesia* proves invaluable. It permits the retention of the idea that the pope acts on behalf of all, but also suggests that on occasions the normal order may be inverted, and the *congregatio fidelium* may act in place of the pope:

bamus de papatu: *potestas enim papalis est in Ecclesia a Deo*, et ideo non potest unquam tolli potestas papalis secundum se, quin semper huiusmodi potestas sit in Ecclesia quae numquam moritur: sed licet creatura non cooperetur ad ipsam potestatem papalem secundum se, quia huiusmodi potestas secundum se est a Deo, sit tamen opere creaturae, quia sit opere humano quod papalis potestas sit in hoc homine. Ideo ex opere humano fieri potest quod talis potestas desinit esse in hoc homine'. This follows Innocent III's opinion that a heretical pope was *ipso facto* deposed by reference to the unfailing *Ecclesia: Consec. serm.*, ii (*PL*, ccxvii. 656), 'propter solum peccatum quod in fide committitur possem ab Ecclesia iudicari'; but this required a public pronouncement by the *populus christianus*: iv (670), '[Romanus pontifex] potest ab hominibus iudicari, vel potius *iudicatus ostendi*, si videlicet evanescat in haeresim, quoniam qui non credit *iam* iudicatus est. *In hoc* siquidem *casu* debet intelligi de illo quod si sal evanuerit ad nihilum valet ultra'.

[1] Complaining that Benedict XI had acted against divine and natural law in usurping complete authority over another bishop's diocese, John de Pouilli urges that a general council should decide whether Benedict had in fact been acting as a true pope or a mere individual: 'Non dixit quod decretalis praedicta non fuit statutum Romanae ecclesiae sed unius singularis personae, scilicet Benedicti papae, qui fuit unus homo. Propter quod generale consilium cassavit decretalem illam praedictam non ut statutum Ecclesiae, sed ut factum unius singularis personae: Koch, 'Der Prozess gegen den Magistro de Polliaco', p. 396. John of Paris also held that it was the task of a general council to decide 'de statu papae, scilicet, an sit papa vel non', *De potestate regia et papali*, ch. 22, p. 248.

[2] In this connection note the use of the idea that it is the will of the subjects which converts a tyranny into a true kingdom (*naturale dominium*) in Augustinus Triumphus, *Summa*, xxvi. 1 ad 2, p. 156. This derived through Tholemy of Lucca, *Determinatio compendiosa*, ch. 31, pp. 63–4, from Thomas Aquinas, *Commentum in Sententias*, II. xliv. ii. 2.

per Ecclesiam potest intelligi praelatus *vel* ipsa congregatio fidelium, qui locum praelati tenet in causa fidei vel in eo quod redundaret in periculum multitudinis et totius reipublicae.[1]

For this purpose the idea of casual or indirect jurisdiction exercised in defence of the common good, hitherto elaborated in favour of the ruler, is applied to the community itself. Since there are always occasions on which human law fails to conform with the higher divine-natural law which embodies the common good, a general council representing this good[2] is morally and legally bound to override the positive law of the society as it stands: 'Ubi autem ius positivum contradicit vel impedit ius naturale vel divinum, servandum non est'.[3] These occasions constitute a case of necessity when the private right possession of superior authority by the pope, as guaranteed by canon law, must give way to the public utility.

Quaedam vero sunt quae redundant in malum totius reipublicae, sicut peccatum haeresis et subversio totius fidei christianae, et in talibus non est talis ordo servandus, sed statim succurrendum est periculo, eo quod bonum commune praeferendum est cuilibet bono privato.[4]

What is normally good is occasionally bad, and what is usually bad, such as a disregard of the law, is justifiable in a case of necessity *ratione status Ecclesiae*.[5] In such conditions the *Ecclesia* is above posi-

[1] Augustinus Triumphus, *Summa*, vii. 3 ad 1, p. 66; cf. c. 1, p. 488, 'doctrina Ecclesiae *et* summorum pontificum est doctrina Christi'.

[2] Augustinus Triumphus, *Summa*, vi. 6 *prop*. 2, p. 61, 'generale concilium repraesentat bonum commune totius Ecclesiae'.

[3] Augustinus Triumphus, *Summa*, ii. 5 ad 1, p. 23.

[4] Augustinus Triumphus, *Summa*, vii. 3, p. 66. The general principle for this can be found in Thomas Aquinas, *Summa theologica*, II. II. xlii. 2 ad 3, 'regimen tyrannicum non est iustum, quia non ordinatur ad bonum commune... Et ideo perturbatio huius regiminis non habet rationem seditionis'.

[5] Augustinus Triumphus, *Summa*, v. 8 ad 3, p. 55, 'ut quando illud bonum quod est mali occasio est bonum necessitatis et publicum totius Ecclesiae'; cf. Thomas Aquinas, *Summa theologica*, II. I. xcvi. 6, 'Unde si emergat *casus* in quo observatio talis legis sit damnosa communi saluti, non est observanda'. He continues, 'Si vero sit subitum periculum non patiens tantam moram ut ad superiorem recurri possit, ipsa necessitas dispensationem habet annexam, quia necessitas non subditur legi'. As the publicists were quick to point out, this was a case when there was no superior. All this was greatly elaborated by Ockham: e.g. *Tractatus pro rege Angliae*, ch. 8, p. 259, 'Item in necessitate omne privilegium cessat, sicut dicunt canonicae sanctiones. Si enim leges non solum

tive law, and all the canonical restrictions upon the convention and activity of a general council without papal consent are null and void. Thus Augustinus Triumphus maintains that any group of people representing the *Ecclesia* may convoke a general council, and its proceedings will be valid in that they are authorised by the *Ecclesia* itself.[1] He suggests that it may be summoned by either the ecclesiastical[2] or the lay princes[3] acting on behalf of all. But it is by

humanae sed etiam divinae in necessitate cessant, et in eis excipitur necessitas... multo fortius privilegia humana in necessitate cessant et in eis necessitas excipi debet'. This is applied directly to the laws which normally safeguard papal immunity: *Tractatus contra Benedictum XII*, vi. 8, p. 290, 'Ergo similiter canones dicentes quod a papa appellare non licet non sunt intelligendi sine omni penitus exceptione, quin *in aliquibus casibus specialibus* liceat appellare a papa, quamvis non sit a papa *regulariter* appellandum. Casus autem in quibus licet appellare a papa sunt censendi illi in quibus papa potest accusari et iudicari... Illi autem casus ad minus sunt duo, scilicet casus haeresis et casus in quo crimen papae esset notorium de quo scandalizaretur Ecclesia, et ipse esset incorrigibilis'.

[1] Augustinus Triumphus, *Summa*, iii. 2 ad 2, p. 28. Ockham refers to the right of free assembly belonging to the members of any corporation, *Dialogus*, I. vi. 84, pp. 602–3.

[2] Augustinus Triumphus, *Summa*, v. 6 ad 1, p. 54, 'Ideo in tali casu eius auctoritas non requiretur, sed sufficeret auctoritas collegii et aliorum episcoporum ac doctorum sacrae scripturae'. It is interesting to note the enhanced role which he gives to the doctors of theology: the opinions of these *venerabiles viri* are to be considered of no less value than that of the pope himself in matters of faith, and whilst they lack the authority of bishops and cardinals, their presence is most necessary at any general council: x. 1 ad 2, p. 77; xiv. 3, p. 97; lx. 5, p. 317; lxvii. 1–2, pp. 352–3; c. 1 ad 2, p. 489. This probably derives from the memory of the 'concilium praelatorum, magistrorum et aliorum eruditorum in sacris litteris' which had decided that the French charges of heresy against Boniface VIII were untenable: see his *Tractatus contra articulos*, i. 7, p. lxxix. The same insistence upon the importance of the doctors can be found with Aegidius Romanus, *De ecclesiastica potestate*, i. 1, p. 5; Conrad of Megenberg, *Tractatus contra Wilhelmum Occam*, ch. 8, p. 373; William of Ockham, *De imperatorum et pontificum potestate*, ch. 9, p. 25, and is significant in view of the influential part played by the Parisian doctors in the Schism.

[3] Augustinus Triumphus, *Summa*, iii. 2 ad 3, p. 29, 'in tali casu imperator et alii reges et principes christianorum possent et deberent concilium episcoporum et praelatorum congregare . . . et puto quod sic posset eos includere . . . ut dicitur *Extra*, *De elect. c. Ubi periculum* [I. vi. 3], et 17 *dist.*, *c.* [6] *Concilia*'. Cf. Nogaret, Dupuy, p. 58, 'Cum igitur in concilio generali omnium consilio deceat et iudicio dictum flagitiosum damnari qui pariter Deum et omnes offendit, peto, requiro quanta possum instantia, et supplico vobis domino regi [Franciae] praedicto ut praelatis, *doctoribus* et populis atque principibus fratribus nostris in Christo, maxime cardinalibus et praelatis omnibus, intimetis ut omnes

now really immaterial who calls it, so long as it comes into being, when it may confirm its own legitimacy.

Although this notion of the supreme right or reason of 'state', the idea that law can be abrogated in special circumstances, suggests that the use of a general council is no more than a necessary evil, the right of the community to act is depicted by Augustinus Triumphus as a public duty of the first order. Indeed, he says, this must be so because there is no other alternative. When the pope becomes heretical only the power of the *congregatio fidelium* is left for use.

Cum igitur potestas Ecclesiae . . . remaneat in tota Ecclesia et in collegio cardinalium: aliter, si nullo modo remaneret mortuo papa, non possent sibi de alio providere.[1]

The *Ecclesia* is *acephala*, and a vacancy may be presumed to exist.[2] Whilst the publicists at the beginning of the century had contented themselves with a vague statement that the *Ecclesia*'s plenitude of power could be used *in certis casibus*,[3] Augustinus Triumphus now proceeds to define several situations in which this is to happen. The

generale concilium convocetis in quo, nefandissimo praedicto damnato, per venerabiles cardinales provideatur Ecclesiae de pastore'. Augustinus Triumphus' view is repeated by William of Ockham, *Dialogus*, I. vi. 84–5, pp. 602–4; and at the end of the century by Zabarella: Tierney, *Foundations of the Conciliar Theory*, pp. 224–5. Gratian, D. 17 c. 6, although asserting papal superiority to a general council, was a favourite basis for conciliar speculation. The decree *Ubi periculum* (*Sextus*, I. vi. 3) of Gregory X said that the college of cardinals was not to engage in any other business during a papal vacancy than the election of a new pope 'except in cases of grave and evident peril'. This made it a familiar quotation in conciliar works.

[1] Augustinus Triumphus, *Summa*, iv. 7, pp. 47–8; cf. v. 6 ad 2, p. 54, 'cum tamen desinit esse papa per crimen haeresis, auctoritas illa remanet in Ecclesia sicut ipso mortuo'; Alvarus Pelagius, *De planctu Ecclesiae*, ch. 68, p. 250, 'Immo vacante Ecclesia per mortem papae, non est dicendum quod remaneat sine capite . . . quia tunc corpus cardinalium et tota Ecclesia habet caput Ecclesiae generale et verum et proprium, Christum scilicet viventem. . . Succedit etiam collegium cardinalium tunc in quibusdam'. See also Aegidius Romanus, *De renuntiatione papae*, x. 5, pp. 26–7; xxiv. 1, p. 59, for the idea that the *Ecclesia* holds a reserve power which remains in being during a vacancy.

[2] Augustinus Triumphus, *Summa*, v. 4, p. 52; cf. Alvarus Pelagius, *De planctu Ecclesiae*, ch. 34, p. 37. The term *acephala* here may be derived from Aegidius Romanus, *De renuntiatione papae*, xxiii, p. 56, or Guido de Baysio, *ad Sext.*, I. vi. 3.

[3] E.g. Aegidius Romanus, *De renuntiatione papae*, ix, p. 21.

first instance is the normal vacancy which ensues upon the death or resignation of a pope. In this event the potential power of the community becomes actual in the college of cardinals, but only to the limited extent of enabling them to elect a new pope. More than this the cardinals cannot do—'omnia alia negotia eis interdicuntur'[1] —nor can the community itself.[2] The *congregatio fidelium* can only move in the second instance, namely, when the cardinals either fail to elect a pope or a double election takes place or when there is doubt cast upon the validity of their election. A general council may then be formed for the purpose of making a new election.

Secundo est hoc congruum propter vitandum futurum periculum. Nam ut ponitur 69 *dist.* c.[8] *Si duo*, Si duo apostolici temeritate concertantium fuerint electi, tunc nullus eorum in sede apostolica sedere debet. Sed ut notatur ibi, convocandum esset *in tali casu* generale concilium, et tunc ex nova ordinatione ille intronizari deberet in cathedra beati Petri quem universitatis consensus eligeret.[3]

On the other hand there are those cases when the behaviour of the

[1] Augustinus Triumphus, *Summa*, lxviii. 3 ad 3, p. 359. He denies that the continuing headship of Christ gives the cardinals further powers than this, unless the pope has specifically delegated other duties to them for exercise during a vacancy: iii. 8, p. 36, 'talis potestas remanet in collegio quantum ad illud quod in papatu est *materiale*, quia papa mortuo potest collegium per electionem personam determinare ad papatum ut sit talis vel talis. . . Sed si nomine potestatis papalis intelligimus actualem administrationem, quod est quid *materiale et formale* in papatu, sic talis actualis administratio bene moritur mortuo papa. Quia nec remanet in collegio actualis administratio potestatis papalis ipso mortuo nisi quantum per statutum praedecessoris est eis commissum; nec remanet isto modo in Christo, quia de *communi lege* Christus post resurrectionem non est executus talem potestatem nisi mediante papa'.

[2] Augustinus Triumphus, *Summa*, iii. 9 ad 1, p. 37, 'Ecclesia non perdit suam *iurisdictionem*, sed bene perdit ad tempus dictae iurisdictionis *actualem administrationem*, quia actualis administratio non sit nisi per papam. Mortuo ergo papa, cessat illa actualis administratio usque ad creationem alterius'.

[3] Augustinus Triumphus, *Summa*, ii. 4, p. 22; cf. iii. 2, pp. 28–9, 'cardinalibus deficientibus . . . puto . . . quod generale concilium ad talem electionem faciendam congregaretur: . . . propter dubium interpretandum . . . magis esse securum quod talis electio ad concilium generale *devolvatur*'. He rejects (ad 1, p. 29) the suggestion that the Roman clergy might replace the cardinals for this purpose, unless a special papal mandate should be issued to this effect. This idea had been put forward by Johannes Andreae, Hostiensis and later Zabarella: Tierney, *op. cit.*, pp. 217, 237. Cf Alvarus Pelagius, *De planctu Ecclesiae*, ch. 1, p. 26, 'Si nullus superesset cardinalis, eligeret clerus Romanus'.

pope himself may properly be termed scandalous, scandal being used in the old medieval sense of an action calculated to endanger the public safety. With Ockham these are carefully subdivided into the separate instances of heresy in matters of faith, criminal activities and tyranny,[1] although Augustinus Triumphus treats them all within the general classification of heresy. Here, although the situation technically comes within the category of a vacancy,[2] the cardinals cannot do anything but convoke a general council. In contrast with his earlier opinion, Augustinus Triumphus does not now permit the cardinals any power to sit in judgement over the pope: if they believe him to be a heretic it is a general council alone which can decide the matter.[3] It is the council which will pass judgement upon him—which it may be presumed will be the death penalty to be carried out by the secular arm[4]—and, he continues, since the cardinals only elect on behalf of all, and since the council is now in being, it may as well appoint the new pope:

> ... per talem igitur potestatem Ecclesia posset illum damnare sicut per talem potestatem potest alium sibi praeficere.[5]

[1] William of Ockham, *Octo quaestiones*, i. 17, pp. 63–6, 'In tribus casibus tenetur papa humanum subire iudicium secundum quosdam: primo in casu haeresis... Secundo quandoque crimen eius est notorium et inde scandalizatur Ecclesia et ipse est incorrigibilis... Tertio si res vel iura aliorum invadit vel detinet minus iuste'.

[2] See also Peter de la Palu, *De causa immediata ecclesiasticae potestatis*, iv. 1, fo. 46: above p. 503 n. 2. Cf. Bernardus Parmensis, *Glossa ordinaria ad Decretales*, V. viii. 1, fo. 459, sv. *Firmitate*, 'Quia dum ecclesia habet pastorem haereticum vel scismaticum vacare intelligitur'. In England in the fifteenth century a usurping ruler was legally presumed to be dead: *KTB*, pp. 370–1.

[3] Augustinus Triumphus, *Summa*, vi. 6 ad 3, p. 62, 'quando papa erraret, in tali casu ... recursus potest haberi ad concilium, quia propter haeresim papa desinit esse papa'.

[4] The death penalty is prescribed as the general remedy for heresy, *Summa*, xxviii. 7, p. 173, although it is not to be carried out by the priesthood. The execution of a tyrant had been approved by Thomas Aquinas, *Commentum in Sententias*, II. xliv. ii. 2; also Alvarus Pelagius, *De planctu Ecclesiae*, ch. 62, p. 194. This was probably inspired by *Dig.*, XI. vii. 35.

[5] Augustinus Triumphus, *Summa*, v. 6, p. 54. Baldus also said that although the cardinals might lose their right to elect, the *Ecclesia* itself always retained it: *ad Decretales*, I. ii. 25, 'Sive per veros cardinales sive per falsos papa eligatur, Ecclesia semper retinet possessionem ... et si expellerentur cardinales, tamen quia ipsi non possident nomine suo sed nomine totius catholicae Ecclesiae, ipsa universalis Ecclesia non perdit possessionem eligendi'. Cf. Thomas Aquinas, *De*

Doubtless the cardinals can elect on the authority of the council,[1] but it is the community of the faithful through which the voice of God directly speaks, and which has full power to take over the government of the society during the vacancy.[2]

Once the idea of a plenitude of power in the members of the society is accepted, the right of a general council to act against a heretical pope is assured. One vital point however has yet to be settled. The council must decide whether the pope is a heretic: but the council can only come together on the presumption that this is already known—it can only act of its own right in a vacancy. At what point then does it become clear to the community in general that a *de iure* vacancy exists? Immediately, says Augustinus Triumphus.[3] But if this is already known, why is it necessary to summon a general council to decide it? In spite of appearances the *ipso facto* argument in itself solves nothing, and to escape from this difficulty the publicists were forced to have recourse to yet another legal fiction, namely, that for all jurisdictional purposes a person accused of heresy can be treated as though he is actually known to be a heretic. Consequently from the time that a written accusation of heresy is lodged against the pope,[4] his power ceases and the imaginary vacancy begins. Bartolus, for example, decided that if a ruler was seen to be a tyrant his acts were to be regarded as null and void from the moment that steps were taken to deprive him of his

regimine principum, i. 6, p. 230, 'Primo quidem, si ad ius multitudinis alicuius pertineat sibi providere de rege, non iniuste ab eadem rex institutus potest destrui vel refrenari eius potestas si potestate regia tyrannice abutatur'.

[1] Peter de la Palu, *De causa immediata ecclesiasticae potestatis*, iv. 1, fo. 44v., would permit either the cardinals or the *Ecclesia* to make the election.

[2] Augustinus Triumphus, *Summa*, iii. 2 ad 2, p. 28, 'posset concilium ordinare et determinare de omnibus quae pertinent ad utilitatem Ecclesiae'.

[3] Augustinus Triumphus, *Summa*, v. 6, p. 54, 'Sic papa in haeresi deprehenso, *statim* ipso facto potestas eius remanet in Ecclesia . . . *statim* universitas fidelium congregari deberet'; vii. 3, p. 66, '*statim* succurrendum est periculo'.

[4] Augustinus Triumphus, *Summa*, vii. 4, p. 67. In their appeals against Boniface VIII in 1297 the Colonna had announced that their tracts constituted a formal written accusation against him (*Memoranda*, i. 514; ii. 518), and that from the time that a cardinal accused the pope of heresy, all papal acts were suspended, and it was no longer necessary to obey him (i. 513; iii. 523–4). Augustinus Triumphus' emphasis upon the need for an *accusatio* (*Summa*, v. 4–5, pp. 52–3; vii. 4, p. 67) follows the general canonistic view of the thirteenth century: Tierney, *op. cit.*, p. 213.

authority, not from the end of the process.[1] This was based on the view that one need not appear before a judge suspected of being hostile, and, according to the author of the *Disquisitio iuridica*, Huguccio had used this argument for the same purpose in the case of an emperor accused of notorious wrong-doing.[2] This device was certainly popular with the lawyers: at the beginning of the thirteenth century the canonist Tancred had maintained that the pope could take over the jurisdiction of any prince under suspicion;[3] and later in the century Hostiensis had supported this idea by pointing out that the power of a proctor was revoked when his status was in doubt.[4] Official approval of the notion came in 1220 when Frederick II laid down that mere suspicion (*sola suspicio*) of heresy incurred outlawry, and was to be followed by automatic condemnation for heresy unless proved otherwise, a ruling subsequently accepted by Honorius III as being valid for all members of the *Ecclesia*.[5] It is perhaps ironic that one of the grounds on which Frederick was himself deposed was suspicion of heresy.[6] Eventually the principle was applied to the pope himself, and in their dispute with Boniface VIII the Colonna asserted that the simple fact that a legitimate accusation had been made against the pontiff, even though based on nothing more than suspicion, was sufficient to deprive the pope of his authority.[7] On this assumption there is no

[1] Woolf, *Bartolus of Sassoferrato*, pp. 166–7.

[2] Anon., *Disquisitio iuridica*, ch. 9, pp. 1388–9, 'Unde notat Huguccio et textus invit iii q.v [c. 15] *Quia suspecti*, quod postea recusatio seu exceptio inite suspitionis propter inimicitiam, desinit esse iudex. . . Igitur iudices suspecti et inimici non debent esse, ut dicto c. *Quia suspecti*'.

[3] Tancred, 'Iste est ergo unus casus in quo iudex ecclesiasticus potest se immiscere saeculari iurisdictioni, scl. . . . cum iudex saecularis est suspectus et recusatur': A. M. Stickler, 'Sacerdozio e Regno nei Decretisti e Decretalisti', *MHP*, xviii (1954), pp. 1–26 at p. 23 n. 80.

[4] Tierney, 'A Conciliar Theory', p. 422.

[5] Ullmann, *Medieval Papalism*, pp. 185–6; G. de Vergottini, *Studi sulla legislazione di Federico II in Italia: Le Leggi del 1220* (Milan, 1952), pp. 159–66.

[6] C. Rodenberg, *Epistolae saeculi xiii e regestris pontificum Romanorum selectae* (*MGH*, 1883–94), ii n. 124, p. 92. In 1289 Philip IV of France complained that Nicholas IV saw fit to correct him 'on bare suspicion'.

[7] Anon., *Colonna memorandum to Philip IV*, p. 226, 'Item post appellationem legitimam legitime ex causis legitimis interpositam, et post *allegationem suspicionis* et recusationem legitimam et ex causis legitimis factam, et petitionem arbitrorum legitimam legitime factam . . . omnis processus post haec habitus, etiam per Romanum pontificem, nullus est ipso iure'.

obstacle to the convocation of a general council without papal authority before it is known whether he is a heretic or not, and regardless of the fact that he may eventually be shown not to have been a heretic at all.

The more closely this theory is scrutinised, the more it shows ominous tendencies towards asserting total conciliar supremacy over the papacy, in spite of the tortuous ways in which its adherents endeavour to retain the immunity of the pope as such. The whole theory is after all little more than the dressing-up of expediency in altruistic legal formulae, and the search for further justification leads slowly but inevitably towards a far more radical attitude. The question of accusation is a case in point. Augustinus Triumphus declares that any man who believes the pope to be a heretic has a duty to lay an accusation against him, even at the peril of his life:[1] and he supports this by reference to the old canonistic maxim that any catholic is superior to a heretical pope.[2] As he points out, if the faith of the pope is, or should be, identical with that of the *congregatio fidelium*, it is logically true that the faith of any member of the community can be seen as the norm against which the faith of a pope under suspicion can be measured.

Fides est communis omnibus fidelibus, et in fide causa uniuscuiusque fidelis agitur. Ergo ad omnes fideles spectat determinare quae sunt fidei.[3]

[1] Augustinus Triumphus, *Summa*, vi. 8 ad 3, p. 63, 'Sed in casu fidei vel pro vitando maiori periculo seu pro utilitate reipublicae tenetur se mortis periculo exponere'. Michael of Cesena said that an accuser was exempt from papal jurisdiction during the time that an accusation was made: *Tractatus contra errores*, pp. 1335–6, 'Et ideo per appellationem interpositam ab eo, ego et adhaerentes mihi essemus ab omni potestate et iurisdictione ipsius domini Iohannis [XXII] exempti': otherwise the pope would be judge in his own case.

[2] Augustinus Triumphus, *Summa*, xviii. 3, p. 115; cf. William of Ockham, *Tractatus contra Benedictum XII*, vi. 8, p. 290; vii. 2, p. 305; *Dialogus*, I. vi. 90, pp. 607–8; *De imperatorum et pontificum potestate*, ch. 27, *additio*, p. 97; Alvarus Pelagius, *De planctu Ecclesiae*, ch. 34, p. 37; Peter Olivi, *Quaestio de infallibilitate*, p. 343; Michael of Cesena, *Tractatus contra errores*, p. 1335; *Litterae ad omnes fratres*, p. 1344; and Nogaret, Dupuy, pp. 243, 262: 'Si papa a fide deviat, minor est quocunque catholico'.

[3] Augustinus Triumphus, *Summa*, x. 1 *prop*. 3, p. 77. Cf. William of Ockham, *Dialogus*, III. 1. iii. 9 and 13, pp. 828, 830.

At this stage he has not reached the point of permitting an individual to depose the pope. The actual measures taken to defend the faith, he comments here, can be left to the *maiores de Ecclesia*. But as far as knowing the content of the faith itself, all Christians must be recognised as capable of deciding that for themselves: 'scire tantummodo quid homo credere debeat propter adipiscendam vitam beatam . . . pertinet communiter ad omnes fideles'.[1] For this purpose any *fidelis* is the *Ecclesia*, and in this sense the *Ecclesia* can consist of only one man, since one may discern the light of the truth when the rest are blinded by it. In that man alone the undying faith would remain.

Ecclesia non potest errare, quia si unus solus catholicus remaneret, ille esset Ecclesia.[2]

To this Ockham could not resist the temptation to add that the *fidelis* concerned might even be a woman or an infant.[3] And it was not to be supposed that when Ockham took over this idea the

[1] Augustinus Triumphus, *Summa*, x. 1 ad 3, p. 77. The distinction between knowing the faith and taking forceful measures to defend it derives from Augustine, *De Trinitate*, xiv. 1 (*PL*, xliii. 1037). Cf. Anon., *Informatio de nullitate processuum papae*, p. 21, 'duplex est iudicium: unum iurisdictionis; hoc non habet homo super papam ut eum pro suis excessibus iudicaliter corrigat. Aliud est iudicium *rationis* vel discretionis; et hoc iudicio *quilibet habet iudicare de factis et maxime de praeceptis sui superioris* an sint iusta vel iniusta, ac bona vel mala, aut in quem finem sint facta. Alias enim semper esset obediendum cuilibet praecepto quandoque contra divinum praeceptum facto'.

[2] Augustinus Triumphus, *Summa*, xx. 6 ad 3, p. 126; also xxv. 1 ad 1, p. 150. Cf. iii. 8 ad 3, p. 36, 'Ecclesia quantum ad congregatio fidelium . . . numquam persecutione tyrannorum deficit vel deficiet. Quia si non remaneret nisi unus fidelis, in eo remaneret Ecclesia'. This probably rests on *Acts*, xiv. 17, but is a logical inversion of the view that the pope alone is the *Ecclesia*. The idea that 'universitas stat in uno' had already been developed by the Decretists: e.g. Huguccio, *ad* D. 65 c. 8, sv. *convocet*, 'et est argumentum quod unus solus clericus superstes omnibus aliis illius ecclesiae mortuis potest eligere, similiter unus consul potest regere totam civitatem aliis defunctis, quia in tali casu universitas tota remanet in uno': Gillet, *La personnalité juridique*, pp. 79–99.

[3] William of Ockham, *Dialogus*, I. v. 29–31, pp. 498–503; *Breviloquium*, v. 4, p. 175. This was supported by the familiar theological idea that the true faith had remained in Mary alone during the crucifixion: e.g. Guido Terrenus, *Quaestio de magisterio infallibilis Romani pontificis*, p. 29. See further Y. M. J. Congar, 'Incidence écclésiologique d'un thème de dévotion mariale', *Mélanges de science religieuse*, viii (1951), pp. 277–92.

matter would be allowed to rest there. In any case the imperialists seized upon the Thomistic version of conciliarism with avidity, and Ockham declares that it completely justifies all Louis of Bavaria's attacks on the papacy.[1] This is borne out by Louis' own denunciation of John XXII, which closely conforms to the procedure outlined by Augustinus Triumphus. In his appeal to a general council of 22 May 1324, and his sentence of deposition against John published at Pisa on 13 December 1328, Louis virtually summarises the whole Thomist position. Having begun with a list of John's alleged heresies in such matters as the doctrine of apostolic poverty, he develops a general attack upon the injustice deriving from papal acts which deprive others of their just rights in contravention of divine and natural law, 'in quo etiam abutitur notorie plenitudine potestatis quae nonnisi ad aedificationem Ecclesiae datur'.[2] But, he continues, since the papal office, the Roman church, is 'inerrabilis in fide et veritate',[3] the only conclusion that can be reached is that John is no longer a true pope, but only says he is: 'qui se dicit Dei vicarium'.[4] In reality, however, he has become a tyrant.

Non haec sunt pontificis opera, non vicarii ut se nominat Ihesu Christi, sed crudelis et dyri tyranni.[5]

Consequently from the moment that he lapsed into heresy he has been *ipso facto* deposed by his own act, and there is strictly speaking no further need for a sentence of deposition against him. Louis' right to make this clear, quite apart from the general equality between popes and emperors, depends upon the fact that John is already less than any catholic.

Quamobrem ex quo *incepit* dicta haereticalia statuta condere et publice divulgare et pertinaciter *defensare*, in haeresim est prolapsus et fuit omni ecclesiastica dignitate, auctoritate et potestate *ipso facto* privatus, *nec est necesse quod accusetur vel dampnetur per aliquem*. Nam sicut legitur in decretis xxiiii, cap. [Gratian, C.24 q.1 c.31], Dicimus omnes haereticos nihil habere potestatis ac iuris, et, Quicunque in haeresim dampnatam labitur, in ipsa dampnatione se ipsum involvit, ubi dicit glos. or., Hic

[1] William of Ockham, *Tractatus contra Benedictum XII*, vi. 8, p. 290.
[2] Baluze, iii. 388. [3] Baluze, iii. 403. [4] Baluze, iii. 392.
[5] Baluze, iii. 394.

enim casus est in quo etiam papa canonem latae sententiae incidit ipso iure. Nec hiis obviat illa regula, *Par in parem* non potest solvere vel ligare, quia papa haereticus *minor est quocunque catholico*.[1]

Since however John refuses to admit to his guilt, the issue must be decided by the *Ecclesia* which 'non potest errare in fide vel in moribus',[2] and Louis announces his intention of accusing the pope before a general council which either he or the cardinals are to convoke.[3]

Underlying the imperial case, as in the matter of the imperial elections, lies a conception of natural human rights and abilities. Every man, according to Ockham, has a natural capacity for the use of right reason, and may always in a case of necessity judge for himself whether the pope ought to be obeyed. If it is argued that there can be no exception to canon law rulings, this, he replies, is true *regulariter*, but not 'ubi scriptura divina excipit vel etiam ubi ius naturale vel ratio evidens naturalis dictat excipiendum'.[4] And once the idea of the natural basis of authority in the community was accepted, the whole theory moves rapidly away in the direction of out-and-out individualism. With Ockham it is virtually impossible to decide where the true source of faith may be found: any

[1] Baluze, iii. 446–7. [2] Baluze, iii. 438.

[3] Baluze, iii. 409–10. The same pattern can be found in most of the lay tracts: e.g. Anon., *Articuli de iuribus imperii*, ch. 11, pp. 596–7; Michael of Cesena, *Tractatus contra errores*, pp. 1335–7; *Litterae ad omnes fratres*, pp. 1339, 1344; *Litterae deprecatoriae*, ch. 12, p. 1360; and with Nogaret and William de Plaisians in Dupuy, pp. 56–8, 237, 259–65, and 106–8 respectively. This may be traced through the appeals of Frederick II and Philip the Fair: Tierney, *Foundations of the Conciliar Theory*, pp. 77–80; Wieruszowski, 'Vom Imperium zum Nationalen Königtum', pp. 175f. The history of imperial appeals to a general council dates back to Frederick I's attempt to convoke councils at Pavia and Avignon in 1160 and 1162 to decide the disputed papal election of 1159: Mansi, xxi. 1111f.; and see also J. T. McNeill, 'The Emergence of Conciliarism', *Medieval and Historiographical Essays in honor of James Westfall Thompson* (ed. J. L. Cate and E. N. Anderson: Chicago, 1938), pp. 269–301 at pp. 275–7.

[4] William of Ockham, *Dialogus*, I. vi. 62, p. 568: this is to apply when 'membrum incurabile totius corporis infectivum est pro salute corporis amputandum'. Nogaret justified Philip IV's actions against Boniface VIII on the grounds that they were taken 'ad conservationem et defensionem corporis universi Ecclesiae catholicae', and added that 'si nulla lex hoc exprimeret, satis hoc *ratio naturalis* ostendit', Dupuy, pp. 243–4; and see the *Informatio de nullitate processuum papae* at p. 515 n. 1 above.

group may be in possession of it,[1] and there is no guarantee that it will be found in the general council. The council may be the *valentior pars* of Christendom, but it is still only a part, and no part can be in permanent possession of the truth. The decisions of general councils are therefore themselves subject to the approval and superior authorisation of all the faithful:

> ... cum Ecclesia universalis sit maior concilio generali sicut totum est maius sua parte, et universalis Ecclesia approbet statuta concilii generalis.[2]

But the same argument applies with even more devastating force to the *congregatio fidelium* itself. May it not be said that the present *congregatio fidelium* is only a part, a minute fraction of the whole Church, the total number of Christians who will be united with God at the end of the world? If the papacy is to be separated into its formal and material elements, its single unending succession of office-holders and its plurality of individual popes, is not this also true of the *Ecclesia* itself? It is certain that *the* congregation of the faithful, the *Ecclesia* in the sense of the eternal succession of the saved, is undying and cannot fail: yet this does not mean that all the actual members of the *Ecclesia* here and now, *a* particular *congregatio fidelium* existing at any one moment in time, is necessarily unerring and perpetually right. According to Augustinus Triumphus the

[1] William of Ockham, *Dialogus*, I. vi. 12, p. 581, 'Ubicunque sunt boni, ibi est Romana ecclesia'. This is taken from Huguccio, *ad* D. 21 c. 3.

[2] William of Ockham, *Tractatus contra Iohannem XXII*, ch. 9, p. 54; also ch. 14, p. 68, 'Dampnatio tamen universalis Ecclesiae videtur esse maioris auctoritatis quam dampnatio concilii generalis, *praesertim dampnatio illius Ecclesiae quae sibimet succedentes praelatos et subditos, clericos et laicos, viros et mulieres per longissima tempora comprehendit*'. Cf. *Tractatus contra Benedictum XII*, iv. 10, p. 260; *Dialogus*, III. II. iii. 13, pp. 829–31. Curiously enough one of the charges of heresy made by Michael of Cesena against John XXII was that he had suggested that the *Ecclesia* acting through its general council could err in matters of faith: *Litterae ad omnes fratres*, pp. 1340–1. Peter de la Palu, *Articulus circa materia confessionum*, fo. 98, stated that the rest of the *Ecclesia* was not to accept the rulings of an erring general council: 'Et si in concilio omnes cardinales et omnes praelati fuissent contrariae opinionis, nulli dubium est quod hoc statuissent. Sed si essent mille millia non est eis credendum, quia si tota Ecclesiae residua teneret unum et Romana ecclesia oppositum, ipsi esset adherendum'. This denial of conciliar infallibility was later upheld by Panormitanus, *Comm. in Decret.*, I. vi. 4.

Ecclesia in its present sense cannot be compared to the unfailing righteousness of the total heavenly Church, of God himself.[1] Again, how is it really to be known which professing Christians are really worthy of salvation and which only appear to be so? It is in no way to be believed, says Ockham, that the mass of Christians cannot err, or that they have never done so. Quite possibly the true faith may be left in possession of a few.

Respondetur quod non est necessarium credere implicite nec explicite multitudinem christianorum non errare nec errasse in fide, nec maiorem [partem] pro eo quod fides catholica in paucis potest servari.[2]

By the time we have traced the twists of this logic to its conclusion we are, as Ockham intends, left quite incapable of knowing who may be right about anything, or if anybody is right at all. And if they are right today, they may well be wrong tomorrow: what is may always be different. Out of this intellectual anarchy only one fact emerges. Every man must be his own priest and his own church: he may be right when everyone else is wrong.[3] The whole structure of society disintegrates. Each man must decide for himself in both faith and government, and be not only his own priest but his own pope. And whilst Ockham is developing this principle primarily for the benefit of the prince who wishes to throw off the

[1] Augustinus Triumphus, *Summa*, xxvii. 4 ad 1, p. 163, 'iudicium Ecclesiae militantis falli potest et fallere. Iudicium vero Dei nec fallere nec falli potest'. The same may be found with Conrad of Megenberg, *Tractatus contra Wilhelmum Occam.*, ch. 11, p. 383, who adds however that normally the decrees of the *Ecclesia* are to be accepted: 'Sed est differentia iudicii Dei a iudicio Ecclesiae militantis quoniam iudicium Dei veritati, quae non fallit neque fallitur, semper innititur. Iudicium autem Ecclesiae nonnumquam opinionem sequitur quam et fallere saepe contingit et falli, propter quod contingit interdum ut qui ligatus est apud Deum, apud Ecclesiam sit solutus, et qui liber est apud Deum, ecclesiastica sit sententia innodatus... Est tamen semper regulariter tenenda sententia Ecclesiae et timenda, alioquin contendens etiam secundum ligatur'.

[2] William of Ockham, *Dialogus*, I. ii. 25, p. 429; also I. v. 8, p. 478; I. v. 12, p. 481; III. II. iii. 13, pp. 829–31. This suggestion of a 'saving remnant' in whom the true faith will persist can also be found in Engelbert of Admont, *De ortu imperii Romani*, ch. 21, p. 771.

[3] William of Ockham, *Dialogus*, III. I. iii. 1, p. 819, 'Quia non frustra esset lex salutis aeternae data Christo quamvis maior pars fidelium, immo omnes praeter paucissimos vel praeter *unum* errarent non solum damnabiliter sed exsecrabiliter'; cf. *Epistola ad Fratres Minores*, p. 15.

fetters of the papal supremacy,[1] it appears that anyone convinced of the pope's deviation from the right way of life may take it upon himself to resist the erring pontiff, seize his person and confiscate his property.[2] But before we dismiss this as the mere pursuit of logic for its own sake, it may well be pointed out that Augustinus Triumphus himself had eventually come to say very much the same thing. In the 'most obvious' cases of papal heresy he questions whether it is really necessary to bother with the process of accusation at all:[3] any catholic can condemn the pope.

Si papa, qui est superior in tota Ecclesia, laberetur in haeresim, quilibet catholicus in tali casu efficeretur maior ipso, et contra eum sententiare posset.[4]

[1] E.g. William of Ockham, *Octo quaestiones*, i. 17, p. 65, 'si autem episcopi vel noluerint vel nequiverint papam haereticum iudicare, alii catholici, maxime imperator si catholicus fuerit, ipsum iudicare valebit'; and note the *Tractatus contra Benedictum XII*, vii. 9, p. 313, where he says that the deposition of a heretical pope 'spectat ad imperatorem si est catholicus et zelator fidei christianae, vel ad dominum temporalem in cuius dominio commoratur, vel istis deficientibus ad quemcunque principem catholicum, qui potest eum per temporalem potentiam cohercere, qui potest contra eum sententiam ferre et dampnare ac punire ablatione rerum et expulsione de apostolica sede et detentione si viderit quod absque detentione ipsius catholici non sunt securi'.

[2] William of Ockham, *Tractatus contra Benedictum XII*, vii. 7, pp. 309–10: this applies to all 'qui *sciunt* eum publicum esse haereticum', although this 'praecipue spectat ad imperatorem, reges et principes et praelatos'. The confiscated goods of the pope are not to be converted to the private use of the lay prince but are to be kept and returned to the next pope. But cf. Anon., *Somnium viridarii*, i. 159, p. 120, 'Respondeo quod non est necessarium universitati fidelium sine omni exceptione obedire sibi in his quae necessaria sunt in congregatione fidelium salvis iuribus et libertatibus aliorum. Et si quaeratur quis habere iudicare quae necessaria sunt regimini fidelium? Respondeo . . . hoc autem auctoritative et iudicaliter spectat principaliter ad Romanum pontificem de consilio sapientum, qui, si iudicando erraverit, sapientes, immo *quicunque* ipsum errare *cognoverint*, resistere obligantur pro loco et tempore et aliis circumstantiis debitis observatis. Et hoc licet *unicuique* pro gradu et statu suo, quia aliter debent ei resistere eruditi, aliter praelati, aliter reges, aliter principes, et aliter *simplices* et temporali potentia destituti'.

[3] Augustinus Triumphus, *Summa*, v. 5, p. 53, 'Sed puto hoc esse intelligendum quando haeresis papae esset sic aperta et manifesta quod non posset tergiversatione aliqua celari, et non indigeat clamore accusatoris; tunc ipso facto esset depositus'; although this does not apply where the papal heresy is more doubtful.

[4] Augustinus Triumphus, *Summa*, xviii. 3, p. 115; cf. vii. 2, p. 65, 'papa in tali

This is the fruit of conciliarism: the 'most extreme defender of the papal monarchy' can be found to have anticipated all that the 'great destroyer' had to say on the subject. Neither Ockham nor Augustinus Triumphus proceed to draw further conclusions beyond this point: that was left to the revolutionaries of the sixteenth and seventeenth centuries. But it is obvious that the implementation of this view, its application to government in general, must mean that all political obligation is at an end. When everyone has authority over everybody else there is logically no authority at all. Society becomes a mere *collectio* of absolute and monolithic individuals, a purely numerical quantity. The structure of the universe is atomistic and unrelated, and man is left as the sole arbiter of his own destiny.

This conflict between the absolutist and conciliar ideals was a reflection of the greater struggle between the claims of faith and the promptings of reason that characterises the intellectual history of the later Middle Ages. According to faith the pope could never be a heretic: but if he could, as reason suggested, then it was only reasonable to consider some means of deposing him. Indeed the idea that a heretical pope should be removed appeared so eminently sensible that the grave constitutional issues involved tended to be completely obscured. Not for the first time reason and faith stood in open opposition to each other, and under the impact of the new learning the writers of the time found it quite impossible to repel the urgings of the human mind. The defenders of the traditional Christian ideal were well aware that they had to face a revival of all the alien conceptions of a pagan antiquity, that the combination of Roman legal with Aristotelian philosophical doctrines was producing a new political ideal, an ideal of humanism, of a *societas*

casu iuste a quocunque fideli posset corrigi'; cf. William of Ockham, *Tractatus pro rege Angliae*, ch. 6, pp. 254–5, 'Sed illi qui per scripturas sacras et *rationem* necessariam *sciunt* ipsum [scil. papam] errare, loco et tempore opportunis, aliis circumstantiis debitis observatis, eum reprobare tenentur, ne erroribus eius dampnabiliter consentire probentur, quia error cui non resistitur, approbatur'. This may be adduced from the principle that one member of a corporation may retain the *iura communitatis* when the rest of the corporation defects: for Hostiensis on this see Gillet, *La personalité juridique*, p. 152; Tierney, 'A Conciliar Theory', p. 421.

humana, of unshackled human liberty, and of a universe in which man rather than God stood at the centre. But they found too much that was useful in the new learning, and too much that was not to be denied. Accordingly they attempted as far as possible to bring it within the framework of the existing system—and in seeking too much, lost all. Beginning with the best of intentions, they were soon unable to stop, and before they realised what was happening the whole hierocratic ideal was in the melting-pot. Perhaps at no other time has a group of political thinkers faced so formidable a complex of problems, and the ingenuity with which the fourteenth-century writers met this situation must compel our admiration. As Augustinus Triumphus and William of Ockham typify, they eventually succeeded in moulding the very idea of popular sovereignty into the traditional concept of papal supremacy itself. Nevertheless, the fact that the name of Augustinus Triumphus can be coupled in the same breath with that of Ockham indicates the extent to which the papalists came to deny the conception of sovereignty which they had so carefully and zealously elaborated. Like so many of his contemporaries, Augustinus Triumphus asserted the supremacy of faith over reason only to attempt to meet reason with reason, to 'explain' the mysteries upon which the hierocratic system was founded. No one could have stressed more emphatically that the pope was an absolute monarch, the repository of all faith and power: he was not even to be considered according to human standards. But as soon as he succumbs to the temptation to rationalise the divine, we are left with a very different picture, virtually a completely contradictory one, of the papal position. The pope cannot err: if he does he is not pope. The pope is only pope while he behaves like one—one slip, and the whole edifice of sovereignty comes crashing to the ground. As the celebrated canonist, Francis Zabarella, commented at the beginning of the next century,

potestatis plenitudo est in papa, ita tamen quod non errat; sed cum errat, habet corrigere concilium.[1]

[1] Francis Zabarella, *De schismate*, p. 703. An interesting comparison might be made here with the power of the magistrate in the later Roman Republic as outlined by Wirszubski, *op. cit.*, pp. 47–9. Here too the original view of the

This aptly illustrates the central problem of authority in later medieval society. The necessity for a strong monarch was not denied; yet it was combined with a constant fear that it would have the worst results: 'unius regimen praeeligendum est, quod est optimum; et contingit ipsum in tyrannidem converti, quod est pessimum'.[1] As Aquinas repeatedly remarked, power corrupts, and the greater the power the more it corrupts,[2] and it is only by limiting the power of the ruler that a measure of security can be guaranteed. This attitude in itself betokens a falling away of faith in favour of reason, a fading of the view that the government of God's kingdom on earth cannot be anything but perfect, and that to question it is to question God himself. There is no longer the climate of belief that had made St. Augustine stipulate the divine right of tyrants. In its place there is now creeping a growing awareness of man's own potentiality. He no longer needs to look to the ruler to perceive divine righteousness, or to gain the good life on earth: he is now capable of looking beyond the prince to find it of his own volition in God himself. And it was the spread of this Christian humanism, of this belief in the human capacity to determine the means of salvation, which in course of time became the mainspring of the Reformation.

magistrate as beyond popular control after his appointment was reduced to the proposition that he was sacrosanct only in so far as he served the people, and automatically deprived himself of office and immunity when, according to the judgement of the Senate, he acted *contra rem publicam*.

[1] Thomas Aquinas, *De regimine principum*, i. 6, p. 229; cf. *Summa theologica*, II. 1. cv. 1 ad 2.

[2] E.g. Thomas Aquinas, *De regimine principum*, i. 9, p. 233.

CONCLUSION

THE main objective of political thought up to the thirteenth century was the inculcation of social virtues and respect for authority. The civilisation of the Middle Ages constantly hovered on the brink of a relapse into barbarism, and was well aware of its situation. There was no lack of examples to point out the results attendant upon the disintegration of unity and the collapse of centralised government. Hence the prevailing belief in the necessity for an inviolate social order, culminating in the institution of absolute monarchy. To this end society was given a religious character: it became a church and its monarch a god. More important, society itself was invested with a personality having a will, needs and existence of its own. This was a perfectly natural process in a world saturated with Roman and Christian beliefs, and has remained a permanent feature of the Western political tradition. It is perhaps essential to all political theory. Man repeatedly demonstrates his inability to survive without his myths, and the most potent of these is the myth of the state. 'Of all things in the world,' remarked the late Ernst Cassirer, 'myth is the most unbridled and immoderate. It exceeds and defies all limits: it is extravagant and exorbitant in its very nature and essence'.[1] The truth of this statement is illustrated by the overwhelming part played by fictions in medieval political thought. That they were fictions does not detract from their vitality and force. They were not static conceptions but living expressions of human ideals, with an organic evolution of their own. If the Greeks had been content to think in terms of an abstract supreme good or *iustitia*, Roman Christianity was impelled to personalise this abstraction. Consequently Augustine and the Church Fathers had identified it with God. As this was an absent God the process was taken a stage further by grafting this personality onto an actually existing being, the ruler seen as the representative of

[1] E. Cassirer, *The Myth of the State* (London, 1946), p. 77.

God and the source of *iustitia*. But with the re-emergence of Greek ways of thought there was a return to the old ideal of an abstract righteousness. If the late medieval ruler still continues to appear *ut Deus*, it is nevertheless true that the political thinkers now tended to think less about the ever-righteous governor and more about abstract notions like natural law. Thomism, the fruit of this reunion of Greek and Roman-Christian ideals, reacted against the hierocratic tendency to see the pope as an abstraction in human form. At the same time it did nothing to lessen the part played by abstractions in political theory. It still saw society as a supreme good. In a sense it enhanced its value as a reality by setting that social entity over and above the ruler himself, and by making its preservation a justification for a denial of the sacred principles of authority and obedience. Eventually it would countenance the destruction of the existing social framework in the cause of society itself, thereby making its own contribution to the development of the idea that the State exists as a force for good.

The modern doctrine of the State, which still retains its fictitious personality, as the embodiment of right living and the supreme power for good, is thus seen to be a direct inheritance from medieval political thought with its emphasis upon the reality of that abstraction, the rightly governed *Ecclesia*, which embraces all the essentials of the Christian way of life. It is here that we must seek the genesis of the theory of State sovereignty. Since few political writers of the thirteenth and fourteenth centuries were prepared to deny the nature of society as an instrument of salvation and a force for good—although they might disagree profoundly over its proper disposition—there was little questioning of the general assumption that society itself was the possessor of sovereignty. Both the Platonic and the Aristotelian traditions agreed that the whole was in one sense or another prior to its parts. Where controversy raged most fiercely was over the problem of precisely which group within society had the practical exercise of this sovereignty. It was acknowledged that the corporation should be represented by a corporation, but which institution, the corporation sole of the head, the *collegia* of the princes, or the whole *communitas fidelium* in the form of a general council, could best represent this whole and wield its plenitude of power? And this could only be answered by a reconsideration of the nature of society itself. Was the *Ecclesia* an ever-present true Reality? If so, its real presence could best be expressed in the person of the ruler, or at least in the continuity of a succession of such rulers descending from Christ himself. From this stemmed the idea that sovereignty was made actual in the papal vicariate of Christ. But in direct contrast to this, purely individualistic and anarchic tendencies were not, as we have seen, entirely absent from later medieval political thought, and there was a growing tendency by the radicals to apply nominalistic dialectic to the problem. Society could indeed be spoken of as existing over and above its members, but it was recognised to exist only as a myth, having no reality apart from the members themselves. The notions of society and abstract sovereignty might be convenient: indeed it was appreciated that they were often of tremendous value in human life. But it remained indisputable that all effective power resided in and derived from the component individuals. Strictly speaking a society was nothing other than the mass of its human members: although it should be added that in practice this inevitably meant a highly artificial arrangement of representation through certain individuals designated as the *maior pars* of the community. Between these two opposed schools of thought, whose basic principles led to logical but terrifying conclusions, stood the exponents of the *via media*. For the Thomists society remained sovereign, but was to be kept as far as possible in its abstract form. This was not to deny its reality: it was by no means a myth. On the other hand it was not sufficient of a reality to be given simple and complete expression by any one human group. This had the effect of proving that the abstract social entity could be either fact or fiction; indeed it was better regarded as both together. In the long run this delicate but involved idea led to the division of the human community into two distinct societies with a dual sovereignty. On one side it became a mystical Reality, a Church, whose true personality was expressed by monarchic government; on the other it was to be seen as a material society, a State, whose will was that of all the members and which had a purely earthly existence. Normally however it could be assumed that both societies would act in unison and be virtually indistinguishable in practice. And of the efficacity of this scheme the continuance of the English constitution bears adequate testimony.

In the thirteenth and fourteenth centuries all this was being expressed by theological as much as legal and philosophical formulae, and it is the use of theological terms which brings out most clearly the stark alternatives which these theories offered. The adherents of all three schools accepted as axiomatic the principle that society was one thing, *unum corpus*, and identifiable with Christ. For the hierocrat, with his unyielding belief in the existence of other-worldly realities, this was tantamount to stipulating the true presence of Christ on earth, cloaked in the human form of his vicar. For the radical lay writer, with his conception of the mythical quality of society, and therefore of Christ, the road led to a purely secular ideal of atheism and to the place of organised religion as nothing more than a useful support for civil government. In the intellectual conditions of the period the first conclusion was becoming untenable: it was still far too early for the overt and unqualified acceptance of the second, although it continued to gain ground beneath the surface. The third solution provided a way of escape from this appalling dilemma. Divine realities need not be questioned, but it was unnecessary to make the political community into a Church and nothing else. The existence of God and the natural capacities of man could be guaranteed with equal certainty: 'God's in his heaven — All's right with the world!' Religion and politics need not interfere with each other, and toleration is a major virtue. It would require several centuries, certainly up until the age of Locke, before this ideal of Christian humanism was fully formulated, but the basic principles had been established by the middle of the fourteenth century. And once having progressed so far, further advance was inevitable. The theory of the *via media* was undeniably attractive: it was well-nigh irresistible. In politics its success was assured, since it appeared to prevent the tyranny of the one as much as it avoided the tyranny of the many. If it still contained serious logical difficulties and seemingly damning inconsistencies, these might be excused on the grounds of evident utility and expediency. Consequently, hardly any writers of the time managed to avoid the lure of the great synthesis propounded by Thomas Aquinas, and the most striking fact that emerges from a study of the publicistic literature is the extent to which they drew upon fundamentally opposed ideas in their eagerness to produce a universal harmony. Each, depending upon his individual predilection, was drawn to one extreme solution or the other, recoiled, and sought refuge in the middle. At the very moment when the influx of Aristotelianism ought to have put a synthesis out of the question, the desire for the old Platonic unity becomes overpowering. But there is a significant difference. The early medieval writer argued from the deeply rooted certainty induced by faith: he knew exactly what conformed to his ideological specifications, and extraneous matter was ruthlessly excised. Underlying the thought of the later Middle Ages is an equally deep-seated instability and capacity for doubt; and in reacting against this the Christian apologist became determined that all ideas should conform, that nothing was to escape the Procrustean bed of ultimate unity, and that if the ideas themselves were stretched or mutilated in the process, no sacrifice was too great for the attainment of overall uniformity. In consequence his work became a compound of irreconcilables, whose net was spread wide enough to catch the imagination of most contemporary theorists. We have seen this reflected in the work of Augustinus Triumphus, in the tendency which he exhibits to adopt two quite different conceptions of papal power, and this dichotomy is symptomatic of every aspect of later medieval political thought. The extreme hierocrat hopelessly compromises himself by confusing logic with reasonableness: there is no power but from the pope, although kings and princes exist in their own right. The extreme anti-hierocrat is similarly confounded—he denies all papal authority except the plenitude of power. The popular basis of government is not seen to accord ill with the most far-reaching exposition of monarchy. This then is the influence of the teachings of Christian Aristotelianism, itself a contradiction in terms. The divisions between the contending ideals are not to be found between mind and mind, but within the same mind. The endemic disease of the scholastic is intellectual schizophrenia. Hence from the Christian point of view the intellectual history of the later medieval period is a story of failure. As the issues between God and man, priest and king, pope and people became increasingly clear-cut, the academic mind shrank back into the comfortable glosses and formulae which covered everything and solved nothing. In the thirteenth and fourteenth centuries the very fundamentals of political society and obligation were being called into question. But all was clouded over with the pale cast of thought. It was this *trahison des clercs* which opened up the way for secularism and lay supremacy. Left to themselves the defenders of the Christian ideal might have prepared better defences against the onrush of the classical resurrection: by attempting to come to terms with it they defeated their own purpose. And in this light Thomism comes to be seen not so much as the last Christian barrier against the pagan floods, but as the catalyst through which the Ages of Faith became transmuted into an Age of Reason.

APPENDIX I

THE SCRIPTURAL BASIS OF THE LAY PAPACY

AUGUSTINUS TRIUMPHUS' theory of the lay pope was a logical development from the distinction between order and office which had become generally accepted since the twelfth century. But it should not be thought that he was content to argue in favour of the legality of a lay pope by process of logic alone. In addition he endeavoured to provide this theory with a scriptural basis. This could be reduced to a simple question of precedent: had St. Peter himself been designated the first pope as a layman, or only after receiving episcopal power? To decide this involved a thorough investigation of the events recorded in the Gospels, and in particular of those texts in which Christ was seen to have committed power to St. Peter and to the other apostles. It may be regarded as a major defect in the hierocratic system that as late as the fourteenth century no complete attempt had been made to bring about a proper integration of these texts, although since the system can be said to have developed round the idea of the Petrine commission it would hardly be possible to exaggerate the importance of knowing exactly when and to whom ecclesiastical power had been granted. On the contrary however, an examination of the work of the publicists reveals that utter confusion reigned over this very point, and the vigorous debate that was in progress during the period only served to make matters worse. Not only did every writer have something different to say, but so many different things could be said that many writers really did not know what to say. Some of the later theorists, like Alvarus Pelagius, were hopelessly at sea, and could do no more than make a compendium of totally contradictory opinions, as if they felt that the only way to insure against error was to quote every possible textual permutation and combination. We cannot therefore hope to investigate the immense ramifications of the dispute here, beyond noting the fact of its existence, and confining our attention to the one writer who seems to have made a genuine attempt to provide a comprehensive solution to the problem.

Augustinus Triumphus is quite emphatic that the vital text is *Matthew*, xvi. 18–19. This constitutes the Petrine commission, the grant of *potestas iurisdictionis* to Peter, and it is important to notice that this precedes the grant of essentially episcopal power, *potestas ordinis*, to all the apostles by *John*, xx. 22–3.

Unde Christus *eligendo* Petrum pastorem Ecclesiae *dedit* sibi singularem potestatem clavium ut dicit iurisdictionem *quando* dixit *Matth.*, 16, Tibi dabo etc... Sed potestatem clavium ut importat ordinis consecrationem tradidit sibi cum aliis quando dixit *Ioan.*, 20, Accipite etc....[1]

Whilst all the apostles received equal sacramental power after the Resurrection, the vicariate of Christ was by that time already established in favour of St. Peter in preparation for Christ's departure from the earth. The other apostles had certainly received *potestas iurisdictionis* before Christ's passion and death, namely by *Matthew*, xviii. 18, but only after the Petrine headship of the community had been affirmed. Consequently it was apparent to Augustinus Triumphus that the apostles could only have derived their jurisdictional power from St. Peter, in the same way that the bishops now

[1] Augustinus Triumphus, *Summa*, xx. 5, p. 125; also *De duplici potestate*, p. 492, 'Unde *Matthaei* xvi, *cum* Christus potestatem iurisdictionis *concessit*, non fuit locutus in plurali sed singulari, dicens soli Petro, Tibi dabo claves regni caelorum, ac si aperte diceret, Quamvis omnibus apostolis *dederim* potestatem ordinis, sic potestatem iurisdictionis *do* tibi soli, per te omnibus aliis dispendendam et distribuendam'. This can also be found in the anonymous French tracts, *Quaestio in utramque partem*, ch. 3, p. 100; ch. 5, p. 105; *Rex pacificus*, ch. 4, p. 679; and with Peter de la Palu, *De causa immediata ecclesiasticae potestatis*, *i.* 1, fo. 24; ii. 7, fo. 33; Alexander de S. Elpidio, *De ecclesiastica potestate*, i. 1, p. 3; Alvarus Pelagius, *De planctu Ecclesiae*, ch. 55, p. 142; *Collirium*, p. 514. I am indebted to Professor Brian Tierney for drawing my attention to the early thirteenth-century *Summa Animal est substantia*, *ad* D. 20 *ante* c. 1, sv. *Quodcunque*, 'Sed Dominus dixit hoc ante passionem, scilicet, Quodcunque ligaveris etc. Ergo et ante passionem *dedit* ei claves'. The author upholds this against Bede, who suggested that 'tunc Dominus non dedit claves sed indicavit se *daturum*. Dedit autem postea cum dixit, Pasces oves meas' (MS Liège 127, fo. 13vb). Support for the *Matthew* text might also be found in Augustine, *Sermo CCXCV*, ii. 2 (*PL*, xxxix. 1349).

derive it from the pope.[1] As Peter de la Palu put it, the eldest son, because he is born first, inherits all. St. Peter was created governor before the rest, and accordingly the *potestas iurisdictionis* of the others can only have been obtained from his plenitude.

Prima conclusio est quod Petrus a Christo habuit potestatem super omnes apostolos tamquam princeps et praelatus eorum. Quod patet quia sicut paterfamilias aliis filiis aliquem unum quem primogenitum praeponit quem facit haeredem universalem, alios vero haeredes particulares . . . sic Christus . . . unum de apostolis, sanctum Petrum, quem primogenitum aliis praeponere voluit. . . Item Petrus prae ceteris a Christo accepit claves, unde super illud *Matt.*, xvi, Tibi dabo. . .[2]

This does not of course mean that Peter had exercised the jurisdictional vicariate of Christ as *caput Ecclesiae* whilst Christ himself was still on earth.[3] As Aegidius Romanus pointed out, the power was for future rather than immediate use,[4] and Augustinus Triumphus agrees that Peter only took over the actual occupation of the vicariate after the Ascension.[5] To understand this however, we

[1] Augustinus Triumphus, *De duplici potestate*, p. 496, 'licet potestas ordinis absolvendi et ligandi a Christo omnibus apostolis sit concessa, iudicariam tamen potestatem solus Petrus accepit, nec alii apostoli talem potestatem receperunt nisi mediante Petro, et per consequens nec episcopi et alii praelati Ecclesiae recipiunt istam potestatem nisi mediante papa'.

[2] Peter de la Palu, *De causa immediata ecclesiasticae potestatis*, i. 1, fo. 24; also ii. 7, fo. 33, 'Solutio sic prius, quia Christus omnibus concessit claves pontificales. Sed Petro per se, aliis per Petrum, non autem aliis per seipsum'. He explains this by making *Matthew*, xviii. 18, into a mere promise of a future grant. This is in agreement with Alexander de S. Elpidio, *De ecclesiastica potestate*, iii. 1, p. 32, who adds, i. 5, pp. 6–7, that the promise was fulfilled by *Mark*, xvi. 15–8.

[3] Peter de la Palu, *De causa immediata ecclesiasticae potestatis*, i. 5, fo. 26, 'quia quamdiu ipse corporaliter inter homines vivens per seipsum Ecclesiam rexit, nulla necessitas nec decentia nec utilitas fuit quod ipse alium loco sui poneret, sed solum quando per ascensionem se absentare debuit, sicut praelati tunc demum quando se absentant ad magnum tempus loco sui constituunt vicarium generalem': as it stands this was an argument in favour of a later occasion—which Peter himself promptly accepts also: 'Unde Petrus non est factus pastor Ecclesiae ante resurrectionem.'

[4] Aegidius Romanus, *De ecclesiastica potestate*, ii. 4, p. 50: commenting on *Matthew*, xvi. 18, he paraphrases it as 'Tu igitur Petrus, qui a me nomen accepisti, totam Ecclesiam super me fundatam *reges* et *gubernabis*'.

[5] Augustinus Triumphus, *Summa*, lxi. 2 ad 3, p. 323, 'Christo praesente cum

must re-emphasise the nature of the papal vicariate of Christ. This vicariate is essentially an office, the headship of the *Ecclesia*. According to Augustinus Triumphus it was set up by the act of *Matthew*, xvi. 18–19, and at the same time its first occupant, St. Peter, was appointed. From now on the jurisdictional power of Christ resided in this office, and it was from the office that the other apostles obtained their own *potestas iurisdictionis* by *Matthew*, xviii. 18: they drew their power from Peter in the sense that they obtained it from the office which was his by right. Christ personally gave them this power, but it was Christ working through the Petrine office in which the power had been deposited by him. In committing jurisdictional power to the apostles Christ had, in a manner of speaking, been acting as his own vicar. But whether Christ personally or Peter personally occupied the office was of no real consequence: it was the office itself which was all-important because it alone contained the power, and because in this capacity as office-holders Christ and St. Peter were identical.

The full significance of this interpretation can only be appreciated when we realise how great an obstacle the text *Matthew*, xviii. 18, had so far proved to any attempt at providing an incontrovertible explanation of the reason for Peter's supremacy over the other apostles. Whilst the passage *Matthew*, xvi. 18–19, was stressed in one form or another with almost monotonous regularity, *Matthew*, xviii. 18, had been tacitly ignored or diplomatically glossed over by most other papal writers.[1] As Alexander of S. Elpidio feebly protested, it was most 'inconveniens' when one acknowledged that all the apostles gained *potestas iurisdictionis* from Christ, and then found that this effectively meant that the pope had no right to depose their

apostolis, Petrus non debebat exercere iurisdictionem suam, principali namque agente praesente, legati iurisdictio cessat... Sed iam Christo absente... nullus umquam fuit exemptus a potestate Petri'; similarly Alexander de S. Elpidio, *De ecclesiastica potestate*, i. 5, p. 7, 'Unde statim assumpto Christo in coelum, Petrus tamquam eius successor Ecclesiam regere coepit'; also Alvarus Pelagius, *De planctu Ecclesiae*, ch. 55, p. 148.

[1] For example it is mentioned in passing by Hervaeus Natalis, *De potestate papae*, ff. 145, 146v, but no conclusions are drawn from it. Aegidius Romanus shows unwonted caution in dealing with it: *De renuntiatione papae*, xi, p. 33, 'et *si* omnes apostoli habuerunt claves, specialiter tamen dictum fuit Petro, Tibi dabo etc....'.

successors.[1] The previous failure to account for this text concealed a dangerous weakness in the papal theory, since the bishops were clearly able to lay claim to a jurisdictional equality with the pope on the strength of it. The episcopalist writers were hard pressed to refute convincingly the view that Christ had in fact granted *potestas iurisdictionis* to Peter by *Matthew*, xvi. 18–19, but *Matthew*, xviii. 18, gave them a sound basis for the assertion that this same power had also been granted to all the apostles, and was therefore inherited by the bishops as their successors. While he left the meaning of *Matthew*, xviii. 18, unexplained, the papalist had no real answer to this claim and was forced to resort to other arguments in favour of a monarchically constituted society. Yet the need to incorporate this text into the papal version of the Petrine commission was urgent, and for this reason Augustinus Triumphus' use and explanation of the two texts in conjunction with each other was by no means the least of the services that he rendered to the vicariate of Christ and the papal-hierocratic theory in general.

At the same time however, this view of *Matthew*, xvi. 18–19, separated Augustinus Triumphus from the opinion held by the papacy itself. As we have said, according to his interpretation the act of *Matthew*, xvi. 18–19, had not only designated Peter as the heir of Christ, but had actually established his vicariate. This office, therefore, although occupied by Christ himself, was already in existence from that time, and with the Ascension Peter succeeded automatically to it. There had to be no formal act of institution. But for the papacy at this time, and for perhaps the majority of other writers, this was not so. We may refer here to a statement of the papal position contemporary with our author. In his condemnation of Marsilius of Padua in 1327 John XXII showed that the

[1] Alexander de S. Elpidio, *De ecclesiastica potestate*, i. 5, pp. 6, 7; i. 7, p. 9; although elsewhere he maintains that all the apostles received *potestas iurisdictionis* by *John*, xx. 22–3: see iii. 1, p. 32; and also Alvarus Pelagius, *De planctu Ecclesiae*, ch. 55, p. 142; William Amidani, *Reprobatio errorum*, ch. 4, p. 27. Ockham refused to commit himself on the question of whether *Matthew*, xvi. 18–19, was meant to be an actual grant or not: *Consultatio de causa matrimoniali*, p. 284; and Peter Olivi, *Ep.*, p. 369, shrugged off all responsibility for making a decision by declaring that what had happened to Peter need not necessarily be regarded as a precedent for succeeding popes, and so the whole dispute was a waste of time and energy.

papacy regarded *Matthew*, xvi. 18–19, as being no more than a promise.

Et secundum hunc modum Christus videtur Petrum *praedixisse futurum* Ecclesiae fundamentum dum dixit, Tu es Petrus etc. . . . Constat enim quod a Christo Petro, et in persona Petri Ecclesiae, potestas coactiva concessa vel saltem *promissa* extitit, *quae quidem promissa fuit postea adimpletur*, cum sibi Christus dixit, Quodcunque ligaveris etc. . . .[1]

It made no change in the situation as it then existed, but simply described the power which would at a future date be granted by Christ to St. Peter.[2] This promise was implemented by *John*, xxi. 15–17, when Christ charged Peter with the care of his flock:

. . . sed a Christo, dicente sibi illud *Ioannis*, Pasce oves meas, pasce agnos meos, *per quae verba* ipsum suum vicarium generalem constituit.[3]

and for John XXII it was this which really established Peter as the vicar of Christ.[4] But from Augustinus Triumphus' point of view

[1] Raynaldus, *Annales Ecclesiastici ad 1327*, xxiv. 324.

[2] Also Peter de la Palu, *De causa immediata ecclesiasticae potestatis*, ii. 8, fo. 36, 'Igitur Christus per illa verba, Tibi dabo claves etc. . . . *promisit* utraque claves, scilicet tam ordinis quam iurisdictionis'. There is a fine selection of views in Alvarus Pelagius, *De planctu Ecclesiae*, ch. 55, pp. 141–2, 'Dicit autem in futuro, Tibi dabo, ut insinuet quod non solum ei *dedit*, sed etiam eius successoribus daturus esset; vel quod *postea plenius dedit* quando dixit ei et aliis post resurrectionem, *Ioan.*, *ult.* [xx. 22–3], Accipite spiritum sanctum etc. . . . quem spiritum sanctum in die Pentecostes plenius receperunt . . . ; vel dixit, dabo, quia haec potestas efficaciam fortitur a Christi passione, quae adhuc futura erat quando hoc dixit'. He then quotes Chrysostom as saying 'quod ante passionem *promisit*, post resurrectionem affirmando dedit cum ei dixit, Pasce oves meas, *Ioan.*, *ult.* [xxi. 15–17]'.

[3] Raynaldus, *Annales Ecclesiastici ad 1327*, xxiv. 323–4. This is almost identical with the statement made a quarter of a century earlier by Henry of Cremona, *De potestate papae*, p. 464, 'et istam potestatem ipse ante mortem *promisit* vicario suo Petro, *Matth.*, xvi [19], cum dixit, Tibi dabo etc. . . . Et istam *promissionem adimplevit* Dominus post resurrectionem quando *Ioh.* xx [xxi. 15–17] dixit Petro . . . Pasce oves meas'. See also Francis de Meyronnes, *Quaestio de subiectione*, i. 11, pp. 84–5; *De principatu regni Siciliae*, ch. 3, p. 112; Durandus de S. Porciano, *De iurisdictione ecclesiastica*, ch. 3, fo. 3.

[4] Also Alvarus Pelagius, *De planctu Ecclesiae*, ch. 13, p. 30, 'terreni simul et coelestis imperii iura commisit *cum* dixit, Pasce oves meas . . . *per quae verba* Christus Petrum fecit pastorem et praelatum mundi'; and Guido Terrenus, *Quaestio de magisterio infallibilis Romani pontificis*, p. 28; Anon., *Somnium viridarii*, i. 61, p. 76; Hervaeus Natalis, *De potestate papae*, ff. 142, 143; Peter

the dangerous aspect of this interpretation was that it left far too many prior occasions when it might be said that Christ had given episcopal power, *potestas ordinis*, to all the apostles. There was his own choice of *John*, xx. 22–3, that is, shortly after the Resurrection.[1] More generally favoured was the occasion of the Last Supper.[2] Whilst there was the testimony of Gratian which seemed to suggest that *potestas ordinis* had been bestowed by *Matthew*, xvi. 18–19, itself, at least on Peter if not on all the apostles.[3] All these suggestions, if taken in conjunction with *John*, xxi. 15–17, would have meant that St. Peter had been created a bishop (by *potestas ordinis*) before he became pope (by *potestas iurisdictionis*), with the implication that a lay or non-episcopal pope was impossible. Hence the obvious wisdom in Augustinus Triumphus' decision to attribute the creation of the papal office to *Matthew*, xvi. 18–19, the

Olivi, *Quaestio de infallibilitate*, p. 337; Peter de la Palu, *De causa immediata ecclesiasticae potestatis*, i. 4, fo. 25v; William Amidani, *Reprobatio errorum*, ch. 4, p. 26.

[1] Guido Terrenus, *Quaestio de magisterio infallibilis Romani pontificis*, p. 28; Hervaeus Natalis, *De potestate papae*, fo. 145. Augustinus Triumphus' choice of texts is upheld by Innocent III, *Reg.*, I. cccliv (*PL*, ccxiv. 328).

[2] *Luke*, xxii. 9; cf. *Matthew*, xxvi. 26–9; *Mark*, xiv. 22–5. E.g. Alexander de S. Elpidio, *De ecclesiastica potestate*, iii. 1, p. 32, 'Nam quantum ad actum principalem qui respicit corpus Christi verum, talis potestas instituta est a Christo et data suis discipulis in coena, quando subtracturus erat ab eis suam praesentiam corporalem, quia tunc facti sunt primo sacerdotes cum impressione sacerdotalis characteris cum dictum est eis, Hoc facite in meam commemorationem, id est, potestatem accipite hoc faciendi. Nam ante illam coenam sacerdotes non erant'; also Alvarus Pelagius, *De planctu Ecclesiae*, ch. 52, p. 127. The danger of this point of view is made apparent by Peter de la Palu, *De causa immediata ecclesiasticae potestatis*, i. 5, fo. 26, 'nullus habet claves ligandi nec solvendi nisi sacerdos... Unde ante coenam in qua fuit institutum eucharistiae sacramentum nullus fuit factus sacerdos ... quia potestas clavium in illo foro quo respicit corpus Christi mysticum fundatur super potestate quae habetur super corpus Christi verum'; also ii. 5, fo. 28. He dismisses *John*, xx. 22–3 as *inconveniens*: ii. 6, fo. 29. This follows the teachings of Huguccio, *ad* D. 21 c. 2, 'Sed forte hunc contulit eis omnes ordines cum dixit, Hoc facite in meam commemorationem': J. F. v. Schulte, *Die Stellung der Concilien, Päpste und Bischöfe* (Prague, 1871), ii. 259; and its acceptance was later authorised under pain of anathema at the Council of Trent (Session 22, canon 2).

[3] Gratian, D. 21 c. 2, 'In novo testamento ... a Petro sacerdotalis coepit ordo quia ipsi primo pontificatus in Ecclesia Christi datus est, Domino dicente ad eum, Tu es, inquit, Petrus etc.'; which is adopted by Alvarus Pelagius, *De planctu Ecclesiae*, ch. 59, p. 178.

earliest possible occasion. Nor did he allow this to deprive *John*, xxi. 15–17, of all significance. On the contrary, he agreed that this text had given jurisdictional power to Peter, but it was jurisdictional power of another order than that given him by *Matthew*, xvi. 18–19. Here was the necessity for the separation of *potestas iurisdictionis* into *potestas administrationis* and *potestas executionis*. All governmental power, it could be shown, had indeed been granted to Peter by *Matthew*, xvi. 18–19, for use after the Ascension, but he could hardly have been given the executive power of a bishop when he had not yet received the *potestas ordinis* which made him a bishop.[1] Peter gained this sacramental power by *John*, xx. 22–3, and so could not have received the power to exercise it until later. This was the meaning of *John*, xxi. 15–17. It was this which enabled the pope to act as the universal bishop as opposed to the supreme governor of the *Ecclesia*. It was true that Christ himself had continued to act as the universal bishop, and had himself authorised the other apostles to begin their episcopal functions—by *Matthew*, xxviii. 19–20, and *Mark*, xvi. 15–18. But this was merely another application of the principle applied to *Matthew*, xviii. 18: it was Christ operating through the Petrine office. Consequently, when Christ commanded the apostles to disperse and take up their episcopal duties in various parts of the world, this too could be said to have been done *auctoritate Petri*.[2] And in this way Augustinus Triumphus once again emphasised the papal identity with Christ: the acts of one could be ascribed to the other.

[1] Augustinus Triumphus, *Summa*, lxxxviii. 1 ad 1, p. 439, 'Verumtamen potestatem iurisdictionis qua possent potestatem ordinis exequi in tanta vel in tali materia non receperunt nisi a Petro post missionem spiritus sancti'; see also Alvarus Pelagius, *De planctu Ecclesiae*, ch. 52, p. 127; Peter de la Palu, *De causa immediata ecclesiasticae potestatis*, ii. 5, fo. 26v.

[2] Augustinus Triumphus, *Summa*, lxxxiv. 1, p. 423; lxxxviii. 1 ad 2, p. 439.

APPENDIX 2

THE HIEROCRATIC INTERPRETATION OF HISTORY

PERHAPS the best weapon in the anti-hierocratic armoury was the *argumentum prioritatis*, namely, the argument that kings had existed long before the time of St. Peter, so that modern lay rulers might have a genuine case for claiming to exist in their own right. Unless it was to be maintained that every king in antiquity was a usurper, it seemed clear that other rulers could be legitimate without papal appointment.[1] Moreover this fitted easily into the idea of the natural law origin of authority, and subsequently exercised a considerable influence upon the Thomistic conception of lay government. As John of Paris asserted, there could be no true priesthood before the Crucifixion, since *potestas ordinis* could not be granted to men before this event: but kings, whose prime function was to provide those things necessary to human life—'officium est ad vitae humanae civilis necessitatem'—must have existed even before the birth of Abraham.[2] The problem was not however new to the thirteenth and fourteenth centuries. Earlier hierocratic writers had already begun to adapt the theological conception of the prefiguration of Christ in the Old Testament, and had converted all the great Jewish leaders into pre-Christian popes.[3] Accordingly, with

[1] This was constantly used by the French writers: see for example the anonymous tract, at one time thought to be the work of Philip the Fair himself, beginning 'Antequam essent clerici rex Franciae habebat custodiam regni sui et poterat statuta facere', Dupuy, p. 21. Also Anon., *Rex pacificus*, ch. 4, pp. 677, 680; Johannes Branchazolus, *De principio imperatoris et papae*, i. 4, p. 47; Ugolinus de Celle, *De electione regis Romanorum*, ch. 9, p. 57.

[2] John of Paris, *De potestate regia et papali*, ch. 4, p. 183; ch. 10, p. 195; ch. 19, p. 233.

[3] This was certainly as old as Augustine, and was stimulated by the setting of Old Testament events in the hierocratic system by Isidore: Ullmann, *The Growth of Papal Government*, especially p. 86 with reference to the Donation of Constantine. Note the development of the idea with Bernard (*PL*, clxxxii.

Augustinus Triumphus, the children of Israel have become the prototype of the *congregatio fidelium*,[1] and their rulers are hailed as the first vicars of Christ.[2] Moses and Aaron, Noah and Abraham are regarded as having carried out the same function as head of God's chosen people before the time of Christ as the popes have done since then.[3] And once the list was pushed back through Melchisedech and Abel to Adam himself,[4] the hierocrats were able to prove

751) as quoted by Augustinus Triumphus, *Summa*, ci. 2, p. 495, 'Solus enim summus pontifex, ut dicit Bernardus ad Eugenium, *lib.* 2 [*De consideratione*, ii. 8], repraesentatione est sacerdos magnus princeps apostolorum primatu Abel, gubernatu Noe, patriarchatu Abraham, ordine Melchisedech, dignitate Aaron, auctoritate Moyses, iudicatu Samuel, potestate Petrus, unctione Christus'; and also by Augustine of Canterbury, whom Augustinus Triumphus follows closely: Ullmann, *op. cit.*, pp. 415–16. Cf. Innocent III, *Prima collectio decretalium* ii. 2 (*PL*, ccxvi. 1183–4); and for Innocent IV see Maccarrone, *Vicarius Christi*, p. 125.

[1] Augustinus Triumphus, *Summa*, i. 5, p. 8; viii. 1, p. 68; viii. 2, p. 69; cf. Anon., *Determinatio compendiosa*, ch. 40 [MS reads ch. 37], p. 551, 'Israhel, id est Ecclesia'.

[2] Augustinus Triumphus, *Summa*, xxxvii. 1, p. 219, '... mediante sacerdotali vel prophetali pronunciatione qui pro illo tempore loco papae vice Dei gerebant'; also vi. 2 ad 2, p. 58; xliv. 1, p. 240; Alvarus Pelagius, *De planctu Ecclesiae*, ch. 36, pp. 40–1. Cf. Aegidius Spiritalis, *Libellus contra infideles*, p. 119, 'In hac autem *vicaria* successerunt patriarchae, iudices, etc.'. This may also be found with Henry of Cremona, *De potestate papae*, p. 461, although he points out (p. 467) that the pre-Christian priesthood was less powerful in that it did not possess the keys of heaven or the power of transubstantiation.

[3] Alvarus Pelagius, *De planctu Ecclesiae*, ch. 68, p. 247, 'Tum quia Moyses et Iosue et Samuel, qui typum tenent papae, sicut rectores populi generales iudicant populum'; Anon., *Somnium viridarii*, i. 61, p. 75, 'Noe fuit monarcha terrestris. Nam [Deus] commisit gubernationem Archae ei, ut scribitur *Gen.*, 5 et 6 *cap.* [13–22]. Unde per Archam significatur militans Ecclesia; in hac autem monarchia successerunt patriarchae, principes et reges sacerdotes, et alii qui pro tempore fuerunt in regimine populi Iudaeorum, et sic duravit usque ad Christum'.

[4] For a full exposition see Aegidius Romanus, *De ecclesiastica potestate*, i. 6, pp. 18–22, which concludes, 'dicere etiam possumus quod in ipso Adam primo parente nostro sacerdotium praecessit'; and for the identification of Adam and Christ see in particular ii. 7, p. 73; iii. 2, pp. 152–3. Cf. Thomas Aquinas, *In symbolum apostolorum*, ch. 9, 'quia haec Ecclesia incoepit a tempore Abel et durabit usque ad finem saeculi'; also Alvarus Pelagius, *De planctu Ecclesiae*, ch. 64, pp. 216–18; *Collirium*, p. 504. With Aegidius Spiritalis, *Libellus contra infideles*, pp. 116, 118–19, there is some confusion over the point whether Abel, Abraham and Melchisedech were popes, or whether God ruled the world by himself up to the Flood—a view put forward by Henry of Cremona, *De*

to their own satisfaction that there never had been a king without a papal contemporary:

Successit enim papatus et sacerdotium Christi sacerdotio Levitico, et sacerdotium Leviticum successit sacerdotio legis naturae. Unde universaliter sacerdotium fuit ante imperium.[1]

For Augustinus Triumphus the so-called natural right of the Old Testament kings to govern is seen to mean only that they had been appointed by the Jewish priesthood in the same way that lay rulers were now set up by the pope.[2] Just as the papacy found it useful to shift some of the burden of administration on to the shoulders of lesser officials, so it could be explained why Moses had instituted others to assist him in the government of his people.[3] But all kings preceding this, even the mighty Nimrod, were to be regarded as the sons of Cain, who usurped the inheritance of pope Abel from the Adam-Christ[4] in the same way that the later Roman emperors

potestate papae, p. 461. The anonymous *Compendium maius*, p. 180, regarded the papacy as beginning with the Levitical priesthood; and Durandus de S. Porciano, *De iurisdictione ecclesiastica*, ch. 3, fo. 4, held that Moses was the first pope.

[1] Augustinus Triumphus, *Summa*, xxxvi. 4, p. 215; and see further civ. 3 and 3 ad 3, p. 514.

[2] Augustinus Triumphus, *Summa*, xxxvi. 1, p. 212, 'Sed dominium naturale et politicum et recto et iusto titulo acquisitum secutum est sacerdotium, et in tuitionem et defensionem Ecclesiae *concessum* est'. And since it is known that 'omnes primogenitos a Noeh usque ad Aaron summos pontifices fuisse: ita ut omnes qui iusto titulo dominio naturali et politico sumpserunt dominium ad reipublicae defensionem et Ecclesiae Dei tuitionem, vere per summos sacerdotes ordinati sunt'. He continues, ad 4, p. 213, 'quantum ad figuram, officium papale praecessit omnes imperatores et omnes reges qui iusto titulo naturaliter et politice dominium sumpserunt'. Since the papal office comprises the eternal power of Christ, there can never have been a time when it did not exist: so that although St. Peter was the first to be actually termed pope, 'nec ante nec post nullus rex vel imperator [iurisdictionem] habere potest nisi a Christo, et per consequens nisi a papa, quia potestas Christi aeterna est'.

[3] Augustinus Triumphus, *Summa*, xix. 3 ad 1, p. 119. Similarly in the *De facto Templariorum*, p. 511, he states that Old Testament kings acted 'de expresso mandato Domini vel summi pontificis qui illo tempore erat, cuius personam papae repraesentat'.

[4] Augustinus Triumphus, *Summa*, xxxvi. 1, p. 212, 'Primum ergo dominium usurpatum et tyrannicum fuit ante sacerdotium, quia primus regum terrae fuit Cain, qui usurpative et tyrannice dominium sibi aquisivit'. This was inspired by Augustine, *De civitate Dei*, xv. 1–8. For the illegitimacy of Nimrod see Alvarus

usurped the papal inheritance of Christ in the first centuries of the Christian era. The legitimisation of kingship by Moses corresponds to the legitimisation of Constantine's emperorship by Silvester I; the unction and institution of Saul and David by Samuel parallels the setting up of Charlemagne by Leo III;[1] and all the medieval translations of imperial power between Romans, Greeks, Franks and Germans had been foreshadowed in the shifting of universal rule between Assyrians, Greeks, Medes and Romans—which Daniel and the prophets had authorised in their capacity as pre-Christian vicars of Christ.[2]

This determination to seek a pattern in history underlines that it is being harnessed for an ideological purpose. The past is held to be an expression of the divine will, and it therefore behoves the priest-

Pelagius, *De planctu Ecclesiae*, ch. 36, p. 41; ch. 41, p. 70. Tholemy of Lucca, *Determinatio compendiosa*, ch. 17, pp. 36–8, declares that all kingship was a *quaedam usurpatio* in that it was not instituted by the priesthood until Saul was instituted by Samuel.

[1] Augustinus Triumphus, *Summa*, i. 7 ad 2, p. 11; xlvi. 3 ad 1, p. 251: Saul, like Charlemagne, received both priestly unction and popular acclamation, although he emphasises that the latter had no constitutive effect. Cf. Francis de Meyronnes, *De principatu temporali*, ch. 4, p. 62; Tholemy of Lucca, *Determinatio compendiosa*, cc. 4–5, pp. 9–12.

[2] Augustinus Triumphus, *Summa*, xxxvii. 1, p. 219, 'vel loquimur de translatione regni Iudaeorum vel de translatione regni gentilium et paganorum, utroque autem modo auctoritate papae vel eius qui gerebant vicem papae secundum conditiones et status illius temporis facta est translatio regnorum... Planum est etiam quod facta est translatio eius mediante auctoritate Dei et prophetica veritate Danielis, qui pro illo tempore personam papae repraesentabat. Scribitur enim *Danielis* 2 quod Nabuchodonosor vidit... visionem, interpretans Daniel sic dicit... Ab Assyriis ergo regnum translatum est ad Graecos, a Graecos ad Medos, vel ad Medos translatum est primum et postmodum a Medis ad Graecos, et a Graecis ad Romanos'; also Alvarus Pelagius, *De planctu Ecclesiae*, ch. 43, p. 76; ch. 64, p. 218. This seems to have been taken straight from Tholemy of Lucca, *Determinatio compendiosa*, ch. 25, pp. 48–9, which appears to be the immediate source of all Augustinus Triumphus' historical passages. Durandus de S. Porciano, *De iurisdictione ecclesiastica*, ch. 1, fo. 1v, on the other hand regarded all four empires as usurpations. The right of the Old Testament priesthood to correct and depose kings followed automatically: e.g. Augustinus Triumphus, *Summa*, i. 7 ad 2, p. 11, 'Vel potest dici quod summi sacerdotes in sacerdotio Levitico habebant potestatem regalem non quidem in executione sed in depositione et confirmatione ipsorum. Unde I *Reg*. Samuel sacerdos David regem constituit et Saul deposuit'; xlvi. 1, p. 250, 'Unde prophetae in veteri lege in quibus erat spiritualis potestas reges cum forefaciabant corrigebant et fortiter increpabant'.

hood to study the past, in particular the past as revealed in the Bible itself, for examples of the divinely approved way of life. And since the cardinal feature of this way of life is the recognition of the papal monarchy of God on earth, history has value only in so far as its interpretation upholds the papal supremacy. Here for Augustinus Triumphus and other hierocratic writers lies the great historical truth which, consciously or unconsciously, must necessarily override the lesser truth of historical accuracy. The study of history, as in other totalitarian regimes based upon a thesis of absolute right, tends to become an instrument of political propaganda, an accessory feature in a governmental system, and for all his genuine belief that the lay argument from priority could be answered, as evidenced in the lengthy passages which he devotes to an 'explanation' of the Old Testament era, it is perhaps true to say that Augustinus Triumphus never quite seems to treat the matter with the sincerity which it deserved. But in any case it was always possible to assert that what had occurred before Christ had no necessary significance afterwards. As another writer remarked, it did not really matter very much what had happened prior to the advent of Christ, since that event had changed the whole order of things. No one could doubt that from birth Christ had been the only true emperor on earth, and that all the power exercised by other rulers had at once fallen, at least *de iure*, into his hands.[1] There was now established the *Ecclesia*, the kingdom of God on earth and the fifth monarchy of Daniel, which was to be governed by Christ and his vicars,[2] and

[1] Anon., *Compendium maius*, p. 180, 'quia verus imperator tunc venit ipse Christus Iesus'; also Alvarus Pelagius, *De planctu Ecclesiae*, ch. 37, p. 46. Reference could always be made to St. Paul's statement that there had been a change in the law (*Heb.*, vii. 12) to cover any very awkward Old Testament events: e.g. Augustinus Triumphus, *Summa*, lx. 2, pp. 313–14; *De facto Templariorum*, p. 512.

[2] Augustinus Triumphus, *Summa*, xxii. 3, p. 131, 'Princeps autem totius principatus mundi est ipse Christus, cuius papa vicarius existit, iuxta illud *Daniel.* 7 [vii. 13–14]; cf. Tholemy of Lucca, *Determinatio compendiosa*, ch. 25, pp. 48–9, 'Prima enim monarchia mundi floruit apud Assirios. . . Secunda translata est ad Medos et Persas. . . Tertia translata est ad Graecos et Aegiptios, quae maxime viguit tempore Alexandri. Quarta translata est ad Romanos. Deinde *redit* ad verum dominum qui contulerat, scilicet Christum, cuius vices summus pontifex gerit'. This was the *quinta monarchia*, which 'adhuc durat et durabit usque ad mundi renovationem', and dated from the birth of Christ:

against this all previous kingdoms paled into insignificance and were superseded.

In conformity with this the hierocratic writers stressed that the events surrounding the Donation of Constantine could only be seen in their correct perspective if they were regarded as constituting the act by which the papacy eventually came into its own. Gone were the days when the papalists needed to point to the Donation as the means by which the Gelasian pope had become his own emperor: with the development of the papal vicariate of Christ it is assumed that every pope since Peter had automatically been the *verus imperator* in succession to Christ. Constantine's handing over of the imperial crown and insignia, the symbols of universal power, to Silvester is seen to be a mere restitution of what the pope already possesses by right.[1] It makes actual, says Augustinus Triumphus, gives him the use of, what has hitherto been only a *potentia im-*

'principatus Christi incoepit statim in ipsa sui nativitate temporali'. *De regimine principum*, iii. 12–14, pp. 261–2; also Bartolus, *Ad reprimendum*, x. 91, '... Quarto fuit imperium Romanorum. Ultimo adveniente Christo istud Romanorum imperium incoepit esse Christi imperium: et ideo apud Christi vicarium est uterque gladius, spiritualis et temporalis': Figgis, *The Divine Right of Kings*, p. 357 n. 1. For this idea with Humbert see now J. J. Ryan, 'Cardinal Humbert *De s. Romana ecclesia*', *Mediaeval Studies*, xx (1958), pp. 206–38 at pp. 230f.

[1] Augustinus Triumphus, *Summa*, i. 1, p. 3, 'Et si inveniatur quandoque aliquos imperatores dedisse aliqua temporalia summis pontificibus, sicut Constantinus dedit Silvestro, hoc non est intelligendum eos dare quod suum est, sed *restituere* quod iniuste et tyrannice ablatum est'; also xliii. 3 ad 1, p. 239; ci. 4 ad 1, p. 497; Alexander de S. Elpidio, *De ecclesiastica potestate*, ii. 8, p. 23, 'ut potestatem, quam habebat Christi vicarius iure divino, liberius ipsam exercere posset de facto quam ante tempora imperatoris praedicti propter tyrannorum persecutionem exercere non poterat'; Tholemy of Lucca, *Determinatio compendiosa*, ch. 26, pp. 50–1; *De regimine principum*, iii. 16, p. 264, 'Constantinus... in dominio cessit vicario Christi, beato videlicet Sylvestro, cui de iure debebatur'. See also Anon., *Compendium maius*, p. 180; Aegidius Spiritalis, *Libellus contra infideles*, p. 111; Alvarus Pelagius, *De planctu Ecclesiae*, ch. 56, pp. 159–60; Henry of Cremona, *De potestate papae*, p. 467. For this interpretation and the events recorded in the Donation see G. Lähr, *Die Konstantinische Schenkung* (Berlin, 1926); W. Ullmann, *The Growth of Papal Government*, pp. 74–86, and here further literature. It may be noted that the Donation did in fact refer to Silvester as *vicarius Christi*: as is pointed out by Augustinus Triumphus, *Summa*, xxxvii. 5, p. 222, 'quem Constantinus vicarium esse Dei Filii firmiter confessus est'. Dr Ullmann informs me that there are many references to the Donation as a *restitutio* in papal letters of the eighth century and it may be suggested that the fourteenth-century theory was already in embryo in the Donation itself.

perialis.[1] The fact that the Donation was initially an imperial grant is irrelevant: Constantine had no right to withhold it. And once made it is irrevocable:[2] the lay argument that what is given may always be retracted has no force.[3] So for Augustinus Triumphus the Donation is no longer a matter of legal, but only of historical, importance. It represents the prototype of the later imperial corona-

[1] Augustinus Triumphus, *Summa*, xxxvi. 7 ad 1, p. 218; xxxvi. 3 *ad argumenta*, p. 215.

[2] Augustinus Triumphus, *Summa*, xliii. 1 ad 1 and 2, pp. 237–8; xliii. 3, p. 239; Alvarus Pelagius, *De planctu Ecclesiae*, ch. 13, pp. 30–1; ch. 68, p. 247; *Collirium*, p. 505; Conrad of Megenberg, *De translatione Romani imperii*, ch. 21, p. 317. Augustinus Triumphus also denies here the view that Constantine had no right to alienate the empire, as maintained by Dante, *Monarchia*, iii. 10, p. 371: on this see further Riesenberg, *Inalienability of Sovereignty*, pp. 145–6.

[3] The lay emphasis upon the Donation as an essentially imperial act is reflected in the remark of Louis of Bavaria, Baluze, iii. 388, 'Item non recogitat quod beato Silvestro papae latenti tunc temporis in spelunca magnificentissime contulit Constantinus quicquid ecclesia libertatis hodie obtinet vel honoris'. Dubois accordingly suggested that either the German or the Greek emperor could revoke it: *Deliberatio super agendis*, p. 46, 'Et sic imperator Constantinopolitanus, qui eidem dedit totum patrimonium quod habebat . . . vel imperator Alemanniae locus eius per papam subrogatus totam huiusmodi donationem posset revocare'. This also illustrates the current attempt to limit the effect of the Donation to Rome itself: e.g. Anon., *Quaestio in utramque partem*, ch. 5, p. 106, 'Sed ex dono Constantini potest ibi esse monarchia sic intelligendo quod, cum papa spiritualem potestatem haberet in urbe et orbe, Constantinus ipse temporalem illam potestatem quae habebat in urbe transtulit in papam, ut in ipsa urbe utraque potestas, quae in duabus personis erat, esset in solo papa . . . Sic ergo concedimus quod papa habet monarchiam utriusque potestatis in urbe, non tamen in orbe'. But most French writers were more concerned to show that the Donation had never included France: John of Paris, *De potestate regia et papali*, ch. 21, p. 243, 'Constantinus non dedit nisi certam provinciam, scilicet Italiam cum quibusdam aliis, ubi Francia non includitur'; *Rex pacificus*, ch. 3, p. 675, 'certum est tamen quod orientale imperium beato Sylvestro non dedit nec suis successoribus, sed illud sibi retinuit. . . Ergo ratione illius donationis non potest dici [dominus] temporalis omnium christianorum, sed saltem illorum christianorum qui sunt de Romano imperio. Quantum ergo ad illa regna quae non subsunt Romano imperio non est papa dominus superior in temporalibus. Regnum autem Franciae non subest Romano imperio'. With the civilians Bartolus acknowledged its character as an imperial concession, but added that it held good and was irrevocable: Ercole, *Da Bartolo all'Althusio*, p. 60. Baldus declared that the Donation was a miracle and that nothing further could be argued from it: 'Nam quicquid dicatur de donatione Constantini quae fuit miraculosa, si similes donationes fierent a regibus non ligarent successores': Riesenberg, *op. cit.*, p. 18, and see further pp. 23–8, 108–10.

tions. When Silvester returned the crown to Constantine he was, according to our author, appointing the first true Roman emperor.[1] The handing over of the imperial crown by the pope was an act of imperial creation. Moreover this event denoted that Constantine had moved his seat from Old Rome to New Rome with papal approval, indeed, in accordance with papal instructions.[2] The Donation then, represents both an imperial coronation and the translation of the empire from the Romans to the Greeks. It thus sets a precedent for 800, when the imperial coronation of Charlemagne again demonstrates the sole right of the pope to set up the Roman emperor, and also constitutes a new translation of the empire from the Greeks to the Franks. From now on the right of the Roman church to institute and control its own protector is a matter

[1] It should be made clear that by handing over the imperial crown to Silvester Constantine gave the pope his universal emperorship: Augustinus Triumphus, *Summa*, xxxviii. 1, p. 224, '*plenum ius totius imperii* est acquisitum summis pontificibus non solum superioris dominationis, verum etiam immediatae administrationis'; and it was this universal power which was returned to Constantine when Silvester conferred the imperial crown on him again: xliii. 2, p. 238, 'et papa hanc *eandem* immediatam administrationem concedit imperatori . . . pro defensione et pacifica gubernatione Ecclesiae'. The handing over of immediate administration in the West to Silvester, which constitutes the actual Donation itself, is a further grant to the pope of part of what Constantine has just received from him: xliii. 3 ad 1, p. 239, 'Constantinus autem *reddidit* Ecclesiae et vicario Christi illa quae ab ipso receperat'; xliii. 1, p. 237, 'illo iure Constantinus potuit concedere partem bonorum temporalium imperii ecclesiae et partem sibi reservare, quo iure homo in lege naturae et in lege scripta partem bonorum temporalium dabat Deo et partem sibi reservabat'. Hence the Donation must be seen as a two stage action. First the emperor's surrender and reacceptance of the imperial crown, which symbolises essentially universal power. Secondly the return to Silvester of imperial power in the West only. This also explains the transfer of Constantine's capital to the East, but this administrative division ceases when the pope takes the administration of the whole empire into his own hands following the supposed vacancy at Constantinople after 797.

[2] Augustinus Triumphus, *Summa*, xxxvii. 3 and 3 ad 1, p. 221, 'postquam imperator Constantinus baptizatus est per beatum Silvestrum imperio occidentali cessit, et urbem sibi in Graecia elegit quae Bizantium vocabatur, quae Romae potentia et meritis coaequavit, ibidemque sedem imperialem constituit, et ex tunc imperium a Romanis ad Graecos translatum est. . . Constantinus huiusmodi translationem fecit auctoritate summi pontificis, qui tamquam vicarius Dei Filii coelestis imperatoris iurisdictionem habet universalem super omnia regna et imperia'; also Tholemy of Lucca, *De regimine principum*, iii. 17, p. 265.

of established fact, and in due course a third translation puts the imperial crown into the hands of the Germans following the papal coronation of Otto I. We need not enter here into the seemingly endless discussions of the publicists about the exact sequence of events in these translations, interesting though they are.[1] It is enough to point out that these examples of past translations are used by Augustinus Triumphus and the hierocratic writers for the prime purpose of underlining the nature of imperial power in a Christian society. For them these historical examples emphasise that the right of a lay ruler to govern in the *Ecclesia* is nothing more than a gift from the pope. No emperor has an intrinsic and imperishable right

[1] Augustinus Triumphus maintains that the empire was transferred from the Greeks to the Franks with the coronation of Charlemagne, but attributes this coronation to Adrian I: *Summa*, xxxvii. 4, p. 222. Charlemagne was therefore crowned twice: xxxviii. 3, p. 226, 'Scribitur enim de Carolo Magno quod . . . per Adrianum et per Leonem successorem eius fuit coronatus', although he does not attempt to explain the meaning of this double coronation. Similarly he credits John XII's coronation of Otto I to Leo VIII: xxxvii. 4, p. 222. Gratian, D. 63 cc. 22–3, would seem to be responsible for this: that these documents were forgeries see Ullmann, *op. cit.*, p. 352–7, but they caused endless trouble to the publicists. Tholemy of Lucca, *De origine Romani imperii*, p. 73 and Alvarus Pelagius, *De planctu Ecclesiae*, ch. 41, p. 68, agree with Augustinus Triumphus that there were two separate translations from Greeks to Franks and from Franks to Germans. Tholemy is probably Augustinus Triumphus' source for all this: he also quotes Leo VIII as crowning Otto I. He also held that Stephen II had given Pippin the Western empire, that Adrian I had completed the translation, but that Charlemagne had no use of the empire until his coronation by Leo III: *Determinatio compendiosa*, ch. 11, pp. 25–6; *De regimine principum*, iii. 10, p. 259; iii. 17–18, pp. 265–6; *De origine Romani imperii*, pp. 68–72. Conrad of Megenberg, *De translatione Romani imperii*, ch. 3, p. 256; ch. 4, pp. 258–9, declared that Stephen II had deprived the Eastern emperor of his power and transferred it to the West, but that it was not given to Charlemagne until 800. The anonymous *Compendium maius*, p. 177, gave the credit for the whole business to Zacharias, who had set up Pippin. The majority of the publicists regarded the translation of the empire to the Franks as holding good for the Germans, following Innocent III in *Decretales*, I. vi. 34. Whilst condemning it, some of the lay writers acknowledged that the translation had been made by Stephen II: e.g. Ugolinus de Celle, *De electione regis Romanorum*, ch. 17, p. 78; Landulfus de Colonna, *De statu Romani imperii*, cc. 3–8, pp. 91–4. Marsilius of Padua, *De translatione imperii*, ch. 5, p. 150; ch. 7, p. 151, said that Stephen II had ordered the translation to be made, and that Leo III had actually carried it out. The canonists were equally uncertain about the real course of events: see Ullmann, *Medieval Papalism*, pp. 169–71. On the whole subject see now W. Goez, *Translatio Imperii* (Tübingen, 1958).

to his office. He rules only by papal authority, and to do so without this authorisation places him in possession of stolen goods. The Roman empire always remains in reality the property of the Roman church, and it follows that the pope may transfer the empire from the Germans when and to whom he wishes.[1] To deny this is to raise up the whole question of how the Germans came to obtain a specifically Roman, that is to say universal, empire. As Conrad of Megenberg argued, unless one accepted that the papacy had transferred the empire from the East to the West, and that it had full right to do so, it must logically be concluded that the Eastern emperor was still the true Roman emperor.[2] There are only two solutions to the *Zweikaiserproblem*. Either the papal thesis is denied and the Eastern ruler remains the legitimate *dominus mundi*—or else the German is recognised as the *imperator Romanorum*, and the papal theory holds good. There is no other explanation of how the Germans came to obtain a universal Roman empire except through the medium of the Roman church, a point which was re-emphasised at each imperial coronation. In the famous words of Innocent III,

> Verum ad apostolicam sedem iampridem fuerat recurrendum, ad quam negotium istud principaliter et finaliter dinoscitur pertinere, principaliter quia ipsa transtulit imperium ab oriente in occidentem, finaliter quia ipsa *concedit* coronam imperii.[3]

And whilst the German emperors continued to maintain their right to rule the world as the direct choice of God, they were, and always would be, unable to give a satisfactory answer to this problem.

[1] Augustinus Triumphus, *Summa*, xxxvii. 5, p. 222; Tholemy of Lucca, *De origine Romani imperii*, pp. 73–4, '. . . Romana ecclesia et ipsam imperialem dignitatem transferret in aliam catholicam devotam nationem'; also Aegidius Romanus, *De ecclesiastica potestate*, ii. 5, p. 59; Francis Toti, *Tractatus contra Bavarum*, pp. 78, 82; Francis de Meyronnes, *De principatu temporali*, ch. 4, p. 62, Alvarus Pelagius, *De planctu Ecclesiae*, ch. 13, p. 31; ch. 21, p. 33. Conrad of Megenberg, *Oeconomica*, II. ii. 5 (Kaeppeli, p. 580 n. 1), stresses that this is an unrestricted right: 'dicto quod ecclesia regulariter transtulit imperium, et non casualiter'.

[2] Conrad of Megenberg, *De translatione Romani imperii*, ch. 2, p. 255; he cites Bernardus Hyspanus and others as accepting this, on which see further Gaines Post, 'Blessed Lady Spain', p. 204. Note Augustinus Triumphus' denial that the Eastern ruler is emperor, *Summa*, xxxvii. 4–5, p. 222.

[3] Innocent III, *RNI*, 18, p. 33 (*Decretales*, I. vi. 34): cited Augustinus Triumphus, *Summa*, xxxv. 5, p. 209.

APPENDIX 3

NOTES ON THE PUBLICISTS AND ANONYMOUS WORKS

Aegidius Romanus (d. 1316). Although generally regarded as a most fervent supporter of the papal supremacy, Aegidius had begun his career as a pupil of Aquinas at Paris, and had been an Aristotelian scholar of some eminence. This is reflected in the *De regimine principum* which he wrote for his own pupil, the future Philip IV of France, in c. 1285, and which was translated into many languages. In 1287 his teaching was officially prescribed for the schools of the Augustinian Hermits, and in 1292 he was elected Prior General of the Order. Three years later he became archbishop of Bourges. Thereafter he spent most of his time at the papal court, where his treatise on the resignation of Celestine V lends support to his supposed family connection with the Colonna. The famous bull *Unam sanctam* is often held to illustrate the importance of his *De ecclesiastica potestate* of 1302. After the death of Boniface VIII he returned to the service of Philip the Fair and is said to have assisted his campaign against the Templars.

Aegidius Spiritalis de Perusio (d. c. 1338). A canonist from Perugia, who had studied under Guido de Baysio, and was one of the few canonists to have the courage to accuse the Decretists of heresy for their dualistic tendencies. He is chiefly known for his elaboration of the theory of papal sovereignty, on the lines laid down by the Elder Durantis, in his attack on Louis of Bavaria and his supporters in 1328.

Alexander de Sancto Elpidio (d. 1326). On the whole one of the most conservative of the theologians, but occasionally coming to terms with Aristotelian principles, probably as a result of his studies at Paris and under the influence of the opinions of James of Viterbo. His support for the papacy was demonstrated by his opposition to Philip the Fair's action against the Templars, his denunciation of Louis of Bavaria, and later in his major work, the *De ecclesiastica potestate* of 1323–4. He was elected Prior General of the Augustinian Hermit Order in 1312, but became bishop of Melfi shortly before his death in 1326.

Alexander of Roes (d. after 1288). A canon of the church of S. Maria in Cologne, who is thought to have added a prologue and conclusion, under the title of *De translatione Romani imperii*, to the *De praerogativa Romani imperii* of Jordan of Osnabruck. This was presented to Cardinal James Colonna whom he was attending at Rome in c. 1281. He is also held responsible for the piece of Teutonic gloom entitled *Notitia saeculi* of 1288.

Alvarus Pelagius (d. 1353). A Spanish Franciscan often regarded as an extreme papalist, but whose most famous work, the *De planctu Ecclesiae* (1330–2, rewritten 1335, third version 1340), is a confused mass of contradictory opinions, deriving notably from Hostiensis, James of Viterbo and Augustinus Triumphus. He was also an expert Roman and canon lawyer. Most of his early life was spent in Italy, where he was in the forefront of the papal opposition to Louis of Bavaria and the anti-pope Nicholas V. In 1329 he became a penitencier of John XXII, and was rewarded with the see of Coron (Greece) in 1332, but was translated to Silves (Portugal) in the following year. Expelled from his see by Alfonso IV c. 1338, he settled in Seville for the remainder of his life.

Andreas de Perusio (d. 1345?). Author of a tract against Louis of Bavaria in which he endeavours to reject the doctrine of apostolic poverty and to clear John XXII of the charge of heresy made against him for denouncing it. Although no certainty attaches to this, he has been identified as the Franciscan master of theology at Naples who became bishop of Gravina (Italy) in 1343–5.

Antequam Essent Clerici (1296). An answer drafted for Philip IV of France, and at one time thought to be by Philip himself, in answer to the papal bull *Clericis laicos*. It is probably the work of Pierre Flotte (d. 1302). There is no evidence that it was ever sent to Boniface VIII.

Articuli de Iuribus Imperii (1338–42). Written in defence of the electoral rights of the German princes after the Declaration of Rhense. It is contained in the collection of documents known as the *Liber de controversia paupertatis Christi* attributed to Nicholas the Minorite.

Colonna Memorandum to Philip IV (1304). One of the most outspoken of the tracts written in defence of the cardinals against Boniface VIII at the beginning of the fourteenth century.

Commentarium in Unam Sanctam (1303). Uses the papal bull as a vehicle for propounding a theory of dualism on the one hand and conciliar supremacy on the other. It has been attributed to Aegidius Romanus, but this is very doubtful, and the author was almost certainly a Frenchman. An abridged version was also current.

Compendium Maius Octo Processuum Papalium (1328). Elaborates the points made in the papal denunciations of Louis of Bavaria. The author, a lawyer, described his attendance at the papal *curia* and in the Roman schools for many years prior to 1328, and claims to have used the records of the papal chancery.

Conrad of Megenberg (d. 1374). Taught at the University of Paris up to 1342, and was for a time proctor of the English nation. He then became rector of the school of St. Stephen at Vienne, and then from 1348 until his death was canon of the church of St. Ulric at Ratisbon (Regensburg). He was a theologian of a firmly conservative frame of mind and a staunch defender of episcopal rights. His great treatise, from amongst about thirty works, is the as yet unprinted *Oeconomica* of c. 1352, although he also wrote an important survey of contemporary opinions on the translation of the Roman empire, and a description of papal power reputedly aimed against William of Ockham.

DANTE ALIGHIERI (d. 1321). The great medieval poet was educated by the Dominicans at Florence, and it was probably from them that he derived the mixture of radical and Thomistic Aristotelianism which is apparent in his political theory. He was expelled from Florence in 1301 for his support of the anti-papal faction, and spent most of his life wandering between the Northern Italian cities. His enthusiasm for the cause of the emperor Henry VII is reflected in his letters and in the *Monarchia*, which was probably written c. 1313. He eventually settled in 1317 at Ravenna.

DE LEGIBUS (attributed to 1329–30, but probably very much earlier). A tract based largely upon Aquinas' discussion of law in the *Summa theologica*, and originally thought to have been written by Durandus de S. Porciano, although this has now been disproved. It is particularly valuable for its discussion of the theory of casual jurisdiction.

DE POTESTATE ECCLESIAE (1324–32). It has been suggested that this was written against Marsilius of Padua, but it is a shrewd and effective piece of work dealing with the deviations of Thomism.

DETERMINATIO COMPENDIOSA (1342). An able defence of papal sovereignty appended to the work of the same title by Tholemy of Lucca (c. 1300), and aimed specifically against the party of Michael of Cesena.

DISPUTATIO INTER CLERICUM ET MILITEM (c. 1296–7). Written during the early stages of the controversy between Boniface VIII and Philip the Fair, apparently by a layman, it takes the form of a dialogue between a knight and a cleric on the royal right to tax the clergy, in which the knight comes off best. There are numerous manuscripts, and it was incorporated into the *Somnium viridarii* in the following century. An English translation was produced in the sixteenth century.

DISQUISITIO THEOLOGICO-IURIDICA (1313), DISQUISITIO PRIOR IURIDICA (1313), DISQUISITIO IURIDICA (1313–14). Three very similar tracts mainly concerned to show that Clement V had a right to impose a truce between Henry VII and Robert of Naples in 1312. Whilst all are pro-papal in character, they are chiefly interesting for their blend of absolute and casual theories of papal power.

DURANDUS DE SANCTO PORCIANO (d. 1332). A gifted but erratic Dominican philosopher and theologian at Paris. Although his work shows pronounced nominalistic tendencies, his political thought is generally Thomistic in approach and favours the papacy. He was successively bishop of Limoux (1317), Le Puy-en-Velay (1318) and Meaux (1326). Soon after his death some of his writings were censured for theological error by a papal commission.

ENGELBERT OF ADMONT (d. 1331). Abbot of Admont in Styria from c. 1297, he was a distinguished theologian and Aristotelian scholar, and a warm supporter of imperial power. Amongst a large number of works his foremost political treatise is the *De ortu, progressu et fine Romani imperii*, probably written in 1307 or shortly afterwards, which bears a close resemblance to the somewhat later *Monarchia* of Dante.

FRANCIS DE MEYRONNES (d. c. 1325–30). A Franciscan theologian originating from Provence, who attended the University of Naples until he became master of theology at Paris in 1323 at the request of John XXII and king Robert of Naples. His work exhibits a mixture of papal and Thomistic theories, and he had a special interest in the situation of the Mediterranean kingdoms. He was papal delegate in Gascony in 1324, but died soon after his return to Italy, probably in 1327.

FRANCIS PETRARCH (d. 1374). A celebrated Italian poet and humanist, he studied law at Bologna and spent much of his earlier life in travelling through France, Italy and the Empire. In 1347 he supported the movement of Cola di Rienzo in Rome, and repeatedly urged Charles IV to recreate the glories of Roman emperorship.

FRANCIS TOTI DE PERUSIO (d. 1350). A Franciscan employed by John XXII as Inquisitor General for Tuscany, and rewarded by promotion to the bishopric of Sarno (Italy) in 1333. He wrote a tract against Louis of Bavaria in 1328 which is mainly full of abuse for Marsilius of Padua and John of Jandun.

GEOFFREY OF FONTAINES (d. after 1303). A master of theology at Paris from at least 1286, but originally from Liège. Amongst his pupils were John de Pouilly and Guido Terrenus, and he is said to have influenced the development of John of Paris' theory of property. He was successively canon at Liège, Paris and Cologne, and in 1300 was elected bishop of Tournai, but withdrew when the election was contested.

GILBERT OF TOURNAI (d. 1284). A Belgian Franciscan at the University of Paris, who was noted as a mystic theologian and liturgist. His work marks him as a papalist with a training in Roman law. He was a friend of Louis IX of France, for whom he wrote the *Eruditio regum et principum* of 1259. He also wrote, amongst various theological treatises, a summary of ecclesiastical abuses for the Council of Lyons of 1274.

GUIDO TERRENUS (d. 1342). A Carmelite from Perpignan, who was a master of theology at Paris and included Sybert of Beek amongst his pupils. He was elected Prior General of his Order in 1318, but became bishop of Majorca in

1321, and subsequently of Elne in 1332. In addition to his work on papal infallibility he wrote an attack on the theories of Marsilius of Padua, and commentaries on the New Testament, Aristotle's *Politics*, and the *Decretum* of Gratian.

GUIDO VERNANI (d. 1348?). A Dominican from Rimini, who lectured at the Dominican *studium* at Bologna between 1310–20, but spent much of his life in the convent of S. Cataldo at Rimini. He has become famous for his attack on the *Monarchia* of Dante, but he also wrote a short treatise *De potestate summi pontificis*. In spite of his hostility to Dante, he was ready to accept Aristotelian principles and wrote a number of commentaries on Aristotle's works, endeavouring to combine these principles with Augustinian teaching by reference to the theories of Aquinas.

GUILIELMUS DURANTIS [THE YOUNGER] (d. 1330). Not to be confused with his uncle of the same name, a famous canonist, whom he succeeded as bishop of Mende in 1296. He is chiefly noted for his proposals for the radical reform of the clergy and papacy which he prepared under the title of *De modo generalis concilii celebrandi* for Clement V in 1310 in readiness for the Council of Vienne.

HENRY OF CREMONA (d. 1312). The author of an influential tract on papal power in 1301, and probably of the earlier treatise beginning with the words *Non ponant laici* (c. 1296). He was an able canon lawyer, and was a canon of Cremona, and then of Bologna c. 1299. He is reputed to have been created bishop of Reggio in 1302 in return for his services to Boniface VIII, but no confirmation of this is available.

HENRY OF GHENT (d. 1293). A Belgian theologian at Paris, generally regarded as one of the leading exponents of Augustinian views in opposition to the teachings of Aquinas. He was concerned in all the major controversies at the University in the 1270s and 1280s, and distinguished himself in the attack on the privileges of the friars in 1282. His *Summa theologica* was never finished, but in his *Quodlibetae* he dealt with most of the theological and philosophical questions in dispute at the time. He became a canon of Tournai in 1267, and later archdeacon of Bruges (1276) and Tournai (1278).

HERMANNUS DE SCHILDIZ (d. 1357). An Augustinian Hermit, canonist and theologian, whose tract against heretics was primarily aimed at Marsilius of Padua. He attended the University of Paris, was a lector at Herford from 1328, and became Prior Provincial for Saxony and Thuringia in 1337. In 1342–5 he was vicar general and penitencier to bishop Otto of Wurzburg, and remained at Wurzburg as a theologian and curial officer.

HERVAEUS NATALIS (d. 1323). A Dominican theologian at Paris, whose *De potestate papae* of 1318 is mainly aimed against the episcopalist arguments put forward by John de Pouilli, but which reveals him as one of the most steadfast believers in papal sovereignty. Thus he was in practice often opposed to the teachings of Aquinas, but went so far as to write a defence of the latter's ideas. He also wrote a tract on the subject of exemption, and made an abridged version of the *Quodlibetae* of Geoffrey of Fontaines. He was concerned in the discussions of the French clergy on the charges of heresy against Boniface VIII and on the affair of the Templars. He became Provincial for France in 1309, and General of the Order from 1318.

INFORMATIO DE NULLITATE PROCESSUUM PAPAE IOHANNIS XXII (1338–42). Written by a Spiritual Franciscan at Munich, at least a decade after the death of John of Jandun to whom it has been attributed. It supports the attacks of the imperial princes on the papal claim to superior jurisdiction over matters concerning the imperial election.

JAMES (d. 1318) and PETER COLONNA (d. 1326). The Cardinals James and his nephew Peter were members of the powerful family which came out into open opposition to Boniface VIII. Their *memoranda* of 1297 sought to show that Boniface could not be pope, since the resignation of his predecessor, Clement V, was illegal. For this, and their defence of Stephen Colonna who had seized a papal treasure convoy, both cardinals were deposed from their offices, the whole family was excommunicated, and their property confiscated: whereupon they sought refuge with Philip the Fair. They were however reinstated by Clement V in 1305.

JAMES OF VITERBO (d. 1308). One of the first of the publicists to elaborate the theory of the papal plenitude of power in terms of the Thomistic principles of grace and nature. His teachings enjoyed considerable popularity in the Augustinian Hermit Order to which he belonged, and his *De regimine christiano* of 1302 was copied wholesale by Alexander de S. Elpidio and Alvarus Pelagius. He was named archbishop of Benevento by Boniface VIII in September, 1302, but was created archbishop of Naples by Charles II a few months later, and his later years were spent at the Neapolitan court.

JOHANNES BRANCHAZOLUS (d. after 1329). Professor of civil law at Pavia and Pisa, and an enthusiastic supporter of Louis of Bavaria's Italian expedition of 1327–9. He had earlier written the *De principio et origine et potentia imperatoris et papae*, a thinly veiled exposition of the *rex-sacerdos* ideal of kingship, which was probably produced for the benefit of Henry VII in 1312.

JOHN DE POUILLI (d. after 1321). A noted theologian at Paris from the end of the thirteenth century, becoming regent master in 1307, when he was also involved in the royal attack on the Templars. He became the spokesman of the French secular clergy, mainly through his bitter opposition to the Mendicant Orders, and took part in a series of celebrated debates with the friars, notably Hervaeus Natalis and Peter de la Palu. He also took a leading part in the discussions of the Council of Vienne of 1311. He was condemned for theological error in 1319.

JOHN OF CALVARUSO. A Neapolitan jurist about whom virtually nothing is known. He was concerned with Clement V's imposition of a truce on Henry VII and Robert of Naples in 1312, which he denounced as illegal on dualistic grounds.

John of Jandun (d. 1328). Leader of the Averro-Aristotelians in the Arts faculty of the University of Paris, he wrote several commentaries on the works of Aristotle, also a tract in praise of Paris and the French monarchy. He fled to the court of Louis of Bavaria with Marsilius of Padua in 1326 after being summoned to Avignon, but was condemned by John XXII in the following year.

John of Paris (d. 1306). A French Dominican whose use of Aristotle made him a most formidable opponent of the papal supremacy, although in many respects he adhered to the teachings of Aquinas. In 1300 he attacked the papally-protected Arnold of Villanova, produced his famous *De potestate regia et papali* in 1302 as part of the French denunciation of Boniface VIII, and in the following year supported the call for a general council against the pope. In 1305 he was condemned by an episcopal court at Paris, and forbidden to teach at the University. He appealed to Clement V, but died before the case was settled.

John of Viterbo. A Roman lawyer whose sole claim to distinction is his authorship of the *De regimine civitatum*, which dealt with the various forms of government adopted by the Italian city-states. This has been ascribed to various dates between 1225 and 1265, but was probably written about 1250.

Jordan of Osnabruck. Little is known about him beyond the fact that he was attached to the cathedral of Osnabruck between 1251 and 1283. His tract, the *De praerogativa Romani imperii*, was continued by Alexander of Roes.

Lambertus Guerrici de Hoyo (d. after 1328). A rather shadowy figure who was a priest in the diocese of Liège. He appears to have been a scribe in the papal penitentiary at Avignon in 1328, when he wrote his *Liber de commendatione Iohannis XXII* against the accusations of Louis of Bavaria in the expressed hope of gaining provision to a benefice at Liège.

Landulfus Colonna (d. 1331?). The eldest of the Colonna brothers who were involved in the conflict with Boniface VIII, Landulfus seems to have been a much more vigorous supporter of the papacy, and was in attendance at the *curia* at Avignon. He wrote a tract on the translation of the Roman empire, and another on the duties of a bishop.

Libellus ad Defensionem Fidei Catholicae (c. 1336–9). Apparently written by a Franciscan, perhaps by Bonagratia of Bergamo (d. 1340), and directed against Benedict XII. It urges conciliar action against an erring pontiff, but without explaining how the council would have a legal right to congregate and act.

Lupold of Bebenburg (d. 1363). One of the leading German ecclesiastics of his day, and attached to the see of Wurzburg in 1325–52. Lupold had studied at

Bologna under the canonist Johannes Andreae, and upheld the papal opposition to Louis of Bavaria until 1338. He then changed over to favour Louis, and was closely concerned with the composition of the Declarations of Rhense and Frankfort in that year and later in the Golden Bull of 1356. His bipartisan attitude is clearly apparent in the tracts which resulted from a brief flurry of literary activity in 1340, of which the most important is the *De iure regni et imperii Romani*. He became bishop of Bamberg in 1353.

Marsilius of Padua (d. 1342–3). The most savage and effective opponent of papal power, whose attack gained force from a skilful exploitation of radical Aristotelian and Roman law doctrines. Marsilius divided his early life between teaching philosophy, theology and medicine at Paris, where he was rector 1312–13, and in military and diplomatic missions in Northern Italy. After the appearance of his celebrated work, the *Defensor pacis*, in 1324, he was forced to flee to the court of Louis of Bavaria, and was condemned for heresy in 1327. He became vicar *in spiritualibus* for Rome during Louis' Italian expedition of 1327–9, but the rest of his life was spent at the imperial court in Bavaria, where he wrote a few minor tracts.

Michael of Cesena (d. 1342). Minister General of the Franciscan Order from 1316, he co-operated with John XXII in the suppression of the Spirituals. But his attitude changed with the papal denial of apostolic poverty in 1323–4, and when he protested, he was summoned to Avignon. He fled however with William of Ockham to the court of Louis of Bavaria in 1328, as a result of which he was deposed from his generalship, and his opinions were denounced as heretical a few years later.

Nicholas de Nonancour (d. 1299). A Parisian theologian who was chancellor, and a deacon of Notre Dame. He was created cardinal-deacon by Celestine V in 1294. He became actively concerned in the dispute between Boniface VIII and the Colonna cardinals, and remained devoted to the pope.

Opicinus de Canistris (d. c. 1352). A priest from Pavia who sought refuge from Louis of Bavaria at Avignon, where he was employed in the papal penitentiary in 1342–52. His *De praeeminentia spiritualis imperii* of 1329 had already marked him out as a most competent political thinker, although his mental instability sometimes led him to emphasise the more bizarre aspects of the papal-hierocratic theory.

Peter Bertrandus (d. 1349). Primarily a lawyer, he wrote glosses on the *Sextus* and the Clementines, and lectured on law at various French universities. His *De iurisdictione ecclesiastica et politica* of c. 1329 is valuable as an account of the proceedings of the Council of Vincennes, but his *De origine iurisdictionum* of the same period is merely an addition to the *De iurisdictione ecclesiastica* of Durandus de S. Porciano. He became bishop of Nevers in 1320, then of Autun later the same year, archbishop of Béziers in 1331, and was eventually created a cardinal.

Peter de la Palu (d. 1342). A French Dominican, theologian and canonist at Paris. He was concerned in the examination of the theses of Durandus de S. Porciano in 1316, was present at the Council of Vincennes of 1329, and was employed on various diplomatic missions for the papacy, including an embassy to the Sultan of Egypt in 1329–31. He was particularly interested in the question of whether the pope or the *congregatio fidelium* was the ultimate possessor of the plenitude of power, and wrote two tracts on the subject, the *De causa immediata ecclesiasticae potestatis* and the *De potestate papae*. He may have been aided in the composition of the former by the Dominican cardinal Guillaume de Pierre de Godin (d. 1336). He was appointed titular patriarch of Jerusalem in 1329, an office which usually carried with it the administration of the see of Limassol (Cyprus) in order to provide revenue, which he held until 1335.

Peter de Lutra (d. c. 1375). A Premonstratensian, prior of Kaiserslauten, about whom little is known beyond the fact that he was involved in the struggle between Baldwin of Triers and the see of Mainz in 1327–35. In about 1328 he wrote an attack on Marsilius of Padua and Michael of Cesena, the 'evil counsellors' of Louis of Bavaria.

Peter Olivi (d. 1298). Lector in theology at Paris (1279), Montpellier (1285), Florence (1288), Montpellier again, and finally Narbonne. He was one of the leading Spiritual Franciscans of the late thirteenth century, and was accused of heresy and censured in 1282–3. In 1287 his orthodoxy was re-established, only to be impugned again after his death, first by the Council of Vienne of 1311, and then by John XXII in 1326. The Spirituals however continued to regard him with the greatest veneration. Most of his work is of a primarily theological nature, but the controversy over the resignation of Celestine V drew him into writing several tracts on the nature of papal power in the closing years of his life.

Peter Roger (d. 1352). A notable Benedictine theologian who distinguished himself at the Council of Vincennes of 1329 by his defence of papal and episcopal rights (as reported by Peter Bertrandus in the *De iurisdictione ecclesiastica et politica*). He was elected abbot of Fécamp in 1326, bishop of Arras in 1328, archbishop of Sens in 1329 and of Rouen in 1330. Created cardinal in 1338, he eventually became pope as Clement VI in 1342.

Pierre Dubois (d. c. 1320). French civil lawyer and royal advocate for Coutances in Normandy up to 1314, when he probably entered the service of the countess of Artois. He was a member of the Estates-General of 1302–3 and 1308. Periodically he bombarded Philip IV with tracts on military and political matters, but his chief concern was with the independence of the French monarchy from papal control during the contest with Boniface VIII. His main work, the *De recuperatione Terrae Sanctae* (c. 1306, with Appendix, 1308) clearly exhibits the dual aim of internal sovereignty and external expansion characteristic of French imperialism at this period.

PSEUDO-THOMAS. The author of the *De eruditione principum* of c. 1260–5 which was for long included with the works of Aquinas. He has been identified as either Vincent of Beauvais or, more probably, William Perrault (d. c. 1275).

QUAESTIO IN UTRAMQUE PARTEM (1302). Originally attributed in error to Aegidius Romanus, this tract is primarily concerned to express the traditional theory of dualism on behalf of the French monarchy. It is said to have been used by John of Paris. The author seems to have been a theologian. A French translation was made by Raoul de Presles c. 1331.

RATIONES EX QUIBUS PROBATUR QUOD BONIFACIUS LEGITIME INGREDI NON POTUIT. This has been attributed to one of the Colonna faction and dated c. 1310, which appears to be much too late. Nor is the style reminiscent of the other Colonna tracts of the period.

REMIGIO DE GIROLAMI (d. 1319). A famous preacher and disciple of Aquinas, trained in Paris, who became lector in theology at the Dominican school in Florence, where he was the master of Dante, and a canon of Sancta Maria Novella. For a short period in 1303 he was made lector in theology to the papal *curia* under Benedict XI. His tract *De bono communi* was written as an exhortation to the Florentines, and he is also noted for his *Contra falsos Ecclesiae professores* of c. 1300, in which he developed the idea of the indirect power of the papacy.

REX PACIFICUS (1302). Perhaps the most effective of the French tracts of the period written in defence of the French monarchy against Boniface VIII. It appears to be the work of a single writer who may well have been a master at the University of Paris.

SOMNIUM VIRIDARII DE IURISDICTIONE REGIA ET SACERDOTALI (c. 1376–7). A long, very popular and influential dialogue addressed to Charles V of France, whose early chapters reproduce the *Disputatio inter clericum et militem*, and which relies heavily upon the views of William of Ockham. Whilst its apparent aim is to champion the independence of the French monarchy, its two disputants frequently find agreement along the lines on the Thomist compromise, and it is a useful compendium of the political ideas of the fourteenth century. Its authorship has often been ascribed to Philippe de Mézières, although Raoul de Presles and Évrart de Trémaugon have also been suggested. A French translation, *Le Songe du Vergier*, appeared soon afterwards.

SYBERT OF BEEK (d. 1332). A Carmelite theologian of Dutch–German origin, and a pupil of Guido Terrenus at Paris. He was the first master of his Order at the University, and became regent master in 1319. He was Provincial for Germany from 1324. He wrote a tract in support of the papal condemnation of Marsilius of Padua in 1327.

THOLEMY OF LUCCA (d. 1326–7). Dominican theologian, Aristotelian scholar, and for long the pupil and companion of Aquinas, Tholemy must be regarded as a moderate on the question of papal sovereignty in spite of a superficial extremism. His chief claim to fame rests on his completion (Books ii–iv) of the *De regimine principum* of Aquinas in c. 1301–3. His other main work on politics, the *Determinatio compendiosa*, was probably written in 1308 or shortly afterwards, and was used by Augustinus Triumphus. By 1295 he had become prior of his house at Lucca, and in 1301 of Sancta Maria Novella at Florence. Between 1309 and 1318 he was more or less continuously at the papal court at Avignon, until in the latter year he was created bishop of Torcello.

THOMAS AQUINAS (d. 1274). Without question the most famous and influential of all late medieval thinkers, Aquinas was above all responsible for assimilating Aristotelian principles with Christian teaching. As a young Dominican he studied under Albertus Magnus at Paris and Cologne, and the greater part of his life was spent in scholastic activities at Paris and in Italy, partly at the papal court. His only purely political work was the unfinished *De regimine principum* of c. 1266, but political and quasi-political passages can be found in many of the enormous number of philosophical and theological works which he wrote, especially in the commentary on the Sentences of 1254–6, the commentaries on Aristotle's *Politics* and *Ethics* of 1269–72, the *Summa contra Gentiles* of 1259–64, and the vast *Summa theologica* (more accurately *Summa theologiae*) which he began in 1266. He is said to have refused the archbishopric of Naples. His work was officially authorised for use by the Dominican Order in 1278, and he was canonised by John XXII in 1323 for his defence of ecclesiastical property ownership.

TRACTATUS CONTRA IOHANNEM XXII ET BENEDICTUM XII (1338). Written to support the imperial princes in their opposition to the papacy at the time of the Declaration of Rhense, and contained in the *Liber de controversia paupertatis Christi* of Nicholas the Minorite.

UGOLINUS DE CELLE (d. after 1323). A Roman lawyer from Florence, who elaborated the idea of imperial rights prior to papal coronation. He may have been at the French court early in the century, but became vicar general for Castruccio Castracani, governor of Lucca, in 1317.

WILLIAM AMIDANI OF CREMONA (d. 1356). Professor of theology at Paris, he was elected Prior General of the Augustinian Hermit Order in 1326, and was much concerned with the reform of the Order until his appointment to the bishopric of Novara in 1342. In addition to several theological works he followed up the papal condemnation of Marsilius of Padua in 1327 with his own denunciation, the *Reprobatio errorum*, in which his hostility to Louis of Bavaria is manifest.

WILLIAM NOGARET (d. 1314). French civil lawyer, chief lieutenant and successor from 1307 of Pierre Flotte (d. 1302) as Keeper of the Great Seal: they were the first laymen to hold the office. He was largely responsible for the attack on

Boniface VIII at Anagni in 1303, for which he was excommunicated. His political views are to be extracted from the flood of pamphlets and letters which he wrote to justify his action. He assisted Philip the Fair in his campaign against the Templars, and the royal favour eventually secured his absolution by Clement V in 1311.

William of Ockham (d. c. 1349). The principal advocate of nominalism in the fourteenth century, and one of the most stimulating and critical thinkers of the later Middle Ages. An English Franciscan, he studied and taught at Oxford until summoned to Avignon to answer charges of heresy in 1324. Here his contact with the Spiritual Franciscans inspired the defence of apostolic poverty which features in many of his works. Shortly before his condemnation in 1328 he escaped to the court of Louis of Bavaria, where he composed a long series of treatises against the papacy. His nominalism comes out most strongly in the individualism of the gigantic but incomplete *Dialogus* of c. 1334–43, but in many of his later works he seems to have been more eager to draw out the principles of the Thomist synthesis in favour of lay government.

BIBLIOGRAPHY

I. ORIGINAL SOURCES

(a) Manuscripts: Augustinus Triumphus

Summa de potestate ecclesiastica
MS Kk.1.2, University Library, Cambridge.
MS 133, Pembroke College Library, Cambridge.
MS 61, Peterhouse Library, Cambridge.
MS 141, Merton College Library, Oxford.
MS 71, St. John's College Library, Oxford.
Tractatus de duplici potestate, Tractatus de potestate collegii, Tractatus contra articulos, Tractatus super facto Templariorum, De origine ac translatione et statu Romani imperii [dubious]
MS Lat. 4046, Bibliothèque National, Paris.

(b) Printed editions: Anonymous Works

Antequam essent clerici, ed. P. Dupuy, *Histoire du différend d'entre le Pape Boniface VIII et Philippe le Bel* (Paris, 1655), pp. 21–3.
Articuli de iuribus imperii, ed. J. F. Boehmer, *Fontes rerum Germanicarum* (Stuttgart, 1843–68), iv pp. 592–7.
Colonna Memorandum to Philip IV, ed. P. Dupuy, *Histoire du différend*, pp. 225–7.
Commentarium in Unam sanctam, ed. P. de Lapparent, 'L'oeuvre politique de François de Meyronnes', *Archives d'histoire doctrinale et littéraire du moyen âge*, xii (1940–2), pp. 126–51.
Compendium maius octo processuum papalium, ed. R. Scholz, *Unbekannte Kirchenpolitische Streitschriften aus der Zeit Ludwigs des Bayern, 1327–54* (Rome, 1911–14), ii pp. 169–87.
De legibus, ed. J. Barbier (Paris, 1506), ff. 10–23 [unnumbered].
De potestate Ecclesiae, ed. R. Scholz, *Unbekannte Kirchenpolitische Streitschriften*, i pp. 250–6.
Determinatio compendiosa, ed. R. Scholz, *Unbekannte Kirchenpolitische Streitschriften*, ii pp. 540–51.
Disputatio inter clericum et militem, ed. M. Goldast, *Monarchia Sancti Romani Imperii* (Hanover, 1612), i pp. 13–18.
Disquisitio iuridica, MGH, Leges iv, *Constitutiones* iv.2, n. 1255, pp. 1379–98.
Disquisitio prior iuridica, MGH, Leges iv, *Constitutiones* iv.2, n. 1250, pp. 1320–41.
Disquisitio theologico-iuridica, MGH, Leges iv, *Constitutiones* iv.2, n. 1251, pp. 1342–62.

Informatio de nullitate processuum papae Iohannis XXII, ed. M. Goldast, *Monarchia*, i pp. 18–21.

Libellus ad defensionem fidei catholicae, ed. R. Scholz, *Unbekannte Kirchenpolitische Streitschriften*, ii pp. 552–62.

Quaestio in utramque partem, ed. M. Goldast, *Monarchia Sancti Romani Imperii* (Frankfort, 1614), ii pp. 96–107.

Rationes ex quibus probatur quod Bonifacius legitime ingredi non potuit, Celestino vivente, ed. P. Dupuy, *Histoire du différend*, pp. 448–66.

Rex pacificus, ed. P. Dupuy, *Histoire du différend*, pp. 663–83, with additions from J. Barbier (Paris, 1506), and S. du Boulay [Bulaeus], *Historia Universitatis Parisiensis* (Paris, 1668), iv pp. 940–1.

Somnium viridarii de iurisdictione regia et sacerdotali, ed. M. Goldast, *Monarchia*, i pp. 58–229.

Tractatus contra Iohannem XXII et Benedictum XII, ed. J. F. Boehmer, *Fontes rerum Germanicarum*, iv pp. 598–605.

(*c*) *Printed editions: Authors*

AEGIDIUS ROMANUS, *De regimine principum* (Rome, 1607).

De renuntiatione papae, ed. J. T. Rocaberti, *Bibliotheca Maxima Pontifica* (Rome, 1698), ii. 1, pp. 1–64.

De ecclesiastica potestate, ed. R. Scholz (Weimar, 1929).

AEGIDIUS SPIRITALIS DE PERUSIO, *Libellus contra infideles et inobedientes et rebelles sanctae Romanae ecclesiae ac summo pontifici*, ed. R. Scholz, *Unbekannte Kirchenpolitische Streitschriften*, ii pp. 105–29.

ALEXANDER OF ROES, *De translatione imperii*, ed. H. Grundmann, *Alexander von Roes, De translatione imperii, und Jordanus von Osnabrück, De praerogativa Romani imperii* (Leipzig and Berlin, 1930), pp. 18–38.

Notitia saeculi, ed. F. Wilhelm, 'Die Schriften des Jordanus Osnabrück. Ein Beitrag zur Geschichte der Publicistik im 13. Jahrhundert', *Mitteilungen des Instituts für österreichische Geschichtsforschung*, xix (1898), pp. 661–75.

ALEXANDER DE SANCTO ELPIDIO, *De ecclesiastica potestate*, ed. J. T. Rocaberti, *Bibliotheca Maxima Pontifica*, ii.7, pp. 1–40.

ALVARUS PELAGIUS, *De planctu Ecclesiae*, ed. J. T. Rocaberti, *Bibliotheca Maxima Pontifica*, iii pp. 23–266.

Speculum regum, ed. R. Scholz, *Unbekannte Kirchenpolitische Streitschriften*, ii pp. 514–29.

Collirium, ed. R. Scholz, *Unbekannte Kirchenpolitische Streitschriften*, ii pp. 491–514.

ANDREAS DE PERUSIO, *Tractatus contra edictum Bavari*, ed. R. Scholz, *Unbekannte Kirchenpolitische Streitschriften*, ii pp. 64–75.

AUGUSTINUS TRIUMPHUS, *Summa de potestate ecclesiastica* (Rome, 1584).

Tractatus brevis de duplici potestate praelatorum et laicorum, ed. R. Scholz,

Die Publizistik zur Zeit Philipps des Schönen und Bonifaz VIII (Stuttgart, 1903), pp. 486–501.

De potestate collegii mortuo papa, ed. R. Scholz, *Die Publizistik*, pp. 501–8.

De facto Templariorum, ed. R. Scholz, *Die Publizistik*, pp. 508–16.

Tractatus contra articulos inventos ad diffamandum sanctissimum patrem dominum Bonifacium papam, ed. H. Finke, *Aus den Tagen Bonifaz VIII* (Münster, 1902), pp. lxix–xcix.

BALDUS DE UBALDIS, *Commentaria in Codicem* (Lyons, 1545).

Commentaria in Digestum (Lyons, 1540).

BARTOLUS OF SASSOFERRATO, *Opera Omnia* (Basle, 1589).

BELLARMINE, *De potestate summi pontificis* (Rome, 1610).

BERNARDUS PARMENSIS, *Glossa Ordinaria ad Decretales* (Paris, 1519).

BONAVENTURE, *Opera Omnia* (ed. Quaracchi, 1898).

BRACTON, *De legibus et consuetudinibus Angliae*, ed. G. E. Woodbine (New Haven, 1915–42).

CONRAD OF MEGENBERG, *Planctus ecclesiae in Germaniam*, ed. R. Scholz, *Unbekannte Kirchenpolitische Streitschriften*, ii pp. 188–248.

De translatione Romani imperii, ed. R. Scholz, *Unbekannte Kirchenpolitische Streitschriften*, ii pp. 249–345.

Tractatus contra Wilhelmum Occam, ed. R. Scholz, *Unbekannte Kirchenpolitische Streitschriften*, ii pp. 346–91.

Oeconomica, ed. B. G. Struve, *Acta litteraria* (Jena, 1706), Fasc. iv, pp. 81–91; and A. Pelzer and T. Kaeppeli, 'L'*Oeconomica* de Conrad de Megenberg retrouvée', *Revue d'histoire ecclésiastique*, xlv (1950), pp. 559–616.

CYNUS, *Super codice et digesto veteri lectura* (Frankfort, 1578).

DANTE ALIGHIERI, *Convivio*, ed. G. Giuliani (Florence, 1874).

Monarchia, ed. E. Moore (Oxford, 1916).

Epistolae, ed. P. Toynbee (Oxford, 1920).

DURANDUS DE SANCTO PORCIANO, *De iurisdictione ecclesiastica*, ed. J. Barbier (Paris, 1506), ff. 1–8 [unnumbered].

ENGELBERT OF ADMONT, *De ortu, progressu et fine imperii Romani*, ed. M. Goldast, *Politica Imperialia* (Frankfort, 1614), pp. 754–73.

De regimine principum, ed. J. G. T. Huffnagl (Ratisbon, 1725).

De officiis et abusionibus eorum, ed. G. B. Fowler, *Essays in Medieval Life and Thought* (ed. J. H. Mundy, R. W. Emery and B. N. Nelson: New York, 1955), pp. 109–22.

FRANCIS DE MEYRONNES, *Quaestio de subiectione*, ed. P. de Lapparent, 'L'oeuvre politique de François de Meyronnes', *Archives d'histoire doctrinale et littéraire du moyen âge*, xiii (1940–2), pp. 75–92.

Tractatus de principatu temporali, ed. P. de Lapparent, 'L'oeuvre politique', pp. 55–74.

Tractatus de principatu regni Siciliae, ed. P. de Lapparent, 'L'oeuvre politique', pp. 93–116.

Francis Petrarch, *Epistolae de iuribus imperii Romani*, ed. M. Goldast, *Monarchia*, ii pp. 1345–65.

Francis Toti de Perusio, *Tractatus contra Bavarum*, ed. R. Scholz, *Unbekannte Kirchenpolitische Streitschriften*, ii pp. 76–88.

Francis Zabarella, *Tractatus de schismate*, ed. S. Schardius, *De iurisdictione, auctoritate et praeeminentia imperiali ac potestate ecclesiastica* (Basle, 1566).

Geoffrey of Fontaines, *Quodlibetae*, ed. M. de Wulf, *Les Philosophes Belges* (Louvain, 1914f.), ii–v, xiv.

Gilbert of Tournai, *Eruditio regum et principum*, ed. M. de Wulf, *Les Philosophes Belges*, ix.

Collectio de scandalis Ecclesiae, ed. A. Stroick, *Archivum Franciscanum Historicum*, xxiv (1931), pp. 33–62.

Guido de Baysio, *Tractatus super haeresi et aliis*, ed. J. D. Mansi, *Sacrorum Conciliorum nova et amplissima collectio* (Venice, 1782), xxv cc. 417–26.

Guido Terrenus, *Quodlibet IV*, ed. B. F. M. Xiberta, *Guiu Terrena, Carmelita de Perpinya* (Barcelona, 1932), pp. 319–20.

Quaestio de magisterio infallibilis Romani pontificis, ed. B. F. M. Xiberta, *Opuscula et Textus*, ii (Münster, 1926).

Guido Vernani, *De reprobatione Monarchiae composita a Dante*, ed. T. Kaeppeli, 'Der Dantegegner Guido Vernani, O.P., von Rimini', *Quellen und Forschungen aus Italienischen Archiven und Bibliotheken*, xxviii (1937–8), pp. 123–46.

Guilielmus Durantis [the Elder], *Speculum iuris* (Basle, 1574).

Guilielmus Durantis [the Younger], *Tractatus de modo generalis concilii celebrandi* (Paris, 1671).

Henry of Cremona, *Non ponant laici*, ed. R. Scholz, *Die Publizistik*, pp. 471–84.

De potestate papae, ed. R. Scholz, *Die Publizistik*, pp. 459–71.

Hermannus de Schildiz, *Contra haereticos negantes immunitatem et iurisdictionem sanctae ecclesiae*, ed. R. Scholz, *Unbekannte Kirchenpolitische Streitschriften*, ii pp. 130–53.

Hervaeus Natalis, *De potestate papae*, ed. J. Barbier (Paris, 1506), ff. 139–73 [unnumbered].

Hostiensis, *Summa aurea super titulis Decretalium* (Lyons, 1588).

Lectura in quinque Decretalium libros (Venice, 1581).

Innocent III, *Opera Omnia*, ed. J. P. Migne, *Patrologia Latina*, ccxiv–ccxvii (Paris, 1890).

Regestum super negotio Romani imperii, ed. W. Holtzmann (Bonn, 1947).

Innocent IV, *Commentaria super libros quinque Decretalium* (Frankfort, 1570).

James and Peter Colonna, *Memoranda*, ed. H. Denifle, 'Die Denkschriften der Colonna gegen Bonifaz VIII, und der Cardinäle gegen die Colonna', *Archiv für Literatur- und Kirchengeschichte*, v (1889), pp. 493–529.

James of Viterbo, *De regimine christiano*, ed. H.-X. Arquillière, *Le plus ancien traité de l'église, Jacques de Viterbo, De Regimine Christiano (1301–2)* (Paris, 1926).

Johannes Andreae, *Glossa ordinaria ad librum Sextum* (Venice, 1567).
Glossa ordinaria ad Clementinas (Venice, 1567).
Novella super Decretalibus (Venice, 1605).
Johannes Branchazolus, *De principio et origine et potentia imperatoris et papae*, ed. E. E. Stengel, *Nova Alamanniae* (Berlin, 1921), i n. 90, pp. 44–52.
Johannes Gerson, *Opera Omnia*, ed. Du Pin (Antwerp, 1706).
Johannes Monachus, *Glossa ordinaria ad Extravagantes Communes* (Venice, 1567).
John of Calvaruso, *Quaestio an Romanus pontifex potuerit treugam inducere principi Romanorum*, *MGH, Leges* iv, *Constitutiones* iv.2, n. 1248, pp. 1308–17.
John of Paris, *Tractatus de potestate regia et papali*, ed. J. Leclercq, *Jean de Paris et l'ecclésiologie du xiiie siècle* (Paris, 1942).
John of Viterbo, *De regimine civitatum*, ed. C. Salvemini, 'Scripta Anecdota Glossatorum', *Bibliotheca Iuridica Medii Aevi* (ed. A. Gaudenzi: Bologna, 1901), iii pp. 217–80.
Jordan of Osnabruck, *De praerogativa Romani imperii*, ed. H. Grundmann, *Alexander von Roes und Jordanus von Osnabrück*, pp. 12–17.
Lambertus Guerrici de Hoyo, *Liber de commendatione Iohannis XXII*, ed. R. Scholz, *Unbekannte Kirchenpolitische Streitschriften*, ii pp. 154–68.
Landulfus Colonna, *De statu et mutatione Romani imperii*, ed. M. Goldast, *Monarchia*, ii pp. 88–95.
De pontificali officio, ed. R. Scholz, *Unbekannte Kirchenpolitische Streitschriften*, ii pp. 530–9.
Lupold of Bebenburg, *De iure regni et imperii Romani*, ed. S. Schardius, *De iurisdictione*, pp. 328–409.
De zelo catholicae fidei veterum principum Germanorum, ed. S. Schardius, *De iurisdictione*, pp. 410–65.
Ritmaticum querulosum et lamentum dictamen, ed. J. F. Boehmer, *Fontes*, i pp. 479–84.
Marsilius of Padua, *Defensor pacis*, ed. R. Scholz (Hanover, 1932–3).
Defensor minor, ed. C. K. Brampton (Birmingham, 1922).
De translatione imperii, ed. M. Goldast, *Monarchia*, ii pp. 147–53.
De iurisdictione imperatoris in causa matrimoniali, ed. M. Goldast, *Monarchia*, ii pp. 1386–91.
Michael of Cesena, *Tractatus contra errores Iohannis XXII*, ed. M. Goldast, *Monarchia*, ii pp. 1236–1338.
Litterae ad omnes fratres Ordinis Minorum, ed. M. Goldast, *Monarchia*, ii pp. 1338–46.
Litterae deprecatoriae, ed. M. Goldast, *Monarchia*, ii pp. 1346–60.
Nicholas of Cues, *De concordantia catholica*, *Opera Omnia*, xviii (Basle, 1566).
Opicinus de Canistris, *De praeeminentia spiritualis imperii*, ed. R. Scholz, *Unbekannte Kirchenpolitische Streitschriften*, ii pp. 89–104.

PETER BERTRANDUS, *De origine iurisdictionum*, *Tractatus Universi Iuris*, iv (Lyons, 1549), ff. 96–9.

De iurisdictione ecclesiastica et politica, ed. M. Goldast, *Monarchia*, ii pp. 1361–83.

PETER DE LA PALU, *De causa immediata ecclesiasticae potestatis*, ed. J. Barbier (Paris, 1506), ff. 24–80 [unnumbered].

Articulus circa materia confessionum, ed. J. Barbier (Paris, 1506), ff. 80–100 [unnumbered].

PETER DE LUTRA, *Tractatus contra Michaelem de Cesena et socios eius*, ed. R. Scholz, *Unbekannte Kirchenpolitische Streitschriften*, ii pp. 29–42.

Liga fratrum, ed. R. Scholz, *Unbekannte Kirchenpolitische Streitschriften*, ii pp. 42–63.

PETER OLIVI, *Quaestio de infallibilitate Romani pontificis*, ed. M. Maccarrone, 'Una questione inedita dell' Olivi sull' infallibilità del papa', *Rivista di Storia della Chiesa in Italia*, iii (1949), pp. 325–42.

De renuntiatione papae, ed. P. L. Oliger, 'Petri Iohannis Olivi De renuntiatione papae Coelestini V, Quaestio et Epistola', *Archivum Franciscanum Historicum*, xi (1918), pp. 340–66.

Epistola ad Conradum de Offida, ed. P. L. Oliger, 'Petri Iohannis Olivi', pp. 366–73.

PIERRE D'AILLY, *De Ecclesiae et cardinalium auctoritate*, in Gerson, *Opera Omnia*, ii.

PIERRE DUBOIS, *Deliberatio super agendis*, ed. P. Dupuy, *Histoire du différend*, pp. 45–7.

La supplication du pueuble de France au Roy contre le pape Boniface le VIII, ed. P. Dupuy, *Histoire du différend*, pp. 214–19.

De recuperatione Terrae Sanctae, ed. C. V. Langlois (Paris, 1891).

PSEUDO-THOMAS, *De eruditione principum*, in Aquinas, *Opera Omnia* (Parma, 1865), xvi pp. 390–475.

SYBERT OF BEEK, *Reprobatio sex errorum*, ed. R. Scholz, *Unbekannte Kirchenpolitische Streitschriften*, ii pp. 3–15.

THOMAS AQUINAS, *Opera Omnia* (Parma, 1852–73).

THOLEMY OF LUCCA, *De regimine principum*, in Aquinas, *Opera Omnia* (Parma, 1865), xvi pp. 240–91.

Determinatio compendiosa de iurisdictione imperii, ed M. Krammer (Hanover and Leipzig, 1909), pp. 1–65.

De origine ac translatione et statu Romani imperii, ed. M. Krammer, pp. 66–75.

UBERTUS DE LAMPUGNANO, *Utrum omnes christiani subsunt Romano imperio*, ed. T. Dolliner, 'Einige Nachrichten über den Rechtsgelehrten Ubertus von Lampugnano', *Zeitschrift für geschichtliche Rechtswissenschaft*, ii (1816), pp. 246–56.

UGOLINUS DE CELLE, *Tractatus de electione et coronatione regis Romanorum*, ed. E. E. Stengel, *Nova Alamanniae*, n. 123, pp. 71–9.

VINCENT OF BEAUVAIS, *Speculum doctrinale* (Douai, 1624).

WILLIAM AMIDANI OF CREMONA, *Reprobatio errorum*, ed. R. Scholz, *Unbekannte Kirchenpolitische Streitschriften*, ii pp. 16–28.

WILLIAM NOGARET, *Appeals, Justifications and Minor Tracts*, ed. P. Dupuy, *Histoire du différend*, pp. 56–9, 237–77, 314–24; and R. Holtzmann, *Wilhelm von Nogaret* (Freiburg im Breisgau, 1898), pp. 246–77.

WILLIAM OF OCKHAM, *Dialogus*, ed. M. Goldast, *Monarchia*, ii pp. 393–957; with addition, ed. R. Scholz, *Unbekannte Kirchenpolitische Streitschriften*, ii pp. 392–5.

Quoniam scriptura testante divina, ed. W. Preger, 'Beiträge und Erörterungen zur Geschichte des Deutschen Reichs in den Jahren 1330–4', *Abhandlungen der bayrischen Akademie der Wissenschaften, Hist. Kl.* (Munich, 1880), xv.2, pp. 76–82.

Epistola ad Fratres Minores, ed. H. S. Offler, *Guillelmi de Ockham Opera Politica*, iii (Manchester, 1956), pp. 2–17.

Opus nonaginta dierum contra errores Iohannis XXII papae, ed. J. G. Sikes and R. F. Bennett, *Guillelmi de Ockham Opera Politica*, i (Manchester, 1940), pp. 287–374; and M. Goldast, *Monarchia*, ii pp. 993–1238.

Tractatus pro rege Angliae, ed. H. S. Offler and R. H. Snape, *Opera Politica.* i pp. 223–71.

Octo quaestiones de potestate papae, ed. J. G. Sikes, *Opera Politica*, i pp. 1-221.

Breviloquium, ed. R. Scholz, *Wilhelm von Ockham als politischer Denker und sein Breviloquium de principatu tyrannico* (Leipzig, 1944).

Tractatus contra Iohannem XXII, ed. H. S. Offler, *Opera Politica*, iii pp. 20–156.

Tractatus contra Benedictum XII, ed. H. S. Offler, *Opera Politica*, iii pp. 158–322.

Allegationes de potestate imperiali, ed. R. Scholz, *Unbekannte Kirchenpolitische Streitschriften*, ii pp. 417–31.

Consultatio de causa matrimoniali, ed. J. G. Sikes, *Opera Politica*, i pp. 273–86.

De imperatorum et pontificum potestate, ed. C. K. Brampton (Oxford, 1930); with addition, ed. W. Mulder, 'Guilielmi Ockham Tractatus de imperatorum et pontificum potestate', *Archivum Franciscanum Historicum*, xvi (1923), pp. 469–92; xvii (1924), pp. 72–97.

ZENZELLINUS DE CASSANIS, *Glossa ordinaria ad Extravagantes Iohannis XXII* (Venice, 1567).

2. SECONDARY AUTHORITIES

AARON, R. I., *The Theory of Universals* (Oxford, 1952).

ALTMANN, W. and BERNHEIM, E., *Ausgewählte Urkunden zur Erlänterung der Verfassungsgeschichte Deutschlands im Mittelalter* (Berlin, 1909).

ARBESMANN, R., 'The *Malleus* metaphor in medieval characterisation', *Traditio*, iii (1945), pp. 389–92.

Arquillière, H.-X., 'L'origine des théories conciliaires', *Séances et Travaux de l'Académie des Sciences Morales et Politiques*, clxxv (1911), pp. 573–86.

'L'appel au concile sous Philippe le Bel et la genèse des théories conciliaires', *Revue des questions historiques*, xlv (1911), pp. 23–55.

Aubert, J. M., *Le droit romain dans l'oeuvre de Saint Thomas* (Paris, 1955).

Baethgen, F., 'Der Anspruch des Papsttums auf das Reichvikariat: Untersuchungen zur Theorie und Praxis der *potestas indirecta in temporalibus*', *Zeitschrift der Savigny-Stiftung für Rechtsgeschichte, Kanonistische Abteilung*, xli (1920), pp. 168–286.

Balogh, J., 'Rex a recte regendo', *Speculum*, iii (1928), pp. 580–2.

Baluzius, S., *Vitae Paparum Avenionensium* (ed. G. Mollat: Paris, 1914–27).

Bayley, C. C., 'Petrarch, Charles IV and the *Renovatio Imperii*', *Speculum*, xvii (1942), pp. 323–41.

'Pivotal Concepts in the Political Philosophy of William of Ockham', *Journal of the History of Ideas*, x (1949), pp. 199–218.

The Formation of the German College of Electors in the Mid-Thirteenth Century (Toronto, 1949).

Berges, W., *Die Fürstenspiegel des hohen und späten Mittelalters* (Leipzig, 1938).

Beumer, J., 'Zur Ekklesiologie der Frühscholastik', *Scholastik*, xxvi (1951), pp. 364–89.

Birdsall, P., '*Non obstante:* A Study of the Dispensing Power of English Kings', *Essays in History and Political Theory in honor of C. H. McIlwain* (Cambridge, Mass., 1936), pp. 37–76.

Bloch, M., *Les rois thaumaturges* (Strasbourg, 1924).

Born, L. K., 'The Perfect Prince', *Speculum*, iii (1928), pp. 470–504.

Boutaric, E., 'Notices et Extraits de documents inédits relatifs à l'histoire de France sous Philippe le Bel', *Notices et Extraits des manuscrits*, xx.2 (1862), pp. 83–237.

Bowe, G., *The Origin of Political Authority* (Dublin, 1955).

Brown, E., *Fasciculus rerum expetendarum et fugiendarum* (London, 1690).

Brys, J., *De dispensatione in Iure Canonico* (Bruges, 1925).

Calasso, F., *I Glossatori e la Teoria della Sovranità* (Milan, 1951).

Carlyle, R. W. and A. J., *History of Medieval Political Theory in the West* (London, 1903–36).

Carré, M. H., *Realists and Nominalists* (Oxford, 1946).

Cassirer, E., *The Myth of the State* (London, 1946).

Chevrier, G., 'Remarques sur l'introduction et les vicissitudes de la distinction du *ius privatum* et du *ius publicum* dans les oeuvres des anciens juristes français', *Archives de philosophie du droit* (1952), pp. 5–77.

Chrimes, S. B., *English Constitutional Ideas in the Fifteenth Century* (Cambridge, 1936).

Chroust, A. H., 'The Corporate Idea and the Body Politic in the Middle Ages', *Review of Politics*, ix (1947), pp. 423–52.

COPLESTONE, F. C., *Aquinas* (London, 1955).

COULON, A., *Jean XXII. Lettres secrètes et curiales* (Paris, 1900 f.).

DABIN, P., *Le Sacerdoce Royal des Fidèles* (Brussels and Paris, 1950).

DARQUENNES, A., *De Juridische Structuur van de Kerk volgens Sint Thomas van Aquino* (Louvain, 1949).

DAVID, M., 'Le serment du sacre du ixe au xve siècle', *Revue du moyen âge latin*, vi (1950), pp. 5–272.

La souveraineté et les limites juridiques du pouvoir monarchique du IXe au XVe siècle (Paris, 1954).

DAVIS, C. T., *Dante and the Idea of Rome* (Oxford, 1957).

DUPUY, P., *Histoire du différend d'entre le pape Boniface VIII et Philippe le Bel, Roy de France* (Paris, 1655).

ECKERMANN, K., *Studien zur Geschichte des monarchischen Gedankens im 15. Jahrhundert* (Berlin, 1933).

EGENTER, R., 'Gemeinnutz vor Eigennutz: Die soziale Leitidee im *Tractatus de bono communi* des Fr. Remigius von Florenz (**1319*)', *Scholastik*, ix (1934), pp. 79–92.

EHRHARDT, A., 'Das *Corpus Christi* und die Korporationen im spät-romischen Recht', *Zeitschrift der Savigny-Stiftung für Rechtsgeschichte, Romanistische Abteilung*, lxx (1953), pp. 299–347.

EICHMANN, E., *Die Kaiserkrönung im Abendlande* (Wurzburg, 1943).

D'ENTREVES, A. P., *The Medieval Contribution to Political Thought* (Oxford, 1939).

Dante as a Political Thinker (Oxford, 1952).

ERCOLE, F., *Il pensiero politico di Dante* (Florence, 1922–8).

Da Bartolo all'Althusio (Florence, 1932).

ERMATINGER, C. J., 'Averroism in Early Fourteenth Century Bologna', *Mediaeval Studies*, xvi (1954), pp. 35–56.

ESCHMANN, I. T., 'A Thomistic Glossary on the Principle of the Preeminence of a Common Good', *Mediaeval Studies*, v (1943), pp. 123–65.

'Bonum commune melior est quam bonum unius', *Mediaeval Studies*, vi (1944), pp. 62–120.

'Studies on the Notion of Society in Thomas Aquinas', *Mediaeval Studies*, viii (1946), pp. 1–42.

'Thomistic Social Philosophy and the Theory of Original Sin', *Mediaeval Studies*, ix (1947), pp. 19–55.

'St. Thomas Aquinas on the Two Powers', *Mediaeval Studies*, xx (1958), pp. 177–205.

ESMEIN, A., 'La Maxime *Princeps legibus solutus est* dans l'ancien droit public français', *Essays in Legal History* (ed. P. Vinogradoff: Oxford, 1913), pp. 201–14.

EUBEL, C., *Hierarchia Catholica Medii Aevi* (Monasterium, 1913).

FEINE, H. E., *Kirchliche Rechtsgeschichte: I. Die Katholische Kirche* (Weimar, 1950).

Figgis, J. N., *Studies of Political Thought from Gerson to Grotius, 1414–1625* (Cambridge, 2nd edition, 1916).

The Divine Right of Kings (Cambridge, 2nd edition, 1934).

Finke, H., *Aus den Tagen Bonifaz VIII* (Münster, 1902).

Folz, R., *Le souvenir et la légende de Charlemagne* (Paris, 1950).

L'idée d'empire en Occident du Ve au XIVe siècle (Paris, 1953).

Fraser, C. M., 'Edward I of England and the Regalian Franchise of Durham', *Speculum*, xxxi (1956), pp. 329–42.

Friedberg, A., *Corpus Iuris Canonici* (Leipzig, 1879).

Frotscher, G., *Die Anschauungen von Papst Johann XXII, 1316–34, über Kirche und Staat* (Jena, 1933).

Gams, P. P. B., *Series Episcoporum Ecclesiae Catholicae* (Ratisbon, 1873).

Genestal, R., *Les origines de l'appel comme d'abus* (Paris, 1950).

Gewirth, A., 'John of Jandun and the *Defensor Pacis*', *Speculum*, xxiii (1948), pp. 267–72.

Marsilius of Padua (New York, 1951–6).

Giannelli, C., 'Un progetto di Barlaam Calabro per l'unione della Chiese', *Miscellanea Giovanni Mercati*, iii (Vatican City, 1946), pp. 157–208.

Gierke, O. von (tr. F. W. Maitland), *Political Theories of the Middle Age* (Cambridge, 1927).

Gilby, T., *Principality and Polity: Aquinas and the Rise of State Theory in the West* (London, 1958).

Gillet, P., *La personnalité juridique en droit ecclésiastique* (Malines, 1927).

Gillmann, F., 'Dominus Deus noster Papa', *Archiv für Katholisches Kirchenrecht*, xcv (1915), pp. 266 f.

'Romanus Pontifex iura omnia in scrinio pectoris sui cervetur habere', *Archiv für Katholisches Kirchenrecht*, xcii (1912), pp. 3f.

'Von wem stammen die Ausdrücke *potestas directa* und *potestas indirecta papae in temporalibus?*' *Archiv für Katholisches Kirchenrecht*, xcviii (1918), pp. 470f.

Gilmore, M. P., *Argument from Roman Law in Political Thought, 1200–1600* (Cambridge, Mass., 1941).

Gilson, E., *Dante the Philosopher* (London, 1948).

La philosophie au moyen âge (Paris, 1952).

Grabmann, M., 'Studien über den Einfluss der aristotelischen Philosophie auf die mittelalterlichen Theorien über das Verhältnis um Kirche und Staat', *Sitzungsberichte der bayrischen Akademie der Wissenschaften, Phil.-Hist. Abt., Heft* 2 (Munich, 1934).

'Der lateinische Averroismus des 13. Jahrhundert und seine Stellung zur christlichen Weltanschauung', *Sitzungsberichte der bayrischen Akademie der Wissenschaften, Phil.-Hist. Abt., Heft* 1 (Munich, 1931).

'Die Erörterung der Frage, ob die Kirche besser durch einen guten Juristen oder durch einen guten Theologen regiert werde bei Gottfried von Fontaines (*1306) und Augustinus Triumphus von Ancona (*1328)', *Eichmann Festschrift* (Paderborn, 1940), pp. 1–19.

'Die mittelalterlichen Kommentare zur Politik des Aristoteles', *Sitzungsberichte der bayrischen Akademie der Wissenschaften, Phil.-Hist. Abt., Band* II, *Heft* 10 (Munich, 1941).

'I Papi del Duecento e l'Aristotelismi: I. I divieti ecclesiastici di Aristotele sotto Innocenzo III e Gregorio IX', *Miscellanea Historiae Pontificiae*, v (Rome, 1941).

GRABOWSKI, S. J., 'Saint Augustine and the Primacy of the Roman Bishops', *Traditio*, iv (1946), pp. 89–113.

The Church: An Introduction to the Theology of Saint Augustine (St Louis, 1957).

GRAF, A., *Roma nella memoria e nelle immaginazioni del medio evo* (Turin, 1923).

GREENHILL, E. S., 'The Child in the Tree: A study of the cosmological tree in Christian tradition', *Traditio*, x (1954), pp. 323–71.

GRIGNASCHI, M., 'Le rôle de l'aristotelisme dans le *Defensor Pacis* de Marsile de Padoue', *Revue d'histoire et de philosophie religieuses*, xxxv (1955), pp. 301–40.

GWYNN, A., *The English Austin Friars in the time of Wyclif* (Oxford, 1940).

HAMMAN, P. A., *La doctrine de l'église et de l'état chez Occam* (Paris, 1942).

HARTUNG, F., 'Die Krone als Symbol der monarchischen Herrschaft im ausgehenden Mittelalter', *Abhandlungen der Preussischen Akademie der Wissenschaften, Phil.-Hist. Kl., Jahr* 1940, xi (Berlin, 1941).

HASKINS, G. L., 'Executive Justice and the Rule of Law', *Speculum*, xxx (1955), pp. 529–38.

HAZELTINE, H. D., 'The Early History of English Equity', *Essays in Legal History* (ed. P. Vinogradoff: Oxford, 1913).

Introduction to W. Ullmann, *The Medieval Idea of Law as represented by Lucas de Penna* (London, 1946), pp. xv–xxxix.

HEARNSHAW, F. J. C. ed., *The Social and Political Ideas of Some Great Medieval Thinkers* (London, 1923).

HOLTZMANN, R., *Wilhelm von Nogaret* (Freiburg im Breisgau, 1898).

HUILLARD-BRÉHOLLES, J. L. A., *Historia diplomatica Frederici Secundi* (Paris, 1852–61).

IUNG, N., *Un Franciscain, théologien du pouvoir pontifical au XIVe siècle, Alvaro Pelayo, évèque et pénitencier de Jean XXII* (Paris, 1931).

JACOB, E. F., *Essays in the Conciliar Epoch* (Manchester, 2nd edition, 1953).

JEDIN, H., *A History of the Council of Trent*, i (tr. E. Graf: London, 1957).

JOLLIFFE, J. E. A., *Angevin Kingship* (London, 1955).

JORDAN, E., 'Dante et la théorie romaine de l'empire', *Revue historique de droit français et étranger*, xlv (1921), pp. 353–96; n.s. i (1922), pp. 191–232, 333–90.

KÄMPF, H., *Pierre Dubois und die Geistigen Grundlagen des Französischen Nationalbewusstseins um 1300* (Leipzig and Berlin, 1935).

KANTOROWICZ, E. H., *Laudes Regiae: A Study in Liturgical Acclamations and Medieval Ruler Worship* (Berkeley and Los Angeles, 1946).

'*Pro Patria Mori* in Medieval Political Thought', *American Historical Review*, lvi (1950–1), pp. 472–92.

'Deus per naturam, Deus per gratiam', *Harvard Theological Review*, xlv (1952), pp. 253–77.

'Inalienability: A Note on Canonical Practice and the English Coronation Oath in the XIIIth. Century', *Speculum*, xxix (1954), pp. 488–502.

'Mysteries of State: An Absolutist Concept and its Late Medieval Origins', *Harvard Theological Review*, xlviii (1955), pp. 65–91.

The King's Two Bodies: A Study in Medieval Political Theology (Princeton, 1957).

KERN, F., *Kingship and Law in the Middle Ages* (tr. S. B. Chrimes: Oxford, 1948).

KLIBANSKY, R., *The Continuity of the Platonic Tradition during the Middle Ages* (London, 1939).

KOCH, J., 'Durandus de S. Porciano, O.P.', *Beiträge zur Geschichte der Philosophie des Mittelalters*, xxvi (1926), pp. 1–436.

'Der Prozess gegen den Magistro de Polliaco und seine Vorgeschichte', *Recherches de théologie ancienne et médiévale*, v (1933), pp. 391–422.

KRUGER, P., *Corpus Iuris Civilis* (Berlin, 1908).

KUTTNER, S., '*Cardinalis*: The History of a Canonical Concept', *Traditio*, iii (1945), pp. 129–214.

LADNER, G. B., 'Aspects of Medieval Thought on Church and State', *Review of Politics*, ix (1947), pp. 403–22.

DE LAGARDE, G., *La naissance de l'esprit laïque au declin du moyen âge* (Paris, 1934–46).

'L'idée de représentation dans les oeuvres de Guillaume d'Ockham', *International Committee of Historical Sciences Bulletin*, ix (1937), pp. 425–51.

'La philosophie sociale d'Henri de Gand et Godefroid de Fontaines', *Archives de l'histoire doctrinale et littéraire du moyen âge*, xiv (1943–5), pp. 73–142.

'Comment Ockham comprend le pouvoir séculier', *Scritti di sociologia e politica in onore di Luigi Sturzo*, i (Bologna, 1953), pp. 593–612.

DE LAPPARENT, P., 'L'oeuvre politique de François de Meyronnes', *Archives d'histoire doctrinale et littéraire du moyen âge*, xiii (1940–2), pp. 5–151.

LASKI, H. J., 'Political Theory in the Later Middle Ages', *Cambridge Medieval History*, viii (Cambridge, 1936), pp. 620–45.

LEAR, F. S., 'The Idea of Majesty in Roman Political Thought', *Essays in History and Political Theory in honor of C. H. McIlwain* (Cambridge, Mass., 1936), pp. 168–98.

LE BRAS, G., 'Le droit romain au service de la domination pontificale', *Revue historique de droit français et étranger*, xxvii (1949), pp. 377–98.

LECLERCQ, J., 'Le rénonciation de Celestin V et l'opinion théologique en France du vivant de Boniface VIII', *Revue de l'histoire de l'Église de France*, xxv (1939), pp. 183–192.

Jean de Paris et l'ecclésiologie du XIIIe siècle (Paris, 1942).

'Un sermon prononcé pendant la guerre de Flandre sous Philippe le Bel', *Revue du moyen âge latin*, i (1948), pp. 165–72.

'L'idée de la royauté du Christ au XIVe siècle', *Miscellanea Pio Paschini*, i (Rome, 1948), pp. 405–25.

LEFF, G., *Bradwardine and the Pelagians* (Cambridge, 1957).

LEMAIRE, A., *Les lois fondamentales de la monarchie française* (Paris, 1907).

LEWIS, E., 'Organic Tendencies in Medieval Political Thought', *American Political Science Review*, xxxii (1938), pp. 849–76.

'Natural Law and Expediency', *Ethics*, l (1939–40), pp. 144–63.

Medieval Political Ideas (London, 1954).

LEWIS, J. D., 'The Genossenschaft-Theory of Otto von Gierke', *University of Wisconsin Studies* (Madison, 1935).

LITTLEJOHN, J. M., *The Political Theory of the Schoolmen and Grotius* (Privately printed, 1896).

DE LUBAC, H., *Corpus Mysticum: L'eucharistie et l'église au moyen âge* (Paris, 1944).

LUCAS, H. S., 'The Low Countries and the Disputed Imperial Election of 1314', *Speculum*, xxi (1946), pp. 72–114.

MACCARRONE, M., 'Teologia e diritto canonico nella *Monarchia*, iii.3', *Rivista di storia della chiesa in Italia*, v (1951), pp. 7–42.

Vicarius Christi (Rome, 1952).

'*Potestas directa* e *potestas indirecta* nei teologi del XII e XIII secolo', *Miscellanea Historiae Pontificiae*, xviii (1954), pp. 27–47.

MAIER, A., 'Due documenti relativi alla lotta dei cardinali Colonna contro Bonifazio VIII', *Rivista di storia della chiesa in Italia*, iii (1949), pp. 344–64.

MAITLAND, F. W., *Roman Canon Law in the Church of England* (London, 1898).

Selected Essays (Cambridge, 1936).

MANSI, J. D., *Sacrorum Conciliorum Nova et Amplissima Collectio* (Florence and Venice, 1759–98).

MARIANI, U., *Chiesa e stato nei teologi agostiniani del secolo xiv* (Rome, 1957).

MARTIN, C., 'Some Medieval Commentaries on Aristotle's *Politics*', *History*, xxxvi (1951), pp. 29–44.

MARTINI, G., 'Regale Sacerdotium', *Archivio della società Romana di storia patria*, n.s. iv (1938), pp. 1–166.

MATHEW, G., 'Boniface VIII to the Council of Constance', *Church and State* (London, 1936).

MAURER, A., 'Boetius of Dacia and the Double Truth', *Mediaeval Studies*, xvii (1955), pp. 233–9.

MCILWAIN, C. H., *The Growth of Political Thought in the West* (London, 1932).

Constitutionalism Ancient and Modern (Ithaca, New York, 1947).

McNeill, J. T., 'The Emergence of Conciliarism', *Medieval and Historiographical Essays in honor of James Westfall Thompson* (ed. J. L. Cate and E. N. Anderson: Chicago, 1938).

Mersch, E., *Le Corps Mystique de Christ* (Paris, 1936).

Merzbacher, F., 'Wandlungen des Kirchenbegriffs im Spätmittelalter', *Zeitschrift der Savigny-Stiftung für Rechtsgeschichte, Kanonistische Abteilung*, xxxix (1953), pp. 274–361.

'Das *Somnium viridarii* von 1376 als Spiegel des gallikanischen Kirchenrechts', *Zeitschrift der Savigny-Stiftung für Rechtsgeschichte, Kanonistische Abteilung*, xlii (1956), pp. 55–72.

Meynial, E., 'Notes sur la formation de la théorie du domaine divisé (domaine direct et domaine utile) du XII au XIV siècle dans les romanistes: Étude de dogmatique juridique', *Mélanges Fitting* ii (Montpellier, 1908).

Michel, A., 'Ordre', *Dictionnaire de théologie catholique*, xi.1 (Paris, 1931), cc. 1194–1406.

Miller, G. J. T., 'The Position of the King in Bracton and Beaumanoir', *Speculum*, xxxi (1956), pp. 263–96.

Ministeri, B., *De Vita et Operibus Augustini de Ancona, O.E.S.A.* (**1328*) (Rome, 1953).

Mitteis, H., *Die deutsche Königswahl* (Brno, 2nd edition, 1944).

Mochi Onory, S., *Fonti canonistiche dell'idea moderna dello stato* (Milan, 1951).

Mollat, G., *Les Papes d'Avignon* (Paris, 6th edition, 1930).

'Le roi de France et la collation plénière, *pleno jure*, des bénéfices ecclésiastiques', *Academie des inscriptions et belles-lettres*, xiv.2 (Paris, 1951).

'Contribution à l'histoire du sacré collège de Clément V à Eugène IV', *Revue d'histoire ecclésiastique*, xlvi (1951), pp. 22–112, 566–94.

Moody, E. A., 'Ockham and Aegidius of Rome', *Franciscan Studies*, ix (1949), pp. 417–42.

Morrall, J. B., 'Some Notes on a Recent Interpretation of Ockham's Political Philosophy', *Franciscan Studies*, ix (1949), pp. 335–69.

Morris, W. A., and Willard, J. F., *The English Government at Work, 1327–36* (Cambridge, Mass., 1940–50).

Most, R., 'Der Reichsgedanke des Lupold von Bebenburg', *Deutsches Archiv für Geschichte des Mittelalters*, iv (1941), pp. 444–85.

Mundy, J. H., Emery, R. W., and Nelson, B. N., ed., *Essays in Medieval Life and Thought* (New York, 1955).

Munz, P., *The Place of Hooker in the History of Thought* (London, 1952).

Nardi, B., 'Il concetto dell' Impero nello svolgimento dell pensiero dantesco', *Saggi di Filosophia Dantesca* (Milan, 1930), pp. 241–305.

Offler, H. S., 'A Political *Collatio* of Pope Clement VI, O.S.B.', *Revue Bénédictine*, lxv (1955), pp. 126–44.

'Empire and Papacy: The Last Struggle', *Transactions of the Royal Historical Society, Vth Series*, vi (1956), pp. 21–47.

PANTIN, W. A., 'Grosseteste's Relations with the Papacy and the Crown', *Robert Grosseteste* (ed. D. A. Callus: Oxford, 1955), pp. 178–215.

The English Church in the Fourteenth Century (Cambridge, 1955).

PELZER, A., and KAEPPELI, T., 'L'*Oeconomica* de Conrad de Megenberg retrouvée', *Revue d'histoire ecclésiastique*, xlv (1950), pp. 559–616.

PILATI, G., 'Bonifacio VIII° e il potere indiretto', *Antonianum*, viii (1933), pp. 350 f.

POLLOCK, F., 'The History of the Law of Nature', *Essays in the Law* (London, 1922), pp. 31–79.

POOLE, R. L., *Illustrations of the History of Medieval Thought and Learning* (London, 1920).

POST, GAINES, 'Roman Law and Early Representation in Spain and Italy', *Speculum*, xviii (1943), pp. 211–32.

'*Plena potestas* and consent in medieval assemblies', *Traditio*, i (1943), pp. 355–408.

'A Romano-canonical maxim *Quod omnes tangit* in Bracton', *Traditio*, iv (1946), pp. 197–251.

'The Theory of Public Law and the State in the Thirteenth Century', *Seminar*, vi (1948), pp. 417–32.

'Two Notes on Nationalism in the Middle Ages', *Traditio*, ix (1953), pp. 281–320.

'Blessed Lady Spain', *Speculum*, xxix (1954), pp. 198–209.

'The Two Laws and the Statute of York', *Speculum*, xxix (1954), pp. 417–32.

POWICKE, F. M., 'Reflections on the Medieval State', *Ways of Medieval Life and Thought* (London, 1949), pp. 130–48.

RAHNER, H., *The Mysteries: Papers from the Eranos Year Books* (ed. J. Campbell: London, 1955), pp. 337–401.

RIESENBERG, P. N., *Inalienability of Sovereignty in Medieval Political Thought* (New York, 1956).

RIEZLER, S., *Die literarischen Widersacher der Päpste zur Zeit Ludwigs des Baiers* (Leipzig, 1874).

RIVIÈRE, J., 'Le Pape est-il 'un Dieu' pour Innocent III?' *Revue des sciences religieuses*, ii (1922), pp. 447–51.

'Sur l'expression 'Papa-Deus' au moyen âge', *Miscellanea Francesco Ehrle*, ii (Rome, 1924), pp. 278–89.

'*In partem sollicitudinis:* évolution d'une formule pontificale', *Revue des sciences religieuses*, v (1925), pp. 210–31.

Le problème de l'église et de l'état au temps de Philippe le Bel (Louvain and Paris, 1926).

'Une première "Somme" du pouvoir pontifical: le pape chez Augustin d'Ancone', *Revue des sciences religieuses*, xviii (1938), pp. 149–83.

ROBERTI, M., 'Il *corpus mysticum* di S. Paolo nella storia della persona giuridica', *Studi di storia e diritto in onore di Enrico Besta*, iv (Milan, 1939), pp. 37–82.

SAEGMULLER, J. B., *Die Thätigkeit und Stellung der Cardinale bis Papst Bonifaz VIII* (Freiburg im Breisgau, 1896).

'Die Idee von der Kirche als *imperium Romanum*', *Theologische Quartalschrift*, lxxx (1898), pp. 50–80.

SALOMON, R. G., *Opicinus de Canistris. Weltbild und Bekentnisse eines Avignonesischen Klerikers des 14. Jahrhunderts* (London, 1936).

'A Newly Discovered Manuscript of Opicinus de Canistris', *Journal of the Warburg and Courtauld Institutes*, xvi (1953), pp. 45–57.

SALTET, L., *Les réordinations* (Paris, 1907).

SAXL, F., 'Macrocosm and Microcosm in Medieval Pictures', *Lectures*, i (London, 1957), pp. 58–72.

SCHLEYER, K., 'Disputes scolastiques sur les états de perfection', *Récherches de théologie ancienne et médiévale*, x (1938), pp. 279–93.

SCHOLZ, R., *Die Publizistik zur Zeit Philippe des Schönen und Bonifaz' VIII* (Stuttgart, 1903).

Unbekannte Kirchenpolitische Streitschriften aus der Zeit Ludwigs des Bayern, 1327–1354 (Rome, 1911–14).

'Marsilius von Padua und die Genesis des modernen Staatsbewusstseins', *Historische Zeitschrift*, clvi (1937), pp. 88–103.

Wilhelm von Ockham als politischer Denker und sein Breviloquium de principatu tyrannico (Leipzig, 1944).

SCHULTE, J. F. von, *Die Stellung der Concilien, Päpste und Bischöfe* (Prague, 1871).

SCHULZ, F., 'Bracton on Kingship', *English Historical Review*, lx (1945), pp. 136–76.

SEZNEC, J., *The Survival of the Pagan Gods* (New York, 1953).

SHEPARD, M. A., 'William of Occam and the Higher Law', *American Political Science Review*, xxvi (1932), pp. 1005–23; xxvii (1933), pp. 24–38.

SIKES, J. G., 'John de Pouilli and Peter de la Palu', *English Historical Review*, xlix (1934), pp. 219–40.

'A Possible Marsilian Source in Ockham', *English Historical Review*, li (1936), pp. 496–504.

SILVERSTEIN, T., 'On the Genesis of *De Monarchia*, II.v', *Speculum*, xiii (1938), pp. 326–49.

'The Throne of the Emperor Henry in Dante's Paradise and the Medieval Conception of Kingship', *Harvard Theological Review*, xxxii (1939), pp. 115–29.

STANLEY, A. P., *Historical Memorials of Westminster Abbey* (London, 1890).

STEENBERGHEN, F. van, *The Philosophical Movement in the Thirteenth Century* (London, 1955).

STENGEL, E. E., *Avignon und Rhens* (Weimar, 1930).

STRAYER, J. R., 'Defense of the Realm and Royal Power in France', *Studi in onore di Gino Luzzatto*, i (Milan, 1949), pp. 289–96.

'The Laicalisation of French and English Society in the Thirteenth and Fourteenth Centuries', *Speculum*, xxv (1950), pp. 76–86.

'Philip the Fair—a "Constitutional" King', *American Historical Review*, lxii (1956), pp. 18–32.

SWEENEY, L., 'Lombard, Augustine and Infinity', *Manuscripta*, ii (1958), pp. 24–40.

THOMSON, S. H., 'Walter Burley's Commentary on the *Politics* of Aristotle', *Mélanges Auguste Pelzer* (Louvain, 1947), pp. 557–78.

TIERNEY, B., 'A Conciliar Theory of the Thirteenth Century', *Catholic Historical Review*, xxxvi (1951), pp. 415–40.

'The Canonists and the Medieval State', *Review of Politics*, xv (1953), pp. 378–88.

'Some Recent Works on the Political Theories of the Medieval Canonists', *Traditio*, x (1954), pp. 594–625.

'Ockham, the Conciliar Theory, and the Canonists', *Journal of the History of Ideas*, xv (1954), pp. 40–70.

'Grosseteste and the Theory of Papal Sovereignty', *Journal of Ecclesiastical History*, vi (1955), pp. 1–17.

Foundations of the Conciliar Theory (Cambridge, 1955).

'Pope and Council: Some New Decretist Texts', *Mediaeval Studies*, xix (1957), pp. 197–218.

TROELTSH, E., *The Social Teaching of the Christian Churches*, i (tr. O. Wyon: London, 1931).

ULLMANN, W., *The Medieval Idea of Law as represented by Lucas de Penna* (London, 1946), with an Introduction by H. D. Hazeltine.

'A Medieval Document on Papal Theories of Government', *English Historical Review*, lxi (1946), pp. 180–201.

'The Delictal Responsibility of Medieval Corporations', *Law Quarterly Review*, lxiv (1948), pp. 77–96.

The Origins of the Great Schism (London, 1948).

'Medieval Views concerning Papal Abdication', *Irish Ecclesiastical Record*, lxxi (1949), pp. 125–33.

'The Development of the Medieval Idea of Sovereignty', *English Historical Review*, lxiv (1949), pp. 1–33.

Medieval Papalism: The Political Theories of the Medieval Canonists (London, 1949).

'Cardinal Humbert and the *ecclesia Romana*', *Studi Gregoriani*, iv (Rome, 1952), pp. 111–27.

'*Nos si aliquid incompetenter . . .*', *Ephemerides Iuris Canonici*, ix (1953), pp. 279–87.

'The Pontificate of Adrian IV', *Cambridge Historical Journal*, xi (1953–5), pp. 233–52.

'Cardinal Roland and the Incident at Besançon', *Miscellanea Historiae Pontificiae*, xviii (1954), pp. 107–25.

The Growth of Papal Government in the Middle Ages (London, 1955).
'The Legal Validity of the Papal Electoral Pacts', *Ephemerides Iuris Canonici*, xii (1956), pp. 3–35.
'Thomas Beckett's Miraculous Oil', *Journal of Theological Studies*, viii (1957), pp. 128–33.

VAN GERVEN, R., *De wereldijke macht van den paus volgens Augustinus Triumphus* (Antwerp and Nijmegen, 1947).

WECKMANN, L., *Las Bulas Alejandrinas de 1493 y la Teoría Política del Papado Medieval: Estudio de la Supremacía Papal sobre Islas, 1091–1493* (Mexico City, 1949).

WENCK, K., *Clemens V und Heinrich VII* (Halle, 1882).

WIERUSZOWSKI, H., 'Vom Imperium zum Nationalen Königtum', *Historische Zeitschrift*, xxx (Munich and Berlin, 1933).

WILKS, M. J., '*Papa est nomen iurisdictionis:* Augustinus Triumphus and the Papal Vicariate of Christ', *Journal of Theological Studies*, viii (1957), pp. 71–91, 256–71.

WILLIAMS, G. H., *The Norman Anonymous of 1100 A.D.* (Cambridge, Mass., 1951).

WILLIAMS, J., *Dante as a Jurist* (Oxford, 1906).

WINKELMANN, E., *Acta imperii inedita saeculi XIII et XIV* (Innsbruck, 1885).

WIRSZUBSKI, C., *Libertas as a Political Idea at Rome during the Late Republic and Early Principate* (Cambridge, 1950).

WOOLF, C. N. S., *Bartolus of Sassoferrato* (Cambridge, 1913).

DE WULF, M., *History of Medieval Philosophy* (tr. E. C. Messenger: London and New York, 1935–8).

ZACOUR, N. P., 'A Note on the Papal Election of 1352: the Candidacy of Jean Birel', *Traditio*, xiii (1957), pp. 456–62.

ZEUMER, K., *Quellen und Studien zur Verfassungsgeschichte des Deutschen Reiches in Mittelalter und Neuzeit. II.2. Die Goldene Bulle Kaiser Karls IV* (Weimar, 1908).

ZELLER, G., 'Les rois de France candidats à l'empire', *Revue Historique*, clxxiii (1934), pp. 273–311, 497–534.

ZUMKELLER, A., 'De doctrina sociali scholae Augustinianae Aevi Medii', *Analecta Augustiniana*, xxii (1951), pp. 57–84.
Hermann von Schildesche, O.E.S.A. (8 Juli, 1357): Zur 600. Wiederkehr seines Todestages (Wurzburg, 1957).

INDEX